Appreciation of Theatre

Deborah C. Mello
Miami Dade College

Kendall Hunt
publishing company

D1219306

Kendall Hunt
publishing company

www.kendallhunt.com
Send all inquiries to:
4050 Westmark Drive
Dubuque, IA 52004-1840

Printed in the United States of America
10 9 8 7 6 5 4 3 2 1

Contents

1

Oedipus Rex

(Greek: Oedipus Tyrannus Latin: *Oedipus Rex; Oedipus the King)*

Play by Sophocles (496–406 B.C.)

Translation by F. Storr, BA

ARGUMENT

To Laius, King of Thebes, an oracle foretold that the child born to him by his queen Jocasta would slay his father and wed his mother. So when in time a son was born the infant's feet were riveted together and he was left to die on Mount Cithaeron. But a shepherd found the babe and tended him, and delivered him to another shepherd who took him to his master, the King or Corinth. Polybus being childless adopted the boy, who grew up believing that he was indeed the King's son. Afterwards doubting his parentage he inquired of the Delphic god and heard himself the weird declared before to Laius. Wherefore he fled from what he deemed his father's house and in his flight he encountered and unwillingly slew his father Laius. Arriving at Thebes he answered the riddle of the Sphinx and the grateful Thebans made their deliverer king. So he reigned in the room of Laius, and espoused the widowed queen. Children were born to them and Thebes prospered under his rule, but again a grievous plague fell upon the city. Again the oracle was consulted and it bade them purge themselves of blood-guiltiness. Oedipus denounces the crime of which he is unaware, and undertakes to track out the criminal. Step by step it is brought home to him that he is the man. The closing scene reveals Jocasta slain by her own hand and Oedipus blinded by his own act and praying for death or exile.

"Oedipus (Rex) the King", 1896

1

DRAMATIS PERSONAE

Oedipus
The Priest of Zeus
Creon
Chorus of Theban Elders
Teiresias
Jocasta
Messenger
Herd of Laius
Second Messenger
Scene: Thebes. Before the Palace of Oedipus.

OEDIPUS REX

Suppliants of all ages are seated round the altar at the palace doors, at their head a PRIEST OF ZEUS. To them enter OEDIPUS.

OEDIPUS

My children, latest born to Cadmus old,
Why sit ye here as suppliants, in your hands
Branches of olive filleted with wool?
What means this reek of incense everywhere,
And everywhere laments and litanies?
Children, it were not meet that I should learn
From others, and am hither come, myself,
I Oedipus, your world-renowned king.
Ho! aged sire, whose venerable locks
Proclaim thee spokesman of this company,
Explain your mood and purport. Is it dread
Of ill that moves you or a boon ye crave?
My zeal in your behalf ye cannot doubt;
Ruthless indeed were I and obdurate
If such petitioners as you I spurned.

PRIEST

Yea, Oedipus, my sovereign lord and king,
Thou seest how both extremes of age besiege
Thy palace altars—fledglings hardly winged,
and greybeards bowed with years; priests, as am I
of Zeus, and these the flower of our youth.
Meanwhile, the common folk, with wreathed
    boughs
Crowd our two market-places, or before
Both shrines of Pallas congregate, or where

Ismenus gives his oracles by fire.
For, as thou seest thyself, our ship of State,
Sore buffeted, can no more lift her head,
Foundered beneath a weltering surge of blood.
A blight is on our harvest in the ear,
A blight upon the grazing flocks and herds,
A blight on wives in travail; and withal
Armèd with his blazing torch the God of Plague
Hath swooped upon our city emptying
The house of Cadmus, and the murky realm
Of Pluto is full fed with groans and tears.
Therefore, O King, here at thy hearth we sit,
I and these children; not as deeming thee
A new divinity, but the first of men;
First in the common accidents of life,
And first in visitations of the Gods.
Art thou not he who coming to the town
of Cadmus freed us from the tax we paid
To the fell songstress? Nor hadst thou received
Prompting from us or been by others schooled;
No, by a god inspired (so all men deem,
And testify) didst thou renew our life.
And now, O Oedipus, our peerless king,
All we thy votaries beseech thee, find
Some succor, whether by a voice from heaven
Whispered, or haply known by human wit.
Tried counselors, methinks, are aptest found [1]
To furnish for the future pregnant rede.
Upraise, O chief of men, upraise our State!
Look to thy laurels! for thy zeal of yore
Our country's savior thou art justly hailed:

O never may we thus record thy reign:—
"He raised us up only to cast us down."
Uplift us, build our city on a rock.
Thy happy star ascendant brought us luck,
O let it not decline! If thou wouldst rule
This land, as now thou reignest, better sure
To rule a peopled than a desert realm.
Nor battlements nor galleys aught avail,
If men to man and guards to guard them tail.

OEDIPUS

Ah! my poor children, known, ah, known too
    well,
The quest that brings you hither and your need.
Ye sicken all, well wot I, yet my pain,
How great soever yours, outtops it all.
Your sorrow touches each man severally,
Him and none other, but I grieve at once
Both for the general and myself and you.
Therefore ye rouse no sluggard from day-dreams.
Many, my children, are the tears I've wept,
And threaded many a maze of weary thought.
Thus pondering one clue of hope I caught,
And tracked it up; I have sent Menoeceus' son,
Creon, my consort's brother, to inquire
Of Pythian Phoebus at his Delphic shrine,
How I might save the State by act or word.
And now I reckon up the tale of days
Since he set forth, and marvel how he fares.
'Tis strange, this endless tarrying, passing strange.
But when he comes, then I were base indeed,
If I perform not all the god declares.

PRIEST

Thy words are well timed; even as thou speakest
That shouting tells me Creon is at hand.

OEDIPUS

O King Apollo! may his joyous looks
Be presage of the joyous news he brings!

PRIEST

As I surmise, 'tis welcome; else his head
Had scarce been crowned with berry-laden bays.

OEDIPUS

We soon shall know; he's now in earshot range.

[Enter CREON]

My royal cousin, say, Menoeceus' child,
What message hast thou brought us from the
    god?

CREON

Good news, for e'en intolerable ills,
Finding right issue, tend to naught but good.

OEDIPUS

How runs the oracle? thus far thy words
Give me no ground for confidence or fear.

CREON

If thou wouldst hear my message publicly,
I'll tell thee straight, or with thee pass within.

OEDIPUS

Speak before all; the burden that I bear
Is more for these my subjects than myself.

CREON

Let me report then all the god declared.
King Phoebus bids us straitly extirpate
A fell pollution that infests the land,
And no more harbor an inveterate sore.

OEDIPUS

What expiation means he? What's amiss?

CREON

Banishment, or the shedding blood for blood.
This stain of blood makes shipwreck of our state.

OEDIPUS

Whom can he mean, the miscreant thus
    denounced?

CREON

Before thou didst assume the helm of State,
The sovereign of this land was Laius.

OEDIPUS

I heard as much, but never saw the man.

CREON

He fell; and now the god's command is plain:
Punish his takers-off, whoe'er they be.

OEDIPUS

Where are they? Where in the wide world to find
The far, faint traces of a bygone crime?

CREON

In this land, said the god; "who seeks shall find;
Who sits with folded hands or sleeps is blind."

OEDIPUS

Was he within his palace, or afield,
Or traveling, when Laius met his fate?

CREON

Abroad; he started, so he told us, bound
For Delphi, but he never thence returned.

OEDIPUS

Came there no news, no fellow-traveler
To give some clue that might be followed up?

CREON

But one escape, who flying for dear life,
Could tell of all he saw but one thing sure.

OEDIPUS

And what was that? One clue might lead us far,
With but a spark of hope to guide our quest.

CREON

Robbers, he told us, not one bandit but
A troop of knaves, attacked and murdered him.

OEDIPUS

Did any bandit dare so bold a stroke,
Unless indeed he were suborned from Thebes?

CREON

So 'twas surmised, but none was found to avenge
His murder mid the trouble that ensued.

OEDIPUS

What trouble can have hindered a full quest,
When royalty had fallen thus miserably?

CREON

The riddling Sphinx compelled us to let slide
The dim past and attend to instant needs.

OEDIPUS

Well, *I* will start afresh and once again
Make dark things clear. Right worthy the concern
Of Phoebus, worthy thine too, for the dead;
I also, as is meet, will lend my aid
To avenge this wrong to Thebes and to the god.
Not for some far-off kinsman, but myself,
Shall I expel this poison in the blood;
For whoso slew that king might have a mind
To strike me too with his assassin hand.
Therefore in righting him I serve myself.
Up, children, haste ye, quit these altar stairs,
Take hence your suppliant wands, go summon
    hither
The Theban commons. With the god's good help
Success is sure; 'tis ruin if we fail.

[Exeunt OEDIPUS and CREON]

PRIEST

Come, children, let us hence; these gracious words
Forestall the very purpose of our suit.
And may the god who sent this oracle
Save us withal and rid us of this pest.

[Exeunt PRIEST and SUPPLIANTS]

CHORUS

(Str. 1)

Sweet-voiced daughter of Zeus from thy gold-
    paved Pythian shrine
Wafted to Thebes divine,
What dost thou bring me? My soul is racked and
    shivers with fear.
(Healer of Delos, hear!)
Hast thou some pain unknown before,
Or with the circling years renewest a penance of
    yore?
Offspring of golden Hope, thou voice immortal,
    O tell me.

(Ant. 1)

First on Athene I call; O Zeus-born goddess,
    defend!
Goddess and sister, befriend,
Artemis, Lady of Thebes, high-throned in the
    midst of our mart!
Lord of the death-winged dart!
Your threefold aid I crave
From death and ruin our city to save.
If in the days of old when we nigh had perished,
    ye drave
From our land the fiery plague, be near us now
    and defend us!

(Str. 2)

Ah me, what countless woes are mine!
All our host is in decline;
Weaponless my spirit lies.
Earth her gracious fruits denies;
Women wail in barren throes;
Life on life downstriken goes,
Swifter than the wind bird's flight,
Swifter than the Fire-God's might,
To the westering shores of Night.

(Ant. 2)

Wasted thus by death on death
All our city perisheth.
Corpses spread infection round;
None to tend or mourn is found.
Wailing on the altar stair
Wives and grandams rend the air—

Long-drawn moans and piercing cries
Blent with prayers and litanies.
Golden child of Zeus, O hear
Let thine angel face appear!
(Str. 3)
And grant that Ares whose hot breath I feel,
Though without targe or steel
He stalks, whose voice is as the battle shout,
May turn in sudden rout,
To the unharbored Thracian waters sped,
Or Amphitrite's bed.
For what night leaves undone,
Smit by the morrow's sun
Perisheth. Father Zeus, whose hand
Doth wield the lightning brand,
Slay him beneath thy levin bold, we pray,
Slay him, O slay!
(Ant. 3)
O that thine arrows too, Lycean King,
From that taut bow's gold string,
Might fly abroad, the champions of our rights;
Yea, and the flashing lights
Of Artemis, wherewith the huntress sweeps
Across the Lycian steeps.
Thee too I call with golden-snooded hair,
Whose name our land doth bear,
Bacchus to whom thy Maenads Evoe shout;
Come with thy bright torch, rout,
Blithe god whom we adore,
The god whom gods abhor.

[Enter OEDIPUS.]

OEDIPUS

Ye pray; 'tis well, but would ye hear my words
And heed them and apply the remedy,
Ye might perchance find comfort and relief.
Mind you, I speak as one who comes a stranger
To this report, no less than to the crime;
For how unaided could I track it far
Without a clue? Which lacking (for too late
Was I enrolled a citizen of Thebes)
This proclamation I address to all:—
Thebans, if any knows the man by whom
Laius, son of Labdacus, was slain,
I summon him to make clean shrift to me.
And if he shrinks, let him reflect that thus
Confessing he shall 'scape the capital charge;
For the worst penalty that shall befall him
Is banishment—unscathed he shall depart.

But if an alien from a foreign land
Be known to any as the murderer,
Let him who knows speak out, and he shall have
Due recompense from me and thanks to boot.
But if ye still keep silence, if through fear
For self or friends ye disregard my hest,
Hear what I then resolve; I lay my ban
On the assassin whosoe'er he be.
Let no man in this land, whereof I hold
The sovereign rule, harbor or speak to him;
Give him no part in prayer or sacrifice
Or lustral rites, but hound him from your homes.
For this is our defilement, so the god
Hath lately shown to me by oracles.
Thus as their champion I maintain the cause
Both of the god and of the murdered King.
And on the murderer this curse I lay
(On him and all the partners in his guilt):—
Wretch, may he pine in utter wretchedness!
And for myself, if with my privity
He gain admittance to my hearth, I pray
The curse I laid on others fall on me.
See that ye give effect to all my hest,
For my sake and the god's and for our land,
A desert blasted by the wrath of heaven.
For, let alone the god's express command,
It were a scandal ye should leave unpurged
The murder of a great man and your king,
Nor track it home. And now that I am lord,
Successor to his throne, his bed, his wife,
(And had he not been frustrate in the hope
Of issue, common children of one womb
Had forced a closer bond twixt him and me,
But Fate swooped down upon him),
        therefore I
His blood-avenger will maintain his cause
As though he were my sire, and leave no stone
Unturned to track the assassin or avenge
The son of Labdacus, of Polydore,
Of Cadmus, and Agenor first of the race.
And for the disobedient thus I pray:
May the gods send them neither timely fruits
Of earth, nor teeming increase of the womb,
But may they waste and pine, as now they waste,
Aye and worse stricken; but to all of you,
My loyal subjects who approve my acts,
May Justice, our ally, and all the gods
Be gracious and attend you evermore.

CHORUS
The oath thou profferest, sire, I take and swear.
I slew him not myself, nor can I name
The slayer. For the quest, 'twere well, methinks
That Phoebus, who proposed the riddle, himself
Should give the answer—who the murderer was.

OEDIPUS
Well argued; but no living man can hope
To force the gods to speak against their will.

CHORUS
May I then say what seems next best to me?

OEDIPUS
Aye, if there be a third best, tell it too.

CHORUS
My liege, if any man sees eye to eye
With our lord Phoebus, 'tis our prophet, lord
Teiresias; he of all men best might guide
A searcher of this matter to the light.

OEDIPUS
Here too my zeal has nothing lagged, for twice
At Creon's instance have I sent to fetch him,
And long I marvel why he is not here.

CHORUS
I mind me too of rumors long ago—
Mere gossip.

OEDIPUS
Tell them, I would fain know all.

CHORUS
'Twas said he fell by travelers.

OEDIPUS
So I heard,
But none has seen the man who saw him fall.

CHORUS
Well, if he knows what fear is, he will quail
And flee before the terror of thy curse.

OEDIPUS
Words scare not him who blenches not at deeds.

CHORUS
But here is one to arraign him. Lo, at length
They bring the god-inspired seer in whom
Above all other men is truth inborn.

[Enter TEIRESIAS, led by a boy.]

OEDIPUS
Teiresias, seer who comprehendest all,
Lore of the wise and hidden mysteries,
High things of heaven and low things of the
     earth,
Thou knowest, though thy blinded eyes see
     naught,
What plague infects our city; and we turn
To thee, O seer, our one defense and shield.
The purport of the answer that the God
Returned to us who sought his oracle,
The messengers have doubtless told thee—how
One course alone could rid us of the pest,
To find the murderers of Laius,
And slay them or expel them from the land.
Therefore begrudging neither augury
Nor other divination that is thine,
O save thyself, thy country, and thy king,
Save all from this defilement of blood shed.
On thee we rest. This is man's highest end,
To others' service all his powers to lend.

TEIRESIAS
Alas, alas, what misery to be wise
When wisdom profits nothing! This old lore
I had forgotten; else I were not here.

OEDIPUS
What ails thee? Why this melancholy mood?

TEIRESIAS
Let me go home; prevent me not; 'twere best
That thou shouldst bear thy burden and I mine.

OEDIPUS
For shame! no true-born Theban patriot
Would thus withhold the word of prophecy.

TEIRESIAS
Thy words, O king, are wide of the mark,
     and I
For fear lest I too trip like thee . . .

OEDIPUS
Oh speak,
Withhold not, I adjure thee, if thou know'st,
Thy knowledge. We are all thy suppliants.

TEIRESIAS
Aye, for ye all are witless, but my voice
Will ne'er reveal my miseries—or thine. [2]

OEDIPUS
What then, thou knowest, and yet willst not
    speak!
Wouldst thou betray us and destroy the State?

TEIRESIAS
I will not vex myself nor thee. Why ask
Thus idly what from me thou shalt not learn?

OEDIPUS
Monster! thy silence would incense a flint.
Will nothing loose thy tongue? Can nothing melt
    thee,
Or shake thy dogged taciturnity?

TEIRESIAS
Thou blam'st my mood and seest not thine own
Wherewith thou art mated; no, thou taxest me.

OEDIPUS
And who could stay his choler when he heard
How insolently thou dost flout the State?

TEIRESIAS
Well, it will come what will, though I be mute.

OEDIPUS
Since come it must, thy duty is to tell me.

TEIRESIAS
I have no more to say; storm as thou willst,
And give the rein to all thy pent-up rage.

OEDIPUS
Yea, I am wroth, and will not stint my words,
But speak my whole mind. Thou methinks thou
    art he,
Who planned the crime, aye, and performed it
    too,
All save the assassination; and if thou
Hadst not been blind, I had been sworn to boot
That thou alone didst do the bloody deed.

TEIRESIAS
Is it so? Then I charge thee to abide
By thine own proclamation; from this day
Speak not to these or me. Thou art the man,
Thou the accursed polluter of this land.

OEDIPUS
Vile slanderer, thou blurtest forth these taunts,
And think'st forsooth as seer to go scot free.

TEIRESIAS
Yea, I am free, strong in the strength of truth.

OEDIPUS
Who was thy teacher? not methinks thy art.

TEIRESIAS
Thou, goading me against my will to speak.

OEDIPUS
What speech? repeat it and resolve my doubt.

TEIRESIAS
Didst miss my sense wouldst thou goad me on?

OEDIPUS
I but half caught thy meaning; say it again.

TEIRESIAS
I say thou art the murderer of the man
Whose murderer thou pursuest.

OEDIPUS
Thou shalt rue it
Twice to repeat so gross a calumny.

TEIRESIAS
Must I say more to aggravate thy rage?

OEDIPUS
Say all thou wilt; it will be but waste of breath.

TEIRESIAS
I say thou livest with thy nearest kin
In infamy, unwitting in thy shame.

OEDIPUS
Think'st thou for aye unscathed to wag thy
    tongue?

TEIRESIAS
Yea, if the might of truth can aught prevail.

OEDIPUS
With other men, but not with thee, for thou
In ear, wit, eye, in everything art blind.

TEIRESIAS
Poor fool to utter gibes at me which all
Here present will cast back on thee ere long.

OEDIPUS
Offspring of endless Night, thou hast no power
O'er me or any man who sees the sun.

TEIRESIAS

No, for thy weird is not to fall by me.
I leave to Apollo what concerns the god.

OEDIPUS

Is this a plot of Creon, or thine own?

TEIRESIAS

Not Creon, thou thyself art thine own bane.

OEDIPUS

O wealth and empiry and skill by skill
Outwitted in the battlefield of life,
What spite and envy follow in your train!
See, for this crown the State conferred on me.
A gift, a thing I sought not, for this crown
The trusty Creon, my familiar friend,
Hath lain in wait to oust me and suborned
This mountebank, this juggling charlatan,
This tricksy beggar-priest, for gain alone
Keen-eyed, but in his proper art stone-blind.
Say, sirrah, hast thou ever proved thyself
A prophet? When the riddling Sphinx was here
Why hadst thou no deliverance for this folk?
And yet the riddle was not to be solved
By guess-work but required the prophet's art;
Wherein thou wast found lacking; neither birds
Nor sign from heaven helped thee, but *I* came,
The simple Oedipus; *I* stopped her mouth
By mother wit, untaught of auguries.
This is the man whom thou wouldst undermine,
In hope to reign with Creon in my stead.
Methinks that thou and thine abettor soon
Will rue your plot to drive the scapegoat out.
Thank thy grey hairs that thou hast still to learn
What chastisement such arrogance deserves.

CHORUS

To us it seems that both the seer and thou,
O Oedipus, have spoken angry words.
This is no time to wrangle but consult
How best we may fulfill the oracle.

TEIRESIAS

King as thou art, free speech at least is mine
To make reply; in this I am thy peer.
I own no lord but Loxias; him I serve
And ne'er can stand enrolled as Creon's man.
Thus then I answer: since thou hast not spared
To twit me with my blindness—thou hast eyes,
Yet see'st not in what misery thou art fallen,
Nor where thou dwellest nor with whom for
     mate.
Dost know thy lineage? Nay, thou know'st it not,
And all unwitting art a double foe
To thine own kin, the living and the dead;
Aye and the dogging curse of mother and sire
One day shall drive thee, like a two-edged sword,
Beyond our borders, and the eyes that now
See clear shall henceforward endless night.
Ah whither shall thy bitter cry not reach,
What crag in all Cithaeron but shall then
Reverberate thy wail, when thou hast found
With what a hymeneal thou wast borne
Home, but to no fair haven, on the gale!
Aye, and a flood of ills thou guessest not
Shall set thyself and children in one line.
Flout then both Creon and my words, for none
Of mortals shall be striken worse than thou.

OEDIPUS

Must I endure this fellow's insolence?
A murrain on thee! Get thee hence! Begone
Avaunt! and never cross my threshold more.

TEIRESIAS

I ne'er had come hadst thou not bidden me.

OEDIPUS

I know not thou wouldst utter folly, else
Long hadst thou waited to be summoned here.

TEIRESIAS

Such am I—as it seems to thee a fool,
But to the parents who begat thee, wise.

OEDIPUS

What sayest thou—"parents"? Who begat me,
     speak?

TEIRESIAS

This day shall be thy birth-day, and thy grave.

OEDIPUS

Thou lov'st to speak in riddles and dark words.

TEIRESIAS

In reading riddles who so skilled as thou?

OEDIPUS

Twit me with that wherein my greatness lies.

TEIRESIAS

And yet this very greatness proved thy bane.

OEDIPUS

No matter if I saved the commonwealth.

TEIRESIAS

'Tis time I left thee. Come, boy, take me home.

OEDIPUS

Aye, take him quickly, for his presence irks
And lets me; gone, thou canst not plague me
    more.

TEIRESIAS

I go, but first will tell thee why I came.
Thy frown I dread not, for thou canst not harm
    me.
Hear then: this man whom thou hast sought to
    arrest
With threats and warrants this long while, the
    wretch
Who murdered Laius—that man is here.
He passes for an alien in the land
But soon shall prove a Theban, native born.
And yet his fortune brings him little joy;
For blind of seeing, clad in beggar's weeds,
For purple robes, and leaning on his staff,
To a strange land he soon shall grope his way.
And of the children, inmates of his home,
He shall be proved the brother and the sire,
Of her who bare him son and husband both,
Co-partner, and assassin of his sire.
Go in and ponder this, and if thou find
That I have missed the mark, henceforth declare
I have no wit nor skill in prophecy.

[*Exeunt TEIRESIAS and OEDIPUS*]

CHORUS
(Str. 1)

Who is he by voice immortal named from Pythia's
    rocky cell,
Doer of foul deeds of bloodshed, horrors that no
    tongue can tell?
A foot for flight he needs
Fleeter than storm-swift steeds,
For on his heels doth follow,
Armed with the lightnings of his Sire, Apollo.
Like sleuth-hounds too
The Fates pursue.

(Ant. 1)

Yea, but now flashed forth the summons from
    Parnassus' snowy peak,

"Near and far the undiscovered doer of this
    murder seek!"
Now like a sullen bull he roves
Through forest brakes and upland groves,
And vainly seeks to fly
The doom that ever nigh
Flits o'er his head,
Still by the avenging Phoebus sped,
The voice divine,
From Earth's mid shrine.

(Str. 2)

Sore perplexed am I by the words of the master
    seer.
Are they true, are they false? I know not and
    bridle my tongue for
fear,
Fluttered with vague surmise; nor present nor
    future is clear.
Quarrel of ancient date or in days still near know
    I none
Twixt the Labdacidan house and our ruler,
    Polybus' son.
Proof is there none: how then can I challenge our
    King's good name,
How in a blood-feud join for an untracked deed
    of shame?

(Ant. 2)

All wise are Zeus and Apollo, and nothing is hid
    from their ken;
They are gods; and in wits a man may surpass his
    fellow men;
But that a mortal seer knows more than I know—
    where
Hath this been proven? Or how without sign
    assured, can I blame
Him who saved our State when the winged
    songstress came,
Tested and tried in the light of us all, like gold
    assayed?
How can I now assent when a crime is on
    Oedipus laid?

CREON

Friends, countrymen, I learn King Oedipus
Hath laid against me a most grievous charge,
And come to you protesting. If he deems
That I have harmed or injured him in aught
By word or deed in this our present trouble,
I care not to prolong the span of life,
Thus ill-reputed; for the calumny

Hits not a single blot, but blasts my name,
If by the general voice I am denounced
False to the State and false by you my friends.

CHORUS
This taunt, it well may be, was blurted out
In petulance, not spoken advisedly.

CREON
Did any dare pretend that it was I
Prompted the seer to utter a forged charge?

CHORUS
Such things were said; with what intent I know
    not.

CREON
Were not his wits and vision all astray
When upon me he fixed this monstrous charge?

CHORUS
I know not; to my sovereign's acts I am blind.
But lo, he comes to answer for himself.

[Enter OEDIPUS.]

OEDIPUS
Sirrah, what mak'st thou here? Dost thou
    presume
To approach my doors, thou brazen-faced rogue,
My murderer and the filcher of my crown?
Come, answer this, didst thou detect in me
Some touch of cowardice or witlessness,
That made thee undertake this enterprise?
I seemed forsooth too simple to perceive
The serpent stealing on me in the dark,
Or else too weak to scotch it when I saw.
This thou art witless seeking to possess
Without a following or friends the crown,
A prize that followers and wealth must win.

CREON
Attend me. Thou hast spoken, 'tis my turn
To make reply. Then having heard me, judge.

OEDIPUS
Thou art glib of tongue, but I am slow to learn
Of thee; I know too well thy venomous hate.

CREON
First I would argue out this very point.

OEDIPUS
O argue not that thou art not a rogue.

CREON
If thou dost count a virtue stubbornness,
Unschooled by reason, thou art much astray.

OEDIPUS
If thou dost hold a kinsman may be wronged,
And no pains follow, thou art much to seek.

CREON
Therein thou judgest rightly, but this wrong
That thou allegest—tell me what it is.

OEDIPUS
Didst thou or didst thou not advise that I
Should call the priest?

CREON
Yes, and I stand to it.

OEDIPUS
Tell me how long is it since Laius . . .

CREON
Since Laius . . .? I follow not thy drift.

OEDIPUS
By violent hands was spirited away.

CREON
In the dim past, a many years agone.

OEDIPUS
Did the same prophet then pursue his craft?

CREON
Yes, skilled as now and in no less repute.

OEDIPUS
Did he at that time ever glance at me?

CREON
Not to my knowledge, not when I was by.

OEDIPUS
But was no search and inquisition made?

CREON
Surely full quest was made, but nothing learnt.

OEDIPUS
Why failed the seer to tell his story then?

CREON
I know not, and not knowing hold my tongue.

OEDIPUS
This much thou knowest and canst surely tell.

CREON
What's mean'st thou? All I know I will declare.

OEDIPUS
But for thy prompting never had the seer
Ascribed to me the death of Laius.

CREON
If so he thou knowest best; but I
Would put thee to the question in my turn.

OEDIPUS
Question and prove me murderer if thou canst.

CREON
Then let me ask thee, didst thou wed my sister?

OEDIPUS
A fact so plain I cannot well deny.

CREON
And as thy consort queen she shares the throne?

OEDIPUS
I grant her freely all her heart desires.

CREON
And with you twain I share the triple rule?

OEDIPUS
Yea, and it is that proves thee a false friend.

CREON
Not so, if thou wouldst reason with thyself,
As I with myself. First, I bid thee think,
Would any mortal choose a troubled reign
Of terrors rather than secure repose,
If the same power were given him? As for me,
I have no natural craving for the name
Of king, preferring to do kingly deeds,
And so thinks every sober-minded man.
Now all my needs are satisfied through thee,
And I have naught to fear; but were I king,
My acts would oft run counter to my will.
How could a title then have charms for me
Above the sweets of boundless influence?
I am not so infatuate as to grasp
The shadow when I hold the substance fast.
Now all men cry me Godspeed! wish me well,
And every suitor seeks to gain my ear,
If he would hope to win a grace from thee.
Why should I leave the better, choose the worse?
That were sheer madness, and I am not mad.
No such ambition ever tempted me,

Nor would I have a share in such intrigue.
And if thou doubt me, first to Delphi go,
There ascertain if my report was true
Of the god's answer; next investigate
If with the seer I plotted or conspired,
And if it prove so, sentence me to death,
Not by thy voice alone, but mine and thine.
But O condemn me not, without appeal,
On bare suspicion. 'Tis not right to adjudge
Bad men at random good, or good men bad.
I would as lief a man should cast away
The thing he counts most precious, his own life,
As spurn a true friend. Thou wilt learn in time
The truth, for time alone reveals the just;
A villain is detected in a day.

CHORUS
To one who walketh warily his words
Commend themselves; swift counsels are not sure.

OEDIPUS
When with swift strides the stealthy plotter stalks
I must be quick too with my counterplot.
To wait his onset passively, for him
Is sure success, for me assured defeat.

CREON
What then's thy will? To banish me the land?

OEDIPUS
I would not have thee banished, no, but dead,
That men may mark the wages envy reaps.

CREON
I see thou wilt not yield, nor credit me.

OEDIPUS
[None but a fool would credit such as thou.] [3]

CREON
Thou art not wise.

OEDIPUS
Wise for myself at least.

CREON
Why not for me too?

OEDIPUS
Why for such a knave?

CREON
Suppose thou lackest sense.

OEDIPUS
Yet kings must rule.

CREON
Not if they rule ill.

OEDIPUS
Oh my Thebans, hear him!

CREON
Thy Thebans? am not I a Theban too?

CHORUS
Cease, princes; lo there comes, and none too
    soon,
Jocasta from the palace. Who so fit
As peacemaker to reconcile your feud?

[Enter JOCASTA.]

JOCASTA
Misguided princes, why have ye upraised
This wordy wrangle? Are ye not ashamed,
While the whole land lies striken, thus to voice
Your private injuries? Go in, my lord;
Go home, my brother, and forebear to make
A public scandal of a petty grief.

CREON
My royal sister, Oedipus, thy lord,
Hath bid me choose (O dread alternative!)
An outlaw's exile or a felon's death.

OEDIPUS
Yes, lady; I have caught him practicing
Against my royal person his vile arts.

CREON
May I ne'er speed but die accursed, if I
In any way am guilty of this charge.

JOCASTA
Believe him, I adjure thee, Oedipus,
First for his solemn oath's sake, then for mine,
And for thine elders' sake who wait on thee.

CHORUS
(Str. 1)
Hearken, King, reflect, we pray thee, but not
    stubborn but relent.

OEDIPUS
Say to what should I consent?

CHORUS
Respect a man whose probity and troth
Are known to all and now confirmed by oath.

OEDIPUS
Dost know what grace thou cravest?

CHORUS
Yea, I know.

OEDIPUS
Declare it then and make thy meaning plain.

CHORUS
Brand not a friend whom babbling tongues assail;
Let not suspicion 'gainst his oath prevail.

OEDIPUS
Bethink you that in seeking this ye seek
In very sooth my death or banishment?

CHORUS
No, by the leader of the host divine!
(Str. 2)
Witness, thou Sun, such thought was never mine,
Unblest, unfriended may I perish,
If ever I such wish did cherish!
But O my heart is desolate
Musing on our striken State,
Doubly fall'n should discord grow
Twixt you twain, to crown our woe.

OEDIPUS
Well, let him go, no matter what it cost me,
Or certain death or shameful banishment,
For your sake I relent, not his; and him,
Where'er he be, my heart shall still abhor.

CREON
Thou art as sullen in thy yielding mood
As in thine anger thou wast truculent.
Such tempers justly plague themselves the most.

OEDIPUS
Leave me in peace and get thee gone.

CREON
I go,
By thee misjudged, but justified by these.

[Exeunt CREON]

CHORUS
(Ant. 1)
Lady, lead indoors thy consort; wherefore longer
    here delay?

JOCASTA
Tell me first how rose the fray.

CHORUS
Rumors bred unjust suspicious and injustice
    rankles sore.

JOCASTA
Were both at fault?

CHORUS
Both.

JOCASTA
What was the tale?

CHORUS
Ask me no more. The land is sore distressed;
'Twere better sleeping ills to leave at rest.

OEDIPUS
Strange counsel, friend! I know thou mean'st me
    well,
And yet would'st mitigate and blunt my zeal.

CHORUS
(Ant. 2)
King, I say it once again,
Witless were I proved, insane,
If I lightly put away
Thee my country's prop and stay,
Pilot who, in danger sought,
To a quiet haven brought
Our distracted State; and now
Who can guide us right but thou?

JOCASTA
Let me too, I adjure thee, know, O king,
What cause has stirred this unrelenting wrath.

OEDIPUS
I will, for thou art more to me than these.
Lady, the cause is Creon and his plots.

JOCASTA
But what provoked the quarrel? make this clear.

OEDIPUS
He points me out as Laius' murderer.

JOCASTA
Of his own knowledge or upon report?

OEDIPUS
He is too cunning to commit himself,
And makes a mouthpiece of a knavish seer.

JOCASTA
Then thou mayest ease thy conscience on that
    score.
Listen and I'll convince thee that no man
Hath scot or lot in the prophetic art.
Here is the proof in brief. An oracle
Once came to Laius (I will not say
'Twas from the Delphic god himself, but from
His ministers) declaring he was doomed
To perish by the hand of his own son,
A child that should be born to him by me.
Now Laius—so at least report affirmed—
Was murdered on a day by highwaymen,
No natives, at a spot where three roads meet.
As for the child, it was but three days old,
When Laius, its ankles pierced and pinned
Together, gave it to be cast away
By others on the trackless mountain side.
So then Apollo brought it not to pass
The child should be his father's murderer,
Or the dread terror find accomplishment,
And Laius be slain by his own son.
Such was the prophet's horoscope. O king,
Regard it not. Whate'er the god deems fit
To search, himself unaided will reveal.

OEDIPUS
What memories, what wild tumult of the soul
Came o'er me, lady, as I heard thee speak!

JOCASTA
What mean'st thou? What has shocked and
    startled thee?

OEDIPUS
Methought I heard thee say that Laius
Was murdered at the meeting of three roads.

JOCASTA
So ran the story that is current still.

OEDIPUS
Where did this happen? Dost thou know the
    place?

JOCASTA
Phocis the land is called; the spot is where
Branch roads from Delphi and from Daulis meet.

OEDIPUS
And how long is it since these things befell?

JOCASTA
'Twas but a brief while were thou wast proclaimed
Our country's ruler that the news was brought.

OEDIPUS
O Zeus, what hast thou willed to do with me!

JOCASTA
What is it, Oedipus, that moves thee so?

OEDIPUS
Ask me not yet; tell me the build and height
Of Laius? Was he still in manhood's prime?

JOCASTA
Tall was he, and his hair was lightly strewn
With silver; and not unlike thee in form.

OEDIPUS
O woe is me! Mehtinks unwittingly
I laid but now a dread curse on myself.

JOCASTA
What say'st thou? When I look upon thee, my
    king,
I tremble.

OEDIPUS
'Tis a dread presentiment
That in the end the seer will prove not blind.
One further question to resolve my doubt.

JOCASTA
I quail; but ask, and I will answer all.

OEDIPUS
Had he but few attendants or a train
Of armed retainers with him, like a prince?

JOCASTA
They were but five in all, and one of them
A herald; Laius in a mule-car rode.

OEDIPUS
Alas! 'tis clear as noonday now. But say,
Lady, who carried this report to Thebes?

JOCASTA
A serf, the sole survivor who returned.

OEDIPUS
Haply he is at hand or in the house?

JOCASTA
No, for as soon as he returned and found
Thee reigning in the stead of Laius slain,
He clasped my hand and supplicated me
To send him to the alps and pastures, where
He might be farthest from the sight of Thebes.
And so I sent him. 'Twas an honest slave
And well deserved some better recompense.

OEDIPUS
Fetch him at once. I fain would see the man.

JOCASTA
He shall be brought; but wherefore summon him?

OEDIPUS
Lady, I fear my tongue has overrun
Discretion; therefore I would question him.

JOCASTA
Well, he shall come, but may not I too claim
To share the burden of thy heart, my king?

OEDIPUS
And thou shalt not be frustrate of thy wish.
Now my imaginings have gone so far.
Who has a higher claim that thou to hear
My tale of dire adventures? Listen then.
My sire was Polybus of Corinth, and
My mother Merope, a Dorian;
And I was held the foremost citizen,
Till a strange thing befell me, strange indeed,
Yet scarce deserving all the heat it stirred.
A roisterer at some banquet, flown with wine,
Shouted "Thou art not true son of thy sire."
It irked me, but I stomached for the nonce
The insult; on the morrow I sought out
My mother and my sire and questioned them.
They were indignant at the random slur
Cast on my parentage and did their best
To comfort me, but still the venomed barb
Rankled, for still the scandal spread and grew.
So privily without their leave I went
To Delphi, and Apollo sent me back
Baulked of the knowledge that I came to seek.
But other grievous things he prophesied,

Woes, lamentations, mourning, portents dire;
To wit I should defile my mother's bed
And raise up seed too loathsome to behold,
And slay the father from whose loins I sprang.
Then, lady,—thou shalt hear the very truth—
As I drew near the triple-branching roads,
A herald met me and a man who sat
In a car drawn by colts—as in thy tale—
The man in front and the old man himself
Threatened to thrust me rudely from the path,
Then jostled by the charioteer in wrath
I struck him, and the old man, seeing this,
Watched till I passed and from his car brought
    down
Full on my head the double-pointed goad.
Yet was I quits with him and more; one stroke
Of my good staff sufficed to fling him clean
Out of the chariot seat and laid him prone.
And so I slew them every one. But if
Betwixt this stranger there was aught in common
With Laius, who more miserable than I,
What mortal could you find more god-abhorred?
Wretch whom no sojourner, no citizen
May harbor or address, whom all are bound
To harry from their homes. And this same curse
Was laid on me, and laid by none but me.
Yea with these hands all gory I pollute
The bed of him I slew. Say, am I vile?
Am I not utterly unclean, a wretch
Doomed to be banished, and in banishment
Forgo the sight of all my dearest ones,
And never tread again my native earth;
Or else to wed my mother and slay my sire,
Polybus, who begat me and upreared?
If one should say, this is the handiwork
Of some inhuman power, who could blame
His judgment? But, ye pure and awful gods,
Forbid, forbid that I should see that day!
May I be blotted out from living men
Ere such a plague spot set on me its brand!

CHORUS

We too, O king, are troubled; but till thou
Hast questioned the survivor, still hope on.

OEDIPUS

My hope is faint, but still enough survives
To bid me bide the coming of this herd.

JOCASTA

Suppose him here, what wouldst thou learn of
    him?

OEDIPUS

I'll tell thee, lady; if his tale agrees
With thine, I shall have 'scaped calamity.

JOCASTA

And what of special import did I say?

OEDIPUS

In thy report of what the herdsman said
Laius was slain by robbers; now if he
Still speaks of robbers, not a robber, I
Slew him not; "one" with "many" cannot square.
But if he says one lonely wayfarer,
The last link wanting to my guilt is forged.

JOCASTA

Well, rest assured, his tale ran thus at first,
Nor can he now retract what then he said;
Not I alone but all our townsfolk heard it.
E'en should he vary somewhat in his story,
He cannot make the death of Laius
In any wise jump with the oracle.
For Loxias said expressly he was doomed
To die by my child's hand, but he, poor babe,
He shed no blood, but perished first himself.
So much for divination. Henceforth I
Will look for signs neither to right nor left.

OEDIPUS

Thou reasonest well. Still I would have thee send
And fetch the bondsman hither. See to it.

JOCASTA

That will I straightway. Come, let us within.
I would do nothing that my lord mislikes.

[Exeunt OEDIPUS and JOCASTA]

CHORUS

(**Str. 1**)
My lot be still to lead
The life of innocence and fly
Irreverence in word or deed,
To follow still those laws ordained on high
Whose birthplace is the bright ethereal sky
No mortal birth they own,
Olympus their progenitor alone:
Ne'er shall they slumber in oblivion cold,

The god in them is strong and grows not old.
(Ant. 1)
Of insolence is bred
The tyrant; insolence full blown,
With empty riches surfeited,
Scales the precipitous height and grasps the
     throne.
Then topples o'er and lies in ruin prone;
No foothold on that dizzy steep.
But O may Heaven the true patriot keep
Who burns with emulous zeal to serve the State.
God is my help and hope, on him I wait.
(Str. 2)
But the proud sinner, or in word or deed,
That will not Justice heed,
Nor reverence the shrine
Of images divine,
Perdition seize his vain imaginings,
If, urged by greed profane,
He grasps at ill-got gain,
And lays an impious hand on holiest things.
Who when such deeds are done
Can hope heaven's bolts to shun?
If sin like this to honor can aspire,
Why dance I still and lead the sacred choir?
(Ant. 2)
No more I'll seek earth's central oracle,
Or Abae's hallowed cell,
Nor to Olympia bring
My votive offering.
If before all God's truth be not bade plain.
O Zeus, reveal thy might,
King, if thou'rt named aright
Omnipotent, all-seeing, as of old;
For Laius is forgot;
His weird, men heed it not;
Apollo is forsook and faith grows cold.

[Enter JOCASTA.]

JOCASTA

My lords, ye look amazed to see your queen
With wreaths and gifts of incense in her hands.
I had a mind to visit the high shrines,
For Oedipus is overwrought, alarmed
With terrors manifold. He will not use
His past experience, like a man of sense,
To judge the present need, but lends an ear
To any croaker if he augurs ill.
Since then my counsels naught avail, I turn
To thee, our present help in time of trouble,

Apollo, Lord Lycean, and to thee
My prayers and supplications here I bring.
Lighten us, lord, and cleanse us from this curse!
For now we all are cowed like mariners
Who see their helmsman dumbstruck in the
     storm.

[Enter Corinthian MESSENGER.]

MESSENGER

My masters, tell me where the palace is
Of Oedipus; or better, where's the king.

CHORUS

Here is the palace and he bides within;
This is his queen the mother of his children.

MESSENGER

All happiness attend her and the house,
Blessed is her husband and her marriage-bed.

JOCASTA

My greetings to thee, stranger; thy fair words
Deserve a like response. But tell me why
Thou comest—what thy need or what thy news.

MESSENGER

Good for thy consort and the royal house.

JOCASTA

What may it be? Whose messenger art thou?

MESSENGER

The Isthmian commons have resolved to make
Thy husband king—so 'twas reported there.

JOCASTA

What! is not aged Polybus still king?

MESSENGER

No, verily; he's dead and in his grave.

JOCASTA

What! is he dead, the sire of Oedipus?

MESSENGER

If I speak falsely, may I die myself.

JOCASTA

Quick, maiden, bear these tidings to my lord.
Ye god-sent oracles, where stand ye now!
This is the man whom Oedipus long shunned,
In dread to prove his murderer; and now
He dies in nature's course, not by his hand.

[Enter OEDIPUS.]

OEDIPUS
My wife, my queen, Jocasta, why hast thou
Summoned me from my palace?

JOCASTA
Hear this man,
And as thou hearest judge what has become
Of all those awe-inspiring oracles.

OEDIPUS
Who is this man, and what his news for me?

JOCASTA
He comes from Corinth and his message this:
Thy father Polybus hath passed away.

OEDIPUS
What? let me have it, stranger, from thy mouth.

MESSENGER
If I must first make plain beyond a doubt
My message, know that Polybus is dead.

OEDIPUS
By treachery, or by sickness visited?

MESSENGER
One touch will send an old man to his rest.

OEDIPUS
So of some malady he died, poor man.

MESSENGER
Yes, having measured the full span of years.

OEDIPUS
Out on it, lady! why should one regard
The Pythian hearth or birds that scream i' the air?
Did they not point at me as doomed to slay
My father? but he's dead and in his grave
And here am I who ne'er unsheathed a sword;
Unless the longing for his absent son
Killed him and so *I* slew him in a sense.
But, as they stand, the oracles are dead—
Dust, ashes, nothing, dead as Polybus.

JOCASTA
Say, did not I foretell this long ago?

OEDIPUS
Thou didst: but I was misled by my fear.

JOCASTA
Then let I no more weigh upon thy soul.

OEDIPUS
Must I not fear my mother's marriage bed.

JOCASTA
Why should a mortal man, the sport of chance,
With no assured foreknowledge, be afraid?
Best live a careless life from hand to mouth.
This wedlock with thy mother fear not thou.
How oft it chances that in dreams a man
Has wed his mother! He who least regards
Such brainsick phantasies lives most at ease.

OEDIPUS
I should have shared in full thy confidence,
Were not my mother living; since she lives
Though half convinced I still must live in dread.

JOCASTA
And yet thy sire's death lights out darkness much.

OEDIPUS
Much, but my fear is touching her who lives.

MESSENGER
Who may this woman be whom thus you fear?

OEDIPUS
Merope, stranger, wife of Polybus.

MESSENGER
And what of her can cause you any fear?

OEDIPUS
A heaven-sent oracle of dread import.

MESSENGER
A mystery, or may a stranger hear it?

OEDIPUS
Aye, 'tis no secret. Loxias once foretold
That I should mate with mine own mother, and
        shed
With my own hands the blood of my own sire.
Hence Corinth was for many a year to me
A home distant; and I trove abroad,
But missed the sweetest sight, my parents' face.

MESSENGER
Was this the fear that exiled thee from home?

OEDIPUS
Yea, and the dread of slaying my own sire.

MESSENGER
Why, since I came to give thee pleasure, King,
Have I not rid thee of this second fear?

OEDIPUS
Well, thou shalt have due guerdon for thy pains.

MESSENGER
Well, I confess what chiefly made me come
Was hope to profit by thy coming home.

OEDIPUS
Nay, I will ne'er go near my parents more.

MESSENGER
My son, 'tis plain, thou know'st not what thou
    doest.

OEDIPUS
How so, old man? For heaven's sake tell me all.

MESSENGER
If this is why thou dreadest to return.

OEDIPUS
Yea, lest the god's word be fulfilled in me.

MESSENGER
Lest through thy parents thou shouldst be
    accursed?

OEDIPUS
This and none other is my constant dread.

MESSENGER
Dost thou not know thy fears are baseless all?

OEDIPUS
How baseless, if I am their very son?

MESSENGER
Since Polybus was naught to thee in blood.

OEDIPUS
What say'st thou? was not Polybus my sire?

MESSENGER
As much thy sire as I am, and no more.

OEDIPUS
My sire no more to me than one who is naught?

MESSENGER
Since I begat thee not, no more did he.

OEDIPUS
What reason had he then to call me son?

MESSENGER
Know that he took thee from my hands, a gift.

OEDIPUS
Yet, if no child of his, he loved me well.

MESSENGER
A childless man till then, he warmed to thee.

OEDIPUS
A foundling or a purchased slave, this child?

MESSENGER
I found thee in Cithaeron's wooded glens.

OEDIPUS
What led thee to explore those upland glades?

MESSENGER
My business was to tend the mountain flocks.

OEDIPUS
A vagrant shepherd journeying for hire?

MESSENGER
True, but thy savior in that hour, my son.

OEDIPUS
My savior? from what harm? what ailed me then?

MESSENGER
Those ankle joints are evidence enow.

OEDIPUS
Ah, why remind me of that ancient sore?

MESSENGER
I loosed the pin that riveted thy feet.

OEDIPUS
Yes, from my cradle that dread brand I bore.

MESSENGER
Whence thou deriv'st the name that still is thine.

OEDIPUS
Who did it? I adjure thee, tell me who
Say, was it father, mother?

MESSENGER
I know not.
The man from whom I had thee may know more.

OEDIPUS
What, did another find me, not thyself?

MESSENGER
Not I; another shepherd gave thee me.

OEDIPUS
Who was he? Would'st thou know again the man?

MESSENGER
He passed indeed for one of Laius' house.

OEDIPUS
The king who ruled the country long ago?

MESSENGER
The same: he was a herdsman of the king.

OEDIPUS
And is he living still for me to see him?

MESSENGER
His fellow-countrymen should best know that.

OEDIPUS
Doth any bystander among you know
The herd he speaks of, or by seeing him
Afield or in the city? answer straight!
The hour hath come to clear this business up.

CHORUS
Methinks he means none other than the hind
Whom thou anon wert fain to see; but that
Our queen Jocasta best of all could tell.

OEDIPUS
Madam, dost know the man we sent to fetch?
Is the same of whom the stranger speaks?

JOCASTA
Who is the man? What matter? Let it be.
'Twere waste of thought to weigh such idle words.

OEDIPUS
No, with such guiding clues I cannot fail
To bring to light the secret of my birth.

JOCASTA
Oh, as thou carest for thy life, give o'er
This quest. Enough the anguish *I* endure.

OEDIPUS
Be of good cheer; though I be proved the son
Of a bondwoman, aye, through three descents
Triply a slave, thy honor is unsmirched.

JOCASTA
Yet humor me, I pray thee; do not this.

OEDIPUS
I cannot; I must probe this matter home.

JOCASTA
'Tis for thy sake I advise thee for the best.

OEDIPUS
I grow impatient of this best advice.

JOCASTA
Ah mayst thou ne'er discover who thou art!

OEDIPUS
Go, fetch me here the herd, and leave yon woman
To glory in her pride of ancestry.

JOCASTA
O woe is thee, poor wretch! With that last word
I leave thee, henceforth silent evermore.

[Exit JOCASTA]

CHORUS
Why, Oedipus, why stung with passionate grief
Hath the queen thus departed? Much I fear
From this dead calm will burst a storm of woes.

OEDIPUS
Let the storm burst, my fixed resolve still holds,
To learn my lineage, be it ne'er so low.
It may be she with all a woman's pride
Thinks scorn of my base parentage. But I
Who rank myself as Fortune's favorite child,
The giver of good gifts, shall not be shamed.
She is my mother and the changing moons
My brethren, and with them I wax and wane.
Thus sprung why should I fear to trace my birth?
Nothing can make me other than I am.

CHORUS
(Str.)
If my soul prophetic err not, if my wisdom aught
    avail,
Thee, Cithaeron, I shall hail,
As the nurse and foster-mother of our Oedipus
    shall greet
Ere tomorrow's full moon rises, and exalt thee as
    is meet.
Dance and song shall hymn thy praises, lover of
    our royal race.
Phoebus, may my words find grace!
(Ant.)
Child, who bare thee, nymph or goddess? sure thy
    sure was more than man,
Haply the hill-roamer Pan.

Of did Loxias beget thee, for he haunts the upland
    wold;
Or Cyllene's lord, or Bacchus, dweller on the
    hilltops cold?
Did some Heliconian Oread give him thee, a new-
    born joy?
Nymphs with whom he love to toy?

OEDIPUS
Elders, if I, who never yet before
Have met the man, may make a guess, methinks
I see the herdsman who we long have sought;
His time-worn aspect matches with the years
Of yonder aged messenger; besides
I seem to recognize the men who bring him
As servants of my own. But you, perchance,
Having in past days known or seen the herd,
May better by sure knowledge my surmise.

CHORUS
I recognize him; one of Laius' house;
A simple hind, but true as any man.

[Enter HERDSMAN.]

OEDIPUS
Corinthian, stranger, I address thee first,
Is this the man thou meanest!

MESSENGER
This is he.

OEDIPUS
And now old man, look up and answer all
I ask thee. Wast thou once of Laius' house?

HERDSMAN
I was, a thrall, not purchased but home-bred.

OEDIPUS
What was thy business? how wast thou employed?

HERDSMAN
The best part of my life I tended sheep.

OEDIPUS
What were the pastures thou didst most frequent?

HERDSMAN
Cithaeron and the neighboring alps.

OEDIPUS
Then there

Thou must have known yon man, at least by
    fame?

HERDSMAN
Yon man? in what way? what man dost thou
    mean?

OEDIPUS
The man here, having met him in past times . . .

HERDSMAN
Off-hand I cannot call him well to mind.

MESSENGER
No wonder, master. But I will revive
His blunted memories. Sure he can recall
What time together both we drove our flocks,
He two, I one, on the Cithaeron range,
For three long summers; I his mate from spring
Till rose Arcturus; then in winter time
I led mine home, he his to Laius' folds.
Did these things happen as I say, or no?

HERDSMAN
'Tis long ago, but all thou say'st is true.

MESSENGER
Well, thou mast then remember giving me
A child to rear as my own foster-son?

HERDSMAN
Why dost thou ask this question? What of that?

MESSENGER
Friend, he that stands before thee was that child.

HERDSMAN
A plague upon thee! Hold thy wanton tongue!

OEDIPUS
Softly, old man, rebuke him not; thy words
Are more deserving chastisement than his.

HERDSMAN
O best of masters, what is my offense?

OEDIPUS
Not answering what he asks about the child.

HERDSMAN
He speaks at random, babbles like a fool.

OEDIPUS
If thou lack'st grace to speak, I'll loose thy tongue.

HERDSMAN
For mercy's sake abuse not an old man.

OEDIPUS
Arrest the villain, seize and pinion him!

HERDSMAN
Alack, alack!
What have I done? what wouldst thou further
          learn?

OEDIPUS
Didst give this man the child of whom he asks?

HERDSMAN
I did; and would that I had died that day!

OEDIPUS
And die thou shalt unless thou tell the truth.

HERDSMAN
But, if I tell it, I am doubly lost.

OEDIPUS
The knave methinks will still prevaricate.

HERDSMAN
Nay, I confessed I gave it long ago.

OEDIPUS
Whence came it? was it thine, or given to thee?

HERDSMAN
I had it from another, 'twas not mine.

OEDIPUS
From whom of these our townsmen, and what
          house?

HERDSMAN
Forbear for God's sake, master, ask no more.

OEDIPUS
If I must question thee again, thou'rt lost.

HERDSMAN
Well then—it was a child of Laius' house.

OEDIPUS
Slave-born or one of Laius' own race?

HERDSMAN
Ah me!
I stand upon the perilous edge of speech.

OEDIPUS
And I of hearing, but I still must hear.

HERDSMAN
Know then the child was by repute his own,
But she within, thy consort best could tell.

OEDIPUS
What! she, she gave it thee?

HERDSMAN
'Tis so, my king.

OEDIPUS
With what intent?

HERDSMAN
To make away with it.

OEDIPUS
What, she its mother.

HERDSMAN
Fearing a dread weird.

OEDIPUS
What weird?

HERDSMAN
'Twas told that he should slay his sire.

OEDIPUS
What didst thou give it then to this old man?

HERDSMAN
Through pity, master, for the babe. I thought
He'd take it to the country whence he came;
But he preserved it for the worst of woes.
For if thou art in sooth what this man saith,
God pity thee! thou wast to misery born.

OEDIPUS
Ah me! ah me! all brought to pass, all true!
O light, may I behold thee nevermore!
I stand a wretch, in birth, in wedlock cursed,
A parricide, incestuously, triply cursed!

[*Exit OEDIPUS*]

CHORUS
(Str. 1)
Races of mortal man
Whose life is but a span,
I count ye but the shadow of a shade!

For he who most doth know
Of bliss, hath but the show;
A moment, and the visions pale and fade.
Thy fall, O Oedipus, thy piteous fall
Warns me none born of women blest to call.
(Ant. 1)
For he of marksmen best,
O Zeus, outshot the rest,
And won the prize supreme of wealth and power.
By him the vulture maid
Was quelled, her witchery laid;
He rose our savior and the land's strong tower.
We hailed thee king and from that day adored
Of mighty Thebes the universal lord.
(Str. 2)
O heavy hand of fate!
Who now more desolate,
Whose tale more sad than thine, whose lot more
 dire?
O Oedipus, discrowned head,
Thy cradle was thy marriage bed;
One harborage sufficed for son and sire.
How could the soil thy father eared so long
Endure to bear in silence such a wrong?
(Ant. 2)
All-seeing Time hath caught
Guilt, and to justice brought
The son and sire commingled in one bed.
O child of Laius' ill-starred race
Would I had ne'er beheld thy face;
I raise for thee a dirge as o'er the dead.
Yet, sooth to say, through thee I drew new breath,
And now through thee I feel a second death.

[Enter SECOND MESSENGER.]

SECOND MESSENGER
Most grave and reverend senators of Thebes,
What Deeds ye soon must hear, what sights
 behold
How will ye mourn, if, true-born patriots,
Ye reverence still the race of Labdacus!
Not Ister nor all Phasis' flood, I ween,
Could wash away the blood-stains from this
 house,
The ills it shrouds or soon will bring to light,
Ills wrought of malice, not unwittingly.
The worst to bear are self-inflicted wounds.

CHORUS
Grievous enough for all our tears and groans
Our past calamities; what canst thou add?

SECOND MESSENGER
My tale is quickly told and quickly heard.
Our sovereign lady queen Jocasta's dead.

CHORUS
Alas, poor queen! how came she by her death?

SECOND MESSENGER
By her own hand. And all the horror of it,
Not having seen, yet cannot comprehend.
Nathless, as far as my poor memory serves,
I will relate the unhappy lady's woe.
When in her frenzy she had passed inside
The vestibule, she hurried straight to win
The bridal-chamber, clutching at her hair
With both her hands, and, once within the room,
She shut the doors behind her with a crash.
"Laius," she cried, and called her husband dead
Long, long ago; her thought was of that child
By him begot, the son by whom the sire
Was murdered and the mother left to breed
With her own seed, a monstrous progeny.
Then she bewailed the marriage bed whereon
Poor wretch, she had conceived a double brood,
Husband by husband, children by her child.
What happened after that I cannot tell,
Nor how the end befell, for with a shriek
Burst on us Oedipus; all eyes were fixed
On Oedipus, as up and down he strode,
Nor could we mark her agony to the end.
For stalking to and fro "A sword!" he cried,
"Where is the wife, no wife, the teeming womb
That bore a double harvest, me and mine?"
And in his frenzy some supernal power
(No mortal, surely, none of us who watched him)
Guided his footsteps; with a terrible shriek,
As though one beckoned him, he crashed against
The folding doors, and from their staples forced
The wrenched bolts and hurled himself within.
Then we beheld the woman hanging there,
A running noose entwined about her neck.
But when he saw her, with a maddened roar
He loosed the cord; and when her wretched
 corpse
Lay stretched on earth, what followed—O 'twas
 dread!

He tore the golden brooches that upheld
Her queenly robes, upraised them high and smote
Full on his eye-balls, uttering words like these:
"No more shall ye behold such sights of woe,
Deeds I have suffered and myself have wrought;
Henceforward quenched in darkness shall ye see
Those ye should ne'er have seen; now blind to
    those
Whom, when I saw, I vainly yearned to know."
Such was the burden of his moan, whereto,
Not once but oft, he struck with his hand uplift
His eyes, and at each stroke the ensanguined orbs
Bedewed his beard, not oozing drop by drop,
But one black gory downpour, thick as hail.
Such evils, issuing from the double source,
Have whelmed them both, confounding man and
    wife.
Till now the storied fortune of this house
Was fortunate indeed; but from this day
Woe, lamentation, ruin, death, disgrace,
All ills that can be named, all, all are theirs.

CHORUS
But hath he still no respite from his pain?

SECOND MESSENGER
He cries, "Unbar the doors and let all Thebes
Behold the slayer of his sire, his mother's—"
That shameful word my lips may not repeat.
He vows to fly self-banished from the land,
Nor stay to bring upon his house the curse
Himself had uttered; but he has no strength
Nor one to guide him, and his torture's more
Than man can suffer, as yourselves will see.
For lo, the palace portals are unbarred,
And soon ye shall behold a sight so sad
That he who must abhorred would pity it.

[Enter OEDIPUS blinded.]

CHORUS
Woeful sight! more woeful none
These sad eyes have looked upon.
Whence this madness? None can tell
Who did cast on thee his spell,
prowling all thy life around,
Leaping with a demon bound.
Hapless wretch! how can I brook
On thy misery to look?
Though to gaze on thee I yearn,

Much to question, much to learn,
Horror-struck away I turn.

OEDIPUS
Ah me! ah woe is me!
Ah whither am I borne!
How like a ghost forlorn
My voice flits from me on the air!
On, on the demon goads. The end, ah where?

CHORUS
An end too dread to tell, too dark to see.

OEDIPUS
(Str. 1)
Dark, dark! The horror of darkness, like a shroud,
Wraps me and bears me on through mist and
    cloud.
Ah me, ah me! What spasms athwart me shoot,
What pangs of agonizing memory?

CHORUS
No marvel if in such a plight thou feel'st
The double weight of past and present woes.

OEDIPUS
(Ant. 1)
Ah friend, still loyal, constant still and kind,
Thou carest for the blind.
I know thee near, and though bereft of eyes,
Thy voice I recognize.

CHORUS
O doer of dread deeds, how couldst thou mar
Thy vision thus? What demon goaded thee?

OEDIPUS
(Str. 2)
Apollo, friend, Apollo, he it was
That brought these ills to pass;
But the right hand that dealt the blow
Was mine, none other. How,
How, could I longer see when sight
Brought no delight?

CHORUS
Alas! 'tis as thou sayest.

OEDIPUS
Say, friends, can any look or voice
Or touch of love henceforth my heart rejoice?
Haste, friends, no fond delay,

Take the twice cursed away
Far from all ken,
The man abhorred of gods, accursed of men.

CHORUS

O thy despair well suits thy desperate case.
Would I had never looked upon thy face!

OEDIPUS

(Ant. 2)

My curse on him whoe'er unrived
The waif's fell fetters and my life revived!
He meant me well, yet had he left me there,
He had saved my friends and me a world of care.

CHORUS

I too had wished it so.

OEDIPUS

Then had I never come to shed
My father's blood nor climbed my mother's bed;
The monstrous offspring of a womb defiled,
Co-mate of him who gendered me, and child.
Was ever man before afflicted thus,
Like Oedipus.

CHORUS

I cannot say that thou hast counseled well,
For thou wert better dead than living blind.

OEDIPUS

What's done was well done. Thou canst never
    shake
My firm belief. A truce to argument.
For, had I sight, I know not with what eyes
I could have met my father in the shades,
Or my poor mother, since against the twain
I sinned, a sin no gallows could atone.
Aye, but, ye say, the sight of children joys
A parent's eyes. What, born as mine were born?
No, such a sight could never bring me joy;
Nor this fair city with its battlements,
Its temples and the statues of its gods,
Sights from which I, now wretchedst of all,
Once ranked the foremost Theban in all Thebes,
By my own sentence am cut off, condemned
By my own proclamation 'gainst the wretch,
The miscreant by heaven itself declared
Unclean—and of the race of Laius.
Thus branded as a felon by myself,
How had I dared to look you in the face?

Nay, had I known a way to choke the springs
Of hearing, I had never shrunk to make
A dungeon of this miserable frame,
Cut off from sight and hearing; for 'tis bliss
to bide in regions sorrow cannot reach.
Why didst thou harbor me, Cithaeron, why
Didst thou not take and slay me? Then I never
Had shown to men the secret of my birth.
O Polybus, O Corinth, O my home,
Home of my ancestors (so wast thou called)
How fair a nursling then I seemed, how foul
The canker that lay festering in the bud!
Now is the blight revealed of root and fruit.
Ye triple high-roads, and thou hidden glen,
Coppice, and pass where meet the three-branched
    ways,
Ye drank my blood, the life-blood these hands
    spilt,
My father's; do ye call to mind perchance
Those deeds of mine ye witnessed and the work
I wrought thereafter when I came to Thebes?
O fatal wedlock, thou didst give me birth,
And, having borne me, sowed again my seed,
Mingling the blood of fathers, brothers, children,
Brides, wives and mothers, an incestuous brood,
All horrors that are wrought beneath the sun,
Horrors so foul to name them were unmeet.
O, I adjure you, hide me anywhere
Far from this land, or slay me straight, or cast me
Down to the depths of ocean out of sight.
Come hither, deign to touch an abject wretch;
Draw near and fear not; I myself must bear
The load of guilt that none but I can share.

[Enter CREON.]

CREON

Lo, here is Creon, the one man to grant
Thy prayer by action or advice, for he
Is left the State's sole guardian in thy stead.

OEDIPUS

Ah me! what words to accost him can I find?
What cause has he to trust me? In the past
I have bee proved his rancorous enemy.

CREON

Not in derision, Oedipus, I come
Nor to upbraid thee with thy past misdeeds.

(To BYSTANDERS)

But shame upon you! if ye feel no sense
Of human decencies, at least revere
The Sun whose light beholds and nurtures all.
Leave not thus nakedly for all to gaze at
A horror neither earth nor rain from heaven
Nor light will suffer. Lead him straight within,
For it is seemly that a kinsman's woes
Be heard by kin and seen by kin alone.

OEDIPUS

O listen, since thy presence comes to me
A shock of glad surprise—so noble thou,
And I so vile—O grant me one small boon.
I ask it not on my behalf, but thine.

CREON

And what the favor thou wouldst crave of me?

OEDIPUS

Forth from thy borders thrust me with all speed;
Set me within some vasty desert where
No mortal voice shall greet me any more.

CREON

This had I done already, but I deemed
It first behooved me to consult the god.

OEDIPUS

His will was set forth fully—to destroy
The parricide, the scoundrel; and I am he.

CREON

Yea, so he spake, but in our present plight
'Twere better to consult the god anew.

OEDIPUS

Dare ye inquire concerning such a wretch?

CREON

Yea, for thyself wouldst credit now his word.

OEDIPUS

Aye, and on thee in all humility
I lay this charge: let her who lies within
Receive such burial as thou shalt ordain;
Such rites 'tis thine, as brother, to perform.
But for myself, O never let my Thebes,
The city of my sires, be doomed to bear
The burden of my presence while I live.
No, let me be a dweller on the hills,
On yonder mount Cithaeron, famed as mine,
My tomb predestined for me by my sire
And mother, while they lived, that I may die

Slain as they sought to slay me, when alive.
This much I know full surely, nor disease
Shall end my days, nor any common chance;
For I had ne'er been snatched from death, unless
I was predestined to some awful doom.
So be it. I reck not how Fate deals with me
But my unhappy children—for my sons
Be not concerned, O Creon, they are men,
And for themselves, where'er they be, can fend.
But for my daughters twain, poor innocent maids,
Who ever sat beside me at the board
Sharing my viands, drinking of my cup,
For them, I pray thee, care, and, if thou willst,
O might I feel their touch and make my moan.
Hear me, O prince, my noble-hearted prince!
Could I but blindly touch them with my hands
I'd think they still were mine, as when I saw.

[ANTIGONE and ISMENE are led in.]

What say I? can it be my pretty ones
Whose sobs I hear? Has Creon pitied me
And sent me my two darlings? Can this be?

CREON

'Tis true; 'twas I procured thee this delight,
Knowing the joy they were to thee of old.

OEDIPUS

God speed thee! and as meed for bringing them
May Providence deal with thee kindlier
Than it has dealt with me! O children mine,
Where are ye? Let me clasp you with these hands,
A brother's hands, a father's; hands that made
Lack-luster sockets of his once bright eyes;
Hands of a man who blindly, recklessly,
Became your sire by her from whom he sprang.
Though I cannot behold you, I must weep
In thinking of the evil days to come,
The slights and wrongs that men will put upon
    you.
Where'er ye go to feast or festival,
No merrymaking will it prove for you,
But oft abashed in tears ye will return.
And when ye come to marriageable years,
Where's the bold wooers who will jeopardize
To take unto himself such disrepute
As to my children's children still must cling,
For what of infamy is lacking here?
"Their father slew his father, sowed the seed
Where he himself was gendered, and begat

These maidens at the source wherefrom he
    sprang."
Such are the gibes that men will cast at you.
Who then will wed you? None, I ween, but ye
Must pine, poor maids, in single barrenness.
O Prince, Menoeceus' son, to thee, I turn,
With the it rests to father them, for we
Their natural parents, both of us, are lost.
O leave them not to wander poor, unwed,
Thy kin, nor let them share my low estate.
O pity them so young, and but for thee
All destitute. Thy hand upon it, Prince.
To you, my children I had much to say,
Were ye but ripe to hear. Let this suffice:
Pray ye may find some home and live content,
And may your lot prove happier than your sire's.

CREON
Thou hast had enough of weeping; pass within.

OEDIPUS
I must obey,
Though 'tis grievous.

CREON
Weep not, everything must have its day.

OEDIPUS
Well I go, but on conditions.

CREON
What thy terms for going, say.

OEDIPUS
Send me from the land an exile.

CREON
Ask this of the gods, not me.

OEDIPUS
But I am the gods' abhorrence.

CREON
Then they soon will grant thy plea.

OEDIPUS
Lead me hence, then, I am willing.

CREON
Come, but let thy children go.

OEDIPUS
Rob me not of these my children!

CREON
Crave not mastery in all,
For the mastery that raised thee was thy bane and
    wrought thy fall.

CHORUS
Look ye, countrymen and Thebans, this is
    Oedipus the great,
He who knew the Sphinx's riddle and was
    mightiest in our state.
Who of all our townsmen gazed not on his fame
    with envious eyes?
Now, in what a sea of troubles sunk and
    overwhelmed he lies!
Therefore wait to see life's ending ere thou count
    one mortal blest;
Wait till free from pain and sorrow he has gained
    his final rest.

Footnotes

1. Dr. Kennedy and others render "Since to men of experience I see that also comparisons of their counsels are in most lively use."
2. Literally "not to call them thine," but the Greek may be rendered "In order not to reveal thine."
3. The Greek text that occurs in this place has been lost.
   - Biblical Stories
   - Celtic Mythology
   - Egyptian Mythology
   - Greek Mythology
   - Japanese Mythology
   - Mayan Mythology
   - Mesopotamian Mythology
   - Norse Mythology
   - Roman Mythology
   - Zoroastrianism

2

Hamlet, Prince of Denmark

Play by William Shakespeare (1564–1616)

PERSONS REPRESENTED

Claudius, King of Denmark.
Hamlet, Son to the former, and Nephew to the present King.
Polonius, Lord Chamberlain.
Horatio, Friend to Hamlet.
Laertes, Son to Polonius.
Voltimand, Courtier.
Cornelius, Courtier.
Rosencrantz, Courtier.
Guildenstern, Courtier.
Osric, Courtier.
A Gentleman, Courtier.
A Priest.
Marcellus, Officer.
Bernardo, Officer.
Francisco, a Soldier.
Reynaldo, Servant to Polonius.
Players.
Two Clowns, Grave-diggers.
Fortinbras, Prince of Norway.
A Captain.
English Ambassadors.

"Hamlet", 1605

Ghost of Hamlet's Father.
Gertrude, Queen of Denmark, and Mother of Hamlet.
Ophelia, Daughter to Polonius.
Lords, Ladies, Officers, Soldiers, Sailors, Messengers, and other Attendants.

SCENE

Elsinore.

HAMLET, PRINCE OF DENMARK

ACT I.

SCENE I. Elsinore. A platform before the Castle.

[Francisco at his post. Enter to him Bernardo.]

BER.
Who's there?

FRAN.
Nay, answer me: stand, and unfold yourself.

BER.
Long live the king!

FRAN.
Bernardo?

BER.
He.

FRAN.
You come most carefully upon your hour.

BER.
'Tis now struck twelve. Get thee to bed, Francisco.

FRAN.
For this relief much thanks: 'tis bitter cold,
And I am sick at heart.

BER.
Have you had quiet guard?

FRAN.
Not a mouse stirring.

BER.
Well, good night.
If you do meet Horatio and Marcellus,
The rivals of my watch, bid them make haste.

FRAN.
I think I hear them.—Stand, ho! Who is there?

[Enter Horatio and Marcellus.]

HOR.
Friends to this ground.

MAR.
And liegemen to the Dane.

FRAN.
Give you good-night.

MAR.
O, farewell, honest soldier;
Who hath reliev'd you?

FRAN.
Bernardo has my place.
Give you good-night.
[Exit.]

MAR.
Holla! Bernardo!

BER.
Say.
What, is Horatio there?

HOR.
A piece of him.

BER.

Welcome, Horatio:—Welcome, good Marcellus.

MAR.

What, has this thing appear'd again to-night?

BER.

I have seen nothing.

MAR.

Horatio says 'tis but our fantasy,
And will not let belief take hold of him
Touching this dreaded sight, twice seen of us:
Therefore I have entreated him along
With us to watch the minutes of this night;
That, if again this apparition come
He may approve our eyes and speak to it.

HOR.

Tush, tush, 'twill not appear.

BER.

Sit down awhile,
And let us once again assail your ears,
That are so fortified against our story,
What we two nights have seen.

HOR.

Well, sit we down,
And let us hear Bernardo speak of this.

BER.

Last night of all,
When yond same star that's westward from the
              pole
Had made his course to illume that part of heaven
Where now it burns, Marcellus and myself,
The bell then beating one,—

MAR.

Peace, break thee off; look where it comes again!

[Enter Ghost, armed.]

BER.

In the same figure, like the king that's dead.

MAR.

Thou art a scholar; speak to it, Horatio.

BER.

Looks it not like the King? mark it, Horatio.

HOR.

Most like:—it harrows me with fear and wonder.

BER.

It would be spoke to.

MAR.

Question it, Horatio.

HOR.

What art thou, that usurp'st this time of night,
Together with that fair and warlike form
In which the majesty of buried Denmark
Did sometimes march? By heaven I charge thee,
              speak!

MAR.

It is offended.

BER.

See, it stalks away!

HOR.

Stay! speak, speak! I charge thee speak!

[Exit Ghost.]

MAR.

'Tis gone, and will not answer.

BER.

How now, Horatio! You tremble and look pale:
Is not this something more than fantasy?
What think you on't?

HOR.

Before my God, I might not this believe
Without the sensible and true avouch
Of mine own eyes.

MAR.

Is it not like the King?

HOR.

As thou art to thyself:
Such was the very armour he had on
When he the ambitious Norway combated;
So frown'd he once when, in an angry parle,
He smote the sledded Polacks on the ice.
'Tis strange.

MAR.

Thus twice before, and jump at this dead hour,
With martial stalk hath he gone by our watch.

HOR.

In what particular thought to work I know not;
But, in the gross and scope of my opinion,
This bodes some strange eruption to our state.

MAR.

Good now, sit down, and tell me, he that knows,
Why this same strict and most observant watch
So nightly toils the subject of the land;

And why such daily cast of brazen cannon,
And foreign mart for implements of war;
Why such impress of shipwrights, whose sore task
Does not divide the Sunday from the week;
What might be toward, that this sweaty haste
Doth make the night joint-labourer with the day:
Who is't that can inform me?

HOR.
That can I;
At least, the whisper goes so. Our last king,
Whose image even but now appear'd to us,
Was, as you know, by Fortinbras of Norway,
Thereto prick'd on by a most emulate pride,
Dar'd to the combat; in which our valiant
        Hamlet,—
For so this side of our known world esteem'd
        him,—
Did slay this Fortinbras; who, by a seal'd compact,
Well ratified by law and heraldry,
Did forfeit, with his life, all those his lands,
Which he stood seiz'd of, to the conqueror:
Against the which, a moiety competent
Was gaged by our king; which had return'd
To the inheritance of Fortinbras,
Had he been vanquisher; as by the same cov'nant,
And carriage of the article design'd,
His fell to Hamlet. Now, sir, young Fortinbras,
Of unimproved mettle hot and full,
Hath in the skirts of Norway, here and there,
Shark'd up a list of lawless resolutes,
For food and diet, to some enterprise
That hath a stomach in't; which is no other,—
As it doth well appear unto our state,—
But to recover of us, by strong hand,
And terms compulsatory, those foresaid lands
So by his father lost: and this, I take it,
Is the main motive of our preparations,
The source of this our watch, and the chief head
Of this post-haste and romage in the land.

BER.
I think it be no other but e'en so:
Well may it sort, that this portentous figure
Comes armed through our watch; so like the king
That was and is the question of these wars.

HOR.
A mote it is to trouble the mind's eye.
In the most high and palmy state of Rome,
A little ere the mightiest Julius fell,
The graves stood tenantless, and the sheeted dead
Did squeak and gibber in the Roman streets;
As, stars with trains of fire and dews of blood,
Disasters in the sun; and the moist star,
Upon whose influence Neptune's empire stands,
Was sick almost to doomsday with eclipse:
And even the like precurse of fierce events,—
As harbingers preceding still the fates,
And prologue to the omen coming on,—
Have heaven and earth together demonstrated
Unto our climature and countrymen.—
But, soft, behold! lo, where it comes again!

[Re-enter Ghost.]

I'll cross it, though it blast me.—Stay, illusion!
If thou hast any sound, or use of voice,
Speak to me:
If there be any good thing to be done,
That may to thee do ease, and, race to me,
Speak to me:
If thou art privy to thy country's fate,
Which, happily, foreknowing may avoid,
O, speak!
Or if thou hast uphoarded in thy life
Extorted treasure in the womb of earth,
For which, they say, you spirits oft walk in death,

[The cock crows.]

Speak of it:—stay, and speak!—Stop it, Marcellus!

MAR.
Shall I strike at it with my partisan?

HOR.
Do, if it will not stand.

BER.
'Tis here!

HOR.
'Tis here!

MAR.
'Tis gone!

[Exit Ghost.]

We do it wrong, being so majestical,
To offer it the show of violence;
For it is, as the air, invulnerable,
And our vain blows malicious mockery.

BER.
It was about to speak, when the cock crew.

HOR.

And then it started, like a guilty thing
Upon a fearful summons. I have heard
The cock, that is the trumpet to the morn,
Doth with his lofty and shrill-sounding throat
Awake the god of day; and at his warning,
Whether in sea or fire, in earth or air,
The extravagant and erring spirit hies
To his confine: and of the truth herein
This present object made probation.

MAR.

It faded on the crowing of the cock.
Some say that ever 'gainst that season comes
Wherein our Saviour's birth is celebrated,
The bird of dawning singeth all night long;
And then, they say, no spirit dare stir abroad;
The nights are wholesome; then no planets strike,
No fairy takes, nor witch hath power to charm;
So hallow'd and so gracious is the time.

HOR.

So have I heard, and do in part believe it.
But, look, the morn, in russet mantle clad,
Walks o'er the dew of yon high eastward hill:
Break we our watch up: and by my advice,
Let us impart what we have seen to-night
Unto young Hamlet; for, upon my life,
This spirit, dumb to us, will speak to him:
Do you consent we shall acquaint him with it,
As needful in our loves, fitting our duty?

MAR.

Let's do't, I pray; and I this morning know
Where we shall find him most conveniently.

[Exeunt.]

SCENE II. Elsinore. A room of state in the Castle.

[Enter the King, Queen, Hamlet, Polonius, Laertes,
    Voltimand, Cornelius, Lords, and Attendant.]

KING.

Though yet of Hamlet our dear brother's death
The memory be green, and that it us befitted
To bear our hearts in grief, and our whole
        kingdom
To be contracted in one brow of woe;
Yet so far hath discretion fought with nature
That we with wisest sorrow think on him,
Together with remembrance of ourselves.
Therefore our sometime sister, now our queen,
Th' imperial jointress to this warlike state,
Have we, as 'twere with a defeated joy,—
With an auspicious and one dropping eye,
With mirth in funeral, and with dirge in
        marriage,
In equal scale weighing delight and dole,—
Taken to wife; nor have we herein barr'd
Your better wisdoms, which have freely gone
With this affair along:—or all, our thanks.
Now follows, that you know, young Fortinbras,
Holding a weak supposal of our worth,
Or thinking by our late dear brother's death
Our state to be disjoint and out of frame,
Colleagued with this dream of his advantage,
He hath not fail'd to pester us with message,
Importing the surrender of those lands
Lost by his father, with all bonds of law,
To our most valiant brother. So much for him,—
Now for ourself and for this time of meeting:
Thus much the business is:—we have here writ
To Norway, uncle of young Fortinbras,—
Who, impotent and bed-rid, scarcely hears
Of this his nephew's purpose,—to suppress
His further gait herein; in that the levies,
The lists, and full proportions are all made
Out of his subject:—and we here dispatch
You, good Cornelius, and you, Voltimand,
For bearers of this greeting to old Norway;
Giving to you no further personal power
To business with the king, more than the scope
Of these dilated articles allow.
Farewell; and let your haste commend your duty.

COR. AND VOLT.

In that and all things will we show our duty.

KING.

We doubt it nothing: heartily farewell.

[Exeunt Voltimand and Cornelius.]

And now, Laertes, what's the news with you?
You told us of some suit; what is't, Laertes?
You cannot speak of reason to the Dane,
And lose your voice: what wouldst thou beg,
        Laertes,
That shall not be my offer, not thy asking?
The head is not more native to the heart,
The hand more instrumental to the mouth,

Than is the throne of Denmark to thy father.
What wouldst thou have, Laertes?

LAER.
Dread my lord,
Your leave and favour to return to France;
From whence though willingly I came to
    Denmark,
To show my duty in your coronation;
Yet now, I must confess, that duty done,
My thoughts and wishes bend again toward
    France,
And bow them to your gracious leave and pardon.

KING.
Have you your father's leave? What says Polonius?

POL.
He hath, my lord, wrung from me my slow leave
By laboursome petition; and at last
Upon his will I seal'd my hard consent:
I do beseech you, give him leave to go.

KING.
Take thy fair hour, Laertes; time be thine,
And thy best graces spend it at thy will!—
But now, my cousin Hamlet, and my son—

HAM.
[Aside.] A little more than kin, and less than kind!

KING.
How is it that the clouds still hang on you?

HAM.
Not so, my lord; I am too much i' the sun.

QUEEN.
Good Hamlet, cast thy nighted colour off,
And let thine eye look like a friend on Denmark.
Do not for ever with thy vailed lids
Seek for thy noble father in the dust:
Thou know'st 'tis common,—all that lives must
    die,
Passing through nature to eternity.

HAM.
Ay, madam, it is common.

QUEEN.
If it be,
Why seems it so particular with thee?

HAM.
Seems, madam! Nay, it is; I know not seems.
'Tis not alone my inky cloak, good mother,
Nor customary suits of solemn black,
Nor windy suspiration of forc'd breath,

No, nor the fruitful river in the eye,
Nor the dejected 'havior of the visage,
Together with all forms, moods, shows of grief,
That can denote me truly: these, indeed, seem;
For they are actions that a man might play;
But I have that within which passeth show;
These but the trappings and the suits of woe.

KING.
'Tis sweet and commendable in your nature,
    Hamlet,
To give these mourning duties to your father;
But, you must know, your father lost a father;
That father lost, lost his; and the survivor bound,
In filial obligation, for some term
To do obsequious sorrow: but to persevere
In obstinate condolement is a course
Of impious stubbornness; 'tis unmanly grief;
It shows a will most incorrect to heaven;
A heart unfortified, a mind impatient;
An understanding simple and unschool'd;
For what we know must be, and is as common
As any the most vulgar thing to sense,
Why should we, in our peevish opposition,
Take it to heart? Fie! 'tis a fault to heaven,
A fault against the dead, a fault to nature,
To reason most absurd; whose common theme
Is death of fathers, and who still hath cried,
From the first corse till he that died to-day,
'This must be so.' We pray you, throw to earth
This unprevailing woe; and think of us
As of a father: for let the world take note
You are the most immediate to our throne;
And with no less nobility of love
Than that which dearest father bears his son
Do I impart toward you. For your intent
In going back to school in Wittenberg,
It is most retrograde to our desire:
And we beseech you bend you to remain
Here in the cheer and comfort of our eye,
Our chiefest courtier, cousin, and our son.

QUEEN.
Let not thy mother lose her prayers, Hamlet:
I pray thee stay with us; go not to Wittenberg.

HAM.
I shall in all my best obey you, madam.

KING.
Why, 'tis a loving and a fair reply:
Be as ourself in Denmark.—Madam, come;
This gentle and unforc'd accord of Hamlet

Sits smiling to my heart: in grace whereof,
No jocund health that Denmark drinks to-day
But the great cannon to the clouds shall tell;
And the king's rouse the heaven shall bruit again,
Re-speaking earthly thunder. Come away.

[Exeunt all but Hamlet.]

HAM.
O that this too too solid flesh would melt,
Thaw, and resolve itself into a dew!
Or that the Everlasting had not fix'd
His canon 'gainst self-slaughter! O God! O God!
How weary, stale, flat, and unprofitable
Seem to me all the uses of this world!
Fie on't! O fie! 'tis an unweeded garden,
That grows to seed; things rank and gross in
        nature
Possess it merely. That it should come to this!
But two months dead!—nay, not so much, not
        two:
So excellent a king; that was, to this,
Hyperion to a satyr; so loving to my mother,
That he might not beteem the winds of heaven
Visit her face too roughly. Heaven and earth!
Must I remember? Why, she would hang on him
As if increase of appetite had grown
By what it fed on: and yet, within a month,—
Let me not think on't,—Frailty, thy name is
        woman!—
A little month; or ere those shoes were old
With which she followed my poor father's body
Like Niobe, all tears;—why she, even she,—
O God! a beast that wants discourse of reason,
Would have mourn'd longer,—married with mine
        uncle,
My father's brother; but no more like my father
Than I to Hercules: within a month;
Ere yet the salt of most unrighteous tears
Had left the flushing in her galled eyes,
She married:— O, most wicked speed, to post
With such dexterity to incestuous sheets!
It is not, nor it cannot come to good;
But break my heart,—for I must hold my tongue!

[Enter Horatio, Marcellus, and Bernardo.]

HOR.
Hail to your lordship!

HAM.
I am glad to see you well:
Horatio,—or I do forget myself.

HOR.
The same, my lord, and your poor Servant. ever.

HAM.
Sir, my good friend; I'll change that name with
        you:
And what make you from Wittenberg, Horatio?—
Marcellus?

MAR.
My good lord,—

HAM.
I am very glad to see you.—Good even, sir.—
But what, in faith, make you from Wittenberg?

HOR.
A truant disposition, good my lord.

HAM.
I would not hear your enemy say so;
Nor shall you do my ear that violence,
To make it truster of your own report
Against yourself: I know you are no truant.
But what is your affair in Elsinore?
We'll teach you to drink deep ere you depart.

HOR.
My lord, I came to see your father's funeral.

HAM.
I prithee do not mock me, fellow-student.
I think it was to see my mother's wedding.

HOR.
Indeed, my lord, it follow'd hard upon.

HAM.
Thrift, thrift, Horatio! The funeral bak'd meats
Did coldly furnish forth the marriage tables.
Would I had met my dearest foe in heaven
Or ever I had seen that day, Horatio!—
My father,—methinks I see my father.

HOR.
Where, my lord?

HAM.
In my mind's eye, Horatio.

HOR.
I saw him once; he was a goodly King.

HAM.
He was a man, take him for all in all,
I shall not look upon his like again.

HOR.
My lord, I think I saw him yesternight.

HAM.
Saw who?

HOR.
My lord, the king your father.

HAM.
The King my father!

HOR.
Season your admiration for awhile
With an attent ear, till I may deliver,
Upon the witness of these gentlemen,
This marvel to you.

HAM.
For God's love let me hear.

HOR.
Two nights together had these gentlemen,
Marcellus and Bernardo, on their watch
In the dead vast and middle of the night,
Been thus encounter'd. A figure like your father,
Armed at point exactly, cap-a-pe,
Appears before them and with solemn march
Goes slow and stately by them: thrice he walk'd
By their oppress'd and fear-surprised eyes,
Within his truncheon's length; whilst they, distill'd
Almost to jelly with the act of fear,
Stand dumb, and speak not to him. This to me
In dreadful secrecy impart they did;
And I with them the third night kept the watch:
Where, as they had deliver'd, both in time,
Form of the thing, each word made true and
       good,
The apparition comes: I knew your father;
These hands are not more like.

HAM.
But where was this?

MAR.
My lord, upon the platform where we watch'd.

HAM.
Did you not speak to it?

HOR.
My lord, I did;
But answer made it none: yet once methought
It lifted up it head, and did address
Itself to motion, like as it would speak:
But even then the morning cock crew loud,
And at the sound it shrunk in haste away,
And vanish'd from our sight.

HAM.
'Tis very strange.

HOR.
As I do live, my honour'd lord, 'tis true;
And we did think it writ down in our duty
To let you know of it.

HAM.
Indeed, indeed, sirs, but this troubles me.
Hold you the watch to-night?

MAR. AND BER.
We do, my lord.

HAM.
Arm'd, say you?
Both.
Arm'd, my lord.

HAM.
From top to toe?
Both.
My lord, from head to foot.

HAM.
Then saw you not his face?

HOR.
O, yes, my lord: he wore his beaver up.

HAM.
What, look'd he frowningly?

HOR.
A countenance more in sorrow than in anger.

HAM.
Pale or red?

HOR.
Nay, very pale.

HAM.
And fix'd his eyes upon you?

HOR.
Most constantly.

HAM.
I would I had been there.

HOR.
It would have much amaz'd you.

HAM.
Very like, very like. Stay'd it long?

HOR.
While one with moderate haste might tell a
       hundred.

MAR. AND BER.

Longer, longer.

HOR.

Not when I saw't.

HAM.

His beard was grizzled,—no?

HOR.

It was, as I have seen it in his life,
A sable silver'd.

HAM.

I will watch to-night;
Perchance 'twill walk again.

HOR.

I warr'nt it will.

HAM.

If it assume my noble father's person,
I'll speak to it, though hell itself should gape
And bid me hold my peace. I pray you all,
If you have hitherto conceal'd this sight,
Let it be tenable in your silence still;
And whatsoever else shall hap to-night,
Give it an understanding, but no tongue:
I will requite your loves. So, fare ye well:
Upon the platform, 'twixt eleven and twelve,
I'll visit you.

ALL.

Our duty to your honour.

HAM.

Your loves, as mine to you: farewell.

[*Exeunt Horatio, Marcellus, and Bernardo.*]

My father's spirit in arms! All is not well;
I doubt some foul play: would the night were
        come!
Till then sit still, my soul: foul deeds will rise,
Though all the earth o'erwhelm them, to men's
        eyes.

[*Exit.*]

SCENE III. A Room in Polonius's house.

[*Enter Laertes and Ophelia.*]

LAER.

My necessaries are embark'd: farewell:
And, sister, as the winds give benefit

And convoy is assistant, do not sleep,
But let me hear from you.

OPH.

Do you doubt that?

LAER.

For Hamlet, and the trifling of his favour,
Hold it a fashion, and a toy in blood:
A violet in the youth of primy nature,
Forward, not permanent, sweet, not lasting;
The perfume and suppliance of a minute;
No more.

OPH.

No more but so?

LAER.

Think it no more:
For nature, crescent, does not grow alone
In thews and bulk; but as this temple waxes,
The inward service of the mind and soul
Grows wide withal. Perhaps he loves you now;
And now no soil nor cautel doth besmirch
The virtue of his will: but you must fear,
His greatness weigh'd, his will is not his own;
For he himself is subject to his birth:
He may not, as unvalu'd persons do,
Carve for himself; for on his choice depends
The safety and health of this whole state;
And therefore must his choice be circumscrib'd
Unto the voice and yielding of that body
Whereof he is the head. Then if he says he loves
        you,
It fits your wisdom so far to believe it
As he in his particular act and place
May give his saying deed; which is no further
Than the main voice of Denmark goes withal.
Then weigh what loss your honour may sustain
If with too credent ear you list his songs,
Or lose your heart, or your chaste treasure open
To his unmaster'd importunity.
Fear it, Ophelia, fear it, my dear sister;
And keep you in the rear of your affection,
Out of the shot and danger of desire.
The chariest maid is prodigal enough
If she unmask her beauty to the moon:
Virtue itself scopes not calumnious strokes:
The canker galls the infants of the spring
Too oft before their buttons be disclos'd:
And in the morn and liquid dew of youth
Contagious blastments are most imminent.

Be wary then; best safety lies in fear:
Youth to itself rebels, though none else near.

OPH.
I shall th' effect of this good lesson keep
As watchman to my heart. But, good my brother,
Do not, as some ungracious pastors do,
Show me the steep and thorny way to heaven;
Whilst, like a puff'd and reckless libertine,
Himself the primrose path of dalliance treads
And recks not his own read.

LAER.
O, fear me not.
I stay too long:—but here my father comes.

[Enter Polonius.]

A double blessing is a double grace;
Occasion smiles upon a second leave.

POL.
Yet here, Laertes! aboard, aboard, for shame!
The wind sits in the shoulder of your sail,
And you are stay'd For. There,—my blessing with
      thee!

[Laying his hand on Laertes's head.]

And these few precepts in thy memory
Look thou character. Give thy thoughts no
      tongue,
Nor any unproportion'd thought his act.
Be thou familiar, but by no means vulgar.
Those friends thou hast, and their adoption tried,
Grapple them unto thy soul with hoops of steel;
But do not dull thy palm with entertainment
Of each new-hatch'd, unfledg'd comrade. Beware
Of entrance to a quarrel; but, being in,
Bear't that the opposed may beware of thee.
Give every man thine ear, but few thy voice:
Take each man's censure, but reserve thy
      judgment.
Costly thy habit as thy purse can buy,
But not express'd in fancy; rich, not gaudy:
For the apparel oft proclaims the man;
And they in France of the best rank and station
Are most select and generous chief in that.
Neither a borrower nor a lender be:
For loan oft loses both itself and friend;
And borrowing dulls the edge of husbandry.
This above all,—to thine own self be true;
And it must follow, as the night the day,

Thou canst not then be false to any man.
Farewell: my blessing season this in thee!

LAER.
Most humbly do I take my leave, my lord.

POL.
The time invites you; go, your Servants tend.

LAER.
Farewell, Ophelia; and remember well
What I have said to you.

OPH.
'Tis in my memory lock'd,
And you yourself shall keep the key of it.

LAER.
Farewell.

[Exit.]

POL.
What is't, Ophelia, he hath said to you?

OPH.
So please you, something touching the Lord
      Hamlet.

POL.
Marry, well bethought:
'Tis told me he hath very oft of late
Given private time to you; and you yourself
Have of your audience been most free and
      bounteous;
If it be so,—as so 'tis put on me,
And that in way of caution,—I must tell you
You do not understand yourself so clearly
As it behooves my daughter and your honour.
What is between you? give me up the truth.

OPH.
He hath, my lord, of late made many tenders
Of his affection to me.

POL.
Affection! pooh! you speak like a green girl,
Unsifted in such perilous circumstance.
Do you believe his tenders, as you call them?

OPH.
I do not know, my lord, what I should think.

POL.
Marry, I'll teach you: think yourself a baby;
That you have ta'en these tenders for true pay,
Which are not sterling. Tender yourself more
      dearly;

Or,—not to crack the wind of the poor phrase,
Wronging it thus,—you'll tender me a fool.

OPH.

My lord, he hath importun'd me with love
In honourable fashion.

POL.

Ay, fashion you may call it; go to, go to.

OPH.

And hath given countenance to his speech, my
    lord,
With almost all the holy vows of heaven.

POL.

Ay, springes to catch woodcocks. I do know,
When the blood burns, how prodigal the soul
Lends the tongue vows: these blazes, daughter,
Giving more light than heat,—extinct in both,
Even in their promise, as it is a-making,—
You must not take for fire. From this time
Be something scanter of your maiden presence;
Set your entreatments at a higher rate
Than a command to parley. For Lord Hamlet,
Believe so much in him, that he is young;
And with a larger tether may he walk
Than may be given you: in few, Ophelia,
Do not believe his vows; for they are brokers,—
Not of that dye which their investments show,
But mere implorators of unholy suits,
Breathing like sanctified and pious bawds,
The better to beguile. This is for all,—
I would not, in plain terms, from this time forth
Have you so slander any moment leisure
As to give words or talk with the Lord Hamlet.
Look to't, I charge you; come your ways.

OPH.

I shall obey, my lord.

[Exeunt.]

SCENE IV. The Platform.

[Enter Hamlet, Horatio, and Marcellus.]

HAM.

The air bites shrewdly; it is very cold.

HOR.

It is a nipping and an eager air.

HAM.

What hour now?

HOR.

I think it lacks of twelve.

MAR.

No, it is struck.

HOR.

Indeed? I heard it not: then draws near the season
Wherein the spirit held his wont to walk.

[A flourish of trumpets, and ordnance shot off
    within.]

What does this mean, my lord?

HAM.

The King doth wake to-night and takes his rouse,
Keeps wassail, and the swaggering up-spring reels;
And, as he drains his draughts of Rhenish down,
The kettle-drum and trumpet thus bray out
The triumph of his pledge.

HOR.

Is it a custom?

HAM.

Ay, marry, is't;
But to my mind,—though I am native here,
And to the manner born,—it is a custom
More honour'd in the breach than the
    observance.
This heavy-headed revel east and west
Makes us traduc'd and tax'd of other nations:
They clepe us drunkards, and with swinish phrase
Soil our addition; and, indeed, it takes
From our achievements, though perform'd at
    height,
The pith and marrow of our attribute.
So oft it chances in particular men
That, for some vicious mole of nature in them,
As in their birth,—wherein they are not guilty,
Since nature cannot choose his origin,—
By the o'ergrowth of some complexion,
Oft breaking down the pales and forts of reason;
Or by some habit, that too much o'er-leavens
The form of plausive manners;—that these
    men,—
Carrying, I say, the stamp of one defect,
Being nature's livery, or fortune's star,—
Their virtues else,—be they as pure as grace,

As infinite as man may undergo,—
Shall in the general censure take corruption
From that particular fault: the dram of eale
Doth all the noble substance often doubt
To his own scandal.

HOR.
Look, my lord, it comes!

[Enter Ghost.]

HAM.
Angels and ministers of grace defend us!—
Be thou a spirit of health or goblin damn'd,
Bring with thee airs from heaven or blasts from
        hell,
Be thy intents wicked or charitable,
Thou com'st in such a questionable shape
That I will speak to thee: I'll call thee Hamlet,
King, father, royal Dane; O, answer me!
Let me not burst in ignorance; but tell
Why thy canoniz'd bones, hearsed in death,
Have burst their cerements; why the sepulchre,
Wherein we saw thee quietly in-urn'd,
Hath op'd his ponderous and marble jaws
To cast thee up again! What may this mean,
That thou, dead corse, again in complete steel,
Revisit'st thus the glimpses of the moon,
Making night hideous, and we fools of nature
So horridly to shake our disposition
With thoughts beyond the reaches of our souls?
Say, why is this? wherefore? what should we do?

[Ghost beckons Hamlet.]

HOR.
It beckons you to go away with it,
As if it some impartment did desire
To you alone.

MAR.
Look with what courteous action
It waves you to a more removed ground:
But do not go with it!

HOR.
No, by no means.

HAM.
It will not speak; then will I follow it.

HOR.
Do not, my lord.

HAM.
Why, what should be the fear?
I do not set my life at a pin's fee;

And for my soul, what can it do to that,
Being a thing immortal as itself?
It waves me forth again;—I'll follow it.

HOR.
What if it tempt you toward the flood, my lord,
Or to the dreadful summit of the cliff
That beetles o'er his base into the sea,
And there assume some other horrible form
Which might deprive your sovereignty of reason,
And draw you into madness? think of it:
The very place puts toys of desperation,
Without more motive, into every brain
That looks so many fadoms to the sea
And hears it roar beneath.

HAM.
It waves me still.—
Go on; I'll follow thee.

MAR.
You shall not go, my lord.

HAM.
Hold off your hands.

HOR.
Be rul'd; you shall not go.

HAM.
My fate cries out,
And makes each petty artery in this body
As hardy as the Nemean lion's nerve.—

[Ghost beckons.]

Still am I call'd;—unhand me, gentlemen;—

[Breaking free from them.]

By heaven, I'll make a ghost of him that lets
        me!—
I say, away!—Go on; I'll follow thee.

[Exeunt Ghost and Hamlet.]

HOR.
He waxes desperate with imagination.

MAR.
Let's follow; 'tis not fit thus to obey him.

HOR.
Have after.—To what issue will this come?

MAR.
Something is rotten in the state of Denmark.

HOR.
Heaven will direct it.

MAR.
Nay, let's follow him.

[Exeunt.]

SCENE V. A more remote part of the Castle.

[Enter Ghost and Hamlet.]

HAM.
Whither wilt thou lead me? speak! I'll go no
    further.

GHOST.
Mark me.

HAM.
I will.

GHOST.
My hour is almost come,
When I to sulph'uous and tormenting flames
Must render up myself.

HAM.
Alas, poor ghost!

GHOST.
Pity me not, but lend thy serious hearing
To what I shall unfold.

HAM.
Speak; I am bound to hear.

GHOST.
So art thou to revenge, when thou shalt hear.

HAM.
What?

GHOST.
I am thy father's spirit;
Doom'd for a certain term to walk the night,
And for the day confin'd to waste in fires,
Till the foul crimes done in my days of nature
Are burnt and purg'd away. But that I am forbid
To tell the secrets of my prison-house,
I could a tale unfold whose lightest word
Would harrow up thy soul; freeze thy young
    blood;
Make thy two eyes, like stars, start from their
    spheres;
Thy knotted and combined locks to part,
And each particular hair to stand on end
Like quills upon the fretful porcupine:
But this eternal blazon must not be
To ears of flesh and blood.—List, list, O, list!—
If thou didst ever thy dear father love—

HAM.
O God!

GHOST.
Revenge his foul and most unnatural murder.

HAM.
Murder!

GHOST.
Murder most foul, as in the best it is;
But this most foul, strange, and unnatural.

HAM.
Haste me to know't, that I, with wings as swift
As meditation or the thoughts of love,
May sweep to my revenge.

GHOST.
I find thee apt;
And duller shouldst thou be than the fat weed
That rots itself in ease on Lethe wharf,
Wouldst thou not stir in this. Now, Hamlet, hear.
'Tis given out that, sleeping in my orchard,
A serpent stung me; so the whole ear of Denmark
Is by a forged process of my death
Rankly abus'd; but know, thou noble youth,
The serpent that did sting thy father's life
Now wears his crown.

HAM.
O my prophetic soul!
Mine uncle!

GHOST.
Ay, that incestuous, that adulterate beast,
With witchcraft of his wit, with traitorous gifts,—
O wicked wit and gifts, that have the power
So to seduce!—won to his shameful lust
The will of my most seeming-virtuous queen:
O Hamlet, what a falling-off was there!
From me, whose love was of that dignity
That it went hand in hand even with the vow
I made to her in marriage; and to decline
Upon a wretch whose natural gifts were poor
To those of mine!
But virtue, as it never will be mov'd,
Though lewdness court it in a shape of heaven;
So lust, though to a radiant angel link'd,
Will sate itself in a celestial bed
And prey on garbage.
But soft! methinks I scent the morning air;
Brief let me be.—Sleeping within my orchard,
My custom always of the afternoon,
Upon my secure hour thy uncle stole,

With juice of cursed hebenon in a vial,
And in the porches of my ears did pour
The leperous distilment; whose effect
Holds such an enmity with blood of man
That, swift as quicksilver, it courses through
The natural gates and alleys of the body;
And with a sudden vigour it doth posset
And curd, like eager droppings into milk,
The thin and wholesome blood; so did it mine;
And a most instant tetter bark'd about,
Most lazar-like, with vile and loathsome crust
All my smooth body.
Thus was I, sleeping, by a brother's hand,
Of life, of crown, of queen, at once dispatch'd:
Cut off even in the blossoms of my sin,
Unhous'led, disappointed, unanel'd;
No reckoning made, but sent to my account
With all my imperfections on my head:
O, horrible! O, horrible! most horrible!
If thou hast nature in thee, bear it not;
Let not the royal bed of Denmark be
A couch for luxury and damned incest.
But, howsoever thou pursu'st this act,
Taint not thy mind, nor let thy soul contrive
Against thy mother aught: leave her to heaven,
And to those thorns that in her bosom lodge,
To prick and sting her. Fare thee well at once!
The glowworm shows the matin to be near,
And 'gins to pale his uneffectual fire:
Adieu, adieu! Hamlet, remember me.

[Exit.]

HAM.
O all you host of heaven! O earth! what else?
And shall I couple hell? O, fie!—Hold, my heart;
And you, my sinews, grow not instant old,
But bear me stiffly up.—Remember thee!
Ay, thou poor ghost, while memory holds a seat
In this distracted globe. Remember thee!
Yea, from the table of my memory
I'll wipe away all trivial fond records,
All saws of books, all forms, all pressures past,
That youth and observation copied there;
And thy commandment all alone shall live
Within the book and volume of my brain,
Unmix'd with baser matter: yes, by heaven!—
O most pernicious woman!
O villain, villain, smiling, damned villain!
My tables,—meet it is I set it down,

That one may smile, and smile, and be a villain;
At least, I am sure, it may be so in Denmark:

[Writing.]

So, uncle, there you are. Now to my word;
It is 'Adieu, adieu! remember me:'
I have sworn't.

HOR.
[Within.] My lord, my lord,—

MAR.
[Within.] Lord Hamlet,—

HOR.
[Within.] Heaven secure him!

HAM.
So be it!

MAR.
[Within.] Illo, ho, ho, my lord!

HAM.
Hillo, ho, ho, boy! Come, bird, come.

[Enter Horatio and Marcellus.]

MAR.
How is't, my noble lord?

HOR.
What news, my lord?

HAM.
O, wonderful!

HOR.
Good my lord, tell it.

HAM.
No; you'll reveal it.

HOR.
Not I, my lord, by heaven.

MAR.
Nor I, my lord.

HAM.
How say you then; would heart of man once
        think it?—
But you'll be secret?

HOR. AND MAR.
Ay, by heaven, my Lord.

HAM.
There's ne'er a villain dwelling in all Denmark
But he's an arrant knave.

HOR.

There needs no ghost, my lord, come from the
	grave
To tell us this.

HAM.

Why, right; you are i' the right;
And so, without more circumstance at all,
I hold it fit that we shake hands and part:
You, as your business and desires shall point
		you,—
For every man hath business and desire,
Such as it is;—and for my own poor part,
Look you, I'll go pray.

HOR.

These are but wild and whirling words, my Lord.

HAM.

I'm sorry they offend you, heartily;
Yes, faith, heartily.

HOR.

There's no offence, my Lord.

HAM.

Yes, by Saint Patrick, but there is, Horatio,
And much offence too. Touching this vision
		here,—
It is an honest ghost, that let me tell you:
For your desire to know what is between us,
O'ermaster't as you may. And now, good friends,
As you are friends, scholars, and soldiers,
Give me one poor request.

HOR.

What is't, my lord? we will.

HAM.

Never make known what you have seen to-night.

HOR. AND MAR.

My lord, we will not.

HAM.

Nay, but swear't.

HOR.

In faith,
My lord, not I.

MAR.

Nor I, my lord, in faith.

HAM.

Upon my sword.

MAR.

We have sworn, my lord, already.

HAM.

Indeed, upon my sword, indeed.

GHOST.

[Beneath.] Swear.

HAM.

Ha, ha boy! say'st thou so? art thou there,
		truepenny?—
Come on!—you hear this fellow in the
		cellarage,—
Consent to swear.

HOR.

Propose the oath, my Lord.

HAM.

Never to speak of this that you have seen,
Swear by my sword.

GHOST.

[Beneath.] Swear.

HAM.

Hic et ubique? then we'll shift our ground.—
Come hither, gentlemen,
And lay your hands again upon my sword:
Never to speak of this that you have heard,
Swear by my sword.

GHOST.

[Beneath.] Swear.

HAM.

Well said, old mole! canst work i' the earth so
		fast?
A worthy pioner!—Once more remove, good
		friends.

HOR.

O day and night, but this is wondrous strange!

HAM.

And therefore as a stranger give it welcome.
There are more things in heaven and earth,
		Horatio,
Than are dreamt of in your philosophy.
But come;—
Here, as before, never, so help you mercy,
How strange or odd soe'er I bear myself,—
As I, perchance, hereafter shall think meet
To put an antic disposition on,—
That you, at such times seeing me, never shall,

With arms encumber'd thus, or this head-shake,
Or by pronouncing of some doubtful phrase,
As 'Well, well, we know'; or 'We could, an if we
    would';—
Or 'If we list to speak'; or 'There be, an if they
    might';—
Or such ambiguous giving out, to note
That you know aught of me:—this is not to do,
So grace and mercy at your most need help you,
Swear.

GHOST.

[*Beneath.*] Swear.

HAM.

Rest, rest, perturbed spirit!—So, gentlemen,
With all my love I do commend me to you:
And what so poor a man as Hamlet is
May do, to express his love and friending to you,
God willing, shall not lack. Let us go in together;
And still your fingers on your lips, I pray.
The time is out of joint:—O cursed spite,
That ever I was born to set it right!—
Nay, come, let's go together.

[*Exeunt.*]

ACT II

SCENE I. A room in Polonius's house.

[*Enter Polonius and Reynaldo.*]

POL.
Give him this money and these notes, Reynaldo.
REY.
I will, my Lord.

POL.
You shall do marvellous wisely, good Reynaldo,
Before You visit him, to make inquiry
Of his behaviour.

REY.
My lord, I did intend it.

POL.
Marry, well said; very well said. Look you, sir,
Enquire me first what Danskers are in Paris;
And how, and who, what means, and where they
    keep,
What company, at what expense; and finding,
By this encompassment and drift of question,

That they do know my son, come you more
    nearer
Than your particular demands will touch it:
Take you, as 'twere, some distant knowledge of
    him;
As thus, I know his father and his friends,
And in part him;—do you mark this, Reynaldo?

REY.
Ay, very well, my lord.

POL.
'And in part him;—but,' you may say, 'not well:
But if't be he I mean, he's very wild;
Addicted so and so;' and there put on him
What forgeries you please; marry, none so rank
As may dishonour him; take heed of that;
But, sir, such wanton, wild, and usual slips
As are companions noted and most known
To youth and liberty.

REY.
As gaming, my lord.

POL.
Ay, or drinking, fencing, swearing, quarrelling,
Drabbing:—you may go so far.

REY.
My lord, that would dishonour him.

POL.
Faith, no; as you may season it in the charge.
You must not put another scandal on him,
That he is open to incontinency;
That's not my meaning: but breathe his faults so
    quaintly
That they may seem the taints of liberty;
The flash and outbreak of a fiery mind;
A savageness in unreclaimed blood,
Of general assault.

REY.
But, my good lord,—

POL.
Wherefore should you do this?

REY.
Ay, my lord,
I would know that.

POL.
Marry, sir, here's my drift;
And I believe it is a fetch of warrant:
You laying these slight sullies on my son

As 'twere a thing a little soil'd i' the working,
Mark you,
Your party in converse, him you would sound,
Having ever seen in the prenominate crimes
The youth you breathe of guilty, be assur'd
He closes with you in this consequence;
'Good sir,' or so; or 'friend,' or 'gentleman'—
According to the phrase or the addition
Of man and country.

REY.
Very good, my lord.

POL.
And then, sir, does he this,—he does—What was I
    about to say?—
By the mass, I was about to say something:—
    Where did I leave?

REY.
At 'closes in the consequence,' at 'friend or so,' and
    'gentleman.'

POL.
At—'closes in the consequence'—ay, marry!
He closes with you thus:—'I know the gentleman;
I saw him yesterday, or t'other day,
Or then, or then; with such, or such; and, as you
    say,
There was he gaming; there o'ertook in's rouse;
There falling out at tennis': or perchance,
'I saw him enter such a house of sale,'—
Videlicet, a brothel,—or so forth.—
See you now;
Your bait of falsehood takes this carp of truth:
And thus do we of wisdom and of reach,
With windlaces, and with assays of bias,
By indirections find directions out:
So, by my former lecture and advice,
Shall you my son. You have me, have you not?

REY.
My lord, I have.

POL.
God b' wi' you, fare you well.

REY.
Good my lord!

POL.
Observe his inclination in yourself.

REY.
I shall, my lord.

POL.
And let him ply his music.

REY.
Well, my lord.

POL.
Farewell!

[Exit Reynaldo.]

[Enter Ophelia.]

How now, Ophelia! what's the matter?

OPH.
Alas, my lord, I have been so affrighted!

POL.
With what, i' the name of God?

OPH.
My lord, as I was sewing in my chamber,
Lord Hamlet,—with his doublet all unbrac'd;
No hat upon his head; his stockings foul'd,
Ungart'red, and down-gyved to his ankle;
Pale as his shirt; his knees knocking each other;
And with a look so piteous in purport
As if he had been loosed out of hell
To speak of horrors,—he comes before me.

POL.
Mad for thy love?

OPH.
My lord, I do not know;
But truly I do fear it.

POL.
What said he?

OPH.
He took me by the wrist, and held me hard;
Then goes he to the length of all his arm;
And with his other hand thus o'er his brow,
He falls to such perusal of my face
As he would draw it. Long stay'd he so;
At last,—a little shaking of mine arm,
And thrice his head thus waving up and down,—
He rais'd a sigh so piteous and profound
As it did seem to shatter all his bulk
And end his being: that done, he lets me go:
And, with his head over his shoulder turn'd
He seem'd to find his way without his eyes;
For out o' doors he went without their help,
And to the last bended their light on me.

POL.

Come, go with me: I will go seek the King.
This is the very ecstasy of love;
Whose violent property fordoes itself,
And leads the will to desperate undertakings,
As oft as any passion under heaven
That does afflict our natures. I am sorry,—
What, have you given him any hard words of late?

OPH.

No, my good lord; but, as you did command,
I did repel his letters and denied
His access to me.

POL.

That hath made him mad.
I am sorry that with better heed and judgment
I had not quoted him: I fear'd he did but trifle,
And meant to wreck thee; but beshrew my
　　jealousy!
It seems it as proper to our age
To cast beyond ourselves in our opinions
As it is common for the younger sort
To lack discretion. Come, go we to the king:
This must be known; which, being kept close,
　　might move
More grief to hide than hate to utter love.

[Exeunt.]

SCENE II. A room in the Castle.

[Enter King, Rosencrantz, Guildenstern, and
　　Attendants.]

KING.

Welcome, dear Rosencrantz and Guildenstern!
Moreover that we much did long to see you,
The need we have to use you did provoke
Our hasty sending. Something have you heard
Of Hamlet's transformation; so I call it,
Since nor the exterior nor the inward man
Resembles that it was. What it should be,
More than his father's death, that thus hath put
　　him
So much from the understanding of himself,
I cannot dream of: I entreat you both
That, being of so young days brought up with
　　him,
And since so neighbour'd to his youth and
　　humour,

That you vouchsafe your rest here in our court
Some little time: so by your companies
To draw him on to pleasures, and to gather,
So much as from occasion you may glean,
Whether aught, to us unknown, afflicts him thus,
That, open'd, lies within our remedy.

QUEEN.

Good gentlemen, he hath much talk'd of you,
And sure I am two men there are not living
To whom he more adheres. If it will please you
To show us so much gentry and good-will
As to expend your time with us awhile,
For the supply and profit of our hope,
Your visitation shall receive such thanks
As fits a king's remembrance.

ROS.

Both your majesties
Might, by the sovereign power you have of us,
Put your dread pleasures more into command
Than to entreaty.

GUIL.

We both obey,
And here give up ourselves, in the full bent,
To lay our service freely at your feet,
To be commanded.

KING.

Thanks, Rosencrantz and gentle Guildenstern.

QUEEN.

Thanks, Guildenstern and gentle Rosencrantz:
And I beseech you instantly to visit
My too-much-changed son.—Go, some of you,
And bring these gentlemen where Hamlet is.

GUIL.

Heavens make our presence and our practices
Pleasant and helpful to him!

QUEEN.

Ay, amen!

[Exeunt Rosencrantz, Guildenstern, and some
　　Attendants].

[Enter Polonius.]

POL.

Th' ambassadors from Norway, my good lord,
Are joyfully return'd.

KING.

Thou still hast been the father of good news.

POL.

Have I, my lord? Assure you, my good liege,
I hold my duty, as I hold my soul,
Both to my God and to my gracious king:
And I do think,—or else this brain of mine
Hunts not the trail of policy so sure
As it hath us'd to do,—that I have found
The very cause of Hamlet's lunacy.

KING.

O, speak of that; that do I long to hear.

POL.

Give first admittance to the ambassadors;
My news shall be the fruit to that great feast.

KING.

Thyself do grace to them, and bring them in.

[Exit Polonius.]

He tells me, my sweet queen, he hath found
The head and source of all your son's distemper.

QUEEN.

I doubt it is no other but the main,—
His father's death and our o'erhasty marriage.

KING.

Well, we shall sift him.

[Enter Polonius, with Voltimand and Cornelius.]

Welcome, my good friends!
Say, Voltimand, what from our brother Norway?

VOLT.

Most fair return of greetings and desires.
Upon our first, he sent out to suppress
His nephew's levies; which to him appear'd
To be a preparation 'gainst the Polack;
But, better look'd into, he truly found
It was against your highness; whereat griev'd,—
That so his sickness, age, and impotence
Was falsely borne in hand,—sends out arrests
On Fortinbras; which he, in brief, obeys;
Receives rebuke from Norway; and, in fine,
Makes vow before his uncle never more
To give th' assay of arms against your majesty.
Whereon old Norway, overcome with joy,
Gives him three thousand crowns in annual fee;
And his commission to employ those soldiers,
So levied as before, against the Polack:
With an entreaty, herein further shown,

[Gives a paper.]

That it might please you to give quiet pass
Through your dominions for this enterprise,
On such regards of safety and allowance
As therein are set down.

KING.

It likes us well;
And at our more consider'd time we'll read,
Answer, and think upon this business.
Meantime we thank you for your well-took
labour:
Go to your rest; at night we'll feast together:
Most welcome home!

[Exeunt Voltimand and Cornelius.]

POL.

This business is well ended.—
My liege, and madam,—to expostulate
What majesty should be, what duty is,
Why day is day, night is night, and time is time.
Were nothing but to waste night, day, and time.
Therefore, since brevity is the soul of wit,
And tediousness the limbs and outward
flourishes,
I will be brief:—your noble son is mad:
Mad call I it; for to define true madness,
What is't but to be nothing else but mad?
But let that go.

QUEEN.

More matter, with less art.

POL.

Madam, I swear I use no art at All.
That he is mad, 'tis true: 'tis true 'tis pity;
And pity 'tis 'tis true: a foolish figure;
But farewell it, for I will use no art.
Mad let us grant him then: and now remains
That we find out the cause of this effect;
Or rather say, the cause of this defect,
For this effect defective comes by cause:
Thus it remains, and the remainder thus.
Perpend.
I have a daughter,—have whilst she is mine,—
Who, in her duty and obedience, mark,
Hath given me this: now gather, and surmise.

[Reads.]

'To the celestial, and my soul's idol, the most
beautified
Ophelia,'—

That's an ill phrase, a vile phrase; 'beautified' is a vile

phrase: but you shall hear. Thus:

[Reads.]

'In her excellent white bosom, these, &c.'

QUEEN.

Came this from Hamlet to her?

POL.

Good madam, stay awhile; I will be faithful.

[Reads.]

'Doubt thou the stars are fire;
Doubt that the sun doth move;
Doubt truth to be a liar;
But never doubt I love.
'O dear Ophelia, I am ill at these numbers; I have
    not art to reckon my groans: but that I love
    thee best, O most best, believe it. Adieu.
'Thine evermore, most dear lady, whilst this
    machine is to him, HAMLET.'
This, in obedience, hath my daughter show'd me;
And more above, hath his solicitings,
As they fell out by time, by means, and place,
All given to mine ear.

KING.

But how hath she
Receiv'd his love?

POL.

What do you think of me?

KING.

As of a man faithful and honourable.

POL.

I would fain prove so. But what might you think,
When I had seen this hot love on the wing,—
As I perceiv'd it, I must tell you that,
Before my daughter told me,— what might you,
Or my dear majesty your queen here, think,
If I had play'd the desk or table-book,
Or given my heart a winking, mute and dumb;
Or look'd upon this love with idle sight;—
What might you think? No, I went round to work,
And my young mistress thus I did bespeak:
'Lord Hamlet is a prince, out of thy sphere;
This must not be:' and then I precepts gave her,
That she should lock herself from his resort,
Admit no messengers, receive no tokens.

Which done, she took the fruits of my advice;
And he, repulsed,—a short tale to make,—
Fell into a sadness; then into a fast;
Thence to a watch; thence into a weakness;
Thence to a lightness; and, by this declension,
Into the madness wherein now he raves,
And all we wail For.

KING.

Do you think 'tis this?

QUEEN.

It may be, very likely.

POL.

Hath there been such a time,—I'd fain know
    that—
That I have positively said 'Tis so,'
When it prov'd otherwise?

KING.

Not that I know.

POL.

Take this from this, if this be otherwise:

[Points to his head and shoulder.]

If circumstances lead me, I will find
Where truth is hid, though it were hid indeed
Within the centre.

KING.

How may we try it further?

POL.

You know sometimes he walks for hours together
Here in the lobby.

QUEEN.

So he does indeed.

POL.

At such a time I'll loose my daughter to him:
Be you and I behind an arras then;
Mark the encounter: if he love her not,
And he not from his reason fall'n thereon
Let me be no assistant for a state,
But keep a farm and carters.

KING.

We will try it.

QUEEN.

But look where sadly the poor wretch comes
    reading.

POL.

Away, I do beseech you, both away
I'll board him presently:—O, give me leave.

[*Exeunt King, Queen, and Attendants.*]

[*Enter Hamlet, reading.*]

How does my good Lord Hamlet?

HAM.

Well, God-a-mercy.

POL.

Do you know me, my lord?

HAM.

Excellent well; you're a fishmonger.

POL.

Not I, my lord.

HAM.

Then I would you were so honest a man.

POL.

Honest, my lord!

HAM.

Ay, sir; to be honest, as this world goes, is to be
one man picked out of ten thousand.

POL.

That's very true, my lord.

HAM.

For if the sun breed maggots in a dead dog, being
a god-kissing carrion,—Have you a
daughter?

POL.

I have, my lord.

HAM.

Let her not walk i' the sun: conception is a
blessing, but not as your daughter may
conceive:—friend, look to't.

POL.

How say you by that?—[*Aside.*] Still harping on
my daughter:—yet he knew me not at first;
he said I was a fishmonger: he is far gone,
far gone: and truly in my youth I suffered
much extremity for love; very near this. I'll
speak to him again.—What do you read, my
lord?

HAM.

Words, words, words.

POL.

What is the matter, my lord?

HAM.

Between who?

POL.

I mean, the matter that you read, my lord.

HAM.

Slanders, sir: for the satirical slave says here that
old men have grey beards; that their faces
are wrinkled; their eyes purging thick amber
and plum-tree gum; and that they have a
plentiful lack of wit, together with most
weak hams: all which, sir, though I most
powerfully and potently believe, yet I hold it
not honesty to have it thus set down; for you
yourself, sir, should be old as I am, if, like a
crab, you could go backward.

POL.

[*Aside.*] Though this be madness, yet there is a
method in't.—
Will you walk out of the air, my lord?

HAM.

Into my grave?

POL.

Indeed, that is out o' the air. [*Aside.*] How
pregnant sometimes his replies are! a
happiness that often madness hits on, which
reason and sanity could not so prosperously
be delivered of. I will leave him and
suddenly contrive the means of meeting
between him and my daughter.—My
honourable lord, I will most humbly take
my leave of you.

HAM.

You cannot, sir, take from me anything that I will
more willingly part withal,—except my life,
except my life, except my life.

POL.

Fare you well, my lord.

HAM.

These tedious old fools!

[*Enter Rosencrantz and Guildenstern.*]

POL.

You go to seek the Lord Hamlet; there he is.

ROS.

[To Polonius.] God save you, sir!

[Exit Polonius.]

GUIL.

My honoured lord!

ROS.

My most dear lord!

HAM.

My excellent good friends! How dost thou,
    Guildenstern? Ah,
Rosencrantz! Good lads, how do ye both?

ROS.

As the indifferent children of the earth.

GUIL.

Happy in that we are not over-happy;
On fortune's cap we are not the very button.

HAM.

Nor the soles of her shoe?

ROS.

Neither, my lord.

HAM.

Then you live about her waist, or in the middle of
    her favours?

GUIL.

Faith, her privates we.

HAM.

In the secret parts of fortune? O, most true; she is
    a strumpet. What's the news?

ROS.

None, my lord, but that the world's grown honest.

HAM.

Then is doomsday near; but your news is not
    true. Let me question more in particular:
    what have you, my good friends, deserved at
    the hands of fortune, that she sends you to
    prison hither?

GUIL.

Prison, my lord!

HAM.

Denmark's a prison.

ROS.

Then is the world one.

HAM.

A goodly one; in which there are many confines,
    wards, and dungeons, Denmark being one o'
    the worst.

ROS.

We think not so, my lord.

HAM.

Why, then 'tis none to you; for there is nothing
    either good or bad but thinking makes it so:
    to me it is a prison.

ROS.

Why, then, your ambition makes it one; 'tis too
    narrow for your mind.

HAM.

O God, I could be bounded in a nutshell, and
    count myself a king of infinite space, were it
    not that I have bad dreams.

GUIL.

Which dreams, indeed, are ambition; for the very
    substance of the ambitious is merely the
    shadow of a dream.

HAM.

A dream itself is but a shadow.

ROS.

Truly, and I hold ambition of so airy and light a
    quality that it is but a shadow's shadow.

HAM.

Then are our beggars bodies, and our monarchs
    and outstretch'd heroes the beggars'
    shadows. Shall we to the court? for, by my
    fay, I cannot reason.

ROS. AND GUILD.

We'll wait upon you.

HAM.

No such matter: I will not sort you with the rest
    of my Servants; for, to speak to you like an
    honest man, I am most dreadfully attended.
    But, in the beaten way of friendship, what
    make you at Elsinore?

ROS.

To visit you, my lord; no other occasion.

HAM.

Beggar that I am, I am even poor in thanks; but I
    thank you: and sure, dear friends, my thanks
    are too dear a halfpenny. Were you not sent
    for? Is it your own inclining? Is it a free
    visitation? Come, deal justly with me: come,
    come; nay, speak.

GUIL.

What should we say, my lord?

HAM.

Why, anything—but to the purpose. You were sent for; and there is a kind of confession in your looks, which your modesties have not craft enough to colour: I know the good king and queen have sent for you.

ROS.

To what end, my lord?

HAM.

That you must teach me. But let me conjure you, by the rights of our fellowship, by the consonancy of our youth, by the obligation of our ever-preserved love, and by what more dear a better proposer could charge you withal, be even and direct with me, whether you were sent for or no.

ROS.

[To Guildenstern.] What say you?

HAM.

[Aside.] Nay, then, I have an eye of you.—If you love me, hold not off.

GUIL.

My lord, we were sent for.

HAM.

I will tell you why; so shall my anticipation prevent your discovery, and your secrecy to the king and queen moult no feather. I have of late,—but wherefore I know not,—lost all my mirth, forgone all custom of exercises; and indeed, it goes so heavily with my disposition that this goodly frame, the earth, seems to me a sterile promontory; this most excellent canopy, the air, look you, this brave o'erhanging firmament, this majestical roof fretted with golden fire,—why, it appears no other thing to me than a foul and pestilent congregation of vapours. What a piece of work is man! How noble in reason! how infinite in faculties! in form and moving, how express and admirable! in action how like an angel! in apprehension, how like a god! the beauty of the world! the paragon of animals! And yet, to me, what is this quintessence of dust? Man delights not me; no, nor woman neither, though by your smiling you seem to say so.

ROS.

My lord, there was no such stuff in my thoughts.

HAM.

Why did you laugh then, when I said 'Man delights not me'?

ROS.

To think, my lord, if you delight not in man, what lenten entertainment the players shall receive from you: we coted them on the way; and hither are they coming to offer you service.

HAM.

He that plays the king shall be welcome,—his majesty shall have tribute of me; the adventurous knight shall use his foil and target; the lover shall not sigh gratis; the humorous man shall end his part in peace; the clown shall make those laugh whose lungs are tickle o' the sere; and the lady shall say her mind freely, or the blank verse shall halt for't. What players are they?

ROS.

Even those you were wont to take such delight in,—the tragedians of the city.

HAM.

How chances it they travel? their residence, both in reputation and profit, was better both ways.

ROS.

I think their inhibition comes by the means of the late innovation.

HAM.

Do they hold the same estimation they did when I was in the city? Are they so followed?

ROS.

No, indeed, are they not.

HAM.

How comes it? do they grow rusty?

ROS.

Nay, their endeavour keeps in the wonted pace: but there is, sir, an aery of children, little eyases, that cry out on the top of question, and are most tyrannically clapped for't: these are now the fashion; and so berattle the common stages,—so they call them,—that many wearing rapiers are afraid of goose-quills and dare scarce come thither.

HAM.

What, are they children? who maintains 'em? How are they escoted? Will they pursue the quality no longer than they can sing? will they not say afterwards, if they should grow themselves to common players,—as it is most like, if their means are no better,— their writers do them wrong to make them exclaim against their own succession?

ROS.
Faith, there has been much to do on both sides; and the nation holds it no sin to tarre them to controversy: there was, for awhile, no money bid for argument unless the poet and the player went to cuffs in the question.

HAM.
Is't possible?

GUIL.
O, there has been much throwing about of brains.

HAM.
Do the boys carry it away?

ROS.
Ay, that they do, my lord; Hercules and his load too.

HAM.
It is not very strange; for my uncle is king of Denmark, and those that would make mouths at him while my father lived, give twenty, forty, fifty, a hundred ducats a-piece for his picture in little. 'Sblood, there is something in this more than natural, if philosophy could find it out.

[Flourish of trumpets within.]

GUIL.
There are the players.

HAM.
Gentlemen, you are welcome to Elsinore. Your hands, come: the appurtenance of welcome is fashion and ceremony: let me comply with you in this garb; lest my extent to the players, which I tell you must show fairly outward, should more appear like entertainment than yours. You are welcome: but my uncle-father and aunt-mother are deceived.

GUIL.
In what, my dear lord?

HAM.
I am but mad north-north-west: when the wind is southerly I know a hawk from a handsaw.

[Enter Polonius.]

POL.
Well be with you, gentlemen!

HAM.
Hark you, Guildenstern;—and you too;—at each ear a hearer: that great baby you see there is not yet out of his swaddling clouts.

ROS.
Happily he's the second time come to them; for they say an old man is twice a child.

HAM.
I will prophesy he comes to tell me of the players; mark it.—You say right, sir: o' Monday morning; 'twas so indeed.

POL.
My lord, I have news to tell you.

HAM.
My lord, I have news to tell you. When Roscius was an actor in
Rome,—

POL.
The actors are come hither, my lord.

HAM.
Buzz, buzz!

POL.
Upon my honour,—

HAM.
Then came each actor on his ass,—

POL.
The best actors in the world, either for tragedy, comedy, history, pastoral, pastoral-comical, historical-pastoral, tragical-historical, tragical-comical-historical-pastoral, scene individable, or poem unlimited: Seneca cannot be too heavy nor Plautus too light. For the law of writ and the liberty, these are the only men.

HAM.
O Jephthah, judge of Israel, what a treasure hadst thou!

POL.

What treasure had he, my lord?

HAM.

Why—

'One fair daughter, and no more,
The which he loved passing well.'

POL.

[*Aside.*] Still on my daughter.

HAM.

Am I not i' the right, old Jephthah?

POL.

If you call me Jephthah, my lord, I have a
daughter that I love passing well.

HAM.

Nay, that follows not.

POL.

What follows, then, my lord?

HAM.

Why—'As by lot, God wot,' and then, you know,
'It came to pass, as most like it was—' The
first row of the pious chanson will show you
more; for look where my abridgment comes.

[*Enter four or five Players.*]

You are welcome, masters; welcome, all:—I am
glad to see thee well.—welcome, good
friends.—O, my old friend! Thy face is
valanc'd since I saw thee last; comest thou to
beard me in Denmark?—What, my young
lady and mistress! By'r lady, your ladyship is
nearer to heaven than when I saw you last,
by the altitude of a chopine. Pray God, your
voice, like a piece of uncurrent gold, be not
cracked within the ring.—Masters, you are
all welcome. We'll e'en to't like French
falconers, fly at anything we see: we'll have a
speech straight: come, give us a taste of your
quality: come, a passionate speech.

I PLAY.

What speech, my lord?

HAM.

I heard thee speak me a speech once,—but it was
never acted; or if it was, not above once; for
the play, I remember, pleased not the
million, 'twas caviare to the general; but it
was,—as I received it, and others, whose
judgments in such matters cried in the top

of mine,—an excellent play, well digested in
the scenes, set down with as much modesty
as cunning. I remember, one said there were
no sallets in the lines to make the matter
savoury, nor no matter in the phrase that
might indite the author of affectation; but
called it an honest method, as wholesome as
sweet, and by very much more handsome
than fine. One speech in it I chiefly loved:
'twas Æneas' tale to Dido, and thereabout
of it especially where he speaks of Priam's
slaughter: if it live in your memory, begin at
this line;—let me see, let me see:—
The rugged Pyrrhus, like th' Hyrcanian beast,—it
is not so:— it begins with Pyrrhus:—
'The rugged Pyrrhus,—he whose sable arms,
Black as his purpose, did the night resemble
When he lay couched in the ominous horse,—
Hath now this dread and black complexion
    smear'd
With heraldry more dismal; head to foot
Now is he total gules; horridly trick'd
With blood of fathers, mothers, daughters, sons,
Bak'd and impasted with the parching streets,
That lend a tyrannous and a damned light
To their vile murders: roasted in wrath and fire,
And thus o'ersized with coagulate gore,
With eyes like carbuncles, the hellish Pyrrhus
Old grandsire Priam seeks.'
So, proceed you.

POL.

'Fore God, my lord, well spoken, with good accent
and good discretion.

I PLAY.

Anon he finds him,
Striking too short at Greeks: his antique sword,
Rebellious to his arm, lies where it falls,
Repugnant to command: unequal match'd,
Pyrrhus at Priam drives; in rage strikes wide;
But with the whiff and wind of his fell sword
The unnerved father falls. Then senseless Ilium,
Seeming to feel this blow, with flaming top
Stoops to his base; and with a hideous crash
Takes prisoner Pyrrhus' ear: for lo! his sword,
Which was declining on the milky head
Of reverend Priam, seem'd i' the air to stick:
So, as a painted tyrant, Pyrrhus stood;
And, like a neutral to his will and matter,
Did nothing.

But as we often see, against some storm,
A silence in the heavens, the rack stand still,
The bold winds speechless, and the orb below
As hush as death, anon the dreadful thunder
Doth rend the region; so, after Pyrrhus' pause,
A roused vengeance sets him new a-work;
And never did the Cyclops' hammers fall
On Mars's armour, forg'd for proof eterne,
With less remorse than Pyrrhus' bleeding sword
Now falls on Priam.—
Out, out, thou strumpet, Fortune! All you gods,
In general synod, take away her power;
Break all the spokes and fellies from her wheel,
And bowl the round nave down the hill of
  heaven,
As low as to the fiends!

POL.
This is too long.

HAM.
It shall to the barber's, with your beard.—Pr'ythee
  say on.—
He's for a jig or a tale of bawdry, or he sleeps:—
  say on; come to Hecuba.

I PLAY.
But who, O who, had seen the mobled queen,—

HAM.
'The mobled queen'?

POL.
That's good! 'Mobled queen' is good.

I PLAY.
Run barefoot up and down, threatening the
  flames
With bisson rheum; a clout upon that head
Where late the diadem stood, and for a robe,
About her lank and all o'erteemed loins,
A blanket, in the alarm of fear caught up;—
Who this had seen, with tongue in venom steep'd,
'Gainst Fortune's state would treason have
  pronounc'd:
But if the gods themselves did see her then,
When she saw Pyrrhus make malicious sport
In mincing with his sword her husband's limbs,
The instant burst of clamour that she made,—
Unless things mortal move them not at all,—
Would have made milch the burning eyes of
  heaven,
And passion in the gods.

POL.
Look, whether he has not turn'd his colour, and
  has tears in's eyes.—Pray you, no more!

HAM.
'Tis well. I'll have thee speak out the rest of this
  soon.— Good my lord, will you see the
  players well bestowed? Do you hear? Let
  them be well used; for they are the abstracts
  and brief chronicles of the time; after your
  death you were better have a bad epitaph
  than their ill report while you live.

POL.
My lord, I will use them according to their desert.

HAM.
Odd's bodikin, man, better: use every man after
  his desert, and who should scape whipping?
  Use them after your own honour and
  dignity: the less they deserve, the more merit
  is in your bounty. Take them in.

POL.
Come, sirs.

HAM.
Follow him, friends: we'll hear a play to-morrow.

[Exeunt Polonius with all the Players but the First.]

Dost thou hear me, old friend? Can you play 'The
  Murder of Gonzago'?

I PLAY.
Ay, my lord.

HAM.
We'll ha't to-morrow night. You could, for a need,
  study a speech of some dozen or sixteen
  lines which I would set down and insert in't?
  could you not?

I PLAY.
Ay, my lord.

HAM.
Very well.—Follow that lord; and look you mock
  him not.

[Exit First Player.]

—My good friends *[to Ros. and Guild.]*, I'll leave
  you till night: you are welcome to Elsinore.

ROS.
Good my lord!

[Exeunt Rosencrantz and Guildenstern.]

HAM.
Ay, so, God b' wi' ye!
Now I am alone.
O, what a rogue and peasant slave am I!
Is it not monstrous that this player here,
But in a fiction, in a dream of passion,
Could force his soul so to his own conceit
That from her working all his visage wan'd;
Tears in his eyes, distraction in's aspect,
A broken voice, and his whole function suiting
With forms to his conceit? And all for nothing!
For Hecuba?
What's Hecuba to him, or he to Hecuba,
That he should weep for her? What would he do,
Had he the motive and the cue for passion
That I have? He would drown the stage with tears
And cleave the general ear with horrid speech;
Make mad the guilty, and appal the free;
Confound the ignorant, and amaze, indeed,
The very faculties of eyes and ears.
Yet I,
A dull and muddy-mettled rascal, peak,
Like John-a-dreams, unpregnant of my cause,
And can say nothing; no, not for a king
Upon whose property and most dear life
A damn'd defeat was made. Am I a coward?
Who calls me villain? breaks my pate across?
Plucks off my beard and blows it in my face?
Tweaks me by the nose? gives me the lie i' the
    throat
As deep as to the lungs? who does me this, ha?
'Swounds, I should take it: for it cannot be
But I am pigeon-liver'd, and lack gall
To make oppression bitter; or ere this
I should have fatted all the region kites
With this slave's offal: bloody, bawdy villain!
Remorseless, treacherous, lecherous, kindless
    villain!
O, vengeance!
Why, what an ass am I! This is most brave,
That I, the son of a dear father murder'd,
Prompted to my revenge by heaven and hell,
Must, like a whore, unpack my heart with words
And fall a-cursing like a very drab,
A scullion!
Fie upon't! foh!—About, my brain! I have heard
That guilty creatures, sitting at a play,
Have by the very cunning of the scene
Been struck so to the soul that presently
They have proclaim'd their malefactions;
For murder, though it have no tongue, will speak
With most miraculous organ, I'll have these
    players
Play something like the murder of my father
Before mine uncle: I'll observe his looks;
I'll tent him to the quick: if he but blench,
I know my course. The spirit that I have seen
May be the devil: and the devil hath power
To assume a pleasing shape; yea, and perhaps
Out of my weakness and my melancholy,—
As he is very potent with such spirits,—
Abuses me to damn me: I'll have grounds
More relative than this.—the play's the thing
Wherein I'll catch the conscience of the King.

[Exit.]

ACT III.

SCENE I. A room in the Castle.

[Enter King, Queen, Polonius, Ophelia,
*   Rosencrantz, and Guildenstern.]*

KING.
And can you, by no drift of circumstance,
Get from him why he puts on this confusion,
Grating so harshly all his days of quiet
With turbulent and dangerous lunacy?

ROS.
He does confess he feels himself distracted,
But from what cause he will by no means speak.

GUIL.
Nor do we find him forward to be sounded,
But, with a crafty madness, keeps aloof
When we would bring him on to some confession
Of his true state.

QUEEN.
Did he receive you well?

ROS.
Most like a gentleman.

GUIL.
But with much forcing of his disposition.

ROS.
Niggard of question; but, of our demands,
Most free in his reply.

QUEEN.
Did you assay him
To any pastime?

ROS.
Madam, it so fell out that certain players
We o'er-raught on the way: of these we told him,
And there did seem in him a kind of joy
To hear of it: they are about the court,
And, as I think, they have already order
This night to play before him.

POL.
'Tis most true;
And he beseech'd me to entreat your majesties
To hear and see the matter.

KING.
With all my heart; and it doth much content me
To hear him so inclin'd.—
Good gentlemen, give him a further edge,
And drive his purpose on to these delights.

ROS.
We shall, my lord.

[Exeunt Rosencrantz and Guildenstern.]

KING.
Sweet Gertrude, leave us too;
For we have closely sent for Hamlet hither,
That he, as 'twere by accident, may here
Affront Ophelia:
Her father and myself,—lawful espials,—
Will so bestow ourselves that, seeing, unseen,
We may of their encounter frankly judge;
And gather by him, as he is behav'd,
If't be the affliction of his love or no
That thus he suffers for.

QUEEN.
I shall obey you:—
And for your part, Ophelia, I do wish
That your good beauties be the happy cause
Of Hamlet's wildness: so shall I hope your virtues
Will bring him to his wonted way again,
To both your honours.

OPH.
Madam, I wish it may.

[Exit Queen.]

POL.
Ophelia, walk you here.—Gracious, so please you,
We will bestow ourselves.—[To Ophelia.] Read on
    this book;

That show of such an exercise may colour
Your loneliness.—We are oft to blame in this,—
'Tis too much prov'd,—that with devotion's
    visage
And pious action we do sugar o'er
The Devil himself.

KING.
[Aside.] O, 'tis too true!
How smart a lash that speech doth give my
    conscience!
The harlot's cheek, beautied with plastering art,
Is not more ugly to the thing that helps it
Than is my deed to my most painted word:
O heavy burden!

POL.
I hear him coming: let's withdraw, my lord.

[Exeunt King and Polonius.]

[Enter Hamlet.]

HAM.
To be, or not to be,—that is the question:—
Whether 'tis nobler in the mind to suffer
The slings and arrows of outrageous fortune
Or to take arms against a sea of troubles,
And by opposing end them?—To die,—to
    sleep,—
No more; and by a sleep to say we end
The heartache, and the thousand natural shocks
That flesh is heir to,—'tis a consummation
Devoutly to be wish'd. To die,—to sleep;—
To sleep! perchance to dream:—ay, there's the
    rub;
For in that sleep of death what dreams may come,
When we have shuffled off this mortal coil,
Must give us pause: there's the respect
That makes calamity of so long life;
For who would bear the whips and scorns of
    time,
The oppressor's wrong, the proud man's
    contumely,
The pangs of despis'd love, the law's delay,
The insolence of office, and the spurns
That patient merit of the unworthy takes,
When he himself might his quietus make
With a bare bodkin? who would these fardels
    bear,
To grunt and sweat under a weary life,
But that the dread of something after death,—
The undiscover'd country, from whose bourn

No traveller returns,—puzzles the will,
And makes us rather bear those ills we have
Than fly to others that we know not of?
Thus conscience does make cowards of us all;
And thus the native hue of resolution
Is sicklied o'er with the pale cast of thought;
And enterprises of great pith and moment,
With this regard, their currents turn awry,
And lose the name of action.—Soft you now!
The fair Ophelia!—Nymph, in thy orisons
Be all my sins remember'd.

OPH.

Good my lord,
How does your honour for this many a day?

HAM.

I humbly thank you; well, well, well.

OPH.

My lord, I have remembrances of yours
That I have longed long to re-deliver.
I pray you, now receive them.

HAM.

No, not I;
I never gave you aught.

OPH.

My honour'd lord, you know right well you did;
And with them words of so sweet breath
    compos'd
As made the things more rich; their perfume lost,
Take these again; for to the noble mind
Rich gifts wax poor when givers prove unkind.
There, my lord.

HAM.

Ha, ha! are you honest?

OPH.

My lord?

HAM.

Are you fair?

OPH.

What means your lordship?

HAM.

That if you be honest and fair, your honesty
    should admit no discourse to your beauty.

OPH.

Could beauty, my lord, have better commerce
    than with honesty?

HAM.

Ay, truly; for the power of beauty will sooner
    transform honesty from what it is to a bawd
    than the force of honesty can translate
    beauty into his likeness: this was sometime a
    paradox, but now the time gives it proof. I
    did love you once.

OPH.

Indeed, my lord, you made me believe so.

HAM.

You should not have believ'd me; for virtue
    cannot so inoculate our old stock but we
    shall relish of it: I loved you not.

OPH.

I was the more deceived.

HAM.

Get thee to a nunnery: why wouldst thou be a
    breeder of sinners? I am myself indifferent
    honest; but yet I could accuse me of such
    things that it were better my mother had not
    borne me: I am very proud, revengeful,
    ambitious; with more offences at my beck
    than I have thoughts to put them in,
    imagination to give them shape, or time to
    act them in. What should such fellows as I
    do crawling between earth and heaven? We
    are arrant knaves, all; believe none of us. Go
    thy ways to a nunnery. Where's your father?

OPH.

At home, my lord.

HAM.

Let the doors be shut upon him, that he may play
    the fool nowhere but in's own house.
    Farewell.

OPH.

O, help him, you sweet heavens!

HAM.

If thou dost marry, I'll give thee this plague for
    thy dowry,— be thou as chaste as ice, as
    pure as snow, thou shalt not escape calumny.
    Get thee to a nunnery, go: farewell. Or, if
    thou wilt needs marry, marry a fool; for wise
    men know well enough what monsters you
    make of them. To a nunnery, go; and quickly
    too. Farewell.

OPH.

O heavenly powers, restore him!

HAM.

I have heard of your paintings too, well enough;
God hath given you one face, and you make
yourselves another: you jig, you amble, and
you lisp, and nickname God's creatures, and
make your wantonness your ignorance. Go
to, I'll no more on't; it hath made me mad. I
say, we will have no more marriages: those
that are married already, all but one, shall
live; the rest shall keep as they are. To a
nunnery, go.

[Exit.]

OPH.

O, what a noble mind is here o'erthrown!
The courtier's, scholar's, soldier's, eye, tongue,
    sword,
The expectancy and rose of the fair state,
The glass of fashion and the mould of form,
The observ'd of all observers,—quite, quite down!
And I, of ladies most deject and wretched
That suck'd the honey of his music vows,
Now see that noble and most sovereign reason,
Like sweet bells jangled, out of tune and harsh;
That unmatch'd form and feature of blown youth
Blasted with ecstasy: O, woe is me,
To have seen what I have seen, see what I see!

[Re-enter King and Polonius.]

KING.

Love! his affections do not that way tend;
Nor what he spake, though it lack'd form a little,
Was not like madness. There's something in his
    soul
O'er which his melancholy sits on brood;
And I do doubt the hatch and the disclose
Will be some danger: which for to prevent,
I have in quick determination
Thus set it down:—he shall with speed to
    England
For the demand of our neglected tribute:
Haply the seas, and countries different,
With variable objects, shall expel
This something-settled matter in his heart;
Whereon his brains still beating puts him thus
From fashion of himself. What think you on't?

POL.

It shall do well: but yet do I believe
The origin and commencement of his grief
Sprung from neglected love.—How now, Ophelia!
You need not tell us what Lord Hamlet said;
We heard it all.—My lord, do as you please;
But if you hold it fit, after the play,
Let his queen mother all alone entreat him
To show his grief: let her be round with him;
And I'll be plac'd, so please you, in the ear
Of all their conference. If she find him not,
To England send him; or confine him where
Your wisdom best shall think.

KING.

It shall be so:
Madness in great ones must not unwatch'd go.

[Exeunt.]

SCENE II. A hall in the Castle.

[Enter Hamlet and certain Players.]

HAM.

Speak the speech, I pray you, as I pronounced it
    to you, trippingly on the tongue: but if you
    mouth it, as many of your players do, I had
    as lief the town crier spoke my lines. Nor do
    not saw the air too much with your hand,
    thus, but use all gently: for in the very
    torrent, tempest, and, as I may say,
    whirlwind of passion, you must acquire and
    beget a temperance that may give it
    smoothness. O, it offends me to the soul, to
    hear a robustious periwig-pated fellow tear a
    passion to tatters, to very rags, to split the
    ears of the groundlings, who, for the most
    part, are capable of nothing but inexplicable
    dumb shows and noise: I would have such a
    fellow whipped for o'erdoing Termagant; it
    out-herods Herod: pray you avoid it.

I PLAYER.

I warrant your honour.

HAM.

Be not too tame neither; but let your own
    discretion be your tutor: suit the action to
    the word, the word to the action; with this
    special observance, that you o'erstep not the
    modesty of nature: for anything so overdone

is from the purpose of playing, whose end, both at the first and now, was and is, to hold, as 'twere, the mirror up to nature; to show virtue her own image, scorn her own image, and the very age and body of the time his form and pressure. Now, this overdone, or come tardy off, though it make the unskilful laugh, cannot but make the judicious grieve; the censure of the which one must in your allowance, o'erweigh a whole theatre of others. O, there be players that I have seen play,—and heard others praise, and that highly,—not to speak it profanely, that, neither having the accent of Christians, nor the gait of Christian, pagan, nor man, have so strutted and bellowed that I have thought some of nature's journeymen had made men, and not made them well, they imitated humanity so abominably.

I PLAYER.

I hope we have reform'd that indifferently with us, sir.

HAM.

O, reform it altogether. And let those that play your clowns speak no more than is set down for them: for there be of them that will themselves laugh, to set on some quantity of barren spectators to laugh too, though in the meantime some necessary question of the play be then to be considered: that's villanous and shows a most pitiful ambition in the fool that uses it. Go make you ready.

[Exeunt Players.]

[Enter Polonius, Rosencrantz, and Guildenstern.]

How now, my lord! will the king hear this piece of work?

POL.

And the queen too, and that presently.

HAM.

Bid the players make haste.

[Exit Polonius.]

Will you two help to hasten them?

ROS. AND GUIL.

We will, my Lord.

[Exeunt Ros. and Guil.]

HAM.

What, ho, Horatio!

[Enter Horatio.]

HOR.

Here, sweet lord, at your service.

HAM.

Horatio, thou art e'en as just a man
As e'er my conversation cop'd withal.

HOR.

O, my dear lord,—

HAM.

Nay, do not think I flatter;
For what advancement may I hope from thee,
That no revenue hast, but thy good spirits,
To feed and clothe thee? Why should the poor be
    flatter'd?
No, let the candied tongue lick absurd pomp;
And crook the pregnant hinges of the knee
Where thrift may follow fawning. Dost thou hear?
Since my dear soul was mistress of her choice,
And could of men distinguish, her election
Hath seal'd thee for herself: for thou hast been
As one, in suffering all, that suffers nothing;
A man that Fortune's buffets and rewards
Hast ta'en with equal thanks: and bles'd are those
Whose blood and judgment are so well
    commingled
That they are not a pipe for Fortune's finger
To sound what stop she please. Give me that man
That is not passion's slave, and I will wear him
In my heart's core, ay, in my heart of heart,
As I do thee.—Something too much of this.—
There is a play to-night before the king;
One scene of it comes near the circumstance,
Which I have told thee, of my father's death:
I pr'ythee, when thou see'st that act a-foot,
Even with the very comment of thy soul
Observe mine uncle: if his occulted guilt
Do not itself unkennel in one speech,
It is a damned ghost that we have seen;
And my imaginations are as foul
As Vulcan's stithy. Give him heedful note;
For I mine eyes will rivet to his face;
And, after, we will both our judgments join
In censure of his seeming.

HOR.

Well, my lord:

If he steal aught the whilst this play is playing,

And scape detecting, I will pay the theft.

HAM.

They are coming to the play. I must be idle:

Get you a place.

[Danish march. A flourish. Enter King, Queen,
Polonius, Ophelia, Rosencrantz, Guildenstern,
and others.]

KING.

How fares our cousin Hamlet?

HAM.

Excellent, i' faith; of the chameleon's dish: I eat
the air, promise-crammed: you cannot feed
capons so.

KING.

I have nothing with this answer, Hamlet; these
words are not mine.

HAM.

No, nor mine now. My lord, you play'd once i' the
university, you say? *[To Polonius.]*

POL.

That did I, my lord, and was accounted a good
actor.

HAM.

What did you enact?

POL.

I did enact Julius Caesar; I was kill'd i' the
Capitol; Brutus killed me.

HAM.

It was a brute part of him to kill so capital a calf
there.—Be the players ready?

ROS.

Ay, my lord; they stay upon your patience.

QUEEN.

Come hither, my dear Hamlet, sit by me.

HAM.

No, good mother, here's metal more attractive.

POL.

O, ho! do you mark that? *[To the King.]*

HAM.

Lady, shall I lie in your lap?

[Lying down at Ophelia's feet.]

OPH.

No, my lord.

HAM.

I mean, my head upon your lap?

OPH.

Ay, my lord.

HAM.

Do you think I meant country matters?

OPH.

I think nothing, my lord.

HAM.

That's a fair thought to lie between maids' legs.

OPH.

What is, my lord?

HAM.

Nothing.

OPH.

You are merry, my lord.

HAM.

Who, I?

OPH.

Ay, my **LORD.**

HAM.

O, your only jig-maker! What should a man do
but be merry? for look you how cheerfully
my mother looks, and my father died within
's two hours.

OPH.

Nay, 'tis twice two months, my lord.

HAM.

So long? Nay then, let the devil wear black, for I'll
have a suit of sables. O heavens! die two
months ago, and not forgotten yet? Then
there's hope a great man's memory may
outlive his life half a year: but, by'r lady, he
must build churches then; or else shall he
suffer not thinking on, with the hobby-
horse, whose epitaph is 'For, O, for, O, the
hobby-horse is forgot!'

[Trumpets sound. The dumb show enters.]

[Enter a King and a Queen very lovingly; the
Queen embracing him and he her. She kneels,
and makes show of protestation unto him. He
takes her up, and declines his head upon her
neck: lays him down upon a bank of flowers:

she, seeing him asleep, leaves him. Anon comes in a fellow, takes off his crown, kisses it, pours poison in the king's ears, and exit. The Queen returns, finds the King dead, and makes passionate action. The Poisoner with some three or four Mutes, comes in again, seeming to lament with her. The dead body is carried away. The Poisoner wooes the Queen with gifts; she seems loth and unwilling awhile, but in the end accepts his love.]

[Exeunt.]

OPH.

What means this, my lord?

HAM.

Marry, this is miching mallecho; it means mischief.

OPH.

Belike this show imports the argument of the play.

[Enter Prologue.]

HAM.

We shall know by this fellow: the players cannot keep counsel; they'll tell qall.

OPH.

Will he tell us what this show meant?

HAM.

Ay, or any show that you'll show him: be not you ashamed to show, he'll not shame to tell you what it means.

OPH.

You are naught, you are naught: I'll mark the play.

PRO.

For us, and for our tragedy,
Here stooping to your clemency,
We beg your hearing patiently.

HAM.

Is this a prologue, or the posy of a ring?

OPH.

'Tis brief, my **LORD.**

HAM.

As woman's love.

[Enter a King and a Queen.]

P. KING.

Full thirty times hath Phoebus' cart gone round
Neptune's salt wash and Tellus' orbed ground,
And thirty dozen moons with borrow'd sheen
About the world have times twelve thirties been,
Since love our hearts, and Hymen did our hands,
Unite commutual in most sacred bands.

P. QUEEN.

So many journeys may the sun and moon
Make us again count o'er ere love be done!
But, woe is me, you are so sick of late,
So far from cheer and from your former state.
That I distrust you. Yet, though I distrust,
Discomfort you, my lord, it nothing must:
For women's fear and love holds quantity;
In neither aught, or in extremity.
Now, what my love is, proof hath made you
          know;
And as my love is siz'd, my fear is so:
Where love is great, the littlest doubts are fear;
Where little fears grow great, great love grows
          there.

P. KING.

Faith, I must leave thee, love, and shortly too;
My operant powers their functions leave to do:
And thou shalt live in this fair world behind,
Honour'd, belov'd, and haply one as kind
For husband shalt thou,—

P. QUEEN.

O, confound the rest!
Such love must needs be treason in my breast:
In second husband let me be accurst!
None wed the second but who kill'd the first.

HAM.

[Aside.] Wormwood, wormwood!

P. QUEEN.

The instances that second marriage move
Are base respects of thrift, but none of love.
A second time I kill my husband dead
When second husband kisses me in bed.

P. KING.

I do believe you think what now you speak;
But what we do determine oft we break.
Purpose is but the slave to memory;
Of violent birth, but poor validity:
Which now, like fruit unripe, sticks on the tree;
But fall unshaken when they mellow be.
Most necessary 'tis that we forget
To pay ourselves what to ourselves is debt:
What to ourselves in passion we propose,
The passion ending, doth the purpose lose.

The violence of either grief or joy
Their own enactures with themselves destroy:
Where joy most revels, grief doth most lament;
Grief joys, joy grieves, on slender accident.
This world is not for aye; nor 'tis not strange
That even our loves should with our fortunes
    change;
For 'tis a question left us yet to prove,
Whether love lead fortune, or else fortune love.
The great man down, you mark his favourite flies,
The poor advanc'd makes friends of enemies;
And hitherto doth love on fortune tend:
For who not needs shall never lack a friend;
And who in want a hollow friend doth try,
Directly seasons him his enemy.
But, orderly to end where I begun,—
Our wills and fates do so contrary run
That our devices still are overthrown;
Our thoughts are ours, their ends none of our
    own:
So think thou wilt no second husband wed;
But die thy thoughts when thy first lord is dead.

P. QUEEN.
Nor earth to me give food, nor heaven light!
Sport and repose lock from me day and night!
To desperation turn my trust and hope!
An anchor's cheer in prison be my scope!
Each opposite that blanks the face of joy
Meet what I would have well, and it destroy!
Both here and hence pursue me lasting strife,
If, once a widow, ever I be wife!

HAM.
If she should break it now! [To Ophelia.]

P. KING.
'Tis deeply sworn. Sweet, leave me here awhile;
My spirits grow dull, and fain I would beguile
The tedious day with sleep.

[Sleeps.]

P. QUEEN.
Sleep rock thy brain,
And never come mischance between us twain!

[Exit.]

HAM.
Madam, how like you this play?

QUEEN.
The lady protests too much, methinks.

HAM.
O, but she'll keep her word.

KING.
Have you heard the argument? Is there no offence
    in't?

HAM.
No, no! They do but jest, poison in jest; no
    offence i' the world.

KING.
What do you call the play?

HAM.
The Mouse-trap. Marry, how? Tropically. This
    play is the image of a murder done in
    Vienna: Gonzago is the duke's name; his
    wife, Baptista: you shall see anon; 'tis a
    knavish piece of work: but what o' that?
    your majesty, and we that have free souls, it
    touches us not: let the gall'd jade wince; our
    withers are unwrung.

[Enter Lucianus.]

This is one Lucianus, nephew to the King.

OPH.
You are a good chorus, my lord.

HAM.
I could interpret between you and your love, if I
    could see the puppets dallying.

OPH.
You are keen, my lord, you are keen.

HAM.
It would cost you a groaning to take off my edge.

OPH.
Still better, and worse.

HAM.
So you must take your husbands.—Begin,
    murderer; pox, leave thy damnable faces,
    and begin. Come:—'The croaking raven
    doth bellow for revenge.'

LUC.
Thoughts black, hands apt, drugs fit, and time
    agreeing;
Confederate season, else no creature seeing;
Thou mixture rank, of midnight weeds collected,
With Hecate's ban thrice blasted, thrice infected,
Thy natural magic and dire property

On wholesome life usurp immediately.

[Pours the poison into the sleeper's ears.]

HAM.

He poisons him i' the garden for's estate. His
    name's Gonzago:
The story is extant, and written in very choice
    Italian; you
shall see anon how the murderer gets the love of
    Gonzago's wife.

OPH.

The King rises.

HAM.

What, frighted with false fire!

QUEEN.

How fares my lord?

POL.

Give o'er the play.

KING.

Give me some light:—away!

ALL.

Lights, lights, lights!

[Exeunt all but Hamlet and Horatio.]

HAM.

Why, let the strucken deer go weep,
The hart ungalled play;
For some must watch, while some must sleep:
So runs the world away.—
Would not this, sir, and a forest of feathers—if the
    rest of my
fortunes turn Turk with me,—with two
    Provincial roses on my
razed shoes, get me a fellowship in a cry of
    players, sir?

HOR.

Half a share.

HAM.

A whole one, I.
For thou dost know, O Damon dear,
This realm dismantled was
Of Jove himself; and now reigns here
A very, very—pajock.

HOR.

You might have rhymed.

HAM.

O good Horatio, I'll take the ghost's word for a
    thousand pound! Didst perceive?

HOR.

Very well, my lord.

HAM.

Upon the talk of the poisoning?—

HOR.

I did very well note him.

HAM.

Ah, ha!—Come, some music! Come, the
    recorders!—
For if the king like not the comedy,
Why then, belike he likes it not, perdy.
Come, some music!

[Enter Rosencrantz and Guildenstern.]

GUIL.

Good my lord, vouchsafe me a word with you.

HAM.

Sir, a whole history.

GUIL.

The king, sir—

HAM.

Ay, sir, what of him?

GUIL.

Is, in his retirement, marvellous distempered.

HAM.

With drink, sir?

GUIL.

No, my lord; rather with choler.

HAM.

Your wisdom should show itself more richer to
    signify this to the doctor; for me to put him
    to his purgation would perhaps plunge him
    into far more choler.

GUIL.

Good my lord, put your discourse into some
    frame, and start not so wildly from my
    affair.

HAM.

I am tame, sir:—pronounce.

GUIL.

The queen, your mother, in most great affliction
    of spirit, hath sent me to you.

HAM.

You are welcome.

GUIL.

Nay, good my lord, this courtesy is not of the right breed. If it shall please you to make me a wholesome answer, I will do your mother's commandment: if not, your pardon and my return shall be the end of my business.

HAM.

Sir, I cannot.

GUIL.

What, my lord?

HAM.

Make you a wholesome answer; my wit's diseased: but, sir, such answer as I can make, you shall command; or rather, as you say, my mother: therefore no more, but to the matter: my mother, you say,—

ROS.

Then thus she says: your behaviour hath struck her into amazement and admiration.

HAM.

O wonderful son, that can so stonish a mother!— But is there no sequel at the heels of this mother's admiration?

ROS.

She desires to speak with you in her closet ere you go to bed.

HAM.

We shall obey, were she ten times our mother. Have you any further trade with us?

ROS.

My lord, you once did love me.

HAM.

And so I do still, by these pickers and stealers.

ROS.

Good my lord, what is your cause of distemper? you do, surely, bar the door upon your own liberty if you deny your griefs to your friend.

HAM.

Sir, I lack advancement.

ROS.

How can that be, when you have the voice of the king himself for your succession in Denmark?

HAM.

Ay, sir, but 'While the grass grows'—the proverb is something musty.

[Re-enter the Players, with recorders.]

O, the recorders:—let me see one.—To withdraw with you:—why do you go about to recover the wind of me, as if you would drive me into a toil?

GUIL.

O my lord, if my duty be too bold, my love is too unmannerly.

HAM.

I do not well understand that. Will you play upon this pipe?

GUIL.

My lord, I cannot.

HAM.

I pray you.

GUIL.

Believe me, I cannot.

HAM.

I do beseech you.

GUIL.

I know, no touch of it, my lord.

HAM.

'Tis as easy as lying: govern these ventages with your finger and thumb, give it breath with your mouth, and it will discourse most eloquent music. Look you, these are the stops.

GUIL.

But these cannot I command to any utterance of harmony; I have not the skill.

HAM.

Why, look you now, how unworthy a thing you make of me! You would play upon me; you would seem to know my stops; you would pluck out the heart of my mystery; you would sound me from my lowest note to the top of my compass; and there is much music, excellent voice, in this little organ, yet cannot you make it speak. 'Sblood, do you think I am easier to be played on than a pipe? Call me what instrument you will, though you can fret me, you cannot play upon me.

[Enter Polonius.]

God bless you, sir!

POL.

My lord, the queen would speak with you, and
    presently.

HAM.

Do you see yonder cloud that's almost in shape of
    a camel?

POL.

By the mass, and 'tis like a camel indeed.

HAM.

Methinks it is like a weasel.

POL.

It is backed like a weasel.

HAM.

Or like a whale.

POL.

Very like a whale.

HAM.

Then will I come to my mother by and by.—They
    fool me to the top of my bent.—I will come
    by and by.

POL.

I will say so.

[Exit.]

HAM.

By-and-by is easily said.

[Exit Polonius.]

—Leave me, friends.

[Exeunt Ros, Guil., Hor., and Players.]

'Tis now the very witching time of night,
When churchyards yawn, and hell itself breathes
    out
Contagion to this world: now could I drink hot
    blood,
And do such bitter business as the day
Would quake to look on. Soft! now to my
    mother.—
O heart, lose not thy nature; let not ever
The soul of Nero enter this firm bosom:
Let me be cruel, not unnatural;
I will speak daggers to her, but use none;
My tongue and soul in this be hypocrites,—
How in my words somever she be shent,

To give them seals never, my soul, consent!
[Exit.]

SCENE III. A room in the Castle.

[Enter King, Rosencrantz, and Guildenstern.]

KING.

I like him not; nor stands it safe with us
To let his madness range. Therefore prepare you;
I your commission will forthwith dispatch,
And he to England shall along with you:
The terms of our estate may not endure
Hazard so near us as doth hourly grow
Out of his lunacies.

GUIL.

We will ourselves provide:
Most holy and religious fear it is
To keep those many many bodies safe
That live and feed upon your majesty.

ROS.

The single and peculiar life is bound,
With all the strength and armour of the mind,
To keep itself from 'noyance; but much more
That spirit upon whose weal depend and rest
The lives of many. The cease of majesty
Dies not alone; but like a gulf doth draw
What's near it with it: it is a massy wheel,
Fix'd on the summit of the highest mount,
To whose huge spokes ten thousand lesser things
Are mortis'd and adjoin'd; which, when it falls,
Each small annexment, petty consequence,
Attends the boisterous ruin. Never alone
Did the king sigh, but with a general groan.

KING.

Arm you, I pray you, to this speedy voyage;
For we will fetters put upon this fear,
Which now goes too free-footed.

ROS AND GUIL.

We will haste us.

[Exeunt Ros. and Guil.]

[Enter Polonius.]

POL.

My lord, he's going to his mother's closet:
Behind the arras I'll convey myself
To hear the process; I'll warrant she'll tax him
    home:

And, as you said, and wisely was it said,
'Tis meet that some more audience than a
    mother,
Since nature makes them partial, should o'erhear
The speech, of vantage. Fare you well, my liege:
I'll call upon you ere you go to bed,
And tell you what I know.

KING.

Thanks, dear my lord.

[Exit Polonius.]

O, my offence is rank, it smells to heaven;
It hath the primal eldest curse upon't,—
A brother's murder!—Pray can I not,
Though inclination be as sharp as will:
My stronger guilt defeats my strong intent;
And, like a man to double business bound,
I stand in pause where I shall first begin,
And both neglect. What if this cursed hand
Were thicker than itself with brother's blood,—
Is there not rain enough in the sweet heavens
To wash it white as snow? Whereto serves mercy
But to confront the visage of offence?
And what's in prayer but this twofold force,—
To be forestalled ere we come to fall,
Or pardon'd being down? Then I'll look up;
My fault is past. But, O, what form of prayer
Can serve my turn? Forgive me my foul
    murder!—
That cannot be; since I am still possess'd
Of those effects for which I did the murder,—
My crown, mine own ambition, and my Queen.
May one be pardon'd and retain the offence?
In the corrupted currents of this world
Offence's gilded hand may shove by justice;
And oft 'tis seen the wicked prize itself
Buys out the law; but 'tis not so above;
There is no shuffling;—there the action lies
In his true nature; and we ourselves compell'd,
Even to the teeth and forehead of our faults,
To give in evidence. What then? what rests?
Try what repentance can: what can it not?
Yet what can it when one cannot repent?
O wretched state! O bosom black as death!
O limed soul, that, struggling to be free,
Art more engag'd! Help, angels! Make assay:
Bow, stubborn knees; and, heart, with strings of
    steel,

Be soft as sinews of the new-born babe!
All may be well.

[Retires and kneels.]

[Enter Hamlet.]

HAM.

Now might I do it pat, now he is praying;
And now I'll do't;—and so he goes to heaven;
And so am I reveng'd.—that would be scann'd:
A villain kills my father; and for that,
I, his sole son, do this same villain send
To heaven.
O, this is hire and salary, not revenge.
He took my father grossly, full of bread;
With all his crimes broad blown, as flush as May;
And how his audit stands, who knows save
    heaven?
But in our circumstance and course of thought,
'Tis heavy with him: and am I, then, reveng'd,
To take him in the purging of his soul,
When he is fit and season'd for his passage?
No.
Up, sword, and know thou a more horrid hent:
When he is drunk asleep; or in his rage;
Or in the incestuous pleasure of his bed;
At gaming, swearing; or about some act
That has no relish of salvation in't;—
Then trip him, that his heels may kick at heaven;
And that his soul may be as damn'd and black
As hell, whereto it goes. My mother stays:
This physic but prolongs thy sickly days.

[Exit.]

[The King rises and advances.]

KING.

My words fly up, my thoughts remain below:
Words without thoughts never to heaven go.

[Exit.]

SCENE IV. Another room in the Castle.

[Enter Queen and Polonius.]

POL.

He will come straight. Look you lay home to him:
Tell him his pranks have been too broad to bear
    with,
And that your grace hath screen'd and stood
    between

Much heat and him. I'll silence me e'en here.
Pray you, be round with him.

HAM.

[*Within.*] Mother, mother, mother!

QUEEN.

I'll warrant you:
Fear me not:—withdraw; I hear him coming.

[*Polonius goes behind the arras.*]

[*Enter Hamlet.*]

HAM.

Now, mother, what's the matter?

QUEEN.

Hamlet, thou hast thy father much offended.

HAM.

Mother, you have my father much offended.

QUEEN.

Come, come, you answer with an idle tongue.

HAM.

Go, go, you question with a wicked tongue.

QUEEN.

Why, how now, Hamlet!

HAM.

What's the matter now?

QUEEN.

Have you forgot me?

HAM.

No, by the rood, not so:
You are the Queen, your husband's brother's wife,
And,—would it were not so!—you are my
    mother.

QUEEN.

Nay, then, I'll set those to you that can speak.

HAM.

Come, come, and sit you down; you shall not
    budge;
You go not till I set you up a glass
Where you may see the inmost part of you.

QUEEN.

What wilt thou do? thou wilt not murder me?—
Help, help, ho!

POL.

[*Behind.*] What, ho! help, help, help!

HAM.

How now? a rat? [*Draws.*]
Dead for a ducat, dead!
[*Makes a pass through the arras.*]

POL.

[*Behind.*] O, I am slain!

[*Falls and dies.*]

QUEEN.

O me, what hast thou done?

HAM.

Nay, I know not: is it the king?

[*Draws forth Polonius.*]

QUEEN.

O, what a rash and bloody deed is this!

HAM.

A bloody deed!—almost as bad, good mother,
As kill a king and marry with his brother.

QUEEN.

As kill a king!

HAM.

Ay, lady, 'twas my word.—
Thou wretched, rash, intruding fool, farewell!

[*To Polonius.*]

I took thee for thy better: take thy fortune;
Thou find'st to be too busy is some danger.—
Leave wringing of your hands: peace! sit you
    down,
And let me wring your heart: for so I shall,
If it be made of penetrable stuff;
If damned custom have not braz'd it so
That it is proof and bulwark against sense.

QUEEN.

What have I done, that thou dar'st wag thy tongue
In noise so rude against me?

HAM.

Such an act
That blurs the grace and blush of modesty;
Calls virtue hypocrite; takes off the rose
From the fair forehead of an innocent love,
And sets a blister there; makes marriage-vows
As false as dicers' oaths: O, such a deed
As from the body of contraction plucks
The very soul, and sweet religion makes
A rhapsody of words: heaven's face doth glow;

Yea, this solidity and compound mass,
With tristful visage, as against the doom,
Is thought-sick at the act.

QUEEN.
Ah me, what act,
That roars so loud, and thunders in the index?

HAM.
Look here upon this picture, and on this,—
The counterfeit presentment of two brothers.
See what a grace was seated on this brow;
Hyperion's curls; the front of Jove himself;
An eye like Mars, to threaten and command;
A station like the herald Mercury
New lighted on a heaven-kissing hill:
A combination and a form, indeed,
Where every god did seem to set his seal,
To give the world assurance of a man;
This was your husband.—Look you now what
       follows:
Here is your husband, like a milldew'd ear
Blasting his wholesome brother. Have you eyes?
Could you on this fair mountain leave to feed,
And batten on this moor? Ha! have you eyes?
You cannot call it love; for at your age
The hey-day in the blood is tame, it's humble,
And waits upon the judgment: and what
       judgment
Would step from this to this? Sense, sure, you
       have,
Else could you not have motion: but sure that
       sense
Is apoplex'd; for madness would not err;
Nor sense to ecstacy was ne'er so thrall'd
But it reserv'd some quantity of choice
To serve in such a difference. What devil was't
That thus hath cozen'd you at hoodman-blind?
Eyes without feeling, feeling without sight,
Ears without hands or eyes, smelling sans all,
Or but a sickly part of one true sense
Could not so mope.
O shame! where is thy blush? Rebellious hell,
If thou canst mutine in a matron's bones,
To flaming youth let virtue be as wax,
And melt in her own fire: proclaim no shame
When the compulsive ardour gives the charge,
Since frost itself as actively doth burn,
And reason panders will.

QUEEN.
O Hamlet, speak no more:
Thou turn'st mine eyes into my very soul;

And there I see such black and grained spots
As will not leave their tinct.

HAM.
Nay, but to live
In the rank sweat of an enseamed bed,
Stew'd in corruption, honeying and making love
Over the nasty sty,—

QUEEN.
O, speak to me no more;
These words like daggers enter in mine ears;
No more, sweet Hamlet.

HAM.
A murderer and a villain;
A slave that is not twentieth part the tithe
Of your precedent lord; a vice of kings;
A cutpurse of the empire and the rule,
That from a shelf the precious diadem stole
And put it in his pocket!

QUEEN.
No more.

HAM.
A king of shreds and patches!—

[Enter Ghost.]

Save me and hover o'er me with your wings,
You heavenly guards!—What would your gracious
       figure?

QUEEN.
Alas, he's mad!

HAM.
Do you not come your tardy son to chide,
That, laps'd in time and passion, lets go by
The important acting of your dread command?
O, say!

GHOST.
Do not forget. This visitation
Is but to whet thy almost blunted purpose.
But, look, amazement on thy mother sits:
O, step between her and her fighting soul,—
Conceit in weakest bodies strongest works,—
Speak to her, Hamlet.

HAM.
How is it with you, lady?

QUEEN.
Alas, how is't with you,
That you do bend your eye on vacancy,
And with the incorporal air do hold discourse?
Forth at your eyes your spirits wildly peep;

And, as the sleeping soldiers in the alarm,
Your bedded hairs, like life in excrements,
Start up and stand an end. O gentle son,
Upon the heat and flame of thy distemper
Sprinkle cool patience! Whereon do you look?

HAM.

On him, on him! Look you how pale he glares!
His form and cause conjoin'd, preaching to
 stones,
Would make them capable.—Do not look upon
 me;
Lest with this piteous action you convert
My stern effects: then what I have to do
Will want true colour; tears perchance for blood.

QUEEN.

To whom do you speak this?

HAM.

Do you see nothing there?

QUEEN.

Nothing at all; yet all that is I see.

HAM.

Nor did you nothing hear?

QUEEN.

No, nothing but ourselves.

HAM.

Why, look you there! look how it steals away!
My father, in his habit as he liv'd!
Look, where he goes, even now out at the portal!

[Exit Ghost.]

QUEEN.

This is the very coinage of your brain:
This bodiless creation ecstasy
Is very cunning in.

HAM.

Ecstasy!
My pulse, as yours, doth temperately keep time,
And makes as healthful music: it is not madness
That I have utter'd: bring me to the test,
And I the matter will re-word; which madness
Would gambol from. Mother, for love of grace,
Lay not that flattering unction to your soul
That not your trespass, but my madness speaks:
It will but skin and film the ulcerous place,
Whilst rank corruption, mining all within,
Infects unseen. Confess yourself to heaven;
Repent what's past; avoid what is to come;
And do not spread the compost on the weeds,

To make them ranker. Forgive me this my virtue;
For in the fatness of these pursy times
Virtue itself of vice must pardon beg,
Yea, curb and woo for leave to do him good.

QUEEN.

O Hamlet, thou hast cleft my heart in twain.

HAM.

O, throw away the worser part of it,
And live the purer with the other half.
Good night: but go not to mine uncle's bed;
Assume a virtue, if you have it not.
That monster custom, who all sense doth eat,
Of habits evil, is angel yet in this,—
That to the use of actions fair and good
He likewise gives a frock or livery
That aptly is put on. Refrain to-night;
And that shall lend a kind of easiness
To the next abstinence: the next more easy;
For use almost can change the stamp of nature,
And either curb the devil, or throw him out
With wondrous potency. Once more, good-night:
And when you are desirous to be bles'd,
I'll blessing beg of you.—For this same lord

[Pointing to Polonius.]

I do repent; but heaven hath pleas'd it so,
To punish me with this, and this with me,
That I must be their scourge and minister.
I will bestow him, and will answer well
The death I gave him. So again, good-night.—
I must be cruel, only to be kind:
Thus bad begins, and worse remains behind.—
One word more, good lady.

QUEEN.

What shall I do?

HAM.

Not this, by no means, that I bid you do:
Let the bloat king tempt you again to bed;
Pinch wanton on your cheek; call you his mouse;
And let him, for a pair of reechy kisses,
Or paddling in your neck with his damn'd fingers,
Make you to ravel all this matter out,
That I essentially am not in madness,
But mad in craft. 'Twere good you let him know;
For who that's but a queen, fair, sober, wise,
Would from a paddock, from a bat, a gib,
Such dear concernings hide? who would do so?
No, in despite of sense and secrecy,
Unpeg the basket on the house's top,

Let the birds fly, and, like the famous ape,
To try conclusions, in the basket creep
And break your own neck down.

QUEEN.
Be thou assur'd, if words be made of breath,
And breath of life, I have no life to breathe
What thou hast said to me.

HAM.
I must to England; you know that?

QUEEN.
Alack,
I had forgot: 'tis so concluded on.

HAM.
There's letters seal'd: and my two schoolfellows,—
Whom I will trust as I will adders fang'd,—
They bear the mandate; they must sweep my way
And marshal me to knavery. Let it work;
For 'tis the sport to have the enginer
Hoist with his own petard: and 't shall go hard
But I will delve one yard below their mines
And blow them at the moon: O, 'tis most sweet,
When in one line two crafts directly meet.—
This man shall set me packing:
I'll lug the guts into the neighbour room.—
Mother, good-night.—Indeed, this counsellor
Is now most still, most secret, and most grave,
Who was in life a foolish peating knave.
Come, sir, to draw toward an end with you:—
Good night, mother.
[Exeunt severally; Hamlet, dragging out
    Polonius.]

ACT IV.

SCENE I. A room in the Castle.

*[Enter King, Queen, Rosencrantz and
    Guildenstern.]*

KING.
There's matter in these sighs. These profound
    heaves
You must translate: 'tis fit we understand them.
Where is your son?

QUEEN.
Bestow this place on us a little while.

[To Rosencrantz and Guildenstern, who go out.]

Ah, my good lord, what have I seen to-night!

KING.
What, Gertrude? How does Hamlet?

QUEEN.
Mad as the sea and wind, when both contend
Which is the mightier: in his lawless fit
Behind the arras hearing something stir,
Whips out his rapier, cries 'A rat, a rat!'
And in this brainish apprehension, kills
The unseen good old man.

KING.
O heavy deed!
It had been so with us, had we been there:
His liberty is full of threats to all;
To you yourself, to us, to every one.
Alas, how shall this bloody deed be answer'd?
It will be laid to us, whose providence
Should have kept short, restrain'd, and out of
    haunt
This mad young man. But so much was our love
We would not understand what was most fit;
But, like the owner of a foul disease,
To keep it from divulging, let it feed
Even on the pith of life. Where is he gone?

QUEEN.
To draw apart the body he hath kill'd:
O'er whom his very madness, like some ore
Among a mineral of metals base,
Shows itself pure: he weeps for what is done.

KING.
O Gertrude, come away!
The sun no sooner shall the mountains touch
But we will ship him hence: and this vile deed
We must with all our majesty and skill
Both countenance and excuse.—Ho,
    Guildenstern!

[Re-enter Rosencrantz and Guildenstern.]

Friends both, go join you with some further aid:
Hamlet in madness hath Polonius slain,
And from his mother's closet hath he dragg'd
    him:
Go seek him out; speak fair, and bring the body
Into the chapel. I pray you, haste in this.

[Exeunt Rosencrantz and Guildenstern.]

Come, Gertrude, we'll call up our wisest friends;
And let them know both what we mean to do
And what's untimely done: so haply slander,—
Whose whisper o'er the world's diameter,
As level as the cannon to his blank,

Transports his poison'd shot,—may miss our name,
And hit the woundless air.—O, come away!
My soul is full of discord and dismay.

[Exeunt.]

SCENE II. Another room in the Castle.

[Enter Hamlet.]

HAM.
Safely stowed.

ROS. AND GUIL.
[Within.] Hamlet! Lord Hamlet!

HAM.
What noise? who calls on Hamlet? O, here they
come.

[Enter Rosencrantz and Guildenstern.]

ROS.
What have you done, my lord, with the dead
body?

HAM.
Compounded it with dust, whereto 'tis kin.

ROS.
Tell us where 'tis, that we may take it thence,
And bear it to the chapel.

HAM.
Do not believe it.

ROS.
Believe what?

HAM.
That I can keep your counsel, and not mine own.
Besides, to be demanded of a sponge!—what
replication should be made by the son of a
king?

ROS.
Take you me for a sponge, my lord?

HAM.
Ay, sir; that soaks up the King's countenance, his
rewards, his authorities. But such officers do
the king best service in the end: he keeps
them, like an ape, in the corner of his jaw;
first mouthed, to be last swallowed: when he
needs what you have gleaned, it is but
squeezing you, and, sponge, you shall be dry
again.

ROS.
I understand you not, my lord.

HAM.
I am glad of it: a knavish speech sleeps in a
foolish ear.

ROS.
My lord, you must tell us where the body is and
go with us to the King.

HAM.
The body is with the king, but the king is not
with the body.
The king is a thing,—

GUIL.
A thing, my lord!

HAM.
Of nothing: bring me to him. Hide fox, and all
after.

[Exeunt.]

SCENE III. Another room in the Castle.

[Enter King, attended.]

KING.
I have sent to seek him and to find the body.
How dangerous is it that this man goes loose!
Yet must not we put the strong law on him:
He's lov'd of the distracted multitude,
Who like not in their judgment, but their eyes;
And where 'tis so, the offender's scourge is
weigh'd,
But never the offence. To bear all smooth and
even,
This sudden sending him away must seem
Deliberate pause: diseases desperate grown
By desperate appliance are reliev'd,
Or not at all.

[Enter Rosencrantz.]

How now! what hath befall'n?

ROS.
Where the dead body is bestow'd, my lord,
We cannot get from him.

KING.
But where is he?

ROS.
Without, my lord; guarded, to know your
pleasure.

KING.
Bring him before us.

ROS.

Ho, Guildenstern! bring in my lord.

[Enter Hamlet and Guildenstern.]

KING.

Now, Hamlet, where's Polonius?

HAM.

At supper.

KING.

At supper! where?

HAM.

Not where he eats, but where he is eaten: a
    certain convocation of politic worms are
    e'en at him. Your worm is your only
    emperor for diet: we fat all creatures else to
    fat us, and we fat ourselves for maggots:
    your fat king and your lean beggar is but
    variable service,—two dishes, but to one
    table: that's the end.

KING.

Alas, alas!

HAM.

A man may fish with the worm that hath eat of a
    king, and eat of the fish that hath fed of that
    worm.

KING.

What dost thou mean by this?

HAM.

Nothing but to show you how a king may go a
    progress through the guts of a beggar.

KING.

Where is Polonius?

HAM.

In heaven: send thither to see: if your messenger
    find him not there, seek him i' the other
    place yourself. But, indeed, if you find him
    not within this month, you shall nose him as
    you go up the stairs into the lobby.

KING.

Go seek him there. *[To some Attendants.]*

HAM.

He will stay till you come.

[Exeunt Attendants.]

KING.

Hamlet, this deed, for thine especial safety,—

Which we do tender, as we dearly grieve
For that which thou hast done,—must send thee
    hence
With fiery quickness: therefore prepare thyself;
The bark is ready, and the wind at help,
The associates tend, and everything is bent
For England.

HAM.

For England!

KING.

Ay, Hamlet.

HAM.

Good.

KING.

So is it, if thou knew'st our purposes.

HAM.

I see a cherub that sees them.—But, come; for
    England!—
Farewell, dear mother.

KING.

Thy loving father, Hamlet.

HAM.

My mother: father and mother is man and wife;
    man and wife is one flesh; and so, my
    mother.—Come, for England!

[Exit.]

KING.

Follow him at foot; tempt him with speed aboard;
Delay it not; I'll have him hence to-night:
Away! for everything is seal'd and done
That else leans on the affair: pray you, make haste.

[Exeunt Rosencrantz and Guildenstern.]

And, England, if my love thou hold'st at aught,—
As my great power thereof may give thee sense,
Since yet thy cicatrice looks raw and red
After the Danish sword, and thy free awe
Pays homage to us,—thou mayst not coldly set
Our sovereign process; which imports at full,
By letters conjuring to that effect,
The present death of Hamlet. Do it, England;
For like the hectic in my blood he rages,
And thou must cure me: till I know 'tis done,
Howe'er my haps, my joys were ne'er begun.

[Exit.]

SCENE IV. A plain in Denmark.

[Enter Fortinbras, and Forces marching.]

FOR.

Go, Captain, from me greet the Danish king:
Tell him that, by his license, Fortinbras
Craves the conveyance of a promis'd march
Over his kingdom. You know the rendezvous.
If that his majesty would aught with us,
We shall express our duty in his eye;
And let him know so.

CAPT.

I will do't, my **LORD.**

FOR.

Go softly on.

[Exeunt all For. and Forces.]

[Enter Hamlet, Rosencrantz, Guildenstern, &c.]

HAM.

Good sir, whose powers are these?

CAPT.

They are of Norway, sir.

HAM.

How purpos'd, sir, I pray you?

CAPT.

Against some part of Poland.

HAM.

Who commands them, sir?

CAPT.

The nephew to old Norway, Fortinbras.

HAM.

Goes it against the main of Poland, sir,
Or for some frontier?

CAPT.

Truly to speak, and with no addition,
We go to gain a little patch of ground
That hath in it no profit but the name.
To pay five ducats, five, I would not farm it;
Nor will it yield to Norway or the Pole
A ranker rate, should it be sold in fee.

HAM.

Why, then the Polack never will defend it.

CAPT.

Yes, it is already garrison'd.

HAM.

Two thousand souls and twenty thousand ducats
Will not debate the question of this straw:
This is the imposthume of much wealth and
     peace,
That inward breaks, and shows no cause without
Why the man dies.—I humbly thank you, sir.

CAPT.

God b' wi' you, sir.

[Exit.]

ROS.

Will't please you go, my lord?

HAM.

I'll be with you straight. Go a little before.

[Exeunt all but Hamlet.]

How all occasions do inform against me
And spur my dull revenge! What is a man,
If his chief good and market of his time
Be but to sleep and feed? a beast, no more.
Sure he that made us with such large discourse,
Looking before and after, gave us not
That capability and godlike reason
To fust in us unus'd. Now, whether it be
Bestial oblivion, or some craven scruple
Of thinking too precisely on the event,—
A thought which, quarter'd, hath but one part
     wisdom
And ever three parts coward,—I do not know
Why yet I live to say 'This thing's to do;'
Sith I have cause, and will, and strength, and
     means
To do't. Examples, gross as earth, exhort me:
Witness this army, of such mass and charge,
Led by a delicate and tender prince;
Whose spirit, with divine ambition puff'd,
Makes mouths at the invisible event;
Exposing what is mortal and unsure
To all that fortune, death, and danger dare,
Even for an egg-shell. Rightly to be great
Is not to stir without great argument,
But greatly to find quarrel in a straw
When honour's at the stake. How stand I, then,
That have a father kill'd, a mother stain'd,
Excitements of my reason and my blood,
And let all sleep? while, to my shame, I see
The imminent death of twenty thousand men

That, for a fantasy and trick of fame,
Go to their graves like beds; fight for a plot
Whereon the numbers cannot try the cause,
Which is not tomb enough and continent
To hide the slain?—O, from this time forth,
My thoughts be bloody, or be nothing worth!

[Exit.]

SCENE V. Elsinore. A room in the Castle.

[Enter Queen and Horatio.]

QUEEN.
I will not speak with her.

GENT.
She is importunate; indeed distract:
Her mood will needs be pitied.

QUEEN.
What would she have?

GENT.
She speaks much of her father; says she hears
There's tricks i' the world, and hems, and beats
    her heart;
Spurns enviously at straws; speaks things in
    doubt,
That carry but half sense: her speech is nothing,
Yet the unshaped use of it doth move
The hearers to collection; they aim at it,
And botch the words up fit to their own thoughts;
Which, as her winks, and nods, and gestures yield
    them,
Indeed would make one think there might be
    thought,
Though nothing sure, yet much unhappily.
'Twere good she were spoken with; for she may
    strew
Dangerous conjectures in ill-breeding minds.

QUEEN.
Let her come in.

[Exit Horatio.]

To my sick soul, as sin's true nature is,
Each toy seems Prologue to some great amiss:
So full of artless jealousy is guilt,
It spills itself in fearing to be spilt.

[Re-enter Horatio with Ophelia.]

OPH.
Where is the beauteous majesty of Denmark?

QUEEN.
How now, Ophelia?

OPH.
[Sings.]
How should I your true love know
From another one?
By his cockle bat and staff
And his sandal shoon.

QUEEN.
Alas, sweet lady, what imports this song?

OPH.
Say you? nay, pray you, mark.

[Sings.]

He is dead and gone, lady,
He is dead and gone;
At his head a grass green turf,
At his heels a stone.

QUEEN.
Nay, but Ophelia—

OPH.
Pray you, mark.

[Sings.]

White his shroud as the mountain snow,

[Enter King.]

QUEEN.
Alas, look here, my lord!

OPH.
[Sings.]
Larded all with sweet flowers;
Which bewept to the grave did go
With true-love showers.

KING.
How do you, pretty lady?

OPH.
Well, God dild you! They say the owl was a
    baker's daughter.
Lord, we know what we are, but know not what
    we may be. God be at your table!

KING.
Conceit upon her father.

OPH.

Pray you, let's have no words of this; but when
    they ask you what
it means, say you this:

[Sings.]

To-morrow is Saint Valentine's day
All in the morning bedtime,
And I a maid at your window,
To be your Valentine.
Then up he rose and donn'd his clothes,
And dupp'd the chamber door,
Let in the maid, that out a maid
Never departed more.

KING.

Pretty Ophelia!

OPH.

Indeed, la, without an oath, I'll make an end on't:

[Sings.]

By Gis and by Saint Charity,
Alack, and fie for shame!
Young men will do't if they come to't;
By cock, they are to blame.
Quoth she, before you tumbled me,
You promis'd me to wed.
So would I ha' done, by yonder sun,
An thou hadst not come to my bed.

KING.

How long hath she been thus?

OPH.

I hope all will be well. We must be patient: but I
    cannot choose but weep, to think they
    would lay him i' the cold ground. My
    brother shall know of it: and so I thank you
    for your good counsel.—Come, my
    coach!—Good night, ladies; good night,
    sweet ladies; good night, good night.

[Exit.]

KING.

Follow her close; give her good watch, I pray you.

[Exit Horatio.]

O, this is the poison of deep grief; it springs
All from her father's death. O Gertrude, Gertrude,
When sorrows come, they come not single spies,
But in battalions! First, her father slain:
Next, your son gone; and he most violent author

Of his own just remove: the people muddied,
Thick and and unwholesome in their thoughts
    and whispers
For good Polonius' death; and we have done but
    greenly
In hugger-mugger to inter him: poor Ophelia
Divided from herself and her fair judgment,
Without the which we are pictures or mere beasts:
Last, and as much containing as all these,
Her brother is in secret come from France;
Feeds on his wonder, keeps himself in clouds,
And wants not buzzers to infect his ear
With pestilent speeches of his father's death;
Wherein necessity, of matter beggar'd,
Will nothing stick our person to arraign
In ear and ear. O my dear Gertrude, this,
Like to a murdering piece, in many places
Give, me superfluous death.

[A noise within.]

QUEEN.

Alack, what noise is this?

KING.

Where are my Switzers? let them guard the door.

[Enter a Gentleman.]

What is the matter?

GENT.

Save yourself, my lord:
The ocean, overpeering of his list,
Eats not the flats with more impetuous haste
Than young Laertes, in a riotous head,
O'erbears your offices. The rabble call him lord;
And, as the world were now but to begin,
Antiquity forgot, custom not known,
The ratifiers and props of every word,
They cry 'Choose we! Laertes shall be king!'
Caps, hands, and tongues applaud it to the
    clouds,
'Laertes shall be king! Laertes king!'

QUEEN.

How cheerfully on the false trail they cry!
O, this is counter, you false Danish dogs!

[A noise within.]

KING.

The doors are broke.

[Enter Laertes, armed; Danes following.]

LAER.
Where is this king?—Sirs, stand you all without.

DANES.
No, let's come in.

LAER.
I pray you, give me leave.

DANES.
We will, we will.

[*They retire without the door.*]

LAER.
I thank you:—keep the door.—O thou vile king,
Give me my father!

QUEEN.
Calmly, good Laertes.

LAER.
That drop of blood that's calm proclaims me
        bastard;
Cries cuckold to my father; brands the harlot
Even here, between the chaste unsmirched brow
Of my true mother.

KING.
What is the cause, Laertes,
That thy rebellion looks so giant-like?—
Let him go, Gertrude; do not fear our person:
There's such divinity doth hedge a king,
That treason can but peep to what it would,
Acts little of his will.—Tell me, Laertes,
Why thou art thus incens'd.—Let him go,
        Gertrude:—
Speak, man.

LAER.
Where is my father?

KING.
Dead.

QUEEN.
But not by him.

KING.
Let him demand his fill.

LAER.
How came he dead? I'll not be juggled with:
To hell, allegiance! vows, to the blackest devil!
Conscience and grace, to the profoundest pit!
I dare damnation:—to this point I stand,—
That both the worlds, I give to negligence,
Let come what comes; only I'll be reveng'd

Most throughly for my father.

KING.
Who shall stay you?

LAER.
My will, not all the world:
And for my means, I'll husband them so well,
They shall go far with little.

KING.
Good Laertes,
If you desire to know the certainty
Of your dear father's death, is't writ in your
        revenge
That, sweepstake, you will draw both friend and
        foe,
Winner and loser?

LAER.
None but his enemies.

KING.
Will you know them then?

LAER.
To his good friends thus wide I'll ope my arms;
And, like the kind life-rendering pelican,
Repast them with my blood.

KING.
Why, now you speak
Like a good child and a true gentleman.
That I am guiltless of your father's death,
And am most sensibly in grief for it,
It shall as level to your judgment pierce
As day does to your eye.

DANES.
[*Within*] Let her come in.

LAER.
How now! What noise is that?

[*Re-enter Ophelia, fantastically dressed with straws
        and flowers.*]

O heat, dry up my brains! tears seven times salt,
Burn out the sense and virtue of mine eye!—
By heaven, thy madness shall be paid by weight,
Till our scale turn the beam. O rose of May!
Dear maid, kind sister, sweet Ophelia!—
O heavens! is't possible a young maid's wits
Should be as mortal as an old man's life?
Nature is fine in love; and where 'tis fine,
It sends some precious instance of itself
After the thing it loves.

OPH.

[Sings.]

> They bore him barefac'd on the bier
> Hey no nonny, nonny, hey nonny
> And on his grave rain'd many a tear.—
> Fare you well, my dove!

LAER.

Hadst thou thy wits, and didst persuade revenge,
It could not move thus.

OPH.

You must sing 'Down a-down, an you call him a-
   down-a.' O, how the wheel becomes it! It is
   the false steward, that stole his master's
   daughter.

LAER.

This nothing's more than matter.

OPH.

There's rosemary, that's for remembrance; pray,
   love, remember: and there is pansies, that's
   for thoughts.

LAER.

A document in madness,—thoughts and
   remembrance fitted.

OPH.

There's fennel for you, and columbines:—there's
   rue for you; and here's some for me:—we
   may call it herb of grace o' Sundays:—O,
   you must wear your rue with a difference.—
   There's a daisy:—I would give you some
   violets, but they wither'd all when my father
   died:—they say he made a good end,—
   [Sings.] For bonny sweet Robin is all my
   joy,—

LAER.

Thought and affliction, passion, hell itself,
She turns to favour and to prettiness.

OPH.

[Sings.]

> And will he not come again?
> And will he not come again?
> No, no, he is dead,
> Go to thy death-bed,
> He never will come again.
> His beard was as white as snow,
> All flaxen was his poll:
> He is gone, he is gone,

> And we cast away moan:
> God ha' mercy on his soul!
> And of all Christian souls, I pray God.—God b'
>   wi' ye.

[Exit.]

LAER.

Do you see this, O God?

KING.

Laertes, I must commune with your grief,
Or you deny me right. Go but apart,
Make choice of whom your wisest friends you
   will,
And they shall hear and judge 'twixt you and me.
If by direct or by collateral hand
They find us touch'd, we will our kingdom give,
Our crown, our life, and all that we call ours,
To you in satisfaction; but if not,
Be you content to lend your patience to us,
And we shall jointly labour with your soul
To give it due content.

LAER.

Let this be so;
His means of death, his obscure burial,—
No trophy, sword, nor hatchment o'er his bones,
No noble rite nor formal ostentation,—
Cry to be heard, as 'twere from heaven to earth,
That I must call't in question.

KING.

So you shall;
And where the offence is let the great axe fall.
I pray you go with me.

[Exeunt.]

SCENE VI. Another room in the Castle.

[Enter Horatio and a Servant.]

HOR.

What are they that would speak with me?

SERVANT.

Sailors, sir: they say they have letters for you.

HOR.

Let them come in.

[Exit Servant.]

I do not know from what part of the world
I should be greeted, if not from Lord Hamlet.

[Enter Sailors.]

I SAILOR.
God bless you, sir.

HOR.
Let him bless thee too.

Sailor. He shall, sir, an't please him. There's a letter
for you, sir,—it comes from the ambassador
that was bound for England; if your name
be Horatio, as I am let to know it is.

HOR.
[Reads.] 'Horatio, when thou shalt have
overlooked this, give these fellows some
means to the king: they have letters for him.
Ere we were two days old at sea, a pirate of
very warlike appointment gave us chase.
Finding ourselves too slow of sail, we put on
a compelled valour, and in the grapple I
boarded them: on the instant they got clear
of our ship; so I alone became their
prisoner. They have dealt with me like
thieves of mercy: but they knew what they
did; I am to do a good turn for them. Let the
king have the letters I have sent; and repair
thou to me with as much haste as thou
wouldst fly death. I have words to speak in
thine ear will make thee dumb; yet are they
much too light for the bore of the matter.
These good fellows will bring thee where I
am. Rosencrantz and Guildenstern hold
their course for England: of them I have
much to tell thee. Farewell. He that thou
knowest thine, Hamlet.'

Come, I will give you way for these your letters;
And do't the speedier, that you may direct me
To him from whom you brought them.

[Exeunt.]

SCENE VII. Another room in the Castle.

[Enter King and Laertes.]

KING.
Now must your conscience my acquittance seal,
And you must put me in your heart for friend,
Sith you have heard, and with a knowing ear,
That he which hath your noble father slain
Pursu'd my life.

LAER.
It well appears:—but tell me
Why you proceeded not against these feats,
So crimeful and so capital in nature,
As by your safety, wisdom, all things else,
You mainly were stirr'd up.

KING.
O, for two special reasons;
Which may to you, perhaps, seem much
          unsinew'd,
But yet to me they are strong. The queen his
          mother
Lives almost by his looks; and for myself,—
My virtue or my plague, be it either which,—
She's so conjunctive to my life and soul,
That, as the star moves not but in his sphere,
I could not but by her. The other motive,
Why to a public count I might not go,
Is the great love the general gender bear him;
Who, dipping all his faults in their affection,
Would, like the spring that turneth wood to stone,
Convert his gyves to graces; so that my arrows,
Too slightly timber'd for so loud a wind,
Would have reverted to my bow again,
And not where I had aim'd them.

LAER.
And so have I a noble father lost;
A sister driven into desperate terms,—
Whose worth, if praises may go back again,
Stood challenger on mount of all the age
For her perfections:—but my revenge will come.

KING.
Break not your sleeps for that:—you must not
          think
That we are made of stuff so flat and dull
That we can let our beard be shook with danger,
And think it pastime. You shortly shall hear more:
I lov'd your father, and we love ourself;
And that, I hope, will teach you to imagine,—

[Enter a Messenger.]

How now! What news?

MESS.
Letters, my lord, from Hamlet:
This to your majesty; this to the Queen.

KING.
From Hamlet! Who brought them?

MESS.

Sailors, my lord, they say; I saw them not:
They were given me by Claudio:—he receiv'd
    them
Of him that brought them.

KING.

Laertes, you shall hear them.
Leave us.

[Exit Messenger.]

[Reads] 'High and mighty,—You shall know I am
    set naked on your kingdom. To-morrow
    shall I beg leave to see your kingly eyes:
    when I shall, first asking your pardon
    thereunto, recount the occasions of my
    sudden and more strange return. Hamlet.'
What should this mean? Are all the rest come
    back?
Or is it some abuse, and no such thing?

LAER.

Know you the hand?

KING.

'Tis Hamlet's character:—'Naked!'—
And in a postscript here, he says 'alone.'
Can you advise me?

LAER.

I am lost in it, my lord. But let him come;
It warms the very sickness in my heart
That I shall live and tell him to his teeth,
'Thus didest thou.'

KING.

If it be so, Laertes,—
As how should it be so? how otherwise?—
Will you be rul'd by me?

LAER.

Ay, my lord;
So you will not o'errule me to a peace.

KING.

To thine own peace. If he be now return'd—
As checking at his voyage, and that he means
No more to undertake it,—I will work him
To exploit, now ripe in my device,
Under the which he shall not choose but fall:
And for his death no wind shall breathe;
But even his mother shall uncharge the practice
And call it accident.

LAER.

My lord, I will be rul'd;
The rather if you could devise it so
That I might be the organ.

KING.

It falls right.
You have been talk'd of since your travel much,
And that in Hamlet's hearing, for a quality
Wherein they say you shine: your sum of parts
Did not together pluck such envy from him
As did that one; and that, in my regard,
Of the unworthiest siege.

LAER.

What part is that, my lord?

KING.

A very riband in the cap of youth,
Yet needful too; for youth no less becomes
The light and careless livery that it wears
Than settled age his sables and his weeds,
Importing health and graveness.—Two months
    since,
Here was a gentleman of Normandy,—
I've seen myself, and serv'd against, the French,
And they can well on horseback: but this gallant
Had witchcraft in't: he grew unto his seat;
And to such wondrous doing brought his horse,
As had he been incorps'd and demi-natur'd
With the brave beast: so far he topp'd my thought
That I, in forgery of shapes and tricks,
Come short of what he did.

LAER.

A Norman was't?

KING.

A Norman.

LAER.

Upon my life, Lamond.

KING.

The very same.

LAER.

I know him well: he is the brooch indeed
And gem of all the nation.

KING.

He made confession of you;
And gave you such a masterly report
For art and exercise in your defence,
And for your rapier most especially,

That he cried out, 'twould be a sight indeed
If one could match you: the scrimers of their
    nation
He swore, had neither motion, guard, nor eye,
If you oppos'd them. Sir, this report of his
Did Hamlet so envenom with his envy
That he could nothing do but wish and beg
Your sudden coming o'er, to play with him.
Now, out of this,—

LAER.
What out of this, my lord?

KING.
Laertes, was your father dear to you?
Or are you like the painting of a sorrow,
A face without a heart?

LAER.
Why ask you this?

KING.
Not that I think you did not love your father;
But that I know love is begun by time,
And that I see, in passages of proof,
Time qualifies the spark and fire of it.
There lives within the very flame of love
A kind of wick or snuff that will abate it;
And nothing is at a like goodness still;
For goodness, growing to a plurisy,
Dies in his own too much: that we would do,
We should do when we would; for this 'would'
    changes,
And hath abatements and delays as many
As there are tongues, are hands, are accidents;
And then this 'should' is like a spendthrift sigh,
That hurts by easing. But to the quick o' the
    ulcer:—
Hamlet comes back: what would you undertake
To show yourself your father's son in deed
More than in words?

LAER.
To cut his throat i' the church.

KING.
No place, indeed, should murder sanctuarize;
Revenge should have no bounds. But, good
    Laertes,
Will you do this, keep close within your chamber.
Hamlet return'd shall know you are come home:

We'll put on those shall praise your excellence
And set a double varnish on the fame
The Frenchman gave you; bring you in fine
    together
And wager on your heads: he, being remiss,
Most generous, and free from all contriving,
Will not peruse the foils; so that with ease,
Or with a little shuffling, you may choose
A sword unbated, and, in a pass of practice,
Requite him for your father.

LAER.
I will do't:
And for that purpose I'll anoint my sword.
I bought an unction of a mountebank,
So mortal that, but dip a knife in it,
Where it draws blood no cataplasm so rare,
Collected from all simples that have virtue
Under the moon, can save the thing from death
This is but scratch'd withal: I'll touch my point
With this contagion, that, if I gall him slightly,
It may be death.

KING.
Let's further think of this;
Weigh what convenience both of time and means
May fit us to our shape: if this should fail,
And that our drift look through our bad
    performance.
'Twere better not assay'd: therefore this project
Should have a back or second, that might hold
If this did blast in proof. Soft! let me see:—
We'll make a solemn wager on your cunnings,—
I ha't:
When in your motion you are hot and dry,—
As make your bouts more violent to that end,—
And that he calls for drink, I'll have prepar'd him
A chalice for the nonce; whereon but sipping,
If he by chance escape your venom'd stuck,
Our purpose may hold there.

[Enter Queen.]

How now, sweet queen!

QUEEN.
One woe doth tread upon another's heel,
So fast they follow:—your sister's drown'd,
    Laertes.

LAER.

Drown'd! O, where?

QUEEN.

There is a willow grows aslant a brook,
That shows his hoar leaves in the glassy stream;
There with fantastic garlands did she come
Of crowflowers, nettles, daisies, and long purples,
That liberal shepherds give a grosser name,
But our cold maids do dead men's fingers call
    them.
There, on the pendant boughs her coronet weeds
Clamb'ring to hang, an envious sliver broke;
When down her weedy trophies and herself
Fell in the weeping brook. Her clothes spread
    wide;
And, mermaid-like, awhile they bore her up;
Which time she chaunted snatches of old tunes;
As one incapable of her own distress,
Or like a creature native and indu'd
Unto that element: but long it could not be
Till that her garments, heavy with their drink,
Pull'd the poor wretch from her melodious lay
To muddy death.

LAER.

Alas, then she is drown'd?

QUEEN.

Drown'd, drown'd.

LAER.

Too much of water hast thou, poor Ophelia,
And therefore I forbid my tears: but yet
It is our trick; nature her custom holds,
Let shame say what it will: when these are gone,
The woman will be out.—Adieu, my lord:
I have a speech of fire, that fain would blaze,
But that this folly douts it.

[*Exit.*]

KING.

Let's follow, Gertrude;
How much I had to do to calm his rage!
Now fear I this will give it start again;
Therefore let's follow.

[*Exeunt.*]

ACT V.

SCENE I. A churchyard.

[*Enter two Clowns, with spades, &c.*]

1 CLOWN.

Is she to be buried in Christian burial when she
    wilfully seeks her own salvation?

2 CLOWN.

I tell thee she is; and therefore make her grave
    straight: the crowner hath sat on her, and
    finds it Christian burial.

1 CLOWN.

How can that be, unless she drowned herself in
    her own defence?

2 CLOWN.

Why, 'tis found so.

1 CLOWN.

It must be se offendendo; it cannot be else. For
    here lies the point: if I drown myself
    wittingly, it argues an act: and an act hath
    three branches; it is to act, to do, and to
    perform: argal, she drowned herself
    wittingly.

2 CLOWN.

Nay, but hear you, goodman delver,—

1 CLOWN.

Give me leave. Here lies the water; good: here
    stands the man; good: if the man go to this
    water and drown himself, it is, will he, nill
    he, he goes,—mark you that: but if the water
    come to him and drown him, he drowns not
    himself; argal, he that is not guilty of his
    own death shortens not his own life.

2 CLOWN.

But is this law?

1 CLOWN.

Ay, marry, is't—crowner's quest law.

2 CLOWN.

Will you ha' the truth on't? If this had not been a
    gentlewoman, she should have been buried
    out o' Christian burial.

1 CLOWN.

Why, there thou say'st: and the more pity that great folk should have countenance in this world to drown or hang themselves more than their even Christian.—Come, my spade. There is no ancient gentlemen but gardeners, ditchers, and grave-makers: they hold up Adam's profession.

2 CLOWN.

Was he a gentleman?

1 CLOWN.

He was the first that ever bore arms.

2 CLOWN.

Why, he had none.

1 CLOWN.

What, art a heathen? How dost thou understand the Scripture? The Scripture says Adam digg'd: could he dig without arms? I'll put another question to thee: if thou answerest me not to the purpose, confess thyself,—

2 CLOWN.

Go to.

1 CLOWN.

What is he that builds stronger than either the mason, the shipwright, or the carpenter?

2 CLOWN.

The gallows-maker; for that frame outlives a thousand tenants.

1 CLOWN.

I like thy wit well, in good faith: the gallows does well; but how does it well? it does well to those that do ill: now, thou dost ill to say the gallows is built stronger than the church; argal, the gallows may do well to thee. To't again, come.

2 CLOWN.

Who builds stronger than a mason, a shipwright, or a carpenter?

1 CLOWN.

Ay, tell me that, and unyoke.

2 CLOWN.

Marry, now I can tell.

1 CLOWN.

To't.

2 CLOWN.

Mass, I cannot tell.

[Enter Hamlet and Horatio, at a distance.]

1 CLOWN.

Cudgel thy brains no more about it, for your dull ass will not mend his pace with beating; and when you are asked this question next, say 'a grave-maker;' the houses he makes last till doomsday. Go, get thee to Yaughan; fetch me a stoup of liquor.

[Exit Second Clown.]

[Digs and sings.]

In youth when I did love, did love,
Methought it was very sweet;
To contract, O, the time for, ah, my behove,
O, methought there was nothing meet.

HAM.

Has this fellow no feeling of his business, that he sings at grave-making?

HOR.

Custom hath made it in him a property of easiness.

HAM.

'Tis e'en so: the hand of little employment hath the daintier sense.

1 CLOWN.

[Sings.]

But age, with his stealing steps,
Hath claw'd me in his clutch,
And hath shipp'd me into the land,
As if I had never been such.

[Throws up a skull.]

HAM.

That skull had a tongue in it, and could sing once: how the knave jowls it to the ground, as if 'twere Cain's jawbone, that did the first murder! This might be the pate of a politician, which this ass now o'erreaches; one that would circumvent God, might it not?

HOR.

It might, my lord.

HAM.

Or of a courtier, which could say 'Good morrow, sweet lord! How dost thou, good lord?' This might be my lord such-a-one, that praised my lord such-a-one's horse when he meant to beg it,—might it not?

HOR.

Ay, my lord.

HAM.

Why, e'en so: and now my Lady Worm's; chapless, and knocked about the mazard with a sexton's spade: here's fine revolution, an we had the trick to see't. Did these bones cost no more the breeding but to play at loggets with 'em? mine ache to think on't.

1 CLOWN.

[Sings.]

A pickaxe and a spade, a spade,
For and a shrouding sheet;
O, a pit of clay for to be made
For such a guest is meet.

[Throws up another skull].

HAM.

There's another: why may not that be the skull of a lawyer? Where be his quiddits now, his quillets, his cases, his tenures, and his tricks? why does he suffer this rude knave now to knock him about the sconce with a dirty shovel, and will not tell him of his action of battery? Hum! This fellow might be in's time a great buyer of land, with his statutes, his recognizances, his fines, his double vouchers, his recoveries: is this the fine of his fines, and the recovery of his recoveries, to have his fine pate full of fine dirt? will his vouchers vouch him no more of his purchases, and double ones too, than the length and breadth of a pair of indentures? The very conveyances of his lands will scarcely lie in this box; and must the inheritor himself have no more, ha?

HOR.

Not a jot more, my lord.

HAM.

Is not parchment made of sheep-skins?

HOR.

Ay, my lord, And of calf-skins too.

HAM.

They are sheep and calves which seek out assurance in that. I will speak to this fellow.—Whose grave's this, sir?

1 CLOWN.

Mine, sir.

[Sings.]

O, a pit of clay for to be made
For such a guest is meet.

HAM.

I think it be thine indeed, for thou liest in't.

1 CLOWN.

You lie out on't, sir, and therefore 'tis not yours: for my part,
I do not lie in't, yet it is mine.

HAM.

Thou dost lie in't, to be in't and say it is thine: 'tis for the dead, not for the quick; therefore thou liest.

1 CLOWN.

'Tis a quick lie, sir; 't will away again from me to you.

HAM.

What man dost thou dig it for?

1 CLOWN.

For no man, sir.

HAM.

What woman then?

1 CLOWN.

For none neither.

HAM.

Who is to be buried in't?

1 CLOWN.

One that was a woman, sir; but, rest her soul, she's dead.

HAM.

How absolute the knave is! We must speak by the card, or equivocation will undo us. By the Lord, Horatio, these three years I have taken note of it, the age is grown so picked that the toe of the peasant comes so near the heel of the courtier he galls his kibe.—How long hast thou been a grave-maker?

1 CLOWN.
Of all the days i' the year, I came to't that day that our last King Hamlet overcame Fortinbras.

HAM.
How long is that since?

1 CLOWN.
Cannot you tell that? every fool can tell that: it was the very day that young Hamlet was born,—he that is mad, and sent into England.

HAM.
Ay, marry, why was be sent into England?

1 CLOWN.
Why, because he was mad: he shall recover his wits there; or, if he do not, it's no great matter there.

HAM.
Why?

1 CLOWN.
'Twill not he seen in him there; there the men are as mad as he.

HAM.
How came he mad?

1 CLOWN.
Very strangely, they say.

HAM.
How strangely?

1 CLOWN.
Faith, e'en with losing his wits.

HAM.
Upon what ground?

1 CLOWN.
Why, here in Denmark: I have been sexton here, man and boy, thirty years.

HAM.
How long will a man lie i' the earth ere he rot?

1 CLOWN.
Faith, if he be not rotten before he die,—as we have many pocky corses now-a-days that will scarce hold the laying in,—he will last you some eight year or nine year: a tanner will last you nine year.

HAM.
Why he more than another?

1 CLOWN.
Why, sir, his hide is so tann'd with his trade that he will keep out water a great while; and your water is a sore decayer of your whoreson dead body. Here's a skull now; this skull hath lain in the earth three-and-twenty years.

HAM.
Whose was it?

1 CLOWN.
A whoreson, mad fellow's it was: whose do you think it was?

HAM.
Nay, I know not.

1 CLOWN.
A pestilence on him for a mad rogue! 'a pour'd a flagon of
Rhenish on my head once. This same skull, sir, was Yorick's skull, the king's jester.

HAM.
This?

1 CLOWN.
E'en that.

HAM.
Let me see. *[Takes the skull.]* Alas, poor Yorick!—I knew him, Horatio; a fellow of infinite jest, of most excellent fancy: he hath borne me on his back a thousand times; and now, how abhorred in my imagination it is! my gorge rises at it. Here hung those lips that I have kiss'd I know not how oft. Where be your gibes now? your gambols? your songs? your flashes of merriment, that were wont to set the table on a roar? Not one now, to mock your own grinning? quite chap-fallen? Now, get you to my lady's chamber, and tell her, let her paint an inch thick, to this favour she must come; make her laugh at that.— Pr'ythee, Horatio, tell me one thing.

HOR.
What's that, my lord?

HAM.
Dost thou think Alexander looked o' this fashion i' the earth?

HOR.
E'en so.

HAM.

And smelt so? Pah!

[Throws down the skull.]

HOR.

E'en so, my lord.

HAM.

To what base uses we may return, Horatio! Why
  may not imagination trace the noble dust of
  Alexander till he find it stopping a bung-
  hole?

HOR.

'Twere to consider too curiously to consider so.

HAM.

No, faith, not a jot; but to follow him thither with
  modesty enough, and likelihood to lead it:
  as thus: Alexander died, Alexander was
  buried, Alexander returneth into dust; the
  dust is earth; of earth we make loam; and
  why of that loam whereto he was converted
  might they not stop a beer-barrel?
  Imperious Caesar, dead and turn'd to clay,
  Might stop a hole to keep the wind away. O,
  that that earth which kept the world in awe
  Should patch a wall to expel the winter's
  flaw! But soft! but soft! aside!—Here comes
  the King.

*[Enter priests, &c, in procession; the corpse of
Ophelia, Laertes, and Mourners following;
King, Queen, their Trains, &c.]*

The queen, the courtiers: who is that they follow?
And with such maimed rites? This doth betoken
The corse they follow did with desperate hand
Fordo it own life: 'twas of some estate.
Couch we awhile and mark.

[Retiring with Horatio.]

LAER.

What ceremony else?

HAM.

That is Laertes,
A very noble youth: mark.

LAER.

What ceremony else?

1 PRIEST.

Her obsequies have been as far enlarg'd
As we have warranties: her death was doubtful;
And, but that great command o'ersways the order,

She should in ground unsanctified have lodg'd
Till the last trumpet; for charitable prayers,
Shards, flints, and pebbles should be thrown on
  her,
Yet here she is allowed her virgin rites,
Her maiden strewments, and the bringing home
Of bell and burial.

LAER.

Must there no more be done?

1 PRIEST.

No more be done;
We should profane the service of the dead
To sing a requiem and such rest to her
As to peace-parted souls.

LAER.

Lay her i' the earth;—
And from her fair and unpolluted flesh
May violets spring!—I tell thee, churlish priest,
A ministering angel shall my sister be
When thou liest howling.

HAM.

What, the fair Ophelia?

QUEEN.

Sweets to the sweet: farewell.

[Scattering flowers.]

I hop'd thou shouldst have been my Hamlet's
  wife;
I thought thy bride-bed to have deck'd, sweet
  maid,
And not have strew'd thy grave.

LAER.

O, treble woe
Fall ten times treble on that cursed head
Whose wicked deed thy most ingenious sense
Depriv'd thee of!—Hold off the earth awhile,
Till I have caught her once more in mine arms:

[Leaps into the grave.]

Now pile your dust upon the quick and dead,
Till of this flat a mountain you have made,
To o'ertop old Pelion or the skyish head
Of blue Olympus.

HAM.

[Advancing.]

What is he whose grief
Bears such an emphasis? whose phrase of sorrow

Conjures the wandering stars, and makes them
    stand
Like wonder-wounded hearers? this is I,
Hamlet the Dane.

[Leaps into the grave.]

LAER.
The devil take thy soul!

[Grappling with him.]

HAM.
Thou pray'st not well.
I pr'ythee, take thy fingers from my throat;
For, though I am not splenetive and rash,
Yet have I in me something dangerous,
Which let thy wiseness fear: away thy hand!

KING.
Pluck them asunder.

QUEEN.
Hamlet! Hamlet!

ALL.
Gentlemen!—

HOR.
Good my lord, be quiet.

*[The Attendants part them, and they come out of
    the grave.]*

HAM.
Why, I will fight with him upon this theme
Until my eyelids will no longer wag.

QUEEN.
O my son, what theme?

HAM.
I lov'd Ophelia; forty thousand brothers
Could not, with all their quantity of love,
Make up my sum.—What wilt thou do for her?

KING.
O, he is mad, Laertes.

QUEEN.
For love of God, forbear him!

HAM.
'Swounds, show me what thou'lt do:
Woul't weep? woul't fight? woul't fast? woul't tear
    thyself?
Woul't drink up eisel? eat a crocodile?
I'll do't.—Dost thou come here to whine?
To outface me with leaping in her grave?
Be buried quick with her, and so will I:

And, if thou prate of mountains, let them throw
Millions of acres on us, till our ground,
Singeing his pate against the burning zone,
Make Ossa like a wart! Nay, an thou'lt mouth,
I'll rant as well as thou.

QUEEN.
This is mere madness:
And thus a while the fit will work on him;
Anon, as patient as the female dove,
When that her golden couplets are disclos'd,
His silence will sit drooping.

HAM.
Hear you, sir;
What is the reason that you use me thus?
I lov'd you ever: but it is no matter;
Let Hercules himself do what he may,
The cat will mew, and dog will have his day.

[Exit.]

KING.
I pray thee, good Horatio, wait upon him.—

[Exit Horatio.]

[To Laertes]

Strengthen your patience in our last night's
    speech;
We'll put the matter to the present push.—
Good Gertrude, set some watch over your son.—
This grave shall have a living monument:
An hour of quiet shortly shall we see;
Till then in patience our proceeding be.

[Exeunt.]

SCENE II. A hall in the Castle.

[Enter Hamlet and Horatio.]

HAM.
So much for this, sir: now let me see the other;
You do remember all the circumstance?

HOR.
Remember it, my lord!

HAM.
Sir, in my heart there was a kind of fighting
That would not let me sleep: methought I lay
Worse than the mutinies in the bilboes. Rashly,
And prais'd be rashness for it,—let us know,
Our indiscretion sometime serves us well,

When our deep plots do fail; and that should
    teach us
There's a divinity that shapes our ends,
Rough-hew them how we will.

HOR.

That is most certain.

HAM.

Up from my cabin,
My sea-gown scarf'd about me, in the dark
Grop'd I to find out them: had my desire;
Finger'd their packet; and, in fine, withdrew
To mine own room again: making so bold,
My fears forgetting manners, to unseal
Their grand commission; where I found, Horatio,
O royal knavery! an exact command,—
Larded with many several sorts of reasons,
Importing Denmark's health, and England's too,
With, ho! such bugs and goblins in my life,—
That, on the supervise, no leisure bated,
No, not to stay the grinding of the axe,
My head should be struck off.

HOR.

Is't possible?

HAM.

Here's the commission: read it at more leisure.
But wilt thou hear me how I did proceed?

HOR.

I beseech you.

HAM.

Being thus benetted round with villanies,—
Or I could make a prologue to my brains,
They had begun the play,—I sat me down;
Devis'd a new commission; wrote it fair:
I once did hold it, as our statists do,
A baseness to write fair, and labour'd much
How to forget that learning; but, sir, now
It did me yeoman's service. Wilt thou know
The effect of what I wrote?

HOR.

Ay, good my lord.

HAM.

An earnest conjuration from the king,—
As England was his faithful tributary;
As love between them like the palm might
    flourish;
As peace should still her wheaten garland wear
And stand a comma 'tween their amities;

And many such-like as's of great charge,—
That, on the view and know of these contents,
Without debatement further, more or less,
He should the bearers put to sudden death,
Not shriving-time allow'd.

HOR.

How was this seal'd?

HAM.

Why, even in that was heaven ordinant.
I had my father's signet in my purse,
Which was the model of that Danish seal:
Folded the writ up in the form of the other;
Subscrib'd it: gave't the impression; plac'd it
    safely,
The changeling never known. Now, the next day
Was our sea-fight; and what to this was sequent
Thou know'st already.

HOR.

So Guildenstern and Rosencrantz go to't.

HAM.

Why, man, they did make love to this
    employment;
They are not near my conscience; their defeat
Does by their own insinuation grow:
'Tis dangerous when the baser nature comes
Between the pass and fell incensed points
Of mighty opposites.

HOR.

Why, what a king is this!

HAM.

Does it not, thinks't thee, stand me now upon,—
He that hath kill'd my king, and whor'd my
    mother;
Popp'd in between the election and my hopes;
Thrown out his angle for my proper life,
And with such cozenage—is't not perfect
    conscience
To quit him with this arm? and is't not to be
    damn'd
To let this canker of our nature come
In further evil?

HOR.

It must be shortly known to him from England
What is the issue of the business there.

HAM.

It will be short: the interim is mine;
And a man's life is no more than to say One.

But I am very sorry, good Horatio,
That to Laertes I forgot myself;
For by the image of my cause I see
The portraiture of his: I'll court his favours:
But, sure, the bravery of his grief did put me
Into a towering passion.

HOR.

Peace; who comes here?

[Enter Osric.]

OSR.

Your lordship is right welcome back to Denmark.

HAM.

I humbly thank you, sir. Dost know this water-fly?

HOR.

No, my good lord.

HAM.

Thy state is the more gracious; for 'tis a vice to
know him. He hath much land, and fertile:
let a beast be lord of beasts, and his crib
shall stand at the king's mess; 'tis a chough;
but, as I say, spacious in the possession of
dirt.

OSR.

Sweet lord, if your lordship were at leisure, I
should impart a thing to you from his
majesty.

HAM.

I will receive it with all diligence of spirit. Put
your bonnet to his right use; 'tis for the
head.

OSR.

I thank your lordship, t'is very hot.

HAM.

No, believe me, 'tis very cold; the wind is
northerly.

OSR.

It is indifferent cold, my lord, indeed.

HAM.

Methinks it is very sultry and hot for my
complexion.

OSR.

Exceedingly, my lord; it is very sultry,—as
'twere—I cannot tell how. But, my lord, his
majesty bade me signify to you that he has
laid a great wager on your head. Sir, this is
the matter,—

HAM.

I beseech you, remember,—

[Hamlet moves him to put on his hat.]

OSR.

Nay, in good faith; for mine ease, in good faith.
Sir, here is newly come to court Laertes;
believe me, an absolute gentleman, full of
most excellent differences, of very soft
society and great showing: indeed, to speak
feelingly of him, he is the card or calendar of
gentry; for you shall find in him the
continent of what part a gentleman would
see.

HAM.

Sir, his definement suffers no perdition in you;—
though, I know, to divide him inventorially
would dizzy the arithmetic of memory, and
yet but yaw neither, in respect of his quick
sail. But, in the verity of extolment, I take
him to be a soul of great article, and his
infusion of such dearth and rareness as, to
make true diction of him, his semblable is
his mirror, and who else would trace him,
his umbrage, nothing more.

OSR.

Your lordship speaks most infallibly of him.

HAM.

The concernancy, sir? why do we wrap the
gentleman in our more rawer breath?

OSR.

Sir?

HOR.

Is't not possible to understand in another tongue?
You will do't, sir, really.

HAM.

What imports the nomination of this gentleman?

OSR.

Of Laertes?

HOR.

His purse is empty already; all's golden words are
spent.

HAM.

Of him, sir.

OSR.

I know, you are not ignorant,—

HAM.

I would you did, sir; yet, in faith, if you did, it would not much approve me.—Well, sir.

OSR.

You are not ignorant of what excellence Laertes is,—

HAM.

I dare not confess that, lest I should compare with him in excellence; but to know a man well were to know himself.

OSR.

I mean, sir, for his weapon; but in the imputation laid on him by them, in his meed he's unfellowed.

HAM.

What's his weapon?

OSR.

Rapier and dagger.

HAM.

That's two of his weapons:—but well.

OSR.

The king, sir, hath wager'd with him six Barbary horses: against the which he has imponed, as I take it, six French rapiers and poniards, with their assigns, as girdle, hangers, and so: three of the carriages, in faith, are very dear to fancy, very responsive to the hilts, most delicate carriages, and of very liberal conceit.

HAM.

What call you the carriages?

HOR.

I knew you must be edified by the margent ere you had done.

OSR.

The carriages, sir, are the hangers.

HAM.

The phrase would be more german to the matter if we could carry cannon by our sides. I would it might be hangers till then. But, on: six Barbary horses against six French swords, their assigns, and three liberal conceited carriages: that's the French bet against the Danish: why is this all imponed, as you call it?

OSR.

The king, sir, hath laid that, in a dozen passes between your and him, he shall not exceed you three hits: he hath laid on twelve for nine; and it would come to immediate trial if your lordship would vouchsafe the answer.

HAM.

How if I answer no?

OSR.

I mean, my lord, the opposition of your person in trial.

HAM.

Sir, I will walk here in the hall: if it please his majesty, it is the breathing time of day with me: let the foils be brought, the gentleman willing, and the king hold his purpose, I will win for him if I can; if not, I will gain nothing but my shame and the odd hits.

OSR.

Shall I re-deliver you e'en so?

HAM.

To this effect, sir; after what flourish your nature will.

OSR.

I commend my duty to your lordship.

HAM.

Yours, yours.

[Exit Osric.]

He does well to commend it himself; there are no tongues else for's turn.

HOR.

This lapwing runs away with the shell on his head.

HAM.

He did comply with his dug before he suck'd it. Thus has he,—and many more of the same bevy that I know the drossy age dotes on,— only got the tune of the time and outward habit of encounter; a kind of yesty collection, which carries them through and through the most fanned and winnowed opinions; and do but blow them to their trial, the bubbles are out,

[Enter a Lord.]

LORD.

My lord, his majesty commended him to you by
 young Osric, who brings back to him that
 you attend him in the hall: he sends to know
 if your pleasure hold to play with Laertes, or
 that you will take longer time.

HAM.

I am constant to my purposes; they follow the
 king's pleasure: if his fitness speaks, mine is
 ready; now or whensoever, provided
I be so able as now.

LORD.

The King and Queen and all are coming down.

HAM.

In happy time.

LORD.

The queen desires you to use some gentle
 entertainment to
Laertes before you fall to play.

HAM.

She well instructs me.

[Exit Lord.]

HOR.

You will lose this wager, my lord.

HAM.

I do not think so; since he went into France I have
 been in continual practice: I shall win at the
 odds. But thou wouldst not think how ill
 all's here about my heart: but it is no matter.

HOR.

Nay, good my lord,—

HAM.

It is but foolery; but it is such a kind of gain-
 giving as would perhaps trouble a woman.

HOR.

If your mind dislike anything, obey it: I will
 forestall their repair hither, and say you are
 not fit.

HAM.

Not a whit, we defy augury: there's a special
 providence in the fall of a sparrow. If it be
 now, 'tis not to come; if it be not to come, it
 will be now; if it be not now, yet it will
 come: the readiness is all: since no man has
 aught of what he leaves, what is't to leave
 betimes?

[Enter King, Queen, Laertes, Lords, Osric, and
 Attendants with foils &c.]

KING.

Come, Hamlet, come, and take this hand from
 me.

[The King puts Laertes' hand into Hamlet's.]

HAM.

Give me your pardon, sir: I have done you wrong:
But pardon't, as you are a gentleman.
This presence knows, and you must needs have
 heard,
How I am punish'd with sore distraction.
What I have done
That might your nature, honour, and exception
Roughly awake, I here proclaim was madness.
Was't Hamlet wrong'd Laertes? Never Hamlet:
If Hamlet from himself be ta'en away,
And when he's not himself does wrong Laertes,
Then Hamlet does it not, Hamlet denies it.
Who does it, then? His madness: if't be so,
Hamlet is of the faction that is wrong'd;
His madness is poor Hamlet's enemy.
Sir, in this audience,
Let my disclaiming from a purpos'd evil
Free me so far in your most generous thoughts
That I have shot my arrow o'er the house
And hurt my brother.

LAER.

I am satisfied in nature,
Whose motive, in this case, should stir me most
To my revenge. But in my terms of honour
I stand aloof; and will no reconcilement
Till by some elder masters of known honour
I have a voice and precedent of peace
To keep my name ungor'd. But till that time
I do receive your offer'd love like love,
And will not wrong it.

HAM.

I embrace it freely;
And will this brother's wager frankly play.—
Give us the foils; come on.

LAER.

Come, one for me.

HAM.

I'll be your foil, Laertes; in mine ignorance
Your skill shall, like a star in the darkest night,
Stick fiery off indeed.

LAER.
You mock me, sir.

HAM.
No, by this hand.

KING.
Give them the foils, young Osric. Cousin Hamlet,
You know the wager?

HAM.
Very well, my lord;
Your grace has laid the odds o' the weaker side.

KING.
I do not fear it; I have seen you both;
But since he's better'd, we have therefore odds.

LAER.
This is too heavy, let me see another.

HAM.
This likes me well. These foils have all a length?

[They prepare to play.]

OSR.
Ay, my good **LORD.**

KING.
Set me the stoups of wine upon that table,—
If Hamlet give the first or second hit,
Or quit in answer of the third exchange,
Let all the battlements their ordnance fire;
The king shall drink to Hamlet's better breath;
And in the cup an union shall he throw,
Richer than that which four successive kings
In Denmark's crown have worn. Give me the
    cups;
And let the kettle to the trumpet speak,
The trumpet to the cannoneer without,
The cannons to the heavens, the heavens to earth,
'Now the king drinks to Hamlet.'—Come,
    begin:—
And you, the judges, bear a wary eye.

HAM.
Come on, sir.

LAER.
Come, my Lord.

[They play.]

HAM.
One.

LAER.
No.

HAM.
Judgment!

OSR.
A hit, a very palpable hit.

LAER.
Well;—again.

KING.
Stay, give me drink.—Hamlet, this pearl is thine;
Here's to thy health.—

[Trumpets sound, and cannon shot off within.]

Give him the cup.

HAM.
I'll play this bout first; set it by awhile.—
Come.—Another hit; what say you?

[They play.]

LAER.
A touch, a touch, I do confess.

KING.
Our son shall win.

QUEEN.
He's fat, and scant of breath.—
Here, Hamlet, take my napkin, rub thy brows:
The queen carouses to thy fortune, Hamlet.

HAM.
Good madam!

KING.
Gertrude, do not drink.

QUEEN.
I will, my lord; I pray you pardon me.

KING.
[Aside.] It is the poison'd cup; it is too late.

HAM.
I dare not drink yet, madam; by-and-by.

QUEEN.
Come, let me wipe thy face.

LAER.
My lord, I'll hit him now.

KING.
I do not think't.

LAER.
[Aside.] And yet 'tis almost 'gainst my conscience.

HAM.
Come, for the third, Laertes: you but dally;

I pray you pass with your best violence:
I am afeard you make a wanton of me.

LAER.
Say you so? come on.

[They play.]

OSR.
Nothing, neither way.

LAER.
Have at you now!

*[Laertes wounds Hamlet; then, in scuffling, they
    change rapiers, and Hamlet wounds Laertes.]*

KING.
Part them; they are incens'd.

HAM.
Nay, come again!

[The Queen falls.]

OSR.
Look to the queen there, ho!

HOR.
They bleed on both sides.—How is it, my lord?

OSR.
How is't, Laertes?

LAER.
Why, as a woodcock to my own springe, Osric;
I am justly kill'd with mine own treachery.

HAM.
How does the Queen?

KING.
She swoons to see them bleed.

QUEEN.
No, no! the drink, the drink!—O my dear
    Hamlet!—
The drink, the drink!—I am poison'd.

[Dies.]

HAM.
O villany!—Ho! let the door be lock'd:
Treachery! seek it out.

[Laertes falls.]

LAER.
It is here, Hamlet: Hamlet, thou art slain;
No medicine in the world can do thee good;
In thee there is not half an hour of life;
The treacherous instrument is in thy hand,

Unbated and envenom'd: the foul practice
Hath turn'd itself on me; lo, here I lie,
Never to rise again: thy mother's poison'd:
I can no more:—the king, the king's to blame.

HAM.
The point envenom'd too!—
Then, venom, to thy work.
[Stabs the King.]
Osric and Lords.
Treason! treason!

KING.
O, yet defend me, friends! I am but hurt.

HAM.
Here, thou incestuous, murderous, damned Dane,
Drink off this potion.—Is thy union here?
Follow my mother.

[King dies.]

LAER.
He is justly serv'd;
It is a poison temper'd by himself.—
Exchange forgiveness with me, noble Hamlet:
Mine and my father's death come not upon thee,
Nor thine on me!

[Dies.]

HAM.
Heaven make thee free of it! I follow thee.—
I am dead, Horatio.—Wretched queen, adieu!—
You that look pale and tremble at this chance,
That are but mutes or audience to this act,
Had I but time,—as this fell sergeant, death,
Is strict in his arrest,—O, I could tell you,—
But let it be.—Horatio, I am dead;
Thou liv'st; report me and my cause aright
To the unsatisfied.

HOR.
Never believe it:
I am more an antique Roman than a Dane.—
Here's yet some liquor left.

HAM.
As thou'rt a man,
Give me the cup; let go; by heaven, I'll have't.—
O good Horatio, what a wounded name,
Things standing thus unknown, shall live behind
    me!
If thou didst ever hold me in thy heart,
Absent thee from felicity awhile,
And in this harsh world draw thy breath in pain,

To tell my story.—

[March afar off, and shot within.]

What warlike noise is this?

OSR.
Young Fortinbras, with conquest come from
    Poland,
To the ambassadors of England gives
This warlike volley.

HAM.
O, I die, Horatio;
The potent poison quite o'er-crows my spirit:
I cannot live to hear the news from England;
But I do prophesy the election lights
On Fortinbras: he has my dying voice;
So tell him, with the occurrents, more and less,
Which have solicited.—the rest is silence.

[Dies.]

HOR.
Now cracks a noble heart.—Good night, sweet
    prince,
And flights of angels sing thee to thy rest!
Why does the drum come hither?

[March within.]

*[Enter Fortinbras, the English Ambassadors, and
    others.]*

FORT.
Where is this sight?

HOR.
What is it you will see?
If aught of woe or wonder, cease your search.

FORT.
This quarry cries on havoc.—O proud death,
What feast is toward in thine eternal cell,
That thou so many princes at a shot
So bloodily hast struck?

1 AMBASSADOR.
The sight is dismal;
And our affairs from England come too late:
The ears are senseless that should give us hearing,
To tell him his commandment is fulfill'd
That Rosencrantz and Guildenstern are dead:
Where should we have our thanks?

HOR.
Not from his mouth,
Had it the ability of life to thank you:
He never gave commandment for their death.
But since, so jump upon this bloody question,
You from the Polack wars, and you from England,
Are here arriv'd, give order that these bodies
High on a stage be placed to the view;
And let me speak to the yet unknowing world
How these things came about: so shall you hear
Of carnal, bloody and unnatural acts;
Of accidental judgments, casual slaughters;
Of deaths put on by cunning and forc'd cause;
And, in this upshot, purposes mistook
Fall'n on the inventors' heads: all this can I
Truly deliver.

FORT.
Let us haste to hear it,
And call the noblest to the audience.
For me, with sorrow I embrace my fortune:
I have some rights of memory in this kingdom,
Which now, to claim my vantage doth invite me.

HOR.
Of that I shall have also cause to speak,
And from his mouth whose voice will draw on
    more:
But let this same be presently perform'd,
Even while men's minds are wild: lest more
    mischance
On plots and errors happen.

FORT.
Let four captains
Bear Hamlet like a soldier to the stage;
For he was likely, had he been put on,
To have prov'd most royally: and, for his passage,
The soldiers' music and the rites of war
Speak loudly for him.—
Take up the bodies.—Such a sight as this
Becomes the field, but here shows much amiss.
Go, bid the soldiers shoot.

[A dead march.]

*[Exeunt, bearing off the dead bodies; after then
    which a peal of ordnance is shot off.]*

3

The Imaginary Invalid

(Le Malade Imaginaire)

Play by Molière (1622–1673)

Translated into English Prose.
With Short Introductions and Explanatory Notes
By Charles Heron Wall

This is the last comedy written by Moliére. He was very ill, nearly dying, at the time he wrote it. It was first acted at the Palais Royal Theatre, on February 10, 1673.

Moliére acted the part of Argan.

Persons Represented

ARGAN, *an imaginary invalid.*
BÉLINE, *second wife to* ARGAN.
ANGÉLIQUE, *daughter to* ARGAN, *in love with* CLÉANTE.
LOUISON, ARGAN'S *young daughter, sister to* ANGÉLIQUE.
BÉRALDE, *brother to* ARGAN.
CLÉANTE, *lover to* ANGÉLIQUE.
MR. DIAFOIRUS, *a physician.*
THOMAS DIAFOIRUS, *his son, in love with* ANGÉLIQUE.
MR. PURGON, *physician to* ARGAN.
MR. FLEURANT, an apothecary.
MR. DE BONNEFOI, *a notary.*
TOINETTE, *maid-servant to* ARGAN.

"The Imaginary Invalid", 1673

THE IMAGINARY INVALID

ACT I.

SCENE I.—ARGAN (*sitting at a table, adding up his apothecary's bill with counters*).

ARG. Three and two make five, and five make ten, and ten make twenty. "Item, on the 24th, a small, insinuative clyster, preparative and gentle, to soften, moisten, and refresh the bowels of Mr. Argan." What I like about Mr. Fleurant, my apothecary, is that his bills are always civil. "The bowels of Mr. Argan." All the same, Mr. Fleurant, it is not enough to be civil, you must also be reasonable, and not plunder sick people. Thirty sous for a clyster! I have already told you, with all due respect to you, that elsewhere you have only charged me twenty sous; and twenty sous, in the language of apothecaries, means only ten sous. Here they are, these ten sous. "Item, on the said day, a good detergent clyster, compounded of double catholicon rhubarb, honey of roses, and other ingredients, according to the prescription, to scour, work, and clear out the bowels of Mr. Argan, thirty sons." With your leave, ten sous. "Item, on the said day, in the evening, a julep, hepatic, soporiferous, and somniferous, intended to promote the sleep of Mr. Argan, thirty-five sous." I do not complain of that, for it made me sleep very well. Ten, fifteen, sixteen, and seventeen sous six deniers. "Item, on the 25th, a good purgative and corroborative mixture, composed of fresh cassia with Levantine senna and other ingredients, according to the prescription of Mr. Purgon, to expel Mr. Argan's bile, four francs." You are joking, Mr. Fleurant; you must learn to be reasonable with patients; Mr. Purgon never ordered you to put four francs. Tut! put three francs, if you please. Twenty; thirty sous.[1] "Item, on the said day, a dose, anodyne and astringent, to make Mr. Argan sleep, thirty sous." Ten sous, Mr. Fleurant. "Item, on the 26th, a carminative clyster to cure the flatulence of Mr. Argan, thirty sous." "Item, the clyster repeated in the evening, as above, thirty sous." Ten sous, Mr. Fleurant. "Item, on the 27th, a good mixture composed for the purpose of driving out the bad humours of Mr. Argan, three francs." Good; twenty and thirty sous; I am glad that you are reasonable. "Item, on the 28th, a dose of clarified and edulcorated whey, to soften, lenify, temper, and refresh the blood of Mr. Argan, twenty sous." Good; ten sous. "Item, a potion, cordial and preservative, composed of twelve grains of bezoar, syrup of citrons and pomegranates, and other ingredients, according to the prescription, five francs." Ah! Mr. Fleurant, gently, if you please; if you go on like that, no one will wish to be unwell. Be satisfied with four francs. Twenty, forty sous. Three and two are five, and five are ten, and ten are twenty. Sixty-three francs four sous six deniers. So that during this month I have taken one, two, three, four, five, six, seven, eight mixtures, and one, two, three, four, five, six, seven, eight, nine, ten, eleven, twelve clysters; and last month there were twelve mixtures and twenty clysters. I am not astonished, therefore, that I am not so well this month as last. I shall speak to Mr. Purgon about it, so that he may set the matter right. Come, let all this be taken away. (*He sees that no one comes, and that he is alone.*) Nobody. It's no use, I am always left alone; there's no way of keeping them here. (*He rings a hand-bell.*) They don't hear, and my bell doesn't make enough noise. (*He rings again.*) No one. (*He rings again.*) Toinette! (*He rings again.*) It's just as if I didn't ring at all. You hussy! you jade! (*He rings again.*) Confound it all! (*He rings and shouts.*) Deuce take you, you wretch!

SCENE II.—Argan, Toinette.

TOI. Coming, coming.

ARG. Ah! you jade, you wretch!

TOI. (*pretending to have knocked her head*). Bother your impatience! You hurry me so much that I have knocked my head against the window-shutter.

ARG. (*angry*). You vixen!

TOI. (*interrupting* ARGAN). Oh!

ARG. There is …

TOI. Oh!

ARG. For the last hour I …

TOI. Oh!

ARG. You have left me …

TOI. Oh!

ARG. Be silent! you baggage, and let me scold you.

TOI. Well! that's too bad after what I have done to myself.

ARG. You make me bawl till my throat is sore, you jade!

TOI. And you, you made me break my head open; one is just as bad as the other; so, with your leave, we are quits.

ARG. What! you hussy. …

TOI. If you go on scolding me, I shall cry.

ARG. To leave me, you …

TOI. (*again interrupting* ARGAN.) Oh!

ARG. You would …

TOI. (*still interrupting him*). Oh!

ARG. What! shall I have also to give up the pleasure of scolding her?

TOI. Well, scold as much as you please; do as you like.

ARG. You prevent me, you hussy, by interrupting me every moment.

TOI. If you have the pleasure of scolding, I surely can have that of crying. Let every one have his fancy; 'tis but right. Oh! oh!

ARG. I must give it up, I suppose. Take this away, take this away, you jade. Be careful to have some broth ready, for the other that I am to take soon.

TOI. This Mr. Fleurant and Mr. Purgon amuse themselves finely with your body. They have a rare milch-cow in you, I must say; and I should like them to tell me what disease it is you have for them to physic you so.

ARG. Hold your tongue, simpleton; it is not for you to control the decrees of the faculty. Ask my daughter Angélique to come to me. I have something to tell her.

TOI. Here she is, coming of her own accord; she must have guessed your thoughts.

SCENE III.—Argan, Angélique, Toinette.

ARG. You come just in time; I want to speak to you.

ANG. I am quite ready to hear you.

ARG. Wait a moment. (*To* TOINETTE) Give me my walking-stick; I'll come back directly.

TOI. Go, Sir, go quickly; Mr. Fleurant gives us plenty to do.

SCENE IV.—Angélique, Toinette.

ANG. Toinette!

TOI. Well! what?

ANG. Look at me a little.

TOI. Well, I am looking at you.

ANG. Toinette!

TOI. Well! what, Toinette?

ANG. Don't you guess what I want to speak about?

TOI. Oh! yes, I have some slight idea that you want to speak of our young lover, for it is of him we have been speaking for the last six days, and you are not well unless you mention him at every turn.

ANG. Since you know what it is I want, why are you not the first to speak to me of him? and why do you not spare me the trouble of being the one to start the conversation?

TOI. You don't give me time, and you are so eager that it is difficult to be beforehand with you on the subject.

ANG. I acknowledge that I am never weary of speaking of him, and that my heart takes eager advantage of every moment I have to open my heart to you. But tell me, Toinette, do you blame the feelings I have towards him?

TOI. I am far from doing so.

ANG. Am I wrong in giving way to these sweet impressions?

TOI. I don't say that you are.

ANG. And would you have me insensible to the tender protestations of ardent love which he shows me?

TOI. Heaven forbid!

ANG. Tell me, do you not see, as I do, something providential, some act of destiny in the unexpected adventure from which our acquaintance originated?

TOI. Yes.

ANG. That it is impossible to act more generously?

TOI. Agreed.

ANG. And that he did all this with the greatest possible grace?

TOI. Oh! yes.

ANG. Do you not think, Toinette, that he is very handsome?

TOI. Certainly.

ANG. That he has the best manners in the world?

TOI. No doubt about it.

ANG. That there is always something noble in what he says and what he does?

TOI. Most certainly.

ANG. That there never was anything more tender than all he says to me?

TOI. True.

ARG. And that there can be nothing more painful than the restraint under which I am kept? for it prevents all sweet intercourse, and puts an end to that mutual love with which Heaven has inspired us.

TOI. You are right.

ANG. But, dear Toinette, tell me, do you think that he loves me as much as he says he does?

TOI. Hum! That's a thing hardly to be trusted at any time. A show of love is sadly like the real thing, and I have met with very good actors in that line.

ANG. Ah! Toinette, what are you saying there? Alas! judging by the manner in which he speaks, is it possible that he is not telling the truth?

TOI. At any rate, you will soon be satisfied on this point, and the resolution which he says he has taken of asking you in marriage, is a sure and ready way of showing you if what he says is true or not. That is the all-sufficient proof.

ANG. Ah! Toinette, if he deceives me, I shall never in all my life believe in any man.

TOI. Here is your father coming back.

SCENE V.—Argan, Angélique, Toinette.

ARG. I say, Angélique, I have a piece of news for yon which, perhaps, you did not expect. You have been asked of me in marriage. Halloa! how is that? You are smiling. It is pleasant, is it not, that word marriage? there is nothing so funny to young girls. Ah! nature! nature! So, from what I see, daughter, there is no need of my asking you if you are willing to marry.

ANG. I ought to obey you in everything, father.

ARG. I am very glad to possess such an obedient daughter; the thing is settled then, and I have promised you.

ANG. It is my duty, father, blindly to follow all you determine upon for me.

ARG. My wife, your mother-in-law, wanted me to make a nun of you and of your little sister Louison also. She has always been bent upon that.

TOI. (*aside*). The excellent creature has her reasons.

ARG. She would not consent to this marriage; but I carried the day, and my word is given.

TOI. (*to ARGAN*). Really, I am pleased with you for that, and it is the wisest thing you ever did in your life.

ARG. I have not seen the person in question; but I am told that I shall be satisfied with him, and that you too will be satisfied.

ANG. Most certainly, father.

ARG. How! have you seen him then?

ANG. Since your consent to our marriage authorises me to open my heart to you, I will not hide from you that chance made us acquainted six days ago, and that the request which has been made to you is the result of the sympathy we felt for one another at first sight.

ARG. They did not tell me that; but I am glad of it; it is much better that things should be so. They say that he is a tall, well-made young fellow.

ANG. Yes, father.

ARG. Of a fine build.

ANG. Yes, indeed.

ARG. Pleasant.

ANG. Certainly.

ARG. A good face.

ANG. Very good.

ARG. Steady and of good family.

ANG. Quite.

ARG. With very good manners.

ANG. The best possible.

ARG. And speaks both Latin and Greek.

ANG. Ah! that I don't know anything about.

ARG. And that he will in three days be made a doctor.

ANG. He, father?

ARG. Yes; did he not tell you?

ANG. No, indeed! who told you?

ARG. Mr. Purgon.

ANG. Does Mr. Purgon know him?

ARG. What a question! Of course he knows him, since he is his nephew.

ANG. Cléante is the nephew of Mr. Purgon?

ARG. What Cléante? We are speaking about him who has asked you in marriage.

ANG. Yes, of course.

ARG. Well, he is the nephew of Mr. Purgon, and the son of his brother-in-law, Mr. Diafoirus; and this son is called Thomas Diafoirus, and not Cléante. Mr. Fleurant and I decided upon this match this morning, and to-morrow this future son-in-law will be brought to me by his father. . . . What is the matter, you look all scared?

ANG. It is because, father, I see that you have been speaking of one person, and I of another.

TOI. What! Sir, you have formed such a queer project as that, and, with all the wealth you possess, you want to marry your daughter to a doctor?

ARG. What business is it of yours, you impudent jade?

TOI. Gently, gently. You always begin by abuse. Can we not reason together without getting into a rage? Come, let us speak quietly. What reason have you, if you please, for such a marriage?

ARG. My reason is, that seeing myself infirm and sick, I wish to have a son-in-law and relatives who are doctors, in order to secure their kind assistance in my illness, to have in my family the fountain-head of those remedies which are necessary to me, and to be within reach of consultations and prescriptions.

TOI. Very well; at least that is giving a reason, and there is a certain pleasure in answering one another calmly. But now, Sir, on your conscience, do you really and truly believe that you are ill?

ARG. Believe that I am ill, you jade? Believe that I am ill, you impudent hussy?

TOI. Very well, then, Sir, you are ill; don't let us quarrel about that. Yes, you are very ill, I agree with you upon that point, more ill even than you think. Now, is that settled? But your daughter is to marry a husband for herself, and as she is not ill, what is the use of giving her a doctor?

ARG. It is for my sake that I give her this doctor, and a good daughter ought to be delighted to marry for the sake of her father's health.

TOI. In good troth, Sir, shall I, as a friend, give you a piece of advice?

ARG. What is this advice?

TOI. Not to think of this match.

ARG. And your reason?

TOI. The reason is that your daughter will never consent to it.

ARG. My daughter will not consent to it?

TOI. No.

ARG. My daughter?

TOI. Your daughter. She will tell you that she has no need of Mr. Diafoirus, nor of his son, Mr. Thomas Diafoirus, nor all the Diafoiruses in the world.

ARG. But I have need of them. Besides, the match is more advantageous than you think. Mr. Diafoirus has only this son for his heir; and, moreover, Mr. Purgon, who has neither wife nor child, gives all he has in favour of this marriage; and Mr. Purgon is a man worth eight thousand francs a year.

TOI. What a lot of people he must have killed to have become so rich!

ARG. Eight thousand francs is something, without counting the property of the father.

TOI. That is very well, Sir, but, all the same, I advise you, between ourselves, to choose another husband for her; she is not of a make to become a Mrs. Diafoirus.

ARG. But I will have it so.

TOI. Fie! nonsense! Don't speak like that.

ARG. Don't speak like that? Why not?

TOI. Dear me, no, don't.

ARG. And why should I not speak like that?

TOI. People will say that you don't know what you are talking about.

ARG. People will say all they like, but I tell you that I will have her make my promise good.

TOI. I feel sure that she won't.

ARG. Then I will force her to do it.

TOI. She will not do it, I tell you.

ARG. She will, or I will shut her up in a convent.

TOI. You?

ARG. I.

TOI. Good!

ARG. How good?

TOI. You will not shut her up in a convent.

ARG. I shall not shut her up in a convent?

TOI. No.

ARG. No?

TOI. No.

ARG. Well, this is cool! I shall not put my daughter in a convent if I like!

TOI. No, I tell you.

ARG. And who will hinder me?

TOI. You yourself.

ARG. Myself?

TOI. You will never have the heart to do it.

ARG. I shall.

TOI. You are joking.

ARG. I am not joking.

TOI. Fatherly love will hinder you.

ARG. It will not hinder me.

TOI. A little tear or two, her arms thrown round your neck, Or "My darling little papa," said very tenderly, will be enough to touch your heart.

ARG. All that will be useless.

TOI. Oh yes!

ARG. I tell you that nothing will move me.

TOI. Rubbish!

ARG. You have no business to say "Rubbish."

TOI. I know you well enough; you are naturally kind-hearted.

ARG. (*angrily*). I am not kind-hearted, and I am ill-natured when I like.

TOI. Gently, Sir, you forget that you are ill.

ARG. I command her to prepare herself to take the husband I have fixed upon.

TOI. And I decidedly forbid her to do anything of the kind.

ARG. What have we come to? And what boldness is this for a scrub of a servant to speak in such a way before her master?

TOI. When a master does not consider what he is doing, a sensible servant should set him right.

ARG. (*running after* TOINETTE). Ah, impudent girl, I will kill you!

TOI. (*avoiding* ARGAN, *and putting the chair between her and him*). It is my duty to oppose what would be a dishonour to you.

ARG. (*running after* TOINETTE *with his cane in his hand*). Come here, come here, let me teach you how to speak.

TOI. (*running to the opposite side of the chair*). I interest myself in your affairs as I ought to do, and I don't wish to see you commit any folly.

ARG. (*as before*). Jade!

TOI. (*as before*). No, I will never consent to this marriage.

ARG. (*as before*). Worthless hussy!

TOI. (*as before*). I won't have her marry your Thomas Diafoirus.

ARG. (*as before*). Vixen!

TOI. (*as before*). She will obey me sooner than you.

ARG. (*stopping*). Angélique, won't you stop that jade for me?

ANG. Ah! father, don't make yourself ill.

ARG. (*to* ANGÉLIQUE). If you don't stop her, I will refuse you my blessing.

TOI. (*going away*). And I will disinherit her if she obeys you.

ARG. (*throwing himself into his chair*). Ah! I am done for. It is enough to kill me!

SCENE VI.—Béline, Argan.

ARG. Ah! come near, my wife.

BEL. What ails you, my poor, dear husband?

ARG. Come to my help.

BEL. What is the matter, my little darling child?

ARG. My love.

BEL. My love.

ARG. They have just put me in a rage.

BEL. Alas! my poor little husband! How was that, my own dear pet?

ARG. That jade of yours, Toinette, has grown more insolent than ever.

BEL. Don't excite yourself.

ARG. She has put me in a rage, my dove.

BEL. Gently, my child.

ARG. She has been thwarting me for the last hour about everything I want to do.

BEL. There, there; never mind.

ARG. And has had the impudence to say that I am not ill.

BEL. She is an impertinent hussy.

ARG. You know, my soul, what the truth is?

BEL. Yes, my darling, she is wrong.

ARG. My own dear, that jade will be the death of me.

BEL. Now, don't, don't.

ARG. She is the cause of all my bile.

BEL. Don't be so angry.

ARG. And I have asked you ever so many times to send her away.

BEL. Alas! my child, there is no servant without defects. We are obliged to put up at times with their bad qualities on account of their good ones. The girl is skilful, careful, diligent, and, above all, honest; and you know that in our days we must be very careful what people we take into our house. I say, Toinette.

SCENE VII.—Argan, Béline, Toinette.

TOI. Madam.

BEL. How is this? Why do you put my husband in a passion?

TOI. (*in a soft tone*). I, Madam? Alas! I don't know what you mean, and my only aim is to please master in everything.

ARG. Ah! the deceitful girl!

TOI. He said to us that he wished to marry his daughter to the son of Mr. Diafoirus. I told him that I thought the match very advantageous for her, but that I believed he would do better to put her in a convent.

BEL. There is not much harm in that, and I think that she is right.

ARG. Ah! deary, do you believe her? She is a vile girl, and has said a hundred insolent things to me.

BEL. Well, I believe you, my dear. Come, compose yourself; and you, Toinette, listen to me. If ever you make my husband angry again, I will send you away. Come, give me his fur cloak and some pillows, that I may make him comfortable in his arm-chair. You are all anyhow. Pull your nightcap right down over your ears; there is nothing that gives people such bad colds as letting in the air through the ears.

ARG. Ah, deary! how much obliged I am to you for all the care you take of me.

BEL. (*adjusting the pillows, which she puts round him*). Raise yourself a little for me to put this under you. Let us put this one for you to lean upon, and this one on the other side; this one behind your back, and this other to support your head.

TOI. (*clapping a pillow rudely on his head*). And this other to keep you from the evening damp.

ARG. (*rising angrily, and throwing the pillows after* TOINETTE, *who runs away*). Ah, wretch! you want to smother me.

SCENE VIII.—Argan, Béline.

BEL. Now, now; what is it again?

ARG. (*throwing himself in his chair*). Ah! I can hold out no longer.

BEL. But why do you fly into such a passion? she thought she was doing right.

ARG. You don't know, darling, the wickedness of that villainous baggage. She has altogether upset me, and I shall want more than eight different mixtures and twelve injections to remedy the evil.

BEL. Come, come, my dearie, compose yourself a little.

ARG. Lovey, you are my only consolation.

BEL. Poor little pet!

ARG. To repay you for all the love you have for me, my darling, I will, as I told you, make my will.

BEL. Ah, my soul! do not let us speak of that, I beseech you. I cannot bear to think of it, and the very word "will" makes me die of grief.

ARG. I had asked you to speak to our notary about it.

BEL. There he is, close at hand; I have brought him with me.

ARG. Make him come in then, my life!

BEL. Alas! my darling, when a woman loves her husband so much, she finds it almost impossible to think of these things.

SCENE IX.—Mr. De Bonnefoi, Béline, Argan.

ARG. Come here, Mr. de Bonnefoi, come here. Take a seat, if you please. My wife tells me, Sir, that you are a very honest man, and altogether one of her friends; I have therefore asked her to speak to you about a will which I wish to make.

BEL. Alas! I cannot speak of those things.

MR. DE BON. She has fully explained to me your intentions, Sir, and what you mean to do for her. But I have to tell you that you can give nothing to your wife by will.

ARG. But why so?

MR. DE BON. It is against custom. If you were in a district where statute law prevailed, the thing could be done; but in Paris, and in almost all places governed by custom, it cannot be done; and the will would be held void. The only settlement that man and wife can make on each other is by mutual donation while they are alive, and even then there must be no children from either that marriage or from any previous marriage at the decease of the first who dies.

ARG. It's a very impertinent custom that a husband can leave nothing to a wife whom he loves, by whom he is tenderly loved, and who takes so much care of him. I should like to consult my own advocate to see what I can do.

MR. DE BON. It is not to an advocate that you must apply; for they are very particular on this point and think it a great crime to bestow one's property contrary to the law. They are people to make difficulties, and are ignorant of the bylaws of conscience. There are others whom you may consult with advantage on that point, and who have expedients for gently overriding the law, and for rendering just that which is not allowed. These know how to smooth over the difficulties of an affair, and to find the means of eluding custom by some indirect advantage. Without that, what would become of us every day? We must make things easy; otherwise we should do nothing, and I wouldn't give a penny for our business.

ARG. My wife had rightly told me, Sir, that you were a very clever and honest man. What can I do, pray, to give her my fortune and deprive my children of it?

MR. DE BON. What you can do? You can discreetly choose a friend of your wife, to whom you will give all you own in due form by your will, and that friend will give it up to her afterwards; or else you can sign a great many safe bonds in favour of various creditors who will lend their names to your wife, and in whose hands they will leave a declaration that what was done was only to serve her. You can also in your lifetime put in her hands ready money and bills which you can make payable to bearer.

BEL. Alas! you must not trouble yourself about all that. If I lose you, my child, I will stay no longer in the world.

ARG. My darling!

BEL. Yes, my pet, if I were unfortunate enough to lose you . . .

ARG. My dear wifey!

BEL. Life would be nothing to me.

ARG. My love!

BEL. And I would follow you to the grave, to show you all the tenderness I feel for you.

ARG. You will break my heart, deary; comfort yourself, I beseech you.

MR. DE BON. (*to* BÉLINE). These tears are unseasonable; things have not come to that yet.

BEL. Ah, Sir! you don't know what it is to have a husband one loves tenderly.

ARG. All the regret I shall have, if I die, my darling, will be to have no child from you. Mr. Purgon told me he would make me have one.

MR. DE BON. That may come still.

ARG. I must make my will, deary, according to what this gentleman advises; but, out of precaution, I will give you the twenty thousand francs in gold which I have in the wainscoting of the recess of my room, and two bills payable to bearer which are due to me, one from Mr. Damon, the other from Mr. Géronte.

BEL. No, no! I will have nothing to do with all that. Ah! How much do you say there is in the recess?

ARG. Twenty thousand francs, darling.

BEL. Don't speak to me of your money, I beseech you. Ah! How much are the two bills for?

ARG. One, my love, is for four thousand francs, and the other for six thousand.

BEL. All the wealth in the world, my soul, is nothing to me compared to you.

MR. DE BON. (*to* ARGAN). Shall we draw up the will?

ARG. Yes, Sir. But we shall be more comfortable in my own little study. Help me, my love.

BEL. Come, my poor, dear child.

SCENE X.—Angélique, Toinette.

TOI. They are shut up with the notary, and I heard something about a will; your mother-in-law doesn't go to sleep; it is, no doubt, some conspiracy of hers against your interests to which she is urging your father.

ANG. Let him dispose of his money as he likes, as long as he does not dispose of my heart in the same way. You see, Toinette, to what violence it is subjected. Do not forsake me, I beseech you, in this my extremity.

TOI. I forsake you! I had rather die. In vain does your stepmother try to take me into her confidence, and make me espouse her interests. I never could like her, and I have always been on your side. Trust me, I will do every thing to serve you. But, in order to serve you more effectually, I shall change my tactics, hide my wish to help you, and affect to enter into the feelings of your father and your stepmother.

ANG. Try, I beseech you, to let Cléante know about the marriage they have decided upon.

TOI. I have nobody to employ for that duty but the old usurer Punchinello, my lover; it will cost me a few honeyed words, which I am most willing to spend for you. To-day it is too late for that, but to-morrow morning early I will send for him, and he will be delighted to . . .

SCENE XI.—Béline (*in the house*), Angélique, Toinette.

BEL. Toinette.

TOI. (*to* ANGÉLIQUE). I am called away. Good night. Trust me.

FIRST INTERLUDE.
ACT II.

SCENE I.—Cléante, Toinette.

TOI. (*not recognizing* CLÉANTE). What is it you want, Sir?

CLE. What do I want?

TOI. Ah! ah! is it you? What a surprise! What are you coming here for?

CLE. To learn my destiny, to speak to the lovely Angélique, to consult the feelings of her heart, and to ask her what she means to do about this fatal marriage of which I have been told.

TOI. Very well; but no one speaks so easily as all that to Angélique; you must take precautions, and you have been told how narrowly she is watched. She never goes out, nor does she see anybody. It was through the curiosity of an old aunt that we obtained leave to go to the play where your love began, and we have taken good care not to say anything about it.

CLE. Therefore am I not here as Cléante, nor as her lover, but as the friend of her music-master, from whom I have obtained leave to say that I have come in his stead.

TOI. Here is her father; withdraw a little, and let me tell him who you are.

SCENE II.—Argan, Toinette.

ARG. (*thinking himself alone*). Mr. Purgon told me that I was to walk twelve times to and fro in my room every morning, but I forgot to ask him whether it should be lengthways or across.

TOI. Sir, here is a gentleman . . .

ARG. Speak in a lower tone, you jade; you split my head open; and you forget that we should never speak so loud to sick people.

TOI. I wanted to tell you, Sir . . .

ARG. Speak low, I tell you.

TOI. Sir . . . (*She moves her lips as if she were speaking.*)

ARG. What?

TOI. I tell you that . . . (*As before.*)

ARG. What is it you say?

TOI. (*aloud*). I say that there is a gentleman here who wants to speak to you.

ARG. Let him come in.

SCENE III.—Argan, Cléante, Toinette.

CLE. Sir.

TOI. (*to* CLÉANTE). Do not speak so loud, for fear of splitting open the head of Mr. Argan.

CLE. Sir, I am delighted to find you up, and to see you better.

TOI. (*affecting to be angry*). How! better? It is false; master is always ill.

CLE. I had heard that your master was better, and I think that he looks well in the face.

TOI. What do you mean by his looking well in the face? He looks very bad, and it is only impertinent folks who say that he is better; he never was so ill in his life.

ARG. She is right.

TOI. He walks, sleeps, eats, and drinks, like other folks, but that does not hinder him from being very ill.

ARG. Quite true.

CLE. I am heartily sorry for it, Sir. I am sent by your daughter's music-master; he was obliged to go into the country for a few days, and as I am his intimate friend, he has asked me to come here in his place, to go on with the lessons, for fear that, if they were discontinued, she should forget what she has already learnt.

ARG. Very well. (*To* TOINETTE) Call Angélique.

TOI. I think, Sir, It would be better to take the gentleman to her room.

ARG. No, make her come here.

TOI. He cannot give her a good lesson if they are not left alone.

ARG. Oh! yes, he can.

TOI. Sir, it will stun you; and you should have nothing to disturb you in the state of health you are in.

ARG. No, no; I like music, and I should be glad to. . . . Ah! here she is. (*To* TOINETTE) Go and see if my wife is dressed.

SCENE IV.—Argan, Angélique, Cléante.

ARG. Come, my daughter, your music-master is gone into the country, and here is a person whom he sends instead, to give you your lesson.

ANG. (*recognizing* CLÉANTE). O heavens!

ARG. What is the matter? Why this surprise?

ANG. It is . . .

ARG. What can disturb you in that manner?

ANG. It is such a strange coincidence.

ARG. How so?

ANG. I dreamt last night that I was in the greatest trouble imaginable, and that some one exactly like this gentleman came to me. I asked him to help me, and presently he saved me from the great trouble I was in. My surprise was very great to meet unexpectedly, on my coming here, him of whom I had been dreaming all night.

CLE. It is no small happiness to occupy your thoughts whether sleeping or waking, and my delight would be great indeed if you were in any trouble out of which you would think me worthy of delivering you. There is nothing that I would not do for . . .

SCENE V.—Argan, Angélique, Cléante, Toinette.

TOI. (*to* ARGAN). Indeed, Sir, I am of your opinion now, and I unsay all that I said yesterday.

Here are Mr. Diafoirus the father, and Mr. Diafoirus the son, who are coming to visit you. How well provided with a son-in-law you will be! You will see the best-made young fellow in the world, and the most intellectual. He said but two words to me, it is true, but I was struck with them, and your daughter will be delighted with him.

ARG. (*to* CLÉANTE, *who moves as if to go*). Do not go, Sir. I am about, as you see, to marry my daughter, and they have just brought her future husband, whom she has not as yet seen.

CLE. You do me great honour, Sir, in wishing me to be witness of such a pleasant interview.

ARG. He is the son of a clever doctor, and the marriage will take place in four days.

CLE. Indeed!

ARG. Please inform her music-master of it, that he may be at the wedding.

CLE. I will not fail to do so.

ARG. And I invite you also.

CLE. You do me too much honour.

TOI. Come, make room; here they are.

SCENE VI.—Mr. Diafoirus, Thomas Diafoirus, Argan, Angélique, Cléante, Toinette, Servants.

ARG. (*putting up his hand to his night-cap without taking it off*). Mr. Purgon has forbidden me to uncover my head. You belong to the profession, and know what would be the consequence if I did so.

MR. DIA. We are bound in all our visits to bring relief to invalids, and not to injure them.

(MR. ARGAN *and* MR. DIAFOIRUS *speak at the same time.*)

ARG. I receive, Sir. . . .

MR. DIA. We come here, Sir. . . .

ARG. With great joy. . . .

MR. DIA. My son Thomas and myself. . . .

ARG. The honour you do me. . . .

MR. DIA. To declare to you, Sir. . . .

ARG. And I wish. . . .

MR. DIA. The delight we are in. . . .

ARG. I could have gone to your house. . . .

MR. DIA. At the favour you do us. . . .

ARG. To assure you of it. . . .

MR. DIA. In so kindly admitting us. . . .

ARG. But you know, Sir. . . .

MR. DIA. To the honour, Sir. . . .

ARG. What it is to be a poor invalid. . . .

MR. DIA. Of your alliance. . . .

ARG. Who can only. . . .

MR. DIA. And assure you. . . .

ARG. Tell you here. . . .

MR. DIA. That in all that depends on our knowledge. . . .

ARG. That he will seize every opportunity. . . .

MR. DIA. As well as in any other way. . . .

ARG. To show you, Sir. . . .

MR. DIA. That we shall ever be ready, Sir. . . .

ARG. That he is entirely at your service. . . .

MR. DIA. To show you our zeal. (*To his son*) Now, Thomas, come forward, and pay your respects.

T. DIA. (*to* MR. DIAFOIRUS). Ought I not to begin with the father?

MR. DIA. Yes.

T. DIA. (*to* ARGAN). Sir, I come to salute, acknowledge, cherish, and revere in you a second father; but a second father to whom I owe more, I make bold to say, than to the first. The first gave me birth; but you have chosen me. He received me by necessity, but you have accepted me by choice. What I have from him is of the body, corporal; what I hold from you is of the will, voluntary; and in so much the more as the mental faculties are above the corporal, in so much the more do I hold precious this future affiliation, for which I come beforehand to-day to render you my most humble and most respectful homage.

TOI. Long life to the colleges which send such clever people into the world!

T. DIA. (*to* MR. DIAFOIRUS). Has this been said to your satisfaction, father?

MR. DIA. *Optime.*

ARG. (*to* ANGÉLIQUE). Come, bow to this gentleman.

T. DIA (*to* MR. DIAFOIRUS). Shall I kiss?

MR. DIA. Yes, yes.

T. DIA. (*to* ANGÉLIQUE). Madam, it is with justice that heaven has given you the name of stepmother, since we see in you steps towards the perfect beauty which . . .[2]

ARG. (*to* THOMAS DIAFOIRUS). It is not to my wife, but to my daughter, that you are speaking.

T. DIA. Where is she?

ARG. She will soon come.

T. DIA. Shall I wait, father, till she comes?

MR. DIA. No; go through your compliments to the young lady in the meantime.

T. DIA. Madam, as the statue of Memnon gave forth a harmonious sound when it was struck by the first rays of the sun, in like manner do I experience a sweet rapture at the apparition of this sun of your beauty. As the naturalists remark that the flower styled heliotrope always turns towards the star of day, so will my heart for ever turn towards the resplendent stars of your adorable eyes as to its only pole. Suffer me, then, Madam, to make to-day on the altar of your charms the offering of a heart which longs for and is ambitious of no greater glory than to be till death, Madam, your most humble, most obedient, most faithful servant and husband.

TOI. Ah! See what it is to study, and how one learns to say fine things!

ARG. (*to* CLÉANTE). Well! what do you say to that?

CLE. The gentleman does wonders, and if he is as good a doctor as he is an orator, it will be most pleasant to be one of his patients.

TOI. Certainly, it will be something admirable if his cures are as wonderful as his speeches.

ARG. Now, quick, my chair; and seats for everybody. (*Servants bring chairs.*) Sit down here, my daughter. (*To* M. DIAFOIRUS) You see, Sir, that everybody admires your son; and I think you very fortunate in being the father of such a fine young man.

MR. DIA. Sir, it is not because I am his father, but I can boast that I have reason to be satisfied with him, and that all those who see him speak of him as of a youth without guile. He has not a very lively imagination, nor that sparkling wit which is found in some others; but it is this which has always made me augur well of his judgment, a quality required for the exercise of our art. As a child he never was what is called sharp or lively. He was always gentle, peaceful, taciturn, never saying a word, and never playing at any of those little pastimes that we call children's games. It was found most difficult to teach him to read, and he was nine years old before he knew his letters. A good omen, I used to say to myself; trees slow of growth bear the best fruit. We engrave on marble with much more difficulty than on sand, but the result is more lasting; and that dulness of apprehension, that heaviness of imagination, is a mark of a sound judgment in the future. When I sent him to college, he found it hard work, but he stuck to his duty, and bore up with obstinacy against all difficulties. His tutors always praised him for his assiduity and the trouble he took. In short, by dint of continual hammering, he at last succeeded gloriously in obtaining his degree; and I can say, without vanity, that from that time till now there has been no candidate who has made more noise than he in all the disputations of our school. There he has rendered himself formidable, and no debate passes but he goes and argues loudly and to the last extreme on the opposite side. He is firm in dispute, strong as a Turk in his principles, never changes his opinion, and pursues an argument to the last recesses of logic. But, above all things, what pleases me in him, and what I am glad to see him follow my example in, is that he is blindly attached to the opinions of the ancients, and that he would never understand nor listen to the reasons and the experiences of the pretended discoveries of our century concerning the circulation of the blood and other opinions of the same stamp.[3]

T. DIA. (*pulling out of his pocket a long paper rolled up, and presenting it to* ANGÉLIQUE). I have upheld against these circulators a thesis which, with the permission (*bowing to* ARGAN) of this gentleman, I venture to present to the young lady as the first-fruits of my genius.

ANG. Sir, it is a useless piece of furniture to me; I do not understand these things.

TOI. (*taking the paper*). Never mind; give it all the same; the picture will be of use, and we will adorn our attic with it.

T. DIA. (*again bowing to* ANGÉLIQUE). With the permission of this gentleman, I invite you to come one of these days to amuse yourself by assisting at the dissection of a woman upon whose body I am to give lectures.

TOI. The treat will be most welcome. There are some who give the pleasure of seeing a play to their lady-love; but a dissection is much more gallant.

MR. DIA. Moreover, in respect to the qualities required for marriage, I assure you that he is all you could wish, and that his children will be strong and healthy.

ARG. Do you not intend, Sir, to push his way at court, and obtain for him the post of physician there?

MR. DIA. To tell you the truth, I have never had any predilection to practice with the great; it never seemed pleasant to me, and I have found that it is better for us to confine ourselves to the ordinary public. Ordinary people are more convenient; you are accountable to nobody for your actions, and as long as you follow the common rules laid down by the faculty, there is no necessity to trouble yourself about the result. What is vexatious among people of rank is that, when they are ill, they positively expect their doctor to cure them.

TOI. How very absurd! How impertinent of them to ask of you doctors to cure them! You are not placed near them for that, but only to receive your fees and to prescribe remedies. It is their own look-out to get well if they can.

MR. DIA. Quite so. We are only bound to treat people according to form.

ARG. (*to* CLÉANTE). Sir, please make my daughter sing before the company.

CLE. I was waiting for your commands, Sir; and I propose, in order to amuse the company, to sing with the young lady an operetta which has lately come out. (*To* ANGÉLIQUE, *giving her a paper*) There is your part.

ANG. Mine?

CLE. (*aside to* ANGÉLIQUE). Don't refuse, pray; but let me explain to you what is the scene we must sing. (*Aloud*) I have no voice; but in this case it is sufficient if I make myself understood; and you must have the goodness to excuse me, because I am under the necessity of making the young lady sing.

ARG. Are the verses pretty?

CLE. It is really nothing but a small extempore opera, and what you will hear is only rhythmical prose or a kind of irregular verse, such as passion and necessity make two people utter.

ARG. Very well; let us hear.

CLE. The subject of the scene is as follows. A shepherd was paying every attention to the beauties of a play, when he was disturbed by a noise close to him, and on turning round he saw a scoundrel who, with insolent language, was annoying a young shepherdess. He immediately espoused the cause of a sex to which all men owe homage; and after having chastised the brute for his insolence, he came near the shepherdess to comfort her. He sees a young girl with the most beautiful eyes he has ever beheld, who is shedding tears which he thinks the most precious in the world. Alas! says he to himself, can any one be capable of insulting such charms? Where is the unfeeling wretch, the barbarous man to be found who will not feel touched by such tears? He endeavours to stop those beautiful tears, and the lovely shepherdess takes the opportunity of thanking him for the slight service he has rendered her. But she does it in a manner so touching, so tender, and so passionate that the shepherd cannot resist it, and each word, each look is a burning shaft which penetrates his heart. Is there anything in the world worthy of such thanks? and what will not one do, what service and what danger will not one be delighted to run to attract upon oneself even for a moment the touching sweetness of so grateful a heart? The whole play was acted without his paying any more attention to it; yet he complains that it was too short, since the end separates him from his lovely shepherdess. From that moment, from that first sight, he carries away with him a love which has the strength of a passion of many years. He now feels all the pangs of absence, and is tormented in no longer seeing what he beheld for so short a time. He tries every means to meet again with a sight so dear to him, and the remembrance of which pursues him day and night. But the great watch which is kept over his shepherdess deprives him of all the power of doing so. The violence of his passion urges him to ask in marriage the adorable beauty without whom he can no longer live, and he obtains from her the permission of doing so, by means of a note that he has succeeded in sending to her. But he is told in the meantime that the father of her whom he loves has decided upon marrying her to another, and that everything is being got ready to celebrate the wedding. Judge what a cruel wound for the heart of that poor shepherd! Behold him suffering from this mortal blow; he cannot bear the dreadful idea of seeing her he loves in the arms of another; and in his despair he finds the means of introducing himself into the house of his shepherdess, in order to learn her feelings and to hear from her the fate he must expect. There he sees everything ready for what he fears; he sees the unworthy rival whom the caprice of a father opposes to the tenderness of his love; he sees that ridiculous rival triumphant near the lovely shepherdess, as if already assured of his conquest. Such a sight fills him with a wrath he can hardly master. He looks despairingly at her whom he adores, but the respect he has for her and the presence of her father prevent him from speaking except with his eyes. At last he breaks through all restraint, and the greatness of his love forces him to speak as follows. (*He sings.*)

Phyllis, too sharp a pain you bid me bear;
Break this stern silence, tell me what to fear;
Disclose your thoughts, and bid them open lie
To tell me if I live or die.

ANG.
The marriage preparations sadden me.
O'erwhelmed with sorrow,
My eyes I lift to heaven; I strive to pray,
Then gaze on you and sigh. No more I say.

CLE.
Tircis, who fain would woo,
Tell him, Phyllis, is it true,
Is he so blest by your sweet grace
As in your heart to find a place?

ANG.

I may not hide it, in this dire extreme,
Tircis, I own for you my love....

CLE.

O blessed words! am I indeed so blest?
Repeat them, Phyllis; set my doubts at rest.

ANG. I love you, Tircis!

CLE. Ah! Phyllis, once again.

ANG. I love you, Tircis!

CLE. Alas! I fain
A hundred times would hearken to that strain.

ANG. I love you! I love you!
Tircis, I love you!

CLE.

Ye kings and gods who, from your eternal seat,
Behold the world of men beneath your feet,
Can you possess a happiness more sweet?
My Phyllis! one dark haunting fear
Our peaceful joy disturbs unsought;
A rival may my homage share.

ANG.

Ah! worse than death is such a thought!
Its presence equal torment is
To both, and mars my bliss.

CLE.

Your father to his vow would subject you.

ANG.

Ah! welcome death before I prove untrue.

ARG. And what does the father say to all that?

CLE. Nothing.

ARG. Then that father is a fool to put up with those silly things, without saying a word!

CLE. (*trying to go on singing*).

Ah! my love....

ARG. No; no; that will do. An opera like that is in very bad taste. The shepherd Tircis is an impertinent fellow, and the shepherdess Phyllis an impudent girl to speak in that way in the presence of her father. (*To* ANGÉLIQUE) Show me that paper. Ah! ah! and where are the words that you have just sung? This is only the music.

CLE. Are you not aware, Sir, that the way of writing the words with the notes themselves has been lately discovered?

ARG. Has it? Good-bye for the present. We could have done very well without your impertinent opera.

CLE. I thought I should amuse you.

ARG. Foolish things do not amuse, Sir. Ah! here is my wife.

SCENE VII.—Béline, Argan, Angélique, Mr. Diafoirus, T. Diafoirus, Toinette.

ARG. My love, here is the son of Mr. Diafoirus.

T. DIA. Madam, it is with justice that heaven has given you the title of stepmother, since we see in you steps . . .

BEL. Sir, I am delighted to have come here just in time to see you.

T. DIA. Since we see in you . . . since we see in you. . . . Madam, you have interrupted me in the middle of my period, and have troubled my memory.

MR. DIA. Keep it for another time.

ARG. I wish, my dear, that you had been here just now.

TOI. Ah! Madam, how much you have lost by not being at the second father, the statue of Memnon, and the flower styled heliotrope.

ARG. Come, my daughter, shake hands with this gentleman, and pledge him your troth.

ANG. Father!

ARG. Well? What do you mean by "Father"?

ANG. I beseech you not to be in such a hurry; give us time to become acquainted with each other, and to see grow in us that sympathy so necessary to a perfect union.

T. DIA. As far as I am concerned, Madam, it is already full-grown within me, and there is no occasion for me to wait.

ANG. I am not so quick as you are, Sir, and I must confess that your merit has not yet made enough impression on my heart.

ARG. Oh! nonsense! There will be time enough for the impression to be made after you are married.

ANG. Ah! my father, give me time, I beseech you! Marriage is a chain which should never be imposed by force. And if this gentleman is a man of honour, he ought not to accept a person who would be his only by force.

T. DIA. *Nego consequentiam.* I can be a man of honour, Madam, and at the same time accept you from the hands of your father.

ANG. To do violence to any one is a strange way of setting about inspiring love.

T. DIA. We read in the ancients, Madam, that it was their custom to carry off by main force from their father's house the maiden they wished to marry, so that the latter might not seem to fly of her own accord into the arms of a man.

ANG. The ancients, Sir, are the ancients; but we are the moderns. Pretences are not necessary in our age; and when a marriage pleases us, we know very well how to go to it without being dragged by force. Have a little patience; if you love me, Sir, you ought to do what I wish.

T. DIA. Certainly, Madam, but without prejudice to the interest of my love.

ANG. But the greatest mark of love is to submit to the will of her who is loved.

T. DIA. *Distinguo*, Madam. In what does not regard the possession of her, concedo; but in what regards it, *nego*.

TOI. (*to* ANGÉLIQUE). It is in vain for you to argue. This gentleman is bran new from college, and will be more than a match for you. Why resist, and refuse the glory of belonging to the faculty?

BEL. She may have some other inclination in her head.

ANG. If I had, Madam, it would be such as reason and honour allow.

ARG. Heyday! I am acting a pleasant part here!

BEL. If I were you, my child, I would not force her to marry; I know very well what I should do.

ANG. I know what you mean, Madam, and how kind you are to me; but it may be hoped that your advice may not be fortunate enough to be followed.

BEL. That is because well-brought-up and good children, like you, scorn to be obedient to the will of their fathers. Obedience was all very well in former times.

ANG. The duty of a daughter has its limits, Madam, and neither reason nor law extend it to all things.

BEL. Which means that your thoughts are all in favour of marriage, but that you will choose a husband for yourself.

ANG. If my father will not give me a husband I like, at least I beseech him not to force me to marry one I can never love.

ARG. Gentlemen, I beg your pardon for all this.

ANG. We all have our own end in marrying. For my part, as I only want a husband that I can love sincerely, and as I intend to consecrate my whole life to him, I feel bound, I confess, to be cautious. There are some who marry simply to free themselves from the yoke of their parents, and to be at liberty to do all they like. There are others, Madam, who see in marriage only a matter of mere interest; who marry only to get a settlement, and to enrich themselves by the death of those they marry. They pass without scruple from husband to husband, with an eye to their possessions. These, no doubt, Madam, are not so difficult to satisfy, and care little what the husband is like.

BEL. You are very full of reasoning to-day. I wonder what you mean by this.

ANG. I, Madam? What can I mean but what I say?

BEL. You are such a simpleton, my dear, that one can hardly bear with you.

ANG. You would like to extract from me some rude answer; but I warn you that you will not have the pleasure of doing so.

BEL. Nothing can equal your impertinence.

ANG. It is of no use, Madam; you will not.

BEL. And you have a ridicuLOU.s pride, an impertinent presumption, which makes you the scorn of everybody.

ANG. All this will be useless, Madam. I shall be quiet in spite of you; and to take away from you all hope of succeeding in what you wish, I will withdraw from your presence.

SCENE VIII.—Argan, Béline, Mr. Diafoirus, T. Diafoirus, Toinette.

ARG. (*to* ANGÉLIQUE, *as she goes away*). Listen to me! Of two things, one. Either you will marry this gentleman or you will go into a convent. I give you four days to consider. (*To* BÉLINE) Don't be anxious; I will bring her to reason.

BEL. I am sorry to leave you, my child; but I have some important business which calls me to town. I shall soon be back.

ARG. Go, my darling; call upon the notary, and tell him to be quick about you know what.

BEL. Good-bye, my child.

ARG. Good-bye, deary.

SCENE IX.—Argan, Mr. Diafoirus, T. Diafoirus, Toinette.

ARG. How much this woman loves me; it is perfectly incredible.

MR. DIA. We shall now take our leave of you, Sir.

ARG. I beg of you, Sir, to tell me how I am.

MR. DIA. (*feeling* ARGAN'S *pulse*). Now, Thomas, take the other arm of the gentleman, so that I may see whether you can form a right judgment on his pulse. *Quid dicis?*

T. DIA. *Dico* that the pulse of this gentleman is the pulse of a man who is not well.

MR. DIA. Good.

T. DIA. That it is *duriusculus*, not to say *durus*.

MR. DIA. Very well.

T. DIA. Irregular.

MR. DIA. *Bene.*

T. DIA. And even a little caprizant.

MR. DIA. *Optime.*

T. DIA. Which speaks of an intemperance in the splenetic *parenchyma;* that is to say, the spleen.

MR. DIA. Quite right.

ARG. It cannot be, for Mr. Purgon says that it is my liver which is out of order.

MR. DIA. Certainly; he who says *parenchyma* says both one and the other, because of the great sympathy which exists between them through the means of the *vas breve,* of the *pylorus,* and often of the *meatus choledici.* He no doubt orders you to eat plenty of roast-meat.

ARG. No; nothing but boiled meat.

MR. DIA. Yes, yes; roast or boiled, it is all the same; he orders very wisely, and you could not have fallen into better hands.

ARG. Sir, tell me how many grains of salt I ought to put to an egg?

MR. DIA. Six, eight, ten, by even numbers; just as in medicines by odd numbers.

ARG. Good-bye, Sir; I hope soon to have the pleasure of seeing you again.

SCENE X.—Béline, Argan.

BEL. Before I go out, I must inform you of one thing you must be careful about. While passing before Angélique's door, I saw with her a young man, who ran away as soon as he noticed me.

ARG. A young man with my daughter!

BEL. Yes; your little girl louison, who was with them, will tell you all about it.

ARG. Send her here, my love, send her here at once. Ah! the brazen-faced girl! (*Alone.*) I no longer wonder at the resistance she showed.

SCENE XI.—Argan, Louison.

LOU. What do you want, papa? My step-mamma told me to come to you.

ARG. Yes; come here. Come nearer. Turn round, and hold up your head. Look straight at me. Well?

LOU. What, papa?

ARG. So?

LOU. What?

ARG. Have you nothing to say to me?

LOU. Yes. I will, to amuse you, tell you, if you like, the story of the Ass's Skin or the fable of the Fox and the Crow, which I have learnt lately.

ARG. That is not what I want of you.

LOU. What is it then?

ARG. Ah! cunning little girl, you know very well what I mean.

LOU. No indeed, papa.

ARG. Is that the way you obey me?

LOU. What, papa?

ARG. Have I not asked you to tell me at once all you see?

LOU. Yes, papa.

ARG. Have you done so?

LOU. Yes, papa. I always come and tell you all I see.

ARG. And have you seen nothing to-day?

LOU. No, papa.

ARG. No?

LOU. No, papa.

ARG. Quite sure?

LOU. Quite sure.

ARG. Ah! indeed! I will make you see something soon.

LOU. (*seeing* ARGAN *take a rod*). Ah! papa!

ARG. Ah! ah! false little girl; you do not tell me that you saw a man in your sister's room!

LOU. (*crying*). Papa!

ARG. (*taking* LOUISON *by the arm*). This will teach you to tell falsehoods.

LOU. (*throwing herself on her knees*). Ah! my dear papa! pray forgive me. My sister had asked me not to say anything to you, but I will tell you everything.

ARG. First you must have a flogging for having told an untruth, then we will see to the rest.

LOU. Forgive me, papa, forgive me!

ARG. No, no!

LOU. My dear papa, don't whip me.

ARG. Yes, you shall be whipped.

LOU. For pity's sake! don't whip me, papa.

ARG. (*going to whip her*). Come, come.

LOU. Ah! papa, you have hurt me; I am dead! (*She feigns to be dead.*)

ARG. How, now! What does this mean? Louison! Louison! Ah! heaven! Louison! My child! Ah!

wretched father! My poor child is dead! What have I done? Ah! villainous rod! A curse on the rod! Ah! my poor child! My dear little Louison!

LOU. Come, come, dear papa; don't weep so. I am not quite dead yet.

ARG. Just see the cunning little wench. Well! I forgive you this once, but you must tell me everything.

LOU. Oh yes, dear papa.

ARG. Be sure you take great care, for here is my little finger that knows everything, and it will tell me if you don't speak the truth.

LOU. But, papa, you won't tell sister that I told you.

ARG. No, no.

LOU. (*after having listened to see if any one can hear*). Papa, a young man came into sister's room while I was there.

ARG. Well?

LOU. I asked him what he wanted; he said that he was her music-master.

ARG. (*aside*). Hm! hm! I see. (*To* LOUISON) Well?

LOU. Then sister came.

ARG. Well?

LOU. She said to him, "Go away, go away, go. Good heavens! you will drive me to despair."

ARG. Well?

LOU. But he would not go away.

ARG. What did he say to her?

LOU. Oh! ever so many things.

ARG. But what?

LOU. He told her this, and that, and the other; that he loved her dearly; that she was the most beautiful person in the world.

ARG. And then, after?

LOU. Then he knelt down before her.

ARG. And then?

LOU. Then he kept on kissing her hands.

ARG. And then?

LOU. Then my mamma came to the door, and, he escaped.

ARG. Nothing else?

LOU. No, dear papa.

ARG. Here is my little finger, which says something though. (*Putting his finger up to his ear.*) Wait. Stay, eh? ah! ah! Yes? oh! oh! here is my little finger, which says that there is something you saw, and which you do not tell me.

LOU. Ah! papa, your little finger is a story-teller.

ARG. Take care.

LOU. No, don't believe him; he tells a story, I assure you.

ARG. Oh! Well, well; we will see to that. Go away now, and pay great attention to what you see. (*Alone.*) Ah! children are no longer children nowadays! What trouble! I have not even enough leisure to attend to my illness. I am quite done up. (*He falls down into his chair.*)

SCENE XII.—Béralde, Argan.

BER. Well, brother! What is the matter? How are you?

ARG. Ah! very bad, brother; very bad.

BER. How is that?

ARG. No one would believe how very feeble I am.

BER. That's a sad thing, indeed.

ARG. I have hardly enough strength to speak.

BER. I came here, brother, to propose a match for my niece, Angélique.

ARG. (*in a rage, speaking with great fury, and starting up from his chair*). Brother, don't speak to me of that wicked, good-for-nothing, insolent, brazen-faced girl. I will put her in a convent before two days are over.

BER. Ah! all right! I am glad to see that you have a little strength still left, and that my visit does you good. Well, well, we will talk of business by-and-by. I have brought you an entertainment, which will dissipate your melancholy, and will dispose you better for what we have to talk about. They are gipsies dressed in Moorish clothes. They perform some dances mixed with songs, which, I am sure, you will like, and which will be as good as a prescription from Mr. Purgon. Come along.

SECOND INTERLUDE.

MEN *and* WOMEN (*dressed as Moors*).

FIRST MOORISH WOMAN.

When blooms the spring of life,
  The golden harvest reap.
Waste not your years in bootless strife,
  Till age upon your bodies creep.
But now, when shines the kindly light,
Give up your soul to love's delight.
No touch of sweetest joy
  This longing heart can know,
No bliss without alloy
  When love does silent show.
Then up, ye lads and lasses gay!
  The spring of life is fair;
  Cloud not these hours with care,
For love must win the day.
Beauty fades,
  Years roll by,
Lowering shades
  Obscure the sky.
And joys so sweet of yore
Shall charm us then no more.
Then up, ye lads and lasses gay!
  The spring of life is fair;
  Cloud not these hours with care,
For love must win the day.

First Entry of the Ballet.

2ND MOORISH WOMAN.

They bid us love, they bid us woo,
  Why seek delay?
To tender sighs and kisses too
  In youth's fair day,
Our hearts are but too true.
The sweetest charms has Cupid's spell.
  No sooner felt, the ready heart
His conquered self would yield him well
  Ere yet the god had winged his dart.
But yet the tale we often hear
  Of tears and sorrows keen,
  To share in them, I ween,
Though sweet, would make us fear!

3RD MOORISH WOMAN.

To love a lover true,
In youth's kind day, I trow,
Is pleasant task enow;
But think how we must rue
If he inconstant show!

4TH MOORISH WOMAN.

The loss of lover false to me
But trifling grief would be,
Yet this is far the keenest smart
That he had stol'n away our heart.

2ND MOORISH WOMAN.

What then shall we do
Whose hearts are so young?

4TH MOORISH WOMAN.

Though cruel his laws,
Attended by woes,
Away with your arms,
Submit to his charms!

TOGETHER.

His whims ye must follow,
  His transports though fleet,
  His pinings too sweet
Though often comes sorrow,
The thousand delights
  The wounds of his darts
Still charm all the hearts.

ACT III.

SCENE I.—Béralde, Argan, Toinette.

BER. Well, brother, what do you say to that? Isn't it as good as a dose of cassia?

TOI. Oh! good cassia is a very good thing, Sir.

BER. Now, shall we have a little chat together.

ARG. Wait a moment, brother, I'll be back directly.

TOI. Here, Sir; you forget that you cannot get about without a stick.

ARG. Ay, to be sure.

SCENE II.—BÉRALDE, TOINETTE.

TOI. Pray, do not give up the interest of your niece.

BER. No, I shall do all in my power to forward her wishes.

TOI. We must prevent this foolish marriage which he has got into his head, from taking place. And I thought to myself that it would be a good thing to introduce a doctor here, having a full understanding of our wishes, to disgust him with his Mr. Purgon, and abuse his mode of treating him. But as we have nobody to act that part for us, I have decided upon playing him a trick of my own.

BER. In what way?

TOI. It is rather an absurd idea, and it may be more fortunate than good. But act your own part. Here is our man.

SCENE III.—Argan, Béralde.

BER. Let me ask you, brother, above all things not to excite yourself during our conversation.

ARG. I agree.

BER. To answer without anger to anything I may mention.

ARG. Very well.

BER. And to reason together upon the business I want to discuss with you without any irritation.

ARG. Dear me! Yes. What a preamble!

BER. How is it, brother, that, with all the wealth you possess, and with only one daughter—for I do not count the little one—you speak of sending her to a convent?

ARG. How is it, brother, that I am master of my family, and that I can do all I think fit?

BER. Your wife doesn't fail to advise you to get rid, in that way, of your two daughters; and I have no doubt that, through a spirit of charity, she would be charmed to see them both good nuns.

ARG. Oh, I see! My poor wife again! It is she who does all the harm, and everybody is against her.

BER. No, brother; let us leave that alone. She is a woman with the best intentions in the world for the good of your family, and is free from all interested motives. She expresses for you the most extraordinary tenderness, and shows towards your children an inconceivable goodness. No, don't let us speak of her, but only of your daughter. What can be your reason for wishing to give her in marriage to the sort of a doctor?

ARG. My reason is that I wish to have a son-in-law who will suit my wants.

BER. But it is not what your daughter requires, and we have a more suitable match for her.

ARG. Yes; but this one is more suitable for me.

BER. But does she marry a husband for herself or for you, brother?

ARG. He must do both for her and for me, brother; and I wish to take into my family people of whom I have need.

BER. So that, if your little girl were old enough, you would give her to an apothecary?

ARG. Why not?

BER. Is it possible that you should always be so infatuated with your apothecaries and doctors, and be so determined to be ill, in spite of men and nature?

ARG. What do you mean by that, brother?

BER. I mean, brother, that I know of no man less sick than you, and that I should be quite satisfied with a constitution no worse than yours. One great proof that you are well, and that you have a body perfectly well made, is that with all the pains you have taken, you have failed as yet in injuring the soundness of your constitution, and that you have not died of all the medicine they have made you swallow.

ARG. But are you aware, brother, that it is these medicines which keep me in good health? Mr. Purgon says that I should go off if he were but three days without taking care of me.

BER. If you are not careful, he will take such care of you that he will soon send you into the next world.

ARG. But let us reason together, brother; don't you believe at all in medicine?

BER. No, brother; and I do not see that it is necessary for our salvation to believe in it.

ARG. What! Do you not hold true a thing acknowledged by everybody, and revered throughout all ages?

BER. Between ourselves, far from thinking it true, I look upon it as one of the greatest follies which exist among men; and to consider things from a philosophical point of view, I don't know of a more absurd piece of mummery, of anything more ridiculous, than a man who takes upon himself to cure another man.

ARG. Why will you not believe that a man can cure another?

BER. For the simple reason, brother, that the springs of our machines are mysteries about which men are as yet completely in the dark, and nature has put too thick a veil before our eyes for us to know anything about it.

ARG. Then, according to you, the doctors know nothing at all.

BER. Oh yes, brother. Most of them have some knowledge of the best classics, can talk fine Latin, can give a Greek name to every disease, can define and distinguish them; but as to curing these diseases, that's out of the question.

ARG. Still, you must agree to this, that doctors know more than others.

BER. They know, brother, what I have told you; and that does not effect many cures. All the excellency of their art consists in pompous gibberish, in a specious babbling, which gives you words instead of reasons, and promises instead of results.

ARG. Still, brother, there exist men as wise and clever as you, and we see that in cases of illness every one has recourse to the doctor.

BER. It is a proof of human weakness, and not of the truth of their art.

ARG. Still, doctors must believe in their art, since they make use of it for themselves.

BER. It is because some of them share the popular error by which they themselves profit, while others profit by it without sharing it. Your Mr. Purgon has no wish to deceive; he is a thorough doctor from head to foot, a man who believes in his rules more than in all the demonstrations of mathematics, and who would think it a crime to question them. He sees nothing obscure in physic, nothing doubtful, nothing difficult, and through an impetuous prepossession, an obstinate confidence, a coarse common sense and reason, orders right and left purgatives and bleedings, and hesitates at nothing. We must bear him no ill-will for the harm he does us; it is with the best intentions in the world that he will send you into the next world, and in killing you he will do no more than he has done to his wife and children, and than he would do to himself, if need be.[4]

ARG. It is because you have a spite against him. But let us come to the point. What is to be done when one is ill?

BER. Nothing, brother.

ARG. Nothing?

BER. Nothing. Only rest. Nature, when we leave her free, will herself gently recover from the disorder into which she has fallen. It is our anxiety, our impatience, which does the mischief, and most men die of their remedies, and not of their diseases.

ARG. Still you must acknowledge, brother, that we can in certain things help nature.

BER. Alas! brother; these are pure fancies, with which we deceive ourselves. At all times, there have crept among men brilliant fancies in which we believe, because they flatter us, and because it would be well if they were true. When a doctor speaks to us of assisting, succouring nature, of removing what is injurious to it, of giving it what it is defective in, of restoring it, and giving back to it the full exercise of its functions, when he speaks of purifying the blood, of refreshing the bowels and the brain, of correcting the spleen, of rebuilding the lungs, of renovating the liver, of fortifying the heart, of re-establishing and keeping up the natural heat, and of possessing secrets wherewith to lengthen life of many years—he repeats to you the romance of physic. But when you test the truth of what he has promised to you, you find that it all ends in nothing; it is like those beautiful dreams which only leave you in the morning the regret of having believed in them.

ARG. Which means that all the knowledge of the world is contained in your brain, and that you think you know more than all the great doctors of our age put together.

BER. When you weigh words and actions, your great doctors are two different kinds of people. Listen to their talk, they are the cleverest people in the world; see them at work, and they are the most ignorant.

ARG. Heyday! You are a great doctor, I see, and I wish that some one of those gentlemen were here to take up your arguments and to check your babble.

BER. I do not take upon myself, brother, to fight against physic; and every one at their own risk and peril may believe what he likes. What I say is only between ourselves; and I should have liked, in order to deliver you from the error into which you have fallen, and in order to amuse you, to take you to see some of Molière's comedies on this subject.

ARG. Your Molière is a fine impertinent fellow with his comedies! I think it mightily pleasant of him to go and take off honest people like the doctors.

BER. It is not the doctors themselves that he takes off, but the absurdity of medicine.

ARG. It becomes him well, truly, to control the faculty! He's a nice simpleton, and a nice impertinent fellow to laugh at consultations and prescriptions, to attack the body of physicians, and to bring on his stage such venerable people as those gentlemen.

BER. What would you have him bring there but the different professions of men? Princes and kings are brought there every day, and they are of as good a stock as your physicians.

ARG. No, by all the devils! if I were a physician, I would be revenged of his impertinence, and when he falls ill, I would let him die without relief. In vain would he beg and pray. I would not prescribe for him the least little bleeding, the least little injection, and I would tell him, "Die, die, like a dog; it will teach you to laugh at us doctors."

BER. You are terribly angry with him.

ARG. Yes, he is an ill-advised fellow, and if the doctors are wise, they will do what I say.

BER. He will be wiser than the doctors, for he will not go and ask their help.

ARG. So much the worse for him, if he has not recourse to their remedies.

BER. He has his reasons for not wishing to have anything to do with them; he is certain that only strong and robust constitutions can bear their remedies in addition to the illness, and he has only just enough strength for his sickness.

ARG. What absurd reasons. Here, brother, don't speak to me anymore about that man; for it makes me savage, and you will give me his complaint.

BER. I will willingly cease, brother; and, to change the subject, allow me to tell you that, because your daughter shows a slight repugnance to the match you propose, it is no reason why you should shut her up in a convent. In your choice of a son-in-law you should not blindly follow the anger which masters you. We should in such a matter yield a little to the inclinations of a daughter, since it is for all her life, and the whole happiness of her married life depends on it.

SCENE IV.—Mr. Fleurant, Argan, Béralde.

ARG. Ah! brother, with your leave.

BER. Eh? What are you going to do?

ARG. To take this little clyster; it will soon be done.

BER. Are you joking? Can you not spend one moment without clysters or physic? Put it off to another time, and be quiet.

ARG. Mr. Fleurant, let it be for to-night or to-morrow morning.

MR. FLEU. (*to* BÉRALDE). What right have you to interfere? How dare you oppose yourself to the prescription of the doctors, and prevent the gentleman from taking my clyster? You are a nice fellow to show such boldness.

BER. Go, Sir, go; it is easy to see that you are not accustomed to speak face to face with men.

MR. FLEU. You ought not thus to sneer at physic, and make me lose my precious time. I came here for a good prescription, and I will go and tell Mr. Purgon that I have been prevented from executing his orders, and that I have been stopped in the performance of my duty. You'll see, you'll see....

SCENE V.—Argan, Béralde.

ARG. Brother, you'll be the cause that some misfortune will happen here.

BER. What a misfortune not to take a clyster prescribed by Mr. Purgon! Once more, brother, is it possible that you can't be cured of this doctor disease, and that you will thus bring yourself under their remedies?

ARG. Ah! brother. You speak like a man who is quite well, but if you were in my place, you would soon change your way of speaking. It is easy to speak against medicine when one is in perfect health.

BER. But what disease do you suffer from?

ARG. You will drive me to desperation. I should like you to have my disease, and then we should see if you would prate as you do. Ah! here is Mr. Purgon.

SCENE VI.—Mr. Purgon, Argan, Béralde, Toinette.

MR. PUR. I have just heard nice news downstairs! You laugh at my prescriptions, and refuse to take the remedy which I ordered.

ARG. Sir, it is not . . .

MR. PUR. What daring boldness, what a strange revolt of a patient against his doctor!

TOI. It is frightful.

MR. PUR. A clyster which I have had the pleasure of composing myself.

ARG. It was not I. . . .

MR. PUR. Invented and made up according to all the rules of art.

TOI. He was wrong.

MR. PUR. And which was to work a marvellous effect on the intestines.

ARG. My brother . . .

MR. PUR. To send it back with contempt!

ARG. (*showing* BÉRALDE). It was he. . . .

MR. PUR. Such conduct is monstrous.

TOI. So it is.

MR. PUR. It is a fearful outrage against medicine.

ARG. (*showing* BÉRALDE). He is the cause. . . .

MR. PUR. A crime of high-treason against the faculty, and one which cannot be too severely punished.

TOI. You are quite right.

MR. PUR. I declare to you that I break off all intercourse with you.

ARG. It is my brother. . . .

MR. PUR. That I will have no more connection with you.

TOI. You will do quite right.

MR. PUR. And to end all association with you, here is the deed of gift which I made to my nephew in favour of the marriage. (*He tears the document, and throws the pieces about furiously.*)

ARG. It is my brother who has done all the mischief.

MR. PUR. To despise my clyster!

ARG. Let it be brought, I will take it directly.

MR. PUR. I would have cured you in a very short time.

TOI. He doesn't deserve it.

MR. PUR. I was about to cleanse your body, and to clear it of its bad humours.

ARG. Ah! my brother!

MR. PUR. And it wanted only a dozen purgatives to cleanse it entirely.

TOI. He is unworthy of your care.

MR. PUR. But since you would not be cured by me . . .

ARG. It was not my fault.

MR. PUR. Since you have forsaken the obedience you owe to your doctor …

TOI. It cries for vengeance.

MR. PUR. Since you have declared yourself a rebel against the remedies I had prescribed for you . . .

ARG. No, no, certainly not.

MR. PUR. I must now tell you that I give you up to your bad constitution, to the imtemperament of your intestines, to the corruption of your blood, to the acrimony of your bile, and to the feculence of your humours.

TOI. It serves you right.

ARG. Alas!

MR. PUR. And I will have you before four days in an incurable state.

ARG. Ah! mercy on me!

MR. PUR. You shall fall into bradypepsia.

ARG. Mr. Purgon!

MR. PUR. From bradypepsia into dyspepsia.

ARG. Mr. Purgon!

MR. PUR. From dyspepsia into apepsy.

ARG. Mr. Purgon!

MR. PUR. From apepsy into lientery.

ARG. Mr. Purgon!

MR. PUR. From lientery into dysentery.

ARG. Mr. Purgon!

MR. PUR. From dysentery into dropsy.

ARG. Mr. Purgon!

MR. PUR. And from dropsy to the deprivation of life into which your folly will bring you.

SCENE VII.—Argan, Béralde.

ARG. Ah heaven! I am dead. Brother, you have undone me.

BER. Why? What is the matter?

ARG. I am undone. I feel already that the faculty is avenging itself.

BER. Really, brother, you are crazy, and I would not for a great deal that you should be seen acting as you are doing. Shake yourself a little, I beg, recover yourself, and do not give way so much to your imagination.

ARG. You hear, brother, with what strange diseases he has threatened me.

BER. What a foolish fellow you are!

ARG. He says that I shall become incurable within four days.

BER. And what does it signify what he says? Is it an oracle that has spoken? To hear you, anyone would think that Mr. Purgon holds in his hands the thread of your life, and that he has supreme authority to prolong it or to cut it short at his will. Remember that the springs of your life are in yourself, and that all the wrath of Mr. Purgon can do as little towards making you die, as his remedies can do to make you live. This is an opportunity, if you like to take it, of getting rid of your doctors; and if you are so constituted that you cannot do without them, it is easy for you, brother, to have another with whom you run less risk.

ARG. Ah, brother! he knows all about my constitution, and the way to treat me.

BER. I must acknowledge that you are greatly infatuated, and that you look at things with strange eyes.

SCENE VIII.—Argan, Toinette, Béralde.

TOI. (*to* ARGAN). There is a doctor, here, Sir, who desires to see you.

ARG. What doctor?

TOI. A doctor of medicine.

ARG. I ask you who he is?

TOI. I don't know who he is, but he is as much like me as two peas, and if I was not sure that my mother was an honest woman, I should say that this is a little brother she has given me since my father's death.

SCENE IX.—Argan, Béralde.

BER. You are served according to your wish. One doctor leaves you, another comes to replace him.

ARG. I greatly fear that you will cause some misfortune.

BER. Oh! You are harping upon that string again?

ARG. Ah! I have on my mind all those diseases that I don't understand, those....

SCENE X.—Argan, Béralde, Toinette (*dressed as a doctor*).

TOI. Allow me, Sir, to come and pay my respects to you, and to offer you my small services for all the bleedings and purging you may require.

ARG. I am much obliged to you, Sir. (*To* BÉRALDE) Toinette herself, I declare!

TOI. I beg you will excuse me one moment, Sir. I forgot to give a small order to my servant.

SCENE XI.—Argan, Béralde.

ARG. Would you not say that this is really Toinette?

BER. It is true that the resemblance is very striking. But it is not the first time that we have seen this kind of thing, and history is full of those freaks of nature.

ARG. For my part, I am astonished, and . . .

SCENE XII.—Argan, Béralde, Toinette.

TOI. What do you want, Sir?

ARG. What?

TOI. Did you not call me?

ARG. I? No.

TOI. My ears must have tingled then.

ARG. Just stop here one moment and see how much that doctor is like you.

TOI. Ah! yes, indeed, I have plenty of time to waste! Besides, I have seen enough of him already.

SCENE XIII.—Argan, Béralde.

ARG. Had I not seen them both together, I should have believed it was one and the same person.

BER. I have read wonderful stories about such resemblances; and we have seen some in our day that have taken in everybody.

ARG. For my part, I should have been deceived this time, and sworn that the two were but one.

SCENE XIV.—Argan, Béralde, Toinette (*as a doctor*).

TOI. Sir, I beg your pardon with all my heart.

ARG. (*to* BÉRALDE). It is wonderful.

TOI. You will not take amiss, I hope, the curiosity I feel to see such an illustrious patient; and your reputation, which reaches the farthest ends of the world, must be my excuse for the liberty I am taking.

ARG. Sir, I am your servant.

TOI. I see, Sir, that you are looking earnestly at me. What age do you think I am?

ARG. I should think twenty-six or twenty-seven at the utmost.

TOI. Ah! ah! ah! ah! ah! I am ninety years old.

ARG. Ninety years old!

TOI. Yes; this is what the secrets of my art have done for me to preserve me fresh and vigorous as you see.

ARG. Upon my word, a fine youthful old fellow of ninety!

TOI. I am an itinerant doctor, and go from town to town, from province to province, from kingdom to kingdom, to seek out illustrious material for my abilities; to find patients worthy of my attention, capable of exercising the great and noble secrets which I have discovered in medicine. I disdain to amuse myself with the small rubbish of common diseases, with the trifles of rheumatism, coughs, fevers, vapours, and headaches. I require diseases of importance, such as good non-intermittent fevers with delirium, good scarlet-fevers, good plagues, good confirmed dropsies, good pleurisies with inflammations of the lungs. These are what I like, what I triumph in, and I wish, Sir, that you had all those diseases combined, that you had been given up, despaired of by all the doctors, and at the point of death, so that I might have the pleasure of showing you the excellency of my remedies, and the desire I have of doing you service!

ARG. I am greatly obliged to you, Sir, for the kind intentions you have towards me.

TOI. Let me feel your pulse. Come, come, beat properly, please. Ah! I will soon make you beat as you should. This pulse is trifling with me; I see that it does not know me yet. Who is your doctor?

ARG. Mr. Purgon.

TOI. That man is not noted in my books among the great doctors. What does he say you are ill of?

ARG. He says it is the liver, and others say it is the spleen.

TOI. They are a pack of ignorant blockheads; you are suffering from the lungs.

ARG. The lungs?

TOI. Yes; what do you feel?

ARG. From time to time great pains in my head.

TOI. Just so; the lungs.

ARG. At times it seems as if I had a mist before my eyes.

TOI. The lungs.

ARG. I feel sick now and then.

TOI. The lungs.

ARG. And I feel sometimes a weariness in all my limbs.

TOI. The lungs.

ARG. And sometimes I have sharp pains in the stomach, as if I had the colic.

TOI. The lungs. Do you eat your food with appetite?

ARG. Yes, Sir.

TOI. The lungs. Do you like to drink a little wine?

ARG. Yes, Sir.

TOI. The lungs. You feel sleepy after your meals, and willingly enjoy a nap?

ARG. Yes, Sir.

TOI. The lungs, the lungs, I tell you. What does your doctor order you for food?

ARG. He orders me soup.

TOI. Ignoramus!

ARG. Fowl.

TOI. Ignoramus!

ARG. Veal.

TOI. Ignoramus!

ARG. Broth.

TOI. Ignoramus!

ARG. New-laid eggs.

TOI. Ignoramus!

ARG. And at night a few prunes to relax the bowels.

TOI. Ignoramus!

ARG. And, above all, to drink my wine well diluted with water.

TOI. *Ignorantus, ignoranta, ignorantum.* You must drink your wine pure; and to thicken your blood, which is too thin, you must eat good fat beef, good fat pork, good Dutch cheese, some gruel, rice puddings, chestnuts, and thin cakes,[5] to make all adhere and conglutinate. Your doctor is an ass. I will send you one of my own school, and will come and examine you from time to time during my stay in this town.

ARG. You will oblige me greatly.

TOI. What the deuce do you want with this arm?

ARG. What?

TOI. If I were you, I should have it cut off on the spot.

ARG. Why?

TOI. Don't you see that it attracts all the nourishment to itself, and hinders this side from growing?

ARG. May be; but I have need of my arm.

TOI. You have also a right eye that I would have plucked out if I were in your place.

ARG. My right eye plucked out?

TOI. Don't you see that it interferes with the other, and robs it of its nourishment? Believe me; have it plucked out as soon as possible; you will see all the clearer with the left eye.

ARG. There is no need to hurry.

TOI. Good-bye. I am sorry to leave you so soon, but I must assist at a grand consultation which is to take place about a man who died yesterday.

ARG. About a man who died yesterday?

TOI. Yes, that we may consider and see what ought to have been done to cure him. Good-bye.

ARG. You know that patients do not use ceremony.

SCENE XV.—Argan, Béralde.

BER. Upon my word, this doctor seems to be a very clever man.

ARG. Yes, but he goes a little too fast.

BER. All great doctors do so.

ARG. Cut off my arm and pluck out my eye, so that the other may be better. I had rather that it were not better. A nice operation indeed, to make me at once one-eyed and one-armed.

SCENE XVI.—Argan, Béralde, Toinette.

TOI. (*pretending to speak to somebody*). Come, come, I am your servant; I'm in no joking humour.

ARG. What is the matter?

TOI. Your doctor, forsooth, who wanted to feel my pulse!

ARG. Just imagine; and that, too, at fourscore and ten years of age.

BER. Now, I say, brother, since you have quarrelled with Mr. Purgon, won't you give me leave to speak of the match which is proposed for my niece?

ARG. No, brother; I will put her in a convent, since she has rebelled against me. I see plainly that there is some love business at the bottom of it all, and I have discovered a certain secret interview which they don't suspect me to know anything about.

BER. Well, brother, and suppose there were some little inclination, where could the harm be? Would it be so criminal when it all tends to what is honourable—marriage?

ARG. Be that as it may, she will be a nun. I have made up my mind.

BER. You intend to please somebody by so doing.

ARG. I understand what you mean. You always come back to that, and my wife is very much in your way.

BER. Well, yes, brother; since I must speak out, it is your wife I mean; for I can no more bear with your infatuation about doctors than with your infatuation about your wife, and see you run headlong into every snare she lays for you.

TOI. Ah! Sir, don't talk so of mistress. She is a person against whom there is nothing to be said;

a woman without deceit, and who loves master ah! who loves him. . . . I can't express how much.

ARG. (*to* BÉRALDE). Just ask her all the caresses she lavishes for me.

TOI. Yes, indeed!

ARG. And all the uneasiness my sickness causes her.

TOI. Certainly.

ARG. And the care and trouble she takes about me.

TOI. Quite right. (*To* BÉRALDE) Will you let me convince you; and to show you at once how my mistress loves my master. (*To* ARGAN) Sir, allow me to undeceive him, and to show him his mistake.

ARG. How?

TOI. My mistress will soon come back. Stretch yourself full-length in this arm-chair, and pretend to be dead. You will see what grief she will be in when I tell her the news.

ARG. Very well, I consent.

TOI. Yes; but don't leave her too long in despair, for she might die of it.

ARG. Trust me for that.

TOI. (*to* BÉRALDE). Hide yourself in that corner.

SCENE XVII.—Argan, Toinette.

ARG. Is there no danger in counterfeiting death?

TOI. No, no. What danger can there be? Only stretch yourself there. It will be so pleasant to put your brother to confusion. Here is my mistress. Mind you keep still.

SCENE XVIII.—Béline, Argan (**stretched out in his chair**), Toinette.

TOI. (*pretending not to see* BÉLINE). Ah heavens! Ah! what a misfortune! What a strange accident!

BEL. What is the matter, Toinette?

TOI. Ah! Madam!

BEL. What ails you?

TOI. Your husband is dead.

BEL. My husband is dead?

TOI. Alas! yes; the poor soul is gone.

BEL. Are you quite certain?

TOI. Quite certain. Nobody knows of it yet. I was all alone here when it happened. He has just breathed his last in my arms. Here, just look at him, full-length in his chair.

BEL. Heaven be praised. I am delivered from a most grievous burden. How silly of you, Toinette, to be so afflicted at his death.

TOI. Ah! Ma'am, I thought I ought to cry.

BEL. Pooh! it is not worth the trouble. What loss is it to anybody, and what good did he do in this world? A wretch, unpleasant to everybody; of nauseous, dirty habits; always a clyster or a dose of physic in his body. Always snivelling, coughing, spitting; a stupid, tedious, ill-natured fellow, who was for ever fatiguing people and scolding night and day at his maids and servants.

TOI. An excellent funeral oration!

BEL. Toinette, you must help me to carry out my design; and you may depend upon it that I will make it worth your while if you serve me. Since, by good luck, nobody is aware of his death, let us put him into his bed, and keep the secret until I have done what I want. There are some papers and some money I must possess myself of. It is not right that I should have passed the best years of my life with him without any kind of advantage. Come along, Toinette, first of all, let us take all the keys.

ARG. (*getting up hastily*). Softly.

BEL. Ah!

ARG. So, my wife, it is thus you love me?

TOI. Ah! the dead man is not dead.

ARG. (*to* BÉLINE, *who goes away*) I am very glad to see how you love me, and to have heard the noble panegyric you made upon me. This is a good warning, which will make me wise for the future, and prevent me from doing many things.

SCENE XIX.—Béralde (*coming out of the place where he was hiding*), Argan, Toinette.

BER. Well, brother, you see. . . .

TOI. Now, really, I could never have believed such a thing. But I hear your daughter coming, place yourself as you were just now, and let us see how she will receive the news. It is not a bad thing to try; and since you have begun, you will be able by this means to know the sentiments of your family towards you.

SCENE XX.—Argan, Angélique, Toinette.

TOI. (*pretending not to see* ANGÉLIQUE). O heavens! what a sad accident! What an unhappy day!

ANG. What ails you, Toinette, and why do you cry?

TOI. Alas! I have such sad news for you.

ANG. What is it?

TOI. Your father is dead.

ANG. My father is dead, Toinette?

TOI. Yes, just look at him there; he died only a moment ago of a fainting fit that came over him.

ANG. O heavens! what a misfortune! What a cruel grief! Alas! why must I lose my father, the only being left me in the world? and why should I lose him, too, at a time when he was angry with me? What will become of me, unhappy girl that I am? What consolation can I find after so great a loss?

SCENE XXI.—Argan, Angélique, Cléante, Toinette.

CLE. What is the matter with you, dear Angélique, and what misfortune makes you weep?

ANG. Alas! I weep for what was most dear and most precious to me. I weep for the death of my father.

CLE. O heaven! what a misfortune! What an unforeseen stroke of fortune! Alas! after I had asked your uncle to ask you in marriage, I was coming to see him, in order to try by my respect and entreaties to incline his heart to grant you to my wishes.

ANG. Ah! Cléante, let us talk no more of this. Let us give up all hopes of marriage. Now my father is dead, I will have nothing to do with the world, and will renounce it for ever. Yes, my dear father, if I resisted your will, I will at least follow out one of your intentions, and will by that make amends for the sorrow I have caused you. (*Kneeling.*) Let me, father, make you this promise here, and kiss you as a proof of my repentance.

ARG. (*kissing* ANGÉLIQUE). Ah! my daughter!

ANG. Ah!

ARG. Come; do not be afraid. I am not dead. Ah! you are my true flesh and blood and my real daughter; I am delighted to have discovered your good heart.

SCENE XXII.—Argan, Béralde, Angélique, Cléante, Toinette.

ANG. Ah! what a delightful surprise! Father, since heaven has given you back to our love, let me here throw myself at your feet to implore one favour of you. If you do not approve of what my heart feels, if you refuse to give me Cléante for a husband, I conjure you, at least, not to force me to marry another. It is all I have to ask of you.

CLE. (*throwing himself at* ARGAN'S *feet*). Ah! Sir, allow your heart to be touched by her entreaties and by mine, and do not oppose our mutual love.

BER. Brother, how can you resist all this?

TOI. Will you remain insensible before such affection?

ARG. Well, let him become a doctor, and I will consent to the marriage. (*To* CLÉANTE) Yes, turn doctor, Sir, and I will give you my daughter.

CLE. Very willingly, Sir, if it is all that is required to become your son-in-law. I will turn doctor; apothecary also, if you like. It is not such a difficult thing after all, and I would do much more to obtain from you the fair Angélique.

BER. But, brother, it just strikes me; why don't you turn doctor yourself? It would be much more convenient to have all you want within yourself.

TOI. Quite true. That is the very way to cure yourself. There is no disease bold enough to dare to attack the person of a doctor.

ARG. I imagine, brother, that you are laughing at me. Can I study at my age?

BER. Study! What need is there? You are clever enough for that; there are a great many who are not a bit more clever than you are.

ARG. But one must be able to speak Latin well, and know the different diseases and the remedies they require.

BER. When you put on the cap and gown of a doctor, all that will come of itself, and you will afterwards be much more clever than you care to be.

ARG. What! We understand how to discourse upon diseases when we have that dress?

BER. Yes; you have only to hold forth; when you have a cap and gown, any stuff becomes learned, and all rubbish good sense.

TOI. Look you, Sir; a beard is something in itself; a beard is half the doctor.

CLE. Anyhow, I am ready for everything.

BER. (*to* ARGAN). Shall we have the thing done immediately?

ARG. How, immediately?

BER. Yes, in your house.

ARG. In my house?

BER. Yes, I know a body of physicians, friends of mine, who will come presently, and will perform the ceremony in your hall. It will cost you nothing.

ARG. But what can I say, what can I answer?

BER. You will be instructed in a few words, and they will give you in writing all you have to say. Go and dress yourself directly, and I will send for them.

ARG. Very well; let it be done.

SCENE XXIII.—Béralde, Angélique, Cléante.

CLE. What is it you intend to do, and what do you mean by this body of physicians?

TOI. What is it you are going to do?

BER. To amuse ourselves a little to-night. The players have made a doctor's admission the subject of an interlude, with dances and music. I want everyone to enjoy it, and my brother to act the principal part in it.

ANG. But, uncle, it seems to me that you are making fun of my father.

BER. But, niece, it is not making too much fun of him to fall in with his fancies. We may each of us take part in it ourselves, and thus perform the comedy for each other's amusement. Carnival time authorises it. Let us go quickly and get everything ready.

CLE. (*to* ANGÉLIQUE). Do you consent to it?

ANG. Yes; since my uncle takes the lead.

THIRD INTERLUDE.[6]

BURLESQUE CEREMONY *representing the Admission of* MR. GERONTE *to the Degree of Doctor of Medicine.*

First Entry of the BALLET.

PRAESES.
Savantissimi doctores,
Medicinae professores,
Qui hic assemblati estis;
Et vos, altri messiores,
Sententiarum Facultatis
Fideles executores,
Chirurgiani et apothicari
Atque tota compagnia aussi,
Salus, honor et argentum,
Atque bonum appetitum.

Non possum, docti confreri,
En moi satis admirari
Qualis bona inventio
Est medici professio;
Quam bella chosa est et bene trovata.
Medicina illa benedicta,
Quae, suo nomine solo,
Surprenanti miraculo,
Depuis si longo tempore,

Facit à gogo vivere
Tant de gens omni genere.

Per totam terram videmus
Grandam vogam ubi sumus;
Et quod grandes et petiti
Sunt de nobis infatuti.
Totus mundus, currens ad nostros remedios,
Nos regardat sicut deos;
Et nostris ordonnanciis
Principes et reges soumissos videtis.

Doncque il est nostrae sapientiae,
Boni sensus atque prudentiae,
De fortement travaillare
A nos bene conservare
In tali credito, voga, et honore;
Et prendere gardam a non recevere
In nostro docto corpore,
Quam personas capabiles,
Et totas dignas remplire
Has plaças honorabiles.

C'est pour cela que nunc convocati estis:
Et credo quod trovabitis
Dignam matieram medici
In savanti homine que voici;
Lequel, in chosis omnibus,
Dono ad interrogandum,
Et à fond examinandum
Vostris capacitatibus.

PRIMUS DOCTOR.
Si mihi licentiam dat dominus praeses,
Et tanti docti doctores,
Et assistantes illustres,
Très savanti bacheliero,
Quem estimo et honoro,
Domandabo causam et rationom quare
Opium facit dormire.

BACHELIERUS.
Mihi a docto doctore
Domandatur causam et rationem quare
Opium facit dormire.
A quoi respondeo,
Quia est in eo
Vertus dormitiva,
Cujus eat natura
Sensus assoupire.

CHORUS.
Bene, bene, bene, bene respondere.
Dignus, dignus est intrare
In nostro docto corpore.
Bene, bene respondere.

SECUNDUS DOCTOR.
Proviso quod non displiceat,
Domino praesidi, lequel n'est pas fat,
Me benigne annuat,
Cum totis doctoribus savantibus,
Et assistantibus bienveillantibus,
Dicat mihi un peu dominus praetendens,
Raison a priori et evidens
Cur rhubarba et le séné
Per nos semper est ordonné
Ad purgandum l'utramque bile?
Si dicit hoc, erit valde habile.

BACHELIERUS.
A docto doctore mihi, qui sum praetendens,
Domandatur raison a priori et evidens
Cur rhubarba et le séné
Per nos semper est ordonné
Ad purgandum l'utramque bile?
Respondeo vobis,
Quia est in illis
Vertus purgativa,
Cujus est natura
Istas duas biles evacuare.

CHORUS.
Bene, bene, bone, bene respondere,
Dignus, dignus est intrare
In nostro docto corpore.

TERTIUS DOCTOR.
Ex responsis, il paraît jam sole clarius
Quod lepidum iste caput bachelierus
Non passavit suam vitam ludendo au trictrac,
Nec in prenando du tabac;
Sed explicit pourquoi furfur macrum et parvum lac,
Cum phlebotomia et purgatione humorum,
Appellantur a medisantibus idolae medicorum,
Nec non pontus asinorum?
Si premièrement grata sit domino praesidi
Nostra libertas quaestionandi,
Pariter dominis doctribus
Atque de tous ordres benignis auditoribus.

BACHELIERUS.
Quaerit a me dominus doctor
Chrysologos, id est, qui dit d'or,
Quare parvum lac et furfur macrum,
Phlebotomia et purgatio humorum
Appellantur a medisantibus idolae medicorum,
Atque pontus asinorum.
Respondeo quia:
Ista ordonnando non requiritur magna scientia,
Et ex illis quatuor rebus
Medici faciunt ludovicos, pistolas, et des quarts
d'écus.

CHORUS.
Bene, bene, bene, bene respondere
Dignus, dignus est intrare
In nostro docto corpore.

QUARTUS DOCTOR.
Cum permissione domini praesidis,
Doctissimae Facultatis,
Et totius his nostris actis
Companiae assistantis,
Domandabo tibi, docte bacheliere,
Quae sunt remedia
Tam in homine quam in muliere
Quae, in maladia
Ditta hydropisia,
In malo caduco, apoplexia, convulsione et
paralysia,
Convenit facere.

BACHELIERUS.
Clysterium donare,
Postea seignare,
Ensuita purgare.

CHORUS.
Bene, bene, bene, bene respondere.
Dignus, dignus est intrare
In nostro docto corpore.

QUINTUS DOCTOR.
Si bonum semblatur domino praesidi.
Doctissimae Facultati,
Et companiae ecoutanti,
Domandabo tibi, erudite bacheliere,
Ut revenir un jour à la maison gravis aegre
Quae remedia colicosis, fievrosis,
Maniacis, nefreticis, freneticis,

Melancolicis, demoniacis,
Asthmaticis atque pulmonicis,
Catharrosis, tussicolisis,
Guttosis, ladris atque gallosis,
In apostemasis plagis et ulcéré,
In omni membro démis aut fracturé
Convenit facere.

BACHELIERUS.
Clysterium donare,
Postea seignare,
Ensuita purgare.

CHORUS.
Bene, bene, bene, bene respondere.
Dignus, dignus est intrare
In nostro docto corpore.

SEXTUS DOCTOR.
Cum bona venia reverendi praesidis,
Filiorum Hippocratis,
Et totius coronae nos admirantis,
Petam tibi, resolute bacheliere,
Non indignus alumnus di Monspeliere,
Quae remedia caecis, surdis, mutis,
Manchotis, claudis, atque omnibus estropiatis,
Pro coris pedum, malum de dentibus, pesta, rabie,
Et nimis magna commotione in omni novo marié
Convenit facere.

BACHELIERUS.
Clysterium donare,
Postea seignare,
Ensuita purgare.

CHORUS.
Bene, bene, bene, bene respondere.
Dignus, dignus est intrare
In nostro docto corpore.

SEPTIMUS DOCTOR.
Super illas maladias,
Dominus bachelierus dixit maravillas;
Mais, si non ennuyo doctissimam facultatem
Et totam honorabilem companiam
Tam corporaliter quam mentaliter hic
        praesentem,
Faciam illi unam quaestionem;
De hiero maladus unus

Tombavit in meas manus,
Homo qualitatis et dives comme un Crésus.
Habet grandam fievram cum redoublamentis,
Grandam dolorem capitis,
Cum troublatione spirii et laxamento ventris.
Grandum insuper malum au côté,
Cum granda difficultate
Et pena a respirare;
Veuillas mihi dire,
Docte bacheliere,
Quid illi facere.

BACHELIERUS.
Clysterium donare,
Postea seignare,
Ensuita purgare.

CHORUS.
Bene, bene, bene, bene respondere.
Dignus, dignus est intrare
In nostro docto corpore.

IDEM DOCTOR.
Mais, si maladia
Opiniatria
Ponendo modicum a quia
Non vult se guarire,
Quid illi facere?

BACHELIERUS.
Clysterium donare,
Postea seignare,
Ensuita purgare,
Reseignare, repurgare, et reclysterizare.

CHORUS.
Bene, bene, bene, bene respondere.
Dignus, dignus est intrare
In nostro docto corpore.

OCTAVUS DOCTOR.
Impetro favorabile congé
A domino praeside,
Ab electa trouppa doctorum,
Tam practicantium quam practica avidorum,
Et a curiosa turba badodorum.
Ingeniose bacheliere
Qui non potuit esse jusqu'ici déferré,
Faciam tibi unam questionem de importantia.
Messiores, detur nobis audiencia.

Isto die bene mane,
Paulo ante mon déjeuné,
Venit ad me una domicella
Italiana jadis bella,
Et ut penso encore un peu pucella,
Quae habebat pallidos colores,
Fievram blancam dicunt magis fini doctores,
Quia plaigniebat se de migraina,
De curta halena,
De granda oppressione,
Jambarum enflatura, et effroyebili lassitudine;
De batimento cordis,
De strangulamento matris,
Alio nomine vapor hystérique,
Quae, sicut omnes maladiae terminatae en ique,
Facit a Galien la nique.
Visagium apparebat bouffietum, et coloris
Tantum vertae quantum merda anseris.
Ex pulsu petito valde frequens, et urina mala
Quam apportaverat in fiola
Non videbatur exempta de febricules;
Au reste, tam debilis quod venerat
De son grabat
In cavallo sur une mule,
Non habuerat menses suos
Ab illa die qui dicitur des grosses eaux;
Sed contabat mihi à l'oreille
Che si non era morta, c'était grand merveille,
Perché in suo negotio
Era un poco d'amore, et troppo di cordoglio;
Che suo galanto sen era andato in Allemagna,
Servire al signor Brandeburg una campagna.
Usque ad maintenant multi charlatani,
Medici, apothicari, et chirurgiani
Pro sua maladia in veno travaillaverunt,
Juxta même las novas gripas istius bouru Van
    Helmont,
Amploiantes ab oculis cancri, ad Alcahest;
Veuillas mihi dire quid superest,
Juxta orthodoxos, illi facere.

BACHELIERUS.
Clysterium donare,
Postea seignare,
Ensuita purgare.

CHORUS.
Bene, bene, bene, bene respondero.
Dignus, dignus est intrare
In nostro docto corpore.

IDEM DOCTOR.

Mais si tam grandum couchamentum
Partium naturalium,
Mortaliter obstinatum,
Per clysterium donare,
Seignare
Et reiterando cent fois purgare,
Non potest se guarire,
Finaliter quid trovaris à propos illi facere?

BACHELIERUS.

In nomine Hippocratis benedictam cum bono
Garçone conjunctionem imperare.

PRAESES.

Juras gardare statuta
Per Facultatem praescripta,
Cum sensu et jugeamento?

BACHELIERUS.

Juro.[7]

PRAESES.

Essere in Omnibus
Consultationibus
Ancieni aviso,
Aut bono,
Aut mauvaiso!

BACHELIERUS.

Juro.

PRAESES.

De non jamais te servire
De remediis aucunis,
Quam de ceuz seulement almae Facultatis,
Maladus dût-il crevare,
Et mori de suo malo?

BACHELIERUS.

Juro.

PRAESES.

Ego, cum isto boneto
Venerabili et docto,
Dono tibi et concedo
Puissanciam, vertutem atque licentiam
Medicinam cum methodo faciendi
Id est,

Clysterizandi,
Seignandi,
Purgandi,
Sangsuandi,
Ventousandi,
Sacrificandi,
Perçandi,
Taillandi,
Coupandi,
Trepanandi,
Brulandi,
Uno verbo, selon les formes, atque impune
    occidendi
Parisiis et per totem terram;
Rendes, Domine, his messioribus gratiam.

Second Entry of the BALLET.

All the DOCTORS *and* APOTHECARIES *come
and do him reverence.*

BACHELIERUS.

Grandes doctres doctrinae
De la rhubarbe et du séné
Ce seroit sans douta à moi chosa folla,
Inepta et ridicula,
Si j'alloibam m'engageare
Vobis Louangeas donare,
Et entreprenoibam ajoutare
Des lumieras au soleillo,
Des etoilas au cielo,
Des flammas à l'inferno
Des ondas à l'oceano,
Et des rosas au printano.
Agreate qu'avec uno moto,
Pro toto remercimento,
Rendam gratias corpori tam docto.
Vobis, vobis debeo
Bien plus qu'à nature et qu'à patri meo:
Natura et pater meus
Hominem me habent factum;
Mais vos me (ce qui est bien plus)
Avetis factum medicum
Honor, favor et gratia,
Qui, in hoc corde que voilà,
Imprimant ressentimenta
Qui dureront in secula.

CHORUS.

Vivat, vivat, vivat, vivat, cent fois vivat,
Novus doctor, qui tam bene parlat!
Mille, mille annis, et manget et bibat,
Et seignet et tuat!

Third Entry of the BALLET.

All the DOCTORS *and* APOTHECARIES *dance to the sound of instruments and voices, the clapping of hands, and the beating of* APOTHECARIES' *mortars.*

CHIRURGUS.

Puisse-t-il voir doctas
Suas ordonnancias,
Omnium chirurgorum,
Et apothicarum
Remplire boutiquas!

CHORUS.

Vivat, vivat, vivat, vivat, cent fois vivat,
Novus doctor, qui tam bene parlat!
Mille, mille annis, et manget et bibat,
Et seignet et tuat!

APOTHICARIUS.

Puissent toti anni
Lui essere boni
Et favorabiles
Et n'habere jamais
Entre ses mains, pestas, epidemias
Quae sunt malas bestias;
Mais semper pluresias, pulmonias
In renibus et vessia pierras,
Rhumatismos d'un anno, et omnis generis fievras,
Fluxus de sanguine, gouttas diabolicas,
Mala de sancto Joanne, Poitevinorum colicas
Scorbutum de Hollandia, verolas parvas et grossas
Bonos chancros atque longas callidopissas.

BACHELIERUS.

Amen.

CHORUS.

Vivat, vivat, vivat, vivat, cent fois vivat,
Novus doctor, qui tam bene parlat!
Mille, mille annis, et manget et bibat,
Et seignet et tuat!

Fourth Entry of the BALLET.

All the DOCTORS *and* APOTHECARIES *go out according to their rank, as they came in.*

THE END

ENDNOTES

1. As usual, Argan only counts half; even after he has reduced the charge.
2. Thomas Diafoirus is evidently going to base some compliment on the *belle-mére.* The only way out of the difficulty in English seems to be to complete the sentence somewhat.
3. Harvey's treatise on the circulation of the blood was published in 1628. His discovery was violently opposed for a long time afterwards.
4. Molière seems to refer to Dr. Guenaut, who was said to have killed with antimony (his favourite remedy) his wife, his daughter, his nephew, and two of his sons-in-law.—AIMÉ MARTIN.
5. *Oubliès;* now called *plaisirs.* "Wafers" would perhaps have been the right rendering in Molière's time.
6. This piece is composed of a mixture of dog-Latin, French, &c. and is utterly untranslateable.
7. It is said that it was when uttering this word that Molière gave way to the illness from which he had long suffered.

4

Major Barbara

Play by George Bernard Shaw (1856–1950)

MAJOR BARBARA

ACT I

It is after dinner on a January night, in the library in Lady Britomart Undershaft's house in Wilton Crescent. A large and comfortable settee is in the middle of the room, upholstered in dark leather. A person sitting on it [it is vacant at present] would have, on his right, Lady Britomart's writing table, with the lady herself busy at it; a smaller writing table behind him on his left; the door behind him on Lady Britomart's side; and a window with a window seat directly on his left. Near the window is an armchair.

Lady Britomart is a woman of fifty or thereabouts, well dressed and yet careless of her dress, well bred and quite reckless of her breeding, well mannered and yet appallingly outspoken and indifferent to the opinion of her interlocutory, amiable and yet peremptory, arbitrary, and high-tempered to the last bearable degree, and withal a very typical managing matron of the upper class, treated as a naughty child until she grew into a scolding mother, and finally settling down with plenty of practical ability and worldly experience, limited in the oddest way with domestic and class limitations, conceiving the universe exactly as if it were a large house in Wilton Crescent, though handling her corner of it very effectively on that assumption, and being quite enlightened and liberal as to the books in the library, the pictures on the walls, the music in the portfolios, and the articles in the papers.

Her son, Stephen, comes in. He is a gravely correct young man under 25, taking himself very seriously, but still in some awe of his mother, from childish habit and bachelor shyness rather than from any weakness of character.

"Major Barbara", 1907

STEPHEN. What's the matter?

LADY BRITOMART. Presently, Stephen.

Stephen submissively walks to the settee and sits down. He takes up The Speaker.

LADY BRITOMART. Don't begin to read, Stephen. I shall require all your attention.

STEPHEN. It was only while I was waiting—

LADY BRITOMART. Don't make excuses, Stephen. [He puts down The Speaker]. Now! [She finishes her writing; rises; and comes to the settee]. I have not kept you waiting very long, I think.

STEPHEN. Not at all, mother.

LADY BRITOMART. Bring me my cushion. [He takes the cushion from the chair at the desk and arranges it for her as she sits down on the settee]. Sit down. [He sits down and fingers his tie nervously]. Don't fiddle with your tie, Stephen: there is nothing the matter with it.

STEPHEN. I beg your pardon. [He fiddles with his watch chain instead].

LADY BRITOMART. Now are you attending to me, Stephen?

STEPHEN. Of course, mother.

LADY BRITOMART. No: it's not of course. I want something much more than your everyday matter-of-course attention. I am going to speak to you very seriously, Stephen. I wish you would let that chain alone.

STEPHEN. [hastily relinquishing the chain] Have I done anything to annoy you, mother? If so, it was quite unintentional.

LADY BRITOMART [astonished] Nonsense! [With some remorse] My poor boy, did you think I was angry with you?

STEPHEN. What is it, then, mother? You are making me very uneasy.

LADY BRITOMART [squaring herself at him rather aggressively] Stephen: may I ask how soon you intend to realize that you are a grown-up man, and that I am only a woman?

STEPHEN. [amazed] Only a—

LADY BRITOMART. Don't repeat my words, please: It is a most aggravating habit. You must learn to face life seriously, Stephen I really cannot bear the whole burden of our family affairs any longer. You must advise me: you must assume the responsibility.

STEPHEN. I!

LADY BRITOMART. Yes, you, of course. You were 24 last June. You've been at Harrow and Cambridge. You've been to India and Japan. You must know a lot of things now; unless you have wasted your time most scandalously. Well, advise me.

STEPHEN. [much perplexed] You know I have never interfered in the household—

LADY BRITOMART. No: I should think not. I don't want you to order the dinner.

STEPHEN. I mean in our family affairs.

LADY BRITOMART. Well, you must interfere now; for they are getting quite beyond me.

STEPHEN. [troubled] I have thought sometimes that perhaps I ought; but really, mother, I know so little about them; and what I do know is so painful—it is so impossible to mention some things to you—[he stops, ashamed].

LADY BRITOMART. I suppose you mean your father.

STEPHEN. [almost inaudibly] Yes.

LADY BRITOMART. My dear: we can't go on all our lives not mentioning him. Of course you were quite right not to open the subject until I asked you to; but you are old enough now to be taken into my confidence, and to help me to deal with him about the girls.

STEPHEN. But the girls are all right. They are engaged.

LADY BRITOMART. [complacently] Yes: I have made a very good match for Sarah. Charles Lomax will be a millionaire at 35. But that is ten years ahead; and in the meantime his trustees cannot under the terms of his father's will allow him more than 800 pounds a year.

STEPHEN. But the will says also that if he increases his income by his own exertions, they may double the increase.

LADY BRITOMART. Charles Lomax's exertions are much more likely to decrease his income than to increase it. Sarah will have to find at least another

800 pounds a year for the next ten years; and even then they will be as poor as church mice. And what about Barbara? I thought Barbara was going to make the most brilliant career of all of you. And what does she do? Joins the Salvation Army; discharges her maid; lives on a pound a week; and walks in one evening with a professor of Greek whom she has picked up in the street, and who pretends to be a Salvationist, and actually plays the big drum for her in public because he has fallen head over ears in love with her.

STEPHEN. I was certainly rather taken aback when I heard they were engaged. Cusins is a very nice fellow, certainly: nobody would ever guess that he was born in Australia; but—

LADY BRITOMART. Oh, Adolphus Cusins will make a very good husband. After all, nobody can say a word against Greek: it stamps a man at once as an educated gentleman. And my family, thank Heaven, is not a pig-headed Tory one. We are Whigs, and believe in liberty. Let snobbish people say what they please: Barbara shall marry, not the man they like, but the man I like.

STEPHEN. Of course I was thinking only of his income. However, he is not likely to be extravagant.

LADY BRITOMART. Don't be too sure of that, Stephen. I know your quiet, simple, refined, poetic people like Adolphus—quite content with the best of everything! They cost more than your extravagant people, who are always as mean as they are second rate. No: Barbara will need at least 2000 pounds a year. You see it means two additional households. Besides, my dear, you must marry soon. I don't approve of the present fashion of philandering bachelors and late marriages; and I am trying to arrange something for you.

STEPHEN. It's very good of you, mother; but perhaps I had better arrange that for myself.

LADY BRITOMART. Nonsense! you are much too young to begin matchmaking: you would be taken in by some pretty little nobody. Of course I don't mean that you are not to be consulted: you know that as well as I do. [Stephen. closes his lips and is silent]. Now don't sulk, Stephen.

STEPHEN. I am not sulking, mother. What has all this got to do with—with—with my father?

LADY BRITOMART. My dear Stephen: where is the money to come from? It is easy enough for you and the other children to live on my income as long as we are in the same house; but I can't keep four families in four separate houses. You know how poor my father is: he has barely seven thousand a year now; and really, if he were not the Earl of Stevenage, he would have to give up society. He can do nothing for us: he says, naturally enough, that it is absurd that he should be asked to provide for the children of a man who is rolling in money. You see, Stephen, your father must be fabulously wealthy, because there is always a war going on somewhere.

STEPHEN. You need not remind me of that, mother. I have hardly ever opened a newspaper in my life without seeing our name in it. The Undershaft torpedo! The Undershaft quick firers! The Undershaft ten inch! the Undershaft disappearing rampart gun! the Undershaft submarine! and now the Undershaft aerial battleship! At Harrow they called me the Woolwich Infant. At Cambridge it was the same. A little brute at King's who was always trying to get up revivals, spoilt my Bible—your first birthday present to me—by writing under my name, "Son and heir to Undershaft and Lazarus, Death and Destruction Dealers: address, Christendom and Judea." But that was not so bad as the way I was kowtowed to everywhere because my father was making millions by selling cannons.

LADY BRITOMART. It is not only the cannons, but the war loans that Lazarus arranges under cover of giving credit for the cannons. You know, Stephen, it's perfectly scandalous. Those two men, Andrew Undershaft and Lazarus, positively have Europe under their thumbs. That is why your father is able to behave as he does. He is above the law. Do you think Bismarck or Gladstone or Disraeli could have openly defied every social and moral obligation all their lives as your father has? They simply wouldn't have dared. I asked Gladstone to take it up. I asked The Times to take it up. I asked the Lord Chamberlain to take it up. But it was just like asking them to declare war on the Sultan. They WOULDN'T. They said they couldn't touch him. I believe they were afraid.

STEPHEN. What could they do? He does not actually break the law.

LADY BRITOMART. Not break the law! He is always breaking the law. He broke the law when he was born: his parents were not married.

STEPHEN. Mother! Is that true?

LADY BRITOMART. Of course it's true: that was why we separated.

STEPHEN. He married without letting you know this!

LADY BRITOMART [rather taken aback by this inference] Oh no. To do Andrew justice, that was not the sort of thing he did. Besides, you know the Undershaft motto: Unashamed. Everybody knew.

STEPHEN. But you said that was why you separated.

LADY BRITOMART. Yes, because he was not content with being a foundling himself: he wanted to disinherit you for another foundling. That was what I couldn't stand.

STEPHEN. [ashamed] Do you mean for—for—for—

LADY BRITOMART. Don't stammer, Stephen. Speak distinctly.

STEPHEN. But this is so frightful to me, mother. To have to speak to you about such things!

LADY BRITOMART. It's not pleasant for me, either, especially if you are still so childish that you must make it worse by a display of embarrassment. It is only in the middle classes, Stephen, that people get into a state of dumb helpless horror when they find that there are wicked people in the world. In our class, we have to decide what is to be done with wicked people; and nothing should disturb our self possession. Now ask your question properly.

STEPHEN. Mother: you have no consideration for me. For Heaven's sake either treat me as a child, as you always do, and tell me nothing at all; or tell me everything and let me take it as best I can.

LADY BRITOMART. Treat you as a child! What do you mean? It is most unkind and ungrateful of you to say such a thing. You know I have never treated any of you as children. I have always made you my companions and friends, and allowed you perfect freedom to do and say whatever you liked, so long as you liked what I could approve of.

STEPHEN. [desperately] I daresay we have been the very imperfect children of a very perfect mother; but I do beg you to let me alone for once, and tell me about this horrible business of my father wanting to set me aside for another son.

Lady Britomart [amazed] Another son! I never said anything of the kind. I never dreamt of such a thing. This is what comes of interrupting me.

STEPHEN. But you said—

LADY BRITOMART [cutting him short] Now be a good boy, Stephen, and listen to me patiently. The Undershafts are descended from a foundling in the parish of St. Andrew Undershaft in the city. That was long ago, in the reign of James the First. Well, this foundling was adopted by an armorer and gun-maker. In the course of time the foundling succeeded to the business; and from some notion of gratitude, or some vow or something, he adopted another foundling, and left the business to him. And that foundling did the same. Ever since that, the cannon business has always been left to an adopted foundling named Andrew Undershaft.

STEPHEN. But did they never marry? Were there no legitimate sons?

LADY BRITOMART. Oh yes: they married just as your father did; and they were rich enough to buy land for their own children and leave them well provided for. But they always adopted and trained some foundling to succeed them in the business; and of course they always quarrelled with their wives furiously over it. Your father was adopted in that way; and he pretends to consider himself bound to keep up the tradition and adopt somebody to leave the business to. Of course I was not going to stand that. There may have been some reason for it when the Undershafts could only marry women in their own class, whose sons were not fit to govern great estates. But there could be no excuse for passing over my son.

STEPHEN. [dubiously] I am afraid I should make a poor hand of managing a cannon foundry.

LADY BRITOMART. Nonsense! you could easily get a manager and pay him a salary.

STEPHEN. My father evidently had no great opinion of my capacity.

LADY BRITOMART. Stuff, child! you were only a baby: it had nothing to do with your capacity. Andrew did it on principle, just as he did every perverse and wicked thing on principle. When my father remonstrated, Andrew actually told him to his face that history tells us of only two successful institutions: one the Undershaft firm, and the other the Roman Empire under the Antonines. That was because the Antonine emperors all adopted their successors. Such rubbish! The Stevenages are as good as the Antonines, I hope; and you are a Stevenage. But that was Andrew all over. There you have the man! Always clever and unanswerable when he was defending nonsense and wickedness: always awkward and sullen when he had to behave sensibly and decently!

STEPHEN. Then it was on my account that your home life was broken up, mother. I am sorry.

LADY BRITOMART. Well, dear, there were other differences. I really cannot bear an immoral man. I am not a Pharisee, I hope; and I should not have minded his merely doing wrong things: we are none of us perfect. But your father didn't exactly do wrong things: he said them and thought them: that was what was so dreadful. He really had a sort of religion of wrongness just as one doesn't mind men practising immorality so long as they own that they are in the wrong by preaching morality; so I couldn't forgive Andrew for preaching immorality while he practised morality. You would all have grown up without principles, without any knowledge of right and wrong, if he had been in the house. You know, my dear, your father was a very attractive man in some ways. Children did not dislike him; and he took advantage of it to put the wickedest ideas into their heads, and make them quite unmanageable. I did not dislike him myself: very far from it; but nothing can bridge over moral disagreement.

STEPHEN. All this simply bewilders me, mother. People may differ about matters of opinion, or even about religion; but how can they differ about right and wrong? Right is right; and wrong is wrong; and if a man cannot distinguish them properly, he is either a fool or a rascal: that's all.

LADY BRITOMART [touched] That's my own boy [she pats his cheek]! Your father never could answer that: he used to laugh and get out of it under cover of some affectionate nonsense. And now that you understand the situation, what do you advise me to do?

STEPHEN. Well, what can you do?

LADY BRITOMART. I must get the money somehow.

STEPHEN. We cannot take money from him. I had rather go and live in some cheap place like Bedford Square or even Hampstead than take a farthing of his money.

LADY BRITOMART. But after all, Stephen, our present income comes from Andrew.

STEPHEN. [shocked] I never knew that.

LADY BRITOMART. Well, you surely didn't suppose your grandfather had anything to give me. The Stevenages could not do everything for you. We gave you social position. Andrew had to contribute something. He had a very good bargain, I think.

STEPHEN. [bitterly] We are utterly dependent on him and his cannons, then!

LADY BRITOMART. Certainly not: the money is settled. But he provided it. So you see it is not a question of taking money from him or not: it is simply a question of how much. I don't want any more for myself.

STEPHEN. Nor do I.

LADY BRITOMART. But Sarah does; and Barbara does. That is, Charles Lomax and Adolphus Cusins will cost them more. So I must put my pride in my pocket and ask for it, I suppose. That is your advice, Stephen, is it not?

STEPHEN. No.

LADY BRITOMART [sharply] Stephen!

STEPHEN. Of course if you are determined—

LADY BRITOMART. I am not determined: I ask your advice; and I am waiting for it. I will not have all the responsibility thrown on my shoulders.

STEPHEN. [obstinately] I would die sooner than ask him for another penny.

LADY BRITOMART [resignedly] You mean that I must ask him. Very well, Stephen: It shall be as you wish. You will be glad to know that your grandfather concurs. But he thinks I ought to ask Andrew to come here and see the girls. After all, he must have some natural affection for them.

STEPHEN. Ask him here!!!

LADY BRITOMART. Do not repeat my words, Stephen. Where else can I ask him?

STEPHEN. I never expected you to ask him at all.

LADY BRITOMART. Now don't tease, Stephen. Come! you see that it is necessary that he should pay us a visit, don't you?

STEPHEN. [reluctantly] I suppose so, if the girls cannot do without his money.

LADY BRITOMART. Thank you, Stephen: I knew you would give me the right advice when it was properly explained to you. I have asked your father to come this evening. [Stephen] bounds from his seat] Don't jump, Stephen: it fidgets me.

STEPHEN. [in utter consternation] Do you mean to say that my father is coming here to-night—that he may be here at any moment?

LADY BRITOMART [looking at her watch] I said nine. [He gasps. She rises]. Ring the bell, please. [Stephen goes to the smaller writing table; presses a button on it; and sits at it with his elbows on the table and his head in his hands, outwitted and overwhelmed]. It is ten minutes to nine yet; and I have to prepare the girls. I asked Charles Lomax and Adolphus to dinner on purpose that they might be here. Andrew had better see them in case he should cherish any delusions as to their being capable of supporting their wives. [The butler enters: Lady Britomart goes behind the settee to speak to him]. Morrison: go up to the drawingroom and tell everybody to come down here at once. [Morrison withdraws. Lady Britomart turns to Stephen]. Now remember, Stephen, I shall need all your countenance and authority. [He rises and tries to recover some vestige of these attributes]. Give me a chair, dear. [He pushes a chair forward from the wall to where she stands, near the smaller writing table. She sits down; and he goes to the armchair, into which he throws himself]. I don't know how Barbara will take it. Ever since they made her a major in the Salvation Army she has developed a propensity to have her own way and order people about which quite cows me sometimes. It's not ladylike: I'm sure I don't know where she picked it up. Anyhow, Barbara shan't bully me; but still it's just as well that your father should be here before she has time to refuse to meet him or make a fuss. Don't look nervous, Stephen, it will only encourage Barbara to make difficulties. I am nervous enough, goodness knows; but I don't show it.

Sarah and Barbara come in with their respective young men, Charles Lomax and Adolphus Cusins. Sarah is slender, bored, and mundane. Barbara is robuster, jollier, much more energetic. Sarah is fashionably dressed: Barbara is in Salvation Army uniform. Lomax, a young man about town, is like many other young men about town. He is affected with a frivolous sense of humor which plunges him at the most inopportune moments into paroxysms of imperfectly suppressed laughter. Cusins is a spectacled student, slight, thin haired, and sweet voiced, with a more complex form of Lomax's complaint. His sense of humor is intellectual and subtle, and is complicated by an appalling temper. The lifelong struggle of a benevolent temperament and a high conscience against impulses of inhuman ridicule and fierce impatience has set up a chronic strain which has visibly wrecked his constitution. He is a most implacable, determined, tenacious, intolerant person who by mere force of character presents himself as—and indeed actually is—considerate, gentle, explanatory, even mild and apologetic, capable possibly of murder, but not of cruelty or coarseness. By the operation of some instinct which is not merciful enough to blind him with the illusions of love, he is obstinately bent on marrying Barbara. Lomax likes Sarah and thinks it will be rather a lark to marry her. Consequently he has not attempted to resist Lady Britomart's arrangements to that end.

All four look as if they had been having a good deal of fun in the drawingroom. The girls enter first, leaving the swains outside. Sarah comes to the settee. Barbara comes in after her and stops at the door.

BARBARA. Are Cholly and Dolly to come in?

LADY BRITOMART [forcibly] Barbara: I will not have Charles called Cholly: the vulgarity of it positively makes me ill.

BARBARA. It's all right, mother. Cholly is quite correct nowadays. Are they to come in?

LADY BRITOMART. Yes, if they will behave themselves.

BARBARA [through the door] Come in, Dolly, and behave yourself.

Barbara comes to her mother's writing table. Cusins enters smiling, and wanders towards Lady Britomart.

SARAH [calling] Come in, Cholly. [Lomax enters, controlling his features very imperfectly, and places himself vaguely between Sarah and Barbara].

LADY BRITOMART [peremptorily] Sit down, all of you. [They sit. Cusins crosses to the window and seats himself there. Lomax takes a chair. Barbara sits at the writing table and Sarah on the settee]. I don't in the least know what you are laughing at, Adolphus. I am surprised at you, though I expected nothing better from Charles Lomax.

CUSINS [in a remarkably gentle voice] Barbara has been trying to teach me the West Ham Salvation March.

LADY BRITOMART. I see nothing to laugh at in that; nor should you if you are really converted.

CUSINS [sweetly] You were not present. It was really funny, I believe.

LOMAX. Ripping.

LADY BRITOMART. Be quiet, Charles. Now listen to me, children. Your father is coming here this evening. [General stupefaction].

LOMAX [remonstrating] Oh I say!

LADY BRITOMART. You are not called on to say anything, Charles.

SARAH. Are you serious, mother?

LADY BRITOMART. Of course I am serious. It is on your account, Sarah, and also on Charles's. [Silence. Charles looks painfully unworthy]. I hope you are not going to object, Barbara.

BARBARA. I! why should I? My father has a soul to be saved like anybody else. He's quite welcome as far as I am concerned.

LOMAX [still remonstrant] But really, don't you know! Oh I say!

LADY BRITOMART [frigidly] What do you wish to convey, Charles?

LOMAX. Well, you must admit that this is a bit thick.

LADY BRITOMART [turning with ominous suavity to Cusins] Adolphus: you are a professor of Greek. Can you translate Charles Lomax's remarks into reputable English for us?

CUSINS [cautiously] If I may say so, Lady Brit, I think Charles has rather happily expressed what we all feel. Homer, speaking of Autolycus, uses the same phrase.

LOMAX [handsomely] Not that I mind, you know, if Sarah don't.

LADY BRITOMART [crushingly] Thank you. Have I your permission, Adolphus, to invite my own husband to my own house?

CUSINS [gallantly] You have my unhesitating support in everything you do.

LADY BRITOMART. Sarah: have you nothing to say?

SARAH. Do you mean that he is coming regularly to live here?

LADY BRITOMART. Certainly not. The spare room is ready for him if he likes to stay for a day or two and see a little more of you; but there are limits.

SARAH. Well, he can't eat us, I suppose. I don't mind.

LOMAX [chuckling] I wonder how the old man will take it.

LADY BRITOMART. Much as the old woman will, no doubt, Charles.

LOMAX [abashed] I didn't mean—at least—

LADY BRITOMART. You didn't think, Charles. You never do; and the result is, you never mean anything. And now please attend to me, children. Your father will be quite a stranger to us.

LOMAX. I suppose he hasn't seen Sarah since she was a little kid.

LADY BRITOMART. Not since she was a little kid, Charles, as you express it with that elegance of diction and refinement of thought that seem never to desert you. Accordingly—er—[impatiently] Now I have forgotten what I was going to say. That comes of your provoking me to be sarcastic, Charles. Adolphus: will you kindly tell me where I was.

CUSINS [sweetly] You were saying that as Mr Undershaft has not seen his children since they were babies, he will form his opinion of the way you have brought them up from their behavior to-night, and that therefore you wish us all to be particularly careful to conduct ourselves well, especially Charles.

LOMAX. Look here: Lady Brit didn't say that.

LADY BRITOMART [vehemently] I did, Charles. Adolphus's recollection is perfectly correct. It is most important that you should be good; and I do beg you for once not to pair off into opposite corners and giggle and whisper while I am speaking to your father.

BARBARA. All right, mother. We'll do you credit.

LADY BRITOMART. Remember, Charles, that Sarah will want to feel proud of you instead of ashamed of you.

LOMAX. Oh I say! There's nothing to be exactly proud of, don't you know.

LADY BRITOMART. Well, try and look as if there was.

Morrison, pale and dismayed, breaks into the room in unconcealed disorder.

MORRISON. Might I speak a word to you, my lady?

LADY BRITOMART. Nonsense! Show him up.

MORRISON. Yes, my lady. [He goes].

LOMAX. Does Morrison know who he is?

LADY BRITOMART. Of course. Morrison has always been with us.

LOMAX. It must be a regular corker for him, don't you know.

LADY BRITOMART. Is this a moment to get on my nerves, Charles, with your outrageous expressions?

LOMAX. But this is something out of the ordinary, really—

MORRISON [at the door] The—er—Mr Undershaft. [He retreats in confusion].

Andrew Undershaft comes in. All rise. Lady Britomart meets him in the middle of the room behind the settee.

Andrew is, on the surface, a stoutish, easygoing elderly man, with kindly patient manners, and an engaging simplicity of character. But he has a watchful, deliberate, waiting, listening face, and formidable reserves of power, both bodily and mental, in his capacious chest and long head. His gentleness is partly that of a strong man who has learnt by experience that his natural grip hurts ordinary people unless he handles them very carefully, and partly the mellowness of age and success. He is also a little shy in his present very delicate situation.

LADY BRITOMART. Good evening, Andrew.

UNDERSHAFT. How d'ye do, my dear.

LADY BRITOMART. You look a good deal older.

UNDERSHAFT [apologetically] I AM somewhat older. [With a touch of courtship] Time has stood still with you.

LADY BRITOMART [promptly] Rubbish! This is your family.

UNDERSHAFT [surprised] Is it so large? I am sorry to say my memory is failing very badly in some things. [He offers his hand with paternal kindness to Lomax].

LOMAX [jerkily shaking his hand] Ahdedoo.

UNDERSHAFT. I can see you are my eldest. I am very glad to meet you again, my boy.

LOMAX [remonstrating] No but look here don't you know—[Overcome] Oh I say!

LADY BRITOMART [recovering from momentary speechlessness] Andrew: do you mean to say that you don't remember how many children you have?

UNDERSHAFT. Well, I am afraid I—. They have grown so much—er. Am I making any ridiculous mistake? I may as well confess: I recollect only one son. But so many things have happened since, of course—er—

LADY BRITOMART [decisively] Andrew: you are talking nonsense. Of course you have only one son.

UNDERSHAFT. Perhaps you will be good enough to introduce me, my dear.

LADY BRITOMART. That is Charles Lomax, who is engaged to Sarah.

UNDERSHAFT. My dear sir, I beg your pardon.

LOMAX. Not at all. Delighted, I assure you.

LADY BRITOMART. This is Stephen.

UNDERSHAFT [bowing] Happy to make your acquaintance, Mr Stephen. Then [going to Cusins] you must be my son. [Taking Cusins' hands in his] How are you, my young friend? [To Lady Britomart] He is very like you, my love.

CUSINS. You flatter me, Mr Undershaft. My name is Cusins: engaged to Barbara. [Very explicitly] That is Major Barbara Undershaft, of the Salvation Army. That is Sarah, your second daughter. This is Stephen. Undershaft, your son.

UNDERSHAFT. My dear Stephen, I beg your pardon.

STEPHEN. Not at all.

UNDERSHAFT. Mr Cusins: I am much indebted to you for explaining so precisely. [Turning to Sarah] Barbara, my dear—

SARAH [prompting him] Sarah.

UNDERSHAFT. Sarah, of course. [They shake hands. He goes over to Barbara] Barbara—I am right this time, I hope.

BARBARA. Quite right. [They shake hands].

LADY BRITOMART [resuming command] Sit down, all of you. Sit down, Andrew. [She comes forward and sits on the settle. Cusins also brings his chair forward on her left. Barbara and Stephen resume their seats. Lomax gives his chair to Sarah and goes for another].

UNDERSHAFT. Thank you, my love.

LOMAX [conversationally, as he brings a chair forward between the writing table and the settee, and offers it to Undershaft] Takes you some time to find out exactly where you are, don't it?

UNDERSHAFT [accepting the chair] That is not what embarrasses me, Mr Lomax. My difficulty is that if I play the part of a father, I shall produce the effect of an intrusive stranger; and if I play the part of a discreet stranger, I may appear a callous father.

LADY BRITOMART. There is no need for you to play any part at all, Andrew. You had much better be sincere and natural.

UNDERSHAFT [submissively] Yes, my dear: I daresay that will be best. [Making himself comfortable] Well, here I am. Now what can I do for you all?

LADY BRITOMART. You need not do anything, Andrew. You are one of the family. You can sit with us and enjoy yourself.

Lomax's too long suppressed mirth explodes in agonized neighings.

LADY BRITOMART [outraged] Charles Lomax: if you can behave yourself, behave yourself. If not, leave the room.

LOMAX. I'm awfully sorry, Lady Brit; but really, you know, upon my soul! [He sits on the settee between Lady Britomart and Undershaft, quite overcome].

BARBARA. Why don't you laugh if you want to, Cholly? It's good for your inside.

LADY BRITOMART. Barbara: you have had the education of a lady. Please let your father see that; and don't talk like a street girl.

UNDERSHAFT. Never mind me, my dear. As you know, I am not a gentleman; and I was never educated.

LOMAX [encouragingly] Nobody'd know it, I assure you. You look all right, you know.

CUSINS. Let me advise you to study Greek, Mr Undershaft. Greek scholars are privileged men. Few of them know Greek; and none of them know anything else; but their position is unchallengeable. Other languages are the qualifications of waiters and commercial travellers: Greek is to a man of position what the hallmark is to silver.

BARBARA. Dolly: don't be insincere. Cholly: fetch your concertina and play something for us.

LOMAX [doubtfully to Undershaft] Perhaps that sort of thing isn't in your line, eh?

UNDERSHAFT. I am particularly fond of music.

LOMAX [delighted] Are you? Then I'll get it. [He goes upstairs for the instrument].

UNDERSHAFT. Do you play, Barbara?

BARBARA. Only the tambourine. But Cholly's teaching me the concertina.

UNDERSHAFT. Is Cholly also a member of the Salvation Army?

BARBARA. No: he says it's bad form to be a dissenter. But I don't despair of Cholly. I made him come yesterday to a meeting at the dock gates, and take the collection in his hat.

LADY BRITOMART. It is not my doing, Andrew. Barbara is old enough to take her own way. She has no father to advise her.

BARBARA. Oh yes she has. There are no orphans in the Salvation Army.

UNDERSHAFT. Your father there has a great many children and plenty of experience, eh?

BARBARA [looking at him with quick interest and nodding] Just so. How did you come to understand that? [Lomax is heard at the door trying the concertina].

LADY BRITOMART. Come in, Charles. Play us something at once.

LOMAX. Righto! [He sits down in his former place, and preludes].

UNDERSHAFT. One moment, Mr Lomax. I am rather interested in the Salvation Army. Its motto might be my own: Blood and Fire.

LOMAX [shocked] But not your sort of blood and fire, you know.

UNDERSHAFT. My sort of blood cleanses: my sort of fire purifies.

BARBARA. So do ours. Come down to-morrow to my shelter—the West Ham shelter—and see what we're doing. We're going to march to a great meeting in the Assembly Hall at Mile End. Come and see the shelter and then march with us: it will do you a lot of good. Can you play anything?

UNDERSHAFT. In my youth I earned pennies, and even shillings occasionally, in the streets and in public house parlors by my natural talent for stepdancing. Later on, I became a member of the Undershaft orchestral society, and performed passably on the tenor trombone.

LOMAX [scandalized] Oh I say!

BARBARA. Many a sinner has played himself into heaven on the trombone, thanks to the Army.

LOMAX [to Barbara, still rather shocked] Yes; but what about the cannon business, don't you know? [To Undershaft] Getting into heaven is not exactly in your line, is it?

LADY BRITOMART. Charles!!!

LOMAX. Well; but it stands to reason, don't it? The cannon business may be necessary and all that: we can't get on without cannons; but it isn't right, you know. On the other hand, there may be a certain amount of tosh about the Salvation Army—I belong to the Established Church myself—but still you can't deny that it's religion; and you can't go against religion, can you? At least unless you're downright immoral, don't you know.

UNDERSHAFT. You hardly appreciate my position, Mr Lomax—

LOMAX [hastily] I'm not saying anything against you personally, you know.

UNDERSHAFT. Quite so, quite so. But consider for a moment. Here I am, a manufacturer of mutilation and murder. I find myself in a specially amiable humor just now because, this morning, down at the foundry, we blew twenty-seven dummy soldiers into fragments with a gun which formerly destroyed only thirteen.

LOMAX [leniently] Well, the more destructive war becomes, the sooner it will be abolished, eh?

UNDERSHAFT. Not at all. The more destructive war becomes the more fascinating we find it. No, Mr Lomax, I am obliged to you for making the usual excuse for my trade; but I am not ashamed of it. I am not one of those men who keep their morals and their business in watertight compartments. All the spare money my trade rivals spend on hospitals, cathedrals and other receptacles for conscience money, I devote to experiments and researches in improved methods of destroying life and property. I have always done so; and I always shall. Therefore your Christmas card moralities of peace on earth and goodwill among men are of no use to me. Your Christianity, which enjoins you to resist not evil, and to turn the other cheek, would make me a bankrupt. My morality—my religion—must have a place for cannons and torpedoes in it.

STEPHEN. [coldly—almost sullenly] You speak as if there were half a dozen moralities and religions to choose from, instead of one true morality and one true religion.

UNDERSHAFT. For me there is only one true morality; but it might not fit you, as you do not manufacture aerial battleships. There is only one true morality for every man; but every man has not the same true morality.

LOMAX [overtaxed] Would you mind saying that again? I didn't quite follow it.

CUSINS. It's quite simple. As Euripides says, one man's meat is another man's poison morally as well as physically.

UNDERSHAFT. Precisely.

LOMAX. Oh, that. Yes, yes, yes. True. True.

STEPHEN. In other words, some men are honest and some are scoundrels.

BARBARA. Bosh. There are no scoundrels.

UNDERSHAFT. Indeed? Are there any good men?

BARBARA. No. Not one. There are neither good men nor scoundrels: there are just children of one Father; and the sooner they stop calling one another names the better. You needn't talk to me: I know them. I've had scores of them through my hands: scoundrels, criminals, infidels, philanthropists, missionaries, county councillors, all sorts. They're all just the same sort of sinner; and there's the same salvation ready for them all.

UNDERSHAFT. May I ask have you ever saved a maker of cannons?

BARBARA. No. Will you let me try?

UNDERSHAFT. Well, I will make a bargain with you. If I go to see you to-morrow in your Salvation Shelter, will you come the day after to see me in my cannon works?

BARBARA. Take care. It may end in your giving up the cannons for the sake of the Salvation Army.

UNDERSHAFT. Are you sure it will not end in your giving up the Salvation Army for the sake of the cannons?

BARBARA. I will take my chance of that.

UNDERSHAFT. And I will take my chance of the other. [They shake hands on it]. Where is your shelter?

BARBARA. In West Ham. At the sign of the cross. Ask anybody in Canning Town. Where are your works?

UNDERSHAFT. In Perivale St Andrews. At the sign of the sword. Ask anybody in Europe.

LOMAX. Hadn't I better play something?

BARBARA. Yes. Give us Onward, Christian Soldiers.

LOMAX. Well, that's rather a strong order to begin with, don't you know. Suppose I sing Thou'rt passing hence, my brother. It's much the same tune.

BARBARA. It's too melancholy. You get saved, Cholly; and you'll pass hence, my brother, without making such a fuss about it.

LADY BRITOMART. Really, Barbara, you go on as if religion were a pleasant subject. Do have some sense of propriety.

UNDERSHAFT. I do not find it an unpleasant subject, my dear. It is the only one that capable people really care for.

LADY BRITOMART [looking at her watch] Well, if you are determined to have it, I insist on having it in a proper and respectable way. Charles: ring for prayers. [General amazement. Stephen rises in dismay].

LOMAX [rising] Oh I say!

UNDERSHAFT [rising] I am afraid I must be going.

LADY BRITOMART. You cannot go now, Andrew: it would be most improper. Sit down. What will the servants think?

UNDERSHAFT. My dear: I have conscientious scruples. May I suggest a compromise? If Barbara will conduct a little service in the drawingroom, with Mr Lomax as organist, I will attend it willingly. I will even take part, if a trombone can be procured.

LADY BRITOMART. Don't mock, Andrew.

UNDERSHAFT [shocked—to Barbara] You don't think I am mocking, my love, I hope.

BARBARA. No, of course not; and it wouldn't matter if you were: half the Army came to their first meeting for a lark. [Rising] Come along. Come, Dolly. Come, Cholly. [She goes out with Undershaft, who opens the door for her. Cusins rises].

LADY BRITOMART. I will not be disobeyed by everybody. Adolphus: sit down. Charles: you may go. You are not fit for prayers: you cannot keep your countenance.

LOMAX. Oh I say! [He goes out].

LADY BRITOMART [continuing] But you, Adolphus, can behave yourself if you choose to. I insist on your staying.

CUSINS. My dear Lady Brit: there are things in the family prayer book that I couldn't bear to hear you say.

LADY BRITOMART. What things, pray?

CUSINS. Well, you would have to say before all the servants that we have done things we ought not to have done, and left undone things we ought to have done, and that there is no health in us. I cannot bear to hear you doing yourself such an unjustice, and Barbara such an injustice. As for myself, I flatly deny it: I have done my best. I shouldn't dare to marry Barbara—I couldn't look you in the face—if it were true. So I must go to the drawingroom.

LADY BRITOMART [offended] Well, go. [He starts for the door]. And remember this, Adolphus [he turns to listen]: I have a very strong suspicion that you went to the Salvation Army to worship Barbara and nothing else. And I quite appreciate the very clever way in which you systematically humbug me. I have found you out. Take care Barbara doesn't. That's all.

CUSINS [with unruffled sweetness] Don't tell on me. [He goes out].

LADY BRITOMART. Sarah: if you want to go, go. Anything's better than to sit there as if you wished you were a thousand miles away.

SARAH [languidly] Very well, mamma. [She goes].

LADY BRITOMART, with a sudden flounce, gives way to a little gust of tears.

STEPHEN. [going to her] Mother: what's the matter?

LADY BRITOMART [swishing away her tears with her handkerchief] Nothing. Foolishness. You can go with him, too, if you like, and leave me with the servants.

STEPHEN. Oh, you mustn't think that, mother. I—I don't like him.

LADY BRITOMART. The others do. That is the injustice of a woman's lot. A woman has to bring up her children; and that means to restrain them, to deny them things they want, to set them tasks, to punish them when they do wrong, to do all the unpleasant things. And then the father, who has nothing to do but pet them and spoil them, comes in when all her work is done and steals their affection from her.

STEPHEN. He has not stolen our affection from you. It is only curiosity.

LADY BRITOMART [violently] I won't be consoled, Stephen. There is nothing the matter with me. [She rises and goes towards the door].

STEPHEN. Where are you going, mother?

LADY BRITOMART. To the drawingroom, of course. [She goes out. Onward, Christian Soldiers, on the concertina, with tambourine accompaniment, is heard when the door opens]. Are you coming, Stephen?

STEPHEN. No. Certainly not. [She goes. He sits down on the settee, with compressed lips and an expression of strong dislike].

ACT II

The yard of the West Ham shelter of the Salvation Army is a cold place on a January morning. The building itself, an old warehouse, is newly whitewashed. Its gabled end projects into the yard in the middle, with a door on the ground floor, and another in the loft above it without any balcony or ladder, but with a pulley rigged over it for hoisting sacks. Those who come from this central gable end into the yard have the gateway leading to the street on their left, with a stone horse-trough just beyond it, and, on the right, a penthouse shielding a table from the weather. There are forms at the table; and on them are seated a man and a woman, both much down on their luck, finishing a meal of bread [one thick slice each, with margarine and golden syrup] and diluted milk.

The man, a workman out of employment, is young, agile, a talker, a poser, sharp enough to be capable of anything in reason except honesty or altruistic considerations of any kind. The woman is a commonplace old bundle of poverty and hard-worn humanity. She looks sixty and probably is forty-five. If they were rich people, gloved and muffed and well wrapped up in furs and overcoats, they would be numbed and miserable; for it is a grindingly cold, raw, January day; and a glance at the background of grimy warehouses and leaden sky visible over the whitewashed walls of the yard would drive any idle rich person straight to the Mediterranean. But these two, being no more troubled with visions of the Mediterranean than of the moon, and being compelled to keep more of their clothes in the pawnshop, and less on their persons, in winter than in summer, are not depressed by the cold: rather are they stung into vivacity, to which their meal has just now given an almost jolly turn. The man takes a pull at his mug, and then gets up and moves about the yard with his hands deep in his pockets, occasionally breaking into a stepdance.

THE WOMAN. Feel better otter your meal, sir?

THE MAN. No. Call that a meal! Good enough for you, props; but wot is it to me, an intelligent workin man.

THE WOMAN. Workin man! Wot are you?

THE MAN. Painter.

THE WOMAN [sceptically] Yus, I dessay.

THE MAN. Yus, you dessay! I know. Every loafer that can't do nothink calls isself a painter. Well, I'm a real painter: grainer, finisher, thirty-eight bob a week when I can get it.

THE WOMAN. Then why don't you go and get it?

THE MAN. I'll tell you why. Fust: I'm intelligent—fffff! it's rotten cold here [he dances a step or two]—yes: intelligent beyond the station o life into which it has pleased the capitalists to call me; and they don't like a man that sees through em. Second, an intelligent bein needs a doo share of appiness; so I drink somethink cruel when I get the chawnce. Third, I stand by my class and do as little as I can so's to leave arf the job for me fellow workers. Fourth, I'm fly enough to know wots inside the law and wots outside it; and inside it I do as the capitalists do: pinch wot I can lay me ands on. In a proper state of society I am sober, industrious and honest: in Rome, so to speak, I do as the Romans do. Wots the consequence? When trade is bad—and it's rotten bad just now—and the employers az to sack arf their men, they generally start on me.

THE WOMAN. What's your name?

THE MAN. Price. Bronterre O'Brien Price. Usually called Snobby Price, for short.

THE WOMAN. Snobby's a carpenter, ain't it? You said you was a painter.

PRICE. Not that kind of snob, but the genteel sort. I'm too uppish, owing to my intelligence, and my father being a Chartist and a reading, thinking man: a stationer, too. I'm none of your common hewers of wood and drawers of water; and don't you forget it. [He returns to his seat at the table, and takes up his mug]. Wots YOUR name?

THE WOMAN. Rummy Mitchens, sir.

PRICE [quaffing the remains of his milk to her] Your elth, Miss Mitchens.

RUMMY [correcting him] Missis Mitchens.

PRICE. Wot! Oh Rummy, Rummy! Respectable married woman, Rummy, gittin rescued by the Salvation Army by pretendin to be a bad un. Same old game!

RUMMY. What am I to do? I can't starve. Them Salvation lasses is dear good girls; but the better you are, the worse they likes to think you were before they rescued you. Why shouldn't they av a bit o credit, poor loves? They're worn to rags by their work. And where would they get the money to rescue us if we was to let on we're no worse than other people? You know what ladies and gentlemen are.

PRICE. Thievin swine! Wish I ad their job, Rummy, all the same. Wot does Rummy stand for? Pet name props?

RUMMY. Short for Romola.

PRICE. For wot!?

RUMMY. Romola. It was out of a new book. Somebody me mother wanted me to grow up like.

PRICE. We're companions in misfortune, Rummy. Both on us got names that nobody cawnt pronounce. Consequently I'm Snobby and you're Rummy because Bill and Sally wasn't good enough for our parents. Such is life!

RUMMY. Who saved you, Mr. Price? Was it Major Barbara?

PRICE. No: I come here on my own. I'm goin to be Bronterre O'Brien Price, the converted painter. I know wot they like. I'll tell em how I blasphemed and gambled and wopped my poor old mother—

RUMMY [shocked] Used you to beat your mother?

PRICE. Not likely. She used to beat me. No matter: you come and listen to the converted painter, and you'll hear how she was a pious woman that taught me me prayers at er knee, an how I used to come home drunk and drag her out o bed be er snow white airs, an lam into er with the poker.

RUMMY. That's what's so unfair to us women. Your confessions is just as big lies as ours: you don't tell what you really done no more than us; but you men can tell your lies right out at the meetins and be made much of for it; while the sort o confessions we az to make az to be wispered to one lady at a time. It ain't right, spite of all their piety.

PRICE. Right! Do you spose the Army'd be allowed if it went and did right? Not much. It combs our air and makes us good little blokes to be robbed and put upon. But I'll play the game as good as any of em. I'll see somebody struck by lightnin, or hear a voice sayin "Snobby Price: where will you spend eternity?" I'll ave a time of it, I tell you.

RUMMY. You won't be let drink, though.

PRICE. I'll take it out in gorspellin, then. I don't want to drink if I can get fun enough any other way.

Jenny Hill, a pale, overwrought, pretty Salvation lass of 18, comes in through the yard gate, leading Peter Shirley, a half hardened, half worn-out elderly man, weak with hunger.

JENNY [supporting him] Come! pluck up. I'll get you something to eat. You'll be all right then.

PRICE [rising and hurrying officiously to take the old man off Jenny's hands] Poor old man! Cheer up, brother: you'll find rest and peace and appiness ere. Hurry up with the food, miss: e's fair done. [Jenny hurries into the shelter]. Ere, buck up, daddy! She's fetchin y'a thick slice o breadn treacle, an a mug o skyblue. [He seats him at the corner of the table].

RUMMY [gaily] Keep up your old art! Never say die!

SHIRLEY. I'm not an old man. I'm only 46. I'm as good as ever I was. The grey patch come in my hair before I was thirty. All it wants is three pennorth o hair dye: am I to be turned on the streets to starve for it? Holy God! I've worked ten to twelve hours a day since I was thirteen, and paid my way all through; and now am I to be thrown into the gutter and my job given to a young man that can do it no better than me because I've black hair that goes white at the first change?

PRICE [cheerfully] No good jawrin about it. You're ony a jumped-up, jerked-off, orspittle-turned-out incurable of an ole workin man: who cares about you? Eh? Make the thievin swine give you a meal: they've stole many a one from you. Get a bit o your own back. [Jenny returns with the usual meal]. There you are, brother. Awsk a blessin an tuck that into you.

SHIRLEY [looking at it ravenously but not touching it, and crying like a child] I never took anything before.

JENNY [petting him] Come, come! the Lord sends it to you: he wasn't above taking bread from his friends; and why should you be? Besides, when we find you a job you can pay us for it if you like.

SHIRLEY [eagerly] Yes, yes: that's true. I can pay you back: it's only a loan. [Shivering] Oh Lord! oh Lord! [He turns to the table and attacks the meal ravenously].

JENNY. Well, Rummy, are you more comfortable now?

RUMMY. God bless you, lovey! You've fed my body and saved my soul, haven't you? [Jenny, touched, kisses her] Sit down and rest a bit: you must be ready to drop.

JENNY. I've been going hard since morning. But there's more work than we can do. I mustn't stop.

RUMMY. Try a prayer for just two minutes. You'll work all the better after.

JENNY [her eyes lighting up] Oh isn't it wonderful how a few minutes prayer revives you! I was quite lightheaded at twelve o'clock, I was so tired; but Major Barbara just sent me to pray for five minutes; and I was able to go on as if I had only just begun. [To Price] Did you have a piece of bread?

PAIGE [with unction] Yes, miss; but I've got the piece that I value more; and that's the peace that passeth hall hannerstennin.

RUMMY [fervently] Glory Hallelujah!

Bill Walker, a rough customer of about 25, appears at the yard gate and looks malevolently at Jenny.

JENNY. That makes me so happy. When you say that, I feel wicked for loitering here. I must get to work again.

She is hurrying to the shelter, when the newcomer moves quickly up to the door and intercepts her. His manner is so threatening that she retreats as he comes at her truculently, driving her down the yard.

BILL. I know you. You're the one that took away my girl. You're the one that set er agen me. Well, I'm goin to av er out. Not that I care a curse for her or you: see? But I'll let er know; and I'll let you know. I'm goin to give er a doin that'll teach er to cut away from me. Now in with you and tell er to come out afore I come in and kick er out. Tell er Bill Walker wants er. She'll know what that means; and if she keeps me waitin it'll be worse. You stop to jaw back at me; and I'll start on you: d'ye hear? There's your way. In you go. [He takes her by the arm and slings her towards the door of the shelter. She falls on her hand and knee. Rummy helps her up again].

PRICE [rising, and venturing irresolutely towards Bill]. Easy there, mate. She ain't doin you no arm.

BILL. Who are you callin mate? [Standing over him threateningly]. You're goin to stand up for her, are you? Put up your ands.

RUMMY [running indignantly to him to scold him]. Oh, you great brute— [He instantly swings his left hand back against her face. She screams and reels back to the trough, where she sits down, covering her bruised face with her hands and rocking and moaning with pain].

JENNY [going to her]. Oh God forgive you! How could you strike an old woman like that?

BILL [seizing her by the hair so violently that she also screams, and tearing her away from the old woman]. You Gawd forgive me again and I'll Gawd forgive you one on the jaw that'll stop you prayin for a week. [Holding her and turning fiercely on Price]. Av you anything to say agen it? Eh?

PRICE [intimidated]. No, matey: she ain't anything to do with me.

BILL. Good job for you! I'd put two meals into you and fight you with one finger after, you starved cur. [To Jenny] Now are you goin to fetch out Mog Habbijam; or am I to knock your face off you and fetch her myself?

JENNY [writhing in his grasp] Oh please someone go in and tell Major Barbara—[she screams again as he wrenches her head down; and Price and Rummy, flee into the shelter].

BILL. You want to go in and tell your Major of me, do you?

JENNY. Oh please don't drag my hair. Let me go.

BILL. Do you or don't you? [She stifles a scream]. Yes or no.

JENNY. God give me strength—

BILL [striking her with his fist in the face] Go and show her that, and tell her if she wants one like it to come and interfere with me. [Jenny, crying with pain, goes into the shed. He goes to the form and addresses the old man]. Here: finish your mess; and get out o my way.

SHIRLEY [springing up and facing him fiercely, with the mug in his hand] You take a liberty with me, and I'll smash you over the face with the mug and cut your eye out. Ain't you satisfied—young whelps like you—with takin the bread out o the mouths of your elders that have brought you up and slaved for you, but you must come shovin and cheekin and bullyin in here, where the bread o charity is sickenin in our stummicks?

BILL [contemptuously, but backing a little] Wot good are you, you old palsy mug? Wot good are you?

SHIRLEY. As good as you and better. I'll do a day's work agen you or any fat young soaker of your age. Go and take my job at Horrockses, where I worked for ten year. They want young men there: they can't afford to keep men over forty-five. They're very sorry—give you a character and happy to help you to get anything suited to your years—sure a steady man won't be long out of a job. Well, let em try you. They'll find the differ. What do you know? Not as much as how to beeyave yourself—layin your dirty fist across the mouth of a respectable woman!

BILL. Don't provoke me to lay it acrost yours: d'ye hear?

SHIRLEY [with blighting contempt] Yes: you like an old man to hit, don't you, when you've finished with the women. I ain't seen you hit a young one yet.

BILL [stung] You lie, you old soupkitchener, you. There was a young man here. Did I offer to hit him or did I not?

SHIRLEY. Was he starvin or was he not? Was he a man or only a crosseyed thief an a loafer? Would you hit my son-in-law's brother?

BILL. Who's he?

SHIRLEY. Todger Fairmile o Balls Pond. Him that won 20 pounds off the Japanese wrastler at the music hall by standin out 17 minutes 4 seconds agen him.

BILL [sullenly] I'm no music hall wrastler. Can he box?

SHIRLEY. Yes: an you can't.

BILL. Wot! I can't, can't I? Wot's that you say [threatening him]?

SHIRLEY [not budging an inch] Will you box Todger Fairmile if I put him on to you? Say the word.

BILL. [subsiding with a slouch] I'll stand up to any man alive, if he was ten Todger Fairmiles. But I don't set up to be a perfessional.

SHIRLEY [looking down on him with unfathomable disdain] YOU box! Slap an old woman with the back o your hand! You hadn't even the sense to hit her where a magistrate couldn't see the mark of it, you silly young lump of conceit and ignorance. Hit a girl in the jaw and ony make her cry! If Todger Fairmile'd done it, she wouldn't a got up inside o ten minutes, no more than you would if he got on to you. Yah! I'd set about you myself if I had a week's feedin in me instead o two months starvation. [He returns to the table to finish his meal].

BILL [following him and stooping over him to drive the taunt in] You lie! you have the bread and treacle in you that you come here to beg.

SHIRLEY [bursting into tears] Oh God! it's true: I'm only an old pauper on the scrap heap. [Furiously] But you'll come to it yourself; and then you'll know. You'll come to it sooner than a teetotaller like me, fillin yourself with gin at this hour o the mornin!

BILL. I'm no gin drinker, you old liar; but when I want to give my girl a bloomin good idin I like to av a bit o devil in me: see? An here I am, talkin to a rotten old blighter like you sted o givin her wot for. [Working himself into a rage] I'm goin in there to fetch her out. [He makes vengefully for the shelter door].

SHIRLEY. You're goin to the station on a stretcher, more likely; and they'll take the gin and the devil out of you there when they get you inside. You mind what you're about: the major here is the Earl o Stevenage's granddaughter.

BILL [checked] Garn!

SHIRLEY. You'll see.

BILL [his resolution oozing] Well, I ain't done nothin to er.

SHIRLEY. Spose she said you did! who'd believe you?

BILL [very uneasy, skulking back to the corner of the penthouse] Gawd! There's no jastice in this country. To think wot them people can do! I'm as good as er.

SHIRLEY. Tell her so. It's just what a fool like you would do.

Barbara, brisk and businesslike, comes from the shelter with a note book, and addresses herself to Shirley. Bill, cowed, sits down in the corner on a form, and turns his back on them.

BARBARA. Good morning.

SHIRLEY [standing up and taking off his hat] Good morning, miss.

BARBARA. Sit down: make yourself at home. [He hesitates; but she puts a friendly hand on his shoulder and makes him obey]. Now then! since you've made friends with us, we want to know all about you. Names and addresses and trades.

SHIRLEY. Peter Shirley. Fitter. Chucked out two months ago because I was too old.

BARBARA [not at all surprised] You'd pass still. Why didn't you dye your hair?

SHIRLEY. I did. Me age come out at a coroner's inquest on me daughter.

BARBARA. Steady?

SHIRLEY. Teetotaller. Never out of a job before. Good worker. And sent to the knockers like an old horse!

BARBARA. No matter: if you did your part God will do his.

SHIRLEY [suddenly stubborn] My religion's no concern of anybody but myself.

BARBARA [guessing] I know. Secularist?

SHIRLEY [hotly] Did I offer to deny it?

BARBARA. Why should you? My own father's a Secularist, I think. Our Father—yours and mine—fulfils himself in many ways; and I daresay he knew what he was about when he made a Secularist of you. So buck up, Peter! we can always find a job for a steady man like you. [Shirley, disarmed, touches his hat. She turns from him to Bill]. What's your name?

BILL [insolently] Wot's that to you?

BARBARA [calmly making a note] Afraid to give his name. Any trade?

BILL. Who's afraid to give his name? [Doggedly, with a sense of heroically defying the House of Lords in the person of Lord Stevenage] If you want to bring a charge agen me, bring it. [She waits, unruffled]. My name's Bill Walker.

BARBARA [as if the name were familiar: trying to remember how] Bill Walker? [Recollecting] Oh, I know: you're the man that Jenny Hill was praying for inside just now. [She enters his name in her note book].

BILL. Who's Jenny Hill? And what call has she to pray for me?

BARBARA. I don't know. Perhaps it was you that cut her lip.

BILL [defiantly] Yes, it was me that cut her lip. I ain't afraid o you.

BARBARA. How could you be, since you're not afraid of God? You're a brave man, Mr. Walker. It takes some pluck to do our work here; but none of us dare lift our hand against a girl like that, for fear of her father in heaven.

BILL [sullenly] I want none o your cantin jaw. I suppose you think I come here to beg from you, like this damaged lot here. Not me. I don't want your bread and scrape and catlap. I don't believe in your Gawd, no more than you do yourself.

BARBARA [sunnily apologetic and ladylike, as on a new footing with him] Oh, I beg your pardon for putting your name down, Mr. Walker. I didn't understand. I'll strike it out.

BILL [taking this as a slight, and deeply wounded by it] Eah! you let my name alone. Ain't it good enough to be in your book?

BARBARA [considering] Well, you see, there's no use putting down your name unless I can do something for you, is there? What's your trade?

BILL [still smarting] That's no concern o yours.

BARBARA. Just so. [very businesslike] I'll put you down as [writing] the man who—struck—poor little Jenny Hill—in the mouth.

BILL [rising threateningly] See here. I've ad enough o this.

BARBARA [quite sunny and fearless] What did you come to us for?

BILL. I come for my girl, see? I come to take her out o this and to break er jaws for her.

BARBARA [complacently] You see I was right about your trade. [Bill, on the point of retorting furiously, finds himself, to his great shame and terror, in danger of crying instead. He sits down again suddenly]. What's her name?

BILL [dogged] Er name's Mog Abbijam: thats wot her name is.

BARBARA. Oh, she's gone to Canning Town, to our barracks there.

BILL [fortified by his resentment of Mog's perfidy] is she? [Vindictively] Then I'm goin to Kennintahn arter her. [He crosses to the gate; hesitates; finally comes back at Barbara]. Are you lyin to me to get shut o me?

BARBARA. I don't want to get shut of you. I want to keep you here and save your soul. You'd better stay: you're going to have a bad time today, Bill.

BILL. Who's goin to give it to me? You, props.

BARBARA. Someone you don't believe in. But you'll be glad afterwards.

BILL [slinking off] I'll go to Kennintahn to be out o the reach o your tongue. [Suddenly turning on her with intense malice] And if I don't find Mog there, I'll come back and do two years for you, selp me Gawd if I don't!

BARBARA [a shade kindlier, if possible] It's no use, Bill. She's got another bloke.

BILL. Wot!

BARBARA. One of her own converts. He fell in love with her when he saw her with her soul saved, and her face clean, and her hair washed.

BILL [surprised] Wottud she wash it for, the carroty slut? It's red.

BARBARA. It's quite lovely now, because she wears a new look in her eyes with it. It's a pity you're too late. The new bloke has put your nose out of joint, Bill.

BILL. I'll put his nose out o joint for him. Not that I care a curse for her, mind that. But I'll teach her to drop me as if I was dirt. And I'll teach him to meddle with my Judy. Wots iz bleedin name?

BARBARA. Sergeant Todger Fairmile.

SHIRLEY [rising with grim joy] I'll go with him, miss. I want to see them two meet. I'll take him to the infirmary when it's over.

BILL [to Shirley, with undissembled misgiving] Is that im you was speakin on?

SHIRLEY. That's him.

BILL. Im that wrastled in the music all?

SHIRLEY. The competitions at the National Sportin Club was worth nigh a hundred a year to him. He's gev em up now for religion; so he's a bit fresh for want of the exercise he was accustomed to. He'll be glad to see you. Come along.

BILL. Wots is weight?

SHIRLEY. Thirteen four. [Bill's last hope expires].

BARBARA. Go and talk to him, Bill. He'll convert you.

SHIRLEY. He'll convert your head into a mashed potato.

BILL [sullenly] I ain't afraid of him. I ain't afraid of ennybody. But he can lick me. She's done me. [He sits down moodily on the edge of the horse trough].

SHIRLEY. You ain't goin. I thought not. [He resumes his seat].

BARBARA [calling] Jenny!

JENNY [appearing at the shelter door with a plaster on the corner of her mouth] Yes, Major.

BARBARA. Send Rummy Mitchens out to clear away here.

JENNY. I think she's afraid.

BARBARA [her resemblance to her mother flashing out for a moment] Nonsense! she must do as she's told.

JENNY [calling into the shelter] Rummy: the Major says you must come.

Jenny comes to Barbara, purposely keeping on the side next Bill, lest he should suppose that she shrank from him or bore malice.

BARBARA. Poor little Jenny! Are you tired? [Looking at the wounded cheek] Does it hurt?

JENNY. No: it's all right now. It was nothing.

BARBARA [critically] It was as hard as he could hit, I expect. Poor Bill! You don't feel angry with him, do you?

JENNY. Oh no, no, no: indeed I don't, Major, bless his poor heart! [Barbara kisses her; and she runs away merrily into the shelter. Bill writhes with an agonizing return of his new and alarming symptoms, but says nothing. Rummy Mitchens comes from the shelter].

BARBARA [going to meet Rummy] Now Rummy, bustle. Take in those mugs and plates to be washed; and throw the crumbs about for the birds.

Rummy takes the three plates and mugs; but Shirley takes back his mug from her, as there it still come milk left in it.

RUMMY. There ain't any crumbs. This ain't a time to waste good bread on birds.

PRICE [appearing at the shelter door] Gentleman come to see the shelter, Major. Says he's your father.

BARBARA. All right. Coming. [Snobby goes back into the shelter, followed by Barbara].

RUMMY [stealing across to Bill and addressing him in a subdued voice, but with intense conviction] I'd av the lor of you, you flat eared pignosed potwalloper, if she'd let me. You're no gentleman, to hit a lady in the face. [Bill, with greater things moving in him, takes no notice].

SHIRLEY [following her] Here! in with you and don't get yourself into more trouble by talking.

RUMMY [with hauteur] I ain't ad the pleasure o being hintroduced to you, as I can remember. [She goes into the shelter with the plates].

BILL [savagely] Don't you talk to me, d'ye hear. You lea me alone, or I'll do you a mischief. I'm not dirt under your feet, anyway.

SHIRLEY [calmly] Don't you be afeerd. You ain't such prime company that you need expect to be sought after. [He is about to go into the shelter when Barbara comes out, with Undershaft on her right].

BARBARA. Oh there you are, Mr Shirley! [Between them] This is my father: I told you he was a Secularist, didn't I? Perhaps you'll be able to comfort one another.

UNDERSHAFT [startled] A Secularist! Not the least in the world: on the contrary, a confirmed mystic.

BARBARA. Sorry, I'm sure. By the way, papa, what is your religion—in case I have to introduce you again?

UNDERSHAFT. My religion? Well, my dear, I am a Millionaire. That is my religion.

BARBARA. Then I'm afraid you and Mr Shirley wont be able to comfort one another after all. You're not a Millionaire, are you, Peter?

SHIRLEY. No; and proud of it.

UNDERSHAFT [gravely] Poverty, my friend, is not a thing to be proud of.

SHIRLEY [angrily] Who made your millions for you? Me and my like. What's kep us poor? Keepin you rich. I wouldn't have your conscience, not for all your income.

UNDERSHAFT. I wouldn't have your income, not for all your conscience, Mr Shirley. [He goes to the penthouse and sits down on a form].

BARBARA [stopping Shirley adroitly as he is about to retort] You wouldn't think he was my father, would you, Peter? Will you go into the shelter and lend the lasses a hand for a while: we're worked off our feet.

SHIRLEY [bitterly] Yes: I'm in their debt for a meal, ain't I?

BARBARA. Oh, not because you're in their debt; but for love of them, Peter, for love of them. [He cannot understand, and is rather scandalized]. There! Don't stare at me. In with you; and give that conscience of yours a holiday [bustling him into the shelter].

SHIRLEY [as he goes in] Ah! it's a pity you never was trained to use your reason, miss. You'd have been a very taking lecturer on Secularism.

Barbara turns to her father.

UNDERSHAFT. Never mind me, my dear. Go about your work; and let me watch it for a while.

BARBARA. All right.

UNDERSHAFT. For instance, what's the matter with that out-patient over there?

BARBARA [looking at Bill, whose attitude has never changed, and whose expression of brooding wrath has deepened] Oh, we shall cure him in no time. Just watch. [She goes over to Bill and waits. He glances up at her and casts his eyes down again, uneasy, but grimmer than ever]. It would be nice to just stamp on Mog Habbijam's face, wouldn't it, Bill?

BILL [starting up from the trough in consternation] It's a lie: I never said so. [She shakes her head]. Who told you wot was in my mind?

BARBARA. Only your new friend.

BILL. Wot new friend?

BARBARA. The devil, Bill. When he gets round people they get miserable, just like you.

BILL [with a heartbreaking attempt at devil-may-care cheerfulness] I ain't miserable. [He sits down again, and stretches his legs in an attempt to seem indifferent].

BARBARA. Well, if you're happy, why don't you look happy, as we do?

BILL [his legs curling back in spite of him] I'm appy enough, I tell you. Why don't you lea me alown? Wot av I done to you? I ain't smashed your face, av I?

BARBARA [softly: wooing his soul] It's not me that's getting at you, Bill.

BILL. Who else is it?

BARBARA. Somebody that doesn't intend you to smash women's faces, I suppose. Somebody or something that wants to make a man of you.

BILL [blustering] Make a man o ME! Ain't I a man? eh? ain't I a man? Who sez I'm not a man?

BARBARA. There's a man in you somewhere, I suppose. But why did he let you hit poor little Jenny Hill? That wasn't very manly of him, was it?

BILL [tormented] Av done with it, I tell you. Chock it. I'm sick of your Jenny Ill and er silly little face.

BARBARA. Then why do you keep thinking about it? Why does it keep coming up against you in your mind? You're not getting converted, are you?

BILL [with conviction] Not ME. Not likely. Not arf.

BARBARA. That's right, Bill. Hold out against it. Put out your strength. Don't let's get you cheap. Todger Fairmile said he wrestled for three nights against his Salvation harder than he ever wrestled with the Jap at the music hall. He gave in to the Jap when his arm was going to break. But he didn't give in to his salvation until his heart was going to break. Perhaps you'll escape that. You haven't any heart, have you?

BILL. Wot dye mean? Wy ain't I got a art the same as ennybody else?

BARBARA. A man with a heart wouldn't have bashed poor little Jenny's face, would he?

BILL [almost crying] Ow, will you lea me alown? Av I ever offered to meddle with you, that you come noggin and provowkin me lawk this? [He writhes convulsively from his eyes to his toes].

BARBARA [with a steady soothing hand on his arm and a gentle voice that never lets him go] It's your soul that's hurting you, Bill, and not me. We've been through it all ourselves. Come with us, Bill. [He looks wildly round]. To brave manhood on earth and eternal glory in heaven. [He is on the point of breaking down]. Come. [A drum is heard in the shelter; and Bill, with a gasp, escapes from the spell as Barbara turns quickly. Adolphus enters from the shelter with a big drum]. Oh! there you are, Dolly. Let me introduce a new friend of mine, Mr Bill Walker. This is my bloke, Bill: Mr Cusins. [Cusins salutes with his drumstick].

BILL. Goin to marry im?

BARBARA. Yes.

BILL [fervently] Gawd elp im! Gawd elp im!

BARBARA. Why? Do you think he won't be happy with me?

BILL. I've only ad to stand it for a mornin: e'll av to stand it for a lifetime.

CUSINS. That is a frightful reflection, Mr Walker. But I can't tear myself away from her.

BILL. Well, I can. [To Barbara] Eah! do you know where I'm goin to, and wot I'm goin to do?

BARBARA. Yes: you're going to heaven; and you're coming back here before the week's out to tell me so.

BILL. You lie. I'm goin to Kennintahn, to spit in Todger Fairmile's eye. I bashed Jenny Ill's face; and now I'll get me own face bashed and come back and show it to er. E'll it me ardern I it er. That'll make us square. [To Adolphus] Is that fair or is it not? You're a genlmn: you oughter know.

BARBARA. Two black eyes wont make one white one, Bill.

BILL. I didn't ast you. Cawn't you never keep your mahth shut? I ast the genlmn.

CUSINS [reflectively] Yes: I think you're right, Mr Walker. Yes: I should do it. It's curious: it's exactly what an ancient Greek would have done.

BARBARA. But what good will it do?

CUSINS. Well, it will give Mr Fairmile some exercise; and it will satisfy Mr Walker's soul.

BILL. Rot! there ain't no sach a thing as a soul. Ah kin you tell wether I've a soul or not? You never seen it.

BARBARA. I've seen it hurting you when you went against it.

BILL [with compressed aggravation] If you was my girl and took the word out o me mahth lawk thet, I'd give you suthink you'd feel urtin, so I would. [To Adolphus] You take my tip, mate. Stop er jawr; or you'll die afore your time. [With intense expression] Wore aht: thets wot you'll be: wore aht. [He goes away through the gate].

CUSINS [looking after him] I wonder!

BARBARA. Dolly! [indignant, in her mother's manner].

CUSINS. Yes, my dear, it's very wearing to be in love with you. If it lasts, I quite think I shall die young.

BARBARA. Should you mind?

CUSINS. Not at all. [He is suddenly softened, and kisses her over the drum, evidently not for the first time, as people cannot kiss over a big drum without practice. Undershaft coughs].

BARBARA. It's all right, papa, we've not forgotten you. Dolly: explain the place to papa: I haven't time. [She goes busily into the shelter].

Undershaft and Adolphus now have the yard to themselves. Undershaft, seated on a form, and still keenly attentive, looks hard at Adolphus. Adolphus looks hard at him.

UNDERSHAFT. I fancy you guess something of what is in my mind, Mr Cusins. [Cusins flourishes his drumsticks as if in the art of beating a lively rataplan, but makes no sound]. Exactly so. But suppose Barbara finds you out!

CUSINS. You know, I do not admit that I am imposing on Barbara. I am quite genuinely

interested in the views of the Salvation Army. The fact is, I am a sort of collector of religions; and the curious thing is that I find I can believe them all. By the way, have you any religion?

UNDERSHAFT. Yes.

CUSINS. Anything out of the common?

UNDERSHAFT. Only that there are two things necessary to Salvation.

CUSINS [disappointed, but polite] Ah, the Church Catechism. Charles Lomax also belongs to the Established Church.

UNDERSHAFT. The two things are—

CUSINS. Baptism and—

UNDERSHAFT. No. Money and gunpowder.

CUSINS [surprised, but interested] That is the general opinion of our governing classes. The novelty is in hearing any man confess it.

UNDERSHAFT. Just so.

CUSINS. Excuse me: is there any place in your religion for honor, justice, truth, love, mercy and so forth?

UNDERSHAFT. Yes: they are the graces and luxuries of a rich, strong, and safe life.

CUSINS. Suppose one is forced to choose between them and money or gunpowder?

UNDERSHAFT. Choose money and gunpowder; for without enough of both you cannot afford the others.

CUSINS. That is your religion?

UNDERSHAFT. Yes.

The cadence of this reply makes a full close in the conversation. Cusins twists his face dubiously and contemplates Undershaft. Undershaft contemplates him.

CUSINS. Barbara won't stand that. You will have to choose between your religion and Barbara.

UNDERSHAFT. So will you, my friend. She will find out that that drum of yours is hollow.

CUSINS. Father Undershaft: you are mistaken: I am a sincere Salvationist. You do not understand the Salvation Army. It is the army of joy, of love, of courage: it has banished the fear and remorse and despair of the old hellridden evangelical sects: it marches to fight the devil with trumpet and drum, with music and dancing, with banner and palm, as becomes a sally from heaven by its happy garrison. It picks the waster out of the public house and makes a man of him: it finds a worm wriggling in a back kitchen, and lo! a woman! Men and women of rank too, sons and daughters of the Highest. It takes the poor professor of Greek, the most artificial and self-suppressed of human creatures, from his meal of roots, and lets loose the rhapsodist in him; reveals the true worship of Dionysos to him; sends him down the public street drumming dithyrambs [he plays a thundering flourish on the drum].

UNDERSHAFT. You will alarm the shelter.

CUSINS. Oh, they are accustomed to these sudden ecstasies of piety. However, if the drum worries you—[he pockets the drumsticks; unhooks the drum; and stands it on the ground opposite the gateway].

UNDERSHAFT. Thank you.

CUSINS. You remember what Euripides says about your money and gunpowder?

UNDERSHAFT. No.

CUSINS [declaiming]

One and another
In money and guns may outpass his brother;
And men in their millions float and flow
And seethe with a million hopes as leaven;
And they win their will; or they miss their will;
And their hopes are dead or are pined for still:
But whoe'er can know
As the long days go
That to live is happy, has found his heaven.
My translation: what do you think of it?

UNDERSHAFT. I think, my friend, that if you wish to know, as the long days go, that to live is happy, you must first acquire money enough for a decent life, and power enough to be your own master.

CUSINS. You are damnably discouraging. [He resumes his declamation].

Is it so hard a thing to see
That the spirit of God—whate'er it be—
The Law that abides and changes not, ages long,
The Eternal and Nature-born: these things be
  strong.
What else is Wisdom? What of Man's endeavor,

Or God's high grace so lovely and so great?
To stand from fear set free? to breathe and wait?
To hold a hand uplifted over Fate?
And shall not Barbara be loved for ever?

UNDERSHAFT. Euripides mentions Barbara, does he?

CUSINS. It is a fair translation. The word means Loveliness.

UNDERSHAFT. May I ask—as Barbara's father— how much a year she is to be loved for ever on?

CUSINS. As Barbara's father, that is more your affair than mine. I can feed her by teaching Greek: that is about all.

UNDERSHAFT. Do you consider it a good match for her?

CUSINS [with polite obstinacy] Mr Undershaft: I am in many ways a weak, timid, ineffectual person; and my health is far from satisfactory. But whenever I feel that I must have anything, I get it, sooner or later. I feel that way about Barbara. I don't like marriage: I feel intensely afraid of it; and I don't know what I shall do with Barbara or what she will do with me. But I feel that I and nobody else must marry her. Please regard that as settled.—Not that I wish to be arbitrary; but why should I waste your time in discussing what is inevitable?

UNDERSHAFT. You mean that you will stick at nothing not even the conversion of the Salvation Army to the worship of Dionysos.

CUSINS. The business of the Salvation Army is to save, not to wrangle about the name of the pathfinder. Dionysos or another: what does it matter?

UNDERSHAFT [rising and approaching him] Professor Cusins you are a young man after my own heart.

CUSINS. Mr Undershaft: you are, as far as I am able to gather, a most infernal old rascal; but you appeal very strongly to my sense of ironic humor.

Undershaft mutely offers his hand. They shake.

UNDERSHAFT [suddenly concentrating himself] And now to business.

CUSINS. Pardon me. We were discussing religion. Why go back to such an uninteresting and unimportant subject as business?

UNDERSHAFT. Religion is our business at present, because it is through religion alone that we can win Barbara.

CUSINS. Have you, too, fallen in love with Barbara?

UNDERSHAFT. Yes, with a father's love.

CUSINS. A father's love for a grown-up daughter is the most dangerous of all infatuations. I apologize for mentioning my own pale, coy, mistrustful fancy in the same breath with it.

UNDERSHAFT. Keep to the point. We have to win her; and we are neither of us Methodists.

CUSINS. That doesn't matter. The power Barbara wields here—the power that wields Barbara herself—is not Calvinism, not Presbyterianism, not Methodism—

UNDERSHAFT. Not Greek Paganism either, eh?

CUSINS. I admit that. Barbara is quite original in her religion.

UNDERSHAFT [triumphantly] Aha! Barbara Undershaft would be. Her inspiration comes from within herself.

CUSINS. How do you suppose it got there?

UNDERSHAFT [in towering excitement] It is the Undershaft inheritance. I shall hand on my torch to my daughter. She shall make my converts and preach my gospel.

CUSINS. What! Money and gunpowder!

UNDERSHAFT. Yes, money and gunpowder; freedom and power; command of life and command of death.

CUSINS [urbanely: trying to bring him down to earth] This is extremely interesting, Mr Undershaft. Of course you know that you are mad.

UNDERSHAFT [with redoubled force] And you?

CUSINS. Oh, mad as a hatter. You are welcome to my secret since I have discovered yours. But I am astonished. Can a madman make cannons?

UNDERSHAFT. Would anyone else than a madman make them? And now [with surging energy] question for question. Can a sane man translate Euripides?

CUSINS. No.

UNDERSHAFT [reining him by the shoulder] Can a sane woman make a man of a waster or a woman of a worm?

CUSINS [reeling before the storm] Father Colossus—Mammoth Millionaire—

UNDERSHAFT [pressing him] Are there two mad people or three in this Salvation shelter to-day?

CUSINS. You mean Barbara is as mad as we are!

UNDERSHAFT [pushing him lightly off and resuming his equanimity suddenly and completely] Pooh, Professor! let us call things by their proper names. I am a millionaire; you are a poet; Barbara is a savior of souls. What have we three to do with the common mob of slaves and idolaters? [He sits down again with a shrug of contempt for the mob].

CUSINS. Take care! Barbara is in love with the common people. So am I. Have you never felt the romance of that love?

UNDERSHAFT [cold and sardonic] Have you ever been in love with Poverty, like St Francis? Have you ever been in love with Dirt, like St Simeon? Have you ever been in love with disease and suffering, like our nurses and philanthropists? Such passions are not virtues, but the most unnatural of all the vices. This love of the common people may please an earl's granddaughter and a university professor; but I have been a common man and a poor man; and it has no romance for me. Leave it to the poor to pretend that poverty is a blessing: leave it to the coward to make a religion of his cowardice by preaching humility: we know better than that. We three must stand together above the common people: how else can we help their children to climb up beside us? Barbara must belong to us, not to the Salvation Army.

CUSINS. Well, I can only say that if you think you will get her away from the Salvation Army by talking to her as you have been talking to me, you don't know Barbara.

UNDERSHAFT. My friend: I never ask for what I can buy.

CUSINS [in a white fury] Do I understand you to imply that you can buy Barbara?

UNDERSHAFT. No; but I can buy the Salvation Army.

CUSINS. Quite impossible.

UNDERSHAFT. You shall see. All religious organizations exist by selling themselves to the rich.

CUSINS. Not the Army. That is the Church of the poor.

UNDERSHAFT. All the more reason for buying it.

CUSINS. I don't think you quite know what the Army does for the poor.

UNDERSHAFT. Oh yes I do. It draws their teeth: that is enough for me—as a man of business—

CUSINS. Nonsense! It makes them sober—

UNDERSHAFT. I prefer sober workmen. The profits are larger.

CUSINS. —honest—

UNDERSHAFT. Honest workmen are the most economical.

CUSINS. —attached to their homes—

UNDERSHAFT. So much the better: they will put up with anything sooner than change their shop.

CUSINS. —happy—

UNDERSHAFT. An invaluable safeguard against revolution.

CUSINS.—unselfish—

UNDERSHAFT. Indifferent to their own interests, which suits me exactly.

CUSINS.—with their thoughts on heavenly things—

UNDERSHAFT [rising] And not on Trade Unionism nor Socialism. Excellent.

CUSINS [revolted] You really are an infernal old rascal.

UNDERSHAFT [indicating Peter Shirley, who has just came from the shelter and strolled dejectedly down the yard between them] And this is an honest man!

SHIRLEY. Yes; and what av I got by it? [he passes on bitterly and sits on the form, in the corner of the penthouse].

Snobby Price, beaming sanctimoniously, and Jenny Hill, with a tambourine full of coppers, come from the shelter and go to the drum, on which Jenny begins to count the money.

UNDERSHAFT [replying to Shirley] Oh, your employers must have got a good deal by it from first to last. [He sits on the table, with one foot on the side form. Cusins, overwhelmed, sits down on the same form nearer the shelter. Barbara comes from the shelter to the middle of the yard. She is excited and a little overwrought].

BARBARA. We've just had a splendid experience meeting at the other gate in Cripps's lane. I've hardly ever seen them so much moved as they were by your confession, Mr Price.

PRICE. I could almost be glad of my past wickedness if I could believe that it would elp to keep hathers stright.

BARBARA. So it will, Snobby. How much, Jenny?

JENNY. Four and tenpence, Major.

BARBARA. Oh Snobby, if you had given your poor mother just one more kick, we should have got the whole five shillings!

PRICE. If she heard you say that, miss, she'd be sorry I didn't. But I'm glad. Oh what a joy it will be to her when she hears I'm saved!

UNDERSHAFT. Shall I contribute the odd twopence, Barbara? The millionaire's mite, eh? [He takes a couple of pennies from his pocket.]

BARBARA. How did you make that twopence?

UNDERSHAFT. As usual. By selling cannons, torpedoes, submarines, and my new patent Grand Duke hand grenade.

BARBARA. Put it back in your pocket. You can't buy your Salvation here for twopence: you must work it out.

UNDERSHAFT. Is twopence not enough? I can afford a little more, if you press me.

BARBARA. Two million millions would not be enough. There is bad blood on your hands; and nothing but good blood can cleanse them. Money is no use. Take it away. [She turns to Cusins]. Dolly: you must write another letter for me to the papers. [He makes a wry face]. Yes: I know you don't like it; but it must be done. The starvation this winter is beating us: everybody is unemployed. The General says we must close this shelter if we cant get more money. I force the collections at the meetings until I am ashamed, don't I, Snobby?

PRICE. It's a fair treat to see you work it, miss. The way you got them up from three-and-six to four-and-ten with that hymn, penny by penny and verse by verse, was a caution. Not a Cheap Jack on Mile End Waste could touch you at it.

BARBARA. Yes; but I wish we could do without it. I am getting at last to think more of the collection than of the people's souls. And what are those hatfuls of pence and halfpence? We want thousands! tens of thousands! hundreds of thousands! I want to convert people, not to be always begging for the Army in a way I'd die sooner than beg for myself.

UNDERSHAFT [in profound irony] Genuine unselfishness is capable of anything, my dear.

BARBARA [unsuspectingly, as she turns away to take the money from the drum and put it in a cash bag she carries] Yes, isn't it? [Undershaft looks sardonically at Cusins].

CUSINS [aside to Undershaft] Mephistopheles! Machiavelli!

BARBARA [tears coming into her eyes as she ties the bag and pockets it] How are we to feed them? I can't talk religion to a man with bodily hunger in his eyes. [Almost breaking down] It's frightful.

JENNY [running to her] Major, dear—

BARBARA [rebounding] No: don't comfort me. It will be all right. We shall get the money.

UNDERSHAFT. How?

JENNY. By praying for it, of course. Mrs Baines says she prayed for it last night; and she has never prayed for it in vain: never once. [She goes to the gate and looks out into the street].

BARBARA [who has dried her eyes and regained her composure] By the way, dad, Mrs Baines has come to march with us to our big meeting this afternoon; and she is very anxious to meet you, for some reason or other. Perhaps she'll convert you.

UNDERSHAFT. I shall be delighted, my dear.

JENNY [at the gate: excitedly] Major! Major! Here's that man back again.

BARBARA. What man?

JENNY. The man that hit me. Oh, I hope he's coming back to join us.

Bill Walker, with frost on his jacket, comes through the gate, his hands deep in his pockets and his chin sunk between his shoulders, like a cleaned-out gambler. He halts between Barbara and the drum.

BARBARA. Hullo, Bill! Back already!

BILL [nagging at her] Bin talkin ever sense, av you?

BARBARA. Pretty nearly. Well, has Todger paid you out for poor Jenny's jaw?

BILL. NO he ain't.

BARBARA. I thought your jacket looked a bit snowy.

BILL. So it is snowy. You want to know where the snow come from, don't you?

BARBARA. Yes.

BILL. Well, it come from off the ground in Parkinses Corner in Kennintahn. It got rubbed off be my shoulders see?

BARBARA. Pity you didn't rub some off with your knees, Bill! That would have done you a lot of good.

BILL [with your mirthless humor] I was saving another man's knees at the time. E was kneelin on my ed, so e was.

JENNY. Who was kneeling on your head?

BILL. Todger was. E was prayin for me: prayin comfortable with me as a carpet. So was Mog. So was the ole bloomin meetin. Mog she sez "O Lord break is stubborn spirit; but don't urt is dear art." That was wot she said. "Don't urt is dear art"! An er bloke—thirteen stun four!—kneelin wiv all is weight on me. Funny, ain't it?

JENNY. Oh no. We're so sorry, Mr Walker.

BARBARA [enjoying it frankly] Nonsense! of course it's funny. Served you right, Bill! You must have done something to him first.

BILL [doggedly] I did wot I said I'd do. I spit in is eye. E looks up at the sky and sez, "O that I should be fahnd worthy to be spit upon for the gospel's sake!" a sez; an Mog sez "Glory Allelloolier!"; an then a called me Brother, an dahned me as if I was a kid and a was me mother washin me a Setterda nawt. I adn't just no show wiv im at all. Arf the street prayed; an the tother arf larfed fit to split theirselves. [To Barbara] There! are you settisfawd nah?

BARBARA [her eyes dancing] Wish I'd been there, Bill.

BILL. Yes: you'd a got in a hextra bit o talk on me, wouldn't you?

JENNY. I'm so sorry, Mr. Walker.

BILL [fiercely] Don't you go bein sorry for me: you've no call. Listen ere. I broke your jawr.

JENNY. No, it didn't hurt me: indeed it didn't, except for a moment. It was only that I was frightened.

BILL. I don't want to be forgive be you, or be ennybody. Wot I did I'll pay for. I tried to get me own jawr broke to settisfaw you—

JENNY [distressed] Oh no—

BILL [impatiently] Tell y'I did: cawn't you listen to wot's bein told you? All I got be it was bein made a sight of in the public street for me pains. Well, if I cawn't settisfaw you one way, I can another. Listen ere! I ad two quid saved agen the frost; an I've a pahnd of it left. A mate n mine last week ad words with the Judy e's goin to marry. E give er wot-for; an e's bin fined fifteen bob. E ad a right to it er because they was goin to be marrid; but I adn't no right to it you; so put anather fawv bob on an call it a pahnd's worth. [He produces a sovereign]. Ere's the money. Take it; and let's av no more o your forgivin an prayin and your Major jawrin me. Let wot I done be done and paid for; and let there be a end of it.

JENNY. Oh, I couldn't take it, Mr. Walker. But if you would give a shilling or two to poor Rummy Mitchens! you really did hurt her; and she's old.

BILL [contemptuously] Not likely. I'd give her anather as soon as look at er. Let her av the lawr o me as she threatened! She ain't forgiven me: not mach. Wot I done to er is not on me mawnd— wot she [indicating Barbara] might call on me conscience—no more than stickin a pig. It's this Christian game o yours that I won't av played agen me: this bloomin forgivin an noggin an jawrin that makes a man that sore that iz lawf's a burdn to im. I won't av it, I tell you; so take your

money and stop throwin your silly bashed face hup agen me.

JENNY. Major: may I take a little of it for the Army?

BARBARA. No: the Army is not to be bought. We want your soul, Bill; and we'll take nothing less.

BILL [bitterly] I know. It ain't enough. Me an me few shillins is not good enough for you. You're a earl's grendorter, you are. Nothin less than a underd pahnd for you.

UNDERSHAFT. Come, Barbara! you could do a great deal of good with a hundred pounds. If you will set this gentleman's mind at ease by taking his pound, I will give the other ninety-nine [Bill, astounded by such opulence, instinctively touches his cap].

BARBARA. Oh, you're too extravagant, papa. Bill offers twenty pieces of silver. All you need offer is the other ten. That will make the standard price to buy anybody who's for sale. I'm not; and the Army's not. [To Bill] You'll never have another quiet moment, Bill, until you come round to us. You can't stand out against your salvation.

BILL [sullenly] I cawn't stend aht agen music all wrastlers and artful tongued women. I've offered to pay. I can do no more. Take it or leave it. There it is. [He throws the sovereign on the drum, and sits down on the horse-trough. The coin fascinates Snobby Price, who takes an early opportunity of dropping his cap on it].

Mrs Baines comes from the shelter. She is dressed as a Salvation Army Commissioner. She is an earnest looking woman of about 40, with a caressing, urgent voice, and an appealing manner.

BARBARA. This is my father, Mrs Baines. [Undershaft comes from the table, taking his hat off with marked civility]. Try what you can do with him. He won't listen to me, because he remembers what a fool I was when I was a baby.

[She leaves them together and chats with Jenny].

MRS BAINES. Have you been shown over the shelter, Mr Undershaft? You know the work we're doing, of course.

UNDERSHAFT [very civilly] The whole nation knows it, Mrs Baines.

MRS BAINES. No, Sir: the whole nation does not know it, or we should not be crippled as we are for want of money to carry our work through the length and breadth of the land. Let me tell you that there would have been rioting this winter in London but for us.

UNDERSHAFT. You really think so?

MRS BAINES. I know it. I remember 1886, when you rich gentlemen hardened your hearts against the cry of the poor. They broke the windows of your clubs in Pall Mall.

UNDERSHAFT [gleaming with approval of their method] And the Mansion House Fund went up next day from thirty thousand pounds to seventy-nine thousand! I remember quite well.

MRS BAINES. Well, won't you help me to get at the people? They won't break windows then. Come here, Price. Let me show you to this gentleman [Price comes to be inspected]. Do you remember the window breaking?

PRICE. My ole father thought it was the revolution, ma'am.

MRS BAINES. Would you break windows now?

PRICE. Oh no ma'm. The windows of eaven av bin opened to me. I know now that the rich man is a sinner like myself.

RUMMY [appearing above at the loft door] Snobby Price!

SNOBBY. Wot is it?

RUMMY. Your mother's askin for you at the other gate in Crippses Lane. She's heard about your confession [Price turns pale].

MRS BAINES. Go, Mr. Price; and pray with her.

JENNY. You can go through the shelter, Snobby.

PRICE [to Mrs Baines] I couldn't face her now; ma'am, with all the weight of my sins fresh on me. Tell her she'll find her son at ome, waitin for her in prayer. [He skulks off through the gate, incidentally stealing the sovereign on his way out by picking up his cap from the drum].

MRS BAINES [with swimming eyes] You see how we take the anger and the bitterness against you out of their hearts, Mr Undershaft.

UNDERSHAFT. It is certainly most convenient and gratifying to all large employers of labor, Mrs Baines.

MRS BAINES. Barbara: Jenny: I have good news: most wonderful news. [Jenny runs to her]. My prayers have been answered. I told you they would, Jenny, didn't I?

JENNY. Yes, yes.

BARBARA [moving nearer to the drum] Have we got money enough to keep the shelter open?

MRS BAINES. I hope we shall have enough to keep all the shelters open. Lord Saxmundham has promised us five thousand pounds—

BARBARA. Hooray!

JENNY. Glory!

MRS BAINES.—if—

BARBARA. "If!" If what?

MRS BAINES. If five other gentlemen will give a thousand each to make it up to ten thousand.

BARBARA. Who is Lord Saxmundham? I never heard of him.

UNDERSHAFT [who has pricked up his ears at the peer's name, and is now watching Barbara curiously] A new creation, my dear. You have heard of Sir Horace Bodger?

BARBARA. Bodger! Do you mean the distiller? Bodger's whisky!

UNDERSHAFT. That is the man. He is one of the greatest of our public benefactors. He restored the cathedral at Hakington. They made him a baronet for that. He gave half a million to the funds of his party: they made him a baron for that.

SHIRLEY. What will they give him for the five thousand?

UNDERSHAFT. There is nothing left to give him. So the five thousand, I should think, is to save his soul.

MRS BAINES. Heaven grant it may! Oh Mr. Undershaft, you have some very rich friends. Can't you help us towards the other five thousand? We are going to hold a great meeting this afternoon at the Assembly Hall in the Mile End Road. If I could only announce that one gentleman had come forward to support Lord

Saxmundham, others would follow. Don't you know somebody? Couldn't you? Wouldn't you? [her eyes fill with tears] oh, think of those poor people, Mr Undershaft: think of how much it means to them, and how little to a great man like you.

UNDERSHAFT [sardonically gallant] Mrs Baines: you are irresistible. I can't disappoint you; and I can't deny myself the satisfaction of making Bodger pay up. You shall have your five thousand pounds.

MRS BAINES. Thank God!

UNDERSHAFT. You don't thank me?

MRS BAINES. Oh sir, don't try to be cynical: don't be ashamed of being a good man. The Lord will bless you abundantly; and our prayers will be like a strong fortification round you all the days of your life. [With a touch of caution] You will let me have the cheque to show at the meeting, won't you? Jenny: go in and fetch a pen and ink. [Jenny runs to the shelter door].

UNDERSHAFT. Do not disturb Miss Hill: I have a fountain pen. [Jenny halts. He sits at the table and writes the cheque. Cusins rises to make more room for him. They all watch him silently].

BILL [cynically, aside to Barbara, his voice and accent horribly debased] Wot prawce Selvytion nah?

BARBARA. Stop. [Undershaft stops writing: they all turn to her in surprise]. Mrs Baines: are you really going to take this money?

MRS BAINES [astonished] Why not, dear?

BARBARA. Why not! Do you know what my father is? Have you forgotten that Lord Saxmundham is Bodger the whisky man? Do you remember how we implored the County Council to stop him from writing Bodger's Whisky in letters of fire against the sky; so that the poor drinkruined creatures on the embankment could not wake up from their snatches of sleep without being reminded of their deadly thirst by that wicked sky sign? Do you know that the worst thing I have had to fight here is not the devil, but Bodger, Bodger, Bodger, with his whisky, his distilleries, and his tied houses? Are you going to make our shelter another tied house for him, and ask me to keep it?

BILL. Rotten drunken whisky it is too.

MRS BAINES. Dear Barbara: Lord Saxmundham has a soul to be saved like any of us. If heaven has found the way to make a good use of his money, are we to set ourselves up against the answer to our prayers?

BARBARA. I know he has a soul to be saved. Let him come down here; and I'll do my best to help him to his salvation. But he wants to send his cheque down to buy us, and go on being as wicked as ever.

UNDERSHAFT [with a reasonableness which Cusins alone perceives to be ironical] My dear Barbara: alcohol is a very necessary article. It heals the sick—

BARBARA. It does nothing of the sort.

UNDERSHAFT. Well, it assists the doctor: that is perhaps a less questionable way of putting it. It makes life bearable to millions of people who could not endure their existence if they were quite sober. It enables Parliament to do things at eleven at night that no sane person would do at eleven in the morning. Is it Bodger's fault that this inestimable gift is deplorably abused by less than one per cent of the poor? [He turns again to the table; signs the cheque; and crosses it].

MRS BAINES. Barbara: will there be less drinking or more if all those poor souls we are saving come to-morrow and find the doors of our shelters shut in their faces? Lord Saxmundham gives us the money to stop drinking—to take his own business from him.

CUSINS [impishly] Pure self-sacrifice on Bodger's part, clearly! Bless dear Bodger! [Barbara almost breaks down as Adolphus, too, fails her].

UNDERSHAFT [tearing out the cheque and pocketing the book as he rises and goes past Cusins to Mrs Baines] I also, Mrs Baines, may claim a little disinterestedness. Think of my business! think of the widows and orphans! the men and lads torn to pieces with shrapnel and poisoned with lyddite [Mrs Baines shrinks; but he goes on remorselessly]! the oceans of blood, not one drop of which is shed in a really just cause! the ravaged crops! the peaceful peasants forced, women and men, to till their fields under the fire of opposing armies on pain of starvation! the bad blood of the fierce little cowards at home who egg on others to fight for the gratification of their national vanity! All this makes money for me: I am never richer, never busier than when the papers are full of it. Well, it is your work to preach peace on earth and goodwill to men. [Mrs Baines's face lights up again]. Every convert you make is a vote against war. [Her lips move in prayer]. Yet I give you this money to help you to hasten my own commercial ruin. [He gives her the cheque].

CUSINS [mounting the form in an ecstasy of mischief] The millennium will be inaugurated by the unselfishness of Undershaft and Bodger. Oh be joyful! [He takes the drumsticks from his pockets and flourishes them].

MRS BAINES [taking the cheque] The longer I live the more proof I see that there is an Infinite Goodness that turns everything to the work of salvation sooner or later. Who would have thought that any good could have come out of war and drink? And yet their profits are brought today to the feet of salvation to do its blessed work. [She is affected to tears].

JENNY [running to Mrs Baines and throwing her arms round her] Oh dear! how blessed, how glorious it all is!

CUSINS [in a convulsion of irony] Let us seize this unspeakable moment. Let us march to the great meeting at once. Excuse me just an instant. [He rushes into the shelter. Jenny takes her tambourine from the drum head].

MRS BAINES. Mr Undershaft: have you ever seen a thousand people fall on their knees with one impulse and pray? Come with us to the meeting. Barbara shall tell them that the Army is saved, and saved through you.

CUSINS [returning impetuously from the shelter with a flag and a trombone, and coming between Mrs Baines and Undershaft] You shall carry the flag down the first street, Mrs Baines [he gives her the flag]. Mr Undershaft is a gifted trombonist: he shall intone an Olympian diapason to the West Ham Salvation March. [Aside to Undershaft, as he forces the trombone on him] Blow, Machiavelli, blow.

UNDERSHAFT [aside to him, as he takes the trombone] The trumpet in Zion! [Cusins rushes to the drum, which he takes up and puts on. Undershaft continues, aloud] I will do my best. I could vamp a bass if I knew the tune.

CUSINS. It is a wedding chorus from one of Donizetti's operas; but we have converted it. We convert everything to good here, including Bodger. You remember the chorus. "For thee immense rejoicing—immenso giubilo—immenso giubilo." [With drum obbligato] Rum tum ti tum tum, tum tum ti ta—

BARBARA. Dolly: you are breaking my heart.

CUSINS. What is a broken heart more or less here? Dionysos Undershaft has descended. I am possessed.

MRS BAINES. Come, Barbara: I must have my dear Major to carry the flag with me.

JENNY. Yes, yes, Major darling.

CUSINS [snatches the tambourine out of Jenny's hand and mutely offers it to Barbara].

BARBARA [coming forward a little as she puts the offer behind her with a shudder, whilst Cusins recklessly tosses the tambourine back to Jenny and goes to the gate] I can't come.

JENNY. Not come!

MRS BAINES [with tears in her eyes] Barbara: do you think I am wrong to take the money?

BARBARA [impulsively going to her and kissing her] No, no: God help you, dear, you must: you are saving the Army. Go; and may you have a great meeting!

JENNY. But arn't you coming?

BARBARA. No. [She begins taking off the silver brooch from her collar].

MRS BAINES. Barbara: what are you doing?

JENNY. Why are you taking your badge off? You can't be going to leave us, Major.

BARBARA [quietly] Father: come here.

UNDERSHAFT [coming to her] My dear! [Seeing that she is going to pin the badge on his collar, he retreats to the penthouse in some alarm].

BARBARA [following him] Don't be frightened. [She pins the badge on and steps back towards the table, showing him to the others] There! It's not much for 5000 pounds is it?

MRS BAINES. Barbara: if you won't come and pray with us, promise me you will pray for us.

BARBARA. I can't pray now. Perhaps I shall never pray again.

MRS BAINES. Barbara!

JENNY. Major!

BARBARA [almost delirious] I can't bear any more. Quick march!

CUSINS [calling to the procession in the street outside] Off we go. Play up, there! Immenso giubilo. [He gives the time with his drum; and the band strikes up the march, which rapidly becomes more distant as the procession moves briskly away].

MRS BAINES. I must go, dear. You're overworked: you will be all right tomorrow. We'll never lose you. Now Jenny: step out with the old flag. Blood and Fire! [She marches out through the gate with her flag].

JENNY. Glory Hallelujah! [flourishing her tambourine and marching].

UNDERSHAFT [to Cusins, as he marches out past him easing the slide of his trombone] "My ducats and my daughter"!

CUSINS [following him out] Money and gunpowder!

BARBARA. Drunkenness and Murder! My God: why hast thou forsaken me?

She sinks on the form with her face buried in her hands. The march passes away into silence. Bill Walker steals across to her.

BILL [taunting] Wot prawce Selvytion nah?

SHIRLEY. Don't you hit her when she's down.

BILL. She it me wen aw wiz dahn. Waw shouldn't I git a bit o me own back?

BARBARA [raising her head] I didn't take your money, Bill. [She crosses the yard to the gate and turns her back on the two men to hide her face from them].

BILL [sneering after her] Naow, it warn't enough for you. [Turning to the drum, he misses the money]. Ellow! If you ain't took it summun else

az. Were's it gorn? Blame me if Jenny Ill didn't take it arter all!

RUMMY [screaming at him from the loft] You lie, you dirty blackguard! Snobby Price pinched it off the drum wen e took ap iz cap. I was ap ere all the time an see im do it.

BILL. Wot! Stowl maw money! Waw didn't you call thief on him, you silly old mucker you?

RUMMY. To serve you aht for ittin me acrost the face. It's cost y'pahnd, that az. [Raising a paean of squalid triumph] I done you. I'm even with you. I've ad it aht o y—. [Bill snatches up Shirley's mug and hurls it at her. She slams the loft door and vanishes. The mug smashes against the door and falls in fragments].

BILL [beginning to chuckle] Tell us, ole man, wot o'clock this morrun was it wen im as they call Snobby Prawce was sived?

BARBARA [turning to him more composedly, and with unspoiled sweetness] About half past twelve, Bill. And he pinched your pound at a quarter to two. I know. Well, you can't afford to lose it. I'll send it to you.

BILL [his voice and accent suddenly improving] Not if I was to starve for it. I ain't to be bought.

SHIRLEY. Ain't you? You'd sell yourself to the devil for a pint o beer; ony there ain't no devil to make the offer.

BILL [unshamed] So I would, mate, and often av, cheerful. But she cawn't buy me. [Approaching Barbara] You wanted my soul, did you? Well, you ain't got it.

BARBARA. I nearly got it, Bill. But we've sold it back to you for ten thousand pounds.

SHIRLEY. And dear at the money!

BARBARA. No, Peter: it was worth more than money.

BILL [salvationproof] It's no good: you cawn't get rahnd me nah. I don't blieve in it; and I've seen today that I was right. [Going] So long, old soupkitchener! Ta, ta, Major Earl's Grendorter! [Turning at the gate] Wot prawce Selvytion nah? Snobby Prawce! Ha! ha!

BARBARA [offering her hand] Goodbye, Bill.

BILL [taken aback, half plucks his cap off then

shoves it on again defiantly] Git aht. [Barbara drops her hand, discouraged. He has a twinge of remorse]. But thet's aw rawt, you knaow. Nathink pasnl. Naow mellice. So long, Judy. [He goes].

BARBARA. No malice. So long, Bill.

SHIRLEY [shaking his head] You make too much of him, miss, in your innocence.

BARBARA [going to him] Peter: I'm like you now. Cleaned out, and lost my job.

SHIRLEY. You've youth an hope. That's two better than me. That's hope for you.

BARBARA. I'll get you a job, Peter, the youth will have to be enough for me. [She counts her money]. I have just enough left for two teas at Lockharts, a Rowton doss for you, and my tram and bus home. [He frowns and rises with offended pride. She takes his arm]. Don't be proud, Peter: it's sharing between friends. And promise me you'll talk to me and not let me cry. [She draws him towards the gate].

SHIRLEY. Well, I'm not accustomed to talk to the like of you—

BARBARA [urgently] Yes, yes: you must talk to me. Tell me about Tom Paine's books and Bradlaugh's lectures. Come along.

SHIRLEY. Ah, if you would only read Tom Paine in the proper spirit, miss! [They go out through the gate together].

ACT III

Next day after lunch Lady Britomart is writing in the library in Wilton Crescent. Sarah is reading in the armchair near the window. Barbara, in ordinary dress, pale and brooding, is on the settee. Charley Lomax enters. Coming forward between the settee and the writing table, he starts on seeing Barbara fashionably attired and in low spirits.

LOMAX. You've left off your uniform!
Barbara says nothing; but an expression of pain passes over her face.

LADY BRITOMART [warning him in low tones to be careful] Charles!

LOMAX [much concerned, sitting down sympathetically on the settee beside Barbara] I'm awfully sorry, Barbara. You know I helped you all I could with the concertina and so forth. [Momentously] Still, I have never shut my eyes to the fact that there is a certain amount of tosh about the Salvation Army. Now the claims of the Church of England—

LADY BRITOMART. That's enough, Charles. Speak of something suited to your mental capacity.

LOMAX. But surely the Church of England is suited to all our capacities.

BARBARA [pressing his hand] Thank you for your sympathy, Cholly. Now go and spoon with Sarah.

LOMAX [rising and going to Sarah] How is my ownest today?

SARAH. I wish you wouldn't tell Cholly to do things, Barbara. He always comes straight and does them. Cholly: we're going to the works at Perivale St. Andrews this afternoon.

LOMAX. What works?

SARAH. The cannon works.

LOMAX. What! Your governor's shop!

SARAH. Yes.

LOMAX. Oh I say!

Cusins enters in poor condition. He also starts visibly when he sees Barbara without her uniform.

BARBARA. I expected you this morning, Dolly. Didn't you guess that?

CUSINS [sitting down beside her] I'm sorry. I have only just breakfasted.

SARAH. But we've just finished lunch.

BARBARA. Have you had one of your bad nights?

CUSINS. No: I had rather a good night: in fact, one of the most remarkable nights I have ever passed.

BARBARA. The meeting?

CUSINS. No: after the meeting.

LADY BRITOMART. You should have gone to bed after the meeting. What were you doing?

CUSINS. Drinking.

LADY BRITOMART. {Adolphus! SARAH. {Dolly! BARBARA. {Dolly! LOMAX. {Oh I say!

LADY BRITOMART. What were you drinking, may I ask?

CUSINS. A most devilish kind of Spanish burgundy, warranted free from added alcohol: a Temperance burgundy in fact. Its richness in natural alcohol made any addition superfluous.

BARBARA. Are you joking, Dolly?

CUSINS [patiently] No. I have been making a night of it with the nominal head of this household: that is all.

LADY BRITOMART. Andrew made you drunk!

CUSINS. No: he only provided the wine. I think it was Dionysos who made me drunk. [To Barbara] I told you I was possessed.

LADY BRITOMART. You're not sober yet. Go home to bed at once.

CUSINS. I have never before ventured to reproach you, Lady Brit; but how could you marry the Prince of Darkness?

LADY BRITOMART. It was much more excusable to marry him than to get drunk with him. That is a new accomplishment of Andrew's, by the way. He usen't to drink.

CUSINS. He doesn't now. He only sat there and completed the wreck of my moral basis, the rout of my convictions, the purchase of my soul. He cares for you, Barbara. That is what makes him so dangerous to me.

BARBARA. That has nothing to do with it, Dolly. There are larger loves and diviner dreams than the fireside ones. You know that, don't you?

CUSINS. Yes: that is our understanding. I know it. I hold to it. Unless he can win me on that holier ground he may amuse me for a while; but he can get no deeper hold, strong as he is.

BARBARA. Keep to that; and the end will be right. Now tell me what happened at the meeting?

CUSINS. It was an amazing meeting. Mrs Baines almost died of emotion. Jenny Hill went stark mad with hysteria. The Prince of Darkness played his trombone like a madman: its brazen roarings were like the laughter of the damned. 117 conversions took place then and there. They prayed with the most touching sincerity and gratitude for Bodger, and for the anonymous donor of the 5000 pounds. Your father would not let his name be given.

LOMAX. That was rather fine of the old man, you know. Most chaps would have wanted the advertisement.

CUSINS. He said all the charitable institutions would be down on him like kites on a battle field if he gave his name.

LADY BRITOMART. That's Andrew all over. He never does a proper thing without giving an improper reason for it.

CUSINS. He convinced me that I have all my life been doing improper things for proper reasons.

LADY BRITOMART. Adolphus: now that Barbara has left the Salvation Army, you had better leave it too. I will not have you playing that drum in the streets.

CUSINS. Your orders are already obeyed, Lady Brit.

BARBARA. Dolly: were you ever really in earnest about it? Would you have joined if you had never seen me?

CUSINS [disingenuously] Well—er—well, possibly, as a collector of religions—

LOMAX [cunningly] Not as a drummer, though, you know. You are a very clearheaded brainy chap, Cholly; and it must have been apparent to you that there is a certain amount of tosh about—

LADY BRITOMART. Charles: if you must drivel, drivel like a grown-up man and not like a schoolboy.

LOMAX [out of countenance] Well, drivel is drivel, don't you know, whatever a man's age.

LADY BRITOMART. In good society in England, Charles, men drivel at all ages by repeating silly formulas with an air of wisdom. Schoolboys make their own formulas out of slang, like you. When they reach your age, and get political private secretaryships and things of that sort, they drop slang and get their formulas out of The Spectator or The Times. You had better confine yourself to The Times. You will find that there is a certain amount of tosh about The Times; but at least its language is reputable.

LOMAX [overwhelmed] You are so awfully strong-minded, Lady Brit—

LADY BRITOMART. Rubbish! [Morrison comes in]. What is it?

MORRISON. If you please, my lady, Mr Undershaft has just drove up to the door.

LADY BRITOMART. Well, let him in. [Morrison hesitates]. What's the matter with you?

MORRISON. Shall I announce him, my lady; or is he at home here, so to speak, my lady?

LADY BRITOMART. Announce him.

MORRISON. Thank you, my lady. You won't mind my asking, I hope. The occasion is in a manner of speaking new to me.

LADY BRITOMART. Quite right. Go and let him in.

MORRISON. Thank you, my lady. [He withdraws].

LADY BRITOMART. Children: go and get ready. [Sarah and Barbara go upstairs for their out-of-door wrap]. Charles: go and tell Stephen to come down here in five minutes: you will find him in the drawing room. [Charles goes]. Adolphus: tell them to send round the carriage in about fifteen minutes. [Adolphus goes].

MORRISON [at the door] Mr Undershaft.

Undershaft comes in. Morrison goes out.

UNDERSHAFT. Alone! How fortunate!

LADY BRITOMART [rising] Don't be sentimental, Andrew. Sit down. [She sits on the settee: he sits beside her, on her left. She comes to the point before he has time to breathe]. Sarah must have 800 pounds a year until Charles Lomax comes into his property. Barbara will need more, and need it permanently, because Adolphus hasn't any property.

UNDERSHAFT [resignedly] Yes, my dear: I will see to it. Anything else? for yourself, for instance?

LADY BRITOMART. I want to talk to you about Stephen.

UNDERSHAFT [rather wearily] Don't, my dear. Stephen doesn't interest me.

LADY BRITOMART. He does interest me. He is our son.

UNDERSHAFT. Do you really think so? He has induced us to bring him into the world; but he chose his parents very incongruously, I think. I see nothing of myself in him, and less of you.

LADY BRITOMART. Andrew: Stephen is an excellent son, and a most steady, capable, highminded young man. YOU are simply trying to find an excuse for disinheriting him.

UNDERSHAFT. My dear Biddy: the Undershaft tradition disinherits him. It would be dishonest of me to leave the cannon foundry to my son.

LADY BRITOMART. It would be most unnatural and improper of you to leave it to anyone else, Andrew. Do you suppose this wicked and immoral tradition can be kept up for ever? Do you pretend that Stephen could not carry on the foundry just as well as all the other sons of the big business houses?

UNDERSHAFT. Yes: he could learn the office routine without understanding the business, like all the other sons; and the firm would go on by its own momentum until the real Undershaft—probably an Italian or a German—would invent a new method and cut him out.

LADY BRITOMART. There is nothing that any Italian or German could do that Stephen could not do. And Stephen at least has breeding.

UNDERSHAFT. The son of a foundling! nonsense!

LADY BRITOMART. My son, Andrew! And even you may have good blood in your veins for all you know.

UNDERSHAFT. True. Probably I have. That is another argument in favor of a foundling.

LADY BRITOMART. Andrew: don't be aggravating. And don't be wicked. At present you are both.

UNDERSHAFT. This conversation is part of the Undershaft tradition, Biddy. Every Undershaft's wife has treated him to it ever since the house was founded. It is mere waste of breath. If the tradition be ever broken it will be for an abler man than Stephen.

LADY BRITOMART [pouting] Then go away.

UNDERSHAFT [deprecatory] Go away!

LADY BRITOMART. Yes: go away. If you will do nothing for Stephen, you are not wanted here. Go to your foundling, whoever he is; and look after him.

UNDERSHAFT. The fact is, Biddy—

LADY BRITOMART. Don't call me Biddy. I don't call you Andy.

UNDERSHAFT. I will not call my wife Britomart: it is not good sense. Seriously, my love, the Undershaft tradition has landed me in a difficulty. I am getting on in years; and my partner Lazarus has at last made a stand and insisted that the succession must be settled one way or the other; and of course he is quite right. You see, I haven't found a fit successor yet.

LADY BRITOMART [obstinately] There is Stephen.

UNDERSHAFT. That's just it: all the foundlings I can find are exactly like Stephen.

LADY BRITOMART. Andrew!!

UNDERSHAFT. I want a man with no relations and no schooling: that is, a man who would be out of the running altogether if he were not a strong man. And I can't find him. Every blessed foundling nowadays is snapped up in his infancy by Barnardo homes, or School Board officers, or Boards of Guardians; and if he shows the least ability, he is fastened on by schoolmasters; trained to win scholarships like a racehorse; crammed with secondhand ideas; drilled and disciplined in docility and what they call good taste; and lamed for life so that he is fit for nothing but teaching. If you want to keep the foundry in the family, you had better find an eligible foundling and marry him to Barbara.

LADY BRITOMART. Ah! Barbara! Your pet! You would sacrifice Stephen to Barbara.

UNDERSHAFT. Cheerfully. And you, my dear, would boil Barbara to make soup for Stephen.

LADY BRITOMART. Andrew: this is not a question of our likings and dislikings: it is a question of duty. It is your duty to make Stephen your successor.

UNDERSHAFT. Just as much as it is your duty to submit to your husband. Come, Biddy! these tricks of the governing class are of no use with me. I am one of the governing class myself; and it is waste of time giving tracts to a missionary. I have the power in this matter; and I am not to be humbugged into using it for your purposes.

LADY BRITOMART. Andrew: you can talk my head off; but you can't change wrong into right. And your tie is all on one side. Put it straight.

UNDERSHAFT [disconcerted] It won't stay unless it's pinned [he fumbles at it with childish grimaces]—

Stephen comes in.

STEPHEN. [at the door] I beg your pardon [about to retire].

LADY BRITOMART. No: come in, Stephen. [Stephen comes forward to his mother's writing table.]

UNDERSHAFT [not very cordially] Good afternoon.

STEPHEN. [coldly] Good afternoon.

UNDERSHAFT [to Lady Britomart] He knows all about the tradition, I suppose?

LADY BRITOMART. Yes. [To Stephen.] It is what I told you last night, Stephen.

UNDERSHAFT [sulkily] I understand you want to come into the cannon business.

STEPHEN. _I_ go into trade! Certainly not.

UNDERSHAFT [opening his eyes, greatly eased in mind and manner] Oh! in that case—!

LADY BRITOMART. Cannons are not trade, Stephen. They are enterprise.

STEPHEN. I have no intention of becoming a man of business in any sense. I have no capacity for business and no taste for it. I intend to devote myself to politics.

UNDERSHAFT [rising] My dear boy: this is an immense relief to me. And I trust it may prove an equally good thing for the country. I was afraid you would consider yourself disparaged and slighted. [He moves towards Stephen as if to shake hands with him].

LADY BRITOMART [rising and interposing] Stephen: I cannot allow you to throw away an enormous property like this.

STEPHEN. [stiffly] Mother: there must be an end of treating me as a child, if you please. [Lady Britomart recoils, deeply wounded by his tone]. Until last night I did not take your attitude seriously, because I did not think you meant it seriously. But I find now that you left me in the dark as to matters which you should have explained to me years ago. I am extremely hurt and offended. Any further discussion of my intentions had better take place with my father, as between one man and another.

LADY BRITOMART. Stephen! [She sits down again; and her eyes fill with tears].

UNDERSHAFT [with grave compassion] You see, my dear, it is only the big men who can be treated as children.

STEPHEN. I am sorry, mother, that you have forced me—

UNDERSHAFT [stopping him] Yes, yes, yes, yes: that's all right, Stephen. She won't interfere with you any more: your independence is achieved: you have won your latchkey. Don't rub it in; and above all, don't apologize. [He resumes his seat]. Now what about your future, as between one man and another—I beg your pardon, Biddy: as between two men and a woman.

LADY BRITOMART [who has pulled herself together strongly] I quite understand, Stephen. By all means go your own way if you feel strong enough. [Stephen sits down magisterially in the chair at the writing table with an air of affirming his majority].

UNDERSHAFT. It is settled that you do not ask for the succession to the cannon business.

STEPHEN. I hope it is settled that I repudiate the cannon business.

UNDERSHAFT. Come, come! Don't be so devilishly sulky: it's boyish. Freedom should be generous. Besides, I owe you a fair start in life in exchange for disinheriting you. You can't become prime minister all at once. Haven't you a turn for something? What about literature, art and so forth?

STEPHEN. I have nothing of the artist about me, either in faculty or character, thank Heaven!

UNDERSHAFT. A philosopher, perhaps? Eh?

STEPHEN. I make no such ridiculous pretension.

UNDERSHAFT. Just so. Well, there is the army, the navy, the Church, the Bar. The Bar requires some ability. What about the Bar?

STEPHEN. I have not studied law. And I am afraid I have not the necessary push—I believe that is the name barristers give to their vulgarity—for success in pleading.

UNDERSHAFT. Rather a difficult case, Stephen. Hardly anything left but the stage, is there? [Stephen makes an impatient movement]. Well, come! is there anything you know or care for?

STEPHEN. [rising and looking at him steadily] I know the difference between right and wrong.

UNDERSHAFT [hugely tickled] You don't say so! What! no capacity for business, no knowledge of law, no sympathy with art, no pretension to philosophy; only a simple knowledge of the secret that has puzzled all the philosophers, baffled all the lawyers, muddled all the men of business, and ruined most of the artists: the secret of right and wrong. Why, man, you're a genius, master of masters, a god! At twenty-four, too!

STEPHEN. [keeping his temper with difficulty] You are pleased to be facetious. I pretend to nothing more than any honorable English gentleman claims as his birthright [he sits down angrily].

UNDERSHAFT. Oh, that's everybody's birthright. Look at poor little Jenny Hill, the Salvation lassie! she would think you were laughing at her if you asked her to stand up in the street and teach grammar or geography or mathematics or even drawingroom dancing; but it never occurs to her to doubt that she can teach morals and religion. You are all alike, you respectable people. You can't tell me the bursting strain of a ten-inch gun, which is a very simple matter; but you all think you can tell me the bursting strain of a man under temptation. You daren't handle high explosives; but you're all ready to handle honesty and truth and justice and the whole duty of man, and kill one another at that game. What a country! what a world!

LADY BRITOMART [uneasily] What do you think he had better do, Andrew?

UNDERSHAFT. Oh, just what he wants to do. He knows nothing; and he thinks he knows everything. That points clearly to a political career. Get him a private secretaryship to someone who can get him an Under

Secretaryship; and then leave him alone. He will find his natural and proper place in the end on the Treasury bench.

STEPHEN. [springing up again] I am sorry, sir, that you force me to forget the respect due to you as my father. I am an Englishman; and I will not hear the Government of my country insulted. [He thrusts his hands in his pockets, and walks angrily across to the window].

UNDERSHAFT [with a touch of brutality] The government of your country! I am the government of your country: I, and Lazarus. Do you suppose that you and half a dozen amateurs like you, sitting in a row in that foolish gabble shop, can govern Undershaft and Lazarus? No, my friend: you will do what pays US. You will make war when it suits us, and keep peace when it doesn't. You will find out that trade requires certain measures when we have decided on those measures. When I want anything to keep my dividends up, you will discover that my want is a national need. When other people want something to keep my dividends down, you will call out the police and military. And in return you shall have the support and applause of my newspapers, and the delight of imagining that you are a great statesman. Government of your country! Be off with you, my boy, and play with your caucuses and leading articles and historic parties and great leaders and burning questions and the rest of your toys. I am going back to my counting house to pay the piper and call the tune.

STEPHEN. [actually smiling, and putting his hand on his father's shoulder with indulgent patronage] Really, my dear father, it is impossible to be angry with you. You don't know how absurd all this sounds to ME. You are very properly proud of having been industrious enough to make money; and it is greatly to your credit that you have made so much of it. But it has kept you in circles where you are valued for your money and deferred to for it, instead of in the doubtless very old fashioned and behind-the-times public school and university where I formed my habits of mind. It is natural for you to think that money governs England; but you must allow me to think I know better.

UNDERSHAFT. And what does govern England, pray?

STEPHEN. Character, father, character.

UNDERSHAFT. Whose character? Yours or mine?

STEPHEN. Neither yours nor mine, father, but the best elements in the English national character.

UNDERSHAFT. Stephen: I've found your profession for you. You're a born journalist. I'll start you with a hightoned weekly review. There!

Stephen goes to the smaller writing table and busies himself with his letters.

Sarah, Barbara, Lomax, and Cusins come in ready for walking. Barbara crosses the room to the window and looks out. Cusins drifts amiably to the armchair, and Lomax remains near the door, whilst Sarah comes to her mother.

SARAH. Go and get ready, mamma: the carriage is waiting. [Lady Britomart leaves the room.]

UNDERSHAFT [to Sarah] Good day, my dear. Good afternoon, Mr. Lomax.

LOMAX [vaguely] Ahdedoo.

UNDERSHAFT [to Cusins] quite well after last night, Euripides, eh?

CUSINS. As well as can be expected.

UNDERSHAFT. That's right. [To Barbara] So you are coming to see my death and devastation factory, Barbara?

BARBARA [at the window] You came yesterday to see my salvation factory. I promised you a return visit.

LOMAX [coming forward between Sarah and Undershaft] You'll find it awfully interesting. I've been through the Woolwich Arsenal; and it gives you a ripping feeling of security, you know, to think of the lot of beggars we could kill if it came to fighting. [To Undershaft, with sudden solemnity] Still, it must be rather an awful reflection for you, from the religious point of view as it were. You're getting on, you know, and all that.

SARAH. You don't mind Cholly's imbecility, papa, do you?

LOMAX [much taken aback] Oh I say!

UNDERSHAFT. Mr Lomax looks at the matter in a very proper spirit, my dear.

LOMAX. Just so. That's all I meant, I assure you.

SARAH. Are you coming, Stephen?

STEPHEN. Well, I am rather busy—er—[Magnanimously] Oh well, yes: I'll come. That is, if there is room for me.

UNDERSHAFT. I can take two with me in a little motor I am experimenting with for field use. You won't mind its being rather unfashionable. It's not painted yet; but it's bullet proof.

LOMAX [appalled at the prospect of confronting Wilton Crescent in an unpainted motor] Oh I say!

SARAH. The carriage for me, thank you. Barbara doesn't mind what she's seen in.

LOMAX. I say, Dolly old chap: do you really mind the car being a guy? Because of course if you do I'll go in it. Still—

CUSINS. I prefer it.

LOMAX. Thanks awfully, old man. Come, Sarah. [He hurries out to secure his seat in the carriage. Sarah follows him].

CUSINS. [moodily walking across to Lady Britomart's writing table] Why are we two coming to this Works Department of Hell? that is what I ask myself.

BARBARA. I have always thought of it as a sort of pit where lost creatures with blackened faces stirred up smoky fires and were driven and tormented by my father? Is it like that, dad?

UNDERSHAFT [scandalized] My dear! It is a spotlessly clean and beautiful hillside town.

CUSINS. With a Methodist chapel? Oh do say there's a Methodist chapel.

UNDERSHAFT. There are two: a primitive one and a sophisticated one. There is even an Ethical Society; but it is not much patronized, as my men are all strongly religious. In the High Explosives Sheds they object to the presence of Agnostics as unsafe.

CUSINS. And yet they don't object to you!

BARBARA. Do they obey all your orders?

UNDERSHAFT. I never give them any orders. When I speak to one of them it is "Well, Jones, is the baby doing well? and has Mrs Jones made a good recovery?" "Nicely, thank you, sir." And that's all.

CUSINS. But Jones has to be kept in order. How do you maintain discipline among your men?

UNDERSHAFT. I don't. They do. You see, the one thing Jones won't stand is any rebellion from the man under him, or any assertion of social equality between the wife of the man with 4 shillings a week less than himself and Mrs Jones! Of course they all rebel against me, theoretically. Practically, every man of them keeps the man just below him in his place. I never meddle with them. I never bully them. I don't even bully Lazarus. I say that certain things are to be done; but I don't order anybody to do them. I don't say, mind you, that there is no ordering about and snubbing and even bullying. The men snub the boys and order them about; the carmen snub the sweepers; the artisans snub the unskilled laborers; the foremen drive and bully both the laborers and artisans; the assistant engineers find fault with the foremen; the chief engineers drop on the assistants; the departmental managers worry the chiefs; and the clerks have tall hats and hymnbooks and keep up the social tone by refusing to associate on equal terms with anybody. The result is a colossal profit, which comes to me.

CUSINS [revolted] You really are a—well, what I was saying yesterday.

BARBARA. What was he saying yesterday?

UNDERSHAFT. Never mind, my dear. He thinks I have made you unhappy. Have I?

BARBARA. Do you think I can be happy in this vulgar silly dress? I! who have worn the uniform. Do you understand what you have done to me? Yesterday I had a man's soul in my hand. I set him in the way of life with his face to salvation. But when we took your money he turned back to drunkenness and derision. [With intense conviction] I will never forgive you that. If I had a child, and you destroyed its body with your explosives—if you murdered Dolly with your horrible guns—I could forgive you if my forgiveness would open the gates of heaven to you. But to take a human soul from me, and turn it into the soul of a wolf! that is worse than any murder.

UNDERSHAFT. Does my daughter despair so easily? Can you strike a man to the heart and leave no mark on him?

BARBARA [her face lighting up] Oh, you are right: he can never be lost now: where was my faith?

CUSINS. Oh, clever clever devil!

BARBARA. You may be a devil; but God speaks through you sometimes. [She takes her father's hands and kisses them]. You have given me back my happiness: I feel it deep down now, though my spirit is troubled.

UNDERSHAFT. You have learnt something. That always feels at first as if you had lost something.

BARBARA. Well, take me to the factory of death, and let me learn something more. There must be some truth or other behind all this frightful irony. Come, Dolly. [She goes out].

CUSINS. My guardian angel! [To Undershaft] Avaunt! [He follows Barbara].

STEPHEN. [quietly, at the writing table] You must not mind Cusins, father. He is a very amiable good fellow; but he is a Greek scholar and naturally a little eccentric.

UNDERSHAFT. Ah, quite so. Thank you, Stephen. Thank you. [He goes out].

Stephen smiles patronizingly; buttons his coat responsibly; and crosses the room to the door. Lady Britomart, dressed for out-of-doors, opens it before he reaches it. She looks round for the others; looks at Stephen; and turns to go without a word.

STEPHEN. [embarrassed] Mother—

LADY BRITOMART. Don't be apologetic, Stephen. And don't forget that you have outgrown your mother. [She goes out].

Perivale St Andrews lies between two Middlesex hills, half climbing the northern one. It is an almost smokeless town of white walls, roofs of narrow green slates or red tiles, tall trees, domes, campaniles, and slender chimney shafts, beautifully situated and beautiful in itself. The best view of it is obtained from the crest of a slope about half a mile to the east, where the high explosives are dealt with. The foundry lies hidden in the depths between, the tops of its chimneys sprouting like huge skittles into the middle distance. Across the crest runs a platform of concrete, with a parapet which suggests a fortification, because there is a huge cannon of the obsolete Woolwich Infant pattern peering across it at the town. The cannon is mounted on an experimental gun carriage: possibly the original model of the Undershaft disappearing rampart gun alluded to by Stephen. The parapet has a high step inside which serves as a seat.

Barbara is leaning over the parapet, looking towards the town. On her right is the cannon; on her left the end of a shed raised on piles, with a ladder of three or four steps up to the door, which opens outwards and has a little wooden landing at the threshold, with a fire bucket in the corner of the landing. The parapet stops short of the shed, leaving a gap which is the beginning of the path down the hill through the foundry to the town. Behind the cannon is a trolley carrying a huge conical bombshell, with a red band painted on it. Further from the parapet, on the same side, is a deck chair, near the door of an office, which, like the sheds, is of the lightest possible construction.

Cusins arrives by the path from the town.

BARBARA. Well?

CUSINS. Not a ray of hope. Everything perfect, wonderful, real. It only needs a cathedral to be a heavenly city instead of a hellish one.

BARBARA. Have you found out whether they have done anything for old Peter Shirley.

CUSINS. They have found him a job as gatekeeper and timekeeper. He's frightfully miserable. He calls the timekeeping brainwork, and says he isn't used to it; and his gate lodge is so splendid that he's ashamed to use the rooms, and skulks in the scullery.

BARBARA. Poor Peter!

Stephen arrives from the town. He carries a fieldglass.

STEPHEN. [enthusiastically] Have you two seen the place? Why did you leave us?

CUSINS. I wanted to see everything I was not intended to see; and Barbara wanted to make the men talk.

STEPHEN. Have you found anything discreditable?

CUSINS. No. They call him Dandy Andy and are proud of his being a cunning old rascal; but it's all horribly, frightfully, immorally, unanswerably perfect.

Sarah arrives.

SARAH. Heavens! what a place! [She crosses to the trolley]. Did you see the nursing home!? [She sits down on the shell].

STEPHEN. Did you see the libraries and schools!?

SARAH. Did you see the ballroom and the banqueting chamber in the Town Hall!?

STEPHEN. Have you gone into the insurance fund, the pension fund, the building society, the various applications of co-operation!?

Undershaft comes from the office, with a sheaf of telegrams in his hands.

UNDERSHAFT. Well, have you seen everything? I'm sorry I was called away. [Indicating the telegrams] News from Manchuria.

STEPHEN. Good news, I hope.

UNDERSHAFT. Very.

STEPHEN. Another Japanese victory?

UNDERSHAFT. Oh, I don't know. Which side wins does not concern us here. No: the good news is that the aerial battleship is a tremendous success. At the first trial it has wiped out a fort with three hundred soldiers in it.

CUSINS [from the platform] Dummy soldiers?

UNDERSHAFT. No: the real thing. [Cusins and Barbara exchange glances. Then Cusins sits on the step and buries his face in his hands. Barbara gravely lays her hand on his shoulder, and he looks up at her in a sort of whimsical desperation]. Well, Stephen, what do you think of the place?

STEPHEN. Oh, magnificent. A perfect triumph of organization. Frankly, my dear father, I have been a fool: I had no idea of what it all meant—of the wonderful forethought, the power of organization, the administrative capacity, the financial genius, the colossal capital it represents. I have been repeating to myself as I came through your streets "Peace hath her victories no less renowned than War." I have only one misgiving about it all.

UNDERSHAFT. Out with it.

STEPHEN. Well, I cannot help thinking that all this provision for every want of your workmen may sap their independence and weaken their sense of responsibility. And greatly as we enjoyed our tea at that splendid restaurant—how they gave us all that luxury and cake and jam and cream for threepence I really cannot imagine!— still you must remember that restaurants break up home life. Look at the continent, for instance! Are you sure so much pampering is really good for the men's characters?

UNDERSHAFT. Well you see, my dear boy, when you are organizing civilization you have to make up your mind whether trouble and anxiety are good things or not. If you decide that they are, then, I take it, you simply don't organize civilization; and there you are, with trouble and anxiety enough to make us all angels! But if you decide the other way, you may as well go through with it. However, Stephen, our characters are safe here. A sufficient dose of anxiety is always provided by the fact that we may be blown to smithereens at any moment.

SARAH. By the way, papa, where do you make the explosives?

UNDERSHAFT. In separate little sheds, like that one. When one of them blows up, it costs very little; and only the people quite close to it are killed.

Stephen, who is quite close to it, looks at it rather scaredly, and moves away quickly to the cannon. At the same moment the door of the shed is thrown abruptly open; and a foreman in overalls and list slippers comes out on the little landing and holds the door open for Lomax, who appears in the doorway.

LOMAX [with studied coolness] My good fellow: you needn't get into a state of nerves. Nothing's going to happen to you; and I suppose it wouldn't be the end of the world if anything did. A little bit of British pluck is what you want, old chap. [He descends and strolls across to Sarah].

UNDERSHAFT [to the foreman] Anything wrong, Bilton?

BILTON [with ironic calm] Gentleman walked into the high explosives shed and lit a cigaret, sir: that's all.

UNDERSHAFT. Ah, quite so. [To Lomax] Do you happen to remember what you did with the match?

LOMAX. Oh come! I'm not a fool. I took jolly good care to blow it out before I chucked it away.

BILTON. The top of it was red hot inside, sir.

LOMAX. Well, suppose it was! I didn't chuck it into any of your messes.

UNDERSHAFT. Think no more of it, Mr Lomax. By the way, would you mind lending me your matches?

LOMAX [offering his box] Certainly.

UNDERSHAFT. Thanks. [He pockets the matches].

LOMAX [lecturing to the company generally] You know, these high explosives don't go off like gunpowder, except when they're in a gun. When they're spread loose, you can put a match to them without the least risk: they just burn quietly like a bit of paper. [Warming to the scientific interest of the subject] Did you know that Undershaft? Have you ever tried?

UNDERSHAFT. Not on a large scale, Mr Lomax. Bilton will give you a sample of gun cotton when you are leaving if you ask him. You can experiment with it at home. [Bilton looks puzzled].

SARAH. Bilton will do nothing of the sort, papa. I suppose it's your business to blow up the Russians and Japs; but you might really stop short of blowing up poor Cholly. [Bilton gives it up and retires into the shed].

LOMAX. My ownest, there is no danger. [He sits beside her on the shell].

Lady Britomart arrives from the town with a bouquet.

LADY BRITOMART [coming impetuously between Undershaft and the deck chair] Andrew: you shouldn't have let me see this place.

UNDERSHAFT. Why, my dear?

LADY BRITOMART. Never mind why: you shouldn't have: that's all. To think of all that [indicating the town] being yours! and that you have kept it to yourself all these years!

UNDERSHAFT. It does not belong to me. I belong to it. It is the Undershaft inheritance.

LADY BRITOMART. It is not. Your ridiculous cannons and that noisy banging foundry may be the Undershaft inheritance; but all that plate and linen, all that furniture and those houses and orchards and gardens belong to us. They belong to me: they are not a man's business. I won't give them up. You must be out of your senses to throw them all away; and if you persist in such folly, I will call in a doctor.

UNDERSHAFT [stooping to smell the bouquet] Where did you get the flowers, my dear?

LADY BRITOMART. Your men presented them to me in your William Morris Labor Church.

CUSINS [springing up] Oh! It needed only that. A Labor Church!

LADY BRITOMART. Yes, with Morris's words in mosaic letters ten feet high round the dome. NO MAN IS GOOD ENOUGH TO BE ANOTHER MAN'S MASTER. The cynicism of it!

UNDERSHAFT. It shocked the men at first, I am afraid. But now they take no more notice of it than of the ten commandments in church.

LADY BRITOMART. Andrew: you are trying to put me off the subject of the inheritance by profane jokes. Well, you shan't. I don't ask it any longer for Stephen he has inherited far too much of your perversity to be fit for it. But Barbara has rights as well as Stephen. Why should not Adolphus succeed to the inheritance? I could manage the town for him; and he can look after the cannons, if they are really necessary.

UNDERSHAFT. I should ask nothing better if Adolphus were a foundling. He is exactly the sort of new blood that is wanted in English business. But he's not a foundling; and there's an end of it.

CUSINS [diplomatically] Not quite. [They all turn and stare at him. He comes from the platform past the shed to Undershaft]. I think—Mind! I am not committing myself in any way as to my future course—but I think the foundling difficulty can be got over.

UNDERSHAFT. What do you mean?

CUSINS. Well, I have something to say which is in the nature of a confession.

SARAH. {Lady Britomart. { Confession! Barbara. { Stephen. {

LOMAX. Oh I say!

CUSINS. Yes, a confession. Listen, all. Until I met Barbara I thought myself in the main an honorable, truthful man, because I wanted the approval of my conscience more than I wanted anything else. But the moment I saw Barbara, I wanted her far more than the approval of my conscience.

LADY BRITOMART. Adolphus!

CUSINS. It is true. You accused me yourself, Lady Brit, of joining the Army to worship Barbara; and so I did. She bought my soul like a flower at a street corner; but she bought it for herself.

UNDERSHAFT. What! Not for Dionysos or another?

CUSINS. Dionysos and all the others are in herself. I adored what was divine in her, and was therefore a true worshipper. But I was romantic about her too. I thought she was a woman of the people, and that a marriage with a professor of Greek would be far beyond the wildest social ambitions of her rank.

LADY BRITOMART. Adolphus!!

LOMAX. Oh I say!!!

CUSINS. When I learnt the horrible truth—

LADY BRITOMART. What do you mean by the horrible truth, pray?

CUSINS. That she was enormously rich; that her grandfather was an earl; that her father was the Prince of Darkness—

UNDERSHAFT. Chut!

CUSINS.—and that I was only an adventurer trying to catch a rich wife, then I stooped to deceive about my birth.

LADY BRITOMART. Your birth! Now Adolphus, don't dare to make up a wicked story for the sake of these wretched cannons. Remember: I have seen photographs of your parents; and the Agent General for South Western Australia knows them personally and has assured me that they are most respectable married people.

CUSINS. So they are in Australia; but here they are outcasts. Their marriage is legal in Australia, but not in England. My mother is my father's deceased wife's sister; and in this island I am consequently a foundling. [Sensation]. Is the subterfuge good enough, Machiavelli?

UNDERSHAFT [thoughtfully] Biddy: this may be a way out of the difficulty.

LADY BRITOMART. Stuff! A man can't make cannons any the better for being his own cousin instead of his proper self [she sits down in the deck chair with a bounce that expresses her downright contempt for their casuistry.]

UNDERSHAFT [to Cusins] You are an educated man. That is against the tradition.

CUSINS. Once in ten thousand times it happens that the schoolboy is a born master of what they try to teach him. Greek has not destroyed my mind: it has nourished it. Besides, I did not learn it at an English public school.

UNDERSHAFT. Hm! Well, I cannot afford to be too particular: you have cornered the foundling market. Let it pass. You are eligible, Euripides: you are eligible.

BARBARA [coming from the platform and interposing between Cusins and Undershaft] Dolly: yesterday morning, when Stephen told us all about the tradition, you became very silent; and you have been strange and excited ever since. Were you thinking of your birth then?

CUSINS. When the finger of Destiny suddenly points at a man in the middle of his breakfast, it makes him thoughtful. [Barbara turns away sadly and stands near her mother, listening perturbedly].

UNDERSHAFT. Aha! You have had your eye on the business, my young friend, have you?

CUSINS. Take care! There is an abyss of moral horror between me and your accursed aerial battleships.

UNDERSHAFT. Never mind the abyss for the present. Let us settle the practical details and leave your final decision open. You know that you will have to change your name. Do you object to that?

CUSINS. Would any man named Adolphus—any man called Dolly!—object to be called something else?

UNDERSHAFT. Good. Now, as to money! I propose to treat you handsomely from the beginning. You shall start at a thousand a year.

CUSINS. [with sudden heat, his spectacles twinkling with mischief] A thousand! You dare offer a miserable thousand to the son-in-law of a millionaire! No, by Heavens, Machiavelli! you shall not cheat me. You cannot do without me; and I can do without you. I must have two thousand five hundred a year for two years. At the end of that time, if I am a failure, I go. But if I am a success, and stay on, you must give me the other five thousand.

UNDERSHAFT. What other five thousand?

CUSINS. To make the two years up to five thousand a year. The two thousand five hundred is only half pay in case I should turn out a failure. The third year I must have ten per cent on the profits.

UNDERSHAFT [taken aback] Ten per cent! Why, man, do you know what my profits are?

CUSINS. Enormous, I hope: otherwise I shall require twenty-five per cent.

UNDERSHAFT. But, Mr Cusins, this is a serious matter of business. You are not bringing any capital into the concern.

CUSINS. What! no capital! Is my mastery of Greek no capital? Is my access to the subtlest thought, the loftiest poetry yet attained by humanity, no capital? my character! my intellect! my life! my career! what Barbara calls my soul! are these no capital? Say another word; and I double my salary.

UNDERSHAFT. Be reasonable—

CUSINS [peremptorily] Mr Undershaft: you have my terms. Take them or leave them.

UNDERSHAFT [recovering himself] Very well. I note your terms; and I offer you half.

CUSINS [disgusted] Half!

UNDERSHAFT [firmly] Half.

CUSINS. You call yourself a gentleman; and you offer me half!!

UNDERSHAFT. I do not call myself a gentleman; but I offer you half.

CUSINS. This to your future partner! your successor! your son-in-law!

BARBARA. You are selling your own soul, Dolly, not mine. Leave me out of the bargain, please.

UNDERSHAFT. Come! I will go a step further for Barbara's sake. I will give you three fifths; but that is my last word.

CUSINS. Done!

LOMAX. Done in the eye. Why, I only get eight hundred, you know.

CUSINS. By the way, Mac, I am a classical scholar, not an arithmetical one. Is three fifths more than half or less?

UNDERSHAFT. More, of course.

CUSINS. I would have taken two hundred and fifty. How you can succeed in business when you are willing to pay all that money to a University don who is obviously not worth a junior clerk's wages!—well! What will Lazarus say?

UNDERSHAFT. Lazarus is a gentle romantic Jew who cares for nothing but string quartets and stalls at fashionable theatres. He will get the credit of your rapacity in money matters, as he has hitherto had the credit of mine. You are a shark of the first order, Euripides. So much the better for the firm!

BARBARA. Is the bargain closed, Dolly? Does your soul belong to him now?

CUSINS. No: the price is settled: that is all. The real tug of war is still to come. What about the moral question?

LADY BRITOMART. There is no moral question in the matter at all, Adolphus. You must simply sell cannons and weapons to people whose cause is right and just, and refuse them to foreigners and criminals.

UNDERSHAFT [determinedly] No: none of that. You must keep the true faith of an Armorer, or you don't come in here.

CUSINS. What on earth is the true faith of an Armorer?

UNDERSHAFT. To give arms to all men who offer an honest price for them, without respect of persons or principles: to aristocrat and republican, to Nihilist and Tsar, to Capitalist and Socialist, to Protestant and Catholic, to burglar and policeman, to black man white man and yellow man, to all sorts and conditions, all nationalities, all faiths, all follies, all causes and all crimes. The first Undershaft wrote up in his shop IF GOD GAVE THE HAND, LET NOT MAN WITHHOLD THE SWORD. The second wrote up ALL HAVE THE RIGHT TO FIGHT: NONE HAVE THE RIGHT TO JUDGE. The third wrote up TO MAN THE WEAPON: TO HEAVEN THE VICTORY. The fourth had no literary turn; so he did not write up anything; but he sold cannons to Napoleon under the nose of George the Third. The fifth wrote up PEACE SHALL NOT PREVAIL SAVE WITH A SWORD IN HER HAND. The sixth, my master, was the best of all. He wrote up NOTHING IS EVER DONE IN THIS WORLD UNTIL MEN ARE PREPARED TO KILL ONE ANOTHER IF IT IS NOT DONE. After that, there was nothing left for the seventh to say. So he wrote up, simply, UNASHAMED.

CUSINS. My good Machiavelli, I shall certainly write something up on the wall; only, as I shall write it in Greek, you won't be able to read it. But as to your Armorer's faith, if I take my neck out of the noose of my own morality I am not going to put it into the noose of yours. I shall sell cannons to whom I please and refuse them to whom I please. So there!

UNDERSHAFT. From the moment when you become Andrew Undershaft, you will never do as you please again. Don't come here lusting for power, young man.

CUSINS. If power were my aim I should not come here for it. YOU have no power.

UNDERSHAFT. None of my own, certainly.

CUSINS. I have more power than you, more will. You do not drive this place: it drives you. And what drives the place?

UNDERSHAFT [enigmatically] A will of which I am a part.

BARBARA [startled] Father! Do you know what you are saying; or are you laying a snare for my soul?

CUSINS. Don't listen to his metaphysics, Barbara. The place is driven by the most rascally part of society, the money hunters, the pleasure hunters, the military promotion hunters; and he is their slave.

UNDERSHAFT. Not necessarily. Remember the Armorer's Faith. I will take an order from a good man as cheerfully as from a bad one. If you good people prefer preaching and shirking to buying my weapons and fighting the rascals, don't blame me. I can make cannons: I cannot make courage and conviction. Bah! You tire me, Euripides, with your morality mongering. Ask Barbara: SHE understands. [He suddenly takes Barbara's hands, and looks powerfully into her eyes]. Tell him, my love, what power really means.

BARBARA [hypnotized] Before I joined the Salvation Army, I was in my own power; and the consequence was that I never knew what to do with myself. When I joined it, I had not time enough for all the things I had to do.

UNDERSHAFT [approvingly] Just so. And why was that, do you suppose?

BARBARA. Yesterday I should have said, because I was in the power of God. [She resumes her self-possession, withdrawing her hands from his with a power equal to his own]. But you came and showed me that I was in the power of Bodger and Undershaft. Today I feel—oh! how can I put it into words? Sarah: do you remember the earthquake at Cannes, when we were little children?—how little the surprise of the first shock mattered compared to the dread and horror of waiting for the second? That is how I feel in this place today. I stood on the rock I thought eternal; and without a word of warning it reeled and crumbled under me. I was safe with an infinite wisdom watching me, an army marching to Salvation with me; and in a moment, at a stroke of your pen in a cheque book, I stood alone; and the heavens were empty. That was the first shock of the earthquake: I am waiting for the second.

UNDERSHAFT. Come, come, my daughter! Don't make too much of your little tinpot tragedy. What do we do here when we spend years of work and thought and thousands of pounds of solid cash on a new gun or an aerial battleship that turns out just a hairsbreadth wrong after all? Scrap it. Scrap it without wasting another hour or another pound on it. Well, you have made for yourself something that you call a morality or a religion or what not. It doesn't fit the facts. Well, scrap it. Scrap it and get one that does fit. That is what is wrong with the world at present. It scraps its obsolete steam engines and dynamos; but it won't scrap its old prejudices and its old moralities and its old religions and its old political constitutions. What's the result? In machinery it does very well; but in morals and religion and politics it is working at a loss that brings it nearer bankruptcy every year. Don't persist in that folly. If your old religion broke down yesterday, get a newer and a better one for tomorrow.

BARBARA. Oh how gladly I would take a better one to my soul! But you offer me a worse one. [Turning on him with sudden vehemence]. Justify yourself: show me some light through the darkness of this dreadful place, with its beautifully clean workshops, and respectable workmen, and model homes.

UNDERSHAFT. Cleanliness and respectability do not need justification, Barbara: they justify themselves. I see no darkness here, no dreadfulness. In your Salvation shelter I saw poverty, misery, cold and hunger. You gave them bread and treacle and dreams of heaven. I give from thirty shillings a week to twelve thousand a year. They find their own dreams; but I look after the drainage.

BARBARA. And their souls?

UNDERSHAFT. I save their souls just as I saved yours.

BARBARA [revolted] You saved my soul! What do you mean?

UNDERSHAFT. I fed you and clothed you and housed you. I took care that you should have money enough to live handsomely—more than enough; so that you could be wasteful, careless, generous. That saved your soul from the seven deadly sins.

BARBARA [bewildered] The seven deadly sins!

UNDERSHAFT. Yes, the deadly seven. [Counting on his fingers] Food, clothing, firing, rent, taxes, respectability and children. Nothing can lift those seven millstones from Man's neck but money; and the spirit cannot soar until the millstones are lifted. I lifted them from your spirit. I enabled Barbara to become Major Barbara; and I saved her from the crime of poverty.

CUSINS. Do you call poverty a crime?

UNDERSHAFT. The worst of crimes. All the other crimes are virtues beside it: all the other dishonors are chivalry itself by comparison. Poverty blights whole cities; spreads horrible pestilences; strikes dead the very souls of all who come within sight, sound or smell of it. What you call crime is nothing: a murder here and a theft there, a blow now and a curse then: what do they matter? they are only the accidents and illnesses of life: there are not fifty genuine professional criminals in London. But there are millions of poor people, abject people, dirty people, ill fed, ill clothed people. They poison us morally and physically: they kill the happiness of society: they force us to do away with our own liberties and to organize unnatural cruelties for fear they should rise against us and drag us down into their abyss. Only fools fear crime: we all fear poverty. Pah! [turning on Barbara] you talk of your half-saved ruffian in West Ham: you accuse me of dragging his soul back to perdition. Well, bring him to me here; and I will drag his soul back again to salvation for you. Not by words and dreams; but by thirty-eight shillings a week, a sound house in a handsome street, and a permanent job. In three weeks he will have a fancy waistcoat; in three months a tall hat and a chapel sitting; before the end of the year he will shake hands with a duchess at a Primrose League meeting, and join the Conservative Party.

BARBARA. And will he be the better for that?

UNDERSHAFT. You know he will. Don't be a hypocrite, Barbara. He will be better fed, better housed, better clothed, better behaved; and his children will be pounds heavier and bigger. That will be better than an American cloth mattress in a shelter, chopping firewood, eating bread and treacle, and being forced to kneel down from time to time to thank heaven for it: knee drill, I think you call it. It is cheap work converting starving men with a Bible in one hand and a slice of bread in the other. I will undertake to convert West Ham to Mahometanism on the same terms. Try your hand on my men: their souls are hungry because their bodies are full.

BARBARA. And leave the east end to starve?

UNDERSHAFT [his energetic tone dropping into one of bitter and brooding remembrance] I was an east ender. I moralized and starved until one day I swore that I would be a fullfed free man at all costs—that nothing should stop me except a bullet, neither reason nor morals nor the lives of other men. I said "Thou shalt starve ere I starve";

and with that word I became free and great. I was a dangerous man until I had my will: now I am a useful, beneficent, kindly person. That is the history of most self-made millionaires, I fancy. When it is the history of every Englishman we shall have an England worth living in.

LADY BRITOMART. Stop making speeches, Andrew. This is not the place for them.

UNDERSHAFT [punctured] My dear: I have no other means of conveying my ideas.

LADY BRITOMART. Your ideas are nonsense. You got oil because you were selfish and unscrupulous.

UNDERSHAFT. Not at all. I had the strongest scruples about poverty and starvation. Your moralists are quite unscrupulous about both: they make virtues of them. I had rather be a thief than a pauper. I had rather be a murderer than a slave. I don't want to be either; but if you force the alternative on me, then, by Heaven, I'll choose the braver and more moral one. I hate poverty and slavery worse than any other crimes whatsoever. And let me tell you this. Poverty and slavery have stood up for centuries to your sermons and leading articles: they will not stand up to my machine guns. Don't preach at them: don't reason with them. Kill them.

BARBARA. Killing. Is that your remedy for everything?

UNDERSHAFT. It is the final test of conviction, the only lever strong enough to overturn a social system, the only way of saying Must. Let six hundred and seventy fools loose in the street; and three policemen can scatter them. But huddle them together in a certain house in Westminster; and let them go through certain ceremonies and call themselves certain names until at last they get the courage to kill; and your six hundred and seventy fools become a government. Your pious mob fills up ballot papers and imagines it is governing its masters; but the ballot paper that really governs is the paper that has a bullet wrapped up in it.

CUSINS. That is perhaps why, like most intelligent people, I never vote.

UNDERSHAFT Vote! Bah! When you vote, you only change the names of the cabinet. When you shoot, you pull down governments, inaugurate new epochs, abolish old orders and set up new. Is that historically true, Mr Learned Man, or is it not?

CUSINS. It is historically true. I loathe having to admit it. I repudiate your sentiments. I abhor your nature. I defy you in every possible way. Still, it is true. But it ought not to be true.

UNDERSHAFT. Ought, ought, ought, ought, ought! Are you going to spend your life saying ought, like the rest of our moralists? Turn your oughts into shalls, man. Come and make explosives with me. Whatever can blow men up can blow society up. The history of the world is the history of those who had courage enough to embrace this truth. Have you the courage to embrace it, Barbara?

LADY BRITOMART. Barbara, I positively forbid you to listen to your father's abominable wickedness. And you, Adolphus, ought to know better than to go about saying that wrong things are true. What does it matter whether they are true if they are wrong?

UNDERSHAFT. What does it matter whether they are wrong if they are true?

LADY BRITOMART [rising] Children: come home instantly. Andrew: I am exceedingly sorry I allowed you to call on us. You are wickeder than ever. Come at once.

BARBARA [shaking her head] It's no use running away from wicked people, mamma.

LADY BRITOMART. It is every use. It shows your disapprobation of them.

BARBARA. It does not save them.

LADY BRITOMART. I can see that you are going to disobey me. Sarah: are you coming home or are you not?

SARAH. I daresay it's very wicked of papa to make cannons; but I don't think I shall cut him on that account.

LOMAX [pouring oil on the troubled waters] The fact is, you know, there is a certain amount of tosh about this notion of wickedness. It doesn't work. You must look at facts. Not that I would say a word in favor of anything wrong; but then, you see, all sorts of chaps are always doing all sorts of things; and we have to fit them in somehow, don't you know. What I mean is that you can't go cutting everybody; and that's about what it comes to. [Their rapt attention to his eloquence makes him nervous] Perhaps I don't make myself clear.

LADY BRITOMART. You are lucidity itself, Charles. Because Andrew is successful and has plenty of money to give to Sarah, you will flatter him and encourage him in his wickedness.

LOMAX [unruffled] Well, where the carcase is, there will the eagles be gathered, don't you know. [To Undershaft] Eh? What?

UNDERSHAFT. Precisely. By the way, may I call you Charles?

LOMAX. Delighted. Cholly is the usual ticket.

UNDERSHAFT [to Lady Britomart] Biddy—

LADY BRITOMART [violently] Don't dare call me Biddy. Charles Lomax: you are a fool. Adolphus Cusins: you are a Jesuit. Stephen: you are a prig. Barbara: you are a lunatic. Andrew: you are a vulgar tradesman. Now you all know my opinion; and my conscience is clear, at all events [she sits down again with a vehemence that almost wrecks the chair].

UNDERSHAFT. My dear, you are the incarnation of morality. [She snorts]. Your conscience is clear and your duty done when you have called everybody names. Come, Euripides! it is getting late; and we all want to get home. Make up your mind.

CUSINS. Understand this, you old demon—

LADY BRITOMART. Adolphus!

UNDERSHAFT. Let him alone, Biddy. Proceed, Euripides.

CUSINS. You have me in a horrible dilemma. I want Barbara.

UNDERSHAFT. Like all young men, you greatly exaggerate the difference between one young woman and another.

BARBARA. Quite true, Dolly.

CUSINS. I also want to avoid being a rascal.

UNDERSHAFT [with biting contempt] You lust for personal righteousness, for self-approval, for what you call a good conscience, for what Barbara calls salvation, for what I call patronizing people who are not so lucky as yourself.

CUSINS. I do not: all the poet in me recoils from being a good man. But there are things in me that I must reckon with: pity—

UNDERSHAFT. Pity! The scavenger of misery.

CUSINS. Well, love.

UNDERSHAFT. I know. You love the needy and the outcast: you love the oppressed races, the negro, the Indian ryot, the Pole, the Irishman. Do you love the Japanese? Do you love the Germans? Do you love the English?

CUSINS. No. Every true Englishman detests the English. We are the wickedest nation on earth; and our success is a moral horror.

UNDERSHAFT. That is what comes of your gospel of love, is it?

CUSINS. May I not love even my father-in-law?

UNDERSHAFT. Who wants your love, man? By what right do you take the liberty of offering it to me? I will have your due heed and respect, or I will kill you. But your love! Damn your impertinence!

CUSINS [grinning] I may not be able to control my affections, Mac.

UNDERSHAFT. You are fencing, Euripides. You are weakening: your grip is slipping. Come! try your last weapon. Pity and love have broken in your hand: forgiveness is still left.

CUSINS. No: forgiveness is a beggar's refuge. I am with you there: we must pay our debts.

UNDERSHAFT. Well said. Come! you will suit me. Remember the words of Plato.

CUSINS [starting] Plato! You dare quote Plato to me!

UNDERSHAFT. Plato says, my friend, that society cannot be saved until either the Professors of Greek take to making gunpowder, or else the makers of gunpowder become Professors of Greek.

CUSINS. Oh, tempter, cunning tempter!

UNDERSHAFT. Come! choose, man, choose.

CUSINS. But perhaps Barbara will not marry me if I make the wrong choice.

BARBARA. Perhaps not.

CUSINS [desperately perplexed] You hear—

BARBARA. Father: do you love nobody?

UNDERSHAFT. I love my best friend.

LADY BRITOMART. And who is that, pray?

UNDERSHAFT. My bravest enemy. That is the man who keeps me up to the mark.

CUSINS. You know, the creature is really a sort of poet in his way. Suppose he is a great man, after all!

UNDERSHAFT. Suppose you stop talking and make up your mind, my young friend.

CUSINS. But you are driving me against my nature. I hate war.

UNDERSHAFT. Hatred is the coward's revenge for being intimidated. Dare you make war on war? Here are the means: my friend Mr Lomax is sitting on them.

LOMAX [springing up] Oh I say! You don't mean that this thing is loaded, do you? My ownest: come off it.

SARAH [sitting placidly on the shell] If I am to be blown up, the more thoroughly it is done the better. Don't fuss, Cholly.

LOMAX [to Undershaft, strongly remonstrant] Your own daughter, you know.

UNDERSHAFT. So I see. [To Cusins] Well, my friend, may we expect you here at six tomorrow morning?

CUSINS [firmly] Not on any account. I will see the whole establishment blown up with its own dynamite before I will get up at five. My hours are healthy, rational hours eleven to five.

UNDERSHAFT. Come when you please: before a week you will come at six and stay until I turn you out for the sake of your health. [Calling] Bilton! [He turns to Lady Britomart, who rises]. My dear: let us leave these two young people to themselves for a moment. [Bilton comes from the shed]. I am going to take you through the gun cotton shed.

BILTON [barring the way] You can't take anything explosive in here, Sir.

LADY BRITOMART. What do you mean? Are you alluding to me?

BILTON [unmoved] No, ma'am. Mr Undershaft has the other gentleman's matches in his pocket.

Lady Britomart [abruptly] Oh! I beg your pardon. [She goes into the shed].

UNDERSHAFT. Quite right, Bilton, quite right: here you are. [He gives Bilton the box of matches]. Come, Stephen. Come, Charles. Bring Sarah. [He passes into the shed].

Bilton opens the box and deliberately drops the matches into the fire-bucket.

LOMAX. Oh I say! [Bilton stolidly hands him the empty box]. Infernal nonsense! Pure scientific ignorance! [He goes in].

SARAH. Am I all right, Bilton?

BILTON. You'll have to put on list slippers, miss: that's all. We've got em inside. [She goes in].

STEPHEN. [very seriously to Cusins] Dolly, old fellow, think. Think before you decide. Do you feel that you are a sufficiently practical man? It is a huge undertaking, an enormous responsibility. All this mass of business will be Greek to you.

CUSINS. Oh, I think it will be much less difficult than Greek.

STEPHEN. Well, I just want to say this before I leave you to yourselves. Don't let anything I have said about right and wrong prejudice you against this great chance in life. I have satisfied myself that the business is one of the highest character and a credit to our country. [Emotionally] I am very proud of my father. I—[Unable to proceed, he presses Cusins' hand and goes hastily into the shed, followed by Bilton].

Barbara and Cusins, left alone together, look at one another silently.

CUSINS. Barbara: I am going to accept this offer.

BARBARA. I thought you would.

CUSINS. You understand, don't you, that I had to decide without consulting you. If I had thrown the burden of the choice on you, you would sooner or later have despised me for it.

BARBARA. Yes: I did not want you to sell your soul for me any more than for this inheritance.

CUSINS. It is not the sale of my soul that troubles me: I have sold it too often to care about that. I have sold it for a professorship. I have sold it for an income. I have sold it to escape being imprisoned for refusing to pay taxes for hangmen's ropes and unjust wars and things that I abhor. What is all human conduct but the daily and hourly sale of our souls for trifles? What I am now selling it for is neither money nor position nor comfort, but for reality and for power.

BARBARA. You know that you will have no power, and that he has none.

CUSINS. I know. It is not for myself alone. I want to make power for the world.

BARBARA. I want to make power for the world too; but it must be spiritual power.

CUSINS. I think all power is spiritual: these cannons will not go off by themselves. I have tried to make spiritual power by teaching Greek. But the world can never be really touched by a dead language and a dead civilization. The people must have power; and the people cannot have Greek. Now the power that is made here can be wielded by all men.

BARBARA. Power to burn women's houses down and kill their sons and tear their husbands to pieces.

CUSINS. You cannot have power for good without having power for evil too. Even mother's milk nourishes murderers as well as heroes. This power which only tears men's bodies to pieces has never been so horribly abused as the intellectual power, the imaginative power, the poetic, religious power that can enslave men's souls. As a teacher of Greek I gave the intellectual man weapons against the common man. I now want to give the common man weapons against the intellectual man. I love the common people. I want to arm them against the lawyer, the doctor, the priest, the literary man, the professor, the artist, and the politician, who, once in authority, are the most dangerous, disastrous, and tyrannical of all the fools, rascals, and impostors. I want a democratic power strong enough to force the intellectual oligarchy to use its genius for the general good or else perish.

BARBARA. Is there no higher power than that [pointing to the shell]?

CUSINS. Yes: but that power can destroy the higher powers just as a tiger can destroy a man: therefore man must master that power first. I admitted this when the Turks and Greeks were last at war. My best pupil went out to fight for Hellas. My parting gift to him was not a copy of Plato's Republic, but a revolver and a hundred Undershaft cartridges. The blood of every Turk he shot—if he shot any—is on my head as well as on Undershaft's. That act committed me to this place for ever. Your father's challenge has beaten me. Dare I make war on war? I dare. I must. I will. And now, is it all over between us?

BARBARA [touched by his evident dread of her answer] Silly baby Dolly! How could it be?

CUSINS [overjoyed] Then you—you—you— Oh for my drum! [He flourishes imaginary drumsticks].

BARBARA [angered by his levity] Take care, Dolly, take care. Oh, if only I could get away from you and from father and from it all! if I could have the wings of a dove and fly away to heaven!

CUSINS. And leave me!

BARBARA. Yes, you, and all the other naughty mischievous children of men. But I can't. I was happy in the Salvation Army for a moment. I escaped from the world into a paradise of enthusiasm and prayer and soul saving; but the moment our money ran short, it all came back to Bodger: it was he who saved our people: he, and the Prince of Darkness, my papa. Undershaft and Bodger: their hands stretch everywhere: when we feed a starving fellow creature, it is with their bread, because there is no other bread; when we tend the sick, it is in the hospitals they endow; if we turn from the churches they build, we must kneel on the stones of the streets they pave. As long as that lasts, there is no getting away from them. Turning our backs on Bodger and Undershaft is turning our backs on life.

CUSINS. I thought you were determined to turn your back on the wicked side of life.

BARBARA. There is no wicked side: life is all one. And I never wanted to shirk my share in whatever evil must be endured, whether it be sin or suffering. I wish I could cure you of middle-class ideas, Dolly.

CUSINS [gasping] Middle cl—! A snub! A social snub to ME! from the daughter of a foundling!

BARBARA. That is why I have no class, Dolly: I come straight out of the heart of the whole people. If I were middle-class I should turn my back on my father's business; and we should both live in an artistic drawingroom, with you reading the reviews in one corner, and I in the other at the piano, playing Schumann: both very superior persons, and neither of us a bit of use. Sooner than that, I would sweep out the guncotton shed, or be one of Bodger's barmaids. Do you know what would have happened if you had refused papa's offer?

CUSINS. I wonder!

BARBARA. I should have given you up and married the man who accepted it. After all, my dear old mother has more sense than any of you. I felt like her when I saw this place—felt that I must have it—that never, never, never could I let it go; only she thought it was the houses and the kitchen ranges and the linen and china, when it was really all the human souls to be saved: not weak souls in starved bodies, crying with gratitude or a scrap of bread and treacle, but fullfed, quarrelsome, snobbish, uppish creatures, all standing on their little rights and dignities, and thinking that my father ought to be greatly obliged to them for making so much money for him—and so he ought. That is where salvation is really wanted. My father shall never throw it in my teeth again that my converts were bribed with bread. [She is transfigured]. I have got rid of the bribe of bread. I have got rid of the bribe of heaven. Let God's work be done for its own sake: the work he had to create us to do because it cannot be done by living men and women. When I die, let him be in my debt, not I in his; and let me forgive him as becomes a woman of my rank.

CUSINS. Then the way of life lies through the factory of death?

BARBARA. Yes, through the raising of hell to heaven and of man to God, through the unveiling of an eternal light in the Valley of The Shadow.

[Seizing him with both hands] Oh, did you think my courage would never come back? did you believe that I was a deserter? that I, who have stood in the streets, and taken my people to my heart, and talked of the holiest and greatest things with them, could ever turn back and chatter foolishly to fashionable people about nothing in a drawingroom? Never, never, never, never: Major Barbara will die with the colors. Oh! and I have my dear little Dolly boy still; and he has found me my place and my work. Glory Hallelujah! [She kisses him].

CUSINS. My dearest: consider my delicate health. I cannot stand as much happiness as you can.

BARBARA. Yes: it is not easy work being in love with me, is it? But it's good for you. [She runs to the shed, and calls, childlike] Mamma! Mamma! [Bilton comes out of the shed, followed by Undershaft]. I want Mamma.

UNDERSHAFT. She is taking off her list slippers, dear. [He passes on to Cusins]. Well? What does she say?

CUSINS. She has gone right up into the skies.

LADY BRITOMART [coming from the shed and stopping on the steps, obstructing Sarah, who follows with Lomax. Barbara clutches like a baby at her mother's skirt]. Barbara: when will you learn to be independent and to act and think for yourself? I know as well as possible what that cry of "Mamma, Mamma," means. Always running to me!

SARAH [touching Lady Britomart's ribs with her finger tips and imitating a bicycle horn] Pip! Pip!

LADY BRITOMART [highly indignant] How dare you say Pip! pip! to me, Sarah? You are both very naughty children. What do you want, Barbara?

BARBARA. I want a house in the village to live in with Dolly. [Dragging at the skirt] Come and tell me which one to take.

UNDERSHAFT [to Cusins] Six o'clock tomorrow morning, my young friend.

5

A Doll's House

Play by Henrik Ibsen (1824–1906)

DRAMATIS PERSONAE

TORVALD HELMER.
NORA, his wife.
DOCTOR RANK.
MRS. LINDE.
NILS KROGSTAD.
HELMER'S THREE YOUNG CHILDREN.
ANNE, their nurse.
A HOUSEMAID.
A PORTER.

(The action takes place in Helmer's house.)

"A Doll's House", 1879

A DOLL'S HOUSE

ACT I

SCENE.

(A room furnished comfortably and tastefully, but not extravagantly. At the back, a door to the right leads to the entrance-hall, another to the left leads to Helmer's study. Between the doors stands a piano. In the middle of the left-hand wall is a door, and beyond it a window. Near the window are a round table, arm-chairs and a small sofa. In the right-hand wall, at the farther end, another door; and on the same side, nearer the footlights, a stove, two easy chairs and a rocking-chair; between the stove and the door, a small table.

Engravings on the walls; a cabinet with china and other small objects; a small book-case with well-bound books. The floors are carpeted, and a fire burns in the stove. It is winter.

A bell rings in the hall; shortly afterwards the door is heard to open. Enter NORA, humming a tune and in high spirits. She is in outdoor dress and carries a number of parcels; these she lays on the table to the right. She leaves the outer door open after her, and through it is seen a PORTER who is carrying a Christmas Tree and a basket, which he gives to the MAID who has opened the door.)

NORA. Hide the Christmas Tree carefully, Helen. Be sure the children do not see it until this evening, when it is dressed. (To the PORTER, taking out her purse.) How much?

PORTER. Sixpence.

NORA. There is a shilling. No, keep the change. (The PORTER thanks her, and goes out. NORA shuts the door. She is laughing to herself, as she takes off her hat and coat. She takes a packet of macaroons from her pocket and eats one or two; then goes cautiously to her husband's door and listens.) Yes, he is in. (Still humming, she goes to the table on the right.)

HELMER (calls out from his room). Is that my little lark twittering out there?

NORA (busy opening some of the parcels). Yes, it is!

HELMER. Is it my little squirrel bustling about?

NORA. Yes!

HELMER. When did my squirrel come home?

NORA. Just now. (Puts the bag of macaroons into her pocket and wipes her mouth.) Come in here, Torvald, and see what I have bought.

HELMER. Don't disturb me. (A little later, he opens the door and looks into the room, pen in hand.) Bought, did you say? All these things? Has my little spendthrift been wasting money again?

NORA. Yes but, Torvald, this year we really can let ourselves go a little. This is the first Christmas that we have not needed to economise.

HELMER. Still, you know, we can't spend money recklessly.

NORA. Yes, Torvald, we may be a wee bit more reckless now, mayn't we? Just a tiny wee bit! You are going to have a big salary and earn lots and lots of money.

HELMER. Yes, after the New Year; but then it will be a whole quarter before the salary is due.

NORA. Pooh! we can borrow until then.

HELMER. Nora! (Goes up to her and takes her playfully by the ear.) The same little featherhead! Suppose, now, that I borrowed fifty pounds today, and you spent it all in the Christmas week, and then on New Year's Eve a slate fell on my head and killed me, and—Nora (putting her hands over his mouth). Oh! don't say such horrid things.

HELMER. Still, suppose that happened,—what then?

NORA. If that were to happen, I don't suppose I should care whether I owed money or not.

HELMER. Yes, but what about the people who had lent it?

NORA. They? Who would bother about them? I should not know who they were.

HELMER. That is like a woman! But seriously, Nora, you know what I think about that. No debt, no borrowing. There can be no freedom or beauty about a home life that depends on borrowing and debt. We two have kept bravely on the straight road so far, and we will go on the same way for the short time longer that there need be any struggle.

NORA (moving towards the stove). As you please, Torvald.

HELMER (following her). Come, come, my little skylark must not droop her wings. What is this! Is my little squirrel out of temper? (Taking out his purse.) Nora, what do you think I have got here?

NORA (turning round quickly). Money!

HELMER. There you are. (Gives her some money.) Do you think I don't know what a lot is wanted for housekeeping at Christmas-time?

NORA (counting). Ten shillings—a pound—two pounds! Thank you, thank you, Torvald; that will keep me going for a long time.

HELMER. Indeed it must.

NORA. Yes, yes, it will. But come here and let me show you what I have bought. And all so cheap! Look, here is a new suit for Ivar, and a sword; and a horse and a trumpet for Bob; and a doll and dolly's bedstead for Emmy,—they are very plain, but anyway she will soon break them in pieces. And here are dress-lengths and handkerchiefs for the maids; old Anne ought really to have something better.

HELMER. And what is in this parcel?

NORA (crying out). No, no! you mustn't see that until this evening.

HELMER. Very well. But now tell me, you extravagant little person, what would you like for yourself?

NORA. For myself? Oh, I am sure I don't want anything.

HELMER. Yes, but you must. Tell me something reasonable that you would particularly like to have.

NORA. No, I really can't think of anything—unless, Torvald—

HELMER. Well?

NORA (playing with his coat buttons, and without raising her eyes to his). If you really want to give me something, you might—you might—

HELMER. Well, out with it!

NORA (speaking quickly). You might give me money, Torvald. Only just as much as you can afford; and then one of these days I will buy something with it.

HELMER. But, Nora—

NORA. Oh, do! dear Torvald; please, please do! Then I will wrap it up in beautiful gilt paper and hang it on the Christmas Tree. Wouldn't that be fun?

HELMER. What are little people called that are always wasting money?

NORA. Spendthrifts—I know. Let us do as you suggest, Torvald, and then I shall have time to think what I am most in want of. That is a very sensible plan, isn't it?

HELMER (smiling). Indeed it is—that is to say, if you were really to save out of the money I give you, and then really buy something for yourself. But if you spend it all on the housekeeping and any number of unnecessary things, then I merely have to pay up again.

NORA. Oh but, Torvald—

HELMER. You can't deny it, my dear little Nora. (Puts his arm round her waist.) It's a sweet little spendthrift, but she uses up a deal of money. One would hardly believe how expensive such little persons are!

NORA. It's a shame to say that. I do really save all I can.

HELMER (laughing). That's very true,—all you can. But you can't save anything!

NORA (smiling quietly and happily). You haven't any idea how many expenses we skylarks and squirrels have, Torvald.

HELMER. You are an odd little soul. Very like your father. You always find some new way of wheedling money out of me, and, as soon as you have got it, it seems to melt in your hands. You never know where it has gone. Still, one must take you as you are. It is in the blood; for indeed it is true that you can inherit these things, Nora.

NORA. Ah, I wish I had inherited many of papa's qualities.

HELMER. And I would not wish you to be anything but just what you are, my sweet little skylark. But, do you know, it strikes me that you are looking rather—what shall I say—rather uneasy today?

NORA. Do I?

HELMER. You do, really. Look straight at me.

NORA (looks at him). Well?

HELMER (wagging his finger at her). Hasn't Miss Sweet Tooth been breaking rules in town today?

NORA. No; what makes you think that?

HELMER. Hasn't she paid a visit to the confectioner's?

NORA. No, I assure you, Torvald—

HELMER. Not been nibbling sweets?

NORA. No, certainly not.

HELMER. Not even taken a bite at a macaroon or two?

NORA. No, Torvald, I assure you really—

HELMER. There, there, of course I was only joking.

NORA (going to the table on the right). I should not think of going against your wishes.

HELMER. No, I am sure of that; besides, you gave me your word—(Going up to her.) Keep your little Christmas secrets to yourself, my darling. They will all be revealed tonight when the Christmas Tree is lit, no doubt.

NORA. Did you remember to invite Doctor Rank?

HELMER. No. But there is no need; as a matter of course he will come to dinner with us. However, I will ask him when he comes in this morning. I have ordered some good wine. Nora, you can't think how I am looking forward to this evening.

NORA. So am I! And how the children will enjoy themselves, Torvald!

HELMER. It is splendid to feel that one has a perfectly safe appointment, and a big enough income. It's delightful to think of, isn't it?

NORA. It's wonderful!

HELMER. Do you remember last Christmas? For a full three weeks beforehand you shut yourself up every evening until long after midnight, making ornaments for the Christmas Tree, and all the other fine things that were to be a surprise to us. It was the dullest three weeks I ever spent!

NORA. I didn't find it dull.

HELMER (smiling). But there was precious little result, Nora.

NORA. Oh, you shouldn't tease me about that again. How could I help the cat's going in and tearing everything to pieces?

HELMER. Of course you couldn't, poor little girl. You had the best of intentions to please us all, and that's the main thing. But it is a good thing that our hard times are over.

NORA. Yes, it is really wonderful.

HELMER. This time I needn't sit here and be dull all alone, and you needn't ruin your dear eyes and your pretty little hands—

NORA (clapping her hands). No, Torvald, I needn't any longer, need I! It's wonderfully lovely to hear you say so! (Taking his arm.) Now I will tell you how I have been thinking we ought to arrange things, Torvald. As soon as Christmas is over—(A bell rings in the hall.) There's the bell. (She tidies the room a little.) There's some one at the door. What a nuisance!

HELMER. If it is a caller, remember I am not at home.

MAID (in the doorway). A lady to see you, ma'am,—a stranger.

NORA. Ask her to come in.

MAID (to HELMER). The doctor came at the same time, sir.

HELMER. Did he go straight into my room?

MAID. Yes, sir.

(HELMER goes into his room. The MAID ushers in Mrs. LINDE, who is in travelling dress, and shuts the door.)

MRS. LINDE (in a dejected and timid voice). How do you do, Nora?

NORA (doubtfully). How do you do—

MRS. LINDE. You don't recognise me, I suppose.

NORA. No, I don't know—yes, to be sure, I seem to—(Suddenly.) Yes!

Christine! Is it really you?

MRS. LINDE. Yes, it is I.

NORA. Christine! To think of my not recognising you! And yet how could I—(In a gentle voice.) How you have altered, Christine!

MRS. LINDE. Yes, I have indeed. In nine, ten long years—

NORA. Is it so long since we met? I suppose it is. The last eight years have been a happy time for me, I can tell you. And so now you have come into the town, and have taken this long journey in winter—that was plucky of you.

MRS. LINDE. I arrived by steamer this morning.

NORA. To have some fun at Christmas-time, of course. How delightful! We will have such fun together! But take off your things. You are not cold, I hope. (Helps her.) Now we will sit down by the stove, and be cosy. No, take this armchair; I will sit here in the rocking-chair. (Takes her hands.) Now you look like your old self again; it was only the first moment—You are a little paler, Christine, and perhaps a little thinner.

MRS. LINDE. And much, much older, Nora.

NORA. Perhaps a little older; very, very little; certainly not much. (Stops suddenly and speaks seriously.) What a thoughtless creature I am, chattering away like this. My poor, dear Christine, do forgive me.

MRS. LINDE. What do you mean, Nora?

NORA (gently). Poor Christine, you are a widow.

MRS. LINDE. Yes; it is three years ago now.

NORA. Yes, I knew; I saw it in the papers. I assure you, Christine, I meant ever so often to write to you at the time, but I always put it off and something always prevented me.

MRS. LINDE. I quite understand, dear.

NORA. It was very bad of me, Christine. Poor thing, how you must have suffered. And he left you nothing?

MRS. LINDE. No.

NORA. And no children?

MRS. LINDE. No.

NORA. Nothing at all, then.

MRS. LINDE. Not even any sorrow or grief to live upon.

NORA (looking incredulously at her). But, Christine, is that possible?

MRS. LINDE (smiles sadly and strokes her hair). It sometimes happens, Nora.

NORA. So you are quite alone. How dreadfully sad that must be. I have three lovely children. You can't see them just now, for they are out with their nurse. But now you must tell me all about it.

MRS. LINDE. No, no; I want to hear about you.

NORA. No, you must begin. I mustn't be selfish today; today I must only think of your affairs. But there is one thing I must tell you. Do you know we have just had a great piece of good luck?

MRS. LINDE. No, what is it?

NORA. Just fancy, my husband has been made manager of the Bank!

MRS. LINDE. Your husband? What good luck!

NORA. Yes, tremendous! A barrister's profession is such an uncertain thing, especially if he won't undertake unsavoury cases; and naturally Torvald has never been willing to do that, and I quite agree with him. You may imagine how pleased we are! He is to take up his work in the Bank at the New Year, and then he will have a big salary and lots of commissions. For the future we can live quite differently—we can do just as we like. I feel so relieved and so happy, Christine! It will be splendid to have heaps of money and not need to have any anxiety, won't it?

MRS. LINDE. Yes, anyhow I think it would be delightful to have what one needs.

NORA. No, not only what one needs, but heaps and heaps of money.

MRS. LINDE (smiling). Nora, Nora, haven't you learned sense yet? In our schooldays you were a great spendthrift.

NORA (laughing). Yes, that is what Torvald says now. (Wags her finger at her.) But "Nora, Nora" is not so silly as you think. We have not been in a position for me to waste money. We have both had to work.

MRS. LINDE. You too?

NORA. Yes; odds and ends, needlework, crotchet-work, embroidery, and that kind of thing. (Dropping her voice.) And other things as well. You know Torvald left his office when we were married? There was no prospect of promotion there, and he had to try and earn more than before. But during the first year he over-worked himself dreadfully. You see, he had to make money every way he could, and he worked early and late; but he couldn't stand it, and fell dreadfully ill, and the doctors said it was necessary for him to go south.

MRS. LINDE. You spent a whole year in Italy, didn't you?

NORA. Yes. It was no easy matter to get away, I can tell you. It was just after Ivar was born; but naturally we had to go. It was a wonderfully beautiful journey, and it saved Torvald's life. But it cost a tremendous lot of money, Christine.

MRS. LINDE. So I should think.

NORA. It cost about two hundred and fifty pounds. That's a lot, isn't it?

MRS. LINDE. Yes, and in emergencies like that it is lucky to have the money.

NORA. I ought to tell you that we had it from papa.

MRS. LINDE. Oh, I see. It was just about that time that he died, wasn't it?

NORA. Yes; and, just think of it, I couldn't go and nurse him. I was expecting little Ivar's birth every day and I had my poor sick Torvald to look after. My dear, kind father—I never saw him again, Christine. That was the saddest time I have known since our marriage.

MRS. LINDE. I know how fond you were of him. And then you went off to Italy?

NORA. Yes; you see we had money then, and the doctors insisted on our going, so we started a month later.

MRS. LINDE. And your husband came back quite well?

NORA. As sound as a bell!

MRS. LINDE. But—the doctor?

NORA. What doctor?

MRS. LINDE. I thought your maid said the gentleman who arrived here just as I did, was the doctor?

NORA. Yes, that was Doctor Rank, but he doesn't come here professionally. He is our greatest friend, and comes in at least once everyday. No, Torvald has not had an hour's illness since then, and our children are strong and healthy and so am I. (Jumps up and claps her hands.) Christine! Christine! it's good to be alive and happy!—But how horrid of me; I am talking of nothing but my own affairs. (Sits on a stool near her, and rests her arms on her knees.) You mustn't be angry with me. Tell me, is it really true that you did not love your husband? Why did you marry him?

MRS. LINDE. My mother was alive then, and was bedridden and helpless, and I had to provide for my two younger brothers; so I did not think I was justified in refusing his offer.

NORA. No, perhaps you were quite right. He was rich at that time, then?

MRS. LINDE. I believe he was quite well off. But his business was a precarious one; and, when he died, it all went to pieces and there was nothing left.

NORA. And then?—

MRS. LINDE. Well, I had to turn my hand to anything I could find—first a small shop, then a small school, and so on. The last three years have seemed like one long working-day, with no rest. Now it is at an end, Nora. My poor mother needs me no more, for she is gone; and the boys do not need me either; they have got situations and can shift for themselves.

NORA. What a relief you must feel if—

MRS. LINDE. No, indeed; I only feel my life unspeakably empty. No one to live for anymore.

(Gets up restlessly.) That was why I could not stand the life in my little backwater any longer. I hope it may be easier here to find something which will busy me and occupy my thoughts. If only I could have the good luck to get some regular work—office work of some kind—

NORA. But, Christine, that is so frightfully tiring, and you look tired out now. You had far better go away to some watering-place.

MRS. LINDE (walking to the window). I have no father to give me money for a journey, Nora.

NORA (rising). Oh, don't be angry with me!

MRS. LINDE (going up to her). It is you that must not be angry with me, dear. The worst of a position like mine is that it makes one so bitter. No one to work for, and yet obliged to be always on the lookout for chances. One must live, and so one becomes selfish. When you told me of the happy turn your fortunes have taken—you will hardly believe it—I was delighted not so much on your account as on my own.

NORA. How do you mean?—Oh, I understand. You mean that perhaps Torvald could get you something to do.

MRS. LINDE. Yes, that was what I was thinking of.

NORA. He must, Christine. Just leave it to me; I will broach the subject very cleverly—I will think of something that will please him very much. It will make me so happy to be of some use to you.

MRS. LINDE. How kind you are, Nora, to be so anxious to help me! It is doubly kind in you, for you know so little of the burdens and troubles of life.

NORA. I—? I know so little of them?

MRS. LINDE (smiling). My dear! Small household cares and that sort of thing!—You are a child, Nora.

NORA (tosses her head and crosses the stage). You ought not to be so superior.

MRS. LINDE. No?

NORA. You are just like the others. They all think that I am incapable of anything really serious—

MRS. LINDE. Come, come—

NORA.—that I have gone through nothing in this world of cares.

MRS. LINDE. But, my dear Nora, you have just told me all your troubles.

NORA. Pooh!—those were trifles. (Lowering her voice.) I have not told you the important thing.

MRS. LINDE. The important thing? What do you mean?

NORA. You look down upon me altogether, Christine—but you ought not to. You are proud, aren't you, of having worked so hard and so long for your mother?

MRS. LINDE. Indeed, I don't look down on anyone. But it is true that I am both proud and glad to think that I was privileged to make the end of my mother's life almost free from care.

NORA. And you are proud to think of what you have done for your brothers?

MRS. LINDE. I think I have the right to be.

NORA. I think so, too. But now, listen to this; I too have something to be proud and glad of.

MRS. LINDE. I have no doubt you have. But what do you refer to?

NORA. Speak low. Suppose Torvald were to hear! He mustn't on any account—no one in the world must know, Christine, except you.

MRS. LINDE. But what is it?

NORA. Come here. (Pulls her down on the sofa beside her.) Now I will show you that I too have something to be proud and glad of. It was I who saved Torvald's life.

MRS. LINDE. "Saved"? How?

NORA. I told you about our trip to Italy. Torvald would never have recovered if he had not gone there—

MRS. LINDE. Yes, but your father gave you the necessary funds.

NORA (smiling). Yes, that is what Torvald and all the others think, but—

MRS. LINDE. But—

NORA. Papa didn't give us a shilling. It was I who procured the money.

MRS. LINDE. You? All that large sum?

NORA. Two hundred and fifty pounds. What do you think of that?

MRS. LINDE. But, Nora, how could you possibly do it? Did you win a prize in the Lottery?

NORA (contemptuously). In the Lottery? There would have been no credit in that.

MRS. LINDE. But where did you get it from, then?

NORA (humming and smiling with an air of mystery). Hm, hm! Aha!

MRS. LINDE. Because you couldn't have borrowed it.

NORA. Couldn't I? Why not?

MRS. LINDE. No, a wife cannot borrow without her husband's consent.

NORA (tossing her head). Oh, if it is a wife who has any head for business—a wife who has the wit to be a little bit clever—

MRS. LINDE. I don't understand it at all, Nora.

NORA. There is no need you should. I never said I had borrowed the money. I may have got it some other way. (Lies back on the sofa.) Perhaps I got it from some other admirer. When anyone is as attractive as I am—

MRS. LINDE. You are a mad creature.

NORA. Now, you know you're full of curiosity, Christine.

MRS. LINDE. Listen to me, Nora dear. Haven't you been a little bit imprudent?

NORA (sits up straight). Is it imprudent to save your husband's life?

MRS. LINDE. It seems to me imprudent, without his knowledge, to—

NORA. But it was absolutely necessary that he should not know! My goodness, can't you understand that? It was necessary he should have no idea what a dangerous condition he was in. It was to me that the doctors came and said that his life was in danger, and that the only thing to save him was to live in the south. Do you suppose I didn't try, first of all, to get what I wanted as if it were for myself? I told him how much I should love to travel abroad like other young wives; I tried tears and entreaties with him; I told him that he ought to remember the condition I was in, and that he ought to be kind and indulgent to me; I even hinted that he might raise a loan. That nearly made him angry, Christine. He said I was

thoughtless, and that it was his duty as my husband not to indulge me in my whims and caprices—as I believe he called them. Very well, I thought, you must be saved—and that was how I came to devise a way out of the difficulty—

MRS. LINDE. And did your husband never get to know from your father that the money had not come from him?

NORA. No, never. Papa died just at that time. I had meant to let him into the secret and beg him never to reveal it. But he was so ill then—alas, there never was any need to tell him.

MRS. LINDE. And since then have you never told your secret to your husband?

NORA. Good Heavens, no! How could you think so? A man who has such strong opinions about these things! And besides, how painful and humiliating it would be for Torvald, with his manly independence, to know that he owed me anything! It would upset our mutual relations altogether; our beautiful happy home would no longer be what it is now.

MRS. LINDE. Do you mean never to tell him about it?

NORA (meditatively, and with a half smile). Yes—someday, perhaps, after many years, when I am no longer as nice-looking as I am now. Don't laugh at me! I mean, of course, when Torvald is no longer as devoted to me as he is now; when my dancing and dressing-up and reciting have palled on him; then it may be a good thing to have something in reserve—(Breaking off.) What nonsense! That time will never come. Now, what do you think of my great secret, Christine? Do you still think I am of no use? I can tell you, too, that this affair has caused me a lot of worry. It has been by no means easy for me to meet my engagements punctually. I may tell you that there is something that is called, in business, quarterly interest, and another thing called payment in installments, and it is always so dreadfully difficult to manage them. I have had to save a little here and there, where I could, you understand. I have not been able to put aside much from my housekeeping money, for Torvald must have a good table. I couldn't let my children be shabbily dressed; I have felt obliged to use up all he gave me for them, the sweet little darlings!

MRS. LINDE. So it has all had to come out of your own necessaries of life, poor Nora?

NORA. Of course. Besides, I was the one responsible for it. Whenever Torvald has given me money for new dresses and such things, I have never spent more than half of it; I have always bought the simplest and cheapest things. Thank Heaven, any clothes look well on me, and so Torvald has never noticed it. But it was often very hard on me, Christine—because it is delightful to be really well dressed, isn't it?

MRS. LINDE. Quite so.

NORA. Well, then I have found other ways of earning money. Last winter I was lucky enough to get a lot of copying to do; so I locked myself up and sat writing every evening until quite late at night. Many a time I was desperately tired; but all the same it was a tremendous pleasure to sit there working and earning money. It was like being a man.

MRS. LINDE. How much have you been able to pay off in that way?

NORA. I can't tell you exactly. You see, it is very difficult to keep an account of a business matter of that kind. I only know that I have paid every penny that I could scrape together. Many a time I was at my wits' end. (Smiles.) Then I used to sit here and imagine that a rich old gentleman had fallen in love with me—

MRS. LINDE. What! Who was it?

NORA. Be quiet!—that he had died; and that when his will was opened it contained, written in big letters, the instruction: "The lovely Mrs. Nora Helmer is to have all I possess paid over to her at once in cash."

MRS. LINDE. But, my dear Nora—who could the man be?

NORA. Good gracious, can't you understand? There was no old gentleman at all; it was only something that I used to sit here and imagine, when I couldn't think of any way of procuring money. But it's all the same now; the tiresome old person can stay where he is, as far as I am concerned; I don't care about him or his will either, for I am free from care now. (Jumps up.) My goodness, it's delightful to think of, Christine!

Free from care! To be able to be free from care, quite free from care; to be able to play and romp with the children; to be able to keep the house beautifully and have everything just as Torvald likes it! And, think of it, soon the spring will come and the big blue sky! Perhaps we shall be able to take a little trip—perhaps I shall see the sea again! Oh, it's a wonderful thing to be alive and be happy. (A bell is heard in the hall.)

MRS. LINDE (rising). There is the bell; perhaps I had better go.

NORA. No, don't go; no one will come in here; it is sure to be for Torvald.

SERVANT (at the hall door). Excuse me, ma'am—there is a gentleman to see the master, and as the doctor is with him—

NORA. Who is it?

KROGSTAD (at the door). It is I, Mrs. Helmer. (Mrs. LINDE starts, trembles, and turns to the window.)

NORA (takes a step towards him, and speaks in a strained, low voice). You? What is it? What do you want to see my husband about?

KROGSTAD. Bank business—in a way. I have a small post in the Bank, and I hear your husband is to be our chief now—

NORA. Then it is—

KROGSTAD. Nothing but dry business matters, Mrs. Helmer; absolutely nothing else.

NORA. Be so good as to go into the study, then. (She bows indifferently to him and shuts the door into the hall; then comes back and makes up the fire in the stove.)

MRS. LINDE. NORA—who was that man?

NORA. A lawyer, of the name of Krogstad.

MRS. LINDE. Then it really was he.

NORA. Do you know the man?

MRS. LINDE. I used to—many years ago. At one time he was a solicitor's clerk in our town.

NORA. Yes, he was.

MRS. LINDE. He is greatly altered.

NORA. He made a very unhappy marriage.

MRS. LINDE. He is a widower now, isn't he?

NORA. With several children. There now, it is burning up. (Shuts the door of the stove and moves the rocking-chair aside.)

MRS. LINDE. They say he carries on various kinds of business.

NORA. Really! Perhaps he does; I don't know anything about it. But don't let us think of business; it is so tiresome.

DOCTOR RANK (comes out of HELMER'S study. Before he shuts the door he calls to him). No, my dear fellow, I won't disturb you; I would rather go in to your wife for a little while. (Shuts the door and sees Mrs. LINDE.) I beg your pardon; I am afraid I am disturbing you too.

NORA. No, not at all. (Introducing him). Doctor Rank, Mrs. Linde.

RANK. I have often heard Mrs. Linde's name mentioned here. I think I passed you on the stairs when I arrived, Mrs. Linde?

MRS. LINDE. Yes, I go up very slowly; I can't manage stairs well.

RANK. Ah! some slight internal weakness?

MRS. LINDE. No, the fact is I have been overworking myself.

RANK. Nothing more than that? Then I suppose you have come to town to amuse yourself with our entertainments?

MRS. LINDE. I have come to look for work.

RANK. Is that a good cure for overwork?

MRS. LINDE. One must live, Doctor Rank.

RANK. Yes, the general opinion seems to be that it is necessary.

NORA. Look here, Doctor Rank—you know you want to live.

RANK. Certainly. However wretched I may feel, I want to prolong the agony as long as possible. All my patients are like that. And so are those who are morally diseased; one of them, and a bad case too, is at this very moment with Helmer—

MRS. LINDE (sadly). Ah!

NORA. Whom do you mean?

RANK. A lawyer of the name of Krogstad, a fellow you don't know at all. He suffers from a diseased moral character, Mrs. Helmer; but even he began talking of its being highly important that he should live.

NORA. Did he? What did he want to speak to Torvald about?

RANK. I have no idea; I only heard that it was something about the Bank.

NORA. I didn't know this—what's his name—Krogstad had anything to do with the Bank.

RANK. Yes, he has some sort of appointment there. (To Mrs. LINDE.) I don't know whether you find also in your part of the world that there are certain people who go zealously snuffing about to smell out moral corruption, and, as soon as they have found some, put the person concerned into some lucrative position where they can keep their eye on him. Healthy natures are left out in the cold.

MRS. LINDE. Still I think the sick are those who most need taking care of.

RANK (shrugging his shoulders). Yes, there you are. That is the sentiment that is turning Society into a sick-house.

(NORA, who has been absorbed in her thoughts, breaks out into smothered laughter and claps her hands.)

RANK. Why do you laugh at that? Have you any notion what Society really is?

NORA. What do I care about tiresome Society? I am laughing at something quite different, something extremely amusing. Tell me, Doctor Rank, are all the people who are employed in the Bank dependent on Torvald now?

RANK. Is that what you find so extremely amusing?

NORA (smiling and humming). That's my affair! (Walking about the room.) It's perfectly glorious to think that we have—that Torvald has so much power over so many people. (Takes the packet from her pocket.) Doctor Rank, what do you say to a macaroon?

RANK. What, macaroons? I thought they were forbidden here.

NORA. Yes, but these are some Christine gave me.

MRS. LINDE. What! I?—

NORA. Oh, well, don't be alarmed! You couldn't know that Torvald had forbidden them. I must tell you that he is afraid they will spoil my teeth. But, bah!—once in a way—That's so, isn't it, Doctor Rank? By your leave! (Puts a macaroon into his mouth.) You must have one too, Christine. And I shall have one, just a little one— or at most two. (Walking about.) I am tremendously happy. There is just one thing in the world now that I should dearly love to do.

RANK. Well, what is that?

NORA. It's something I should dearly love to say, if Torvald could hear me.

RANK. Well, why can't you say it?

NORA. No, I daren't; it's so shocking.

MRS. LINDE. Shocking?

RANK. Well, I should not advise you to say it. Still, with us you might. What is it you would so much like to say if Torvald could hear you?

NORA. I should just love to say—Well, I'm damned!

RANK. Are you mad?

MRS. LINDE. Nora, dear—!

RANK. Say it, here he is!

NORA (hiding the packet). Hush! Hush! Hush! (HELMER comes out of his room, with his coat over his arm and his hat in his hand.)

NORA. Well, Torvald dear, have you got rid of him?

HELMER. Yes, he has just gone.

NORA. Let me introduce you—this is Christine, who has come to town.

HELMER. Christine—? Excuse me, but I don't know—

NORA. Mrs. Linde, dear; Christine Linde.

HELMER. Of course. A school friend of my wife's, I presume?

MRS. LINDE. Yes, we have known each other since then.

NORA. And just think, she has taken a long journey in order to see you.

HELMER. What do you mean? Mrs. Linde. No, really, I—

NORA. Christine is tremendously clever at book-keeping, and she is frightfully anxious to work under some clever man, so as to perfect herself—

HELMER. Very sensible, Mrs. Linde.

NORA. And when she heard you had been appointed manager of the Bank—the news was telegraphed, you know—she travelled here as quick as she could. Torvald, I am sure you will be able to do something for Christine, for my sake, won't you?

HELMER. Well, it is not altogether impossible. I presume you are a widow, Mrs. Linde?

MRS. LINDE. Yes.

HELMER. And have had some experience of book-keeping?

MRS. LINDE. Yes, a fair amount.

HELMER. Ah! well, it's very likely I may be able to find something for you—

NORA (clapping her hands). What did I tell you? What did I tell you?

HELMER. You have just come at a fortunate moment, Mrs. Linde.

MRS. LINDE. How am I to thank you?

HELMER. There is no need. (Puts on his coat.) But today you must excuse me—

RANK. Wait a minute; I will come with you. (Brings his fur coat from the hall and warms it at the fire.)

NORA. Don't be long away, Torvald dear.

HELMER. About an hour, not more.

NORA. Are you going too, Christine?

MRS. LINDE (putting on her cloak). Yes, I must go and look for a room.

HELMER. Oh, well then, we can walk down the street together.

NORA (helping her). What a pity it is we are so short of space here; I am afraid it is impossible for us—

MRS. LINDE. Please don't think of it! Goodbye, Nora dear, and many thanks.

NORA. Goodbye for the present. Of course you will come back this evening. And you too, Dr. Rank. What do you say? If you are well enough?

Oh, you must be! Wrap yourself up well. (They go to the door all talking together. Children's voices are heard on the staircase.)

NORA. There they are! There they are! (She runs to open the door. The NURSE comes in with the children.) Come in! Come in! (Stoops and kisses them.) Oh, you sweet blessings! Look at them, Christine! Aren't they darlings?

RANK. Don't let us stand here in the draught.

HELMER. Come along, Mrs. Linde; the place will only be bearable for a mother now!

(RANK, HELMER, and Mrs. LINDE go downstairs. The NURSE comes forward with the children; NORA shuts the hall door.)

NORA. How fresh and well you look! Such red cheeks like apples and roses. (The children all talk at once while she speaks to them.) Have you had great fun? That's splendid! What, you pulled both Emmy and Bob along on the sled?—both at once?—that was good. You are a clever boy, Ivar. Let me take her for a little, Anne. My sweet little baby doll! (Takes the baby from the MAID and dances it up and down.) Yes, yes, mother will dance with Bob too. What! Have you been snowballing? I wish I had been there too! No, no, I will take their things off, Anne; please let me do it, it is such fun. Go in now, you look half frozen. There is some hot coffee for you on the stove.

(The NURSE goes into the room on the left. NORA takes off the children's things and throws them about, while they all talk to her at once.)

NORA. Really! Did a big dog run after you? But it didn't bite you? No, dogs don't bite nice little dolly children. You mustn't look at the parcels, Ivar. What are they? Ah, I daresay you would like to know. No, no—it's something nasty! Come, let us have a game! What shall we play at? Hide and Seek? Yes, we'll play Hide and Seek. Bob shall hide first. Must I hide? Very well, I'll hide first. (She and the children laugh and shout, and romp in and out of the room; at last NORA hides under the table, the children rush in and out for her, but do not see her; they hear her smothered laughter, run to the table, lift up the cloth and find her. Shouts of laughter. She crawls forward and pretends to frighten them. Fresh laughter. Meanwhile there has been a knock at the hall

door, but none of them has noticed it. The door is half opened, and KROGSTAD appears, lie waits a little; the game goes on.)

KROGSTAD. Excuse me, Mrs. Helmer.

NORA (with a stifled cry, turns round and gets up on to her knees). Ah! what do you want?

KROGSTAD. Excuse me, the outer door was ajar; I suppose someone forgot to shut it.

NORA (rising). My husband is out, Mr. Krogstad.

KROGSTAD. I know that.

NORA. What do you want here, then?

KROGSTAD. A word with you.

NORA. With me?—(To the children, gently.) Go in to nurse. What? No, the strange man won't do mother any harm. When he has gone we will have another game. (She takes the children into the room on the left, and shuts the door after them.) You want to speak to me?

KROGSTAD. Yes, I do.

NORA. Today? It is not the first of the month yet.

KROGSTAD. No, it is Christmas Eve, and it will depend on yourself what sort of a Christmas you will spend.

NORA. What do you mean? Today it is absolutely impossible for me—

KROGSTAD. We won't talk about that until later on. This is something different. I presume you can give me a moment?

NORA. Yes—yes, I can—although—

KROGSTAD. Good. I was in Olsen's Restaurant and saw your husband going down the street—

NORA. Yes?

KROGSTAD. With a lady.

NORA. What then?

KROGSTAD. May I make so bold as to ask if it was a Mrs. Linde?

NORA. It was.

KROGSTAD. Just arrived in town?

NORA. Yes, today.

KROGSTAD. She is a great friend of yours, isn't she?

NORA. She is. But I don't see—

KROGSTAD. I knew her too, once upon a time.

NORA. I am aware of that.

KROGSTAD. Are you? So you know all about it; I thought as much. Then I can ask you, without beating about the bush—is Mrs. Linde to have an appointment in the Bank?

NORA. What right have you to question me, Mr. Krogstad?—You, one of my husband's subordinates! But since you ask, you shall know. Yes, Mrs. Linde is to have an appointment. And it was I who pleaded her cause, Mr. Krogstad, let me tell you that.

KROGSTAD. I was right in what I thought, then.

NORA (walking up and down the stage). Sometimes one has a tiny little bit of influence, I should hope. Because one is a woman, it does not necessarily follow that—. When anyone is in a subordinate position, Mr. Krogstad, they should really be careful to avoid offending anyone who—who—

KROGSTAD. Who has influence?

NORA. Exactly.

KROGSTAD (changing his tone). Mrs. Helmer, you will be so good as to use your influence on my behalf.

NORA. What? What do you mean?

KROGSTAD. You will be so kind as to see that I am allowed to keep my subordinate position in the Bank.

NORA. What do you mean by that? Who proposes to take your post away from you?

KROGSTAD. Oh, there is no necessity to keep up the pretence of ignorance. I can quite understand that your friend is not very anxious to expose herself to the chance of rubbing shoulders with me; and I quite understand, too, whom I have to thank for being turned off.

NORA. But I assure you—

KROGSTAD. Very likely; but, to come to the point, the time has come when I should advise you to use your influence to prevent that.

NORA. But, Mr. Krogstad, I have no influence.

KROGSTAD. Haven't you? I thought you said yourself just now—

NORA. Naturally I did not mean you to put that construction on it. I! What should make you think I have any influence of that kind with my husband?

KROGSTAD. Oh, I have known your husband from our student days. I don't suppose he is any more unassailable than other husbands.

NORA. If you speak slightingly of my husband, I shall turn you out of the house.

KROGSTAD. You are bold, Mrs. Helmer.

NORA. I am not afraid of you any longer. As soon as the New Year comes, I shall in a very short time be free of the whole thing.

KROGSTAD (controlling himself). Listen to me, Mrs. Helmer. If necessary, I am prepared to fight for my small post in the Bank as if I were fighting for my life.

NORA. So it seems.

KROGSTAD. It is not only for the sake of the money; indeed, that weighs least with me in the matter. There is another reason—well, I may as well tell you. My position is this. I daresay you know, like everybody else, that once, many years ago, I was guilty of an indiscretion.

NORA. I think I have heard something of the kind.

KROGSTAD. The matter never came into court; but every way seemed to be closed to me after that. So I took to the business that you know of. I had to do something; and, honestly, I don't think I've been one of the worst. But now I must cut myself free from all that. My sons are growing up; for their sake I must try and win back as much respect as I can in the town. This post in the Bank was like the first step up for me—and now your husband is going to kick me downstairs again into the mud.

NORA. But you must believe me, Mr. Krogstad; it is not in my power to help you at all.

KROGSTAD. Then it is because you haven't the will; but I have means to compel you.

NORA. You don't mean that you will tell my husband that I owe you money?

KROGSTAD. Hm!—suppose I were to tell him?

NORA. It would be perfectly infamous of you. (Sobbing.) To think of his learning my secret, which has been my joy and pride, in such an ugly, clumsy way—that he should learn it from you! And it would put me in a horribly disagreeable position—

KROGSTAD. Only disagreeable?

NORA (impetuously). Well, do it, then!—and it will be the worse for you. My husband will see for himself what a blackguard you are, and you certainly won't keep your post then.

KROGSTAD. I asked you if it was only a disagreeable scene at home that you were afraid of?

NORA. If my husband does get to know of it, of course he will at once pay you what is still owing, and we shall have nothing more to do with you.

KROGSTAD (coming a step nearer). Listen to me, Mrs. Helmer. Either you have a very bad memory or you know very little of business. I shall be obliged to remind you of a few details.

NORA. What do you mean?

KROGSTAD. When your husband was ill, you came to me to borrow two hundred and fifty pounds.

NORA. I didn't know anyone else to go to.

KROGSTAD. I promised to get you that amount—

NORA. Yes, and you did so.

KROGSTAD. I promised to get you that amount, on certain conditions. Your mind was so taken up with your husband's illness, and you were so anxious to get the money for your journey, that you seem to have paid no attention to the conditions of our bargain. Therefore it will not be amiss if I remind you of them. Now, I promised to get the money on the security of a bond which I drew up.

NORA. Yes, and which I signed.

KROGSTAD. Good. But below your signature there were a few lines constituting your father a surety for the money; those lines your father should have signed.

NORA. Should? He did sign them.

KROGSTAD. I had left the date blank; that is to say, your father should himself have inserted the date on which he signed the paper. Do you remember that?

NORA. Yes, I think I remember—

KROGSTAD. Then I gave you the bond to send by post to your father. Is that not so?

NORA. Yes.

KROGSTAD. And you naturally did so at once, because five or six days afterwards you brought me the bond with your father's signature. And then I gave you the money.

NORA. Well, haven't I been paying it off regularly?

KROGSTAD. Fairly so, yes. But—to come back to the matter in hand—that must have been a very trying time for you, Mrs. Helmer?

NORA. It was, indeed.

KROGSTAD. Your father was very ill, wasn't he?

NORA. He was very near his end.

KROGSTAD. And died soon afterwards?

NORA. Yes.

KROGSTAD. Tell me, Mrs. Helmer, can you by any chance remember what day your father died?—on what day of the month, I mean.

NORA. Papa died on the 29th of September.

KROGSTAD. That is correct; I have ascertained it for myself. And, as that is so, there is a discrepancy (taking a paper from his pocket) which I cannot account for.

NORA. What discrepancy? I don't know—

KROGSTAD. The discrepancy consists, Mrs. Helmer, in the fact that your father signed this bond three days after his death.

NORA. What do you mean? I don't understand—

KROGSTAD. Your father died on the 29th of September. But, look here; your father has dated his signature the 2nd of October. It is a discrepancy, isn't it? (NORA is silent.) Can you explain it to me? (NORA is still silent.) It is a remarkable thing, too, that the words "2nd of October," as well as the year, are not written in your father's handwriting but in one that I think I know. Well, of course it can be explained; your father may have forgotten to date his signature, and someone else may have dated it haphazard before they knew of his death. There is no harm in that. It all depends on the signature of the name; and that is genuine, I suppose, Mrs. Helmer? It was your father himself who signed his name here?

NORA (after a short pause, throws her head up and looks defiantly at him). No, it was not. It was I that wrote papa's name.

KROGSTAD. Are you aware that is a dangerous confession?

NORA. In what way? You shall have your money soon.

KROGSTAD. Let me ask you a question; why did you not send the paper to your father?

NORA. It was impossible; papa was so ill. If I had asked him for his signature, I should have had to tell him what the money was to be used for; and when he was so ill himself I couldn't tell him that my husband's life was in danger—it was impossible.

KROGSTAD. It would have been better for you if you had given up your trip abroad.

NORA. No, that was impossible. That trip was to save my husband's life; I couldn't give that up.

KROGSTAD. But did it never occur to you that you were committing a fraud on me?

NORA. I couldn't take that into account; I didn't trouble myself about you at all. I couldn't bear you, because you put so many heartless difficulties in my way, although you knew what a dangerous condition my husband was in.

KROGSTAD. Mrs. Helmer, you evidently do not realise clearly what it is that you have been guilty of. But I can assure you that my one false step, which lost me all my reputation, was nothing more or nothing worse than what you have done.

NORA. You? Do you ask me to believe that you were brave enough to run a risk to save your wife's life?

KROGSTAD. The law cares nothing about motives.

NORA. Then it must be a very foolish law.

KROGSTAD. Foolish or not, it is the law by which you will be judged, if I produce this paper in court.

NORA. I don't believe it. Is a daughter not to be allowed to spare her dying father anxiety and care? Is a wife not to be allowed to save her husband's life? I don't know much about law; but I am certain that there must be laws permitting such things as that. Have you no knowledge of such laws—you who are a lawyer? You must be a very poor lawyer, Mr. Krogstad.

KROGSTAD. Maybe. But matters of business—such business as you and I have had together—do you think I don't understand that? Very well. Do as you please. But let me tell you this—if I lose my position a second time, you shall lose yours with me. (He bows, and goes out through the hall.)

NORA (appears buried in thought for a short time, then tosses her head). Nonsense! Trying to frighten me like that!—I am not so silly as he thinks. (Begins to busy herself putting the children's things in order.) And yet—? No, it's impossible! I did it for love's sake.

THE CHILDREN (in the doorway on the left). Mother, the stranger man has gone out through the gate.

NORA. Yes, dears, I know. But, don't tell anyone about the stranger man. Do you hear? Not even papa.

CHILDREN. No, mother; but will you come and play again?

NORA. No, no,—not now.

CHILDREN. But, mother, you promised us.

NORA. Yes, but I can't now. Run away in; I have such a lot to do. Run away in, my sweet little darlings. (She gets them into the room by degrees and shuts the door on them; then sits down on the sofa, takes up a piece of needlework and sews a few stitches, but soon stops.) No! (Throws down the work, gets up, goes to the hall door and calls out.) Helen! bring the Tree in. (Goes to the table on the left, opens a drawer, and stops again.) No, no! it is quite impossible!

MAID (coming in with the Tree). Where shall I put it, ma'am?

NORA. Here, in the middle of the floor.

MAID. Shall I get you anything else?

NORA. No, thank you. I have all I want. [Exit MAID.]

NORA (begins dressing the tree). A candle here— and flowers here—The horrible man! It's all nonsense—there's nothing wrong. The tree shall be splendid! I will do everything I can think of to please you, Torvald!—I will sing for you, dance for you—(HELMER comes in with some papers under his arm.) Oh! are you back already?

HELMER. Yes. Has anyone been here?

NORA. Here? No.

HELMER. That is strange. I saw Krogstad going out of the gate.

NORA. Did you? Oh yes, I forgot, Krogstad was here for a moment.

HELMER. Nora, I can see from your manner that he has been here begging you to say a good word for him.

NORA. Yes.

HELMER. And you were to appear to do it of your own accord; you were to conceal from me the fact of his having been here; didn't he beg that of you too?

NORA. Yes, Torvald, but—

HELMER. Nora, Nora, and you would be a party to that sort of thing? To have any talk with a man like that, and give him any sort of promise? And to tell me a lie into the bargain?

NORA. A lie—?

HELMER. Didn't you tell me no one had been here? (Shakes his finger at her.) My little songbird must never do that again. A songbird must have a clean beak to chirp with—no false notes! (Puts his arm round her waist.) That is so, isn't it? Yes, I am sure it is. (Lets her go.) We will say no more about it. (Sits down by the stove.) How warm and snug it is here! (Turns over his papers.)

NORA (after a short pause, during which she busies herself with the Christmas Tree.) Torvald!

HELMER. Yes.

NORA. I am looking forward tremendously to the fancy-dress ball at the Stenborgs' the day after tomorrow.

HELMER. And I am tremendously curious to see what you are going to surprise me with.

NORA. It was very silly of me to want to do that.

HELMER. What do you mean?

NORA. I can't hit upon anything that will do; everything I think of seems so silly and insignificant.

HELMER. Does my little Nora acknowledge that at last?

NORA (standing behind his chair with her arms on the back of it). Are you very busy, Torvald?

HELMER. Well—

NORA. What are all those papers?

HELMER. Bank business.

NORA. Already?

HELMER. I have got authority from the retiring manager to undertake the necessary changes in the staff and in the rearrangement of the work; and I must make use of the Christmas week for that, so as to have everything in order for the new year.

NORA. Then that was why this poor Krogstad—

HELMER. Hm!

NORA (leans against the back of his chair and strokes his hair). If you hadn't been so busy I should have asked you a tremendously big favour, Torvald.

HELMER. What is that? Tell me.

NORA. There is no one has such good taste as you. And I do so want to look nice at the fancy-dress ball. Torvald, couldn't you take me in hand and decide what I shall go as, and what sort of a dress I shall wear?

HELMER. Aha! so my obstinate little woman is obliged to get someone to come to her rescue?

NORA. Yes, Torvald, I can't get along a bit without your help.

HELMER. Very well, I will think it over, we shall manage to hit upon something.

NORA. That is nice of you. (Goes to the Christmas Tree. A short pause.) How pretty the red flowers look—. But, tell me, was it really something very bad that this Krogstad was guilty of?

HELMER. He forged someone's name. Have you any idea what that means?

NORA. Isn't it possible that he was driven to do it by necessity?

HELMER. Yes; or, as in so many cases, by imprudence. I am not so heartless as to condemn a man altogether because of a single false step of that kind.

NORA. No, you wouldn't, would you, Torvald?

HELMER. Many a man has been able to retrieve his character, if he has openly confessed his fault and taken his punishment.

NORA. Punishment—?

HELMER. But Krogstad did nothing of that sort; he got himself out of it by a cunning trick, and that is why he has gone under altogether.

NORA. But do you think it would—?

HELMER. Just think how a guilty man like that has to lie and play the hypocrite with every one, how he has to wear a mask in the presence of those near and dear to him, even before his own wife and children. And about the children—that is the most terrible part of it all, Nora.

NORA. How?

HELMER. Because such an atmosphere of lies infects and poisons the whole life of a home. Each breath the children take in such a house is full of the germs of evil.

NORA (coming nearer him). Are you sure of that?

HELMER. My dear, I have often seen it in the course of my life as a lawyer. Almost everyone who has gone to the bad early in life has had a deceitful mother.

NORA. Why do you only say—mother?

HELMER. It seems most commonly to be the mother's influence, though naturally a bad father's would have the same result. Every lawyer is familiar with the fact. This Krogstad, now, has been persistently poisoning his own children with lies and dissimulation; that is why I say he has lost all moral character. (Holds out his hands to her.) That is why my sweet little Nora must promise me not to plead his cause. Give me your hand on it. Come, come, what is this? Give me your hand. There now, that's settled. I assure you it would be quite impossible for me to work with him; I literally feel physically ill when I am in the company of such people.

NORA (takes her hand out of his and goes to the opposite side of the Christmas Tree). How hot it is in here; and I have such a lot to do.

HELMER (getting up and putting his papers in order). Yes, and I must try and read through some of these before dinner; and I must think about your costume, too. And it is just possible I may have something ready in gold paper to hang up on the Tree. (Puts his hand on her head.) My precious little singing-bird! (He goes into his room and shuts the door after him.)

NORA (after a pause, whispers). No, no—it isn't true. It's impossible; it must be impossible.

(The NURSE opens the door on the left.)

NURSE. The little ones are begging so hard to be allowed to come in to mamma.

NORA. No, no, no! Don't let them come in to me! You stay with them, Anne.

NURSE. Very well, ma'am. (Shuts the door.)

NORA (pale with terror). Deprave my little children? Poison my home? (A short pause. Then she tosses her head.) It's not true. It can't possibly be true.

ACT II

THE SAME SCENE.

(The Christmas Tree is in the corner by the piano, stripped of its ornaments and with burnt-down candle-ends on its dishevelled branches. NORA'S cloak and hat are lying on the sofa. She is alone in the room, walking about uneasily. She stops by the sofa and takes up her cloak.)

NORA (drops her cloak). Someone is coming now! (Goes to the door and listens.) No—it is no one. Of course, no one will come today, Christmas Day—nor tomorrow either. But, perhaps—(opens the door and looks out). No, nothing in the letterbox; it is quite empty. (Comes forward.) What rubbish! of course he can't be in earnest about it. Such a thing couldn't happen; it is impossible—I have three little children.

(Enter the NURSE from the room on the left, carrying a big cardboard box.)

NURSE. At last I have found the box with the fancy dress.

NORA. Thanks; put it on the table.

NURSE (doing so). But it is very much in want of mending.

NORA. I should like to tear it into a hundred thousand pieces.

NURSE. What an idea! It can easily be put in order—just a little patience.

NORA. Yes, I will go and get Mrs. Linde to come and help me with it.

NURSE. What, out again? In this horrible weather? You will catch cold, ma'am, and make yourself ill.

NORA. Well, worse than that might happen. How are the children?

NURSE. The poor little souls are playing with their Christmas presents, but—

NORA. Do they ask much for me?

NURSE. You see, they are so accustomed to have their mamma with them.

NORA. Yes, but, nurse, I shall not be able to be so much with them now as I was before.

NURSE. Oh well, young children easily get accustomed to anything.

NORA. Do you think so? Do you think they would forget their mother if she went away altogether?

NURSE. Good heavens!—went away altogether?

NORA. Nurse, I want you to tell me something I have often wondered about—how could you have the heart to put your own child out among strangers?

NURSE. I was obliged to, if I wanted to be little Nora's nurse.

NORA. Yes, but how could you be willing to do it?

NURSE. What, when I was going to get such a good place by it? A poor girl who has got into trouble should be glad to. Besides, that wicked man didn't do a single thing for me.

NORA. But I suppose your daughter has quite forgotten you.

NURSE. No, indeed she hasn't. She wrote to me when she was confirmed, and when she was married.

NORA (putting her arms round her neck). Dear old Anne, you were a good mother to me when I was little.

NURSE. Little Nora, poor dear, had no other mother but me. Nora. And if my little ones had no other mother, I am sure you would—What nonsense I am talking! (Opens the box.) Go in to them. Now I must—. You will see tomorrow how charming I shall look.

NURSE. I am sure there will be no one at the ball so charming as you, ma'am. (Goes into the room on the left.)

NORA (begins to unpack the box, but soon pushes it away from her). If only I dared go out. If only no one would come. If only I could be sure nothing would happen here in the meantime. Stuff and nonsense! No one will come. Only I mustn't think about it. I will brush my muff. What lovely, lovely gloves! Out of my thoughts, out of my thoughts! One, two, three, four, five, six— (Screams.) Ah! there is someone coming—. Makes a movement towards the door, but stands irresolute.)

(Enter MRS. LINDE from the hall, where she has taken off her cloak and hat.)

NORA. Oh, it's you, Christine. There is no one else out there, is there? How good of you to come!

MRS. LINDE. I heard you were up asking for me.

NORA. Yes, I was passing by. As a matter of fact, it is something you could help me with. Let us sit down here on the sofa. Look here. Tomorrow evening there is to be a fancy-dress ball at the Stenborgs', who live above us; and Torvald wants me to go as a Neapolitan fisher-girl, and dance the Tarantella that I learned at Capri.

MRS. LINDE. I see; you are going to keep up the character.

NORA. Yes, Torvald wants me to. Look, here is the dress; Torvald had it made for me there, but now it is all so torn, and I haven't any idea—

MRS. LINDE. We will easily put that right. It is only some of the trimming come unsewn here and there. Needle and thread? Now then, that's all we want.

NORA. It is nice of you.

MRS. LINDE (sewing). So you are going to be dressed up tomorrow Nora. I will tell you what—I shall come in for a moment and see you in your fine feathers. But I have completely forgotten to thank you for a delightful evening yesterday.

NORA (gets up, and crosses the stage). Well, I don't think yesterday was as pleasant as usual. You ought to have come to town a little earlier, Christine. Certainly Torvald does understand how to make a house dainty and attractive.

MRS. LINDE. And so do you, it seems to me; you are not your father's daughter for nothing. But tell me, is Doctor Rank always as depressed as he was yesterday?

NORA. No; yesterday it was very noticeable. I must tell you that he suffers from a very dangerous disease. He has consumption of the spine, poor creature. His father was a horrible man who committed all sorts of excesses; and that is why his son was sickly from childhood, do you understand?

MRS. LINDE (dropping her sewing). But, my dearest Nora, how do you know anything about such things?

NORA (walking about). Pooh! When you have three children, you get visits now and then from—from married women, who know something of medical matters, and they talk about one thing and another.

MRS. LINDE (goes on sewing. A short silence). Does Doctor Rank come here everyday?

NORA. Everyday regularly. He is Torvald's most intimate friend, and a great friend of mine too. He is just like one of the family.

MRS. LINDE. But tell me this—is he perfectly sincere? I mean, isn't he the kind of man that is very anxious to make himself agreeable?

NORA. Not in the least. What makes you think that?

MRS. LINDE. When you introduced him to me yesterday, he declared he had often heard my name mentioned in this house; but afterwards I noticed that your husband hadn't the slightest idea who I was. So how could Doctor Rank—?

NORA. That is quite right, Christine. Torvald is so absurdly fond of me that he wants me absolutely to himself, as he says. At first he used to seem almost jealous if I mentioned any of the dear folk at home, so naturally I gave up doing so. But I often talk about such things with Doctor Rank, because he likes hearing about them.

MRS. LINDE. Listen to me, Nora. You are still very like a child in many things, and I am older than you in many ways and have a little more experience. Let me tell you this—you ought to make an end of it with Doctor Rank.

NORA. What ought I to make an end of?

MRS. LINDE. Of two things, I think. Yesterday you talked some nonsense about a rich admirer who was to leave you money—

NORA. An admirer who doesn't exist, unfortunately! But what then?

MRS. LINDE. Is Doctor Rank a man of means?

NORA. Yes, he is.

MRS. LINDE. And has no one to provide for?

NORA. No, no one; but—

MRS. LINDE. And comes here everyday?

NORA. Yes, I told you so.

MRS. LINDE. But how can this well-bred man be so tactless?

NORA. I don't understand you at all.

MRS. LINDE. Don't prevaricate, Nora. Do you suppose I don't guess who lent you the two hundred and fifty pounds?

NORA. Are you out of your senses? How can you think of such a thing! A friend of ours, who comes here everyday! Do you realise what a horribly painful position that would be?

MRS. LINDE. Then it really isn't he?

NORA. No, certainly not. It would never have entered into my head for a moment. Besides, he had no money to lend then; he came into his money afterwards.

MRS. LINDE. Well, I think that was lucky for you, my dear Nora.

NORA. No, it would never have come into my head to ask Doctor Rank. Although I am quite sure that if I had asked him—

MRS. LINDE. But of course you won't.

NORA. Of course not. I have no reason to think it could possibly be necessary. But I am quite sure that if I told Doctor Rank—

MRS. LINDE. Behind your husband's back?

NORA. I must make an end of it with the other one, and that will be behind his back too. I must make an end of it with him.

MRS. LINDE. Yes, that is what I told you yesterday, but—

NORA (walking up and down). A man can put a thing like that straight much easier than a woman—

MRS. LINDE. One's husband, yes.

NORA. Nonsense! (Standing still.) When you pay off a debt you get your bond back, don't you?

MRS. LINDE. Yes, as a matter of course.

NORA. And can tear it into a hundred thousand pieces, and burn it up—the nasty dirty paper!

MRS. LINDE (looks hard at her, lays down her sewing and gets up slowly).

NORA, you are concealing something from me.

NORA. Do I look as if I were?

MRS. LINDE. Something has happened to you since yesterday morning. Nora, what is it?

NORA (going nearer to her). Christine! (Listens.) Hush! there's Torvald come home. Do you mind going in to the children for the present? Torvald can't bear to see dressmaking going on. Let Anne help you.

MRS. LINDE (gathering some of the things together). Certainly—but I am not going away from here until we have had it out with one another. (She goes into the room on the left, as HELMER comes in from the hall.)

NORA (going up to HELMER). I have wanted you so much, Torvald dear.

HELMER. Was that the dressmaker?

NORA. No, it was Christine; she is helping me to put my dress in order. You will see I shall look quite smart.

HELMER. Wasn't that a happy thought of mine, now?

NORA. Splendid! But don't you think it is nice of me, too, to do as you wish?

HELMER. Nice?—because you do as your husband wishes? Well, well, you little rogue, I am sure you did not mean it in that way. But I am not going to disturb you; you will want to be trying on your dress, I expect.

NORA. I suppose you are going to work.

HELMER. Yes. (Shows her a bundle of papers.) Look at that. I have just been into the bank. (Turns to go into his room.)

NORA. Torvald.

HELMER. Yes.

NORA. If your little squirrel were to ask you for something very, very prettily—?

HELMER. What then?

NORA. Would you do it?

HELMER. I should like to hear what it is, first.

NORA. Your squirrel would run about and do all her tricks if you would be nice, and do what she wants.

HELMER. Speak plainly.

NORA. Your skylark would chirp about in every room, with her song rising and falling—

HELMER. Well, my skylark does that anyhow.

NORA. I would play the fairy and dance for you in the moonlight, Torvald.

HELMER. Nora—you surely don't mean that request you made to me this morning?

NORA (going near him). Yes, Torvald, I beg you so earnestly—

HELMER. Have you really the courage to open up that question again?

NORA. Yes, dear, you must do as I ask; you must let Krogstad keep his post in the bank.

HELMER. My dear Nora, it is his post that I have arranged Mrs. Linde shall have.

NORA. Yes, you have been awfully kind about that; but you could just as well dismiss some other clerk instead of Krogstad.

HELMER. This is simply incredible obstinacy! Because you chose to give him a thoughtless promise that you would speak for him, I am expected to—

NORA. That isn't the reason, Torvald. It is for your own sake. This fellow writes in the most scurrilous newspapers; you have told me so yourself. He can do you an unspeakable amount of harm. I am frightened to death of him—

HELMER. Ah, I understand; it is recollections of the past that scare you.

NORA. What do you mean?

HELMER. Naturally you are thinking of your father.

NORA. Yes—yes, of course. Just recall to your mind what these malicious creatures wrote in the papers about papa, and how horribly they slandered him. I believe they would have procured his dismissal if the Department had not sent you over to inquire into it, and if you had not been so kindly disposed and helpful to him.

HELMER. My little Nora, there is an important difference between your father and me. Your father's reputation as a public official was not above suspicion. Mine is, and I hope it will continue to be so, as long as I hold my office.

NORA. You never can tell what mischief these men may contrive. We ought to be so well off, so snug and happy here in our peaceful home, and have no cares—you and I and the children, Torvald! That is why I beg you so earnestly—

HELMER. And it is just by interceding for him that you make it impossible for me to keep him. It is already known at the Bank that I mean to dismiss Krogstad. Is it to get about now that the new manager has changed his mind at his wife's bidding—

NORA. And what if it did?

HELMER. Of course!—if only this obstinate little person can get her way! Do you suppose I am going to make myself ridiculous before my whole staff, to let people think that I am a man to be swayed by all sorts of outside influence? I should very soon feel the consequences of it, I can tell you! And besides, there is one thing that makes it quite impossible for me to have Krogstad in the Bank as long as I am manager.

NORA. Whatever is that?

HELMER. His moral failings I might perhaps have overlooked, if necessary—

NORA. Yes, you could—couldn't you?

HELMER. And I hear he is a good worker, too. But I knew him when we were boys. It was one of those rash friendships that so often prove an incubus in afterlife. I may as well tell you plainly, we were once on very intimate terms with one another. But this tactless fellow lays no restraint on himself when other people are present. On the contrary, he thinks it gives him the right to adopt a familiar tone with me, and every minute it is "I say, Helmer, old fellow!" and that sort of thing. I assure you it is extremely painful for me. He would make my position in the Bank intolerable.

NORA. Torvald, I don't believe you mean that.

HELMER. Don't you? Why not?

NORA. Because it is such a narrow-minded way of looking at things.

HELMER. What are you saying? Narrow-minded? Do you think I am narrow-minded?

NORA. No, just the opposite, dear—and it is exactly for that reason.

HELMER. It's the same thing. You say my point of view is narrow-minded, so I must be so too. Narrow-minded! Very well—I must put an end to this. (Goes to the hall door and calls.) Helen!

NORA. What are you going to do?

HELMER (looking among his papers). Settle it. (Enter MAID.) Look here; take this letter and go downstairs with it at once. Find a messenger and tell him to deliver it, and be quick. The address is on it, and here is the money.

MAID. Very well, sir. (Exit with the letter.)

HELMER (putting his papers together). Now then, little Miss Obstinate.

NORA (breathlessly). Torvald—what was that letter?

HELMER. Krogstad's dismissal.

NORA. Call her back, Torvald! There is still time. Oh Torvald, call her back! Do it for my sake—for your own sake—for the children's sake! Do you hear me, Torvald? Call her back! You don't know what that letter can bring upon us.

HELMER. It's too late.

NORA. Yes, it's too late.

HELMER. My dear Nora, I can forgive the anxiety you are in, although really it is an insult to me. It is, indeed. Isn't it an insult to think that I should be afraid of a starving quill-driver's vengeance? But I forgive you nevertheless, because it is such eloquent witness to your great love for me. (Takes her in his arms.) And that is as it should be, my own darling Nora. Come what will, you may be sure I shall have both courage and strength if they be needed. You will see I am man enough to take everything upon myself.

NORA (in a horror-stricken voice). What do you mean by that?

HELMER. Everything, I say—

NORA (recovering herself). You will never have to do that.

HELMER. That's right. Well, we will share it, Nora, as man and wife should. That is how it shall be. (Caressing her.) Are you content now? There! There!—not these frightened dove's eyes! The whole thing is only the wildest fancy!—Now, you must go and play through the Tarantella and practise with your tambourine. I shall go into the inner office and shut the door, and I shall hear nothing; you can make as much noise as you please. (Turns back at the door.) And when Rank comes, tell him where he will find me. (Nods to her, takes his papers and goes into his room, and shuts the door after him.)

NORA (bewildered with anxiety, stands as if rooted to the spot, and whispers). He was capable of doing it. He will do it. He will do it in spite of everything.—No, not that! Never, never! Anything rather than that! Oh, for some help, some way out of it! (The door-bell rings.) Doctor Rank! Anything rather than that—anything, whatever it is! (She puts her hands over her face, pulls herself together, goes to the door and opens it. RANK is standing without, hanging up his coat. During the following dialogue it begins to grow dark.)

NORA. Good day, Doctor Rank. I knew your ring. But you mustn't go in to Torvald now; I think he is busy with something.

RANK. And you?

NORA (brings him in and shuts the door after him). Oh, you know very well I always have time for you.

RANK. Thank you. I shall make use of as much of it as I can.

NORA. What do you mean by that? As much of it as you can?

RANK. Well, does that alarm you?

NORA. It was such a strange way of putting it. Is anything likely to happen?

RANK. Nothing but what I have long been prepared for. But I certainly didn't expect it to happen so soon.

NORA (gripping him by the arm). What have you found out? Doctor Rank, you must tell me.

RANK (sitting down by the stove). It is all up with me. And it can't be helped.

NORA (with a sigh of relief). Is it about yourself?

RANK. Who else? It is no use lying to one's self. I am the most wretched of all my patients, Mrs. Helmer. Lately I have been taking stock of my internal economy. Bankrupt! Probably within a month I shall lie rotting in the churchyard.

NORA. What an ugly thing to say!

RANK. The thing itself is cursedly ugly, and the worst of it is that I shall have to face so much more that is ugly before that. I shall only make one more examination of myself; when I have done that, I shall know pretty certainly when it will be that the horrors of dissolution will begin. There is something I want to tell you. Helmer's refined nature gives him an unconquerable disgust at everything that is ugly; I won't have him in my sick-room.

NORA. Oh, but, Doctor Rank—

RANK. I won't have him there. Not on any account. I bar my door to him. As soon as I am quite certain that the worst has come, I shall send you my card with a black cross on it, and then you will know that the loathsome end has begun.

NORA. You are quite absurd today. And I wanted you so much to be in a really good humour.

RANK. With death stalking beside me?—To have to pay this penalty for another man's sin? Is there any justice in that? And in every single family, in one way or another, some such inexorable retribution is being exacted—

NORA (putting her hands over her ears). Rubbish! Do talk of something cheerful.

RANK. Oh, it's a mere laughing matter, the whole thing. My poor innocent spine has to suffer for my father's youthful amusements.

NORA (sitting at the table on the left). I suppose you mean that he was too partial to asparagus and pate de foie gras, don't you?

RANK. Yes, and to truffles.

NORA. Truffles, yes. And oysters too, I suppose?

RANK. Oysters, of course, that goes without saying.

NORA. And heaps of port and champagne. It is sad that all these nice things should take their revenge on our bones.

RANK. Especially that they should revenge themselves on the unlucky bones of those who have not had the satisfaction of enjoying them.

NORA. Yes, that's the saddest part of it all.

RANK (with a searching look at her). Hm!—

NORA (after a short pause). Why did you smile?

RANK. No, it was you that laughed.

NORA. No, it was you that smiled, Doctor Rank!

RANK (rising). You are a greater rascal than I thought.

NORA. I am in a silly mood today.

RANK. So it seems.

NORA (putting her hands on his shoulders). Dear, dear Doctor Rank, death mustn't take you away from Torvald and me.

RANK. It is a loss you would easily recover from. Those who are gone are soon forgotten.

NORA (looking at him anxiously). Do you believe that?

RANK. People form new ties, and then—

NORA. Who will form new ties?

RANK. Both you and Helmer, when I am gone. You yourself are already on the high road to it, I think. What did that Mrs. Linde want here last night?

NORA. Oho!—you don't mean to say you are jealous of poor Christine?

RANK. Yes, I am. She will be my successor in this house. When I am done for, this woman will—

NORA. Hush! don't speak so loud. She is in that room.

RANK. Today again. There, you see.

NORA. She has only come to sew my dress for me. Bless my soul, how unreasonable you are! (Sits down on the sofa.) Be nice now, Doctor Rank, and tomorrow you will see how beautifully I shall dance, and you can imagine I am doing it all for you—and for Torvald too, of course. (Takes various things out of the box.) Doctor Rank, come and sit down here, and I will show you something.

RANK (sitting down). What is it?

NORA. Just look at those!

RANK. Silk stockings.

NORA. Flesh-coloured. Aren't they lovely? It is so dark here now, but tomorrow—. No, no, no! you must only look at the feet. Oh well, you may have leave to look at the legs too.

RANK. Hm!—

NORA. Why are you looking so critical? Don't you think they will fit me?

RANK. I have no means of forming an opinion about that.

NORA (looks at him for a moment). For shame! (Hits him lightly on the ear with the stockings.) That's to punish you. (Folds them up again.)

RANK. And what other nice things am I to be allowed to see?

NORA. Not a single thing more, for being so naughty. (She looks among the things, humming to herself.)

RANK (after a short silence). When I am sitting here, talking to you as intimately as this, I cannot imagine for a moment what would have become of me if I had never come into this house.

NORA (smiling). I believe you do feel thoroughly at home with us.

RANK (in a lower voice, looking straight in front of him). And to be obliged to leave it all—

NORA. Nonsense, you are not going to leave it.

RANK (as before). And not be able to leave behind one the slightest token of one's gratitude, scarcely even a fleeting regret—nothing but an empty place which the first comer can fill as well as any other.

NORA. And if I asked you now for a—? No!

RANK. For what?

NORA. For a big proof of your friendship—

RANK. Yes, yes!

NORA. I mean a tremendously big favour—

RANK. Would you really make me so happy for once?

NORA. Ah, but you don't know what it is yet.

RANK. No—but tell me.

NORA. I really can't, Doctor Rank. It is something out of all reason; it means advice, and help, and a favour—

RANK. The bigger a thing it is the better. I can't conceive what it is you mean. Do tell me. Haven't I your confidence?

NORA. More than anyone else. I know you are my truest and best friend, and so I will tell you what it is. Well, Doctor Rank, it is something you must help me to prevent. You know how devotedly, how inexpressibly deeply Torvald loves me; he would never for a moment hesitate to give his life for me.

RANK (leaning towards her). Nora—do you think he is the only one—?

NORA (with a slight start). The only one—?

RANK. The only one who would gladly give his life for your sake.

NORA (sadly). Is that it?

RANK. I was determined you should know it before I went away, and there will never be a better opportunity than this. Now you know it, Nora. And now you know, too, that you can trust me as you would trust no one else.

NORA (rises, deliberately and quietly). Let me pass.

RANK (makes room for her to pass him, but sits still). Nora!

NORA (at the hall door). Helen, bring in the lamp. (Goes over to the stove.) Dear Doctor Rank, that was really horrid of you.

RANK. To have loved you as much as anyone else does? Was that horrid?

NORA. No, but to go and tell me so. There was really no need—

RANK. What do you mean? Did you know—? (MAID enters with lamp, puts it down on the table, and goes out.) Nora—Mrs. Helmer—tell me, had you any idea of this?

NORA. Oh, how do I know whether I had or whether I hadn't? I really can't tell you—To think you could be so clumsy, Doctor Rank! We were getting on so nicely.

RANK. Well, at all events you know now that you can command me, body and soul. So won't you speak out?

NORA (looking at him). After what happened?

RANK. I beg you to let me know what it is.

NORA. I can't tell you anything now.

RANK. Yes, yes. You mustn't punish me in that way. Let me have permission to do for you whatever a man may do.

NORA. You can do nothing for me now. Besides, I really don't need any help at all. You will find that the whole thing is merely fancy on my part. It really is so—of course it is! (Sits down in the rocking-chair, and looks at him with a smile.) You are a nice sort of man, Doctor Rank!—don't you feel ashamed of yourself, now the lamp has come?

RANK. Not a bit. But perhaps I had better go—for ever?

NORA. No, indeed, you shall not. Of course you must come here just as before. You know very well Torvald can't do without you.

RANK. Yes, but you?

NORA. Oh, I am always tremendously pleased when you come.

RANK. It is just that, that put me on the wrong track. You are a riddle to me. I have often thought that you would almost as soon be in my company as in Helmer's.

NORA. Yes—you see there are some people one loves best, and others whom one would almost always rather have as companions.

RANK. Yes, there is something in that.

NORA. When I was at home, of course I loved papa best. But I always thought it tremendous fun if I could steal down into the maids' room, because they never moralised at all, and talked to each other about such entertaining things.

RANK. I see—it is their place I have taken.

NORA (jumping up and going to him). Oh, dear, nice Doctor Rank, I never meant that at all. But surely you can understand that being with Torvald is a little like being with papa—(Enter MAID from the hall.)

MAID. If you please, ma'am. (Whispers and hands her a card.)

NORA (glancing at the card). Oh! (Puts it in her pocket.)

RANK. Is there anything wrong?

NORA. No, no, not in the least. It is only something—it is my new dress—

RANK. What? Your dress is lying there.

NORA. Oh, yes, that one; but this is another. I ordered it. Torvald mustn't know about it—

RANK. Oho! Then that was the great secret.

NORA. Of course. Just go in to him; he is sitting in the inner room. Keep him as long as—

RANK. Make your mind easy; I won't let him escape.

(Goes into HELMER'S room.)

NORA (to the MAID). And he is standing waiting in the kitchen?

MAID. Yes; he came up the back stairs.

NORA. But didn't you tell him no one was in?

MAID. Yes, but it was no good.

NORA. He won't go away?

MAID. No; he says he won't until he has seen you, ma'am.

NORA. Well, let him come in—but quietly. Helen, you mustn't say anything about it to anyone. It is a surprise for my husband.

MAID. Yes, ma'am, I quite understand. (Exit.)

NORA. This dreadful thing is going to happen! It will happen in spite of me! No, no, no, it can't happen—it shan't happen! (She bolts the door of HELMER'S room. The MAID opens the hall door for KROGSTAD and shuts it after him. He is wearing a fur coat, high boots and a fur cap.)

NORA (advancing towards him). Speak low—my husband is at home.

KROGSTAD. No matter about that.

NORA. What do you want of me?

KROGSTAD. An explanation of something.

NORA. Make haste then. What is it?

KROGSTAD. You know, I suppose, that I have got my dismissal.

NORA. I couldn't prevent it, Mr. Krogstad. I fought as hard as I could on your side, but it was no good.

KROGSTAD. Does your husband love you so little, then? He knows what I can expose you to, and yet he ventures—

NORA. How can you suppose that he has any knowledge of the sort?

KROGSTAD. I didn't suppose so at all. It would not be the least like our dear Torvald Helmer to show so much courage—

NORA. Mr. Krogstad, a little respect for my husband, please.

KROGSTAD. Certainly—all the respect he deserves. But since you have kept the matter so carefully to yourself, I make bold to suppose that you have a little clearer idea, than you had yesterday, of what it actually is that you have done?

NORA. More than you could ever teach me.

KROGSTAD. Yes, such a bad lawyer as I am.

NORA. What is it you want of me?

KROGSTAD. Only to see how you were, Mrs. Helmer. I have been thinking about you all day long. A mere cashier, a quill-driver, a—well, a man like me—even he has a little of what is called feeling, you know.

NORA. Show it, then; think of my little children.

KROGSTAD. Have you and your husband thought of mine? But never mind about that. I only wanted to tell you that you need not take this matter too seriously. In the first place there will be no accusation made on my part.

NORA. No, of course not; I was sure of that.

KROGSTAD. The whole thing can be arranged amicably; there is no reason why anyone should know anything about it. It will remain a secret between us three.

NORA. My husband must never get to know anything about it.

KROGSTAD. How will you be able to prevent it? Am I to understand that you can pay the balance that is owing?

NORA. No, not just at present.

KROGSTAD. Or perhaps that you have some expedient for raising the money soon?

NORA. No expedient that I mean to make use of.

KROGSTAD. Well, in any case, it would have been of no use to you now. If you stood there with ever so much money in your hand, I would never part with your bond.

NORA. Tell me what purpose you mean to put it to.

KROGSTAD. I shall only preserve it—keep it in my possession. No one who is not concerned in the matter shall have the slightest hint of it. So that if the thought of it has driven you to any desperate resolution—

NORA. It has.

KROGSTAD. If you had it in your mind to run away from your home—

NORA. I had.

KROGSTAD. Or even something worse—

NORA. How could you know that?

KROGSTAD. Give up the idea.

NORA. How did you know I had thought of that?

KROGSTAD. Most of us think of that at first. I did, too—but I hadn't the courage.

NORA (faintly). No more had I.

KROGSTAD (in a tone of relief). No, that's it, isn't it—you hadn't the courage either?

NORA. No, I haven't—I haven't.

KROGSTAD. Besides, it would have been a great piece of folly. Once the first storm at home is over—. I have a letter for your husband in my pocket.

NORA. Telling him everything?

KROGSTAD. In as lenient a manner as I possibly could.

NORA (quickly). He mustn't get the letter. Tear it up. I will find some means of getting money.

KROGSTAD. Excuse me, Mrs. Helmer, but I think I told you just now—

NORA. I am not speaking of what I owe you. Tell me what sum you are asking my husband for, and I will get the money.

KROGSTAD. I am not asking your husband for a penny.

NORA. What do you want, then?

KROGSTAD. I will tell you. I want to rehabilitate myself, Mrs. Helmer; I want to get on; and in that your husband must help me. For the last year and a half I have not had a hand in anything dishonourable, amid all that time I have been struggling in most restricted circumstances. I was content to work my way up step by step. Now I am turned out, and I am not going to be satisfied with merely being taken into favour again. I want to get on, I tell you. I want to get into the Bank again, in a higher position. Your husband must make a place for me—

NORA. That he will never do!

KROGSTAD. He will; I know him; he dare not protest. And as soon as I am in there again with him, then you will see! Within a year I shall be the manager's right hand. It will be Nils Krogstad and not Torvald Helmer who manages the Bank.

NORA. That's a thing you will never see!

KROGSTAD. Do you mean that you will—?

NORA. I have courage enough for it now.

KROGSTAD. Oh, you can't frighten me. A fine, spoilt lady like you—

NORA. You will see, you will see.

KROGSTAD. Under the ice, perhaps? Down into the cold, coal-black water? And then, in the spring, to float up to the surface, all horrible and unrecognisable, with your hair fallen out—

NORA. You can't frighten me.

KROGSTAD. Nor you me. People don't do such things, Mrs. Helmer. Besides, what use would it be? I should have him completely in my power all the same.

NORA. Afterwards? When I am no longer—

KROGSTAD. Have you forgotten that it is I who have the keeping of your reputation? (NORA stands speechlessly looking at him.) Well, now, I have warned you. Do not do anything foolish. When Helmer has had my letter, I shall expect a message from him. And be sure you remember that it is your husband himself who has forced me into such ways as this again. I will never forgive him for that. Goodbye, Mrs. Helmer. (Exit through the hall.)

NORA (goes to the hall door, opens it slightly and listens.) He is going. He is not putting the letter in the box. Oh no, no! that's impossible! (Opens the door by degrees.) What is that? He is standing outside. He is not going downstairs. Is he hesitating? Can he—? (A letter drops into the box; then KROGSTAD'S footsteps are heard, until they die away as he goes downstairs. NORA utters a stifled cry, and runs across the room to the table by the sofa. A short pause.)

NORA. In the letter-box. (Steals across to the hall door.) There it lies—Torvald, Torvald, there is no hope for us now!

(Mrs. LINDE comes in from the room on the left, carrying the dress.)

MRS. LINDE. There, I can't see anything more to mend now. Would you like to try it on—?

NORA (in a hoarse whisper). Christine, come here.

MRS. LINDE (throwing the dress down on the sofa). What is the matter with you? You look so agitated!

NORA. Come here. Do you see that letter? There, look—you can see it through the glass in the letter-box.

MRS. LINDE. Yes, I see it.

NORA. That letter is from Krogstad.

MRS. LINDE. Nora—it was Krogstad who lent you the money!

NORA. Yes, and now Torvald will know all about it.

MRS. LINDE. Believe me, Nora, that's the best thing for both of you.

NORA. You don't know all. I forged a name.

MRS. LINDE. Good heavens—!

NORA. I only want to say this to you, Christine—you must be my witness.

MRS. LINDE. Your witness? What do you mean? What am I to—?

NORA. If I should go out of my mind—and it might easily happen—

MRS. LINDE. Nora!

NORA. Or if anything else should happen to me—anything, for instance, that might prevent my being here—

MRS. LINDE. Nora! Nora! you are quite out of your mind.

NORA. And if it should happen that there were some one who wanted to take all the responsibility, all the blame, you understand—

MRS. LINDE. Yes, yes—but how can you suppose—?

NORA. Then you must be my witness, that it is not true, Christine. I am not out of my mind at all; I am in my right senses now, and I tell you no one else has known anything about it; I, and I alone, did the whole thing. Remember that.

MRS. LINDE. I will, indeed. But I don't understand all this.

NORA. How should you understand it? A wonderful thing is going to happen!

MRS. LINDE. A wonderful thing?

NORA. Yes, a wonderful thing!—But it is so terrible, Christine; it mustn't happen, not for all the world.

MRS. LINDE. I will go at once and see Krogstad.

NORA. Don't go to him; he will do you some harm.

MRS. LINDE. There was a time when he would gladly do anything for my sake.

NORA. He?

MRS. LINDE. Where does he live?

NORA. How should I know—? Yes (feeling in her pocket), here is his card. But the letter, the letter—!

HELMER (calls from his room, knocking at the door). Nora! Nora (cries out anxiously). Oh, what's that? What do you want?

HELMER. Don't be so frightened. We are not coming in; you have locked the door. Are you trying on your dress?

NORA. Yes, that's it. I look so nice, Torvald.

MRS. LINDE (who has read the card). I see he lives at the corner here.

NORA. Yes, but it's no use. It is hopeless. The letter is lying there in the box.

MRS. LINDE. And your husband keeps the key?

NORA. Yes, always.

MRS. LINDE. Krogstad must ask for his letter back unread, he must find some pretence—

NORA. But it is just at this time that Torvald generally—

MRS. LINDE. You must delay him. Go in to him in the meantime. I will come back as soon as I can. (She goes out hurriedly through the hall door.)

NORA (goes to HELMER'S door, opens it and peeps in). Torvald!

HELMER (from the inner room). Well? May I venture at last to come into my own room again? Come along, Rank, now you will see— (Halting in the doorway.) But what is this?

NORA. What is what, dear?

HELMER. Rank led me to expect a splendid transformation.

RANK (in the doorway). I understood so, but evidently I was mistaken.

NORA. Yes, nobody is to have the chance of admiring me in my dress until tomorrow.

HELMER. But, my dear Nora, you look so worn out. Have you been practising too much?

NORA. No, I have not practised at all.

HELMER. But you will need to—

NORA. Yes, indeed I shall, Torvald. But I can't get on a bit without you to help me; I have absolutely forgotten the whole thing.

HELMER. Oh, we will soon work it up again.

NORA. Yes, help me, Torvald. Promise that you will! I am so nervous about it—all the people—. You must give yourself up to me entirely this evening. Not the tiniest bit of business—you mustn't even take a pen in your hand. Will you promise, Torvald dear?

HELMER. I promise. This evening I will be wholly and absolutely at your service, you helpless little mortal. Ah, by the way, first of all I will just— (Goes towards the hall door.)

NORA. What are you going to do there?

HELMER. Only see if any letters have come.

NORA. No, no! don't do that, Torvald!

HELMER. Why not?

NORA. Torvald, please don't. There is nothing there.

HELMER. Well, let me look. (Turns to go to the letter-box. NORA, at the piano, plays the first bars of the Tarantella. HELMER stops in the doorway.) Aha!

NORA. I can't dance tomorrow if I don't practise with you.

HELMER (going up to her). Are you really so afraid of it, dear?

NORA. Yes, so dreadfully afraid of it. Let me practise at once; there is time now, before we go to dinner. Sit down and play for me, Torvald dear; criticise me, and correct me as you play.

HELMER. With great pleasure, if you wish me to. (Sits down at the piano.)

NORA (takes out of the box a tambourine and a long variegated shawl. She hastily drapes the shawl round her. Then she springs to the front of the stage and calls out). Now play for me! I am going to dance!

(HELMER plays and NORA dances. RINK stands by the piano behind HELMER, and looks on.)

HELMER (as he plays). Slower, slower!

NORA. I can't do it any other way.

HELMER. Not so violently, Nora!

NORA. This is the way.

HELMER (stops playing). No, no—that is not a bit right.

NORA (laughing and swinging the tambourine). Didn't I tell you so?

RANK. Let me play for her.

HELMER (getting up). Yes, do. I can correct her better then.

(RANK sits down at the piano and plays. NORA dances more and more wildly. HELMER has taken up a position beside the stove, and during her dance gives her frequent instructions. She does not seem to hear him; her hair comes down and falls over her shoulders; she pays no attention to it, but goes on dancing. Enter Mrs. LINDE.)

MRS. LINDE (standing as if spell-bound in the doorway). Oh!—

NORA (as she dances). Such fun, Christine!

HELMER. My dear darling Nora, you are dancing as if your life depended on it.

NORA. So it does.

HELMER. Stop, Rank; this is sheer madness. Stop, I tell you! (RANK stops playing, and NORA suddenly stands still. HELMER goes up to her.) I could never have believed it. You have forgotten everything I taught you.

NORA (throwing away the tambourine). There, you see.

HELMER. You will want a lot of coaching.

NORA. Yes, you see how much I need it. You must coach me up to the last minute. Promise me that, Torvald!

HELMER. You can depend on me.

NORA. You must not think of anything but me, either today or tomorrow; you mustn't open a single letter—not even open the letter-box—

HELMER. Ah, you are still afraid of that fellow—

NORA. Yes, indeed I am.

HELMER. Nora, I can tell from your looks that there is a letter from him lying there.

NORA. I don't know; I think there is; but you must not read anything of that kind now. Nothing horrid must come between us until this is all over.

RANK (whispers to HELMER). You mustn't contradict her.

HELMER (taking her in his arms). The child shall have her way. But tomorrow night, after you have danced—

NORA. Then you will be free. (The MAID appears in the doorway to the right.)

MAID. Dinner is served, ma'am.

NORA. We will have champagne, Helen.

MAID. Very good, ma'am. [Exit.]

HELMER. Hullo!—are we going to have a banquet?

NORA. Yes, a champagne banquet until the small hours. (Calls out.) And a few macaroons, Helen—lots, just for once!

HELMER. Come, come, don't be so wild and nervous. Be my own little skylark, as you used.

NORA. Yes, dear, I will. But go in now and you too, Doctor Rank. Christine, you must help me to do up my hair.

RANK (whispers to HELMER as they go out). I suppose there is nothing—she is not expecting anything?

HELMER. Far from it, my dear fellow; it is simply nothing more than this childish nervousness I was telling you of. (They go into the right-hand room.)

NORA. Well!

MRS. LINDE. Gone out of town.

NORA. I could tell from your face.

MRS. LINDE. He is coming home tomorrow evening. I wrote a note for him.

NORA. You should have let it alone; you must prevent nothing. After all, it is splendid to be waiting for a wonderful thing to happen.

MRS. LINDE. What is it that you are waiting for?

NORA. Oh, you wouldn't understand. Go in to them, I will come in a moment. (Mrs. LINDE goes into the dining-room. NORA stands still for a little while, as if to compose herself. Then she looks at her watch.) Five o'clock. Seven hours until midnight; and then four-and-twenty hours until the next midnight. Then the Tarantella will be over. Twenty-four and seven? Thirty-one hours to live.

HELMER (from the doorway on the right). Where's my little skylark?

NORA (going to him with her arms outstretched). Here she is!

ACT III

THE SAME SCENE.

The table has been placed in the middle of the stage, with chairs around it. A lamp is burning on the table. The door into the hall stands open. Dance music is heard in the room above. Mrs. LINDE is sitting at the table idly turning over the leaves of a book; she tries to read, but does not seem able to collect her thoughts. Every now and then she listens intently for a sound at the outer door.)

MRS. LINDE (looking at her watch). Not yet—and the time is nearly up. If only he does not—. (Listens again.) Ah, there he is. (Goes into the hall and opens the outer door carefully. Light footsteps are heard on the stairs. She whispers.) Come in. There is no one here.

KROGSTAD (in the doorway). I found a note from you at home. What does this mean?

MRS. LINDE. It is absolutely necessary that I should have a talk with you.

KROGSTAD. Really? And is it absolutely necessary that it should be here?

MRS. LINDE. It is impossible where I live; there is no private entrance to my rooms. Come in; we are quite alone. The maid is asleep, and the Helmers are at the dance upstairs.

KROGSTAD (coming into the room). Are the Helmers really at a dance tonight?

MRS. LINDE. Yes, why not?

KROGSTAD. Certainly—why not?

MRS. LINDE. Now, Nils, let us have a talk.

KROGSTAD. Can we two have anything to talk about?

MRS. LINDE. We have a great deal to talk about.

KROGSTAD. I shouldn't have thought so.

MRS. LINDE. No, you have never properly understood me.

KROGSTAD. Was there anything else to understand except what was obvious to all the world—a heartless woman jilts a man when a more lucrative chance turns up?

MRS. LINDE. Do you believe I am as absolutely heartless as all that? And do you believe that I did it with a light heart?

KROGSTAD. Didn't you?

MRS. LINDE. Nils, did you really think that?

KROGSTAD. If it were as you say, why did you write to me as you did at the time?

MRS. LINDE. I could do nothing else. As I had to break with you, it was my duty also to put an end to all that you felt for me.

KROGSTAD (wringing his hands). So that was it. And all this—only for the sake of money!

MRS. LINDE. You must not forget that I had a helpless mother and two little brothers. We couldn't wait for you, Nils; your prospects seemed hopeless then.

KROGSTAD. That may be so, but you had no right to throw me over for anyone else's sake.

MRS. LINDE. Indeed I don't know. Many a time did I ask myself if I had the right to do it.

KROGSTAD (more gently). When I lost you, it was as if all the solid ground went from under my feet. Look at me now—I am a shipwrecked man clinging to a bit of wreckage.

MRS. LINDE. But help may be near.

KROGSTAD. It was near; but then you came and stood in my way.

MRS. LINDE. Unintentionally, Nils. It was only today that I learned it was your place I was going to take in the Bank.

KROGSTAD. I believe you, if you say so. But now that you know it, are you not going to give it up to me?

MRS. LINDE. No, because that would not benefit you in the least.

KROGSTAD. Oh, benefit, benefit—I would have done it whether or no.

MRS. LINDE. I have learned to act prudently. Life, and hard, bitter necessity have taught me that.

KROGSTAD. And life has taught me not to believe in fine speeches.

MRS. LINDE. Then life has taught you something very reasonable. But deeds you must believe in?

KROGSTAD. What do you mean by that?

MRS. LINDE. You said you were like a shipwrecked man clinging to some wreckage.

KROGSTAD. I had good reason to say so.

MRS. LINDE. Well, I am like a shipwrecked woman clinging to some wreckage—no one to mourn for, no one to care for.

KROGSTAD. It was your own choice.

MRS. LINDE. There was no other choice—then.

KROGSTAD. Well, what now?

MRS. LINDE. Nils, how would it be if we two shipwrecked people could join forces?

KROGSTAD. What are you saying?

MRS. LINDE. Two on the same piece of wreckage would stand a better chance than each on their own.

KROGSTAD. Christine I . . .

MRS. LINDE. What do you suppose brought me to town?

KROGSTAD. Do you mean that you gave me a thought?

MRS. LINDE. I could not endure life without work. All my life, as long as I can remember, I have worked, and it has been my greatest and only pleasure. But now I am quite alone in the world—my life is so dreadfully empty and I feel so forsaken. There is not the least pleasure in working for one's self. Nils, give me someone and something to work for.

KROGSTAD. I don't trust that. It is nothing but a woman's overstrained sense of generosity that prompts you to make such an offer of yourself.

MRS. LINDE. Have you ever noticed anything of the sort in me?

KROGSTAD. Could you really do it? Tell me—do you know all about my past life?

MRS. LINDE. Yes.

KROGSTAD. And do you know what they think of me here?

MRS. LINDE. You seemed to me to imply that with me you might have been quite another man.

KROGSTAD. I am certain of it.

MRS. LINDE. Is it too late now?

KROGSTAD. Christine, are you saying this deliberately? Yes, I am sure you are. I see it in your face. Have you really the courage, then—?

MRS. LINDE. I want to be a mother to someone, and your children need a mother. We two need each other. Nils, I have faith in your real character—I can dare anything together with you.

KROGSTAD (grasps her hands). Thanks, thanks, Christine! Now I shall find a way to clear myself in the eyes of the world. Ah, but I forgot—

MRS. LINDE (listening). Hush! The Tarantella! Go, go!

KROGSTAD. Why? What is it?

MRS. LINDE. Do you hear them up there? When that is over, we may expect them back.

KROGSTAD. Yes, yes—I will go. But it is all no use. Of course you are not aware what steps I have taken in the matter of the Helmers.

MRS. LINDE. Yes, I know all about that.

KROGSTAD. And in spite of that have you the courage to—?

MRS. LINDE. I understand very well to what lengths a man like you might be driven by despair.

KROGSTAD. If I could only undo what I have done!

MRS. LINDE. You cannot. Your letter is lying in the letter-box now.

KROGSTAD. Are you sure of that?

MRS. LINDE. Quite sure, but—

KROGSTAD (with a searching look at her). Is that what it all means?—that you want to save your friend at any cost? Tell me frankly. Is that it?

MRS. LINDE. Nils, a woman who has once sold herself for another's sake, doesn't do it a second time.

KROGSTAD. I will ask for my letter back.

MRS. LINDE. No, no.

KROGSTAD. Yes, of course I will. I will wait here until Helmer comes; I will tell him he must give me my letter back—that it only concerns my dismissal—that he is not to read it—

MRS. LINDE. No, Nils, you must not recall your letter.

KROGSTAD. But, tell me, wasn't it for that very purpose that you asked me to meet you here?

MRS. LINDE. In my first moment of fright, it was. But twenty-four hours have elapsed since then, and in that time I have witnessed incredible things in this house. Helmer must know all about it. This unhappy secret must be disclosed; they must have a complete understanding between them, which is impossible with all this concealment and falsehood going on.

KROGSTAD. Very well, if you will take the responsibility. But there is one thing I can do in any case, and I shall do it at once.

MRS. LINDE (listening). You must be quick and go! The dance is over; we are not safe a moment longer.

KROGSTAD. I will wait for you below.

MRS. LINDE. Yes, do. You must see me back to my door . . .

KROGSTAD. I have never had such an amazing piece of good fortune in my life! (Goes out through the outer door. The door between the room and the hall remains open.)

MRS. LINDE (tidying up the room and laying her hat and cloak ready). What a difference! what a difference! Someone to work for and live for—a home to bring comfort into. That I will do, indeed. I wish they would be quick and come—(Listens.) Ah, there they are now. I must put on my things. (Takes up her hat and cloak. HELMER'S and NORA'S voices are heard outside; a key is turned, and HELMER brings NORA almost by force into the hall. She is in an Italian costume with a large black shawl around her; he is in evening dress, and a black domino which is flying open.)

NORA (hanging back in the doorway, and struggling with him). No, no, no!—don't take me in. I want to go upstairs again; I don't want to leave so early.

HELMER. But, my dearest Nora—

NORA. Please, Torvald dear—please, please—only an hour more.

HELMER. Not a single minute, my sweet Nora. You know that was our agreement. Come along into the room; you are catching cold standing there. (He brings her gently into the room, in spite of her resistance.)

MRS. LINDE. Good evening.

NORA. Christine!

HELMER. You here, so late, Mrs. Linde?

MRS. LINDE. Yes, you must excuse me; I was so anxious to see Nora in her dress.

NORA. Have you been sitting here waiting for me?

MRS. LINDE. Yes, unfortunately I came too late, you had already gone upstairs; and I thought I couldn't go away again without having seen you.

HELMER (taking off NORA'S shawl). Yes, take a good look at her. I think she is worth looking at. Isn't she charming, Mrs. Linde?

MRS. LINDE. Yes, indeed she is.

HELMER. Doesn't she look remarkably pretty? Everyone thought so at the dance. But she is terribly self-willed, this sweet little person. What are we to do with her? You will hardly believe that I had almost to bring her away by force.

NORA. Torvald, you will repent not having let me stay, even if it were only for half an hour.

HELMER. Listen to her, Mrs. Linde! She had danced her Tarantella, and it had been a tremendous success, as it deserved—although possibly the performance was a trifle too realistic—a little more so, I mean, than was strictly compatible with the limitations of art. But never mind about that! The chief thing is, she had made a success—she had made a tremendous success. Do you think I was going to let her remain there after that, and spoil the effect? No, indeed! I took my charming little Capri maiden—my capricious little Capri maiden, I should say—on my arm; took one quick turn round the room; a curtsey on either side, and, as they say in novels, the beautiful apparition disappeared. An exit ought always to be effective, Mrs. Linde; but that is what I cannot make Nora understand. Pooh! this room is hot. (Throws his domino on a chair, and opens the door of his room.) Hullo! it's all dark in here. Oh, of course—excuse me—. (He goes in, and lights some candles.)

NORA (in a hurried and breathless whisper). Well?

MRS. LINDE (in a low voice). I have had a talk with him.

NORA. Yes, and—

MRS. LINDE. Nora, you must tell your husband all about it.

NORA (in an expressionless voice). I knew it.

MRS. LINDE. You have nothing to be afraid of as far as Krogstad is concerned; but you must tell him.

NORA. I won't tell him.

MRS. LINDE. Then the letter will.

NORA. Thank you, Christine. Now I know what I must do. Hush—!

HELMER (coming in again). Well, Mrs. Linde, have you admired her?

MRS. LINDE. Yes, and now I will say goodnight.

HELMER. What, already? Is this yours, this knitting?

MRS. LINDE (taking it). Yes, thank you, I had very nearly forgotten it.

HELMER. So you knit?

MRS. LINDE. Of course.

HELMER. Do you know, you ought to embroider.

MRS. LINDE. Really? Why?

HELMER. Yes, it's far more becoming. Let me show you. You hold the embroidery thus in your left hand, and use the needle with the right—like this—with a long, easy sweep. Do you see?

MRS. LINDE. Yes, perhaps—

HELMER. But in the case of knitting—that can never be anything but ungraceful; look here—the arms close together, the knitting-needles going up and down—it has a sort of Chinese effect—. That was really excellent champagne they gave us.

MRS. LINDE. Well,—goodnight, Nora, and don't be self-willed any more.

HELMER. That's right, Mrs. Linde.

MRS. LINDE. Goodnight, Mr. Helmer.

HELMER (accompanying her to the door). Goodnight, goodnight. I hope you will get home all right. I should be very happy to—but you haven't any great distance to go. Goodnight, goodnight. (She goes out; he shuts the door after her, and comes in again.) Ah!—at last we have got rid of her. She is a frightful bore, that woman.

NORA. Aren't you very tired, Torvald?

HELMER. No, not in the least.

NORA. Nor sleepy?

HELMER. Not a bit. On the contrary, I feel extraordinarily lively. And you?—you really look both tired and sleepy.

NORA. Yes, I am very tired. I want to go to sleep at once.

HELMER. There, you see it was quite right of me not to let you stay there any longer.

NORA. Everything you do is quite right, Torvald.

HELMER (kissing her on the forehead). Now my little skylark is speaking reasonably. Did you notice what good spirits Rank was in this evening?

NORA. Really? Was he? I didn't speak to him at all.

HELMER. And I very little, but I have not for a long time seen him in such good form. (Looks for a while at her and then goes nearer to her.) It is delightful to be at home by ourselves again, to be all alone with you—you fascinating, charming little darling!

NORA. Don't look at me like that, Torvald.

HELMER. Why shouldn't I look at my dearest treasure?—at all the beauty that is mine, all my very own?

NORA (going to the other side of the table). You mustn't say things like that to me tonight.

HELMER (following her). You have still got the Tarantella in your blood, I see. And it makes you more captivating than ever. Listen—the guests are beginning to go now. (In a lower voice.) Nora—soon the whole house will be quiet.

NORA. Yes, I hope so.

HELMER. Yes, my own darling Nora. Do you know, when I am out at a party with you like this, why I speak so little to you, keep away from you, and only send a stolen glance in your direction now and then?—do you know why I do that? It is because I make believe to myself that we are secretly in love, and you are my secretly promised bride, and that no one suspects there is anything between us.

NORA. Yes, yes—I know very well your thoughts are with me all the time.

HELMER. And when we are leaving, and I am putting the shawl over your beautiful young shoulders—on your lovely neck—then I imagine that you are my young bride and that we have just come from the wedding, and I am bringing you for the first time into our home—to be alone with you for the first time—quite alone with my shy little darling! All this evening I have longed for nothing but you. When I watched the seductive figures of the Tarantella, my blood was on fire; I could endure it no longer, and that was why I brought you down so early—

NORA. Go away, Torvald! You must let me go. I won't—

HELMER. What's that? You're joking, my little Nora! You won't—you won't? Am I not your husband—? (A knock is heard at the outer door.)

NORA (starting). Did you hear—?

HELMER (going into the hall). Who is it?

RANK (outside). It is I. May I come in for a moment?

HELMER (in a fretful whisper). Oh, what does he want now? (Aloud.) Wait a minute! (Unlocks the door.) Come, that's kind of you not to pass by our door.

RANK. I thought I heard your voice, and felt as if I should like to look in. (With a swift glance round.) Ah, yes!—these dear familiar rooms. You are very happy and cosy in here, you two.

HELMER. It seems to me that you looked after yourself pretty well upstairs too.

RANK. Excellently. Why shouldn't I? Why shouldn't one enjoy everything in this world?—at any rate as much as one can, and as long as one can. The wine was capital—

HELMER. Especially the champagne.

RANK. So you noticed that too? It is almost incredible how much I managed to put away!

NORA. Torvald drank a great deal of champagne tonight too.

RANK. Did he?

NORA. Yes, and he is always in such good spirits afterwards.

RANK. Well, why should one not enjoy a merry evening after a well-spent day?

HELMER. Well spent? I am afraid I can't take credit for that.

RANK (clapping him on the back). But I can, you know!

NORA. Doctor Rank, you must have been occupied with some scientific investigation today.

RANK. Exactly.

HELMER. Just listen!—little Nora talking about scientific investigations!

NORA. And may I congratulate you on the result?

RANK. Indeed you may.

NORA. Was it favourable, then?

RANK. The best possible, for both doctor and patient—certainty.

NORA (quickly and searchingly). Certainty?

RANK. Absolute certainty. So wasn't I entitled to make a merry evening of it after that?

NORA. Yes, you certainly were, Doctor Rank.

HELMER. I think so too, so long as you don't have to pay for it in the morning.

RANK. Oh well, one can't have anything in this life without paying for it.

NORA. Doctor Rank—are you fond of fancy-dress balls?

RANK. Yes, if there is a fine lot of pretty costumes.

NORA. Tell me—what shall we two wear at the next?

HELMER. Little featherbrain!—are you thinking of the next already?

RANK. We two? Yes, I can tell you. You shall go as a good fairy—

HELMER. Yes, but what do you suggest as an appropriate costume for that?

RANK. Let your wife go dressed just as she is in everyday life.

HELMER. That was really very prettily turned. But can't you tell us what you will be?

RANK. Yes, my dear friend, I have quite made up my mind about that.

HELMER. Well?

RANK. At the next fancy-dress ball I shall be invisible.

HELMER. That's a good joke!

RANK. There is a big black hat—have you never heard of hats that make you invisible? If you put one on, no one can see you.

HELMER (suppressing a smile). Yes, you are quite right.

RANK. But I am clean forgetting what I came for. Helmer, give me a cigar—one of the dark Havanas.

HELMER. With the greatest pleasure. (Offers him his case.)

RANK (takes a cigar and cuts off the end). Thanks.

NORA (striking a match). Let me give you a light.

RANK. Thank you. (She holds the match for him to light his cigar.) And now goodbye!

HELMER. Goodbye, goodbye, dear old man!

NORA. Sleep well, Doctor Rank.

RANK. Thank you for that wish.

NORA. Wish me the same.

RANK. You? Well, if you want me to sleep well! And thanks for the light.

(He nods to them both and goes out.)

HELMER (in a subdued voice). He has drunk more than he ought.

NORA (absently). Maybe. (HELMER takes a bunch of keys out of his pocket and goes into the hall.) Torvald! what are you going to do there?

HELMER. Emptying the letter-box; it is quite full; there will be no room to put the newspaper in tomorrow morning.

NORA. Are you going to work tonight?

HELMER. You know quite well I'm not. What is this? Someone has been at the lock.

NORA. At the lock—?

HELMER. Yes, someone has. What can it mean? I should never have thought the maid—. Here is a broken hairpin. Nora, it is one of yours.

NORA (quickly). Then it must have been the children—

HELMER. Then you must get them out of those ways. There, at last I have got it open. (Takes out the contents of the letter-box, and calls to the kitchen.) Helen!—Helen, put out the light over the front door. (Goes back into the room and shuts the door into the hall. He holds out his hand full of letters.) Look at that—look what a heap of them there are. (Turning them over.) What on earth is that?

NORA (at the window). The letter—No! Torvald, no!

HELMER. Two cards—of Rank's.

NORA. Of Doctor Rank's?

HELMER (looking at them). Doctor Rank. They were on the top. He must have put them in when he went out.

NORA. Is there anything written on them?

HELMER. There is a black cross over the name. Look there—what an uncomfortable idea! It looks as if he were announcing his own death.

NORA. It is just what he is doing.

HELMER. What? Do you know anything about it? Has he said anything to you?

NORA. Yes. He told me that when the cards came it would be his leave-taking from us. He means to shut himself up and die.

HELMER. My poor old friend! Certainly I knew we should not have him very long with us. But so soon! And so he hides himself away like a wounded animal.

NORA. If it has to happen, it is best it should be without a word—don't you think so, Torvald?

HELMER (walking up and down). He had so grown into our lives. I can't think of him as having gone out of them. He, with his sufferings and his loneliness, was like a cloudy background to our sunlit happiness. Well, perhaps it is best so. For him, anyway. (Standing still.) And perhaps for us too, Nora. We two are thrown quite upon each other now. (*Puts his arms round her.*) My darling wife, I don't feel as if I could hold you tight enough. Do you know, Nora, I have often wished that you might be threatened by some great danger, so that I might risk my life's blood, and everything, for your sake.

NORA (*disengages herself, and says firmly and decidedly*). Now you must read your letters, Torvald.

HELMER. No, no; not tonight. I want to be with you, my darling wife.

NORA. With the thought of your friend's death—

HELMER. You are right, it has affected us both. Something ugly has come between us—the thought of the horrors of death. We must try and rid our minds of that. Until then—we will each go to our own room.

NORA (*hanging on his neck*). Goodnight, Torvald—Goodnight!

HELMER (*kissing her on the forehead*). Goodnight, my little singing-bird. Sleep sound, Nora. Now I will read my letters through. (*He takes his letters and goes into his room, shutting the door after him.*)

NORA (*gropes distractedly about, seizes HELMER'S domino, throws it round her, while she says in quick, hoarse, spasmodic whispers*). Never to see him again. Never! Never! (*Puts her shawl over her head.*) Never to see my children again either—never again. Never! Never!—Ah! the icy, black water—the unfathomable depths—If only it were over! He has got it now—now he is reading it. Goodbye, Torvald and my children! (*She is about to rush out through the hall, when HELMER opens his door hurriedly and stands with an open letter in his hand.*)

HELMER. Nora!

NORA. Ah!—

HELMER. What is this? Do you know what is in this letter?

NORA. Yes, I know. Let me go! Let me get out!

HELMER (*holding her back*). Where are you going?

NORA (*trying to get free*). You shan't save me, Torvald!

HELMER (*reeling*). True? Is this true, that I read here? Horrible! No, no—it is impossible that it can be true.

NORA. It is true. I have loved you above everything else in the world.

HELMER. Oh, don't let us have any silly excuses.

NORA (*taking a step towards him*). Torvald—!

HELMER. Miserable creature—what have you done?

NORA. Let me go. You shall not suffer for my sake. You shall not take it upon yourself.

HELMER. No tragic airs, please. (*Locks the hall door.*) Here you shall stay and give me an explanation. Do you understand what you have done? Answer me! Do you understand what you have done?

NORA (*looks steadily at him and says with a growing look of coldness in her face*). Yes, now I am beginning to understand thoroughly.

HELMER (*walking about the room*). What a horrible awakening! All these eight years—she who was my joy and pride—a hypocrite, a liar—worse, worse—a criminal! The unutterable ugliness of it all!—For shame! For shame! (*NORA is silent and looks steadily at him. He stops in front of her.*) I ought to have suspected that something of the sort would happen. I ought to have foreseen it. All your father's want of principle—be silent!—all your father's want of principle has come out in you. No religion, no morality, no sense of duty—. How I am punished for having winked at what he did! I did it for your sake, and this is how you repay me.

NORA. Yes, that's just it.

HELMER. Now you have destroyed all my happiness. You have ruined all my future. It is horrible to think of! I am in the power of an unscrupulous man; he can do what he likes with me, ask anything he likes of me, give me any orders he pleases—I dare not refuse. And I must sink to such miserable depths because of a thoughtless woman!

NORA. When I am out of the way, you will be free.

HELMER. No fine speeches, please. Your father had always plenty of those ready, too. What good would it be to me if you were out of the way, as you say? Not the slightest. He can make the affair known everywhere; and if he does, I may be falsely suspected of having been a party to your criminal action. Very likely people will think I was behind it all—that it was I who prompted you! And I have to thank you for all this—you whom I have cherished during the whole of our married life. Do you understand now what it is you have done for me?

NORA (coldly and quietly). Yes.

HELMER. It is so incredible that I can't take it in. But we must come to some understanding. Take off that shawl. Take it off, I tell you. I must try and appease him some way or another. The matter must be hushed up at any cost. And as for you and me, it must appear as if everything between us were just as before—but naturally only in the eyes of the world. You will still remain in my house, that is a matter of course. But I shall not allow you to bring up the children; I dare not trust them to you. To think that I should be obliged to say so to one whom I have loved so dearly, and whom I still—. No, that is all over. From this moment happiness is not the question; all that concerns us is to save the remains, the fragments, the appearance—

(A ring is heard at the front-door bell.)

HELMER (with a start). What is that? So late! Can the worst—? Can he—? Hide yourself, Nora. Say you are ill.

(NORA stands motionless. HELMER goes and unlocks the hall door.)

MAID (half-dressed, comes to the door). A letter for the mistress.

HELMER. Give it to me. (Takes the letter, and shuts the door.) Yes, it is from him. You shall not have it; I will read it myself.

NORA. Yes, read it.

HELMER (standing by the lamp). I scarcely have the courage to do it. It may mean ruin for both of us. No, I must know. (Tears open the letter, runs his eye over a few lines, looks at a paper enclosed, and gives a shout of joy.) Nora! (She looks at him questioningly.) Nora!—No, I must read it once again—. Yes, it is true! I am saved! Nora, I am saved!

NORA. And I?

HELMER. You too, of course; we are both saved, both you and I. Look, he sends you your bond back. He says he regrets and repents—that a happy change in his life—never mind what he says! We are saved, Nora! No one can do anything to you. Oh, Nora, Nora!—no, first I must destroy these hateful things. Let me see—. (Takes a look at the bond.) No, no, I won't look at it. The whole thing shall be nothing but a bad dream to me. (Tears up the bond and both letters, throws them all into the stove, and watches them burn.) There—now it doesn't exist any longer. He says that since Christmas Eve you—. These must have been three dreadful days for you, Nora.

NORA. I have fought a hard fight these three days.

HELMER. And suffered agonies, and seen no way out but—. No, we won't call any of the horrors to mind. We will only shout with joy, and keep saying, "It's all over! It's all over!" Listen to me, Nora. You don't seem to realise that it is all over. What is this?—such a cold, set face! My poor little Nora, I quite understand; you don't feel as if you could believe that I have forgiven you. But it is true, Nora, I swear it; I have forgiven you everything. I know that what you did, you did out of love for me.

NORA. That is true.

HELMER. You have loved me as a wife ought to love her husband. Only you had not sufficient knowledge to judge of the means you used. But do you suppose you are any the less dear to me, because you don't understand how to act on your own responsibility? No, no; only lean on me; I will advise you and direct you. I should not be a man if this womanly helplessness did not just give you a double attractiveness in my eyes. You must not think anymore about the hard things I said in my first moment of consternation, when I thought everything was going to overwhelm me. I have forgiven you, Nora; I swear to you I have forgiven you.

NORA. Thank you for your forgiveness. (She goes out through the door to the right.)

HELMER. No, don't go—. (Looks in.) What are you doing in there?

NORA (from within). Taking off my fancy dress.

HELMER (standing at the open door). Yes, do. Try and calm yourself, and make your mind easy again, my frightened little singing-bird. Be at rest, and feel secure; I have broad wings to shelter you under. (Walks up and down by the door.) How warm and cosy our home is, Nora. Here is shelter for you; here I will protect you like a hunted dove that I have saved from a hawk's claws; I will bring peace to your poor beating heart. It will come, little by little, Nora, believe me. Tomorrow morning you will look upon it all quite differently; soon everything will be just as it was before. Very soon you won't need me to assure you that I have forgiven you; you will yourself feel the certainty that I have done so. Can you suppose I should ever think of such a thing as repudiating you, or even reproaching you? You have no idea what a true man's heart is like, Nora. There is something so indescribably sweet and satisfying, to a man, in the knowledge that he has forgiven his wife—forgiven her freely, and with all his heart. It seems as if that had made her, as it were, doubly his own; he has given her a new life, so to speak; and she has in a way become both wife and child to him. So you shall be for me after this, my little scared, helpless darling. Have no anxiety about anything, Nora; only be frank and open with me, and I will serve as will and conscience both to you—. What is this? Not gone to bed? Have you changed your things?

NORA (in everyday dress). Yes, Torvald, I have changed my things now.

HELMER. But what for?—so late as this.

NORA. I shall not sleep tonight.

HELMER. But, my dear Nora—

NORA (looking at her watch). It is not so very late. Sit down here, Torvald. You and I have much to say to one another. (She sits down at one side of the table.)

HELMER. Nora—what is this?—this cold, set face?

NORA. Sit down. It will take some time; I have a lot to talk over with you.

HELMER (sits down at the opposite side of the table). You alarm me, Nora!—and I don't understand you.

NORA. No, that is just it. You don't understand me, and I have never understood you either—

before tonight. No, you mustn't interrupt me. You must simply listen to what I say. Torvald, this is a settling of accounts.

HELMER. What do you mean by that?

NORA (after a short silence). Isn't there one thing that strikes you as strange in our sitting here like this?

HELMER. What is that?

NORA. We have been married now eight years. Does it not occur to you that this is the first time we two, you and I, husband and wife, have had a serious conversation?

HELMER. What do you mean by serious?

NORA. In all these eight years—longer than that—from the very beginning of our acquaintance, we have never exchanged a word on any serious subject.

HELMER. Was it likely that I would be continually and forever telling you about worries that you could not help me to bear?

NORA. I am not speaking about business matters. I say that we have never sat down in earnest together to try and get at the bottom of anything.

HELMER. But, dearest Nora, would it have been any good to you?

NORA. That is just it; you have never understood me. I have been greatly wronged, Torvald—first by papa and then by you.

HELMER. What! By us two—by us two, who have loved you better than anyone else in the world?

NORA (shaking her head). You have never loved me. You have only thought it pleasant to be in love with me.

HELMER. Nora, what do I hear you saying?

NORA. It is perfectly true, Torvald. When I was at home with papa, he told me his opinion about everything, and so I had the same opinions; and if I differed from him I concealed the fact, because he would not have liked it. He called me his doll-child, and he played with me just as I used to play with my dolls. And when I came to live with you—

HELMER. What sort of an expression is that to use about our marriage?

NORA (undisturbed). I mean that I was simply transferred from papa's hands into yours. You arranged everything according to your own taste, and so I got the same tastes as your else I pretended to, I am really not quite sure which—I think sometimes the one and sometimes the other. When I look back on it, it seems to me as if I had been living here like a poor woman—just from hand to mouth. I have existed merely to perform tricks for you, Torvald. But you would have it so. You and papa have committed a great sin against me. It is your fault that I have made nothing of my life.

HELMER. How unreasonable and how ungrateful you are, Nora! Have you not been happy here?

NORA. No, I have never been happy. I thought I was, but it has never really been so.

HELMER. Not—not happy!

NORA. No, only merry. And you have always been so kind to me. But our home has been nothing but a playroom. I have been your doll-wife, just as at home I was papa's doll-child; and here the children have been my dolls. I thought it great fun when you played with me, just as they thought it great fun when I played with them. That is what our marriage has been, Torvald.

HELMER. There is some truth in what you say—exaggerated and strained as your view of it is. But for the future it shall be different. Playtime shall be over, and lesson-time shall begin.

NORA. Whose lessons? Mine, or the children's?

HELMER. Both yours and the children's, my darling Nora.

NORA. Alas, Torvald, you are not the man to educate me into being a proper wife for you.

HELMER. And you can say that!

NORA. And I—how am I fitted to bring up the children?

HELMER. Nora!

NORA. Didn't you say so yourself a little while ago—that you dare not trust me to bring them up?

HELMER. In a moment of anger! Why do you pay any heed to that?

NORA. Indeed, you were perfectly right. I am not fit for the task. There is another task I must undertake first. I must try and educate myself—you are not the man to help me in that. I must do that for myself. And that is why I am going to leave you now.

HELMER (springing up). What do you say?

NORA. I must stand quite alone, if I am to understand myself and everything about me. It is for that reason that I cannot remain with you any longer.

HELMER. Nora, Nora!

NORA. I am going away from here now, at once. I am sure Christine will take me in for the night—

HELMER. You are out of your mind! I won't allow it! I forbid you!

NORA. It is no use forbidding me anything any longer. I will take with me what belongs to myself. I will take nothing from you, either now or later.

HELMER. What sort of madness is this!

NORA. Tomorrow I shall go home—I mean, to my old home. It will be easiest for me to find something to do there.

HELMER. You blind, foolish woman!

NORA. I must try and get some sense, Torvald.

HELMER. To desert your home, your husband and your children! And you don't consider what people will say!

NORA. I cannot consider that at all. I only know that it is necessary for me.

HELMER. It's shocking. This is how you would neglect your most sacred duties.

NORA. What do you consider my most sacred duties?

HELMER. Do I need to tell you that? Are they not your duties to your husband and your children?

NORA. I have other duties just as sacred.

HELMER. That you have not. What duties could those be?

NORA. Duties to myself.

HELMER. Before all else, you are a wife and a mother.

NORA. I don't believe that any longer. I believe that before all else I am a reasonable human being, just as you are—or, at all events, that I must try and become one. I know quite well, Torvald, that most people would think you right, and that views of that kind are to be found in books; but I can no longer content myself with what most people say, or with what is found in books. I must think over things for myself and get to understand them.

HELMER. Can you not understand your place in your own home? Have you not a reliable guide in such matters as that?—have you no religion?

NORA. I am afraid, Torvald, I do not exactly know what religion is.

HELMER. What are you saying?

NORA. I know nothing but what the clergyman said, when I went to be confirmed. He told us that religion was this, and that, and the other. When I am away from all this, and am alone, I will look into that matter too. I will see if what the clergyman said is true, or at all events if it is true for me.

HELMER. This is unheard of in a girl of your age! But if religion cannot lead you aright, let me try and awaken your conscience. I suppose you have some moral sense? Or—answer me—am I to think you have none?

NORA. I assure you, Torvald, that is not an easy question to answer. I really don't know. The thing perplexes me altogether. I only know that you and I look at it in quite a different light. I am learning, too, that the law is quite another thing from what I supposed; but I find it impossible to convince myself that the law is right. According to it a woman has no right to spare her old dying father, or to save her husband's life. I can't believe that.

HELMER. You talk like a child. You don't understand the conditions of the world in which you live.

NORA. No, I don't. But now I am going to try. I am going to see if I can make out who is right, the world or I.

HELMER. You are ill, Nora; you are delirious; I almost think you are out of your mind.

NORA. I have never felt my mind so clear and certain as tonight.

HELMER. And is it with a clear and certain mind that you forsake your husband and your children?

NORA. Yes, it is.

HELMER. Then there is only one possible explanation.

NORA. What is that?

HELMER. You do not love me anymore.

NORA. No, that is just it.

HELMER. Nora!—and you can say that?

NORA. It gives me great pain, Torvald, for you have always been so kind to me, but I cannot help it. I do not love you any more.

HELMER (regaining his composure). Is that a clear and certain conviction too?

NORA. Yes, absolutely clear and certain. That is the reason why I will not stay here any longer.

HELMER. And can you tell me what I have done to forfeit your love?

NORA. Yes, indeed I can. It was tonight, when the wonderful thing did not happen; then I saw you were not the man I had thought you were.

HELMER. Explain yourself better. I don't understand you.

NORA. I have waited so patiently for eight years; for, goodness knows, I knew very well that wonderful things don't happen every day. Then this horrible misfortune came upon me; and then I felt quite certain that the wonderful thing was going to happen at last. When Krogstad's letter was lying out there, never for a moment did I imagine that you would consent to accept this man's conditions. I was so absolutely certain that you would say to him: Publish the thing to the whole world. And when that was done—

HELMER. Yes, what then?—when I had exposed my wife to shame and disgrace?

NORA. When that was done, I was so absolutely certain, you would come forward and take everything upon yourself, and say: I am the guilty one.

HELMER. Nora—!

NORA. You mean that I would never have accepted such a sacrifice on your part? No, of course not. But what would my assurances have been worth against yours? That was the wonderful thing which I hoped for and feared; and it was to prevent that, that I wanted to kill myself.

HELMER. I would gladly work night and day for you, Nora—bear sorrow and want for your sake. But no man would sacrifice his honour for the one he loves.

NORA. It is a thing hundreds of thousands of women have done.

HELMER. Oh, you think and talk like a heedless child.

NORA. Maybe. But you neither think nor talk like the man I could bind myself to. As soon as your fear was over—and it was not fear for what threatened me, but for what might happen to you—when the whole thing was past, as far as you were concerned it was exactly as if nothing at all had happened. Exactly as before, I was your little skylark, your doll, which you would in future treat with doubly gentle care, because it was so brittle and fragile. (Getting up.) Torvald—it was then it dawned upon me that for eight years I had been living here with a strange man, and had borne him three children—. Oh, I can't bear to think of it! I could tear myself into little bits!

HELMER (sadly). I see, I see. An abyss has opened between us—there is no denying it. But, Nora, would it not be possible to fill it up?

NORA. As I am now, I am no wife for you.

HELMER. I have it in me to become a different man.

NORA. Perhaps—if your doll is taken away from you.

HELMER. But to part!—to part from you! No, no, Nora, I can't understand that idea.

NORA (going out to the right). That makes it all the more certain that it must be done. (She comes back with her cloak and hat and a small bag which she puts on a chair by the table.)

HELMER. Nora, Nora, not now! Wait until tomorrow.

NORA (putting on her cloak). I cannot spend the night in a strange man's room.

HELMER. But can't we live here like brother and sister—?

NORA (putting on her hat). You know very well that would not last long. (Puts the shawl round her.) Goodbye, Torvald. I won't see the little ones. I know they are in better hands than mine. As I am now, I can be of no use to them.

HELMER. But some day, Nora—some day?

NORA. How can I tell? I have no idea what is going to become of me.

HELMER. But you are my wife, whatever becomes of you.

NORA. Listen, Torvald. I have heard that when a wife deserts her husband's house, as I am doing now, he is legally freed from all obligations towards her. In any case, I set you free from all your obligations. You are not to feel yourself bound in the slightest way, any more than I shall. There must be perfect freedom on both sides. See, here is your ring back. Give me mine.

HELMER. That too?

NORA. That too.

HELMER. Here it is.

NORA. That's right. Now it is all over. I have put the keys here. The maids know all about everything in the house—better than I do. Tomorrow, after I have left her, Christine will come here and pack up my own things that I brought with me from home. I will have them sent after me.

HELMER. All over! All over! Nora, shall you never think of me again?

NORA. I know I shall often think of you, the children, and this house.

HELMER. May I write to you, Nora?

NORA. No—never. You must not do that.

HELMER. But at least let me send you—

NORA. Nothing—nothing—

HELMER. Let me help you if you are in want.

NORA. No. I can receive nothing from a stranger.

HELMER. Nora—can I never be anything more than a stranger to you?

NORA (taking her bag). Ah, Torvald, the most wonderful thing of all would have to happen.

HELMER. Tell me what that would be!

NORA. Both you and I would have to be so changed that—. Oh, Torvald, I don't believe any longer in wonderful things happening.

HELMER. But I will believe in it. Tell me! So changed that—?

NORA. That our life together would be a real wedlock. Goodbye. (She goes out through the hall.)

HELMER (sinks down on a chair at the door and buries his face in his hands). Nora! Nora! (Looks round, and rises.) Empty. She is gone. (A hope flashes across his mind.) The most wonderful thing of all—?

(The sound of a door shutting is heard from below.)

6

The Three Sisters

A DRAMA IN FOUR ACTS

Play by Anton Pavlovich-Chekov (1860–1904)

CHARACTERS

ANDREY SERGEYEVITCH PROSOROV
NATALIA IVANOVA (NATASHA), his fiancée, later his wife (28)
His sisters:
OLGA
MASHA
IRINA
FEODOR ILITCH KULIGIN, high school teacher, married to MASHA (20)
ALEXANDER IGNATEYEVITCH VERSHININ, lieutenant-colonel in charge of a battery (42)
NICOLAI LVOVITCH TUZENBACH, baron, lieutenant in the army (30)
VASSILI VASSILEVITCH SOLENI, captain
IVAN ROMANOVITCH CHEBUTIKIN, army doctor (60)
ALEXEY PETROVITCH FEDOTIK, sub-lieutenant
VLADIMIR CARLOVITCH RODE, sub-lieutenant
FERAPONT, door-keeper at local council offices, an old man
ANFISA, nurse (80)

The action takes place in a provincial town.

[Ages are stated in brackets.]

"The Three Sisters", 1914.

THE THREE SISTERS

ACT I

[In PROSOROV'S house. A sitting-room with pillars; behind is seen a large dining-room. It is midday, the sun is shining brightly outside. In the dining-room the table is being laid for lunch.]

[OLGA, in the regulation blue dress of a teacher at a girl's high school, is walking about correcting exercise books; MASHA, in a black dress, with a hat on her knees, sits and reads a book; IRINA, in white, stands about, with a thoughtful expression.]

OLGA. It's just a year since father died last May the fifth, on your name-day, Irina. It was very cold then, and snowing. I thought I would never survive it, and you were in a dead faint. And now a year has gone by and we are already thinking about it without pain, and you are wearing a white dress and your face is happy. [Clock strikes twelve] And the clock struck just the same way then. [Pause] I remember that there was music at the funeral, and they fired a volley in the cemetery. He was a general in command of a brigade but there were few people present. Of course, it was raining then, raining hard, and snowing.

IRINA. Why think about it!

[BARON TUZENBACH, CHEBUTIKIN and SOLENI appear by the table in the dining-room, behind the pillars.]

OLGA. It's so warm to-day that we can keep the windows open, though the birches are not yet in flower. Father was put in command of a brigade, and he rode out of Moscow with us eleven years ago. I remember perfectly that it was early in May and that everything in Moscow was flowering then. It was warm too, everything was bathed in sunshine. Eleven years have gone, and I remember everything as if we rode out only yesterday. Oh, God! When I awoke this morning and saw all the light and the spring, joy entered my heart, and I longed passionately to go home.

CHEBUTIKIN. Will you take a bet on it?

TUZENBACH. Oh, nonsense.

[MASHA, lost in a reverie over her book, whistles softly.]

OLGA. Don't whistle, Masha. How can you! [Pause] I'm always having headaches from having to go to the High School every day and then teach till evening. Strange thoughts come to me, as if I were already an old woman. And really, during these four years that I have been working here, I have been feeling as if every day my strength and youth have been squeezed out of me, drop by drop. And only one desire grows and gains in strength . . .

IRINA. To go away to Moscow. To sell the house, drop everything here, and go to Moscow . . .

OLGA. Yes! To Moscow, and as soon as possible.

[CHEBUTIKIN and TUZENBACH laugh.]

IRINA. I expect Andrey will become a professor, but still, he won't want to live here. Only poor Masha must go on living here.

OLGA. Masha can come to Moscow every year, for the whole summer.

[MASHA is whistling gently.]

IRINA. Everything will be arranged, please God. [Looks out of the window] It's nice out to-day. I don't know why I'm so happy: I remembered this morning that it was my name-day, and I suddenly felt glad and remembered my childhood, when mother was still with us. What beautiful thoughts I had, what thoughts!

OLGA. You're all radiance to-day, I've never seen you look so lovely. And Masha is pretty, too. Andrey wouldn't be bad-looking, if he wasn't so stout; it does spoil his appearance. But I've grown old and very thin, I suppose it's because I get angry with the girls at school. To-day I'm free. I'm at home. I haven't got a headache, and I feel younger than I was yesterday. I'm only twenty-eight. . . . All's well, God is everywhere, but it seems to me that if only I were married and could stay at home all day, it would be even better. [Pause] I should love my husband.

TUZENBACH. [To SOLENI] I'm tired of listening to the rot you talk. [Entering the sitting-room] I forgot to say that Vershinin, our new lieutenant-colonel of artillery, is coming to see us to-day. [Sits down to the piano.]

OLGA. That's good. I'm glad.

IRINA. Is he old?

TUZENBACH. Oh, no. Forty or forty-five, at the very outside. [Plays softly] He seems rather a good sort. He's certainly no fool, only he likes to hear himself speak.

IRINA. Is he interesting?

TUZENBACH. Oh, he's all right, but there's his wife, his mother-in-law, and two daughters. This is his second wife. He pays calls and tells everybody that he's got a wife and two daughters. He'll tell you so here. The wife isn't all there, she does her hair like a flapper and gushes extremely. She talks philosophy and tries to commit suicide every now and again, apparently in order to annoy her husband. I should have left her long ago, but he bears up patiently, and just grumbles.

SOLENI. [Enters with CHEBUTIKIN from the dining-room] With one hand I can only lift fifty-four pounds, but with both hands I can lift 180, or even 200 pounds. From this I conclude that two men are not twice as strong as one, but three times, perhaps even more. . . .

CHEBUTIKIN. [Reads a newspaper as he walks] If your hair is coming out . . . take an ounce of naphthaline and hail a bottle of spirit . . . dissolve and use daily. . . . [Makes a note in his pocket diary] When found make a note of! Not that I want it though. . . . [Crosses it out] It doesn't matter.

IRINA. Ivan Romanovitch, dear Ivan Romanovitch!

CHEBUTIKIN. What does my own little girl want?

IRINA. Ivan Romanovitch, dear Ivan Romanovitch! I feel as if I were sailing under the broad blue sky with great white birds around me. Why is that? Why?

CHEBUTIKIN. [Kisses her hands, tenderly] My white bird. . . .

IRINA. When I woke up to-day and got up and dressed myself, I suddenly began to feel as if everything in this life was open to me, and that I knew how I must live. Dear Ivan Romanovitch, I know everything. A man must work, toil in the sweat of his brow, whoever he may be, for that is the meaning and object of his life, his happiness, his enthusiasm. How fine it is to be a workman who gets up at daybreak and breaks stones in the street, or a shepherd, or a schoolmaster, who teaches children, or an engine-driver on the railway. . . . My God, let alone a man, it's better to be an ox, or just a horse, so long as it can work, than a young woman who wakes up at twelve o'clock, has her coffee in bed, and then spends two hours dressing. . . . Oh it's awful! Sometimes when it's hot, your thirst can be just as tiresome as my need for work. And if I don't get up early in future and work, Ivan Romanovitch, then you may refuse me your friendship.

CHEBUTIKIN. [Tenderly] I'll refuse, I'll refuse. . . .

OLGA. Father used to make us get up at seven. Now Irina wakes at seven and lies and meditates about something till nine at least. And she looks so serious! [Laughs.]

IRINA. You're so used to seeing me as a little girl that it seems queer to you when my face is serious. I'm twenty!

TUZENBACH. How well I can understand that craving for work, oh God! I've never worked once in my life. I was born in Petersburg, a chilly, lazy place, in a family which never knew what work or worry meant. I remember that when I used to come home from my regiment, a footman used to have to pull off my boots while I fidgeted and my mother looked on in adoration and wondered why other people didn't see me in the same light. They shielded me from work; but only just in time! A new age is dawning, the people are marching on us all, a powerful, health-giving storm is gathering, it is drawing near, soon it will be upon us and it will drive away laziness, indifference, the prejudice against labour, and rotten dullness from our society. I shall work, and in twenty-five or thirty years, every man will have to work. Every one!

CHEBUTIKIN. I shan't work.

TUZENBACH. You don't matter.

SOLENI. In twenty-five years' time, we shall all be dead, thank the Lord. In two or three years' time apoplexy will carry you off, or else I'll blow your brains out, my pet. [Takes a scent-bottle out of his pocket and sprinkles his chest and hands.]

CHEBUTIKIN. [Laughs] It's quite true, I never have worked. After I came down from the university I never stirred a finger or opened a book, I just read the papers. . . . [Takes another newspaper out of his pocket] Here we are. . . . I've learnt from the papers that there used to be one, Dobrolubov [Note: Dobroluboy (1836–81), in spite of the shortness of his career, established himself as one of the classic literary critics of Russia], for instance, but what he wrote—I don't know . . . God only knows. . . . [Somebody is heard tapping on the floor from below] There. . . . They're calling me downstairs, somebody's come to see me. I'll be back in a minute . . . won't be long. . . . [Exit hurriedly, scratching his beard.]

IRINA. He's up to something.

TUZENBACH. Yes, he looked so pleased as he went out that I'm pretty certain he'll bring you a present in a moment.

IRINA. How unpleasant!

OLGA. Yes, it's awful. He's always doing silly things.

MASHA.
"There stands a green oak by the sea.
And a chain of bright gold is around it . . .
And a chain of bright gold is around it. . . ."

[Gets up and sings softly.]

OLGA. You're not very bright to-day, Masha. [MASHA sings, putting on her hat] Where are you off to?

MASHA. Home.

IRINA. That's odd. . . .

TUZENBACH. On a name-day, too!

MASHA. It doesn't matter. I'll come in the evening. Good-bye, dear. [Kisses MASHA] Many happy returns, though I've said it before. In the old days when father was alive, every time we had a name-day, thirty or forty officers used to come, and there was lots of noise and fun, and to-day there's only a man and a half, and it's as quiet as a desert . . . I'm

off . . . I've got the hump to-day, and am not at all cheerful, so don't you mind me. [Laughs through her tears] We'll have a talk later on, but good-bye for the present, my dear; I'll go somewhere.

IRINA. [Displeased] You are queer. . . .

OLGA. [Crying] I understand you, Masha.

SOLENI. When a man talks philosophy, well, it is philosophy or at any rate sophistry; but when a woman, or two women, talk philosophy—it's all my eye.

MASHA. What do you mean by that, you very awful man?

SOLENI. Oh, nothing. You came down on me before I could say . . . help! [Pause.]

MASHA. [Angrily, to OLGA] Don't cry!

[Enter ANFISA and FERAPONT with a cake.]

ANFISA. This way, my dear. Come in, your feet are clean. [To IRINA] From the District Council, from Mihail Ivanitch Protopopov . . . a cake.

IRINA. Thank you. Please thank him. [Takes the cake.]

FERAPONT. What?

IRINA. [Louder] Please thank him.

OLGA. Give him a pie, nurse. Ferapont, go, she'll give you a pie.

FERAPONT. What?

ANFISA. Come on, gran'fer, Ferapont Spiridonitch. Come on. [Exeunt.]

MASHA. I don't like this Mihail Potapitch or Ivanitch, Protopopov. We oughtn't to invite him here.

IRINA. I never asked him.

MASHA. That's all right.

[Enter CHEBUTIKIN followed by a soldier with a silver samovar; there is a rumble of dissatisfied surprise.]

OLGA. [Covers her face with her hands] A samovar! That's awful! [Exit into the dining-room, to the table.]

IRINA. My dear Ivan Romanovitch, what are you doing!

TUZENBACH. [Laughs] I told you so!

MASHA. Ivan Romanovitch, you are simply shameless!

CHEBUTIKIN. My dear good girl, you are the only thing, and the dearest thing I have in the world. I'll soon be sixty. I'm an old man, a lonely worthless old man. The only good thing in me is my love for you, and if it hadn't been for that, I would have been dead long ago. . . . [To IRINA] My dear little girl, I've known you since the day of your birth, I've carried you in my arms . . . I loved your dead mother. . . .

MASHA. But your presents are so expensive!

CHEBUTIKIN. [Angrily, through his tears] Expensive presents. . . . You really, are! . . . [To the orderly] Take the samovar in there. . . . [Teasing] Expensive presents!

[The orderly goes into the dining-room with the samovar.]

ANFISA. [Enters and crosses stage] My dear, there's a strange Colonel come! He's taken off his coat already. Children, he's coming here. Irina darling, you'll be a nice and polite little girl, won't you. . . . Should have lunched a long time ago. . . . Oh, Lord. . . . [Exit.]

TUZENBACH. It must be Vershinin. [Enter VERSHININ] Lieutenant-Colonel Vershinin!

VERSHININ. [To MASHA and IRINA] I have the honour to introduce myself, my name is Vershinin. I am very glad indeed to be able to come at last. How you've grown! Oh! oh!

IRINA. Please sit down. We're very glad you've come.

VERSHININ. [Gaily] I am glad, very glad! But there are three sisters, surely. I remember—three little girls. I forget your faces, but your father, Colonel Prosorov, used to have three little girls, I remember that perfectly, I saw them with my own eyes. How time does fly! Oh, dear, how it flies!

TUZENBACH. Alexander Ignateyevitch comes from Moscow.

IRINA. From Moscow? Are you from Moscow?

VERSHININ. Yes, that's so. Your father used to be in charge of a battery there, and I was an officer in the same brigade. [To MASHA] I seem to remember your face a little.

MASHA. I don't remember you.

IRINA. Olga! Olga! [Shouts into the dining-room] Olga! Come along! [OLGA enters from the dining-room] Lieutenant Colonel Vershinin comes from Moscow, as it happens.

VERSHININ. I take it that you are Olga Sergeyevna, the eldest, and that you are Maria . . . and you are Irina, the youngest. . . .

OLGA. So you come from Moscow?

VERSHININ. Yes. I went to school in Moscow and began my service there; I was there for a long time until at last I got my battery and moved over here, as you see. I don't really remember you, I only remember that there used to be three sisters. I remember your father well; I have only to shut my eyes to see him as he was. I used to come to your house in Moscow. . . .

OLGA. I used to think I remembered everybody, but . . .

VERSHININ. My name is Alexander Ignateyevitch.

IRINA. Alexander Ignateyevitch, you've come from Moscow. That is really quite a surprise!

OLGA. We are going to live there, you see.

IRINA. We think we may be there this autumn. It's our native town, we were born there. In Old Basmanni Road. . . . [They both laugh for joy.]

MASHA. We've unexpectedly met a fellow countryman. [Briskly] I remember: Do you remember, Olga, they used to speak at home of a "lovelorn Major." You were only a Lieutenant then, and in love with somebody, but for some reason they always called you a Major for fun.

VERSHININ. [Laughs] That's it . . . the lovelorn Major, that's got it!

MASHA. You only wore moustaches then. You have grown older! [Through her tears] You have grown older!

VERSHININ. Yes, when they used to call me the lovelorn Major, I was young and in love. I've grown out of both now.

OLGA. But you haven't a single white hair yet. You're older, but you're not yet old.

VERSHININ. I'm forty-two, anyway. Have you been away from Moscow long?

IRINA. Eleven years. What are you crying for, Masha, you little fool. . . . [Crying] And I'm crying too.

MASHA. It's all right. And where did you live?

VERSHININ. Old Basmanni Road.

OLGA. Same as we.

VERSHININ. Once I used to live in German Street. That was when the Red Barracks were my headquarters. There's an ugly bridge in between, where the water rushes underneath. One gets melancholy when one is alone there. [Pause] Here the river is so wide and fine! It's a splendid river!

OLGA. Yes, but it's so cold. It's very cold here, and the midges. . . .

VERSHININ. What are you saying! Here you've got such a fine healthy Russian climate. You've a forest, a river . . . and birches. Dear, modest birches, I like them more than any other tree. It's good to live here. Only it's odd that the railway station should be thirteen miles away. . . . Nobody knows why.

SOLENI. I know why. [All look at him] Because if it was near it wouldn't be far off, and if it's far off, it can't be near. [An awkward pause.]

TUZENBACH. Funny man.

OLGA. Now I know who you are. I remember.

VERSHININ. I used to know your mother.

CHEBUTIKIN. She was a good woman, rest her soul.

IRINA. Mother is buried in Moscow.

OLGA. At the Novo-Devichi Cemetery.

MASHA. Do you know, I'm beginning to forget her face. We'll be forgotten in just the same way.

VERSHININ. Yes, they'll forget us. It's our fate, it can't be helped. A time will come when everything that seems serious, significant, or very important to us will be forgotten, or considered trivial. [Pause] And the curious thing is that we can't possibly find out what will come to be regarded as great and important, and what will be feeble, or silly. Didn't the discoveries of Copernicus, or Columbus, say, seem unnecessary and ludicrous at first, while wasn't it thought that some rubbish written by a fool, held all the truth? And it may so happen that our present existence, with which we are so satisfied, will in time appear strange, inconvenient, stupid, unclean, perhaps even sinful. . . .

TUZENBACH. Who knows? But on the other hand, they may call our life noble and honour its memory. We've abolished torture and capital punishment, we live in security, but how much suffering there is still!

SOLENI. [In a feeble voice] There, there. . . . The Baron will go without his dinner if you only let him talk philosophy.

TUZENBACH. Vassili Vassilevitch, kindly leave me alone. [Changes his chair] You're very dull, you know.

SOLENI. [Feebly] There, there, there.

TUZENBACH. [To VERSHININ] The sufferings we see to-day—there are so many of them!—still indicate a certain moral improvement in society.

VERSHININ. Yes, yes, of course.

CHEBUTIKIN. You said just now, Baron, that they may call our life noble; but we are very petty. . . . [Stands up] See how little I am. [Violin played behind.]

MASHA. That's Andrey playing—our brother.

IRINA. He's the learned member of the family. I expect he will be a professor some day. Father was a soldier, but his son chose an academic career for himself.

MASHA. That was father's wish.

OLGA. We ragged him to-day. We think he's a little in love.

IRINA. To a local lady. She will probably come here to-day.

MASHA. You should see the way she dresses! Quite prettily, quite fashionably too, but so badly! Some queer bright yellow skirt with a wretched little fringe and a red bodice. And such a complexion! Andrey isn't in love. After all he has taste, he's simply making fun of us. I heard yesterday that she was going to marry Protopopov, the chairman of the Local Council. That would do her nicely. . . . [At the side door] Andrey, come here! Just for a minute, dear! [Enter Andrey.]

OLGA. My brother, Andrey Sergeyevitch.

VERSHININ. My name is Vershinin.

ANDREY. Mine is Prosorov. [Wipes his perspiring hands] You've come to take charge of the battery?

OLGA. Just think, Alexander Ignateyevitch comes from Moscow.

ANDREY. That's all right. Now my little sisters won't give you any rest.

VERSHININ. I've already managed to bore your sisters.

IRINA. Just look what a nice little photograph frame Andrey gave me to-day. [Shows it] He made it himself.

VERSHININ. [Looks at the frame and does not know what to say] Yes. . . . It's a thing that . . .

IRINA. And he made that frame there, on the piano as well. [Andrey waves his hand and walks away.]

OLGA. He's got a degree, and plays the violin, and cuts all sorts of things out of wood, and is really a domestic Admirable Crichton. Don't go away, Andrey! He's got into a habit of always going away. Come here!

[MASHA and IRINA take his arms and laughingly lead him back.]

MASHA. Come on, come on!

ANDREY. Please leave me alone.

MASHA. You are funny. Alexander Ignateyevitch used to be called the lovelorn Major, but he never minded.

VERSHININ. Not the least.

MASHA. I'd like to call you the lovelorn fiddler!

IRINA. Or the lovelorn professor!

OLGA. He's in love! little Andrey is in love!

IRINA. [Applauds] Bravo, Bravo! Encore! Little Andrey is in love.

CHEBUTIKIN. [Goes up behind ANDREY and takes him round the waist with both arms] Nature only brought us into the world that we should love! [Roars with laughter, then sits down and reads a newspaper which he takes out of his pocket.]

ANDREY. That's enough, quite enough. . . . [Wipes his face] I couldn't sleep all night and now I can't quite find my feet, so to speak. I read until four o'clock, then tried to sleep, but nothing happened. I thought about one thing and another, and then it dawned and the sun crawled into my bedroom. This summer, while I'm here, I want to translate a book from the English. . . .

VERSHININ. Do you read English?

ANDREY. Yes father, rest his soul, educated us almost violently. It may seem funny and silly, but it's nevertheless true, that after his death I began to fill out and get rounder, as if my body had had some great pressure taken off it. Thanks to father, my sisters and I know French, German, and English, and Irina knows Italian as well. But we paid dearly for it all!

MASHA. A knowledge of three languages is an unnecessary luxury in this town. It isn't even a luxury but a sort of useless extra, like a sixth finger. We know a lot too much.

VERSHININ. Well, I say! [Laughs] You know a lot too much! I don't think there can really be a town so dull and stupid as to have no place for a clever, cultured person. Let us suppose even that among the hundred thousand inhabitants of this backward and uneducated town, there are only three persons like yourself. It stands to reason that you won't be able to conquer that dark mob around you; little by little as you grow older you will be bound to give way and lose yourselves in this crowd of a hundred thousand human beings; their life will suck you up in itself, but still, you won't disappear having influenced nobody; later on, others like you will come, perhaps six of them, then twelve, and so on, until at last your sort will be in the majority. In two or three hundred years' time life on this earth will be unimaginably beautiful and wonderful. Mankind needs such a life, and if it is not ours to-day then we must look ahead for it, wait, think, prepare for it. We must see and know more than our fathers and grandfathers saw and knew. [Laughs] And you complain that you know too much.

MASHA. [Takes off her hat] I'll stay to lunch.

IRINA. [Sighs] Yes, all that ought to be written down.

[ANDREY has gone out quietly.]

TUZENBACH. You say that many years later on, life on this earth will be beautiful and wonderful. That's true. But to share in it now, even though at a distance, we must prepare by work. . . .

VERSHININ. [Gets up] Yes. What a lot of flowers you have. [Looks round] It's a beautiful flat. I envy you! I've spent my whole life in rooms with two chairs, one sofa, and fires which always smoke. I've never had flowers like these in my life. . . . [Rubs his hands] Well, well!

TUZENBACH. Yes, we must work. You are probably thinking to yourself: the German lets himself go. But I assure you I'm a Russian, I can't even speak German. My father belonged to the Orthodox Church. . . . [Pause.]

VERSHININ. [Walks about the stage] I often wonder: suppose we could begin life over again, knowing what we were doing? Suppose we could use one life, already ended, as a sort of rough draft for another? I think that every one of us would try, more than anything else, not to repeat himself, at the very least he would rearrange his manner of life, he would make sure of rooms like these, with flowers and light . . . I have a wife and two daughters, my wife's health is delicate and so on and so on, and if I had to begin life all over again I would not marry. . . . No, no!

[Enter KULIGIN in a regulation jacket.]

KULIGIN. [Going up to IRINA] Dear sister, allow me to congratulate you on the day sacred to your good angel and to wish you, sincerely and from the bottom of my heart, good health and all that one can wish for a girl of your years. And then let me offer you this book as a present. [Gives it to her] It is the history of our High School during the last fifty years, written by myself. The book is worthless, and written because I had nothing to do, but read it all the same. Good day, gentlemen! [To VERSHININ] My name is Kuligin, I am a master of the local High School. [Note: He adds that he is a *Nadvorny Sovetnik* (almost the same as a German *Hofrat*), an undistinguished civilian title with no English equivalent.] [To IRINA] In this book you will find a list of all those who have taken the full course at our High School during these fifty years. *Feci quod potui, faciant meliora potentes.* [Kisses Masha.]

IRINA. But you gave me one of these at Easter.

KULIGIN. [Laughs] I couldn't have, surely! You'd better give it back to me in that case, or else give it to the Colonel. Take it, Colonel. You'll read it some day when you're bored.

VERSHININ. Thank you. [Prepares to go] I am extremely happy to have made the acquaintance of . . .

OLGA. Must you go? No, not yet?

IRINA. You'll stop and have lunch with us. Please do.

OLGA. Yes, please!

VERSHININ. [Bows] I seem to have dropped in on your name-day. Forgive me, I didn't know, and I didn't offer you my congratulations. [Goes with OLGA into the dining-room.]

KULIGIN. To-day is Sunday, the day of rest, so let us rest and rejoice, each in a manner compatible with his age and disposition. The carpets will have to be taken up for the summer and put away till the winter . . . Persian powder or naphthaline. . . . The Romans were healthy because they knew both how to work and how to rest, they had *mens sana in corpore sano.* Their life ran along certain recognized patterns. Our director says: "The chief thing about each life is its pattern. Whoever loses his pattern is lost himself"—and it's just the same in our daily life. [Takes MASHA by the waist, laughing] Masha loves me. My wife loves me. And you ought to put the window curtains away with the carpets. . . . I'm feeling awfully pleased with life to-day. Masha, we've got to be at the director's at four. They're getting up a walk for the pedagogues and their families.

MASHA. I shan't go.

KULIGIN. [Hurt] My dear Masha, why not?

MASHA. I'll tell you later. . . . [Angrily] All right, I'll go, only please stand back. . . . [Steps away.]

KULIGIN. And then we're to spend the evening at the director's. In spite of his ill-health that man tries, above everything else, to be sociable. A splendid, illuminating personality. A wonderful man. After yesterday's committee he said to me: "I'm tired, Feodor Ilitch, I'm tired!" [Looks at the clock, then at his watch] Your clock is seven minutes fast. "Yes," he said, "I'm tired." [Violin played off.]

OLGA. Let's go and have lunch! There's to be a masterpiece of baking!

KULIGIN. Oh my dear Olga, my dear. Yesterday I was working till eleven o'clock at night, and got awfully tired. To-day I'm quite happy. [Goes into dining-room] My dear . . .

CHEBUTIKIN. [Puts his paper into his pocket, and combs his beard] A pie? Splendid!

MASHA. [Severely to CHEBUTIKIN] Only mind; you're not to drink anything to-day. Do you hear? It's bad for you.

CHEBUTIKIN. Oh, that's all right. I haven't been drunk for two years. And it's all the same, anyway!

MASHA. You're not to dare to drink, all the same. [Angrily, but so that her husband should not hear] Another dull evening at the Director's, confound it!

TUZENBACH. I shouldn't go if I were you. . . . It's quite simple.

CHEBUTIKIN. Don't go.

MASHA. Yes, "don't go. . . ." It's a cursed, unbearable life. . . . [Goes into dining-room.]

CHEBUTIKIN. [Follows her] It's not so bad.

SOLENI. [Going into the dining-room] There, there, there. . . .

TUZENBACH. Vassili Vassilevitch, that's enough. Be quiet!

SOLENI. There, there, there. . . .

KULIGIN. [Gaily] Your health, Colonel! I'm a pedagogue and not quite at home here. I'm Masha's husband. . . . She's a good sort, a very good sort.

VERSHININ. I'll have some of this black vodka. . . . [Drinks] Your health! [To OLGA] I'm very comfortable here!

[Only IRINA and TUZENBACH are now left in the sitting-room.]

IRINA. Masha's out of sorts to-day. She married when she was eighteen, when he seemed to her the wisest of men. And now it's different. He's the kindest man, but not the wisest.

OLGA. [Impatiently] Andrey, when are you coming?

ANDREY. [Off] One minute. [Enters and goes to the table.]

TUZENBACH. What are you thinking about?

IRINA. I don't like this Soleni of yours and I'm afraid of him. He only says silly things.

TUZENBACH. He's a queer man. I'm sorry for him, though he vexes me. I think he's shy. When there are just the two of us he's quite all right and very good company; when other people are about he's rough and hectoring. Don't let's go in, let them have their meal without us. Let me stay with you. What are you thinking of? [Pause] You're twenty. I'm not yet thirty. How many years are there left to us, with their long, long lines of days, filled with my love for you. . . .

IRINA. Nicolai Lvovitch, don't speak to me of love.

TUZENBACH. [Does not hear] I've a great thirst for life, struggle, and work, and this thirst has united with my love for you, Irina, and you're so beautiful, and life seems so beautiful to me! What are you thinking about?

IRINA. You say that life is beautiful. Yes, if only it seems so! The life of us three hasn't been beautiful yet; it has been stifling us as if it was weeds . . . I'm crying. I oughtn't. . . . [Dries her tears, smiles] We must work, work. That is why we are unhappy and look at the world so sadly; we don't know what work is. Our parents despised work. . . .

[Enter NATALIA IVANOVA; she wears a pink dress and a green sash.]

NATASHA. They're already at lunch . . . I'm late . . . [Carefully examines herself in a mirror, and puts herself straight] I think my hair's done all right. . . . [Sees IRINA] Dear Irina Sergeyevna, I congratulate you! [Kisses her firmly and at length] You've so many visitors, I'm really ashamed. . . . How do you do, Baron!

OLGA. [Enters from dining-room] Here's Natalia Ivanovna. How are you, dear! [They kiss.]

NATASHA. Happy returns. I'm awfully shy, you've so many people here.

OLGA. All our friends. [Frightened, in an undertone] You're wearing a green sash! My dear, you shouldn't!

NATASHA. Is it a sign of anything?

OLGA. No, it simply doesn't go well . . . and it looks so queer.

NATASHA. [In a tearful voice] Yes? But it isn't really green, it's too dull for that. [Goes into dining-room with Olga.]

[They have all sat down to lunch in the dining-room, the sitting-room is empty.]

KULIGIN. I wish you a nice fiancée, Irina. It's quite time you married.

CHEBUTIKIN. Natalia Ivanovna, I wish you the same.

KULIGIN. Natalia Ivanovna has a fiancé already.

MASHA. [Raps with her fork on a plate] Let's all get drunk and make life purple for once!

KULIGIN. You've lost three good conduct marks.

VERSHININ. This is a nice drink. What's it made of?

SOLENI. Blackbeetles.

IRINA. [Tearfully] Phoo! How disgusting!

OLGA. There is to be a roast turkey and a sweet apple pie for dinner. Thank goodness I can spend all day and the evening at home. You'll come in the evening, ladies and gentlemen. . . .

VERSHININ. And please may I come in the evening!

IRINA. Please do.

NATASHA. They don't stand on ceremony here.

CHEBUTIKIN. Nature only brought us into the world that we should love! [Laughs.]

ANDREY. [Angrily] Please don't! Aren't you tired of it?

[Enter FEDOTIK and RODE with a large basket of flowers.]

FEDOTIK. They're lunching already.

RODE. [Loudly and thickly] Lunching? Yes, so they are. . . .

FEDOTIK. Wait a minute! [Takes a photograph] That's one. No, just a moment. . . . [Takes another] That's two. Now we're ready!

[They take the basket and go into the dining-room, where they have a noisy reception.]

RODE. [Loudly] Congratulations and best wishes! Lovely weather to-day, simply perfect. Was out walking with the High School students all the morning. I take their drills.

FEDOTIK. You may move, Irina Sergeyevna! [Takes a photograph] You look well to-day. [Takes a humming-top out of his pocket] Here's a humming-top, by the way. It's got a lovely note!

IRINA. How awfully nice!

MASHA.
"There stands a green oak by the sea,
And a chain of bright gold is around it . . .
And a chain of bright gold is around it . . ."

[Tearfully] What am I saying that for? I've had those words running in my head all day. . . .

KULIGIN. There are thirteen at table!

RODE. [Aloud] Surely you don't believe in that superstition? [Laughter.]

KULIGIN. If there are thirteen at table then it means there are lovers present. It isn't you, Ivan Romanovitch, hang it all. . . . [Laughter.]

CHEBUTIKIN. I'm a hardened sinner, but I really don't see why Natalia Ivanovna should blush. . . .

[Loud laughter; NATASHA runs out into the sitting-room, followed by ANDREY.]

ANDREY. Don't pay any attention to them! Wait . . . do stop, please. . . .

NATASHA. I'm shy . . . I don't know what's the matter with me and they're all laughing at me. It wasn't nice of me to leave the table like that, but I can't . . . I can't. [Covers her face with her hands.]

ANDREY. My dear, I beg you. I implore you not to excite yourself. I assure you they're only joking, they're kind people. My dear, good girl, they're all kind and sincere people, and they like both you and me. Come here to the window, they can't see us here. . . . [Looks round.]

NATASHA. I'm so unaccustomed to meeting people!

ANDREY. Oh your youth, your splendid, beautiful youth! My darling, don't be so excited! Believe me, believe me . . . I'm so happy, my soul is full of love, of ecstasy. . . . They don't see us! They can't! Why, why or when did I fall in love with you— Oh, I can't understand anything. My dear, my pure darling, be my wife! I love you, love you . . . as never before. . . . [They kiss.]

[Two officers come in and, seeing the lovers kiss, stop in astonishment.]

Curtain.

ACT II

[Scene as before. It is 8 p.m. Somebody is heard playing a concertina outside in the street. There is no fire. NATALIA IVANOVNA enters in indoor dress carrying a candle; she stops by the door which leads into ANDREY'S room.]

NATASHA. What are you doing, Andrey? Are you reading? It's nothing, only I. . . . [She opens another door, and looks in, then closes it] Isn't there any fire. . . .

ANDREY. [Enters with book in hand] What are you doing, Natasha?

NATASHA. I was looking to see if there wasn't a fire. It's Shrovetide, and the servant is simply beside herself; I must look out that something doesn't happen. When I came through the dining-room yesterday midnight, there was a candle burning. I couldn't get her to tell me who had lighted it. [Puts down her candle] What's the time?

ANDREY. [Looks at his watch] A quarter past eight.

NATASHA. And Olga and Irina aren't in yet. The poor things are still at work. Olga at the teacher's council, Irina at the telegraph office. . . . [Sighs] I said to your sister this morning, "Irina, darling, you must take care of yourself." But she pays no attention. Did you say it was a quarter past eight? I am afraid little Bobby is quite ill. Why is he so cold? He was feverish yesterday, but to-day he is quite cold . . . I am so frightened!

ANDREY. It's all right, Natasha. The boy is well.

NATASHA. Still, I think we ought to put him on a diet. I am so afraid. And the entertainers were to be here after nine; they had better not come, Audrey.

ANDREY. I don't know. After all, they were asked.

NATASHA. This morning, when the little boy woke up and saw me he suddenly smiled; that means he knew me. "Good morning, Bobby!" I said, "good morning, darling." And he laughed. Children understand, they understand very well. So I'll tell them, Andrey dear, not to receive the entertainers.

ANDREY. [Hesitatingly] But what about my sisters. This is their flat.

NATASHA. They'll do as I want them. They are so kind. . . . [Going] I ordered sour milk for supper. The doctor says you must eat sour milk and nothing else, or you won't get thin. [Stops] Bobby is so cold. I'm afraid his room is too cold for him. It would be nice to put him into another room till the warm weather comes. Irina's room, for instance, is just right for a child: it's dry and has the sun all day. I must tell her, she can share Olga's room. It isn't as if she was at home in the daytime, she only sleeps here. . . . [A pause] Andrey, darling, why are you so silent?

ANDREY. I was just thinking. . . . There is really nothing to say. . . .

NATASHA. Yes . . . there was something I wanted to tell you. . . . Oh, yes. Ferapont has come from the Council offices, he wants to see you.

ANDREY. [Yawns] Call him here.

[NATASHA goes out; ANDREY reads his book, stooping over the candle she has left behind. FERAPONT enters; he wears a tattered old coat with the collar up. His ears are muffled.]

ANDREY. Good morning, grandfather. What have you to say?

FERAPONT. The Chairman sends a book and some documents or other. Here. . . . [Hands him a book and a packet.]

ANDREY. Thank you. It's all right. Why couldn't you come earlier? It's past eight now.

FERAPONT. What?

ANDREY. [Louder]. I say you've come late, it's past eight.

FERAPONT. Yes, yes. I came when it was still light, but they wouldn't let me in. They said you were busy. Well, what was I to do. If you're busy, you're busy, and I'm in no hurry. [He thinks that ANDREY is asking him something] What?

ANDREY. Nothing. [Looks through the book] To-morrow's Friday. I'm not supposed to go to work, but I'll come—all the same . . . and do some work. It's dull at home. [Pause] Oh, my dear old man, how strangely life changes, and how it deceives! To-day, out of sheer boredom, I took up this book—old university lectures, and I couldn't help laughing. My God, I'm secretary of the local district council, the council which has Protopopov for its chairman, yes, I'm the secretary, and the summit of my ambitions is—to become a member of the council! I to be a member of the local district council, I, who dream every night that I'm a professor of Moscow University, a famous scholar of whom all Russia is proud!

FERAPONT. I can't tell . . . I'm hard of hearing. . . .

ANDREY. If you weren't, I don't suppose I should talk to you. I've got to talk to somebody, and my wife doesn't understand me, and I'm a bit afraid of my sisters—I don't know why unless it is that they may make fun of me and make me feel ashamed . . . I don't drink, I don't like public-houses, but how I should like to be sitting just now in Tyestov's place in Moscow, or at the Great Moscow, old fellow!

FERAPONT. Moscow? That's where a contractor was once telling that some merchants or other were eating pancakes; one ate forty pancakes and he went and died, he was saying. Either forty or fifty, I forget which.

ANDREY. In Moscow you can sit in an enormous restaurant where you don't know anybody and where nobody knows you, and you don't feel all the same that you're a stranger. And here you know everybody and everybody knows you, and you're a stranger . . . and a lonely stranger.

FERAPONT. What? And the same contractor was telling—perhaps he was lying—that there was a cable stretching right across Moscow.

ANDREY. What for?

FERAPONT. I can't tell. The contractor said so.

ANDREY. Rubbish. [He reads] Were you ever in Moscow?

FERAPONT. [After a pause] No. God did not lead me there. [Pause] Shall I go?

ANDREY. You may go. Good-bye. [FERAPONT goes] Good-bye. [Reads] You can come to-morrow and fetch these documents. . . . Go along. . . . [Pause] He's gone. [A ring] Yes, yes. . . . [Stretches himself and slowly goes into his own room.]

[Behind the scene the nurse is singing a lullaby to the child. MASHA and VERSHININ come in. While they talk, a maidservant lights candles and a lamp.]

MASHA. I don't know. [Pause] I don't know. Of course, habit counts for a great deal. After father's death, for instance, it took us a long time to get used to the absence of orderlies. But, apart from habit, it seems to me in all fairness that, however it may be in other towns, the best and most-educated people are army men.

VERSHININ. I'm thirsty. I should like some tea.

MASHA. [Glancing at her watch] They'll bring some soon. I was given in marriage when I was eighteen, and I was afraid of my husband because he was a teacher and I'd only just left school. He then seemed to me frightfully wise and learned and important. And now, unfortunately, that has changed.

VERSHININ. Yes . . . yes.

MASHA. I don't speak of my husband, I've grown used to him, but civilians in general are so often coarse, impolite, uneducated. Their rudeness offends me, it angers me. I suffer when I see that a man isn't quite sufficiently refined, or delicate, or polite. I simply suffer agonies when I happen to be among schoolmasters, my husband's colleagues.

VERSHININ. Yes. . . . It seems to me that civilians and army men are equally interesting, in this town, at any rate. It's all the same! If you listen to a member of the local intelligentsia, whether to civilian or military, he will tell you that he's sick of his wife, sick of his house, sick of his estate, sick of his horses. . . . We Russians are extremely gifted in the direction of thinking on an exalted plane, but, tell me, why do we aim so low in real life? Why?

MASHA. Why?

VERSHININ. Why is a Russian sick of his children, sick of his wife? And why are his wife and children sick of him?

MASHA. You're a little downhearted to-day.

VERSHININ. Perhaps I am. I haven't had any dinner, I've had nothing since the morning. My daughter is a little unwell, and when my girls are ill, I get very anxious and my conscience tortures me because they have such a mother. Oh, if you had seen her to-day! What a trivial personality! We began quarrelling at seven in the morning and at nine I slammed the door and went out. [Pause] I never speak of her, it's strange that I bear my complaints to you alone. [Kisses her hand] Don't be angry with me. I haven't anybody but you, nobody at all. . . . [Pause.]

MASHA. What a noise in the oven. Just before father's death there was a noise in the pipe, just like that.

VERSHININ. Are you superstitious?

MASHA. Yes.

VERSHININ. That's strange. [Kisses her hand] You are a splendid, wonderful woman. Splendid, wonderful! It is dark here, but I see your sparkling eyes.

MASHA. [Sits on another chair] There is more light here.

VERSHININ. I love you, love you, love you . . . I love your eyes, your movements, I dream of them. . . . Splendid, wonderful woman!

MASHA. [Laughing] When you talk to me like that, I laugh; I don't know why, for I'm afraid. Don't repeat it, please. . . . [In an undertone] No, go on, it's all the same to me. . . . [Covers her face with her hands] Somebody's coming, let's talk about something else.

[IRINA and TUZENBACH come in through the dining-room.]

TUZENBACH. My surname is really triple. I am called Baron Tuzenbach-Krone-Altschauer, but I am Russian and Orthodox, the same as you. There is very little German left in me, unless perhaps it is the patience and the obstinacy with which I bore you. I see you home every night.

IRINA. How tired I am!

TUZENBACH. And I'll come to the telegraph office to see you home every day for ten or twenty years, until you drive me away. [He sees MASHA and VERSHININ; joyfully] Is that you? How do you do.

IRINA. Well, I am home at last. [To MASHA] A lady came to-day to telegraph to her brother in Saratov that her son died to-day, and she couldn't remember the address anyhow. So she sent the telegram without an address, just to Saratov. She was crying. And for some reason or other I was rude to her. "I've no time," I said. It was so stupid. Are the entertainers coming to-night?

MASHA. Yes.

IRINA. [Sitting down in an armchair] I want a rest. I am tired.

TUZENBACH. [Smiling] When you come home from your work you seem so young, and so unfortunate. . . . [Pause.]

IRINA. I am tired. No, I don't like the telegraph office, I don't like it.

MASHA. You've grown thinner. . . . [Whistles a little] And you look younger, and your face has become like a boy's.

TUZENBACH. That's the way she does her hair.

IRINA. I must find another job, this one won't do for me. What I wanted, what I hoped to get, just that is lacking here. Labour without poetry, without ideas. . . . [A knock on the floor] The doctor is knocking. [To TUZENBACH] Will you knock, dear. I can't . . . I'm tired. . . . [TUZENBACH knocks] He'll come in a minute. Something ought to be done. Yesterday the doctor and Andrey played cards at the club and lost money. Andrey seems to have lost 200 roubles.

MASHA. [With indifference] What can we do now?

IRINA. He lost money a fortnight ago, he lost money in December. Perhaps if he lost everything we should go away from this town. Oh, my God, I dream of Moscow every night. I'm just like a lunatic. [Laughs] We go there in June, and before June there's still . . . February, March, April, May . . . nearly half a year!

MASHA. Only Natasha mustn't get to know of these losses.

IRINA. I expect it will be all the same to her.

[CHEBUTIKIN, who has only just got out of bed—he was resting after dinner—comes into the dining-room and combs his beard. He then sits by the table and takes a newspaper from his pocket.]

MASHA. Here he is. . . . Has he paid his rent?

IRINA. [Laughs] No. He's been here eight months and hasn't paid a copeck. Seems to have forgotten.

MASHA. [Laughs] What dignity in his pose! [They all laugh. A pause.]

IRINA. Why are you so silent, Alexander Ignateyevitch?

VERSHININ. I don't know. I want some tea. Half my life for a tumbler of tea: I haven't had anything since morning.

CHEBUTIKIN. Irina Sergeyevna!

IRINA. What is it?

CHEBUTIKIN. Please come here, Venez ici. [IRINA goes and sits by the table] I can't do without you. [IRINA begins to play patience.]

VERSHININ. Well, if we can't have any tea, let's philosophize, at any rate.

TUZENBACH. Yes, let's. About what?

VERSHININ. About what? Let us meditate . . . about life as it will be after our time; for example, in two or three hundred years.

TUZENBACH. Well? After our time people will fly about in balloons, the cut of one's coat will change, perhaps they'll discover a sixth sense and develop it, but life will remain the same, laborious, mysterious, and happy. And in a thousand years' time, people will still be sighing: "Life is hard!"—and at the same time they'll be just as afraid of death, and unwilling to meet it, as we are.

VERSHININ. [Thoughtfully] How can I put it? It seems to me that everything on earth must change, little by little, and is already changing under our very eyes. After two or three hundred years, after a thousand—the actual time doesn't matter—a new and happy age will begin. We, of course, shall not take part in it, but we live and work and even suffer to-day that it should come.

We create it—and in that one object is our destiny and, if you like, our happiness.

[MASHA laughs softly.]

TUZENBACH. What is it?

MASHA. I don't know. I've been laughing all day, ever since morning.

VERSHININ. I finished my education at the same point as you, I have not studied at universities; I read a lot, but I cannot choose my books and perhaps what I read is not at all what I should, but the longer I love, the more I want to know. My hair is turning white, I am nearly an old man now, but I know so little, oh, so little! But I think I know the things that matter most, and that are most real. I know them well. And I wish I could make you understand that there is no happiness for us, that there should not and cannot be. . . . We must only work and work, and happiness is only for our distant posterity. [Pause] If not for me, then for the descendants of my descendants.

[FEDOTIK and RODE come into the dining-room; they sit and sing softly, strumming on a guitar.]

TUZENBACH. According to you, one should not even think about happiness! But suppose I am happy!

VERSHININ. No.

TUZENBACH. [Moves his hands and laughs] We do not seem to understand each other. How can I convince you? [MASHA laughs quietly, TUZENBACH continues, pointing at her] Yes, laugh! [To VERSHININ] Not only after two or three centuries, but in a million years, life will still be as it was; life does not change, it remains for ever, following its own laws which do not concern us, or which, at any rate, you will never find out. Migrant birds, cranes for example, fly and fly, and whatever thoughts, high or low, enter their heads, they will still fly and not know why or where. They fly and will continue to fly, whatever philosophers come to life among them; they may philosophize as much as they like, only they will fly. . . .

MASHA. Still, is there a meaning?

TUZENBACH. A meaning. . . . Now the snow is falling. What meaning? [Pause.]

MASHA. It seems to me that a man must have faith, or must search for a faith, or his life will be empty, empty. . . . To live and not to know why the cranes fly, why babies are born, why there are stars in the sky. . . . Either you must know why you live, or everything is trivial, not worth a straw. [A pause.]

VERSHININ. Still, I am sorry that my youth has gone.

MASHA. Gogol says: life in this world is a dull matter, my masters!

TUZENBACH. And I say it's difficult to argue with you, my masters! Hang it all.

CHEBUTIKIN. [Reading] Balzac was married at Berdichev. [IRINA is singing softly] That's worth making a note of. [He makes a note] Balzac was married at Berdichev. [Goes on reading.]

IRINA. [Laying out cards, thoughtfully] Balzac was married at Berdichev.

TUZENBACH. The die is cast. I've handed in my resignation, Maria Sergeyevna.

MASHA. So I heard. I don't see what good it is; I don't like civilians.

TUZENBACH. Never mind. . . . [Gets up] I'm not handsome; what use am I as a soldier? Well, it makes no difference . . . I shall work. If only just once in my life I could work so that I could come home in the evening, fall exhausted on my bed, and go to sleep at once. [Going into the dining-room] Workmen, I suppose, do sleep soundly!

FEDOTIK. [To IRINA] I bought some coloured pencils for you at Pizhikov's in the Moscow Road, just now. And here is a little knife.

IRINA. You have got into the habit of behaving to me as if I am a little girl, but I am grown up. [Takes the pencils and the knife, then, with joy] How lovely!

FEDOTIK. And I bought myself a knife . . . look at it . . . one blade, another, a third, an ear-scoop, scissors, nail-cleaners.

RODE. [Loudly] Doctor, how old are you?

CHEBUTIKIN. I? Thirty-two. [Laughter]

FEDOTIK. I'll show you another kind of patience. . . . [Lays out cards.]

[A samovar is brought in; ANFISA attends to it; a little later NATASHA enters and helps by the table; SOLENI arrives and, after greetings, sits by the table.]

VERSHININ. What a wind!

MASHA. Yes. I'm tired of winter. I've already forgotten what summer's like.

IRINA. It's coming out, I see. We're going to Moscow.

FEDOTIK. No, it won't come out. Look, the eight was on the two of spades. [Laughs] That means you won't go to Moscow.

CHEBUTIKIN. [Reading paper] Tsitsigar. Smallpox is raging here.

ANFISA. [Coming up to MASHA] Masha, have some tea, little mother. [To VERSHININ] Please have some, sir . . . excuse me, but I've forgotten your name. . . .

MASHA. Bring some here, nurse. I shan't go over there.

IRINA. Nurse!

ANFISA. Coming, coming!

NATASHA. [To SOLENI] Children at the breast understand perfectly. I said "Good morning, Bobby; good morning, dear!" And he looked at me in quite an unusual way. You think it's only the mother in me that is speaking; I assure you that isn't so! He's a wonderful child.

SOLENI. If he was my child I'd roast him on a frying-pan and eat him. [Takes his tumbler into the drawing-room and sits in a corner.]

NATASHA. [Covers her face in her hands] Vulgar, ill-bred man!

MASHA. He's lucky who doesn't notice whether it's winter now, or summer. I think that if I were in Moscow, I shouldn't mind about the weather.

VERSHININ. A few days ago I was reading the prison diary of a French minister. He had been sentenced on account of the Panama scandal. With what joy, what delight, he speaks of the birds he saw through the prison windows, which he had never noticed while he was a minister. Now, of course, that he is at liberty, he notices birds no more than he did before. When you go to live in Moscow you'll not notice it, in just the same way. There can be no happiness for us, it only exists in our wishes.

TUZENBACH. [Takes cardboard box from the table] Where are the pastries?

IRINA. Soleni has eaten them.

TUZENBACH. All of them?

ANFISA. [Serving tea] There's a letter for you.

VERSHININ. For me? [Takes the letter] From my daughter. [Reads] Yes, of course . . . I will go quietly. Excuse me, Maria Sergeyevna. I shan't have any tea. [Stands up, excited] That eternal story. . . .

MASHA. What is it? Is it a secret?

VERSHININ. [Quietly] My wife has poisoned herself again. I must go. I'll go out quietly. It's all awfully unpleasant. [Kisses MASHA'S hand] My dear, my splendid, good woman . . . I'll go this way, quietly. [Exit.]

ANFISA. Where has he gone? And I'd served tea. . . . What a man.

MASHA. [Angrily] Be quiet! You bother so one can't have a moment's peace. . . . [Goes to the table with her cup] I'm tired of you, old woman!

ANFISA. My dear! Why are you offended!

ANDREY'S VOICE. Anfisa!

ANFISA. [Mocking] Anfisa! He sits there and . . . [Exit.]

MASHA. [In the dining-room, by the table angrily] Let me sit down! [Disturbs the cards on the table] Here you are, spreading your cards out. Have some tea!

IRINA. You are cross, Masha.

MASHA. If I am cross, then don't talk to me. Don't touch me!

CHEBUTIKIN. Don't touch her, don't touch her. . . .

MASHA. You're sixty, but you're like a boy, always up to some beastly nonsense.

NATASHA. [Sighs] Dear Masha, why use such expressions? With your beautiful exterior you would be simply fascinating in good society, I tell you so directly, if it wasn't for your words. *Je vous prie, pardonnez moi, Marie, mais vous avez des manières un peu grossières.*

TUZENBACH. [Restraining his laughter] Give me . . . give me . . . there's some cognac, I think.

NATASHA. *Il parait, que mon Bobick déjà ne dort pas,* he has awakened. He isn't well to-day. I'll go to him, excuse me . . . [Exit.]

IRINA. Where has Alexander Ignateyevitch gone?

MASHA. Home. Something extraordinary has happened to his wife again.

TUZENBACH. [Goes to SOLENI with a cognac-flask in his hands] You go on sitting by yourself, thinking of something—goodness knows what. Come and let's make peace. Let's have some cognac. [They drink] I expect I'll have to play the piano all night, some rubbish most likely . . . well, so be it!

SOLENI. Why make peace? I haven't quarrelled with you.

TUZENBACH. You always make me feel as if something has taken place between us. You've a strange character, you must admit.

SOLENI. [Declaims] "I am strange, but who is not? Don't be angry, Aleko!"

TUZENBACH. And what has Aleko to do with it? [Pause.]

SOLENI. When I'm with one other man I behave just like everybody else, but in company I'm dull and shy and . . . talk all manner of rubbish. But I'm more honest and more honourable than very, very many people. And I can prove it.

TUZENBACH. I often get angry with you, you always fasten on to me in company, but I like you all the same. I'm going to drink my fill to-night, whatever happens. Drink, now!

SOLENI. Let's drink. [They drink] I never had anything against you, Baron. But my character is like Lermontov's [In a low voice] I even rather resemble Lermontov, they say. . . . [Takes a scent-bottle from his pocket, and scents his hands.]

TUZENBACH. I've sent in my resignation. Basta! I've been thinking about it for five years, and at last made up my mind. I shall work.

SOLENI. [Declaims] "Do not be angry, Aleko . . . forget, forget, thy dreams of yore. . . ."

[While he is speaking ANDREY enters quietly with a book, and sits by the table.]

TUZENBACH. I shall work.

CHEBUTIKIN. [Going with IRINA into the dining-room] And the food was also real Caucasian onion soup, and, for a roast, some chehartma.

SOLENI. Cheremsha [Note: A variety of garlic.] isn't meat at all, but a plant something like an onion.

CHEBUTIKIN. No, my angel. Chehartma isn't onion, but roast mutton.

SOLENI. And I tell you, chehartma—is a sort of onion.

CHEBUTIKIN. And I tell you, chehartma—is mutton.

SOLENI. And I tell you, cheremsha—is a sort of onion.

CHEBUTIKIN. What's the use of arguing! You've never been in the Caucasus, and never ate any chehartma.

SOLENI. I never ate it, because I hate it. It smells like garlic.

ANDREY. [Imploring] Please, please! I ask you!

TUZENBACH. When are the entertainers coming?

IRINA. They promised for about nine; that is, quite soon.

TUZENBACH. [Embraces ANDREY]

"Oh my house, my house, my new-built house."

ANDREY. [Dances and sings] "Newly-built of maple-wood."

CHEBUTIKIN. [Dances]

"Its walls are like a sieve!" [Laughter.]

TUZENBACH. [Kisses ANDREY] Hang it all, let's drink. Andrey, old boy, let's drink with you. And I'll go with you, Andrey, to the University of Moscow.

SOLENI. Which one? There are two universities in Moscow.

ANDREY. There's one university in Moscow.

SOLENI. Two, I tell you.

ANDREY. Don't care if there are three. So much the better.

SOLENI. There are two universities in Moscow! [There are murmurs and "hushes"] There are two universities in Moscow, the old one and the new

one. And if you don't like to listen, if my words annoy you, then I need not speak. I can even go into another room. . . . [Exit.]

TUZENBACH. Bravo, bravo! [Laughs] Come on, now. I'm going to play. Funny man, Soleni. . . . [Goes to the piano and plays a waltz.]

MASHA. [Dancing solo] The Baron's drunk, the Baron's drunk, the Baron's drunk!

[NATASHA comes in.]

NATASHA. [To CHEBUTIKIN] Ivan Romanovitch!

[Says something to CHEBUTIKIN, then goes out quietly; CHEBUTIKIN touches TUZENBACH on the shoulder and whispers something to him.]

IRINA. What is it?

CHEBUTIKIN. Time for us to go. Good-bye.

TUZENBACH. Good-night. It's time we went.

IRINA. But, really, the entertainers?

ANDREY. [In confusion] There won't be any entertainers. You see, dear, Natasha says that Bobby isn't quite well, and so. . . . In a word, I don't care, and it's absolutely all one to me.

IRINA. [Shrugging her shoulders] Bobby ill!

MASHA. What is she thinking of! Well, if they are sent home, I suppose they must go. [To IRINA] Bobby's all right, it's she herself. . . . Here! [Taps her forehead] Little bourgeoise!

[ANDREY goes to his room through the right-hand door, CHEBUTIKIN follows him. In the dining-room they are saying good-bye.]

FEDOTIK. What a shame! I was expecting to spend the evening here, but of course, if the little baby is ill . . . I'll bring him some toys to-morrow.

RODE. [Loudly] I slept late after dinner to-day because I thought I was going to dance all night. It's only nine o'clock now!

MASHA. Let's go into the street, we can talk there. Then we can settle things.

(Good-byes and good nights are heard. TUZENBACH'S merry laughter is heard. [All go out] ANFISA and the maid clear the table, and put out the lights. [The nurse sings] ANDREY, wearing an overcoat and a hat, and CHEBUTIKIN enter silently.)

CHEBUTIKIN. I never managed to get married because my life flashed by like lightning, and because I was madly in love with your mother, who was married.

ANDREY. One shouldn't marry. One shouldn't, because it's dull.

CHEBUTIKIN. So there I am, in my loneliness. Say what you will, loneliness is a terrible thing, old fellow. . . . Though really . . . of course, it absolutely doesn't matter!

ANDREY. Let's be quicker.

CHEBUTIKIN. What are you in such a hurry for? We shall be in time.

ANDREY. I'm afraid my wife may stop me.

CHEBUTIKIN. Ah!

ANDREY. I shan't play to-night, I shall only sit and look on. I don't feel very well. . . . What am I to do for my asthma, Ivan Romanovitch?

CHEBUTIKIN. Don't ask me! I don't remember, old fellow, I don't know.

ANDREY. Let's go through the kitchen. [They go out.]

[A bell rings, then a second time; voices and laughter are heard.]

IRINA. [Enters] What's that?

ANFISA. [Whispers] The entertainers! [Bell.]

IRINA. Tell them there's nobody at home, nurse. They must excuse us.

[ANFISA goes out. IRINA walks about the room deep in thought; she is excited. SOLENI enters.]

SOLENI. [In surprise] There's nobody here. . . . Where are they all?

IRINA. They've gone home.

SOLENI. How strange. Are you here alone?

IRINA. Yes, alone. [A pause] Good-bye.

SOLENI. Just now I behaved tactlessly, with insufficient reserve. But you are not like all the others, you are noble and pure, you can see the truth. . . . You alone can understand me. I love you, deeply, beyond measure, I love you.

IRINA. Good-bye! Go away.

SOLENI. I cannot live without you. [Follows her] Oh, my happiness! [Through his tears] Oh, joy!

Wonderful, marvellous, glorious eyes, such as I have never seen before. . . .

IRINA. [Coldly] Stop it, Vassili Vassilevitch!

SOLENI. This is the first time I speak to you of love, and it is as if I am no longer on the earth, but on another planet. [Wipes his forehead] Well, never mind. I can't make you love me by force, of course . . . but I don't intend to have any more-favoured rivals. . . . No . . . I swear to you by all the saints, I shall kill my rival. . . . Oh, beautiful one!

[NATASHA enters with a candle; she looks in through one door, then through another, and goes past the door leading to her husband's room.]

NATASHA. Here's Andrey. Let him go on reading. Excuse me, Vassili Vassilevitch, I did not know you were here; I am engaged in domesticities.

SOLENI. It's all the same to me. Good-bye! [Exit.]

NATASHA. You're so tired, my poor dear girl! [Kisses IRINA] If you only went to bed earlier.

IRINA. Is Bobby asleep?

NATASHA. Yes, but restlessly. By the way, dear, I wanted to tell you, but either you weren't at home, or I was busy . . . I think Bobby's present nursery is cold and damp. And your room would be so nice for the child. My dear, darling girl, do change over to Olga's for a bit!

IRINA. [Not understanding] Where?

[The bells of a troika are heard as it drives up to the house.]

NATASHA. You and Olga can share a room, for the time being, and Bobby can have yours. He's such a darling; to-day I said to him, "Bobby, you're mine! Mine!" And he looked at me with his dear little eyes. [A bell rings] It must be Olga. How late she is! [The maid enters and whispers to NATASHA] Protopopov? What a queer man to do such a thing. Protopopov's come and wants me to go for a drive with him in his troika. [Laughs] How funny these men are. . . . [A bell rings] Somebody has come. Suppose I did go and have half an hour's drive. . . . [To the maid] Say I shan't be long. [Bell rings] Somebody's ringing, it must be OLGA. [Exit.]

[The maid runs out; IRINA sits deep in thought; KULIGIN and OLGA enter, followed by VERSHININ.]

KULIGIN. Well, there you are. And you said there was going to be a party.

VERSHININ. It's queer; I went away not long ago, half an hour ago, and they were expecting entertainers.

IRINA. They've all gone.

KULIGIN. Has Masha gone too? Where has she gone? And what's Protopopov waiting for downstairs in his troika? Whom is he expecting?

IRINA. Don't ask questions . . . I'm tired.

KULIGIN. Oh, you're all whimsies. . . .

OLGA. My committee meeting is only just over. I'm tired out. Our chairwoman is ill, so I had to take her place. My head, my head is aching. . . . [Sits] Andrey lost 200 roubles at cards yesterday . . . the whole town is talking about it. . . .

KULIGIN. Yes, my meeting tired me too. [Sits.]

VERSHININ. My wife took it into her head to frighten me just now by nearly poisoning herself. It's all right now, and I'm glad; I can rest now. . . . But perhaps we ought to go away? Well, my best wishes, Feodor Ilitch, let's go somewhere together! I can't, I absolutely can't stop at home. . . . Come on!

KULIGIN. I'm tired. I won't go. [Gets up] I'm tired. Has my wife gone home?

IRINA. I suppose so.

KULIGIN. [Kisses IRINA'S hand] Good-bye, I'm going to rest all day to-morrow and the day after. Best wishes! [Going] I should like some tea. I was looking forward to spending the whole evening in pleasant company and—o, fallacem hominum spem! . . . Accusative case after an interjection. . . .

VERSHININ. Then I'll go somewhere by myself. [Exit with KULIGIN, whistling.]

OLGA. I've such a headache . . . Andrey has been losing money. . . . The whole town is talking. . . . I'll go and lie down. [Going] I'm free to-morrow. . . . Oh, my God, what a mercy! I'm free to-morrow, I'm free the day after. . . . Oh my head, my head. . . . [Exit.]

IRINA. [alone] They've all gone. Nobody's left.

[A concertina is being played in the street. The nurse sings.]

NATASHA. [in fur coat and cap, steps across the dining-room, followed by the maid] I'll be back in half an hour. I'm only going for a little drive. [Exit.]

IRINA. [Alone in her misery] To Moscow! Moscow! Moscow!

Curtain.

ACT III

[The room shared by OLGA and IRINA. Beds, screened off, on the right and left. It is past 2 a.m. Behind the stage a fire-alarm is ringing; it has apparently been going for some time. Nobody in the house has gone to bed yet. MASHA is lying on a sofa dressed, as usual, in black. Enter OLGA and ANFISA.]

ANFISA. Now they are downstairs, sitting under the stairs. I said to them, "Won't you come up," I said, "You can't go on like this," and they simply cried, "We don't know where father is." They said, "He may be burnt up by now." What an idea! And in the yard there are some people . . . also undressed.

OLGA. [Takes a dress out of the cupboard] Take this grey dress. . . . And this . . . and the blouse as well. . . . Take the skirt, too, nurse. . . . My God! How awful it is! The whole of the Kirsanovsky Road seems to have burned down. Take this . . . and this. . . . [Throws clothes into her hands] The poor Vershinins are so frightened. . . . Their house was nearly burnt. They ought to come here for the night. . . . They shouldn't be allowed to go home. . . . Poor Fedotik is completely burnt out, there's nothing left. . . .

ANFISA. Couldn't you call Ferapont, Olga dear. I can hardly manage. . . .

OLGA. [Rings] They'll never answer. . . . [At the door] Come here, whoever there is! [Through the open door can be seen a window, red with flame: afire-engine is heard passing the house] How awful this is. And how I'm sick of it! [FERAPONT enters] Take these things down. . . . The Kolotilin girls are down below . . . and let them have them. This, too.

FERAPONT. Yes'm. In the year twelve Moscow was burning too. Oh, my God! The Frenchmen were surprised.

OLGA. Go on, go on. . . .

FERAPONT. Yes'm. [Exit.]

OLGA. Nurse, dear, let them have everything. We don't want anything. Give it all to them, nurse. . . . I'm tired, I can hardly keep on my legs. . . . The Vershinins mustn't be allowed to go home. . . . The girls can sleep in the drawing-room, and Alexander Ignateyevitch can go downstairs to the Baron's flat . . . Fedotik can go there, too, or else into our dining-room. . . . The doctor is drunk, beastly drunk, as if on purpose, so nobody can go to him. Vershinin's wife, too, may go into the drawing-room.

ANFISA. [Tired] Olga, dear girl, don't dismiss me! Don't dismiss me!

OLGA. You're talking nonsense, nurse. Nobody is dismissing you.

ANFISA. [Puts OLGA'S head against her bosom] My dear, precious girl, I'm working, I'm toiling away . . . I'm growing weak, and they'll all say go away! And where shall I go? Where? I'm eighty. Eighty-one years old. . . .

OLGA. You sit down, nurse dear. . . . You're tired, poor dear. . . . [Makes her sit down] Rest, dear. You're so pale!

[NATASHA comes in.]

NATASHA. They are saying that a committee to assist the sufferers from the fire must be formed at once. What do you think of that? It's a beautiful idea. Of course the poor ought to be helped, it's the duty of the rich. Bobby and little Sophy are sleeping, sleeping as if nothing at all was the matter. There's such a lot of people here, the place is full of them, wherever you go. There's influenza in the town now. I'm afraid the children may catch it.

OLGA. [Not attending] In this room we can't see the fire, it's quiet here.

NATASHA. Yes . . . I suppose I'm all untidy. [Before the looking-glass] They say I'm growing stout . . . it isn't true! Certainly it isn't! Masha's asleep; the poor thing is tired out. . . . [Coldly, to ANFISA] Don't dare to be seated in my presence! Get up! Out of this! [Exit ANFISA; a pause] I don't understand what makes you keep on that old woman!

OLGA. [Confusedly] Excuse me, I don't understand either . . .

NATASHA. She's no good here. She comes from the country, she ought to live there. . . . Spoiling her, I call it! I like order in the house! We don't want any unnecessary people here. [Strokes her cheek] You're tired, poor thing! Our head mistress is tired! And when my little Sophie grows up and goes to school I shall be so afraid of you.

OLGA. I shan't be head mistress.

NATASHA. They'll appoint you, OLGA. It's settled.

OLGA. I'll refuse the post. I can't . . . I'm not strong enough. . . . [Drinks water] You were so rude to nurse just now . . . I'm sorry. I can't stand it . . . everything seems dark in front of me. . . .

NATASHA. [Excited] Forgive me, Olga, forgive me . . . I didn't want to annoy you.

[MASHA gets up, takes a pillow and goes out angrily.]

OLGA. Remember, dear . . . we have been brought up, in an unusual way, perhaps, but I can't bear this. Such behaviour has a bad effect on me, I get ill . . . I simply lose heart!

NATASHA. Forgive me, forgive me. . . . [Kisses her.]

OLGA. Even the least bit of rudeness, the slightest impoliteness, upsets me.

NATASHA. I often say too much, it's true, but you must agree, dear, that she could just as well live in the country.

OLGA. She has been with us for thirty years.

NATASHA. But she can't do any work now. Either I don't understand, or you don't want to understand me. She's no good for work, she can only sleep or sit about.

OLGA. And let her sit about.

NATASHA. [Surprised] What do you mean? She's only a servant. [Crying] I don't understand you, OLGA. I've got a nurse, a wet-nurse, we've a cook, a housemaid . . . what do we want that old woman for as well? What good is she? [Fire-alarm behind the stage.]

OLGA. I've grown ten years older to-night.

NATASHA. We must come to an agreement, OLGA. Your place is the school, mine—the home. You devote yourself to teaching, I, to the household. And if I talk about servants, then I do know what I am talking about; I do know what I am talking about . . . And to-morrow there's to be no more of that old thief, that old hag . . . [Stamping] that witch! And don't you dare to annoy me! Don't you dare! [Stopping short] Really, if you don't move downstairs, we shall always be quarrelling. This is awful.

[Enter KULIGIN.]

KULIGIN. Where's Masha? It's time we went home. The fire seems to be going down. [Stretches himself] Only one block has burnt down, but there was such a wind that it seemed at first the whole town was going to burn. [Sits] I'm tired out. My dear OLGA. I often think that if it hadn't been for Masha, I should have married you. You are awfully nice. . . . I am absolutely tired out. [Listens.]

OLGA. What is it?

KULIGIN. The doctor, of course, has been drinking hard; he's terribly drunk. He might have done it on purpose! [Gets up] He seems to be coming here. . . . Do you hear him? Yes, here. . . . [Laughs] What a man . . . really . . . I'll hide myself. [Goes to the cupboard and stands in the corner] What a rogue.

OLGA. He hadn't touched a drop for two years, and now he suddenly goes and gets drunk. . . .

[Retires with NATASHA to the back of the room. CHEBUTIKIN enters; apparently sober, he stops, looks round, then goes to the wash-stand and begins to wash his hands.]

CHEBUTIKIN. [Angrily] Devil take them all . . . take them all. . . . They think I'm a doctor and can cure everything, and I know absolutely nothing, I've forgotten all I ever knew, I remember nothing, absolutely nothing. [OLGA and NATASHA go out, unnoticed by him] Devil take it. Last Wednesday I attended a woman in Zasip— and she died, and it's my fault that she died. Yes . . . I used to know a certain amount five-and-twenty years ago, but I don't remember anything now. Nothing. Perhaps I'm not really a man, and am only pretending that I've got arms and legs and a head; perhaps I don't exist at all, and only imagine that I walk, and eat, and sleep. [Cries] Oh, if only I didn't exist! [Stops crying; angrily] The devil only knows. . . . Day before yesterday they were talking in the club; they said, Shakespeare, Voltaire . . . I'd never read, never read at all, and I put on an expression as if I had read. And so did the others. Oh, how beastly! How petty! And then I remembered the woman I killed on Wednesday . . . and I couldn't get her out of my mind, and everything in my mind became crooked, nasty, wretched. . . . So I went and drank. . . .

[IRINA, VERSHININ and TUZENBACH enter; TUZENBACH is wearing new and fashionable civilian clothes.]

IRINA. Let's sit down here. Nobody will come in here.

VERSHININ. The whole town would have been destroyed if it hadn't been for the soldiers. Good men! [Rubs his hands appreciatively] Splendid people! Oh, what a fine lot!

KULIGIN. [Coming up to him] What's the time?

TUZENBACH. It's past three now. It's dawning.

IRINA. They are all sitting in the dining-room, nobody is going. And that Soleni of yours is sitting there. [To CHEBUTIKIN] Hadn't you better be going to sleep, doctor?

CHEBUTIKIN. It's all right . . . thank you. . . . [Combs his beard.]

KULIGIN. [Laughs] Speaking's a bit difficult, eh, Ivan Romanovitch! [Pats him on the shoulder] Good man! *In vino veritas,* the ancients used to say.

TUZENBACH. They keep on asking me to get up a concert in aid of the sufferers.

IRINA. As if one could do anything. . . .

TUZENBACH. It might be arranged, if necessary. In my opinion Maria Sergeyevna is an excellent pianist.

KULIGIN. Yes, excellent!

IRINA. She's forgotten everything. She hasn't played for three years . . . or four.

TUZENBACH. In this town absolutely nobody understands music, not a soul except myself, but I do understand it, and assure you on my word of honour that Maria Sergeyevna plays excellently, almost with genius.

KULIGIN. You are right, Baron, I'm awfully fond of Masha. She's very fine.

TUZENBACH. To be able to play so admirably and to realize at the same time that nobody, nobody can understand you!

KULIGIN. [Sighs] Yes. . . . But will it be quite all right for her to take part in a concert? [Pause] You see, I don't know anything about it. Perhaps it will even be all to the good. Although I must admit that our Director is a good man, a very good man even, a very clever man, still he has such views. . . . Of course it isn't his business but still, if you wish it, perhaps I'd better talk to him.

[CHEBUTIKIN takes a porcelain clock into his hands and examines it.]

VERSHININ. I got so dirty while the fire was on, I don't look like anybody on earth. [Pause] Yesterday I happened to hear, casually, that they want to transfer our brigade to some distant place. Some said to Poland, others, to Chita.

TUZENBACH. I heard so, too. Well, if it is so, the town will be quite empty.

IRINA. And we'll go away, too!

CHEBUTIKIN. [Drops the clock which breaks to pieces] To smithereens!

[A pause; everybody is pained and confused.]

KULIGIN. [Gathering up the pieces] To smash such a valuable object—oh, Ivan Romanovitch, Ivan Romanovitch! A very bad mark for your misbehaviour!

IRINA. That clock used to belong to our mother.

CHEBUTIKIN. Perhaps. . . . To your mother, your mother. Perhaps I didn't break it; it only looks as if I broke it. Perhaps we only think that we exist, when really we don't. I don't know anything, nobody knows anything. [At the door] What are you looking at? Natasha has a little romance with Protopopov, and you don't see it. . . . There you sit and see nothing, and Natasha has a little romance with Protopovov. . . . [Sings] Won't you please accept this date. . . . [Exit.]

VERSHININ. Yes. [Laughs] How strange everything really is! [Pause] When the fire broke out, I hurried off home; when I get there I see the house is whole, uninjured, and in no danger, but my two girls are standing by the door in just their underclothes, their mother isn't there, the crowd is excited, horses and dogs are running about, and the girls' faces are so agitated, terrified, beseeching, and I don't know what else. My heart was pained when I saw those faces. My God, I thought, what these girls will have to put up with if they live long! I caught them up and ran, and still kept on thinking the one thing: what they will have to live through in this world! [Fire-alarm; a pause] I come here and find their mother shouting and angry. [MASHA enters with a pillow and sits on the sofa] And when my girls were standing by the door in just their underclothes, and the street was red from the fire, there was a dreadful noise, and I thought that something of the sort used to happen many years ago when an enemy made a sudden attack, and looted, and burned. . . . And at the same time what a difference there really is between the present and the past! And when a little more time has gone by, in two or three hundred years perhaps, people will look at our present life with just the same fear, and the same contempt, and the whole past will seem clumsy and dull, and very uncomfortable, and strange. Oh, indeed, what a life there will be, what a life! [Laughs] Forgive me, I've dropped into philosophy again. Please let me continue. I do awfully want to philosophize, it's just how I feel at present. [Pause] As if they are all asleep. As I was saying: what a life there will be! Only just imagine. . . . There are only three persons like yourselves in the town just now, but in future generations there will be more and more, and still more, and the time will come when everything will change and become as you would have it, people will live as you do, and then you too will go out of date; people will be born who are better than you. . . . [Laughs] Yes, to-day I am quite exceptionally in the vein. I am devilishly keen on living. . . . [Sings.]

"The power of love all ages know,
From its assaults great good does grow." [Laughs.]

MASHA. Trum-tum-tum . . .

VERSHININ. Tum-tum . . .

MASHA. Tra-ra-ra?

VERSHININ. Tra-ta-ta. [Laughs.]

[Enter Fedotik.]

FEDOTIK. [Dancing] I'm burnt out, I'm burnt out! Down to the ground! [Laughter.]

IRINA. I don't see anything funny about it. Is everything burnt?

FEDOTIK. [Laughs] Absolutely. Nothing left at all. The guitar's burnt, and the photographs are burnt, and all my correspondence. . . . And I was going to make you a present of a note-book, and that's burnt too.

[SOLENI comes in.]

IRINA. No, you can't come here, Vassili Vassilevitch. Please go away.

SOLENI. Why can the Baron come here and I can't?

VERSHININ. We really must go. How's the fire?

SOLENI. They say it's going down. No, I absolutely don't see why the Baron can, and I can't? [Scents his hands.]

VERSHININ. Trum-tum-tum.

MASHA. Trum-tum.

VERSHININ. [Laughs to SOLENI] Let's go into the dining-room.

SOLENI. Very well, we'll make a note of it. "If I should try to make this clear, the geese would be annoyed, I fear." [Looks at TUZENBACH] There, there, there. . . . [Goes out with VERSHININ and FEDOTIK.]

IRINA. How Soleni smelt of tobacco. . . . [In surprise] The Baron's asleep! Baron! Baron!

TUZENBACH. [Waking] I am tired, I must say. . . . The brickworks. . . . No, I'm not wandering, I

mean it; I'm going to start work soon at the brickworks . . . I've already talked it over. [Tenderly, to IRINA] You're so pale, and beautiful, and charming. . . . Your paleness seems to shine through the dark air as if it was a light. . . . You are sad, displeased with life. . . . Oh, come with me, let's go and work together!

MASHA. Nicolai Lvovitch, go away from here.

TUZENBACH. [Laughs] Are you here? I didn't see you. [Kisses IRINA'S hand] good-bye, I'll go . . . I look at you now and I remember, as if it was long ago, your name-day, when you, cheerfully and merrily, were talking about the joys of labour. . . . And how happy life seemed to me, then! What has happened to it now? [Kisses her hand] There are tears in your eyes. Go to bed now; it is already day . . . the morning begins. . . . If only I was allowed to give my life for you!

MASHA. Nicolai Lvovitch, go away! What business . . .

TUZENBACH. I'm off. [Exit.]

MASHA. [Lies down] Are you asleep, Feodor?

KULIGIN. Eh?

MASHA. Shouldn't you go home.

KULIGIN. My dear Masha, my darling Masha. . . .

IRINA. She's tired out. You might let her rest, Fedia.

KULIGIN. I'll go at once. My wife's a good, splendid . . . I love you, my only one. . . .

MASHA. [Angrily] Amo, amas, amat, amamus, amatis, amant.

KULIGIN. [Laughs] No, she really is wonderful. I've been your husband seven years, and it seems as if I was only married yesterday. On my word. No, you really are a wonderful woman. I'm satisfied, I'm satisfied, I'm satisfied!

MASHA. I'm bored, I'm bored, I'm bored. . . . [Sits up] But I can't get it out of my head. . . . It's simply disgraceful. It has been gnawing away at me . . . I can't keep silent. I mean about Andrey. . . . He has mortgaged this house with the bank, and his wife has got all the money; but the house doesn't belong to him alone, but to the four of us! He ought to know that, if he's an honourable man.

KULIGIN. What's the use, Masha? Andrey is in debt all round; well, let him do as he pleases.

MASHA. It's disgraceful, anyway. [Lies down]

KULIGIN. You and I are not poor. I work, take my classes, give private lessons . . . I am a plain, honest man . . . *Omnia mea mecum porto*, as they say.

MASHA. I don't want anything, but the unfairness of it disgusts me. [Pause] You go, Feodor.

KULIGIN. [Kisses her] You're tired, just rest for half an hour, and I'll sit and wait for you. Sleep. . . . [Going] I'm satisfied, I'm satisfied, I'm satisfied. [Exit.]

IRINA. Yes, really, our Andrey has grown smaller; how he's snuffed out and aged with that woman! He used to want to be a professor, and yesterday he was boasting that at last he had been made a member of the district council. He is a member, and Protopopov is chairman. . . . The whole town talks and laughs about it, and he alone knows and sees nothing. . . . And now everybody's gone to look at the fire, but he sits alone in his room and pays no attention, only just plays on his fiddle. [Nervily] Oh, it's awful, awful, awful. [Weeps] I can't, I can't bear it any longer! . . . I can't, I can't! . . . [OLGA comes in and clears up at her little table. IRINA is sobbing loudly] Throw me out, throw me out, I can't bear any more!

OLGA. [Alarmed] What is it, what is it? Dear!

IRINA. [Sobbing] Where? Where has everything gone? Where is it all? Oh my God, my God! I've forgotten everything, everything . . . I don't remember what is the Italian for window or, well, for ceiling . . . I forget everything, every day I forget it, and life passes and will never return, and we'll never go away to Moscow . . . I see that we'll never go. . . .

OLGA. Dear, dear. . . .

IRINA. [Controlling herself] Oh, I am unhappy . . . I can't work, I shan't work. Enough, enough! I used to be a telegraphist, now I work at the town council offices, and I have nothing but hate and contempt for all they give me to do . . . I am already twenty-three, I have already been at work for a long while, and my brain has dried up, and I've grown thinner, plainer, older, and there is no relief of any sort, and time goes and it seems all the while as if I am going away from the real, the beautiful life, farther and farther away, down some precipice. I'm in despair and I can't understand how it is that I am still alive, that I haven't killed myself.

OLGA. Don't cry, dear girl, don't cry . . . I suffer, too.

IRINA. I'm not crying, not crying. . . . Enough. . . . Look, I'm not crying any more. Enough . . . enough!

OLGA. Dear, I tell you as a sister and a friend if you want my advice, marry the Baron. [IRINA cries softly] You respect him, you think highly of him. . . . It is true that he is not handsome, but he is so honourable and clean . . . people don't marry from love, but in order to do one's duty. I think so, at any rate, and I'd marry without being in love. Whoever he was, I should marry him, so long as he was a decent man. Even if he was old. . . .

IRINA. I was always waiting until we should be settled in Moscow, there I should meet my true love; I used to think about him, and love him. . . . But it's all turned out to be nonsense, all nonsense. . . .

OLGA. [Embraces her sister] My dear, beautiful sister, I understand everything; when Baron Nicolai Lvovitch left the army and came to us in evening dress, [Note: I.e. in the correct dress for making a proposal of marriage.] he seemed so bad-looking to me that I even started crying. . . . He asked, "What are you crying for?" How could I tell him! But if God brought him to marry you, I should be happy. That would be different, quite different.

[NATASHA with a candle walks across the stage from right to left without saying anything.]

MASHA. [Sitting up] She walks as if she's set something on fire.

OLGA. Masha, you're silly, you're the silliest of the family. Please forgive me for saying so. [Pause.]

MASHA. I want to make a confession, dear sisters. My soul is in pain. I will confess to you, and never again to anybody . . . I'll tell you this minute. [Softly] It's my secret but you must know everything . . . I can't be silent. . . . [Pause] I love, I love . . . I love that man. . . . You saw him only just now. . . . Why don't I say it . . . in one word. I love Vershinin.

OLGA. [Goes behind her screen] Stop that, I don't hear you in any case.

MASHA. What am I to do? [Takes her head in her hands] First he seemed queer to me, then I was sorry for him . . . then I fell in love with him . . . fell in love with his voice, his words, his misfortunes, his two daughters.

OLGA. [Behind the screen] I'm not listening. You may talk any nonsense you like, it will be all the same, I shan't hear.

MASHA. Oh, Olga, you are foolish. I am in love— that means that is to be my fate. It means that is to be my lot. . . . And he loves me. . . . It is all awful. Yes; it isn't good, is it? [Takes IRINA'S hand and draws her to her] Oh, my dear. . . . How are we going to live through our lives, what is to become of us. . . . When you read a novel it all seems so old and easy, but when you fall in love yourself, then you learn that nobody knows anything, and each must decide for himself. . . . My dear ones, my sisters . . . I've confessed, now I shall keep silence. . . . Like the lunatics in Gogol's story, I'm going to be silent . . . silent . . .

[ANDREY enters, followed by FERAPONT.]

ANDREY. [Angrily] What do you want? I don't understand.

FERAPONT. [At the door, impatiently] I've already told you ten times, Andrey Sergeyevitch.

ANDREY. In the first place I'm not Andrey Sergeyevitch, but sir. [Note: Quite literally, "your high honour," to correspond to Andrey's rank as a civil servant.]

FERAPONT. The firemen, sir, ask if they can go across your garden to the river. Else they go right round, right round; it's a nuisance.

ANDREY. All right. Tell them it's all right. [Exit FERAPONT] I'm tired of them. Where is Olga? [OLGA comes out from behind the screen] I came to you for the key of the cupboard. I lost my own. You've got a little key. [OLGA gives him the key; IRINA goes behind her screen; pause] What a huge fire! It's going down now. Hang it all, that

Ferapont made me so angry that I talked nonsense to him. . . . Sir, indeed. . . . [A pause] Why are you so silent, Olga? [Pause] It's time you stopped all that nonsense and behaved as if you were properly alive. . . . You are here, Masha. Irina is here, well, since we're all here, let's come to a complete understanding, once and for all. What have you against me? What is it?

OLGA. Please don't, Audrey dear. We'll talk to-morrow. [Excited] What an awful night!

ANDREY. [Much confused] Don't excite yourself. I ask you in perfect calmness; what have you against me? Tell me straight.

VERSHININ'S VOICE. Trum-tum-tum!

MASHA. [Stands; loudly] Tra-ta-ta! [To OLGA] Goodbye, Olga, God bless you. [Goes behind screen and kisses IRINA] Sleep well. . . . Good-bye, Andrey. Go away now, they're tired . . . you can explain to-morrow. . . . [Exit.]

ANDREY. I'll only say this and go. Just now. . . . In the first place, you've got something against Natasha, my wife; I've noticed it since the very day of my marriage. Natasha is a beautiful and honest creature, straight and honourable—that's my opinion. I love and respect my wife; understand it, I respect her, and I insist that others should respect her too. I repeat, she's an honest and honourable person, and all your disapproval is simply silly . . . [Pause] In the second place, you seem to be annoyed because I am not a professor, and am not engaged in study. But I work for the zemstvo, I am a member of the district council, and I consider my service as worthy and as high as the service of science. I am a member of the district council, and I am proud of it, if you want to know. [Pause] In the third place, I have still this to say . . . that I have mortgaged the house without obtaining your permission. . . . For that I am to blame, and ask to be forgiven. My debts led me into doing it . . . thirty-five thousand . . . I do not play at cards any more, I stopped long ago, but the chief thing I have to say in my defence is that you girls receive a pension, and I don't . . . my wages, so to speak. . . . [Pause.]

KULIGIN. [At the door] Is Masha there? [Excitedly] Where is she? It's queer. . . . [Exit.]

ANDREY. They don't hear. Natasha is a splendid, honest person. [Walks about in silence, then stops] When I married I thought we should be happy . . . all of us. . . . But, my God. . . . [Weeps] My dear, dear sisters, don't believe me, don't believe me. . . . [Exit.]

[Fire-alarm. The stage is clear.]

IRINA. [behind her screen] Olga, who's knocking on the floor?

OLGA. It's doctor Ivan Romanovitch. He's drunk.

IRINA. What a restless night! [Pause] Olga! [Looks out] Did you hear? They are taking the brigade away from us; it's going to be transferred to some place far away.

OLGA. It's only a rumour.

IRINA. Then we shall be left alone. . . . Olga!

OLGA. Well?

IRINA. My dear, darling sister, I esteem, I highly value the Baron, he's a splendid man; I'll marry him, I'll consent, only let's go to Moscow! I implore you, let's go! There's nothing better than Moscow on earth! Let's go, Olga, let's go!

Curtain

ACT IV

[The old garden at the house of the PROSOROVS. There is a long avenue of firs, at the end of which the river can be seen. There is a forest on the far side of the river. On the right is the terrace of the house: bottles and tumblers are on a table here; it is evident that champagne has just been drunk. It is midday. Every now and again passers-by walk across the garden, from the road to the river; five soldiers go past rapidly. CHEBUTIKIN, in a comfortable frame of mind which does not desert him throughout the act, sits in an armchair in the garden, waiting to be called. He wears a peaked cap and has a stick. IRINA, KULIGIN with a cross hanging from his neck and without his moustaches, and TUZENBACH are standing on the terrace seeing off FEDOTIK and RODE, who are coming down into the garden; both officers are in service uniform.]

TUZENBACH. [Exchanges kisses with FEDOTIK] You're a good sort, we got on so well together. [Exchanges kisses with RODE] Once again. . . . Good-bye, old man!

IRINA. Au revoir!

FEDOTIK. It isn't au revoir, it's good-bye; we'll never meet again!

KULIGIN. Who knows! [Wipes his eyes; smiles] Here I've started crying!

IRINA. We'll meet again sometime.

FEDOTIK. After ten years—or fifteen? We'll hardly know one another then; we'll say, "How do you do?" coldly. . . . [Takes a snapshot] Keep still. . . . Once more, for the last time.

RODE. [Embracing TUZENBACH] We shan't meet again. . . . [Kisses IRINA'S hand] Thank you for everything, for everything!

FEDOTIK. [Grieved] Don't be in such a hurry!

TUZENBACH. We shall meet again, if God wills it. Write to us. Be sure to write.

RODE. [Looking round the garden] Good-bye, trees! [Shouts] Yo-ho! [Pause] Good-bye, echo!

KULIGIN. Best wishes. Go and get yourselves wives there in Poland. . . . Your Polish wife will clasp you and call you "kochanku!" [Note: Darling.] [Laughs.]

FEDOTIK. [Looking at the time] There's less than an hour left. Soleni is the only one of our battery who is going on the barge; the rest of us are going with the main body. Three batteries are leaving to-day, another three to-morrow and then the town will be quiet and peaceful.

TUZENBACH. And terribly dull.

RODE. And where is Maria Sergeyevna?

KULIGIN. Masha is in the garden.

FEDOTIK. We'd like to say good-bye to her.

RODE. Good-bye, I must go, or else I'll start weeping. . . . [Quickly embraces KULIGIN and TUZENBACH, and kisses IRINA'S hand] We've been so happy here. . . .

FEDOTIK. [To KULIGIN] Here's a keepsake for you . . . a note-book with a pencil. . . . We'll go to the river from here. . . . [They go aside and both look round.]

RODE. [Shouts] Yo-ho!

KULIGIN. [Shouts] Good-bye!

[At the back of the stage FEDOTIK and RODE meet MASHA; they say good-bye and go out with her.]

IRINA. They've gone. . . . [Sits on the bottom step of the terrace.]

CHEBUTIKIN. And they forgot to say good-bye to me.

IRINA. But why is that?

CHEBUTIKIN. I just forgot, somehow. Though I'll soon see them again, I'm going to-morrow. Yes . . . just one day left. I shall be retired in a year, then I'll come here again, and finish my life near you. I've only one year before I get my pension. . . . [Puts one newspaper into his pocket and takes another out] I'll come here to you and change my life radically . . . I'll be so quiet . . . so agree . . . agreeable, respectable. . . .

IRINA. Yes, you ought to change your life, dear man, somehow or other.

CHEBUTIKIN. Yes, I feel it. [Sings softly.] "Tarara-boom-deay. . . ."

KULIGIN. We won't reform Ivan Romanovitch! We won't reform him!

CHEBUTIKIN. If only I was apprenticed to you! Then I'd reform.

IRINA. Feodor has shaved his moustache! I can't bear to look at him.

KULIGIN. Well, what about it?

CHEBUTIKIN. I could tell you what your face looks like now, but it wouldn't be polite.

KULIGIN. Well! It's the custom, it's modus vivendi. Our Director is clean-shaven, and so I too, when I received my inspectorship, had my moustaches removed. Nobody likes it, but it's all one to me. I'm satisfied. Whether I've got moustaches or not, I'm satisfied. . . . [Sits.]

[At the back of the stage ANDREY is wheeling a perambulator containing a sleeping infant.]

IRINA. Ivan Romanovitch, be a darling. I'm awfully worried. You were out on the boulevard last night; tell me, what happened?

CHEBUTIKIN. What happened? Nothing. Quite a trifling matter. [Reads paper] Of no importance!

KULIGIN. They say that Soleni and the Baron met yesterday on the boulevard near the theatre. . . .

TUZENBACH. Stop! What right . . . [Waves his hand and goes into the house.]

KULIGIN. Near the theatre . . . Soleni started behaving offensively to the Baron, who lost his temper and said something nasty. . . .

CHEBUTIKIN. I don't know. It's all bunkum.

KULIGIN. At some seminary or other a master wrote "bunkum" on an essay, and the student couldn't make the letters out—thought it was a Latin word "luckum." [Laughs] Awfully funny, that. They say that Soleni is in love with Irina and hates the Baron. . . . That's quite natural. Irina is a very nice girl. She's even like Masha, she's so thoughtful. . . . Only, Irina your character is gentler. Though Masha's character, too, is a very good one. I'm very fond of Masha. [Shouts of "Yo-ho!" are heard behind the stage.]

IRINA. [Shudders] Everything seems to frighten me today. [Pause] I've got everything ready, and I send my things off after dinner. The Baron and I will be married to-morrow, and to-morrow we go away to the brickworks, and the next day I go to the school, and the new life begins. God will help me! When I took my examination for the teacher's post, I actually wept for joy and gratitude. . . . [Pause] The cart will be here in a minute for my things. . . .

KULIGIN. Somehow or other, all this doesn't seem at all serious. As if it was all ideas, and nothing really serious. Still, with all my soul I wish you happiness.

CHEBUTIKIN. [With deep feeling] My splendid . . . my dear, precious girl. . . . You've gone on far ahead, I won't catch up with you. I'm left behind like a migrant bird grown old, and unable to fly. Fly, my dear, fly, and God be with you! [Pause] It's a pity you shaved your moustaches, Feodor Ilitch.

KULIGIN. Oh, drop it! [Sighs] To-day the soldiers will be gone, and everything will go on as in the old days. Say what you will, Masha is a good, honest woman. I love her very much, and thank my fate for her. People have such different fates.

There's a Kosirev who works in the excise department here. He was at school with me; he was expelled from the fifth class of the High School for being entirely unable to understand *ut consecutivum*. He's awfully hard up now and in very poor health, and when I meet him I say to him, "How do you do, *ut consecutivum*." "Yes," he says, "precisely *consecutivum* . . ." and coughs. But I've been successful all my life, I'm happy, and I even have a Stanislaus Cross, of the second class, and now I myself teach others that *ut consecutivum*. Of course, I'm a clever man, much cleverer than many, but happiness doesn't only lie in that. . . .

["The Maiden's Prayer" is being played on the piano in the house.]

IRINA. To-morrow night I shan't hear that "Maiden's Prayer" any more, and I shan't be meeting Protopopov. . . . [Pause] Protopopov is sitting there in the drawing-room; and he came to-day . . .

KULIGIN. Hasn't the head-mistress come yet?

IRINA. No. She has been sent for. If you only knew how difficult it is for me to live alone, without OLGA. . . . She lives at the High School; she, a head-mistress, busy all day with her affairs and I'm alone, bored, with nothing to do, and hate the room I live in. . . . I've made up my mind: if I can't live in Moscow, then it must come to this. It's fate. It can't be helped. It's all the will of God, that's the truth. Nicolai Lvovitch made me a proposal. . . . Well? I thought it over and made up my mind. He's a good man . . . it's quite remarkable how good he is. . . . And suddenly my soul put out wings, I became happy, and light-hearted, and once again the desire for work, work, came over me. . . . Only something happened yesterday, some secret dread has been hanging over me. . . .

CHEBUTIKIN. Luckum. Rubbish.

NATASHA. [At the window] The head-mistress.

KULIGIN. The head-mistress has come. Let's go. [Exit with IRINA into the house.]

CHEBUTIKIN. "It is my washing day. . . . Tara-ra . . . boom-deay."

[MASHA approaches, ANDREY is wheeling a perambulator at the back.]

MASHA. Here you are, sitting here, doing nothing.

CHEBUTIKIN. What then?

MASHA. [Sits] Nothing. . . . [Pause] Did you love my mother?

CHEBUTIKIN. Very much.

MASHA. And did she love you?

CHEBUTIKIN. [After a pause] I don't remember that.

MASHA. Is my man here? When our cook Martha used to ask about her gendarme, she used to say my man. Is he here?

CHEBUTIKIN. Not yet.

MASHA. When you take your happiness in little bits, in snatches, and then lose it, as I have done, you gradually get coarser, more bitter. [Points to her bosom] I'm boiling in here. . . . [Looks at ANDREY with the perambulator] There's our brother Andrey. . . . All our hopes in him have gone. There was once a great bell, a thousand persons were hoisting it, much money and labour had been spent on it, when it suddenly fell and was broken. Suddenly, for no particular reason. . . . Andrey is like that. . . .

ANDREY. When are they going to stop making such a noise in the house? It's awful.

CHEBUTIKIN. They won't be much longer. [Looks at his watch] My watch is very old-fashioned, it strikes the hours. . . . [Winds the watch and makes it strike] The first, second, and fifth batteries are to leave at one o'clock precisely. [Pause] And I go to-morrow.

ANDREY. For good?

CHEBUTIKIN. I don't know. Perhaps I'll return in a year. The devil only knows . . . it's all one. . . . [Somewhere a harp and violin are being played.]

ANDREY. The town will grow empty. It will be as if they put a cover over it. [Pause] Something happened yesterday by the theatre. The whole town knows of it, but I don't.

CHEBUTIKIN. Nothing. A silly little affair. Soleni started irritating the Baron, who lost his temper and insulted him, and so at last Soleni had to challenge him. [Looks at his watch] It's about time, I think. . . . At half-past twelve, in the public wood, that one you can see from here across the river. . . . Piff-paff. [Laughs] Soleni thinks he's Lermontov, and even writes verses. That's all very well, but this is his third duel.

MASHA. Whose?

CHEBUTIKIN. Soleni's.

MASHA. And the Baron?

CHEBUTIKIN. What about the Baron? [Pause.]

MASHA. Everything's all muddled up in my head. . . . But I say it ought not to be allowed. He might wound the Baron or even kill him.

CHEBUTIKIN. The Baron is a good man, but one Baron more or less—what difference does it make? It's all the same! [Beyond the garden somebody shouts "Co-ee! Hallo!"] You wait. That's Skvortsov shouting; one of the seconds. He's in a boat. [Pause.]

ANDREY. In my opinion it's simply immoral to fight in a duel, or to be present, even in the quality of a doctor.

CHEBUTIKIN. It only seems so. . . . We don't exist, there's nothing on earth, we don't really live, it only seems that we live. Does it matter, anyway!

MASHA. You talk and talk the whole day long. [Going] You live in a climate like this, where it might snow any moment, and there you talk. . . . [Stops] I won't go into the house, I can't go there. . . . Tell me when Vershinin comes. . . . [Goes along the avenue] The migrant birds are already on the wing. . . . [Looks up] Swans or geese. . . . My dear, happy things. . . . [Exit.]

ANDREY. Our house will be empty. The officers will go away, you are going, my sister is getting married, and I alone will remain in the house.

CHEBUTIKIN. And your wife?

[FERAPONT enters with some documents.]

ANDREY. A wife's a wife. She's honest, well-bred, yes; and kind, but with all that there is still something about her that degenerates her into a petty, blind, even in some respects misshapen animal. In any case, she isn't a man. I tell you as a friend, as the only man to whom I can lay bare my soul. I love Natasha, it's true, but sometimes she seems extraordinarily vulgar, and then I lose myself and can't understand why I love her so much, or, at any rate, used to love her. . . .

CHEBUTIKIN. [Rises] I'm going away to-morrow, old chap, and perhaps we'll never meet again, so here's my advice. Put on your cap, take a stick in your hand, go . . . go on and on, without looking round. And the farther you go, the better.

[SOLENI goes across the back of the stage with two officers; he catches sight of CHEBUTIKIN, and turns to him, the officers go on.]

SOLENI. Doctor, it's time. It's half-past twelve already. [Shakes hands with Andrey.]

CHEBUTIKIN. Half a minute. I'm tired of the lot of you. [To ANDREY] If anybody asks for me, say I'll be back soon. . . . [Sighs] Oh, oh, oh!

SOLENI. "He didn't have the time to sigh. The bear sat on him heavily." [Goes up to him] What are you groaning about, old man?

CHEBUTIKIN. Stop it!

SOLENI. How's your health?

CHEBUTIKIN. [Angry] Mind your own business.

SOLENI. The old man is unnecessarily excited. I won't go far, I'll only just bring him down like a snipe. [Takes out his scent-bottle and scents his hands] I've poured out a whole bottle of scent to-day and they still smell . . . of a dead body. [Pause] Yes. . . . You remember the poem

"But he, the rebel seeks the storm,
As if the storm will bring him rest . . ."?

CHEBUTIKIN. Yes.

"He didn't have the time to sigh,
The bear sat on him heavily."

[Exit with SOLENI.]

[Shouts are heard. ANDREY and FERAPONT come in.]

FERAPONT. Documents to sign. . . .

ANDREY. [Irritated]. Go away! Leave me! Please! [Goes away with the perambulator.]

FERAPONT. That's what documents are for, to be signed. [Retires to back of stage.]

[Enter IRINA, with TUZENBACH in a straw hat; KULIGIN walks across the stage, shouting "Co-ee, Masha, co-ee!"]

TUZENBACH. He seems to be the only man in the town who is glad that the soldiers are going.

IRINA. One can understand that. [Pause] The town will be empty.

TUZENBACH. My dear, I shall return soon.

IRINA. Where are you going?

TUZENBACH. I must go into the town and then . . . see the others off.

IRINA. It's not true . . . Nicolai, why are you so absentminded to-day? [Pause] What took place by the theatre yesterday?

TUZENBACH. [Making a movement of impatience] In an hour's time I shall return and be with you again. [Kisses her hands] My darling . . . [Looking her closely in the face] it's five years now since I fell in love with you, and still I can't get used to it, and you seem to me to grow more and more beautiful. What lovely, wonderful hair! What eyes! I'm going to take you away to-morrow. We shall work, we shall be rich, my dreams will come true. You will be happy. There's only one thing, one thing only: you don't love me!

IRINA. It isn't in my power! I shall be your wife, I shall be true to you, and obedient to you, but I can't love you. What can I do! [Cries] I have never been in love in my life. Oh, I used to think so much of love, I have been thinking about it for so long by day and by night, but my soul is like an expensive piano which is locked and the key lost. [Pause] You seem so unhappy.

TUZENBACH. I didn't sleep at night. There is nothing in my life so awful as to be able to frighten me, only that lost key torments my soul and does not let me sleep. Say something to me [Pause] say something to me. . . .

IRINA. What can I say, what?

TUZENBACH. Anything.

IRINA. Don't! don't! [Pause.]

TUZENBACH. It is curious how silly trivial little things, sometimes for no apparent reason, become significant. At first you laugh at these things, you think they are of no importance, you go on and you feel that you haven't got the strength to stop yourself. Oh don't let's talk about it! I am happy. It is as if for the first time in my life I see these firs, maples, beeches, and they all look at me inquisitively and wait. What beautiful trees and how beautiful, when one comes to think of it, life must be near them! [A shout of Co-ee! in the distance] It's time I went. . . . There's a tree which has dried up but it still sways in the breeze with the others. And so it seems to me that if I die, I shall still take part in life in one way or another. Good-bye, dear. . . . [Kisses her hands] The papers which you gave me are on my table under the calendar.

IRINA. I am coming with you.

TUZENBACH. [Nervously] No, no! [He goes quickly and stops in the avenue] Irina!

IRINA. What is it?

TUZENBACH. [Not knowing what to say] I haven't had any coffee to-day. Tell them to make me some. . . . [He goes out quickly.]

[IRINA stands deep in thought. Then she goes to the back of the stage and sits on a swing. ANDREY comes in with the perambulator and FERAPONT also appears.]

FERAPONT. Andrey Sergeyevitch, it isn't as if the documents were mine, they are the government's. I didn't make them.

ANDREY. Oh, what has become of my past and where is it? I used to be young, happy, clever, I used to be able to think and frame clever ideas, the present and the future seemed to me full of hope. Why do we, almost before we have begun to live, become dull, grey, uninteresting, lazy, apathetic, useless, unhappy. . . . This town has already been in existence for two hundred years and it has a hundred thousand inhabitants, not one of whom is in any way different from the others. There has never been, now or at any other time, a single leader of men, a single scholar, an artist, a man of even the slightest eminence who might arouse envy or a passionate desire to be imitated. They only eat, drink, sleep, and then they die . . . more people are born and also eat, drink, sleep, and so as not to go silly from boredom, they try to make life many-sided with their beastly backbiting, vodka, cards, and litigation. The wives deceive their husbands, and the husbands lie, and pretend they see nothing and hear nothing, and the evil influence irresistibly oppresses the children and the divine spark in them is extinguished, and they become just as pitiful corpses and just as much like one another as their fathers and mothers. . . . [Angrily to FERAPONT] What do you want?

FERAPONT. What? Documents want signing.

ANDREY. I'm tired of you.

FERAPONT. [Handing him papers] The hall-porter from the law courts was saying just now that in the winter there were two hundred degrees of frost in Petersburg.

ANDREY. The present is beastly, but when I think of the future, how good it is! I feel so light, so free; there is a light in the distance, I see freedom. I see myself and my children freeing ourselves from vanities, from kvass, from goose baked with cabbage, from after-dinner naps, from base idleness. . . .

FERAPONT. He was saying that two thousand people were frozen to death. The people were frightened, he said. In Petersburg or Moscow, I don't remember which.

ANDREY. [Overcome by a tender emotion] My dear sisters, my beautiful sisters! [Crying] Masha, my sister. . . .

NATASHA. [At the window] Who's talking so loudly out here? Is that you, Andrey? You'll wake little Sophie. *Il ne faut pas faire du bruit, la Sophie est dormée deja. Vous êtes un ours.* [Angrily] If you want to talk, then give the perambulator and the baby to somebody else. Ferapont, take the perambulator!

FERAPONT. Yes'm. [Takes the perambulator.]

ANDREY. [Confused] I'm speaking quietly.

NATASHA. [At the window, nursing her boy] Bobby! Naughty Bobby! Bad little Bobby!

ANDREY. [Looking through the papers] All right, I'll look them over and sign if necessary, and you can take them back to the offices. . . .

[Goes into house reading papers; FERAPONT takes the perambulator to the back of the garden.]

NATASHA. [At the window] Bobby, what's your mother's name? Dear, dear! And who's this? That's Aunt OLGA. Say to your aunt, "How do you do, Olga!"

[Two wandering musicians, a man and a girl, are playing on a violin and a harp. VERSHININ, OLGA, and ANFISA come out of the house and listen for a minute in silence; IRINA comes up to them.]

OLGA. Our garden might be a public thoroughfare, from the way people walk and ride across it. Nurse, give those musicians something!

ANFISA. [Gives money to the musicians] Go away with God's blessing on you. [The musicians bow and go away] A bitter sort of people. You don't play on a full stomach. [To IRINA] How do you do, Arisha! [Kisses her] Well, little girl, here I am, still alive! Still alive! In the High School, together with little Olga, in her official apartments . . . so the Lord has appointed for my old age. Sinful woman that I am, I've never lived like that in my life before. . . . A large flat, government property, and I've a whole room and bed to myself. All government property. I wake up at nights and, oh God, and Holy Mother, there isn't a happier person than I!

VERSHININ. [Looks at his watch] We are going soon, Olga Sergeyevna. It's time for me to go. [Pause] I wish you every . . . every. . . . Where's Maria Sergeyevna?

IRINA. She's somewhere in the garden. I'll go and look for her.

VERSHININ. If you'll be so kind. I haven't time.

ANFISA. I'll go and look, too. [Shouts] Little Masha, co-ee! [Goes out with IRINA down into the garden] Co-ee, co-ee!

VERSHININ. Everything comes to an end. And so we, too, must part. [Looks at his watch] The town gave us a sort of farewell breakfast, we had champagne to drink and the mayor made a speech, and I ate and listened, but my soul was here all the time. . . . [Looks round the garden] I'm so used to you now.

OLGA. Shall we ever meet again?

VERSHININ. Probably not. [Pause] My wife and both my daughters will stay here another two months. If anything happens, or if anything has to be done . . .

OLGA. Yes, yes, of course. You need not worry. [Pause] To-morrow there won't be a single soldier left in the town, it will all be a memory, and, of course, for us a new life will begin. . . . [Pause] None of our plans are coming right. I didn't want to be a head-mistress, but they made me one, all the same. It means there's no chance of Moscow. . . .

VERSHININ. Well . . . thank you for everything. Forgive me if I've . . . I've said such an awful lot—forgive me for that too, don't think badly of me.

OLGA. [Wipes her eyes] Why isn't Masha coming . . .

VERSHININ. What else can I say in parting? Can I philosophize about anything? [Laughs] Life is heavy. To many of us it seems dull and hopeless, but still, it must be acknowledged that it is getting lighter and clearer, and it seems that the time is not far off when it will be quite clear. [Looks at his watch] It's time I went! Mankind used to be absorbed in wars, and all its existence was filled with campaigns, attacks, defeats, now we've outlived all that, leaving after us a great waste place, which there is nothing to fill with at present; but mankind is looking for something, and will certainly find it. Oh, if it only happened more quickly. [Pause] If only education could be added to industry, and industry to education. [Looks at his watch] It's time I went. . . .

OLGA. Here she comes.

[Enter MASHA.]

VERSHININ. I came to say good-bye. . . .

[OLGA steps aside a little, so as not to be in their way.]

MASHA. [Looking him in the face] Good-bye. [Prolonged kiss.]

OLGA. Don't, don't. [MASHA is crying bitterly]

VERSHININ. Write to me. . . . Don't forget! Let me go. . . . It's time. Take her, Olga Sergeyevna . . . it's time . . . I'm late . . .

[He kisses OLGA'S hand in evident emotion, then embraces MASHA once more and goes out quickly.]

OLGA. Don't, Masha! Stop, dear. . . . [KULIGIN enters.]

KULIGIN. [Confused] Never mind, let her cry, let her. . . . My dear Masha, my good Masha. . . . You're my wife, and I'm happy, whatever happens . . . I'm not complaining, I don't reproach you at all. . . . Olga is a witness to it. Let's begin to live again as we used to, and not by a single word, or hint . . .

MASHA. [Restraining her sobs] *"There stands a green oak by the sea,*
And a chain of bright gold is around it. . . .
And a chain of bright gold is around it. . . ."

I'm going off my head . . . "There stands . . . a green oak . . . by the sea." . . .

OLGA. Don't, Masha, don't . . . give her some water. . . .

MASHA. I'm not crying any more. . . .

KULIGIN. She's not crying any more . . . she's a good . . . [A shot is heard from a distance.]

MASHA. *"There stands a green oak by the sea,*
And a chain of bright gold is around it . . .
An oak of green gold. . . ."

I'm mixing it up. . . . [Drinks some water] Life is dull . . . I don't want anything more now . . . I'll be all right in a moment. . . . It doesn't matter. . . . What do those lines mean? Why do they run in my head? My thoughts are all tangled.

[IRINA enters.]

OLGA. Be quiet, Masha. There's a good girl. . . . Let's go in.

MASHA. [Angrily] I shan't go in there. [Sobs, but controls herself at once] I'm not going to go into the house, I won't go. . . .

IRINA. Let's sit here together and say nothing. I'm going away to-morrow. . . . [Pause.]

KULIGIN. Yesterday I took away these whiskers and this beard from a boy in the third class. . . . [He puts on the whiskers and beard] Don't I look like the German master. . . . [Laughs] Don't I? The boys are amusing.

MASHA. You really do look like that German of yours.

OLGA. [Laughs] Yes. [MASHA weeps.]

IRINA. Don't, Masha!

KULIGIN. It's a very good likeness. . . .

[Enter Natasha.]

NATASHA. [To the maid] What? Mihail Ivanitch Protopopov will sit with little Sophie, and Andrey Sergeyevitch can take little Bobby out. Children are such a bother. . . . [To IRINA] Irina, it's such a pity you're going away to-morrow. Do stop just another week. [Sees KULIGIN and screams; he laughs and takes off his beard and whiskers] How you frightened me! [To IRINA] I've grown used to you and do you think it will be easy for me to part from you? I'm going to have Andrey and his violin put into your room—let him fiddle away in there!—and we'll put little Sophie into his room. The beautiful, lovely child! What a little girlie! To-day she looked at me with such pretty eyes and said "Mamma!"

KULIGIN. A beautiful child, it's quite true.

NATASHA. That means I shall have the place to myself to-morrow. [Sighs] In the first place I shall have that avenue of fir-trees cut down, then that maple. It's so ugly at nights. . . . [To IRINA] That belt doesn't suit you at all, dear. . . . It's an error of taste. And I'll give orders to have lots and lots of little flowers planted here, and they'll smell. . . . [Severely] Why is there a fork lying about here on the seat? [Going towards the house, to the maid] Why is there a fork lying about here on the seat, I say? [Shouts] Don't you dare to answer me!

KULIGIN. Temper! temper! [A march is played off; they all listen.]

OLGA. They're going.

[CHEBUTIKIN comes in.]

MASHA. They're going. Well, well. . . . Bon voyage! [To her husband] We must be going home. . . . Where's my coat and hat?

KULIGIN. I took them in . . . I'll bring them, in a moment.

OLGA. Yes, now we can all go home. It's time.

CHEBUTIKIN. Olga Sergeyevna!

OLGA. What is it? [Pause] What is it?

CHEBUTIKIN. Nothing . . . I don't know how to tell you. . . . [Whispers to her.]

OLGA. [Frightened] It can't be true!

CHEBUTIKIN. Yes . . . such a story . . . I'm tired out, exhausted, I won't say any more. . . . [Sadly] Still, it's all the same!

MASHA. What's happened?

OLGA. [Embraces IRINA] This is a terrible day . . . I don't know how to tell you, dear. . . .

IRINA. What is it? Tell me quickly, what is it? For God's sake! [Cries.]

CHEBUTIKIN. The Baron was killed in the duel just now.

IRINA. [Cries softly] I knew it, I knew it. . . .

CHEBUTIKIN. [Sits on a bench at the back of the stage] I'm tired. . . . [Takes a paper from his pocket] Let 'em cry. . . . [Sings softly] "Tarara-boom-deay, it is my washing day. . . ." Isn't it all the same!

[The three sisters are standing, pressing against one another.]

MASHA. Oh, how the music plays! They are leaving us, one has quite left us, quite and for ever. We remain alone, to begin our life over again. We must live . . . we must live. . . .

IRINA. [Puts her head on OLGA's bosom] There will come a time when everybody will know why, for what purpose, there is all this suffering, and there will be no more mysteries. But now we must live . . . we must work, just work! To-morrow, I'll go away alone, and I'll teach and give my whole life to those who, perhaps, need it. It's autumn now, soon it will be winter, the snow will cover everything, and I shall be working, working. . . .

OLGA. [Embraces both her sisters] The bands are playing so gaily, so bravely, and one does so want to live! Oh, my God! Time will pass on, and we shall depart for ever, we shall be forgotten; they will forget our faces, voices, and even how many there were of us, but our sufferings will turn into joy for those who will live after us, happiness and peace will reign on earth, and people will remember with kindly words, and bless those who are living now. Oh dear sisters, our life is not yet at an end. Let us live. The music is so gay, so joyful, and, it seems that in a little while we shall know why we are living, why we are suffering. . . . If we could only know, if we could only know!

[The music has been growing softer and softer; KULIGIN, smiling happily, brings out the hat and coat; ANDREY wheels out the perambulator in which BOBBY is sitting.]

CHEBUTIKIN. [Sings softly] "Tara . . . ra-boom-deay. . . . It is my washing-day." . . . [Reads a paper] It's all the same! It's all the same!

OLGA. If only we could know, if only we could know!

Curtain.

7

Six Characters in Search of an Author

by Luigi Pirandello (translated by Edward Storer) (1887–1936)

A COMEDY IN THE MAKING

CHARACTERS of the Comedy in the Making

The Father
The Mother
The Step-Daughter
The Boy
The Child
(The last two do not speak)
The Son
Madame Pace
Actors of the Company
The Manager
Leading Lady
Leading Man
Second Lady
L'ingénue
Juvenile Lead
Other Actors and Actresses
Property Man
Prompter
Machinist
Manager's Secretary
Door-Keeper
Scene-Shifters

"Six Characters in Search of an Author" by Luigi Pirandello, English Version Translated by Edward Storer, 1922.

DAYTIME. The Stage of a Theatre

N. B. The Comedy is without acts or scenes. The performance is interrupted once, without the curtain being lowered, when the manager and the chief characters withdraw to arrange the scenario. A second interruption of the action takes place when, by mistake, the stage hands let the curtain down.

SIX CHARACTER IN SEARCH OF AN AUTHOR

ACT I

The spectators will find the curtain raised and the stage as it usually is during the day time. It will be half dark, and empty, so that from the beginning the public may have the impression of an impromptu performance. Prompter's box and a small table and chair for the manager.

Two other small tables and several chairs scattered about as during rehearsals.

The ACTORS *and* ACTRESSES *of the company enter from the back of the stage: first one, then another, then two together; nine or ten in all. They are about to rehearse a Pirandello play:* Mixing it Up. [Il giuoco delle parti.] *Some of the company move off towards their dressing rooms. The* PROMPTER *who has the "book" under his arm, is waiting for the manager in order to begin the rehearsal.*

The ACTORS *and* ACTRESSES, *some standing, some sitting, chat and smoke. One perhaps reads a paper; another cons his part.*

Finally, the MANAGER *enters and goes to the table prepared for him. His* SECRETARY *brings him his mail, through which he glances. The* PROMPTER *takes his seat, turns on a light, and opens the "book."*

THE MANAGER [*throwing a letter down on the table*]. I can't see [*To* PROPERTY MAN.] Let's have a little light, please!

PROPERTY MAN. Yes sir, yes, at once. [*A light comes down on to the stage.*]

THE MANAGER [*clapping his hands*]. Come along! Come along! Second act of "Mixing It Up." [*Sits down.*] [*The* ACTORS *and* ACTRESSES *go from the front of the stage to the wings, all except the three who are to begin the rehearsal.*]

THE PROMPTER [*reading the "book"*]. "Leo Gala's house. A curious room serving as dining-room and study."

THE MANAGER [*to* PROPERTY MAN]. Fix up the old red room.

PROPERTY MAN [*noting it down*]. Red set. All right!

THE PROMPTER [*continuing to read from the "book"*]. "Table already laid and writing desk with books and papers. Book-shelves. Exit rear to Leo's bedroom. Exit left to kitchen. Principal exit to right."

THE MANAGER [*energetically*]. Well, you understand: The principal exit over there; here, the kitchen. [*Turning to actor who is to play the part of* SOCRATES.] You make your entrances and exits here. [*To* PROPERTY MAN.] The baize doors at the rear, and curtains.

PROPERTY MAN [*noting it down*]. Right!

PROMPTER [*reading as before*]. "When the curtain rises, Leo Gala, dressed in cook's cap and apron is busy beating an egg in a cup. Philip, also dressed as a cook, is beating another egg. Guido Venanzi is seated and listening."

LEADING MAN [*To* MANAGER]. Excuse me, but must I absolutely wear a cook's cap?

THE MANAGER [*annoyed*]. I imagine so. It says so there anyway. [*Pointing to the "book."*]

LEADING MAN. But it's ridiculous!

THE MANAGER [*jumping up in a rage*]. Ridiculous? Ridiculous? Is it my fault if France won't send us any more good comedies, and we are reduced to putting on Pirandello's works, where nobody understands anything, and where the author plays the fool with us all? [*The* ACTORS *grin. The* MANAGER *goes to* LEADING MAN *and shouts.*] Yes sir, you put on the cook's cap and beat eggs. Do you suppose that with all this egg-beating business you are on an ordinary stage? Get that out of your head. You represent the shell of the eggs you are beating! [*Laughter and comments among the* ACTORS.] Silence! and listen to my explanations, please! [*To* LEADING MAN.] "The empty form of reason without the fullness of instinct, which is blind."— You stand for reason, your wife is instinct. It's a mixing up of the parts, according to which you who act your own part become the puppet of yourself. Do you understand?

LEADING MAN. I'm hanged if I do.

THE MANAGER. Neither do I. But let's get on with it. It's sure to be a glorious failure anyway. [*Confidentially.*] But I say, please face three-quarters. Otherwise, what with the abstruseness of the dialogue, and the public that won't be able to hear you, the whole thing will go to hell. Come on! come on!

PROMPTER. Pardon sir, may I get into my box? There's a bit of a draught.

THE MANAGER. Yes, yes, of course!

At this point, the DOOR-KEEPER *has entered from the stage door and advances towards the manager's table, taking off his braided cap. During this manoeuvre, the Six* CHARACTERS *enter, and stop by the door at back of stage, so that when the* DOOR-KEEPER *is about to announce their coming to the* MANAGER, *they are already on the stage. A tenuous light surrounds them, almost as if irradiated by them—the faint breath of their fantastic reality.*

This light will disappear when they come forward towards the actors. They preserve, however, something of the dream lightness in which they seem almost suspended; but this does not detract from the essential reality of their forms and expressions.

He who is known as THE FATHER *is a man of about 50: hair, reddish in colour, thin at the temples; he is not bald, however; thick moustaches,* *falling over his still fresh mouth, which often opens in an empty and uncertain smile. He is fattish, pale; with an especially wide forehead. He has blue, oval-shaped eyes, very clear and piercing. Wears light trousers and a dark jacket. He is alternatively mellifluous and violent in his manner.*

THE MOTHER *seems crushed and terrified as if by an intolerable weight of shame and abasement. She is dressed in modest black and wears a thick widow's veil of crêpe. When she lifts this, she reveals a wax-like face. She always keeps her eyes downcast.*

THE STEP-DAUGHTER, *is dashing, almost impudent, beautiful. She wears mourning too, but with great elegance. She shows contempt for the timid half-frightened manner of the wretched* BOY *(14 years old, and also dressed in black); on the other hand, she displays a lively tenderness for her little sister,* THE CHILD *(about four), who is dressed in white, with a black silk sash at the waist.*

THE SON *(22) tall, severe in his attitude of contempt for* THE FATHER, *supercilious and indifferent to* THE MOTHER. *He looks as if he had come on the stage against his will.*

DOOR-KEEPER [*cap in hand*]. Excuse me, sir . . .

THE MANAGER [*rudely*]. Eh? What is it?

DOOR-KEEPER [*timidly*]. These people are asking for you, sir.

THE MANAGER [*furious*]. I am rehearsing, and you know perfectly well no one's allowed to come in during rehearsals! [*Turning to the* CHARACTERS.] Who are you, please? What do you want?

THE FATHER [*coming forward a little, followed by the others who seem embarrassed*]. As a matter of fact . . . we have come here in search of an author . . .

THE MANAGER [*half angry, half amazed*]. An author? What author?

THE FATHER. Any author, sir.

THE MANAGER. But there's no author here. We are not rehearsing a new piece.

THE STEP-DAUGHTER [*vivaciously*]. So much the better, so much the better! We can be your new piece.

AN ACTOR [*coming forward from the others*]. Oh, do you hear that?

THE FATHER [*to* STEP-DAUGHTER].Yes, but if the author isn't here . . . [*To* MANAGER.] unless you would be willing. . .

THE MANAGER. You are trying to be funny.

THE FATHER. No, for Heaven's sake, what are you saying? We bring you a drama, sir.

THE STEP-DAUGHTER. We may be your fortune.

THE MANAGER. Will you oblige me by going away? We haven't time to waste with mad people.

THE FATHER [*mellifluously*]. Oh sir, you know well that life is full of infinite absurdities, which, strangely enough, do not even need to appear plausible, since they are true.

THE MANAGER. What the devil is he talking about?

THE FATHER. I say that to reverse the ordinary process may well be considered a madness: that is, to create credible situations, in order that they may appear true. But permit me to observe that if this be madness, it is the sole *raison d'être* of your profession, gentlemen. [*The* ACTORS *look hurt and perplexed.*]

THE MANAGER [*getting up and looking at him*]. So our profession seems to you one worthy of madmen then?

THE FATHER. Well, to make seem true that which isn't true . . . without any need . . . for a joke as it were . . . Isn't that your mission, gentlemen: to give life to fantastic characters on the stage?

THE MANAGER [*interpreting the rising anger of the* COMPANY]. But I would beg you to believe, my dear sir, that the profession of the comedian is a noble one. If today, as things go, the playwrights give us stupid comedies to play and puppets to represent instead of men, remember we are proud to have given life to immortal works here on these very boards! [*The* ACTORS, *satisfied, applaud their* MANAGER.]

THE FATHER [*interrupting furiously*]. Exactly, perfectly, to living beings more alive than those who breathe and wear clothes: beings less real perhaps, but truer! I agree with you entirely. [*The* ACTORS *look at one another in amazement.*]

THE MANAGER. But what do you mean? Before, you said . . .

THE FATHER. No, excuse me, I meant it for you, sir, who were crying out that you had no time to lose with madmen, while no one better than yourself knows that nature uses the instrument of human fantasy in order to pursue her high creative purpose.

THE MANAGER. Very well,—but where does all this take us?

THE FATHER. Nowhere! It is merely to show you that one is born to life in many forms, in many shapes, as tree, or as stone, as water, as butterfly, or as woman. So one may also be born a character in a play.

THE MANAGER [*with feigned comic dismay*]. So you and these other friends of yours have been born characters?

THE FATHER. Exactly, and alive as you see! [MANAGER *and* ACTORS *burst out laughing.*]

THE FATHER [*hurt*]. I am sorry you laugh, because we carry in us a drama, as you can guess from this woman here veiled in black.

THE MANAGER [*losing patience at last and almost indignant*]. Oh, chuck it! Get away please! Clear out of here! [*To* PROPERTY MAN.] For Heaven's sake, turn them out!

THE FATHER [*resisting*]. No, no, look here, we . . .

THE MANAGER [*roaring*]. We come here to work, you know.

LEADING ACTOR. One cannot let oneself be made such a fool of.

THE FATHER [*determined, coming forward*]. I marvel at your incredulity, gentlemen. Are you not accustomed to see the characters created by an author spring to life in yourselves and face each other? Just because there is no "book" [*Pointing to the* PROMPTER'S *box.*] which contains us, you refuse to believe . . .

THE STEP-DAUGHTER [*advances towards* MANAGER, *smiling and coquettish*]. Believe me, we are really six most interesting characters, sir; side-tracked however.

THE FATHER. Yes, that is the word! [*To* MANAGER *all at once.*] In the sense, that is, that the author who created us alive no longer wished, or was no longer able, materially to put us into a work of art. And this was a real crime, sir; because he who has had the luck to be born a character can laugh even at death. He cannot die. The man, the writer, the instrument of the creation will die, but his creation does not die. And to live for ever, it does not need to have extraordinary gifts or to be able to work wonders. Who was Sancho Panza? Who was Don Abbondio? Yet they live eternally because—live germs as they were—they had the fortune to find a fecundating matrix, a fantasy which could raise and nourish them: make them live for ever!

THE MANAGER. That is quite all right. But what do you want here, all of you?

THE FATHER. We want to live.

THE MANAGER [*ironically*]. For Eternity?

THE FATHER. No, sir, only for a moment . . . in you.

AN ACTOR. Just listen to him!

LEADING LADY. They want to live, in us . . .

JUVENILE LEAD [*pointing to the STEP-DAUGHTER*]. I've no objection, as far as that one is concerned!

THE FATHER. Look here! Look here! The comedy has to be made. [*To the MANAGER.*] But if you and your actors are willing, we can soon concert it among ourselves.

THE MANAGER [*annoyed*]. But what do you want to concert? We don't go in for concerts here. Here we play dramas and comedies!

THE FATHER. Exactly! That is just why we have come to you.

THE MANAGER. And where is the "book"?

THE FATHER. It is in us! [*The ACTORS laugh.*] The drama is in us, and we are the drama. We are impatient to play it. Our inner passion drives us on to this.

THE STEP-DAUGHTER [*disdainful, alluring, treacherous, full of impudence*]. My passion, sir! Ah, if you only knew! My passion for him! [*Points to the FATHER and makes a pretence of embracing him. Then she breaks out into a loud laugh.*]

THE FATHER [*angrily*]. Behave yourself! And please don't laugh in that fashion.

THE STEP-DAUGHTER. With your permission, gentlemen, I, who am a two months' orphan, will show you how I can dance and sing. [*Sings and then dances* Prenez garde à Tchou-Tchin-Tchou.]

Les chinois sont un peuple malin,
De Shangal à Pekin,
Ils ont mis des écriteaux partout:
Prenez garde àTchou-Tchin-Tchou.

ACTORS AND ACTRESSES. Bravo! Well done! Tip-top!

THE MANAGER. Silence! This isn't a café concert, you know! [*Turning to the FATHER in consternation.*] Is she mad?

THE FATHER. Mad? No, she's worse than mad.

THE STEP-DAUGHTER [*to MANAGER*]. Worse? Worse? Listen! Stage this drama for us at once! Then you will see that at a certain moment I . . . when this little darling here . . . [*Takes the CHILD by the hand and leads her to the MANAGER.*] Isn't she a dear? [*Takes her up and kisses her.*] Darling! Darling! [*Puts her down again and adds feelingly.*] Well, when God suddenly takes this dear little child away from that poor mother there; and this imbecile here [*Seizing hold of the BOY roughly and pushing him forward.*] does the stupidest things, like the fool he is, you will see me run away. Yes, gentlemen, I shall be off. But the moment hasn't arrived yet. After what has taken place between him and me [*indicates the FATHER with a horrible wink.*] I can't remain any longer in this society, to have to witness the anguish of this mother here for that fool . . . [*Indicates the SON.*] Look at him! Look at him! See how indifferent, how frigid he is, because he is the legitimate son. He despises me, despises him [*Pointing to the BOY.*], despises this baby here; because . . . we are bastards. [*Goes to the MOTHER and embraces her.*] And he doesn't want to recognize her as his mother—she who is the common mother of us all. He looks down upon her as if she were only the mother of us three bastards. Wretch! [*She says all this very rapidly, excitedly. At the word "bastards" she raises her voice, and almost spits out the final "Wretch!"*]

THE MOTHER [*to the* MANAGER, *in anguish*]. In the name of these two little children, I beg you . . . [*She grows faint and is about to fall.*] Oh God!

THE FATHER [*coming forward to support her as do some of the* ACTORS]. Quick, a chair, a chair for this poor widow!

THE ACTORS. Is it true? Has she really fainted?

THE MANAGER. Quick, a chair! Here! [*One of the* ACTORS *brings a chair, the* OTHERS *proffer assistance. The* MOTHER *tries to prevent the* FATHER *from lifting the veil which covers her face.*]

THE FATHER. Look at her! Look at her!

THE MOTHER. No, no; stop it please!

THE FATHER [*raising her veil*]. Let them see you!

THE MOTHER [*rising and covering her face with her hands, in desperation*]. I beg you, sir, to prevent this man from carrying out his plan which is loathsome to me.

THE MANAGER [*dumbfounded*]. I don't understand at all. What is the situation? Is this lady your wife? [*To the* FATHER.]

THE FATHER. Yes, gentlemen: my wife!

THE MANAGER. But how can she be a widow if you are alive? [*The* ACTORS *find relief for their astonishment in a loud laugh.*]

THE FATHER. Don't laugh! Don't laugh like that, for Heaven's sake. Her drama lies just here in this: she has had a lover, a man who ought to be here.

THE MOTHER [*with a cry*]. No! No!

THE STEP-DAUGHTER. Fortunately for her, he is dead. Two months ago as I said. We are in mourning, as you see.

THE FATHER. He isn't here you see, not because he is dead. He isn't here—look at her a moment and you will understand—because her drama isn't a drama of the love of two men for whom she was incapable of feeling anything except possibly a little gratitude—gratitude not for me but for the other. She isn't a woman, she is a mother, and her drama—powerful sir, I assure you—lies, as a matter of fact, all in these four children she has had by two men.

THE MOTHER. I had them? Have you got the courage to say that I wanted them? [*To the* COMPANY.] It was his doing. It was he who gave me that other man, who forced me to go away with him.

THE STEP-DAUGHTER. It isn't true.

THE MOTHER [*startled*]. Not true, isn't it?

THE STEP-DAUGHTER. No, it isn't true, it just isn't true.

THE MOTHER. And what can you know about it?

THE STEP-DAUGHTER. It isn't true. Don't believe it. [*To* MANAGER.] Do you know why she says so? For that fellow there. [*Indicates the* SON.] She tortures herself, destroys herself on account of the neglect of that son there; and she wants him to believe that if she abandoned him when he was only two years old, it was because he [*Indicates the* FATHER.] made her do so.

THE MOTHER [*vigorously*]. He forced me to it, and I call God to witness it. [*To the* MANAGER.] Ask him [*Indicates* HUSBAND.] if it isn't true. Let him speak. You [*To* DAUGHTER.] are not in a position to know anything about it.

THE STEP-DAUGHTER. I know you lived in peace and happiness with my father while he lived. Can you deny it?

THE MOTHER. No, I don't deny it . . .

THE STEP-DAUGHTER. He was always full of affection and kindness for you. [*To the* BOY, *angrily.*] It's true, isn't it? Tell them! Why don't you speak, you little fool?

THE MOTHER. Leave the poor boy alone. Why do you want to make me appear ungrateful, daughter? I don't want to offend your father. I have answered him that I didn't abandon my house and my son through any fault of mine, nor from any wilful passion.

THE FATHER. It is true. It was my doing.

LEADING MAN [*to the* COMPANY]. What a spectacle!

LEADING LADY. We are the audience this time.

JUVENILE LEAD. For once, in a way.

THE MANAGER [*beginning to get really interested*]. Let's hear them out. Listen!

THE SON. Oh yes, you're going to hear a fine bit now. He will talk to you of the Demon of Experiment.

THE FATHER. You are a cynical imbecile. I've told you so already a hundred times. [*To the* MANAGER.] He tries to make fun of me on account of this expression which I have found to excuse myself with.

THE SON [*with disgust*]. Yes, phrases! phrases!

THE FATHER. Phrases! Isn't everyone consoled when faced with a trouble or fact he doesn't understand, by a word, some simple word, which tells us nothing and yet calms us?

THE STEP-DAUGHTER. Even in the case of remorse. In fact, especially then.

THE FATHER. Remorse? No, that isn't true. I've done more than use words to quieten the remorse in me.

THE STEP-DAUGHTER. Yes, there was a bit of money too. Yes, yes, a bit of money. There were the hundred lire he was about to offer me in payment, gentlemen. . . [*Sensation of horror among the* ACTORS.]

THE SON [*to the* STEP-DAUGHTER]. This is vile.

THE STEP-DAUGHTER. Vile? There they were in a pale blue envelope on a little mahogany table in the back of Madame Pace's shop. You know Madame Pace—one of those ladies who attract poor girls of good family into their ateliers, under the pretext of their selling *robes et manteaux*.

THE SON. And he thinks he has bought the right to tyrannize over us all with those hundred lire he was going to pay; but which, fortunately—note this, gentlemen—he had no chance of paying.

THE STEP-DAUGHTER. It was a near thing, though, you know! [*Laughs ironically*.]

THE MOTHER [*protesting*]. Shame, my daughter, shame!

THE STEP-DAUGHTER. Shame indeed! This is my revenge! I am dying to live that scene . . . The room . . . I see it . . . Here is the window with the mantles exposed, there the divan, the looking-glass, a screen, there in front of the window the little mahogany table with the blue envelope containing one hundred lire. I see it. I see it. I could take hold of it . . . But you, gentlemen, you ought to turn your backs now: I am almost nude, you know. But I don't blush: I leave that to him. [*Indicating* FATHER.]

THE MANAGER. I don't understand this at all.

THE FATHER. Naturally enough. I would ask you, sir, to exercise your authority a little here, and let me speak before you believe all she is trying to blame me with. Let me explain.

THE STEP-DAUGHTER. Ah yes, explain it in your own way.

THE FATHER. But don't you see that the whole trouble lies here. In words, words. Each one of us has within him a whole world of things, each man of us his own special world. And how can we ever come to an understanding if I put in the words I utter the sense and value of things as I see them; while you who listen to me must inevitably translate them according to the conception of things each one of you has within himself. We think we understand each other, but we never really do. Look here! This woman [*Indicating the* MOTHER.] takes all my pity for her as a specially ferocious form of cruelty.

THE MOTHER. But you drove me away.

THE FATHER. Do you hear her? I drove her away! She believes I really sent her away.

THE MOTHER. You know how to talk, and I don't; but, believe me, sir [*To* MANAGER.], after he had married me . . . who knows why? . . . I was a poor insignificant woman . . .

THE FATHER. But, good Heavens! It was just for your humility that I married you. I loved this simplicity in you. [*He stops when he sees she makes signs to contradict him, opens his arms wide in sign of desperation, seeing how hopeless it is to make himself understood.*] You see she denies it. Her mental deafness, believe me, is phenomenal, the limit: [*Touches his forehead.*] deaf, deaf, mentally deaf! She has plenty of feeling. Oh yes, a good heart for the children; but the brain—deaf, to the point of desperation.

THE STEP-DAUGHTER. Yes, but ask him how his intelligence has helped us.

THE FATHER. If we could see all the evil that may spring from good, what should we do? [*At this point the* LEADING LADY *who is biting her lips with rage at seeing the* LEADING MAN *flirting with the* STEP-DAUGHTER, *comes forward and says to the* MANAGER.]

LEADING LADY. Excuse me, but are we going to rehearse today?

MANAGER. Of course, of course; but let's hear them out.

JUVENILE LEAD. This is something quite new.

L'INGÉNUE. Most interesting!

LEADING LADY. Yes, for the people who like that kind of thing. [*Casts a glance at* LEADING MAN.]

THE MANAGER [*to* FATHER]. You must please explain yourself quite clearly. [*Sits down.*]

THE FATHER. Very well then: listen! I had in my service a poor man, a clerk, a secretary of mine, full of devotion, who became friends with her. [*Indicating the* MOTHER.] They understood one another, were kindred souls in fact, without, however, the least suspicion of any evil existing. They were incapable even of thinking of it.

THE STEP-DAUGHTER. So he thought of it—for them!

THE FATHER. That's not true. I meant to do good to them—and to myself, I confess, at the same time. Things had come to the point that I could not say a word to either of them without their making a mute appeal, one to the other, with their eyes. I could see them silently asking each other how I was to be kept in countenance, how I was to be kept quiet. And this, believe me, was just about enough of itself to keep me in a constant rage, to exasperate me beyond measure.

THE MANAGER. And why didn't you send him away then—this secretary of yours?

THE FATHER. Precisely what I did, sir. And then I had to watch this poor woman drifting forlornly about the house like an animal without a master, like an animal one has taken in out of pity.

THE MOTHER. Ah yes . . .

THE FATHER [*suddenly turning to the* MOTHER]. It's true about the son anyway, isn't it?

THE MOTHER. He took my son away from me first of all.

THE FATHER. But not from cruelty. I did it so that he should grow up healthy and strong by living in the country.

THE STEP-DAUGHTER [*pointing to him ironically*]. As one can see.

THE FATHER [*quickly*]. Is it my fault if he has grown up like this? I sent him to a wet nurse in the country, a peasant, as she did not seem to me strong enough, though she is of humble origin. That was, anyway, the reason I married her. Unpleasant all this may be, but how can it be helped? My mistake possibly, but there we are! All my life I have had these confounded aspirations towards a certain moral sanity. [*At this point the* STEP-DAUGHTER *bursts into a noisy laugh.*] Oh, stop it! Stop it! I can't stand it.

THE MANAGER. Yes, please stop it, for Heaven's sake.

THE STEP-DAUGHTER. But imagine moral sanity from him, if you please—the client of certain ateliers like that of Madame Pace!

THE FATHER. Fool! That is the proof that I am a man! This seeming contradiction, gentlemen, is the strongest proof that I stand here a live man before you. Why, it is just for this very incongruity in my nature that I have had to suffer what I have. I could not live by the side of that woman [*Indicating the* MOTHER.] any longer; but not so much for the boredom she inspired me with as for the pity I felt for her.

THE MOTHER. And so he turned me out—.

THE FATHER.—well provided for! Yes, I sent her to that man, gentlemen . . . to let her go free of me.

THE MOTHER. And to free himself.

THE FATHER. Yes, I admit it. It was also a liberation for me. But great evil has come of it. I meant well when I did it; and I did it more for her sake than mine. I swear it. [*Crosses his arms on his chest; then turns suddenly to the* MOTHER.] Did I ever lose sight of you until that other man carried you off to another town, like the angry fool he was? And on account of my pure interest in you . . . my pure interest, I repeat, that had no base motive in it . . . I watched with the tenderest concern the new family that grew up around her. She can bear witness to this. [*Points to the* STEP-DAUGHTER.]

THE STEP-DAUGHTER. Oh yes, that's true enough. When I was a kiddie, so so high, you know, with plaits over my shoulders and knickers longer than my skirts, I used to see him waiting outside the school for me to come out. He came to see how I was growing up.

THE FATHER. This is infamous, shameful!

THE STEP-DAUGHTER. No. Why?

THE FATHER. Infamous! infamous! [*Then excitedly to* MANAGER *explaining.*] After she [*Indicating* MOTHER.] went away, my house seemed suddenly empty. She was my incubus, but she filled my house. I was like a dazed fly alone in the empty rooms. This boy here [*Indicating the* SON.] was educated away from home, and when he came back, he seemed to me to be no more mine. With no mother to stand between him and me, he grew up entirely for himself, on his own, apart, with no tie of intellect or affection binding him to me. And then—strange but true—I was driven, by curiosity at first and then by some tender sentiment, towards her family, which had come into being through my will. The thought of her began gradually to fill up the emptiness I felt all around me. I wanted to know if she were happy in living out the simple daily duties of life. I wanted to think of her as fortunate and happy because far away from the complicated torments of my spirit. And so, to have proof of this, I used to watch that child coming out of school.

THE STEP-DAUGHTER. Yes, yes. True. He used to follow me in the street and smiled at me, waved his hand, like this. I would look at him with interest, wondering who he might be. I told my mother, who guessed at once. [*The* MOTHER *agrees with a nod.*] Then she didn't want to send me to school for some days; and when I finally went back, there he was again—looking so ridiculous—with a paper parcel in his hands. He came close to me, caressed me, and drew out a fine straw hat from the parcel, with a bouquet of flowers—all for me!

THE MANAGER. A bit discursive this, you know!

THE SON [*contemptuously*]. Literature! Literature!

THE FATHER. Literature indeed! This is life, this is passion!

THE MANAGER. It may be, but it won't act.

THE FATHER. I agree. This is only the part leading up. I don't suggest this should be staged. She [*Pointing to the* STEP-DAUGHTER.], as you see, is no longer the flapper with plaits down her back—.

THE STEP-DAUGHTER.—and the knickers showing below the skirt!

THE FATHER. The drama is coming now, sir; something new, complex, most interesting.

THE STEP-DAUGHTER. As soon as my father died. . .

THE FATHER.—there was absolute misery for them. They came back here, unknown to me. Through her stupidity! [*Pointing to the* MOTHER.] It is true she can barely write her own name; but she could anyhow have got her daughter to write to me that they were in need . . .

THE MOTHER. And how was I to divine all this sentiment in him?

THE FATHER. That is exactly your mistake, never to have guessed any of my sentiments.

THE MOTHER. After so many years apart, and all that had happened . . .

THE FATHER. Was it my fault if that fellow carried you away? It happened quite suddenly; for after he had obtained some job or other, I could find no trace of them; and so, not unnaturally, my interest in them dwindled. But the drama culminated unforeseen and violent on their return, when I was impelled by my miserable flesh that still lives . . . Ah! what misery, what wretchedness is that of the man who is alone and disdains debasing liaisons! Not old enough to do without women, and not young enough to go and look for one without shame. Misery? It's worse than misery; it's a horror; for no woman can any longer give him love; and when a man feels this . . . One ought to do without, you say? Yes, yes. I know. Each of us when he appears before his fellows is clothed in a certain dignity. But every man knows what unconfessable things pass within the secrecy of his own heart. One gives way to the temptation, only to rise from it again, afterwards, with a great eagerness to re-establish one's dignity, as if it were a tombstone to place on the grave of one's shame, and a monument to hide and sign the memory of our weaknesses. Everybody's in the same case. Some folks haven't the courage to say certain things, that's all!

THE STEP-DAUGHTER. All appear to have the courage to do them though.

THE FATHER. Yes, but in secret. Therefore, you want more courage to say these things. Let a man but speak these things out, and folks at once label him a cynic. But it isn't true. He is like all the others, better indeed, because he isn't afraid to reveal with the light of the intelligence the red shame of human bestiality on which most men close their eyes so as not to see it. Woman—for example, look at her case! She turns tantalizing inviting glances on you. You seize her. No sooner does she feel herself in your grasp than she closes her eyes. It is the sign of her mission, the sign by which she says to man: "Blind yourself, for I am blind."

THE STEP-DAUGHTER. Sometimes she can close them no more: when she no longer feels the need of hiding her shame to herself, but dry-eyed and dispassionately, sees only that of the man who has blinded himself without love. Oh, all these intellectual complications make me sick, disgust me—all this philosophy that uncovers the beast in man, and then seeks to save him, excuse him. . . . I can't stand it, sir. When a man seeks to "simplify" life bestially, throwing aside every relic of humanity, every chaste aspiration, every pure feeling, all sense of ideality, duty, modesty, shame . . . then nothing is more revolting and nauseous than a certain kind of remorse—crocodiles' tears, that's what it is.

THE MANAGER. Let's come to the point. This is only discussion.

THE FATHER. Very good, sir! But a fact is like a sack which won't stand up when it is empty. In order that it may stand up, one has to put into it the reason and sentiment which have caused it to exist. I couldn't possibly know that after the death of that man, they had decided to return here, that they were in misery, and that she [*Pointing to the* MOTHER.] had gone to work as a modiste, and at a shop of the type of that of Madame Pace.

THE STEP-DAUGHTER. A real high-class modiste, you must know, gentlemen. In appearance, she works for the leaders of the best society; but she arranges matters so that these elegant ladies serve her purpose . . . without prejudice to other ladies who are . . . well . . . only so so.

THE MOTHER. You will believe me, gentlemen, that it never entered my mind that the old hag offered me work because she had her eye on my daughter.

THE STEP-DAUGHTER. Poor mamma! Do you know, sir, what that woman did when I brought her back the work my mother had finished? She would point out to me that I had torn one of my frocks, and she would give it back to my mother to mend. It was I who paid for it, always I; while this poor creature here believed she was sacrificing herself for me and these two children here, sitting up at night sewing Madame Pace's robes.

THE MANAGER. And one day you met there . . .

THE STEP-DAUGHTER. Him, him. Yes sir, an old client. There's a scene for you to play! Superb!

THE FATHER. She, the Mother arrived just then . . .

THE STEP-DAUGHTER [*treacherously*]. Almost in time!

THE FATHER [*crying out*]. No, in time! in time! Fortunately I recognized her . . . in time. And I took them back home with me to my house. You can imagine now her position and mine; she, as you see her; and I who cannot look her in the face.

THE STEP-DAUGHTER. Absurd! How can I possibly be expected—after that—to be a modest young miss, a fit person to go with his confounded aspirations for "a solid moral sanity"?

THE FATHER. For the drama lies all in this—in the conscience that I have, that each one of us has. We believe this conscience to be a single thing, but it is many-sided. There is one for this person, and another for that. Diverse consciences. So we have this illusion of being one person for all, of having a personality that is unique in all our acts. But it isn't true. We perceive this when, tragically perhaps, in something we do, we are as it were, suspended, caught up in the air on a kind of hook. Then we perceive that all of us was not in that act, and that it would be an atrocious injustice to judge us by that action alone, as if all our existence were summed up in that one deed. Now do you understand the perfidy of this girl? She surprised me in a place, where she ought not to have known me, just as I could not exist for her; and she now seeks to attach to me a reality such as I could never suppose I should have to assume for her in a shameful and fleeting moment of my life. I feel this above all else. And the drama, you will see, acquires a tremendous value from this point. Then there is the position of the others . . . his . . . [*Indicating the* SON.]

THE SON [*shrugging his shoulders scornfully*]. Leave me alone! I don't come into this.

THE FATHER. What? You don't come into this?

THE SON. I've got nothing to do with it, and don't want to have; because you know well enough I wasn't made to be mixed up in all this with the rest of you.

THE STEP-DAUGHTER. We are only vulgar folk! He is the fine gentleman. You may have noticed, Mr. Manager, that I fix him now and again with a look of scorn while he lowers his eyes—for he knows the evil he has done me.

THE SON [*scarcely looking at her*]. I?

THE STEP-DAUGHTER. You! you! I owe my life on the streets to you. Did you or did you not deny us, with your behaviour, I won't say the intimacy of home, but even that mere hospitality which makes guests feel at their ease? We were intruders who had come to disturb the kingdom of your legitimacy. I should like to have you witness, Mr. Manager, certain scenes between him and me. He says I have tyrannized over everyone. But it was just his behaviour which made me insist on the reason for which I had come into the house,—this reason he calls "vile"—into his house, with my mother who is his mother too. And I came as mistress of the house.

THE SON. It's easy for them to put me always in the wrong. But imagine, gentlemen, the position of a son, whose fate it is to see arrive one day at his home a young woman of impudent bearing, a young woman who inquires for his father, with whom who knows what business she has. This young man has then to witness her return bolder than ever, accompanied by that child there. He is obliged to watch her treat his father in an equivocal and confidential manner. She asks money of him in a way that lets one suppose he must give it her, must, do you understand, because he has every obligation to do so.

THE FATHER. But I have, as a matter of fact, this obligation. I owe it to your mother.

THE SON. How should I know? When had I ever seen or heard of her? One day there arrive with her [*Indicating* STEP-DAUGHTER.] that lad and this baby here. I am told: "This is your mother too, you know." I divine from her manner [*Indicating* STEP-DAUGHTER *again*.] why it is they have come home. I had rather not say what I feel and think about it. I shouldn't even care to confess to myself. No action can therefore be hoped for from me in this affair. Believe me, Mr. Manager, I am an "unrealized" character, dramatically speaking; and I find myself not at all at ease in their company. Leave me out of it, I beg you.

THE FATHER. What? It is just because you are so that . . .

THE SON. How do you know what I am like? When did you ever bother your head about me?

THE FATHER. I admit it. I admit it. But isn't that a situation in itself? This aloofness of yours which is so cruel to me and to your mother, who returns home and sees you almost for the first time grown up, who doesn't recognize you but knows you are her son . . . [*Pointing out the* MOTHER *to the* MANAGER.] See, she's crying!

THE STEP-DAUGHTER [*angrily, stamping her foot*]. Like a fool!

THE FATHER [*indicating* STEP-DAUGHTER]. She can't stand him you know. [*Then referring again to the* SON.] He says he doesn't come into the affair, whereas he is really the hinge of the whole action. Look at that lad who is always clinging to his mother, frightened and humiliated. It is on account of this fellow here. Possibly his situation is the most painful of all. He feels himself a stranger more than the others. The poor little chap feels mortified, humiliated at being brought into a home out of charity as it were. [*In confidence.*] He is the image of his father. Hardly talks at all. Humble and quiet.

THE MANAGER. Oh, we'll cut him out. You've no notion what a nuisance boys are on the stage . . .

THE FATHER. He disappears soon, you know. And the baby too. She is the first to vanish from the scene. The drama consists finally in this: when that mother re-enters my house, her family born outside of it, and shall we say superimposed on the original, ends with the death of the little girl, the tragedy of the boy and the flight of the elder daughter. It cannot go on, because it is foreign to its surroundings. So after much torment, we three remain: I, the mother, that son. Then, owing to the disappearance of that extraneous family, we too find ourselves strange to one another. We find we are living in an atmosphere of mortal desolation which is the revenge, as he [*Indicating* SON.] scornfully said of the Demon of Experiment, that unfortunately hides in me. Thus, sir, you see when faith is lacking, it becomes impossible to create certain states of happiness, for we lack the necessary humility. Vaingloriously, we try to substitute ourselves for this faith, creating thus for the rest of the world a reality which we believe after their fashion, while, actually, it doesn't exist. For each one of us has his own reality to be respected before God, even when it is harmful to one's very self.

THE MANAGER. There is something in what you say. I assure you all this interests me very much. I begin to think there's the stuff for a drama in all this, and not a bad drama either.

THE STEP-DAUGHTER [*coming forward*]. When you've got a character like me.

THE FATHER [*shutting her up, all excited to learn the decision of the* MANAGER]. You be quiet!

THE MANAGER [*reflecting, heedless of interruption*]. It's new . . . hem . . . yes . . .

THE FATHER. Absolutely new!

THE MANAGER. You've got a nerve though, I must say, to come here and fling it at me like this . . .

THE FATHER. You will understand, sir, born as we are for the stage . . .

THE MANAGER. Are you amateur actors then?

THE FATHER. No. I say born for the stage, because . . .

THE MANAGER. Oh, nonsense. You're an old hand, you know.

THE FATHER. No sir, no. We act that rôle for which we have been cast, that rôle which we are given in life. And in my own case, passion itself, as usually happens, becomes a trifle theatrical when it is exalted.

THE MANAGER. Well, well, that will do. But you see, without an author . . . I could give you the address of an author if you like . . .

THE FATHER. No, no. Look here! You must be the author.

THE MANAGER. I? What are you talking about?

THE FATHER. Yes, you, you! Why not?

THE MANAGER. Because I have never been an author: that's why.

THE FATHER. Then why not turn author now? Everybody does it. You don't want any special qualities. Your task is made much easier by the fact that we are all here alive before you . . .

THE MANAGER. It won't do.

THE FATHER. What? When you see us live our drama . . .

THE MANAGER. Yes, that's all right. But you want someone to write it.

THE FATHER. No, no. Someone to take it down, possibly, while we play it, scene by scene! It will be enough to sketch it out at first, and then try it over.

THE MANAGER. Well. . . . I am almost tempted. It's a bit of an idea. One might have a shot at it.

THE FATHER. Of course. You'll see what scenes will come out of it. I can give you one, at once . . .

THE MANAGER. By Jove, it tempts me. I'd like to have a go at it. Let's try it out. Come with me to my office. [*Turning to the* ACTORS.] You are at liberty for a bit, but don't step out of the theatre for long. In a quarter of an hour, twenty minutes, all back here again! [*To the* FATHER.] We'll see what can be done. Who knows if we don't get something really extraordinary out of it?

THE FATHER. There's no doubt about it. They [*Indicating the* CHARACTERS.] had better come with us too, hadn't they?

THE MANAGER. Yes, yes. Come on! come on! [*Moves away and then turning to the* ACTORS.] Be punctual, please! [MANAGER *and the Six* CHARACTERS *cross the stage and go off. The other* ACTORS *remain, looking at one another in astonishment.*]

LEADING MAN. Is he serious? What the devil does be want to do?

JUVENILE LEAD. This is rank madness.

THIRD ACTOR. Does he expect to knock up a drama in five minutes?

JUVENILE LEAD. Like the improvisers!

LEADING LADY. If he thinks I'm going to take part in a joke like this . . .

JUVENILE LEAD. I'm out of it anyway.

FOURTH ACTOR. I should like to know who they are. [*Alludes to* CHARACTERS].

THIRD ACTOR. What do you suppose? Madmen or rascals!

JUVENILE LEAD. And he takes them seriously!

L'INGÉNUE. Vanity! He fancies himself as an author now.

LEADING MAN. It's absolutely unheard of. If the stage has come to this . . . well I'm . . .

FIFTH ACTOR. It's rather a joke.

THIRD ACTOR. Well, we'll see what's going to happen next.

[*Thus talking, the* ACTORS *leave the stage; some going out by the little door at the back; others retiring to their dressing-rooms.*

The curtain remains up.

The action of the play is suspended for twenty minutes].

ACT II

The stage call-bells ring to warn the company that the play is about to begin again.

THE STEP-DAUGHTER comes out of the MANAGER'S office along with the CHILD and the BOY. As she comes out of the office, she cries:— Nonsense! nonsense! Do it yourselves! I'm not going to mix myself up in this mess. [*Turning to the* CHILD *and coming quickly with her on to the stage.*] Come on, Rosetta, let's run! [*The* BOY *follows them slowly, remaining a little behind and seeming perplexed.*]

THE STEP-DAUGHTER [*stops, bends over the* CHILD *and takes the latter's face between her hands*]. My little darling! You're frightened, aren't you? You don't know where we are, do you?

[*Pretending to reply to a question of the* CHILD.] What is the stage? It's a place, baby, you know, where people play at being serious, a place where they act comedies. We've got to act a comedy now, dead serious, you know; and you're in it also, little one. [*Embraces her, pressing the little head to her breast, and rocking the* CHILD *for a moment.*] Oh darling, darling, what a horrid comedy you've got to play! What a wretched part they've found for you! A garden . . . a fountain . . . look . . . just suppose, kiddie, it's here. Where, you say? Why, right here in the middle. It's all pretence you know. That's the trouble, my pet: it's all make-believe here. It's better to imagine it though, because if they fix it up for you, it'll only be painted cardboard, painted cardboard for the rockery, the water, the plants . . . Ah, but I think a baby like this one would sooner have a make-believe fountain than a real one, so she could play with it. What a joke it'll be for the others! But for you, alas! not quite such a joke: you who are real, baby dear, and really play by a real fountain that is big and green and beautiful, with ever so many bamboos around it that are reflected in the water, and a whole lot of little ducks swimming about . . . No, Rosetta, no, your mother doesn't bother about you on account of that wretch of a son there. I'm in the devil of a temper, and as for that lad . . . [*Seizes* BOY *by the arm to force him to take one of his hands out of his pockets.*] What have you got there? What are you hiding? [*Pulls his hand out of his pocket, looks into it and catches the glint of a revolver.*] Ah! where did you get this? [*The* BOY, *very pale in the face, looks at her, but does not answer*]. Idiot! If I'd been in your place, instead of killing myself, I'd have shot one of those two, or both of them: father and son. [*The* FATHER *enters from the office, all excited from his work. The* MANAGER *follows him.*]

THE FATHER. Come on, come on dear! Come here for a minute! We've arranged everything. It's all fixed up.

THE MANAGER [*also excited*]. If you please, young lady, there are one or two points to settle still. Will you come along?

THE STEP-DAUGHTER [*following him towards the office*]. Ouff! what's the good, if you've arranged everything. [*The* FATHER, MANAGER *and* STEP-DAUGHTER *go back into the office again (off) for* *a moment. At the same time, The* SON *followed by* The MOTHER, *comes out.*]

THE SON [*looking at the three entering office*]. Oh this is fine, fine! And to think I can't even get away! [*The* MOTHER *attempts to look at him, but lowers her eyes immediately when* HE *turns away from her.* SHE *then sits down. The* BOY *and The* CHILD *approach her.* SHE *casts a glance again at the* SON, *and speaks with humble tones, trying to draw him into conversation.*]

THE MOTHER. And isn't my punishment the worst of all? [*Then seeing from the* SON's *manner that he will not bother himself about her.*] My God! Why are you so cruel? Isn't it enough for one person to support all this torment? Must you then insist on others seeing it also?

THE SON [*half to himself, meaning the* MOTHER *to hear, however*]. And they want to put it on the stage! If there was at least a reason for it! He thinks he has got at the meaning of it all. Just as if each one of us in every circumstance of life couldn't find his own explanation of it! [*Pauses.*] He complains he was discovered in a place where he ought not to have been seen, in a moment of his life which ought to have remained hidden and kept out of the reach of that convention which he has to maintain for other people. And what about my case? Haven't I had to reveal what no son ought ever to reveal: how father and mother live and are man and wife for themselves quite apart from that idea of father and mother which we give them? When this idea is revealed, our life is then linked at one point only to that man and that woman; and as such it should shame them, shouldn't it?

[*The* MOTHER *hides her face in her hands. From the dressing-rooms and the little door at the back of the stage the* ACTORS *and* STAGE MANAGER *return, followed by the* PROPERTY MAN, *and the* PROMPTER. *At the same moment, The* MANAGER *comes out of his office, accompanied by the* FATHER *and the* STEP-DAUGHTER.]

THE MANAGER. Come on, come on, ladies and gentlemen! Heh! you there, machinist!

MACHINIST. Yes sir?

THE MANAGER. Fix up the white parlor with the floral decorations. Two wings and a drop with a door will do. Hurry up!

[*The* MACHINIST *runs off at once to prepare the scene, and arranges it while The* MANAGER *talks with the* STAGE MANAGER, *the* PROPERTY MAN, *and the* PROMPTER *on matters of detail.*]

THE MANAGER [*to* PROPERTY MAN]. Just have a look, and see if there isn't a sofa or divan in the wardrobe . . .

PROPERTY MAN. There's the green one.

THE STEP-DAUGHTER. No no! Green won't do. It was yellow, ornamented with flowers—very large! and most comfortable!

PROPERTY MAN. There isn't one like that.

THE MANAGER. It doesn't matter. Use the one we've got.

THE STEP-DAUGHTER. Doesn't matter? it's most important!

THE MANAGER. We're only trying it now. Please don't interfere. [*To* PROPERTY MAN.] See if we've got a shop window—long and narrowish.

THE STEP-DAUGHTER. And the little table! The little mahogany table for the pale blue envelope!

PROPERTY MAN [*to* MANAGER]. There's that little gilt one.

THE MANAGER. That'll do fine.

THE FATHER. A mirror.

THE STEP-DAUGHTER. And the screen! We must have a screen. Otherwise how can I manage?

PROPERTY MAN. That's all right, Miss. We've got any amount of them.

THE MANAGER [*to the* STEP-DAUGHTER]. We want some clothes pegs too, don't we?

THE STEP-DAUGHTER. Yes, several, several!

THE MANAGER. See how many we've got and bring them all.

PROPERTY MAN. All right!

[*The* PROPERTY MAN *hurries off to obey his orders. While he is putting the things in their places, the* MANAGER *talks to the* PROMPTER *and then with the* CHARACTERS *and the* ACTORS.]

THE MANAGER [*to* PROMPTER]. Take your seat. Look here: this is the outline of the scenes, act by act. [*Hands him some sheets of paper.*] And now I'm going to ask you to do something out of the ordinary.

PROMPTER. Take it down in shorthand?

THE MANAGER [*pleasantly surprised*]. Exactly! Can you do shorthand?

PROMPTER. Yes, a little.

THE MANAGER. Good! [*Turning to a STAGE HAND.*] Go and get some paper from my office, plenty, as much as you can find. [*The STAGE HAND goes off, and soon returns with a handful of paper which he gives to the PROMPTER.*]

THE MANAGER [*to PROMPTER*]. You follow the scenes as we play them, and try and get the points down, at any rate the most important ones. [*Then addressing the ACTORS.*] Clear the stage, ladies and gentlemen! Come over here. [*Pointing to the left.*] and listen attentively.

LEADING LADY. But, excuse me, we . . .

THE MANAGER [*guessing her thought*]. Don't worry! You won't have to improvise.

LEADING MAN. What have we to do then?

THE MANAGER. Nothing. For the moment you just watch and listen. Everybody will get his part written out afterwards. At present we're going to try the thing as best we can. They're going to act now.

THE FATHER [*as if fallen from the clouds into the confusion of the stage*]. We? What do you mean, if you please, by a rehearsal?

THE MANAGER. A rehearsal for them. [*Points to the ACTORS.*]

THE FATHER. But since we are the characters . . .

THE MANAGER. All right: "characters" then, if you insist on calling yourselves such. But here, my dear sir, the characters don't act. Here the actors do the acting. The characters are there, in the "book" [*Pointing towards PROMPTER'S box.*]— when there is a "book"!

THE FATHER. I won't contradict you; but excuse me, the actors aren't the characters. They want to be, they pretend to be, don't they? Now if these gentlemen here are fortunate enough to have us alive before them . . .

THE MANAGER. Oh this is grand! You want to come before the public yourselves then?

THE FATHER. As we are . . .

THE MANAGER. I can assure you it would be a magnificent spectacle!

LEADING MAN. What's the use of us here anyway then?

THE MANAGER. You're not going to pretend that you can act? It makes me laugh! [*The ACTORS laugh.*] There, you see, they are laughing at the notion. But, by the way, I must cast the parts. That won't be difficult. They cast themselves. [*To the SECOND LADY LEAD.*] You play the Mother. [*To the FATHER.*] We must find her a name.

THE FATHER. Amalia, sir.

THE MANAGER. But that is the real name of your wife. We don't want to call her by her real name.

THE FATHER. Why ever not, if it is her name? . . . Still, perhaps, if that lady must . . . [*Makes a slight motion of the hand to indicate the SECOND LADY LEAD.*] I see this woman here [*Means the MOTHER.*] as Amalia. But do as you like. [*Gets more and more confused.*] I don't know what to say to you. Already, I begin to hear my own words ring false, as if they had another sound . . .

THE MANAGER. Don't you worry about it. It'll be our job to find the right tones. And as for her name, if you want her Amalia, Amalia it shall be; and if you don't like it, we'll find another! For the moment though, we'll call the characters in this way: [*To JUVENILE LEAD.*] You are the Son. [*To the LEADING LADY.*] You naturally are the Step-Daughter . . .

THE STEP-DAUGHTER [*excitedly*]. What? what? I, that woman there? [*Bursts out laughing.*]

THE MANAGER [*angry*]. What is there to laugh at?

LEADING LADY. [*indignant*]. Nobody has ever dared to laugh at me. I insist on being treated with respect; otherwise I go away.

THE STEP-DAUGHTER. No, no, excuse me . . . I am not laughing at you . . .

THE MANAGER [*to STEP-DAUGHTER*]. You ought to feel honored to be played by . . .

LEADING LADY. [*at once, contemptuously*]. "That woman there" . . .

THE STEP-DAUGHTER. But I wasn't speaking of you, you know. I was speaking of myself— whom I can't see at all in you! That is all. I don't know . . . but . . . you . . . aren't in the least like me . . .

THE FATHER. True. Here's the point. Look here, sir, our temperaments, our souls . . .

THE MANAGER. Temperament, soul, be hanged! Do you suppose the spirit of the piece is in you? Nothing of the kind!

THE FATHER. What, haven't we our own temperaments, our own souls?

THE MANAGER. Not at all. Your soul or whatever you like to call it takes shape here. The actors give body and form to it, voice and gesture. And my actors—I may tell you—have given expression to much more lofty material than this little drama of yours, which may or may not hold up on the stage. But if it does, the merit of it, believe me, will be due to my actors.

THE FATHER. I don't dare contradict you, sir; but, believe me, it is a terrible suffering for us who are as we are, with these bodies of ours, these features to see . . .

THE MANAGER [cutting him short and out of patience]. Good heavens! The make-up will remedy all that, man, the make-up . . .

THE FATHER. Maybe. But the voice, the gestures . . .

THE MANAGER. Now, look here! On the stage, you as yourself, cannot exist. The actor here acts you, and that's an end to it!

THE FATHER. I understand. And now I think I see why our author who conceived us as we are, all alive, didn't want to put us on the stage after all. I haven't the least desire to offend your actors. Far from it! But when I think that I am to be acted by . . . I don't know by whom . . .

LEADING MAN [on his dignity]. By me, if you've no objection!

THE FATHER [humbly, mellifluously]. Honored, I assure you, sir. [Bows.] Still, I must say that try as this gentleman may, with all his good will and wonderful art, to absorb me into himself . . .

LEADING MAN. Oh chuck it! "Wonderful art!" Withdraw that, please!

THE FATHER. The performance he will give, even doing his best with make-up to look like me . . .

LEADING MAN. It will certainly be a bit difficult! [The ACTORS laugh.]

THE FATHER. Exactly! It will be difficult to act me as I really am. The effect will be rather—apart from the make-up—according as to how he supposes I am, as he senses me—if he does sense me—and not as I inside of myself feel myself to be. It seems to me then that account should be taken of this by everyone whose duty it may become to criticize us . . .

THE MANAGER. Heavens! The man's starting to think about the critics now! Let them say what they like. It's up to us to put on the play if we can. [Looking around.] Come on! come on! Is the stage set? [To the ACTORS and CHARACTERS.] Stand back—stand back! Let me see, and don't let's lose any more time! [To the STEP-DAUGHTER.] Is it all right as it is now?

THE STEP-DAUGHTER. Well, to tell the truth, I don't recognize the scene.

THE MANAGER. My dear lady, you can't possibly suppose that we can construct that shop of Madame Pace piece by piece here? [To the FATHER.] You said a white room with flowered wall paper, didn't you?

THE FATHER. Yes.

THE MANAGER. Well then. We've got the furniture right more or less. Bring that little table a bit further forward. [The STAGE HANDS obey the order. To PROPERTY MAN.] You go and find an envelope, if possible, a pale blue one; and give it to that gentleman. [Indicates FATHER.]

PROPERTY MAN. An ordinary envelope?

MANAGER AND FATHER. Yes, yes, an ordinary envelope.

PROPERTY MAN. At once, sir. [Exit.]

THE MANAGER. Ready, everyone! First scene—the Young Lady. [The LEADING LADY comes forward.] No, no, you must wait. I meant her [Indicating the STEP-DAUGHTER.] You just watch—

THE STEP-DAUGHTER [adding at once]. How I shall play it, how I shall live it! . . .

LEADING LADY. [offended]. I shall live it also, you may be sure, as soon as I begin!

THE MANAGER [*with his hands to his head*]. Ladies and gentlemen, if you please! No more useless discussions! Scene I: the young lady with Madame Pace: Oh! [*Looks around as if lost.*] And this Madame Pace, where is she?

THE FATHER. She isn't with us, sir.

THE MANAGER. Then what the devil's to be done?

THE FATHER. But she is alive too.

THE MANAGER. Yes, but where is she?

THE FATHER. One minute. Let me speak! [*Turning to the* ACTRESSES.] If these ladies would be so good as to give me their hats for a moment . . .

THE ACTRESSES [*half surprised, half laughing, in chorus*]. What?

Why?

Our hats?

What does he say?

THE MANAGER. What are you going to do with the ladies' hats? [*The* ACTORS *laugh.*]

THE FATHER. Oh nothing. I just want to put them on these pegs for a moment. And one of the ladies will be so kind as to take off her mantle . . .

THE ACTORS. Oh, what d' you think of that? Only the mantle?

He must be mad.

SOME ACTRESSES. But why?

Mantles as well?

THE FATHER. To hang them up here for a moment. Please be so kind, will you?

THE ACTRESSES [*taking off their hats, one or two also their cloaks, and going to hang them on the racks*]. After all, why not?

There you are!

This is really funny.

We've got to put them on show.

THE FATHER. Exactly; just like that, on show.

THE MANAGER. May we know why?

THE FATHER. I'll tell you. Who knows if, by arranging the stage for her, she does not come here herself, attracted by the very articles of her trade? [*Inviting the* ACTORS *to look towards the exit at back of stage.*] Look! Look!

[*The door at the back of stage opens and* MADAME PACE *enters and takes a few steps forward. She is a fat, oldish woman with puffy oxygenated hair. She is rouged and powdered, dressed with a comical elegance in black silk. Round her waist is a long silver chain from which hangs a pair of scissors. The* STEPDAUGHTER *runs over to her at once amid the stupor of the actors.*]

THE STEP-DAUGHTER [*turning towards her*]. There she is! There she is!

THE FATHER [*radiant*]. It's she! I said so, didn't I? There she is!

THE MANAGER [*conquering his surprise, and then becoming indignant*]. What sort of a trick is this?

LEADING MAN [*almost at the same time*]. What's going to happen next?

JUVENILE LEAD. Where does she come from?

L'INGÉNUE. They've been holding her in reserve, I guess.

LEADING LADY. A vulgar trick!

THE FATHER [*dominating the protests*]. Excuse me, all of you! Why are you so anxious to destroy in the name of a vulgar, commonplace sense of truth, this reality which comes to birth attracted and formed by the magic of the stage itself, which has indeed more right to live here than you, since it is much truer than you—if you don't mind my saying so? Which is the actress among you who is to play Madame Pace? Well, here is Madame Pace herself. And you will allow, I fancy, that the actress who acts her will be less true than this woman here, who is herself in person. You see my daughter recognized her and went over to her at once. Now you're going to witness the scene!

[*But the scene between the* STEP-DAUGHTER *and* MADAME PACE *has already begun despite the protest of the actors and the reply of The* FATHER. *It has begun quietly, naturally, in a manner impossible for the stage. So when the actors, called to attention by The* FATHER, *turn round and see* MADAME PACE, *who has placed one hand under the* STEP-DAUGHTER'S *chin to raise her head, they observe her at first with great attention, but hearing her speak in an unintelligible manner their interest begins to wane.*]

THE MANAGER. Well? well?

LEADING MAN. What does she say?

LEADING LADY. One can't hear a word.

JUVENILE LEAD. Louder! Louder please!

THE STEP-DAUGHTER [*leaving* MADAME PACE, *who smiles a Sphinx-like smile, and advancing towards the actors*]. Louder? Louder? What are you talking about? These aren't matters which can be shouted at the top of one's voice. If I have spoken them out loud, it was to shame him and have my revenge. [*Indicates* FATHER.] But for Madame it's quite a different matter.

THE MANAGER. Indeed? indeed? But here, you know, people have got to make themselves heard, my dear. Even we who are on the stage can't hear you. What will it be when the public's in the theatre? And anyway, you can very well speak up now among yourselves, since we shan't be present to listen to you as we are now. You've got to pretend to be alone in a room at the back of a shop where no one can hear you.

[*The* STEP-DAUGHTER *coquettishly and with a touch of malice makes a sign of disagreement two or three times with her finger.*]

THE MANAGER. What do you mean by no?

THE STEP-DAUGHTER [*sotto voce, mysteriously*]. There's someone who will hear us if she [*Indicating* MADAME PACE.] speaks out loud.

THE MANAGER [*in consternation*]. What? Have you got someone else to spring on us now? [*The* ACTORS *burst out laughing.*]

THE FATHER. No, no sir. She is alluding to me. I've got to be here—there behind that door, in waiting; and Madame Pace knows it. In fact, if you will allow me, I'll go there at once, so I can be quite ready. [*Moves away.*]

THE MANAGER [*stopping him*]. No! Wait! wait! We must observe the conventions of the theatre. Before you are ready . . .

THE STEP-DAUGHTER [*interrupting him*]. No, get on with it at once! I'm just dying, I tell you, to act this scene. If he's ready, I'm more than ready.

THE MANAGER [*shouting*]. But, my dear young lady, first of all, we must have the scene between you and this lady . . . [*Indicates* MADAME PACE.] Do you understand? . . .

THE STEP-DAUGHTER. Good Heavens! She's been telling me what you know already: that mamma's work is badly done again, that the material's ruined; and that if I want her to continue to help us in our misery I must be patient . . .

Madame Pace [*coming forward with an air of great importance*]. Yes indeed, sir, I no wanta take advantage of her, I no wanta be hard . . .

[Note. MADAME PACE is supposed to talk in a jargon half Italian, half English.]

THE MANAGER [*alarmed*]. What? What? She talks like that? [*The* ACTORS *burst out laughing again.*]

THE STEP-DAUGHTER [*also laughing*].Yes yes, that's the way she talks, half English, half Italian! Most comical it is!

MADAME PACE. Itta seem not verra polite gentlemen laugha atta me eef I trya best speaka English.

THE MANAGER. *Diamine!* Of course! Of course! Let her talk like that! Just what we want. Talk just like that, Madame, if you please! The effect will be certain. Exactly what was wanted to put a little comic relief into the crudity of the situation. Of course she talks like that! Magnificent!

THE STEP-DAUGHTER. Magnificent? Certainly! When certain suggestions are made to one in language of that kind, the effect is certain, since it seems almost a joke. One feels inclined to laugh when one hears her talk about an "old signore" "who wanta talka nicely with you." Nice old signore, eh, Madame?

MADAME PACE. Not so old my dear, not so old! And even if you no lika him, he won't make any scandal!

THE MOTHER [*jumping up amid the amazement and consternation of the actors who had not been noticing her.* THEY *move to restrain her*]. You old devil! You murderess!

THE STEP-DAUGHTER [*running over to calm her* MOTHER]. Calm yourself, Mother, calm yourself! Please don't . . .

THE FATHER [*going to her also at the same time*]. Calm yourself! Don't get excited! Sit down now!

THE MOTHER. Well then, take that woman away out of my sight!

THE STEP-DAUGHTER [*to* MANAGER]. It is impossible for my mother to remain here.

THE FATHER [*to* MANAGER]. They can't be here together. And for this reason, you see: that woman there was not with us when we came . . . If they are on together, the whole thing is given away inevitably, as you see.

THE MANAGER. It doesn't matter. This is only a first rough sketch—just to get an idea of the various points of the scene, even confusedly . . . [*Turning to the* MOTHER *and leading her to her chair.*] Come along, my dear lady, sit down now, and let's get on with the scene . . .

[*Meanwhile, the* STEP-DAUGHTER, *coming forward again, turns to* MADAME PACE.]

THE STEP-DAUGHTER. Come on, Madame, come on!

MADAME PACE [*offended*]. No, no, grazie. I not do anything with a your mother present.

THE STEP-DAUGHTER. Nonsense! Introduce this "old signore" who wants to talk nicely to me. [*Addressing the* COMPANY *imperiously.*] We've got to do this scene one way or another, haven't we? Come on! [*To* MADAME PACE.] You can go!

MADAME PACE. Ah yes! I go'way! I go'way! Certainly! [*Exits furious.*]

THE STEP-DAUGHTER [*to the* FATHER]. Now you make your entry. No, you needn't go over here. Come here. Let's suppose you've already come in. Like that, yes! I'm here with bowed head, modest like. Come on! Out with your voice! Say "Good morning, Miss" in that peculiar tone, that special tone . . .

THE MANAGER. Excuse me, but are you the Manager, or am I? [*To the* FATHER, *who looks undecided and perplexed.*] Get on with it, man! Go down there to the back of the stage. You needn't go off. Then come right forward here.

[*The* FATHER *does as he is told, looking troubled and perplexed at first. But as soon as he begins to move, the reality of the action affects him, and he begins to smile and to be more natural. The* ACTORS *watch intently.*]

THE MANAGER [*sotto voce, quickly to the* PROMPTER *in his box*]. Ready! ready? Get ready to write now.

THE FATHER [*coming forward and speaking in a different tone*]. Good afternoon, Miss!

THE STEP-DAUGHTER [*head bowed down slightly, with restrained disgust*]. Good afternoon!

THE FATHER [*looks under her hat which partly covers her face. Perceiving she is very young, he makes an exclamation, partly of surprise, partly of fear lest he compromise himself in a risky adventure*]. Ah . . . but . . . ah . . . I say . . . this is not the first time that you have come here, is it?

THE STEP-DAUGHTER [*modestly*]. No sir.

THE FATHER. You've been here before, eh?

[*Then seeing her nod agreement.*] More than once? [*Waits for her to answer, looks under her hat, smiles, and then says.*] Well then, there's no need to be so shy, is there? May I take off your hat?

THE STEP-DAUGHTER [*anticipating him and with veiled disgust*]. No sir . . . . I'll do it myself. [*Takes it off quickly.*]

[*The* MOTHER, *who watches the progress of the scene with The* SON *and the other two children who cling to her, is on thorns; and follows with varying expressions of sorrow, indignation, anxiety, and horror the words and actions of the other two. From time to time* SHE *hides her face in her hands and sobs.*]

THE MOTHER. Oh, my God, my God!

THE FATHER [*playing his part with a touch of gallantry*]. Give it to me! I'll put it down. [*Takes hat from her hands.*] But a dear little head like yours ought to have a smarter hat. Come and help me choose one from the stock, won't you?

L'INGÉNUE [*interrupting*]. I say . . . those are our hats you know.

THE MANAGER [*furious*]. Silence! silence! Don't try and be funny, if you please. . . . We're playing the scene now I'd have you notice. [*To the* STEP-DAUGHTER.] Begin again, please!

THE STEP-DAUGHTER [*continuing*]. No thank you, sir.

THE FATHER. Oh, come now. Don't talk like that. You must take it. I shall be upset if you don't. There are some lovely little hats here; and then—Madame will be pleased. She expects it, anyway, you know.

THE STEP-DAUGHTER. No, no! I couldn't wear it!

THE FATHER. Oh, you're thinking about what they'd say at home if they saw you come in with a new hat? My dear girl, there's always a way round these little matters, you know.

THE STEP-DAUGHTER [*all keyed up*]. No, it's not that—I couldn't wear it because I am . . . as you see . . . you might have noticed . . . [*Showing her black dress.*]

THE FATHER. . . . in mourning! Of course: I beg your pardon: I'm frightfully sorry . . .

THE STEP-DAUGHTER [*forcing herself to conquer her indignation and nausea*]. Stop! Stop! It's I who must thank you. There's no need for you to feel mortified or specially sorry. Don't think any more of what I've said. [*Tries to smile.*] I must forget that I am dressed so . . .

THE MANAGER [*interrupting and turning to the* PROMPTER]. Stop a minute! Stop! Don't write that down. Cut out that last bit. [*Then to the* FATHER *and* STEP-DAUGHTER.] Fine! It's going fine! [*To the* FATHER *only.*] And now you can go on as we arranged. [*To the* ACTORS.] Pretty good that scene, where he offers her the hat, eh?

THE STEP-DAUGHTER. The best's coming now. Why can't we go on?

THE MANAGER. Have a little patience! [*To the* ACTORS.] Of course, it must be treated rather lightly.

LEADING MAN. Still, with a bit of go in it!

LEADING LADY. Of course! It's easy enough! [*To* LEADING MAN.] Shall you and I try it now?

LEADING MAN. Why, yes! I'll prepare my entrance. [*Exit in order to make his entrance.*]

THE MANAGER [*to* LEADING LADY]. See here! The scene between you and Madame Pace is finished. I'll have it written out properly after. You remain here . . . oh, where are you going?

LEADING LADY. One minute. I want to put my hat on again. [*Goes over to hat-rack and puts her hat on her head.*]

THE MANAGER. Good! You stay here with your head bowed down a bit.

THE STEP-DAUGHTER. But she isn't dressed in black.

LEADING LADY. But I shall be, and much more effectively than you.

THE MANAGER [*to* STEP-DAUGHTER]. Be quiet please, and watch! You'll be able to learn something. [*Clapping his hands.*] Come on! come on! Entrance, please! [*The door at rear of stage opens, and the* LEADING MAN *enters with the lively manner of an old gallant. The rendering of the scene by the* ACTORS *from the very first words is seen to be quite a different thing, though it has not in any way the air of a parody. Naturally, the* STEP-DAUGHTER *and the* FATHER, *not being able to recognize themselves in the* LEADING LADY *and the* LEADING MAN, *who deliver their words in different tones and with a different psychology, express, sometimes with smiles, sometimes with gestures, the impression they receive.*]

LEADING MAN. Good afternoon, Miss . . .

THE FATHER [*at once unable to contain himself*]. No! no! [*The* STEP-DAUGHTER *noticing the way the* LEADING MAN *enters, bursts out laughing.*]

THE MANAGER [*furious*]. Silence! And you please just stop that laughing. If we go on like this, we shall never finish.

THE STEP-DAUGHTER. Forgive me, sir, but it's natural enough. This lady [*Indicating* LEADING LADY.] stands there still; but if she is supposed to be me, I can assure you that if I heard anyone say "Good afternoon" in that manner and in that tone, I should burst out laughing as I did.

THE FATHER. Yes, yes, the manner, the tone . . .

THE MANAGER. Nonsense! Rubbish! Stand aside and let me see the action.

LEADING MAN. If I've got to represent an old fellow who's coming into a house of an equivocal character . . .

THE MANAGER. Don't listen to them, for Heaven's sake! Do it again! It goes fine. [*Waiting for the* ACTORS *to begin again.*] Well?

LEADING MAN. Good afternoon, Miss.

LEADING LADY. Good afternoon.

LEADING MAN [*imitating the gesture of the* FATHER *when he looked under the hat, and then expressing quite clearly first satisfaction and then fear*]. Ah, but . . . I say . . . this is not the first time that you have come here, is it?

THE MANAGER. Good, but not quite so heavily. Like this. [*Acts himself.*] "This isn't the first time that you have come here" . . . [*To* LEADING LADY.] And you say: "No, sir."

LEADING LADY. No, sir.

LEADING MAN. You've been here before, more than once.

THE MANAGER. No, no, stop! Let her nod "yes" first. "You've been here before, eh?" [*The* LEADING LADY *lifts up her head slightly and closes her eyes as though in disgust. Then* SHE *inclines her head twice.*]

THE STEP-DAUGHTER [*unable to contain herself*]. Oh my God! [*Puts a hand to her mouth to prevent herself from laughing.*]

THE MANAGER [*turning round*]. What's the matter?

THE STEP-DAUGHTER. Nothing, nothing!

THE MANAGER [*to* LEADING MAN]. Go on!

LEADING MAN. You've been here before, eh? Well then, there's no need to be so shy, is there? May I take off your hat?

[*The* LEADING MAN *says this last speech in such a tone and with such gestures that the* STEP-DAUGHTER, *though she has her hand to her mouth, cannot keep from laughing.*]

LEADING LADY. [*indignant*]. I'm not going to stop here to be made a fool of by that woman there.

LEADING MAN. Neither am I! I'm through with it!

THE MANAGER [*shouting to* STEP-DAUGHTER]. Silence! for once and all, I tell you!

THE STEP-DAUGHTER. Forgive me! forgive me!

THE MANAGER. You haven't any manners: that's what it is! You go too far.

THE FATHER [*endeavouring to intervene*]. Yes, it's true, but excuse her . . .

THE MANAGER. Excuse what? It's absolutely disgusting.

THE FATHER. Yes, sir, but believe me, it has such a strange effect when . . .

THE MANAGER. Strange? Why strange? Where is it strange?

THE FATHER. No, sir; I admire your actors—this gentleman here, this lady; but they are certainly not us!

THE MANAGER. I should hope not. Evidently they cannot be you, if they are actors.

THE FATHER. Just so: actors! Both of them act our parts exceedingly well. But, believe me, it produces quite a different effect on us. They want to be us, but they aren't, all the same.

THE MANAGER. What is it then anyway?

THE FATHER. Something that is . . . that is theirs—and no longer ours . . .

THE MANAGER. But naturally, inevitably. I've told you so already.

THE FATHER. Yes, I understand . . . I understand . . .

THE MANAGER. Well then, let's have no more of it! [*Turning to the* ACTORS.] We'll have the rehearsals by ourselves, afterwards, in the ordinary way. I never could stand rehearsing with the author present. He's never satisfied! [*Turning to* FATHER *and* STEP-DAUGHTER.] Come on! Let's get on with it again; and try and see if you can't keep from laughing.

THE STEP-DAUGHTER. Oh, I shan't laugh any more. There's a nice little bit coming for me now: you'll see.

THE MANAGER. Well then: when she says "Don't think any more of what I've said. I must forget, etc.," you [*Addressing the* FATHER.] come in sharp with "I understand, I understand"; and then you ask her . . .

THE STEP-DAUGHTER [*interrupting*]. What?

THE MANAGER. Why she is in mourning.

THE STEP-DAUGHTER. Not at all! See here: when I told him that it was useless for me to be thinking about my wearing mourning, do you know how he answered me? "Ah well," he said, "then let's take off this little frock."

THE MANAGER. Great! Just what we want, to make a riot in the theatre!

THE STEP-DAUGHTER. But it's the truth!

THE MANAGER. What does that matter? Acting is our business here. Truth up to a certain point, but no further.

THE STEP-DAUGHTER. What do you want to do then?

THE MANAGER. You'll see, you'll see! Leave it to me.

THE STEP-DAUGHTER. No sir! What you want to do is to piece together a little romantic sentimental scene out of my disgust, out of all the reasons, each more cruel and viler than the other, why I am what I am. He is to ask me why I'm in mourning; and I'm to answer with tears in my eyes, that it is just two months since papa died. No sir, no! He's got to say to me; as he did say: "Well, let's take off this little dress at once." And I; with my two months' mourning in my heart, went there behind that screen, and with these fingers tingling with shame . . .

THE MANAGER [*running his hands through his hair*]. For Heaven's sake! What are you saying?

THE STEP-DAUGHTER [*crying out excitedly*]. The truth! The truth!

THE MANAGER. It may be. I don't deny it, and I can understand all your horror; but you must surely see that you can't have this kind of thing on the stage. It won't go.

THE STEP-DAUGHTER. Not possible, eh? Very well! I'm much obliged to you—but I'm off!

THE MANAGER. Now be reasonable! Don't lose your temper!

THE STEP-DAUGHTER. I won't stop here! I won't! I can see you've fixed it all up with him in your office. All this talk about what is possible for the stage . . . I understand! He wants to get at his complicated "cerebral drama," to have his famous remorses and torments acted; but I want to act my part, my part!

THE MANAGER [*annoyed, shaking his shoulders*]. Ah! Just your part! But, if you will pardon me, there are other parts than yours: His [*Indicating the* FATHER.] and hers! [*Indicating the* MOTHER.] On the stage you can have a character becoming too prominent and overshadowing all the others. The thing is to pack them all into a neat little framework and then act what is actable. I am aware of the fact that everyone has his own interior life which he wants very much to put forward. But the difficulty lies in this fact: to set out just so much as is necessary for the stage, taking the other characters into consideration, and at the same time hint at the unrevealed interior life of each. I am willing to admit, my dear young lady, that from your point of view it would be a fine idea if each character could tell the public all his troubles in a nice monologue or a regular one hour lecture. [*Good humoredly.*] You must restrain yourself, my dear, and in your own interest, too; because this fury of yours, this exaggerated disgust you show, may make a bad impression, you know. After you have confessed to me that there were others before him at Madame Pace's and more than once . . .

THE STEP-DAUGHTER [*bowing her head, impressed*]. It's true. But remember those others mean him for me all the same.

THE MANAGER [*not understanding*]. What? The others? What do you mean?

THE STEP-DAUGHTER. For one who has gone wrong, sir, he who was responsible for the first fault is responsible for all that follow. He is responsible for my faults, was, even before I was born. Look at him, and see if it isn't true!

THE MANAGER. Well, well! And does the weight of so much responsibility seem nothing to you? Give him a chance to act it, to get it over!

THE STEP-DAUGHTER. How? How can he act all his "noble remorses," all his "moral torments," if you want to spare him the horror of being discovered one day—after he had asked her what he did ask her—in the arms of her, that already fallen woman, that child, sir, that child he used to watch come out of school? [SHE *is moved.*] [*The* MOTHER *at this point is overcome with emotion, and breaks out into a fit of crying. ALL are touched. A long pause.*]

THE STEP-DAUGHTER [*as soon as the* MOTHER *becomes a little quieter, adds resolutely and gravely*]. At present, we are unknown to the public. Tomorrow, you will act us as you wish, treating us in your own manner. But do you really want to see drama, do you want to see it flash out as it really did?

THE MANAGER. Of course! That's just what I do want, so I can use as much of it as is possible.

THE STEP-DAUGHTER. Well then, ask that Mother there to leave us.

THE MOTHER [*changing her low plaint into a sharp cry*]. No! No! Don't permit it, sir, don't permit it!

THE MANAGER. But it's only to try it.

THE MOTHER. I can't bear it. I can't.

THE MANAGER. But since it has happened already . . . I don't understand!

THE MOTHER. It's taking place now. It happens all the time. My torment isn't a pretended one. I live and feel every minute of my torture. Those two children there—have you heard them speak? They can't speak any more. They cling to me to keep up my torment actual and vivid for me. But for themselves, they do not exist, they aren't any more. And she [*Indicating the STEP-DAUGHTER.*] has run away, she has left me, and is lost. If I now see her here before me, it is only to renew for me the tortures I have suffered for her too.

THE FATHER. The eternal moment! She [*Indicating the STEP-DAUGHTER.*] is here to catch me, fix me, and hold me eternally in the stocks for that one fleeting and shameful moment of my life. She can't give it up! And you sir, cannot either fairly spare me it.

THE MANAGER. I never said I didn't want to act it. It will form, as a matter of fact, the nucleus of the whole first act right up to her surprise. [*Indicates the MOTHER.*]

THE FATHER. Just so! This is my punishment: the passion in all of us that must culminate in her final cry.

THE STEP-DAUGHTER. I can hear it still in my ears. It's driven me mad, that cry!—You can put me on as you like; it doesn't matter. Fully dressed, if you like—provided I have at least the arm bare; because, standing like this [*She goes close to the FATHER and leans her head on his breast.*] with my head so, and my arms round his neck, I saw a view in pulsing in my arm here; and then, as if that live vein had awakened disgust in me, I closed my eyes like this, and let my head sink on his breast. [*Turning to the MOTHER.*] Cry out mother! Cry out! [*Buries head in FATHER'S breast, and with her shoulders raised as if to prevent her hearing the cry, adds in tones of intense emotion.*] Cry out as you did then!

THE MOTHER [*coming forward to separate them*]. No! My daughter, my daughter! [*And after having pulled her away from him.*] You brute! you brute! She is my daughter! Don't you see she's my daughter?

THE MANAGER [*walking backwards towards footlights*]. Fine! fine! Damned good! And then, of course—curtain!

THE FATHER [*going towards him excitedly*]. Yes, of course, because that's the way it really happened.

THE MANAGER [*convinced and pleased*]. Oh, yes, no doubt about it. Curtain here, curtain! [*At the reiterated cry of* The MANAGER, *The* MACHINIST *lets the curtain down, leaving The* MANAGER *and* The FATHER *in front of it before the footlights.*]

THE MANAGER. The darned idiot! I said "curtain" to show the act should end there, and he goes and lets it down in earnest. [*To the* FATHER, *while he pulls the curtain back to go on to the stage again.*] Yes, yes, it's all right. Effect certain! That's the right ending. I'll guarantee the first act at any rate.

ACT III

When the curtain goes up again, it is seen that the stagehands have shifted the bit of scenery used in the last part, and have rigged up instead at the back of the stage a drop, with some trees, and one or two wings. A portion of a fountain basin is visible. The MOTHER *is sitting on the right with the two children by her side. The* SON *is on the same side, but away from the others. He seems bored, angry, and full of shame. The* FATHER *and the* STEP-DAUGHTER *are also seated towards the right front. On the other side (left) are the* ACTORS, *much in the positions they occupied before the curtain was lowered. Only the* MANAGER *is standing up in the middle of the stage, with his hand closed over his mouth in the act of meditating.*

THE MANAGER [*shaking his shoulders after a brief pause*]. Ah yes: the second act! Leave it to me, leave it all to me as we arranged, and you'll see! It'll go fine!

THE STEP-DAUGHTER. Our entry into his house [*Indicates* FATHER.] in spite of him . . . [*Indicates the* SON.]

THE MANAGER [*out of patience*]. Leave it to me, I tell you!

THE STEP-DAUGHTER. Do let it be clear, at any rate, that it is in spite of my wishes.

THE MOTHER [*from her corner, shaking her head*]. For all the good that's come of it . . .

THE STEP-DAUGHTER [*turning towards her quickly*]. It doesn't matter. The more harm done us, the more remorse for him.

THE MANAGER [*impatiently*]. I understand! Good Heavens! I understand! I'm taking it into account.

THE MOTHER [*supplicatingly*]. I beg you, sir, to let it appear quite plain that for conscience' sake I did try in everyway . . .

THE STEP-DAUGHTER [*interrupting indignantly and continuing for the* MOTHER]. . . . to pacify me, to dissuade me from spiting him. [*To* MANAGER.] Do as she wants: satisfy her, because it is true! I enjoy it immensely. Any how, as you can see, the meeker she is, the more she tries to get at his heart, the more distant and aloof does he become.

THE MANAGER. Are we going to begin this second act or not?

THE STEP-DAUGHTER. I'm not going to talk any more now—But I must tell you this: you can't have the whole action take place in the garden, as you suggest. It isn't possible!

THE MANAGER. Why not?

THE STEP-DAUGHTER. Because he [*Indicates the* SON *again.*] is always shut up alone in his room. And then there's all the part of that poor dazed-looking boy there which takes place indoors.

THE MANAGER. Maybe! On the other hand, you will understand—we can't change scenes three or four times in one act.

THE LEADING MAN. They used to once.

THE MANAGER. Yes, when the public was up to the level of that child there.

THE LEADING LADY. It makes the illusion easier.

THE FATHER [*irritated*]. The illusion! For Heaven's sake, don't say illusion. Please don't use that word, which is particularly painful for us.

THE MANAGER [*astounded*]. And why, if you please?

THE FATHER. It's painful, cruel, really cruel; and you ought to understand that.

THE MANAGER. But why? What ought we to say then? The illusion, I tell you, sir, which we've got to create for the audience . . .

THE LEADING MAN. With our acting.

THE MANAGER. The illusion of a reality.

THE FATHER. I understand; but you, perhaps, do not understand us. Forgive me! You see . . . here for you and your actors, the thing is only—and rightly so . . . a kind of game . . .

THE LEADING LADY [*interrupting indignantly*]. A game! We're not children here, if you please! We are serious actors.

THE FATHER. I don't deny it. What I mean is the game, or play, of your art, which has to give, as the gentleman says, a perfect illusion of reality.

THE MANAGER. Precisely—!

THE FATHER. Now, if you consider the fact that we [*Indicates himself and the other five* CHARACTERS.], as we are, have no other reality outside of this illusion . . .

THE MANAGER [*astonished, looking at his* ACTORS, *who are also amazed*]. And what does that mean?

THE FATHER [*after watching them for a moment with a wan smile*]. As I say, sir, that which is a game of art for you is our sole reality. [*Brief pause. He goes a step or two nearer the* MANAGER *and adds.*] But not only for us, you know, by the way. Just you think it over well. [*Looks him in the eyes.*] Can you tell me who you are?

THE MANAGER [*perplexed, half smiling*]. What? Who am I? I am myself.

THE FATHER. And if I were to tell you that that isn't true, because you and I . . .

THE MANAGER. I should say you were mad—! [*The* ACTORS *laugh.*]

THE FATHER. You're quite right to laugh: because we are all making believe here. [*To* MANAGER.]

And you can therefore object that it's only for a joke that that gentleman there [*Indicates the* LEADING MAN.], who naturally is himself, has to be me, who am on the contrary myself—this thing you see here. You see I've caught you in a trap! [*The* ACTORS *laugh.*]

THE MANAGER [*annoyed*]. But we've had all this over once before. Do you want to begin again?

THE FATHER. No, no! That wasn't my meaning! In fact, I should like to request you to abandon this game of art [*Looking at the* LEADING LADY *as if anticipating her.*] which you are accustomed to play here with your actors, and to ask you seriously once again: who are you?

THE MANAGER [*astonished and irritated, turning to his* ACTORS]. If this fellow here hasn't got a nerve! A man who calls himself a character comes and asks me who I am!

THE FATHER [*with dignity, but not offended*]. A character, sir, may always ask a man who he is. Because a character has really a life of his own, marked with his especial characteristics; for which reason he is always "somebody." But a man—I'm not speaking of you now—may very well be "nobody."

THE MANAGER. Yes, but you are asking these questions of me, the boss, the manager! Do you understand?

THE FATHER. But only in order to know if you, as you really are now, see yourself as you once were with all the illusions that were yours then, with all the things both inside and outside of you as they seemed to you—as they were then indeed for you. Well, sir, if you think of all those illusions that mean nothing to you now, of all those things which don't even seem to you to exist any more, while once they were for you, don't you feel that—I won't say these boards—but the very earth under your feet is sinking away from you when you reflect that in the same way this you as you feel it today—all this present reality of yours—is fated to seem a mere illusion to you tomorrow?

THE MANAGER [*without having understood much, but astonished by the specious argument*]. Well, well! And where does all this take us anyway?

THE FATHER. Oh, nowhere! It's only to show you that if we [*Indicating the* CHARACTERS.] have no other reality beyond the illusion, you too must not count overmuch on your reality as you feel it today, since, like that of yesterday, it may prove an illusion for you tomorrow.

THE MANAGER [*determining to make fun of him*]. Ah. excellent! Then you'll be saying next that you, with this comedy of yours that you brought here to act, are truer and more real than I am.

THE FATHER [*with the greatest seriousness*]. But of course; without doubt!

THE MANAGER. Ah, really?

THE FATHER. Why, I thought you'd understand that from the beginning.

THE MANAGER. More real than I?

THE FATHER. If your reality can change from one day to another . . .

THE MANAGER. But everyone knows it can change. It is always changing, the same as anyone else's.

THE FATHER [*with a cry*]. No, sir, not ours! Look here! That is the very difference! Our reality doesn't change: it can't change! It can't be other than what it is, because it is already fixed for ever. It's terrible. Ours is an immutable reality which should make you shudder when you approach us if you are really conscious of the fact that your reality is a mere transitory and fleeting illusion, taking this form today and that tomorrow, according to the conditions, according to your will, your sentiments, which in turn are controlled by an intellect that shows them to you today in one manner and tomorrow . . . who knows how? . . . Illusions of reality represented in this fatuous comedy of life that never ends, nor can ever end! Because if tomorrow it were to end . . . then why, all would be finished.

THE MANAGER. Oh for God's sake, will you at least finish with this philosophizing and let us try and shape this comedy which you yourself have brought me here? You argue and philosophize a bit too much, my dear sir. You know you seem to me almost, almost . . . [*Stops and looks him over from head to foot.*] Ah, by the way, I think you introduced yourself to me as a—what shall . . . we say—a "character," created by an author who did not afterward care to make a drama of his own creations.

THE FATHER. It is the simple truth, sir.

THE MANAGER. Nonsense! Cut that out, please! None of us believes it, because it isn't a thing, as you must recognize yourself, which one can believe seriously. If you want to know, it seems to me you are trying to imitate the manner of a certain author whom I heartily detest—I warn you—although I have unfortunately bound myself to put on one of his works. As a matter of fact, I was just starting to rehearse it, when you arrived. [*Turning to the* ACTORS.] And this is what we've gained—out of the frying-pan into the fire!

THE FATHER. I don't know to what author you may be alluding, but believe me I feel what I think; and I seem to be philosophizing only for those who do not think what they feel, because they blind themselves with their own sentiment. I know that for many people this self-blinding seems much more "human"; but the contrary is really true. For man never reasons so much and becomes so introspective as when he suffers; since he is anxious to get at the cause of his sufferings, to learn who has produced them, and whether it is just or unjust that he should have to bear them. On the other hand, when he is happy, he takes his happiness as it comes and doesn't analyze it, just as if happiness were his right. The animals suffer without reasoning about their sufferings. But take the case of a man who suffers and begins to reason about it. Oh no! it can't be allowed! Let him suffer like an animal, and then—ah yet, he is "human"!

THE MANAGER. Look here! Look here! You're off again, philosophizing worse than ever.

THE FATHER. Because I suffer, sir! I'm not philosophizing: I'm crying aloud the reason of my sufferings.

THE MANAGER [*makes brusque movement as he is taken with a new idea*]. I should like to know if anyone has ever heard of a character who gets right out of his part and perorates and speechifies as you do. Have you ever heard of a case? I haven't.

THE FATHER. You have never met such a case, sir, because authors, as a rule, hide the labour of their creations. When the characters are really alive before their author, the latter does nothing but follow them in their action, in their words, in the situations which they suggest to him; and he has to will them the way they will themselves—for there's trouble if he doesn't. When a character is born, he acquires at once such an independence, even of his own author, that he can be imagined by everybody even in many other situations where the author never dreamed of placing him; and so he acquires for himself a meaning which the author never thought of giving him.

THE MANAGER. Yes, yes, I know this.

THE FATHER. What is there then to marvel at in us? Imagine such a misfortune for characters as I have described to you: to be born of an author's fantasy, and be denied life by him; and then answer me if these characters left alive, and yet without life, weren't right in doing what they did do and are doing now, after they have attempted everything in their power to persuade him to give them their stage life. We've all tried him in turn, I, she [*Indicating the* STEP-DAUGHTER.] and she. [*Indicating the* MOTHER.]

THE STEP-DAUGHTER. It's true. I too have sought to tempt him, many, many times, when he has been sitting at his writing table, feeling a bit melancholy, at the twilight hour. He would sit in his armchair too lazy to switch on the light, and all the shadows that crept into his room were full of our presence coming to tempt him. [*As if she saw herself still there by the writing table, and was annoyed by the presence of the* ACTORS.] Oh, if you would only go away, go away and leave us alone—mother here with that son of hers—I with that Child—that Boy there always alone—and then I with him [*Just hints at the* FATHER.]—and then I alone, alone . . . in those shadows! [*Makes a sudden movement as if in the vision she has of herself illuminating those shadows she wanted to seize hold of herself.*] Ah! my life! my life! Oh, what scenes we proposed to him—and I tempted him more than any of the others!

THE FATHER. Maybe. But perhaps it was your fault that he refused to give us life: because you were too insistent, too troublesome.

THE STEP-DAUGHTER. Nonsense! Didn't he make me so himself? [*Goes close to the* MANAGER *to tell him, as if in confidence.*] In my opinion he abandoned us in a fit of depression, of disgust for the ordinary theatre as the public knows it and likes it.

THE SON. Exactly what it was, sir; exactly that!

THE FATHER. Not at all! Don't believe it for a minute. Listen to me! You'll be doing quite right to modify, as you suggest, the excesses both of this girl here, who wants to do too much, and of this young man, who won't do anything at all.

THE SON. No, nothing!

THE MANAGER. You too get over the mark occasionally, my dear sir, if I may say so.

THE FATHER. I? When? Where?

THE MANAGER. Always! Continuously! Then there's this insistence of yours in trying to make us believe you are a character. And then too, you must really argue and philosophize less, you know, much less.

THE FATHER. Well, if you want to take away from me the possibility of representing the torment of my spirit which never gives me peace, you will be suppressing me: that's all. Every true man, sir, who is a little above the level of the beasts and plants does not live for the sake of living, without knowing how to live; but he lives so as to give a meaning and a value of his own to life. For me this is everything. I cannot give up this, just to represent a mere fact as she [*Indicating the* STEP-DAUGHTER.] wants. It's all very well for her, since her "vendetta" lies in the "fact." I'm not going to do it. It destroys my raison d'être.

THE MANAGER. Your raison d'être! Oh, we're going ahead fine! First she starts off, and then you jump in. At this rate, we'll never finish.

THE FATHER. Now, don't be offended! Have it your own way—provided, however, that within the limits of the parts you assign us each one's sacrifice isn't too great.

THE MANAGER. You've got to understand that you can't go on arguing at your own pleasure. Drama is action, sir, action and not confounded philosophy.

THE FATHER. All right. I'll do just as much arguing and philosophizing as everybody does when he is considering his own torments.

THE MANAGER. If the drama permits! But for Heaven's sake, man, let's get along and come to the scene.

THE STEP-DAUGHTER. It seems to me we've got too much action with our coming into his house. [*Indicating* FATHER.] You said, before, you couldn't change the scene every five minutes.

THE MANAGER. Of course not. What we've got to do is to combine and group up all the facts in one simultaneous, close-knit, action. We can't have it as you want, with your little brother wandering like a ghost from room to room, hiding behind doors and meditating a project which—what did you say it did to him?

THE STEP-DAUGHTER. Consumes him, sir, wastes him away!

THE MANAGER. Well, it may be. And then at the same time, you want the little girl there to be playing in the garden . . . one in the house, and the other in the garden: isn't that it?

THE STEP-DAUGHTER. Yes, in the sun, in the sun! That is my only pleasure: to see her happy and careless in the garden after the misery and squalor of the horrible room where we all four slept together. And I had to sleep with her—I, do you understand?—with my vile contaminated body next to hers; with her folding me fast in her loving little arms. In the garden, whenever she spied me, she would run to take me by the hand. She didn't care for the big flowers, only the little ones; and she loved to show me them and pet me.

THE MANAGER. Well then, we'll have it in the garden. Everything shall happen in the garden; and we'll group the other scenes there. [*Calls a* STAGE HAND.] Here, a backcloth with trees and something to do as a fountain basin. [*Turning round to look at the back of the stage.*] Ah, you've fixed it up. Good! [*To* STEP-DAUGHTER.] This is just to give an idea, of course. The Boy, instead of hiding behind the doors, will wander about here in the garden, hiding behind the trees. But it's going to be rather difficult to find a child to do that scene with you where she shows you the flowers. [*Turning to the* BOY.] Come forward a little, will you please? Let's try it now! Come along! come along! [*Then seeing him come shyly forward, full of fear and looking lost.*] It's a nice business, this lad here. What's the matter with him? We'll have to give him a word or two to say. [*Goes close to him, puts a hand on his shoulders, and Leads him behind one of the trees.*] Come on! come on! Let me see you a little! Hide here . . . yes, like that. Try and show your head just a little as if you were looking for someone . . . [*Goes back to observe the effect, when the* BOY *at once goes through the action.*] Excellent! fine! [*Turning to* STEP-DAUGHTER.] Suppose the little girl there were to surprise him as he looks round and run over to him, so we could give him a word or two to say?

THE STEP-DAUGHTER. It's useless to hope he will speak, as long as that fellow there is here . . . [*indicates the* SON.] You must send him away first.

THE SON [*jumping up*]. Delighted! Delighted! I don't ask for anything better. [*Begins to move away.*]

THE MANAGER [at once stopping him]. No! No! Where are you going? Wait a bit!

[*The* MOTHER *gets up alarmed and terrified at the thought that he is really about to go away. Instinctively she lifts her arms to prevent him, without, however, leaving her seat.*]

THE SON [*to* MANAGER *who stops him*]. I've got nothing to do with this affair. Let me go please! Let me go!

THE MANAGER. What do you mean by saying you've got nothing to do with this?

THE STEP-DAUGHTER [*calmly, with irony*]. Don't bother to stop him: he won't go away.

THE FATHER. He has to act the terrible scene in the garden with his mother.

THE SON [*suddenly resolute and with dignity*]. I shall act nothing at all. I've said so from the very beginning. [*To the* MANAGER.] Let me go!

THE STEP-DAUGHTER [*going over to the* MANAGER]. Allow me? [*Puts down the* MANAGER'S *arm which is restraining the* SON.] Well, go away then, if you want to! [*The* SON

looks at her with contempt and hatred. She laughs and says.] You see, he can't, he can't go away! He is obliged to stay here, indissolubly bound to the chain. If I, who fly off when that happens which has to happen, because I can't bear him—if I am still here and support that face and expression of his, you can well imagine that he is unable to move. He has to remain here, has to stop with that nice father of his, and that mother whose only son he is. [*Turning to the* MOTHER.] Come on, mother, come along! [*Turning to* MANAGER *to indicate her.*] You see, she was getting up to keep him back. [*To the* MOTHER, *beckoning her with her hand.*] Come on! come on! [*Then to* MANAGER.] You can imagine how little she wants to show these actors of yours what she really feels; but so eager is she to get near him that . . . There, you see? She is willing to act her part. [*And in fact, the* MOTHER *approaches him; and as soon as the* STEP-DAUGHTER *has finished speaking, opens her arms to signify that she consents.*]

THE SON [*suddenly*]. No! no! If I can't go away, then I'll stop here; but I repeat: I act nothing!

THE FATHER [*to* MANAGER *excitedly*]. You can force him, sir.

THE SON. Nobody can force me.

THE FATHER. I can.

THE STEP-DAUGHTER. Wait a minute, wait . . . First of all, the baby has to go to the fountain . . . [*Runs to take the* CHILD *and leads her to the fountain.*]

THE MANAGER. Yes, yes of course; that's it. Both at the same time.

[*The second* LADY LEAD *and the* JUVENILE LEAD *at this point separate themselves from the group of* ACTORS. *One watches the* MOTHER *attentively; the other moves about studying the movements and manner of the* SON *whom he will have to act.*]

THE SON [*to* MANAGER]. What do you mean by both at the same time? It isn't right. There was no scene between me and her. [*Indicates the* MOTHER.] Ask her how it was!

THE MOTHER. Yes, it's true. I had come into his room . . .

THE SON. Into my room, do you understand? Nothing to do with the garden.

THE MANAGER. It doesn't matter. Haven't I told you we've got to group the action?

THE SON [*observing the* JUVENILE LEAD *studying him*]. What do you want?

THE JUVENILE LEAD. Nothing! I was just looking at you.

THE SON [*turning towards the second* LADY LEAD]. Ah! she's at it too: to re-act her part! [*Indicating the* MOTHER.]

THE MANAGER. Exactly! And it seems to me that you ought to be grateful to them for their interest.

THE SON. Yes, but haven't you yet perceived that it isn't possible to live in front of a mirror which not only freezes us with the image of ourselves, but throws our likeness back at us with a horrible grimace?

THE FATHER. That is true, absolutely true. You must see that.

THE MANAGER [*to second* LADY LEAD *and* JUVENILE LEAD]. He's right! Move away from them!

THE SON. Do as you like. I'm out of this!

THE MANAGER. Be quiet, you, will you? And let me hear your mother! [*To* MOTHER.] You were saying you had entered . . .

THE MOTHER. Yes, into his room, because I couldn't stand it any longer. I went to empty my heart to him of all the anguish that tortures me . . . But as soon as he saw me come in . . .

THE SON. Nothing happened! There was no scene. I went away, that's all! I don't care for scenes!

THE MOTHER. It's true, true. That's how it was.

THE MANAGER. Well now, we've got to do this bit between you and him. It's indispensable.

THE MOTHER. I'm ready . . . when you are ready. If you could only find a chance for me to tell him what I feel here in my heart.

THE FATHER [*going to* SON *in a great rage*]. You'll do this for your mother, for your mother, do you understand?

THE SON [*quite determined*]. I do nothing!

THE FATHER [*taking hold of him and shaking him*]. For God's sake, do as I tell you! Don't you hear your mother asking you for a favor? Haven't you even got the guts to be a son?

THE SON [*taking hold of the* FATHER]. No! No! And for God's sake stop it, or else . . . [*General agitation.*]

[*The* MOTHER, *frightened, tries to separate them.*]

THE MOTHER [*pleading*]. Please! please!

THE FATHER [*not leaving hold of the* SON]. You've got to obey, do you hear?

THE SON [*almost crying from rage*]. What does it mean, this madness you've got? [*They separate.*] Have you no decency, that you insist on showing everyone our shame? I won't do it! I won't! And I stand for the will of our author in this. He didn't want to put us on the stage, after all!

THE MANAGER. Man alive! You came here . . .

THE SON [*indicating* FATHER]. He did! I didn't!

THE MANAGER. Aren't you here now?

THE SON. It was his wish, and he dragged us along with him. He's told you not only the things that did happen, but also things that have never happened at all.

THE MANAGER. Well, tell me then what did happen. You went out of your room without saying a word?

THE SON. Without a word, so as to avoid a scene!

THE MANAGER. And then what did you do?

THE SON. Nothing . . . walking in the garden . . . [*Hesitates for a moment with expression of gloom.*]

THE MANAGER [*coming closer to him, interested by his extraordinary reserve*]. Well, well . . . walking in the garden . . .

THE SON [*exasperated*]. Why on earth do you insist? It's horrible! [*The* MOTHER *trembles, sobs, and looks towards the fountain.*]

THE MANAGER [*slowly observing the glance and turning towards the* SON *with increasing apprehension*]. The baby?

THE SON. There in the fountain . . .

THE FATHER [*pointing with tender pity to the* MOTHER]. She was following him at the moment . . .

THE MANAGER [*to the* SON *anxiously*]. And then you . . .

THE SON. I ran over to her; I was jumping in to drag her out when I saw something that froze my blood . . . the boy standing stock still, with eyes like a madman's, watching his little drowned sister, in the fountain! [*The* STEP-DAUGHTER *bends over the fountain to hide the* CHILD. *She sobs.*] Then . . . [*A revolver shot rings out behind the trees where the* BOY *is hidden.*]

THE MOTHER [*with a cry of terror runs over in that direction together with several of the* ACTORS *amid general confusion*]. My son! My son! [*Then amid the cries and exclamations one hears her voice.*] Help! Help!

THE MANAGER [*pushing the* ACTORS *aside while* THEY *lift up the* BOY *and carry him off.*] Is he really wounded?

SOME ACTORS. He's dead! dead!

OTHER ACTORS. No, no, it's only make believe, it's only pretence!

THE FATHER [*with a terrible cry*]. Pretence? Reality, sir, reality!

THE MANAGER. Pretence? Reality? To hell with it all! Never in my life has such a thing happened to me. I've lost a whole day over these people, a whole day!

Curtain.

8

Cat on a Hot Tin Roof

Play by Tennessee Williams (1911–1983)

ACT ONE

At the rise of the curtain someone is taking a shower in the bathroom, the door of which is half open. A pretty young woman, with anxious lines in her face, enters the bedroom and crosses to the bathroom door.

MARGARET (*shouting above roar of water*). One of those no-neck monsters hit me with a hot buttered biscuit so I have t' change!

Margaret's voice is both rapid and drawling. In her long speeches she has the vocal tricks of a priest delivering a liturgical chant, the lines are almost sung, always continuing a little beyond her breath so she has to gasp for another. Sometimes she intersperses the lines with a little wordless singing, such as "Da-da-daaaa!"

Water turns off and BRICK *calls out to her, but is still unseen. A tone of politely feigned interest, masking indifference, or worse, is characteristic of his speech with Margaret.*

BRICK. Wha'd you say, Maggie? Water was on s' loud I couldn't hearya. . . .

MARGARET. Well, I!—just remarked that!—one of th' no-neck monsters messed up m' lovely lace dress so I got t'—cha-a-ange. . . .

She opens and kicks shut drawers of the dresser.

BRICK. Why d'ya call Gooper's kiddies no-neck monsters?

MARGARET. Because they've got no necks! Isn't that a good enough reason?

BRICK. Don't they have any necks?

MARGARET. None visible. Their fat little heads are set on their fat little bodies without a bit of connection.

BRICK. That's too bad.

MARGARET. Yes, it's too bad because you can't wring their necks if they've got no necks to wring! Isn't that right, honey?

She steps out of her dress, stands in a slip of ivory satin and lace.

Yep, they're no-neck monsters, all no-neck people are monsters . . .

Children shriek downstairs.

By Tennessee Williams, from *"Cat on a Hot Tin Roof"*, Copyright © 1954, 1955, 1971, 1975 by The University of the South. Reprinted by permission of New Directions Publishing Corp.

Hear them? Hear them screaming? I don't know where their voice boxes are located since they don't have necks. I tell you I got so nervous at that table tonight I thought I would throw back my head and utter a scream you could hear across the Arkansas border an' parts of Louisiana an' Tennessee. I said to your charming sister-in-law, Mae, honey, couldn't you feed those precious little things at a separate table with an oilcloth cover? They make such a mess an' the lace cloth looks *so* pretty! She made enormous eyes at me and said, "Ohhh, noooooo! On Big Daddy's birthday? Why, he would never forgive me!" Well, I want you to know, Big Daddy hadn't been at the table two minutes with those five no-neck monsters slobbering and drooling over their food before he' threw down his fork an' shouted, "Fo' God's sake, Gooper, why don't you put them pigs at a trough in th' kitchen?"—Well, I swear, I simply could have di-ieed!

Think of it, Brick, they've got five of them and number six is coming. They've brought the whole bunch down here like animals to display at a county fair. Why, they have those children doin' tricks all the time! "Junior, show Big Daddy how you do this, show Big Daddy how you do that, say your little piece fo' Big Daddy, Sister. Show your dimples, Sugar. Brother, show Big Daddy how you stand on your head!"—It goes on all the time, along with constant little remarks and innuendos about the fact that you and I have not produced any children, are totally childless and therefore totally useless!—Of course it's comical but it's also disgusting since it's so obvious what they're up to!

BRICK. (*without interest*). What are they up to, Maggie?

MARGARET. Why, you know what they're up to!

BRICK. (*appearing*). No, I don't know what they're up to.

He stands there in the bathroom doorway drying his hair with a towel and hanging onto the towel rack because one ankle is broken, plastered and bound. He is still slim and firm as a boy. His liquor hasn't started tearing him down outside. He has the additional charm of that cool air of detachment that people have who have given up the struggle. But now and then, when disturbed, something

flashes behind it, like lightning in a fair sky, which shows that at some deeper level he is far from peaceful. Perhaps in a stronger light he would show some signs of deliquescence, but the fading, still warm, light from the gallery treats him gently.

MARGARET. I'll tell you what they're up to, boy of mine!—They're up to cutting you out of your father's estate, and—

She freezes momentarily before her next remark. Her voice drops as if it were somehow a personally embarrassing admission.

—Now we know that Big Daddy's dyin' of—*cancer. . . .*

There are voices on the lawn below: long-drawn calls across distance. Margaret raises her lovely bare arms and powders her armpits with a light sigh.

She adjusts the angle of a magnifying mirror to straighten an eyelash, then rises fretfully saying:

There's so much light in the room it—

BRICK. (*softly but sharply*). Do we?

MARGARET. Do we what?

BRICK. Know Big Daddy's dyin' of cancer?

MARGARET. Got the report today.

BRICK. Oh . . .

MARGARET (*letting down bamboo blinds which cast long, gold-fretted shadows over the room*). Yep, got th' report just now . . . it didn't surprise me, Baby. . . .

Her voice has range, and music; sometimes it drops low as a boy's and you have a sudden image of her playing boy's games as a child.

I recognized the symptoms soon's we got here last spring and I'm willin' to bet you that Brother Man and his wife were pretty sure of it, too. That more than likely explains why their usual summer migration to the coolness of the Great Smokies was passed up this summer in favor of—hustlin' down here ev'ry whipstitch with their whole screamin' tribe! And why so many allusions have been made to Rainbow Hill lately. You know what Rainbow Hill is? Place that's famous for treatin' alcoholics an dope fiends in the movies!

BRICK. I'm not in the movies.

MARGARET. No, and you don't take dope.

Otherwise you're a perfect candidate for Rainbow Hill, Baby, and that's where they aim to ship you—over my dead body! Yep, over my dead body they'll ship you there, but nothing would please them better. Then Brother Man could get a-hold of the purse strings and dole out remittances to us, maybe get power of attorney and sign checks for us and cut off our credit wherever, whenever he wanted! Son-of-a-bitch!—How'd you like that, Baby?—Well, you've been doin' just about ev'rything in your power to bring it about, you've just been doin' ev'rything you can think of to aid and abet them in this scheme of theirs! Quittin' work, devoting yourself to the occupation of drinkin'!—Breakin' your ankle last night on the high school athletic field: doin' what? Jumpin' hurdles? At two or three in the morning? Just fantastic! Got in the paper. *Clarksdale Register* carried a nice little item about it, human interest story about a well-known former athlete stagin' a one-man track meet on the Glorious Hill High School athletic field last night, but was slightly out of condition and didn't clear the first hurdle! Brother Man Gooper claims he exercised his influence t' keep it from goin' out over AP or UP or every goddam "P."

But, Brick? You still have one big advantage!

During the above swift flood of words, BRICK has reclined with contrapuntal leisure on the snowy surface of the bed and has rolled over carefully on his side or belly.

BRICK. *(wryly).* Did you *say* something, Maggie?

MARGARET. Big Daddy dotes on you, honey. And he can't stand Brother Man and Brother Man's wife, that monster of fertility, Mae. Know how I know? By little expressions that flicker over his face when that woman is holding fo'th on one of her choice topics such as—how she refused twilight sleep!—when the twins were delivered! Because she feels motherhood's an experience that a woman ought to experience fully!—in order to fully appreciate the wonder and beauty of it! HAH!—and how she made Brother Man come in an' stand beside her in the delivery room so he would not miss out on the "wonder and beauty" of it either!—producin' those no-neck monsters. . . .

A speech of this kind would be antipathetic from almost anybody but MARGARET; she makes it oddly funny, because her eyes constantly twinkle and her voice shakes with laughter which is basically indulgent.

—Big Daddy shares my attitude toward those two! As for me, well—I give him a laugh now and then and he tolerates me. In fact!—I sometimes suspect that Big Daddy harbors a little unconscious "lech" fo' me. . . .

BRICK. What makes you think that Big Daddy has a lech for you, Maggie?

MARGARET. Way he always drops his eyes down my body when I'm talkin' to him, drops his eyes to my boobs an' licks his old chops! Ha ha!

BRICK. That kind of talk is disgusting.

MARGARET. Did anyone ever tell you that you're an ass-aching Puritan, Brick?

I think it's mighty fine that that ole fellow, on the doorstep of death, still takes in my shape with what I think is deserved appreciation!

And you wanta know something else? Big Daddy didn't know how many little Maes and Goopers had been produced! "How many kids have you got?" he asked at the table, just like Brother Man and his wife were new acquaintances to him! Big Mama said he was jokin', but that ole boy wasn't jokin', Lord, no!

And when they infawmed him that they had five already and were turning out number six!—the news seemed to come as a sort of unpleasant surprise. . . .

Children yell below.

Scream, monsters!

Turns to BRICK with a sudden, gay, charming smile which fades as she notices that be is not looking at her but into fading gold space with a troubled expression.

It is constant rejection that makes her humor "bitchy."

Yes, you should have been at that supper-table, Baby.

Whenever she calls him "baby" the word is a soft caress.

Y'know, Big Daddy, bless his ole sweet soul, he's the dearest ole thing in the world, but he does hunch over his food as if he preferred not to notice anything else. Well, Mae an' Gooper were side by side at the table, direckly across from Big Daddy, watchin' his face like hawks while they jawed an' jabbered about the cuteness an' brillance of th' no-neck monsters!

She giggles with a hand fluttering at her throat and her breast and her long throat arched.

She comes downstage and recreates the scene with voice and gesture.

And the no-neck monsters were ranged around the table, some in high chairs and some on th' *Books of Knowledge*, all in fancy little paper caps in honor of Big Daddy's birthday, and all through dinner, well, I want you to know that Brother Man an' his partner never once, for one moment, stopped exchanging pokes an' pinches an' kicks an' signs an' signals!—Why, they were like a couple of cardsharps fleecing a sucker.—Even Big Mama, bless her ole sweet soul, she isn't th' quickest an' brightest thing in the world, she finally noticed, at last, an' said to Gooper, "Gooper, what are you an' Mae makin' all these signs at each other about?"—I swear t' goodness, I nearly choked on my chicken!

Margaret, back at the dressing table, still doesn't see Brick. He is watching her with a look that is not quite definable—Amused? shocked? contemptuous?—part of those and part of something else.

Y'know—your brother Gooper still cherishes the illusion he took a giant step up on the social ladder when he married Miss Mae Flynn of the Memphis Flynns.

But I have a piece of Spanish news for Gooper. The Flynns never had a thing in this world but money and they lost that, they were nothing at all but fairly successful climbers. Of course, Mae Flynn came out in Memphis eight years before I made my debut in Nashville, but I had friends at Ward-Belmont who came from Memphis and they used to come to see me and I used to go to see them for Christmas and spring vacations, and so I know who rates an' who doesn't rate in Memphis society. Why, y'know ole Papa Flynn, he barely escaped doing time in the Federal pen for shady manipulations on th' stock market when his chain stores crashed, and as for Mae having been a cotton carnival queen, as they remind us so often, lest we forget, well, that's one honor that I don't envy her for!—Sit on a brass throne on a tacky float an' ride down Main Street, smilin', bowin', and blowin' kisses to all the trash on the street—

She picks out a pair of jeweled sandals and rushes to the dressing table.

Why, year before last, when Susan McPheeters was singled out fo' that honor, y' know what happened to her? Y'know what happened to poor little Susie McPheeters?

BRICK. [*absently*]. No. What happened to little Susie McPheeters?

MARGARET. Somebody spit tobacco juice in her face.

BRICK. (*dreamily*). Somebody spit tobacco juice in her face?

MARGARET. That's right, some old drunk leaned out of a window in the Hotel Gayoso and yelled, "Hey, Queen, hey, hey, there, Queenie!" Poor Susie looked up and flashed him a radiant smile and he shot out a squirt of tobacco juice right in poor Susie's face.

BRICK. Well, what d'you know about that.

MARGARET. (*gaily*). What do I know about it? I was there, I saw it!

BRICK. (*absently*). Must have been kind of funny.

MARGARET. Susie didn't think so. Had hysterics. Screamed like a banshee. They had to stop th' parade an' remove her from her throne an' go on with—

She catches sight of him in the mirror, gasps slightly, wheels about to face him. Count ten.

—Why are you looking at me like that?

BRICK. (*whistling softly, now*). Like what, Maggie?

MARGARET. (*intensely, fearfully*). The way y' were lookin' at me just now, befo' I caught your eye in the mirror and you started t' whistle! I don't know how t' d escribe it but it froze my blood!—I've caught you lookin' at me like that so often lately. What are you thinkin' of when you look at me like that?

BRICK. I wasn't conscious of lookin' at you, Maggie.

MARGARET. Well, I *was* conscious of it! What were you thinkin'?

BRICK. I don't remember thinking of anything, Maggie.

MARGARET. Don't you think I know that—? Don't you—?—Think I know that—?

BRICK. *(coolly).* Know *what,* Maggie?

MARGARET. *(struggling for expression).* That I've gone through this—*hideous!*—transformation, become—hard! Frantic!

Then she adds, almost tenderly.

—cruel!!

That's what you've been observing in me lately. How could y' help but observe it? That's all right. I'm not—thin-skinned any more, can't afford t' be thin-skinned any more.

She is now recovering her power.

—But Brick? Brick?

BRICK. Did you say something?

MARGARET. I was *goin'* t' say something: that I get—lonely. Very!

BRICK. Ev'rybody gets that . . .

MARGARET. Living with someone you love can be lonelier—than living entirely *alone!*—if the one that y' love doesn't love you. . . .

There is a pause. BRICK *bobbles downstage and asks, without looking at her.*

BRICK. Would you like to live alone, Maggie?

Another pause: then—after she has caught a quick, hurt breath:

MARGARET. No!—God!—I wouldn't!

Another gasping breath. She forcibly controls what must have been an impulse to cry out. We see her deliberately, very forcibly, going all the way back to the world in which you can talk about ordinary matters.

Did you have a nice shower?

BRICK. Uh-huh.

MARGARET. Was the water cool?

BRICK. No.

MARGARET. But it made y' feel fresh, huh?

BRICK. Fresher. . . .

MARGARET. I know something would make y' feel *much* fresher!

BRICK. What?

MARGARET. An alcohol rub. Or cologne, a rub with cologne!

BRICK. That's good after a workout but I haven't been workin' out, Maggie.

MARGARET. You've kept in good shape, though.

BRICK. *(indifferently).* You think so, Maggie?

MARGARET. I always thought drinkin' men lost their looks, but I was plainly mistaken.

BRICK. *(wryly).* Why, thanks, Maggie.

MARGARET. You're the only drinkin' man I know that it never seems t' put fat on.

BRICK. I'm gettin' softer, Maggie.

MARGARET. Well, sooner or later it's bound to soften you up. It was just beginning to soften up Skipper when—

She stops short.

I'm sorry. I never could keep my fingers off a sore—I wish you *would* lose your looks. If you did it would make the martyrdom of Saint Maggie a little more bearable. But no such goddam luck. I actually believe you've gotten better looking since you've gone on the bottle. Yeah, a person who didn't know you would think you'd never had a tense nerve in your body or a strained muscle.

There are sounds of croquet on the lawn below: the click of mallets, light voices, near and distant.

Of course, you always had that detached quality as if you were playing a game without much concern over whether you won or lost, and now that you've lost the game, not lost but just quit playing, you have that rare sort of charm that usually only happens in very old or hopelessly sick people, the charm of the defeated.—You look so cool, so cool, so enviably cool.

REVEREND TOOKER. *(off stage right).* Now looka here, boy, lemme show you how to get outa that!

MARGARET. They're playing croquet. The moon has appeared and it's white, just beginning to turn a little bit yellow. . . .

You were a wonderful lover.

Such a wonderful person to go to bed with, and I think mostly because you were really indifferent to it. Isn't that right? Never had any anxiety about it, did it naturally, easily, slowly, with absolute confidence and perfect calm, more like opening a door for a lady or seating her at a table than giving expression to any longing for her. Your indifference made you wonderful at lovemaking—*strange?*—but true.

REVEREND TOOKER. Oh! That's a beauty.

DOCTOR BAUGH. Yeah. I got you boxed.

MARGARET. You know, if I thought you would never, never, *never* make love to me again—I would go downstairs to the kitchen and pick out the longest and sharpest knife I could find and stick it straight into my heart, I swear that I would!

REVEREND TOOKER. Watch out, you're gonna miss it.

DOCTOR BAUGH. You just don't know me, boy!

MARGARET. But one thing I don't have is the charm of the defeated, my hat is still in the ring, and I am determined to win!

There is the sound of croquet mallets hitting croquet balls.

REVEREND TOOKER. Mmm—You're too slippery for me.

MARGARET. —What is the victory of a cat on a hot tin roof?—I wish I knew. . . .

Just staying on it, I guess, as long as she can. . . .

DOCTOR BAUGH. Jus' like an eel, boy, jus' like an eel!

More croquet sounds.

MARGARET. Later tonight I'm going to tell you I love you an' maybe by that time you'll be drunk enough to believe me. Yes, they're playing croquet. . . .

Big Daddy is dying of cancer.

What were you thinking of when I caught you looking at me like that? Were you thinking of Skipper?

BRICK takes up his crutch, rises.

Oh, excuse me, forgive me, but laws of silence don't work! No, laws of silence don't work.

BRICK crosses to the bar, takes a quick drink, and rubs his head with a towel.

Laws of silence don't work.

When something is festering in your memory or your imagination, laws of silence don't work, it's just like shutting a door and locking it on a house on fire in hope of forgetting that the house is burning. But not facing a fire doesn't put it out. Silence about a thing just magnifies it. It grows and festers in silence, becomes malignant. . . .

He drops his crutch.

BRICK. Give me my crutch.

He has stopped rubbing his hair dry but still stands hanging onto the towel rack in a white towel-cloth robe.

MARGARET. Lean on me.

BRICK. No, just give me my crutch.

MARGARET. Lean on my shoulder.

BRICK. *I don't want to lean on your shoulder, I want my crutch!*
This is spoken like sudden lightning.

Are you going to give me my crutch or do I have to get down on my knees on the floor and—

MARGARET. *Here, here, take it, take it!*

She has thrust the crutch at him.

BRICK (*bobbling out*). Thanks. . . .

MARGARET. We mustn't scream at each other, the walls in this house have ears. . . .

He bobbles directly to liquor cabinet to get a new drink.

—but that's the first time I've heard you raise your voice in a long time, Brick. A crack in the wall?—Of composure?

—I think that's a good sign. . . .

A sign of nerves in a player on the defensive!

Brick turns and smiles at her coolly over his fresh drink.

BRICK. It just hasn't happened yet, Maggie.

MARGARET. What?

BRICK. The click I get in my head when I've had enough of this stuff to make me peaceful. . . . Will you do me a favor?

MARGARET. Maybe I will. What favor?

BRICK. Just, just keep your voice down!

MARGARET (*in a hoarse whisper*). I'll do you that favor, I'll speak in a whisper, if not shut up completely, if *you* will do *me* a favor and make that drink your last one till after the party.

BRICK. What party?

MARGARET. Big Daddy's birthday party.

BRICK. Is this Big Daddy's birthday?

MARGARET. You know this is Big Daddy's birthday!

BRICK. No, I don't, I forgot it.

MARGARET. Well, I remembered it for you. . . .

They are both speaking as breathlessly as a pair of kids after a fight, drawing deep exhausted breaths and looking at each other with faraway eyes, shaking and panting together as if they had broken apart from a violent struggle.

BRICK. Good for you, Maggie.

MARGARET. You just have to scribble a few lines on this card.

BRICK. You scribble something, Maggie.

MARGARET. It's got to be your handwriting; it's your present, I've given him my present; it's got to be your handwriting!

The tension between them is building again, the voices becoming shrill once more.

BRICK. I didn't get him a present.

MARGARET. I got one for you.

BRICK. All right. You write the card, then.

MARGARET. And have him know you didn't remember his birthday?

BRICK. I didn't remember his birthday.

MARGARET. You don't have to prove you didn't!

BRICK. I don't want to fool him about it.

MARGARET. Just write "Love, Brick!" for God's—

BRICK. No.

MARGARET. You've *got* to!

BRICK. I don't have to do anything I don't want to do. You keep forgetting the conditions on which I agreed to stay on living with you.

MARGARET. (*out before she knows it*). I'm not living with you. We occupy the same cage.

BRICK. You've got to remember the conditions agreed on.

SONNY. (*off stage*). Mommy, give it to me. I had it first.

MAE. Hush.

MARGARET. They're impossible conditions!

BRICK. Then why don't you—?

SONNY. I want it, I want it!

MAE. Get away!

MARGARET. HUSH! Who is out there? Is somebody at the door?

There are footsteps in hall.

MAE. (*outside*). May I enter a moment?

MARGARET. Oh, *you!* Sure. Come in, Mae.

MAE enters bearing aloft the bow of a young lady's archery set.

MAE. Brick, is this thing yours?

MARGARET. Why, Sister Woman—that's my Diana Trophy. Won it at the intercollegiate archery contest on the Ole Miss campus.

MAE. It's a mighty dangerous thing to leave exposed round a house full of nawmal rid-blooded children attracted t'weapons.

MARGARET. "Nawmal rid-blooded children attracted t'weapons" ought t'be taught to keep their hands off things that don't belong to them.

MAE. Maggie, honey, if you had children of your own you'd know how funny that is. Will you please lock this up and put the key out of reach?

MARGARET. Sister Woman, nobody is plotting the destruction of your kiddies.—Brick and I still have our special archers' license. We're goin' deer-huntin' on Moon Lake as soon as the season starts. I love to run with dogs through chilly woods, run, run leap over obstructions—

She goes into the closet carrying the bow.

MAE. How's the injured ankle, Brick?

BRICK. Doesn't hurt. Just itches.

MAE. Oh, my! Brick—Brick, you should've been downstairs after supper! Kiddies put on a show. Polly played the piano, Buster an' Sonny drums, an' then they turned out the lights an' Dixie an' Trixie puhfawmed a toe dance in fairy costume with *spahkluhs!* Big Daddy just beamed! He just beamed!

MARGARET. (*from the closet with a sharp laugh*). Oh, I bet. It breaks my heart that we missed it!

She reenters.

But Mae? Why did y' give dawgs' names to all your kiddies?

MAE. *Dogs'* names?

MARGARET. (*sweetly*). Dixie, Trixie, Buster, Sonny, Polly!—Sounds like four dogs and a parrot . . .

MAE. Maggie?

MARGARET. *turns with a smile.* Why are you so catty?

MARGARET. Cause I'm a cat! But why can't *you* take a joke, Sister Woman?

MAE. Nothin' pleases me more than a joke that's funny. You know the real names of our kiddies. Buster's real name is Robert. Sonny's real name is Saunders. Trixie's real name is Marlene and Dixie's—

GOOPER *downstairs calls for her.* "Hey, Mae! Sister Woman, intermission is over!"—*She rushes to door, saying:*

Intermission is over! See ya later!

MARGARET. I wonder what Dixie's real name is?

BRICK. Maggie, being catty doesn't help things any.

MARGARET. I know! *WHY!*—Am I so catty?—Cause I'm consumed with envy an' eaten up with longing?—Brick, I'm going to lay out your beautiful Shantung silk suit from Rome and one of your monogrammed silk shirts. I'll put your cuff links in it, those lovely star sapphires I get you to wear so rarely.

BRICK. I can't get trousers on over this plaster cast.

MARGARET. Yes, you can, I'll help you.

BRICK. I'm not going to get dressed, Maggie.

MARGARET. Will you just put on a pair of white silk pajamas?

BRICK. Yes, I'll do that, Maggie.

MARGARET. *Thank* you, thank you so *much!*

BRICK. Don't mention it.

MARGARET. *Oh, Brick!* How long does it have t' go on? This punishment? Haven't I done time enough, haven't I served my term, can't I apply for a—pardon?

BRICK. Maggie, you're spoiling my liquor. Lately your voice always sounds like you'd been running upstairs to warn somebody that the house was on fire!

MARGARET. Well, no wonder, no wonder. Y'know what I feel like, Brick?

I feel all the time like a cat on a hot tin roof!

BRICK. Then jump off the roof, jump off it, cats can jump off roofs and land on their four feet uninjured!

MARGARET. Oh, yes!

BRICK. Do it!—fo' God's sake, do it . . .

MARGARET. Do what?

BRICK. Take a lover!

MARGARET. I can't see a man but you! Even with my eyes closed, I just see you! Why don't you get ugly, Brick, why don't you please get fat or ugly or something so I could stand it?

She rushes to ball door, opens it, listens.

The concert is still going on! Bravo, no-necks, bravo!

She slams and locks door fiercely.

BRICK. What did you lock the door for?

MARGARET. To give us a little privacy for a while.

BRICK. You know better, Maggie.

MARGARET. No, I don't know better.

She rushes to gallery doors, draws the rose-silk drapes across them.

BRICK. Don't make a fool of yourself.

MARGARET. I don't mind makin' a fool of myself over you!

BRICK. I mind, Maggie. I feel embarrassed for you.

MARGARET. Feel embarrassed! But don't continue my torture. I can't live on and on under these circumstances.

BRICK. You agreed to——

MARGARET. I know but——

BRICK. ——Accept that condition!

MARGARET. I CAN'T! CAN'T! CAN'T!

She seizes his shoulder.

BRICK. Let go!

He breaks away from her and seizes the small boudoir chair and raises it like a lion-tamer facing a big circus cat.

Count five. She stares at him with her fist pressed to her mouth, then bursts into shrill, almost hysterical laughter. He remains grave for a moment, then grins and puts the chair down.

BIG MAMA *calls through closed door.*

BIG MAMA. Son? Son? Son?

BRICK. What is it, Big Mama?

BIG MAMA. *(outside).* Oh, son! We got the most wonderful news about Big Daddy. I just had t' run up an' tell you right this——

She rattles the knob.

——What's this door doin', locked, faw? You all think there's robbers in the house?

MARGARET. Big Mama, Brick is dressin', he's not dressed yet.

BIG MAMA. That's all right, it won't be the first time I've seen Brick not dressed. Come on, open this door!

MARGARET, with a grimace, goes to unlock and open the hall door, as BRICK hobbles rapidly to the bathroom and kicks the door shut. BIG MAMA has disappeared from the hall.

MARGARET. Big Mama?

BIG MAMA appears through the opposite gallery doors behind MARGARET, huffing and puffing like an old bulldog. She is a short, stout woman; her sixty years and 170 pounds have left her somewhat breathless most of the time; she's always tensed like a boxer, or rather, a Japanese wrestler. Her "family" was maybe a little superior to BIG DADDY'S, but not much. She wears a black or silver lace dress and at

least half a million in flashy gems. She is very sincere.

BIG MAMA. *(loudly, startling Margaret).* Here—I come through Gooper's and Mae's gall'ry door. Where's Brick? *Brick*—Hurry on out of there, son, I just have a second and want to give you the news about Big Daddy.—I hate locked doors in a house.

MARGARET. *(with affected lightness).* I've noticed you do, Big Mama, but people have got to have *some* moments of privacy, don't they?

BIG MAMA. No, ma'ma, not in *my* house. *(without pause)* Whacha took off you' dress faw? I thought that little lace dress was so sweet on yuh, honey.

MARGARET. I thought it looked sweet on me, too, but one of m' cute little table-partners used it for a napkin so—!

BIG MAMA. *(picking up stockings on floor).* What?

MARGARET. You know, Big Mama, Mae and Gooper's so touchy about those children—thanks, Big Mama . . .

BIG MAMA *has thrust the picked-up stockings in* MARGARET's *hand with a grunt.*

—that you just don't dare to suggest there's any room for improvement in their—

BIG MAMA. Brick, hurry out!—Shoot, Maggie, you just don't like children.

MARGARET. I do SO like children! Adore them!—well brought up!

BIG MAMA *(gentle—loving).* Well, why don't you have some and bring them up well, then, instead of all the time pickin' on Gooper's an' Mae's?

GOOPER. *(shouting up the stairs).* Hey, hey, Big Mama, Betsy an' Hugh got to go, waitin' t' tell yuh g'by!

BIG MAMA. Tell 'em to hold their hawses, I'll be right down in a jiffy!

GOOPER. Yes ma'am!

She turns to the bathroom door and calls out.

BIG MAMA. Son? Can you hear me in there?

There is a muffled answer.

We just got the full report from the laboratory at the Ochsner Clinic, completely negative, son, ev'rything negative, right on down the line! Nothin' a-tall's wrong with him but some little functional thing called a spastic colon. Can you hear me, son?

MARGARET. He can hear you, Big Mama.

BIG MAMA. Then why don't he say something? God Almighty, a piece of news like that should make him shout. It made *me* shout, I can tell you. I shouted and sobbed and fell right down on my knees!—Look!

She pulls up her skirt.

See the bruises where I hit my kneecaps? Took both doctors to haul me back on my feet! *She laughs—she always laughs like hell at herself.* Big Daddy was furious with me! But ain't that wonderful news?

Facing bathroom again, she continues:

After all the anxiety we been through to git a report like that on Big Daddy's birthday? Big Daddy tried to hide how much of a load that news took off his mind, but didn't fool *me*. He was mighty close to crying about it *himself!*

Goodbyes are shouted downstairs, and she rushes to door.

GOOPER. Big Mama!

BIG MAMA. *Hold those people down there, don't let them go!*—Now, git dressed, we're all comin' up to this room fo' Big Daddy's birthday party because of your ankle.—How's his ankle, Maggie!

MARGARET. Well, he broke it, Big Mama.

BIG MAMA. I know he broke it.

A phone is ringing in hall. A Negro voice answers: "Mistuh Polly's res'dence."

I mean does it hurt him much still.

MARGARET. I'm afraid I can't give you that information, Big Mama. You'll have to ask Brick if it hurts much still or not.

SOOKEY. *(in the hall).* It's Memphis, Mizz Polly, it's Miss Sally in Memphis.

BIG MAMA. Awright, Sookey.

BIG MAMA *rushes into the hall and is heard shouting on the phone:*

Hello, Miss Sally. How are you, Miss Sally?—Yes, well, I was just gonna call you about it. *Shoot!*—

MARGARET. Brick, don't!

Big Mama raises her voice to a bellow.

BIG MAMA. *Miss Sally? Don't ever call me from the Gayoso Lobby, too much talk goes on in that hotel lobby, no wonder you can't hear me!* Now listen, Miss Sally. They's nothin' serious wrong with BIG DADDY. We got the report just now, they's nothin' wrong but a thing called a—spastic! SPASTIC!—colon . . .

She appears at the hall door and calls to Margaret.

—Maggie, come out here and talk to that fool on the phone. I'm shouted breathless!

MARGARET *(goes out and is heard sweetly at phone).* Miss Sally? This is Brick's wife, Maggie. So nice to hear your voice. Can you hear *mine?* Well, good!—Big Mama just wanted you to know that they've got the report from the Ochsner Clinic and what Big Daddy has is a spastic colon. Yes. Spastic colon, Miss Sally. That's right, spastic colon. *G'bye, Miss Sally, hope I'll see you real soon!*

Hangs up a little before MISS SALLY *was probably ready to terminate the talk. She returns through the hall door.*

She heard me perfectly. I've discovered with deaf people the thing to do is not shout at them but just enunciate clearly. My rich old Aunt Cornelia was deaf as the dead but I could make her hear me just by sayin' each word slowly, distinctly, close to her ear. I read her the *Commercial Appeal* ev'ry night, read her the classified ads in it, even, she never missed a word of it. But was she a mean ole thing! Know what I got when she died? Her unexpired subscriptions to five magazines and the Book-of-the-Month Club and a LIBRARY full of ev'ry dull book ever written! All else went to her hellcat of a sister . . . meaner than she was, even!

BIG MAMA has been straightening things up in the room during this speech.

BIG MAMA *(closing closet door on discarded clothes).* Miss Sally sure is a case! Big Daddy says she's always got her hand out fo' something. He's not mistaken. That poor ole thing always has her hand out fo' somethin'. I don't think Big Daddy gives her as much as he should.

GOOPER. Big Mama! Come on now! Betsy and Hugh can't wait no longer!

BIG MAMA (*shouting*). I'm comin'!

She starts out. At the hall door, turns and jerks a forefinger, first toward the bathroom door, then toward the liquor cabinet, meaning: "Has BRICK *been drinking?"* MARGARET *pretends not to understand, cocks her head and raises her brows as if the pantomimic performance was completely mystifying to her.*

BIG MAMA *rushes back to* MARGARET:

Shoot! Stop playin' so dumb!—I mean has he been drinkin' that stuff much yet?

MARGARET [*with a little laugh*]. Oh! I think he had a highball after supper.

BIG MAMA. Don't laugh about it!—Some single men stop drinkin' when they git married and others start! Brick never touched liquor before he—!

MARGARET (*crying out*). *THAT'S NOT FAIR!*

BIG MAMA. Fair or not fair I want to ask you a question, one question: D'you make Brick happy in bed?

MARGARET. Why don't you ask if he makes *me* happy in bed?

BIG MAMA. Because I know that—

MARGARET. *It works both ways!*

BIG MAMA. Something's not right! You're childless and my son drinks!

GOOPER. Come on, Big Mama!

GOOPER *has called her downstairs and she has rushed to the door on the line above. She turns at the door and points at the bed.*

—When a marriage goes on the rocks, the rocks are *there,* right *there!*

MARGARET. *That's—*

BIG MAMA *has swept out of the room and slammed the door.*

—not—*fair . . .*

MARGARET *is alone, completely alone, and she feels it. She draws in, hunches her shoulders, raises her arms with fists clenched, shuts her eyes tight as a child about to be stabbed with a vaccination needle. When she opens her eyes again, what she sees is the long oval mirror and she rushes straight to it, stares into it with a grimace and says: "Who are you?"—*

Then she crouches a little and answers herself in a different voice which is high, thin, mocking: "I am Maggie the Cat!"—Straightens quickly as bathroom door opens a little and Bricks calls out to her.

BRICK. Has Big Mama gone?

MARGARET. She's gone.

He opens the bathroom door and hobbles out, with his liquor glass now empty, straight to the liquor cabinet. He is whistling softly. MARGARET's *head pivots on her long, slender throat to watch him.*

She raises a hand uncertainly to the base of her throat, as if it was difficult for her to swallow, before she speaks.

You know, our sex life didn't just peter out in the usual way, it was cut off short, long before the natural time for it to, and it's going to revive again, just as sudden as that. I'm confident of it. That's what I'm keeping myself attractive for. For the time when you'll see me again like other men see me. Yes, like other men see me. They still see me, Brick, and they like what they see. Uh-huh. Some of them would give their—

Look, Brick!

She stands before the long oval mirror, touches her breast and then her hips with her two hands.

How high my body stays on me!—Nothing has fallen on me—not a fraction. . . .

Her voice is soft and trembling: a pleading child's. At this moment as he turns to glance at her—a look which is like a player passing a ball to another player, third down and goal to go—she has to capture the audience in a grip so tight that she can hold it till the first intermission without any lapse of attention.

Other men still want me. My face looks strained, sometimes, but I've kept my figure as well as you've kept yours, and men admire it. I still turn heads on the street. Why, last week in Memphis everywhere that I went men's eyes burned holes in my clothes, at the country club and in restaurants and department stores, there wasn't a man I met or walked by that didn't just eat me up with his eyes and turn around when I passed him and look back at me. Why, at Alice's party for her New York cousins, the best-lookin' man in the crowd— followed me upstairs and tried to force his way in the powder room with me, followed me to the door and tried to force his way in!

BRICK. Why didn't you let him, Maggie?

MARGARET. Because I'm not that common, for one thing. Not that I wasn't almost tempted to. You like to know who it was? It was Sonny Boy Maxwell, that's who!

BRICK. Oh, yeah, Sonny Boy Maxwell, he was a good end-runner but had a little injury to his back and had to quit.

MARGARET. He has no injury now and has no wife and still has a lech for me!

BRICK. I see no reason to lock him out of a powder room in that case.

MARGARET. And have someone catch me at it? I'm not that stupid. Oh, I might sometime cheat on you with someone, since you're so insultingly eager to have me do it!—But if I do, you can be damned sure it will be in a place and a time where no one but me and the man could possibly know. Because I'm not going to give you any excuse to divorce me for being unfaithful or anything else....

BRICK. Maggie, I wouldn't divorce you for being unfaithful or anything else. Don't you know that? Hell. I'd be relieved to know that you'd found yourself a lover.

MARGARET. Well, I'm taking no chances. No, I'd rather stay on this hot tin roof.

BRICK. A hot tin roof's 'n uncomfo'table place t' stay on....

He starts to whistle softly.

MARGARET. *(through his whistle).* Yeah, but I can stay on it just as long as I have to.

BRICK. You could leave me, Maggie.

He resumes whistle. She wheels about to glare at him.

MARGARET. *Don't want to and will not!* Besides if I did, you don't have a cent to pay for it but what you get from Big Daddy and he's dying of cancer!

For the first time a realization of Big Daddy's doom seems to penetrate to Brick's consciousness, visibly, and he looks at Margaret.

BRICK. Big Mama just said he *wasn't,* that the report was okay.

MARGARET. That's what she thinks because she got the same story that they gave Big Daddy. And was just as taken in by it as he was, poor ole things.... But tonight they're going to tell her the truth about it. When Big Daddy goes to bed, they're going to tell her that he is dying of cancer.

She slams the dresser drawer.

—It's malignant and it's terminal.

BRICK. Does Big Daddy know it?

MARGARET. Hell, do they *ever* know it? Nobody says, "You're dying." You have to fool them. They have to fool *themselves.*

BRICK. Why?

MARGARET. *Why?* Because human beings dream of life everlasting, that's the reason! But most of them want it on earth and not in heaven.

He gives a short, hard laugh at her touch of humor.

Well.... *(She touches up her mascara).* That's how it is, anyhow.... *(She looks about).* Where did I put down my cigarette? Don't want to burn up the home-place, at least not with Mae and Gooper and their five monsters in it!

She has found it and sucks at it greedily. Blows out smoke and continues:

So this is Big Daddy's last birthday. And Mae and Gooper, they know it, oh, *they* know it, all right. They got the first information from the Ochsner Clinic. That's why they rushed down here with their no-neck monsters. Because. Do you know something? Big Daddy's made no will? Big Daddy's never made out any will in his life, and so this campaign's afoot to impress him, forcibly as possible, with the fact that you drink and I've borne no children!

He continues to stare at her a moment, then mutters something sharp but not audible and hobbles rather rapidly out onto the long gallery in the fading, much faded, gold light.

MARGARET. *(continuing her liturgical chant).* Y'know, I'm *fond* of Big Daddy, I am genuinely fond of that old man, I really *am,* you know....

BRICK *(faintly, vaguely).* Yes, I know you are....

MARGARET. I've always sort of admired him in spite of his coarseness, his four-letter words and so forth. Because Big Daddy *is* what he *is*, and he makes no bones about it. He hasn't turned gentleman farmer, he's still a Mississippi redneck, as much of a redneck as he must have been when he was just overseer here on the old Jack Straw and Peter Ochello place. But he got hold of it an' built it into th' biggest an' finest plantation in the Delta.—I've always *liked* Big Daddy. . . .

She crosses to the proscenium.

Well, this is Big Daddy's last birthday. I'm sorry about it. But I'm facing the facts. It takes money to take care of a drinker and that's the office that I've been elected to lately.

BRICK. You don't have to take care of me.

MARGARET. Yes, I do. Two people in the same boat have got to take care of each other. At least you want money to buy more Echo Spring when this supply is exhausted, or will you be satisfied with a ten-cent beer?

Mae an' Gooper are plannin' to freeze us out of Big Daddy's estate because you drink and I'm childless. But we can defeat that plan. We're *going* to defeat that plan!

Brick, y'know, I've been so God damn disgustingly poor all my life!—That's the *truth*, Brick!

BRICK. I'm not sayin' it isn't.

MARGARET. Always had to suck up to people I couldn't stand because they had money and I was poor as Job's turkey. You don't know what that's like. Well, I'll tell you, it's like you would feel a thousand miles away from Echo Spring!—And had to get back to it on that broken ankle without a crutch!

That's how it feels to be as poor as Job's turkey and have to suck up to relatives that you hated because they had money and all you had was a bunch of hand-me-down clothes and a few old moldly three-per-cent government bonds. My daddy loved his liquor, he fell in love with his liquor the way you've fallen in love with Echo Spring!—And my poor Mama, having to maintain some semblance of social position, to keep appearances up, on an income of one hundred and fifty dollars a month on those old government bonds!

When I came out, the year that I made my debut, I had just two evening dresses! One Mother made me from a pattern in *Vogue*, the other a hand-me-down from a snotty rich cousin I hated!

—The dress that I married you in was my grandmother's weddin' gown. . . .

So that's why I'm like a cat on a hot tin roof!

BRICK is still on the gallery. Someone below calls up to him in a warm Negro voice, "Hiya, Mistuh BRICK, how yuh feelin'?" BRICK raises his liquor glass as if that answered the question.

MARGARET. You can be young without money, but you can't be old without it. You've got to be old *with* money because to be old without it is just too awful, you've got to be one or the other, either *young* or *with money*, you can't be old and *without* it.—That's the *truth*, Brick. . . .

BRICK *whistles softly, vaguely.*

Well, now I'm dressed, I'm all dressed, there's nothing else for me to do.

Forlornly, almost fearfully.

I'm dressed, all dressed, nothing else for me to do. . . .

She moves about restlessly, aimlessly, and speaks, as if to herself.

What am I——? Oh!——my bracelets.

She starts working a collection of bracelets over her hands onto her wrists, about six on each, as she talks.

I've thought a whole lot about it and now I know when I made my mistake. Yes, I made my mistake when I told you the truth about that thing with Skipper. Never should have confessed it, a fatal error, tellin' you about that thing with Skipper.

BRICK. Maggie, shut up about Skipper. I mean it, Maggie; you got to shut up about Skipper.

MARGARET. You ought to understand that Skipper and I—

BRICK. You don't think I'm serious, Maggie? You're fooled by the fact that I am saying this quiet? Look, Maggie. What you're doing is a dangerous thing to do. You're—you're—you're—foolin' with something that nobody ought to fool with.

MARGARET. This time I'm going to finish what I have to say to you. Skipper and I made love, if love you could call it, because it made both of us feel a little bit closer to you. You see, you son of a bitch, you asked too much of people, of me, of him, of all the unlucky poor damned sons of bitches that happen to love you, and there was a whole pack of them, yes, there was a pack of them besides me and Skipper, you asked too goddam much of people that loved you, you—superior creature!—you godlike being!—And so we made love to each other to dream it was you, both of us! Yes, yes, yes! Truth, truth! What's so awful about it? I like it, I think the truth is—yeah! I shouldn't have told you.…

BRICK (*holding his head unnaturally still and uptilted a bit*). It was Skipper that told me about it. Not you, Maggie.

MARGARET. I told you!

BRICK. After he told me!

MARGARET. What does it matter who—?

DIXIE. I got your mallet, I got your mallet.

TRIXIE. Give it to me, give it to me. IT's mine.

BRICK turns suddenly out upon the gallery and calls:

BRICK. Little girl! Hey, little girl!

LITTLE GIRL (*at a distance*). What, Uncle Brick?

BRICK. Tell the folks to come up!—Bring everybody upstairs!

TRIXIE. It's mine, it's mine.

MARGARET. I can't stop myself! I'd go on telling you this in front of them all, if I had to!

BRICK. Little girl! Go on, go on, will you? Do what I told you, call them!

DIXIE. Okay.

MARGARET. Because it's got to be told and you, you!—you never let me!

She sobs, then controls herself, and continues almost calmly.

It was one of those beautiful, ideal things they tell about in the Greek legends, it couldn't be anything else, you being you, and that's what made it so sad, that's what made it so awful, because it was love that never could be carried through to anything satisfying or even talked about plainly.

BRICK. Maggie, you gotta stop this.

MARGARET. Brick, I tell you, you got to believe me, Brick, I *do* understand all about it! I—I think it was—*noble!* Can't you tell I'm sincere when I say I respect it? My only point, the only point that I'm making, is life has got to be allowed to continue even after the *dream* of life is—all— over.

BRICK *is without his crutch. Leaning on furniture, he crosses to pick it up as she continues as if possessed by a will outside herself.*

Why I remember when we double-dated at college, Gladys Fitzgerald and I and you and Skipper, it was more like a date between you and Skipper. Gladys and I were just sort of tagging along as if it was necessary to chaperone you!—to make a good public impression—

BRICK (*turns to face her, half lifting his crutch*). Maggie, you want me to hit you with this crutch? Don't you know I could kill you with this crutch?

MARGARET. Good Lord, man, d' you think I'd care if you did?

BRICK. One man has one great good true thing in his life. One great good thing which is true!—I had friendship with Skipper.—You are naming it dirty!

MARGARET. I'm not naming it dirty! I am naming it clean.

BRICK. Not love with you, Maggie, but friendship with Skipper was that one great true thing, and you are naming it dirty!

MARGARET. Then you haven't been listenin', not understood what I'm saying! I'm naming it so damn clean that it killed poor Skipper!—You two had something that had to be kept on ice, yes, incorruptible, yes!—and death was the only icebox where you could keep it.…

BRICK. I married you, Maggie. Why would I marry you, Maggie, if I was—?

MARGARET. Brick, let me finish!—I know, believe me I know, that it was only Skipper that harbored even any *unconscious* desire for anything not perfectly pure between you two!—Now let me skip a little. You married me early that summer we graduated out of Ole Miss, and we were happy, weren't we, we were blissful, yes, hit heaven together ev'ry time that we loved! But that fall you an' Skipper turned down wonderful offers of jobs in order to keep on bein' football heroes—pro-football heroes. You organized the Dixie Stars that fall, so you could keep on bein' teammates forever! But somethin' was not right with it!—*Me included!*—between you. Skipper began hittin' the bottle . . . you got a spinal injury—couldn't play the Thanks-givin' game in Chicago, watched it on TV from a traction bed in Toledo. I joined Skipper. The Dixie Stars lost because poor Skipper was drunk. We drank together that night all night in the bar of the Blackstone and when cold day was comin' up over the Lake an' we were comin' out drunk to take a dizzy look at it, I said, "SKIPPER! STOP LOVIN' MY HUSBAND OR TELL HIM HE'S GOT TO LET YOU ADMIT IT TO HIM!"—one way or another!

HE SLAPPED ME HARD ON THE MOUTH!—then turned and ran without stopping once, I am sure, all the way back into his room at the Blackstone.

—When I came to his room that night, with a little scratch like a shy little mouse at his door, he made that pitiful, ineffectual little attempt to prove that what I had said wasn't true. . . .
Brick strikes at her with crutch, a blow that shatters the gemlike lamp on the table.

—In this way, I destroyed him, by telling him truth that he and his world which he was born and raised in, your and his world, had told him could not be told?

—From then on Skipper was nothing at all but a receptacle for liquor and drugs. . . .
—*Who shot cock robin? I with my—*
She throws back her head with tight shut eyes.
—*merciful arrow!*
Brick strikes at her; misses.

Missed me!—Sorry,—I'm not tryin' to whitewash my behavior, Christ, no! Brick, I'm not good. I don't know why people have to pretend to be good, nobody's good. The rich or the well-to-do can afford to respect moral patterns, conventional moral patterns, but I could never afford to, yeah, but—I'm honest! Give me credit for just that, will you *please*?—Born poor, raised poor, expect to die poor unless I manage to get us something out of

what Big Daddy leaves when he dies of cancer! But Brick?!—*Skipper is dead! I'm alive!* Maggie the cat is—
Brick hops awkwardly forward and strikes at her again with his crutch.
—alive! I am alive, alive! I am . . .
He hurls the crutch at her, across the bed she took refuge behind, and pitches forward on the floor as she completes her speech.
—alive!
A little girl, Dixie, bursts into the room, wearing an Indian war bonnet and firing a cap pistol at Margaret and shouting: "Bang, bang, bang!"
Laughter downstairs floats through the open hall door. MARGARET had crouched gasping to bed at child's entrance. She now rises and says with cool fury:

Little girl, your mother or someone should teach you—(*gasping*)—to knock at a door before you come into a room. Otherwise people might think that you—lack—good breeding. . . .

DIXIE. Yanh, yanh, yanh, what is Uncle Brick doin' on th' floor?

BRICK. I tried to kill your Aunt Maggie, but I failed—and I fell. Little girl, give me my crutch so I can get up off th' floor.

MARGARET. Yes, give your uncle his crutch, he's a cripple, honey, he broke his ankle last night jumping hurdles on the high school athletic field!

DIXIE. What were you jumping hurdles for, Uncle Brick?

BRICK. Because I used to jump them, and people like to do what they used to do, even after they've stopped being able to do it. . . .

MARGARET. That's right, that's your answer, now go away, little girl.

DIXIE fires cap pistol at MARGARET three times.
Stop, you stop that, monster! You little no-neck monster!
She seizes the cap pistol and hurls it through gallery doors.

DIXIE (*with a precocious instinct for the cruelest thing*). You're *jealous*!—You're just jealous because you can't have babies!

She sticks out her tongue at MARGARET *as she sashays past her with her stomach stuck out, to the gallery.* MARGARET *slams the gallery doors and leans panting against them. There is a pause. Brick has replaced his spilt drink and sits, faraway, on the great four-poster bed.*

MARGARET. You see?—they gloat over us being childless, even in front of their five little no-neck monsters!

Pause. Voices approach on the stairs.

Brick?—I've been to a doctor in Memphis, a—a gynecologist. . . .
I've been completely examined, and there is no reason why we can't have a child whenever we want one. And this is my time by the calendar to conceive. Are you listening to me? Are you? Are you LISTENING TO ME!

BRICK. Yes. I hear you, Maggie.

His attention returns to her inflamed face.

—But how in hell on earth do you imagine—that you're going to have a child by a man that can't stand you?

MARGARET. That's a problem that I will have to work out.

She wheels about to face the hall door.

MAE (*off stage left*). Come on, Big Daddy. We're all goin' up to Brick's room.

From off stage left, voices: REVEREND TOOKER, DOCTOR BAUGH, *Mae.*

MARGARET. *Here they come!*

The lights dim.

CURTAIN.

ACT TWO

There is no lapse of time. Margaret and Brick are in the same positions they held at the end of Act I.

MARGARET. (*at door*). Here they come!

BIG DADDY *appears first, a tall man with a fierce, anxious look, moving carefully not to betray his weakness even, or especially, to himself.*

GOOPER. I read in the *Register* that you're getting a new memorial window.

Some of the people are approaching through the hall, others along the gallery: voices from both directions. Gooper and Reverend Tooker become visible outside gallery doors, and their voices come in clearly.

They pause outside as GOOPER *lights a cigar.*

REVEREND TOOKER (*vivaciously*). Oh, but St. Paul's in Grenada has three memorial windows, and the latest one is a Tiffany stained-glass window that cost twenty-five hundred dollars, a picture of Christ the Good Shepherd with a Lamb in His arms.

MARGARET. Big Daddy.

BIG DADDY. Well, Brick.

BRICK. Hello Big Daddy.—Congratulations!

BIG DADDY. —Crap. . . .

GOOPER. Who give that window, Preach?

REVEREND TOOKER. Clyde Fletcher's widow. Also presented St. Paul's with a baptismal font.

GOOPER. Y'know what somebody ought t' give your church is a *coolin'* system, Preach.

MAE (*almost religiously*). —Let's see now, they've had their *tyyy*-phoid shots, and their tetanus shots, their diphtheria shots and their hepatitis shots and their polio shots, they got *those* shots every month from May through September, and—Gooper? Hey! Gooper!—What all have the kiddies been shot faw?

REVEREND TOOKER. Yes, siree, Bob! And y'know what Gus Hamma's family gave in his memory to the church at Two Rivers? A complete new stone parish-house with a basketball court in the basement and a—

BIG DADDY (*uttering a loud barking laugh which is far from truly mirthful*). Hey, Preach! What's all this talk about memorials, Preach? Y 'think somebody's about t' kick off around here? 'S that it?

Startled by this interjection, REVEREND TOOKER *decides to laugh at the question almost as loud as he can.*

How he would answer the question we'll never know, as he's spared that embarrassment by the voice of GOOPER'S *wife,* MAE, *rising high and clear as she appears with "Doc" Baugh, the family doctor, through the hall door.*

MARGARET. (*overlapping a bit*). Turn on the hi-fi, Brick! Let's have some music t' start off th' party with!

BRICK. You turn it on, Maggie.

The talk becomes so general that the room sounds like a great aviary of chattering birds. Only BRICK *remains unengaged, leaning upon the liquor cabinet with his faraway smile, an ice cube in a paper napkin with which he now and then rubs his forehead. He doesn't respond to* MARGARET'S *command. She bounds forward and stoops over the instrument panel of the console.*

GOOPER. We gave 'em that thing for a third anniversary present, got three speakers in it.

The room is suddenly blasted by the climax of a Wagnerian opera or a Beethoven symphony.

BIG DADDY. *Turn that dam thing off!*

Almost instant silence, almost instantly broken by the shouting charge of BIG MAMA, *entering through hall door like a charging rhino.*

BIG MAMA. *Wha's my Brick, wha's mah precious baby!!*

BIG DADDY. *Sorry! Turn it back on!*

Everyone laughs very loud. BIG DADDY *is famous for his jokes at* BIG MAMA'S *expense, and nobody laughs louder at these jokes than Big Mama herself, though sometimes they're pretty cruel and* BIG MAMA *has to pick up or fuss with something to cover the hurt that the loud laugh doesn't quite cover.*

On this occasion, a happy occasion because the dread in her heart has also been lifted by the false report on Big Daddy's condition, she giggles, grotesquely, coyly, in BIG DADDY'S *direction and bears down upon* BRICK, *all very quick and alive.*

BIG MAMA. Here he is, here's my precious baby! What's that you've got in your hand? You put that liquor down, son, your hand was made fo' holdin' somethin' better than that!

GOOPER. Look at Brick put it down!

BRICK *has obeyed* BIG MAMA *by draining the glass and handing it to her. Again everyone laughs, some high, some low.*

BIG MAMA. Oh, you bad boy, you, you're my bad little boy. Give Big Mama a kiss, you bad boy, you!—Look at him shy away, will you? Brick never liked bein' kissed or made a fuss over, I guess because he's always had too much of it! Son, you turn that thing off!

BRICK *has switched on the TV set.*

I can't stand TV, radio was bad enough but TV has gone it one better, I mean—(*plops wheezing in chair*)—one worse, ha ha! Now what'm I sittin' down here faw? I want t' sit next to my sweetheart on the sofa, hold hands with him and love him up a little!

BIG MAMA *has on a black and white figured chiffon. The large irregular patterns, like the markings of some massive animal, the luster of her great diamonds and many pearls, the brilliants set in the silver frames of her glasses, her riotous voice, booming laugh, have dominated the room since she entered.* BIG DADDY *has been regarding her with a steady grimace of chronic annoyance.*

BIG MAMA (*still louder*). Preacher, Preacher, hey, Preach! Give me you' hand an' help me up from this chair!

REVEREND TOOKER. None of your tricks, Big Mama!

BIG MAMA. What tricks? You give me you' hand so I can get up an'—

REVEREND TOOKER *extends her his hand. She grabs it and pulls him into her lap with a shrill laugh that spans an octave in two notes.*

Ever seen a preacher in a fat lady's lap? Hey, hey, folks! Ever seen a preacher in a fat lady's lap?

BIG MAMA *is notorious throughout the Delta for this sort of inelegant horseplay.* MARGARET *looks on with indulgent humor, sipping Dubonnet "on the rocks" and watching Brick, but* MAE *and* GOOPER *exchange signs of humorless anxiety over these antics, the sort of behavior which* MAE *thinks may account for their failure to quite get in with the smartest young married set in Memphis, despite all. One of the Negroes,* LACY *or* SOOKEY, *peeks in, cackling. They are waiting for a sign to bring in the cake and champagne. But* BIG DADDY'S *not amused. He doesn't understand why, in spite of the infinite mental relief he's received from the doctor's report, he still has these same old fox teeth in his guts. "This spastic condition is something else," he says to himself, but aloud he roars at* BIG MAMA.

BIG DADDY. *BIG MAMA, WILL YOU QUIT HORSIN'?—*You're too old an' too fat fo' that sort of crazy kid stuff an' besides a woman with your blood pressure—she had two hundred last spring!—is riskin' a stroke when you mess around like that.

MAE blows on a pitch pipe.

BIG MAMA. *Here comes Big Daddy's birthday!*

Negroes in white jackets enter with an enormous birthday cake ablaze with candles and carrying buckets of champagne with satin ribbons about the bottle necks.

MAE and GOOPER strike up song, and everybody, including the Negroes and Children, joins in. Only BRICK remains aloof.

EVERYONE. Happy birthday to you.
Happy birthday to you.
Happy birthday, Big Daddy—

Some sing: "Dear, Big Daddy!"
Happy birthday to you.

Some sing: "How old are you?"

MAE has come down center and is organizing her children like a chorus. She gives them a barely audible: "One, two, three!" and they are off in the new tune.

CHILDREN. Skinamarinka—dinka—dink
Skinamarinka—do
We love you.
Skinamarinka—dinka—dink
Skinamarinka—do.

All together, they turn to Big Daddy.
Big Daddy, you!

They turn back front, like a musical comedy chorus.

We love you in the morning;
We love you in the night.
We love you when we're with you,
And we love you out of sight.
Skinamarinka—dinka—dink
Skinamarinka—do.

MAE turns to BIG MAMA.
Big Mama, too!

BIG MAMA bursts into tears. The Negroes leave.

BIG DADDY. Now Ida, what the hell is the matter with you?

MAE. She's just so happy.

BIG MAMA. I'm just so happy, Big Daddy, I have to cry or something.

Sudden and loud in the hush:

Brick, do you know the wonderful news that Doc Baugh got from the clinic about Big Daddy? Big Daddy's one hundred per cent!

MARGARET. Isn't that wonderful?

BIG MAMA. He's just one hundred per cent. Passed the examination with flying colors. Now that we know there's nothing wrong with Big Daddy but a spastic colon, I can tell you something. I was worried sick, half out of my mind, for fear that Big Daddy might have a thing like—

MARGARET cuts through this speech, jumping up and exclaiming shrilly.

MARGARET. Brick, honey, aren't you going to give Big Daddy his birthday present?

Passing by him, she snatches his liquor glass from him.

She picks up a fancily wrapped package.

Here it is, Big Daddy, this is from Brick!

BIG MAMA. This is the biggest birthday Big Daddy's ever had, a hundred presents and bushels of telegrams from—

MAE *(at same time).* What is it, Brick?

GOOPER. I bet 500 to 50 that Brick don't *know* what it is.

BIG MAMA. The fun of presents is not knowing what they are till you open the package. Open your present, Big Daddy.

BIG DADDY. Open it you'self. I want to ask Brick something! Come here, Brick.

MARGARET. Big Daddy's callin' you, Brick.

She is opening the package.

BRICK. Tell Big Daddy I'm crippled.

BIG DADDY. I see you're crippled. I want to know how you got crippled.

MARGARET *(making diversionary tactics).* Oh, look, oh, look, why, it's a cashmere robe!

She holds the robe up for all to see.

MAE. You sound surprised, Maggie.

MARGARET. I never saw one before.

MAE. That's funny.—*Hah!*

MARGARET. *(turning on her fiercely, with a brilliant smile).* Why is it funny? All my family ever had was family—and luxuries such as cashmere robes still surprise me!

BIG DADDY *(ominously).* Quiet!

MAE *(heedless in her fury).* I don't see how you could be so surprised when you bought it yourself at Loewenstein's in Memphis last Saturday. You know how I know?

BIG DADDY. I said, Quiet!

MAE. —I know because the salesgirl that sold it to you waited on me and said, Oh, Mrs. Pollitt, your sister-in-law just bought a cashmere robe for your husband's father!

MARGARET. Sister Woman! Your talents are wasted as a housewife and mother, you really ought to be with the FBI or——

BIG DADDY. QUIET!

REVEREND TOOKER's reflexes are slower than the others'. He finishes a sentence after the bellow.

REVEREND TOOKER *(To Doc Baugh).* —the Stork and the Reaper are running neck and neck!

He starts to laugh gaily when he notices the silence and BIG DADDY'S glare. His laugh dies falsely.

BIG DADDY. Preacher, I hope I'm not butting in on more talk about memorial stained-glass windows, am I, Preacher?

REVEREND TOOKER laughs feebly, then coughs dryly in the embarrassed silence.

Preacher?

BIG MAMA. Now, Big Daddy, don't you pick on Preacher!

BIG DADDY *(raising his voice).* You ever hear that expression all hawk and no spit? You bring that expression to mind with that little dry cough of yours, all hawk an' no spit. . . .

The pause is broken only by a short startled laugh from MARGARET, the only one there who is conscious of and amused by the grotesque.

MAE *(raising her arms and jangling her bracelets).* I wonder if the mosquitoes are active tonight?

BIG DADDY. What's that, Little Mama? Did you make some remark?

MAE. Yes, I said I wondered if the mosquitoes would eat us alive if we went out on the gallery for a while.

BIG DADDY. Well, if they do, I'll have your bones pulverized for fertilizer!

BIG MAMA *(quickly).* Last week we had an airplane spraying the place and I think it done some good, at least I haven't had a——

BIG DADDY *(cutting her speech).* Brick, they tell me, if what they tell me is true, that you done some jumping last night on the high school athletic field?

BIG MAMA. Brick, Big Daddy is talking to you, son.

BRICK *(smiling vaguely over his drink).* What was that, Big Daddy?

BIG DADDY. They said you done some jumping on the high school track field last night.

BRICK. That's what they told me, too.

BIG DADDY. Was it jumping or humping that you were doing out there? What were doing out there at three A.M., layin' a woman on that cinder track?

BIG MAMA. Big Daddy, you are off the sick-list, now, and I'm not going to excuse you for talkin' so——

BIG DADDY. Quiet!

BIG MAMA. —nasty in front of Preacher and——

BIG DADDY. QUIET!—I ast you, Brick, if you was cuttin' you'self a piece o' poon-tang last night on that cinder track? I thought maybe you were chasin' poon-tang on that track an' tripped over something in the heat of the chase—'sthat it?

GOOPER laughs, loud and false, others nervously following suit. BIG MAMA stamps her foot, and purses her lips, crossing to MAE and whispering something to her as BRICK meets his father's hard, intent, grinning stare with a slow, vague smile that he offers all situations from behind the screen of his liquor.

BRICK. No, sir, I don't think so. . . .

MAE *(at the same time, sweetly).* Reverend Tooker, let's you and I take a stroll on the widow's walk.

She and the preacher go out on the gallery as BIG DADDY *says:*

BIG DADDY. Then what the hell were you doing out there at three o'clock in the morning?

BRICK. Jumping the hurdles, Big Daddy, runnin' and jumpin' the hurdles, but those high hurdles have gotten too high for me, now.

BIG DADDY. Cause you was drunk?

BRICK (*his vague smile fading a little*). Sober I wouldn't have tried to jump the *low* ones. . . .

BIG MAMA (*quickly*). Big Daddy, blow out the candles on your birthday cake!

MARGARET. (*at the same time*). I want to propose a toast to Big Daddy Pollitt on his sixty-fifth birthday, the biggest cotton planter in—

BIG DADDY (*bellowing with fury and disgust*). I told you to stop it, now stop it, quit this—!

BIG MAMA (*coming in front of Big Daddy with the cake*). Big Daddy, I will not allow you to talk that way, not even on your birthday, I—

BIG DADDY. I'll talk like I want to on my birthday, Ida, or any other goddam day of the year and anybody here that don't like it knows what they can do!

BIG MAMA. You don't mean that!

BIG DADDY. What makes you think I don't mean it?

Meanwhile various discreet signals have been exchanged and GOOPER *has also gone out on the gallery.*

BIG MAMA. I just know you don't mean it.

BIG DADDY. You don't know a goddam thing and you never did!

BIG MAMA. Big Daddy, you don't mean that.

BIG DADDY. Oh, yes, I do, oh, yes, I do, I mean it! I put up with a whole lot of crap around here because I thought I was dying. And you thought I was dying and you started taking over, well, you can stop taking over now, Ida, because I'm not gonna die, you can just stop now this business of taking over because you're not taking over because I'm not dying, I went through the laboratory and the goddam exploratory operation and there's nothing wrong with me but a spastic

colon. And I'm not dying of cancer which you thought I was dying of. Ain't that so? Didn't you think that I was dying of cancer, Ida?

Almost everybody is out on the gallery but the two old people glaring at each other across the blazing cake.

BIG MAMA's *chest heaves and she presses a fat fist to her mouth.*

BIG DADDY *continues, hoarsely:*

Ain't that so, Ida? Didn't you have an idea I was dying of cancer and now you could take control of this place and everything on it? I got that impression, I seemed to get that impression. Your loud voice everywhere, your fat old body butting in here and there!

BIG MAMA. Hush! The Preacher!

BIG DADDY. Fuck the goddam preacher!

BIG MAMA *gasps loudly and sits down on the sofa which is almost too small for her.*

Did you hear what I said? I said fuck the goddam preacher!

Somebody closes the gallery doors from outside just as there is a burst of fireworks and excited cries from the children.

BIG MAMA. I never seen you act like this before and I can't think what's got in you!

BIG DADDY. I went through all that laboratory and operation and all just so I would know if you or me was boss here! Well, now it turns out that I am and you ain't—and that's my birthday present—and my cake and champagne!—because for three years now you been gradually taking over. Bossing. Talking. Sashaying your fat old body around the place I made! I made this place! I was overseer on it! I was the overseer on the old Straw and Ochello plantation. I quit school at ten! I quit school at ten years old and went to work like a nigger in the fields. And I rose to be overseer of the Straw and Ochello plantation. And old Straw died and I was Ochello's partner and the place got bigger and bigger and bigger and bigger and bigger! I did all that myself with no goddam help from you, and now you think you're just about to take over. Well, I am just about to tell you that you are not just about to take over, you are not just about to take over a God damn thing. Is that clear to you, Ida? Is that very plain to you, now? Is that understood completely? I been through the laboratory from A to Z. I've had the goddam exploratory operation, and nothing is wrong with me but a spastic colon——made spastic, I guess, by *disgust!* By all the goddam lies and liars that I have had to put up with, and all the goddam hypocrisy that I lived with all these forty years that we been livin' together! Hey! Ida!! Blow out the candles on the birthday cake! Purse up your lips and draw a deep breath and blow out the goddam candles on the cake!

BIG MAMA. Oh, Big Daddy, oh, oh, oh, Big Daddy!

BIG DADDY. What's the matter with you?

BIG MAMA. *In all these years you never believed that I loved You??*

BIG DADDY. Huh?

BIG MAMA. *And I did, I did so much, I did love you!*—I even loved your hate and your hardness, Big Daddy!

She sobs and rushes awkwardly out onto the gallery.

BIG DADDY (*to himself*). *Wouldn't it be funny if that was true. . . .*

A pause is followed by a burst of light in the sky from the fireworks.

BRICK! HEY, BRICK!

He stands over his blazing birthday cake.

After some moments, BRICK *hobbles in on his crutch, holding his glass.*

MARGARET *follows him with a bright, anxious smile.*

I didn't call you, Maggie. I called Brick.

MARGARET. I'm just delivering him to you.

She kisses BRICK *on the mouth which he immediately wipes with the back of his hand. She flies girlishly back out.* BRICK *and his father are alone.*

BIG DADDY. Why did you do that?

BRICK. Do what, Big Daddy?

BIG DADDY. Wipe her kiss off your mouth like she'd spit on you.

BRICK. I don't know. I wasn't conscious of it.

BIG DADDY. That woman of yours has a better shape on her than Gooper's but somehow or other they got the same look about them.

BRICK. What sort of look is that, Big Daddy?

BIG DADDY. I don't know how to describe it but it's the same look.

BRICK. They don't look peaceful, do they?

BIG DADDY. No, they sure in hell don't.

BRICK. They look nervous as cats?

BIG DADDY. That's right, they look nervous as cats.

BRICK. Nervous as a couple of cats on a hot tin roof?

BIG DADDY. That's right, boy, they look like a couple of cats on a hot tin roof. It's funny that you and Gooper being so different would pick out the same type of woman.

BRICK. Both of us married into society, Big Daddy.

BIG DADDY. Crap . . . . I wonder what gives them both that look?

BRICK. Well. They're sittin' in the middle of a big piece of land, Big Daddy, twenty-eight thousand acres is a pretty big piece of land and so they're squaring off on it, each determined to knock off a bigger piece of it than the other whenever you let it go.

BIG DADDY. I got a surprise for those women. I'm not gonna let it go for a long time yet if that's what they're waiting for.

BRICK. That's right, Big Daddy. You just sit tight and let them scratch each other's eyes out. . . .

BIG DADDY. You bet your life I'm going to sit tight on it and let those sons of bitches scratch their eyes out, ha ha ha. . . .

But Gooper's wife's a good breeder, you got to admit she's fertile. Hell, at supper tonight she had them all at the table and they had to put a couple of extra leafs in the table to make room for them, she's got five head of them, now, and another one's comin'.

BRICK. Yep, number six is comin'. . . .

BIG DADDY. Six hell, she'll probably drop a litter next time. Brick, you know, I swear to God, I don't know the way it happens?

BRICK. The way what happens, Big Daddy?

BIG DADDY. You git you a piece of land, by hook or crook, an' things start growin' on it, things accumulate on it, and the first thing you know it's completely out of hand, completely out of hand!

BRICK. Well, they say nature hates a vacuum, Big Daddy.

BIG DADDY. That's what they say, but sometimes I think that a vacuum is a hell of a lot better than some of the stuff that nature replaces it with.

Is someone out there by that door?

GOOPER. Hey Mae.

BRICK. Yep.

BIG DADDY. Who?

He has lowered his voice.

BRICK. Someone int'rested in what we say to each other.

BIG DADDY. Gooper?——*GOOPER!*

After a discreet pause, MAE appears in the gallery door.

MAE. Did you call Gooper, Big Daddy?

BIG DADDY. Aw, it was you.

MAE. Do you want Gooper, Big Daddy?

BIG DADDY. No, and I don't want you. I want some privacy here, while I'm having a confidential talk with my son Brick. Now it's too hot in here to close them doors, but if I have to close those fuckin' doors in order to have a private talk with my son Brick, just let me know and I'll close 'em. Because I hate eavesdroppers, I don't like any kind of sneakin' an' spyin'.

MAE. Why, Big Daddy—

BIG DADDY. You stood on the wrong side of the moon, it threw your shadow!

MAE. I was just——

BIG DADDY. You was just nothing but *spyin'* an' you *know* it!

MAE (*begins to sniff and sob*). Oh, Big Daddy, you're so unkind for some reason to those that really love you!

BIG DADDY. Shut up, shut up, shut up! I'm going to move you and Gooper out of that room next to this! It's none of your goddam business what goes on in here at night between Brick an' Maggie. You listen at night like a couple of rutten peekhole spies and go and give a report on what you hear to Big Mama an' she comes to me and says they say such and such and so and so about what they heard goin' on between Brick an' Maggie, and Jesus, it makes me sick. I'm goin' to move you an' Gooper out of that room, I can't stand sneakin' an' spyin', it makes me puke.

MAE throws back her head and rolls her eyes heavenward and extends her arms as if invoking God's pity for this unjust martyrdom; then she presses a handkerchief to her nose and flies from the room with a loud swish of skirts.

BRICK (*now at the liquor cabinet*). They listen, do they?

BIG DADDY. Yeah. They listen and give reports to Big Mama on what goes on in here between you and Maggie. They say that—

He stops as if embarrassed.

—You won't sleep with her, that you sleep on the sofa. Is that true or not true? If you don't like Maggie, get rid of Maggie!—What are you doin' there now?

BRICK. Fresh'nin' up my drink.

BIG DADDY. Son, you know you got a real liquor problem?

BRICK. Yes, sir, yes, I know.

BIG DADDY. Is that why you quit sports-announcing, because of this liquor problem?

BRICK. Yes, sir, yes, sir, I guess so.

He smiles vaguely and amiably at his father across his replenished drink.

BIG DADDY. Son, don't guess about it, it's too important.

BRICK (*vaguely*). Yes, sir.

BIG DADDY. And listen to me, don't look at the damn chandelier. . . .

Pause. BIG DADDY's voice is husky.

—Somethin' else we picked up at th' big fire sale in Europe.

Another pause.

Life is important. There's nothing else to hold onto. A man that drinks is throwing his life away. Don't do it, hold onto your life. There's nothing else to hold onto. . . .

Sit down over here so we don't have to raise our voices, the walls have ears in this place.

BRICK (*hobbling over to sit on the sofa beside him*). All right, Big Daddy.

BIG DADDY. Quit!—how'd that come about? Some disappointment?

BRICK. I don't know. Do you?

BIG DADDY. I'm askin' you, God damn it! How in hell would I know if you don't?

BRICK. I just got out there and found that I had a mouth full of cotton. I was always two or three beats behind what was goin' on on the field and so I—

BIG DADDY. Quit!

BRICK (*amiably*). Yes, quit.

BIG DADDY. Son?

BRICK. Huh?

BIG DADDY (*inhales loudly and deeply from his cigar; then bends suddenly a little forward, exhaling loudly and raising a hand to his forehead*). — Whew!—ha ha!—I took in too much smoke, it made me a little lightheaded. . . .

The mantel clock chimes.

Why is it so damn hard for people to talk?

BRICK. Yeah. . . .

The clock goes on sweetly chiming till it has completed the stroke of ten.

—Nice peaceful-soundin' clock, I like to hear it all night. . . .

He slides low and comfortable on the sofa; BIG DADDY sits up straight and rigid with some unspoken anxiety. All his gestures are tense and jerky as he talks. He wheezes and pants and sniffs through his nervous speech, glancing quickly, shyly, from time to time, at his son.

BIG DADDY. We got that clock the summer we wint to Europe, me an' Big Mama on that damn Cook's Tour, never had such an awful time in my life, I'm tellin' you, son, those gooks over there, they gouge your eyeballs out in their grand hotels. And Big Mama bought more stuff than you could haul in a couple of boxcars, that's no crap. Everywhere she wint on this whirlwind tour, she bought, bought, bought. Why, half that stuff she bought is still crated up in the cellar, under water last spring!

He laughs.

That Europe is nothin' on earth but a great big auction, that's all it is, that bunch of old worn-out places, it's just a big fire-sale, the whole fuckin' thing, an' Big Mama wint wild in it, why, you couldn't hold that woman with a mule's harness! Bought, bought, bought!—lucky I'm a rich man, yes siree, Bob, an' half that stuff is mildewin' in th' basement. It's lucky I'm a rich man, it sure is lucky, well, I'm a rich man, Brick, yep, I'm a mighty rich man.

His eyes light up for a moment.

Y'know how much I'm worth? Guess, Brick! Guess how much I'm worth!

BRICK smiles vaguely over his drink.

Close on ten million in cash an' blue-chip stocks, outside, mind you, of twenty-eight thousand acres of the richest land this side of the valley Nile!

But a man can't buy his life with it, he can't buy back his life with it when his life has been spent, that's one thing not offered in the Europe fire-sale or in the American markets or any markets on earth, a man can't buy his life with it, he can't buy back his life when his life is finished. . . .

That's a sobering thought, a very sobering thought, and that's a thought that I was turning over in my head, over and over and over—until today. . . .

I'm wiser and sadder, Brick, for this experience which I just gone through. They's one thing else that I remember in Europe.

BRICK. What is that, Big Daddy?

BIG DADDY. The hills around Barcelona in the country of Spain and the children running over those bare hills in their bare skins beggin' like starvin' dogs with howls and screeches, and how fat the priests are on the streets of Barcelona, so many of them and so fat and so pleasant, ha ha!—Y'know I could feed that country? I got money enough to feed that goddam country, but the human animal is a selfish beast and I don't reckon the money I passed out there to those howling children in the hills around Barcelona would more than upholster the chairs in this room, I mean pay to put a new cover on this chair!

Hell, I threw them money like you'd scatter feed corn for chickens, I threw money at them just to get rid of them long enough to climb back into th' car and—drive away. . . .

And then in Morocco, them Arabs, why, I remember one day in Marrakech, that old walled Arab city, I set on a broken-down wall to have a cigar, it was fearful hot there and this Arab woman stood in the road and looked at me till I was embarrassed, she stood stock still in the dusty hot road and looked at me till I was embarrassed. But listen to this. She had a naked child with her, a little naked girl with her, barely able to toddle, and after a while she set this child on the ground and give her a push and whispered something to her.

This child come toward me, barely able t' walk, come toddling up to me and—

Jesus, it makes you sick t' remember a thing like this! It stuck out its hand and tried to unbutton my trousers!

That child was not yet five! Can you believe me? Or do you think that I am making this up? I wint back to the hotel and said to Big Mama, Git packed! We're clearing out of this country. . . .

BRICK. Big Daddy, you're on a talkin' jag tonight.

BIG DADDY (*ignoring this remark*). Yes, sir, that's how it is, the human animal is a beast that dies but the fact that he's dying don't give him pity for others, no, sir, it—

—Did you say something?

BRICK. Yes.

BIG DADDY. What?

BRICK. Hand me over that crutch so I can get up.

BIG DADDY. Where you goin'?

BRICK. I'm takin' a little short trip to Echo Spring.

BIG DADDY. To where?

BRICK. Liquor cabinet. . . .

BIG DADDY. Yes, sir, boy—

He hands BRICK *the crutch.*

—the human animal is a beast that dies and if he's got money he buys and buys and buys I think the reason he buys everything he can buy is that in the back of his mind he has the crazy hope that one of his purchases will be life everlasting!—Which it never can be. . . . The human animal is a beast that—

BRICK (*at the liquor cabinet*). Big Daddy, you sure are shootin' th' breeze here tonight.

There is a pause and voices are heard outside.

BIG DADDY. I been quiet here lately, spoke not a word, just sat and stared into space. I had something heavy weighing on my mind but tonight that load was took off me. That's why I'm talking.—The sky looks diff'rent to me. . . .

BRICK. You know what I like to hear most?

BIG DADDY. What?

BRICK. Solid quiet. Perfect unbroken quiet.

BIG DADDY. Why?

BRICK. Because it's more peaceful.

BIG DADDY. Man, you'll hear a lot of that in the grave.

He chuckles agreeably.

BRICK. Are you through talkin' to me?

BIG DADDY. Why are you so anxious to shut me up?

BRICK. Well, sir, ever so often you say to me, Brick, I want to have a talk with you, but when we talk, it never materializes. Nothing is said. You sit in a chair and gas about this and that and I look like I listen. I try to look like I listen, but I don't listen, not much. Communication is—awful hard between people an'—somehow between you and me, it just don't—happen.

BIG DADDY. Have you ever been scared? I mean have you ever felt downright terror of something?

He gets up.

Just one moment.

He looks off as if he were going to tell an important secret.

BIG DADDY. Brick?

BRICK. What?

BIG DADDY. Son, I thought I had it!

BRICK. Had what? Had what, Big Daddy?

BIG DADDY. Cancer!

BRICK. Oh . . .

BIG DADDY. I thought the old man made out of bones had laid his cold and heavy hand on my shoulder!

BRICK. Well, Big Daddy, you kept a tight mouth about it.

BIG DADDY. A pig squeals. A man keeps a tight mouth about it, in spite of a man not having a pig's advantage.

BRICK. What advantage is that?

BIG DADDY. Ignorance—of mortality—is a comfort. A man don't have that comfort, he's the only living thing that conceives of death, that knows what it is. The others go without knowing which is the way that anything living should go, go without knowing, without any knowledge of it, and yet a pig squeals, but a man sometimes, he can keep a tight mouth about it. Sometimes he—

There is a deep, smoldering ferocity in the old man.

—can keep a tight mouth about it. I wonder if—

BRICK. What, Big Daddy?

BIG DADDY. A whiskey highball would injure this spastic condition?

BRICK. No, sir, it might do it good.

BIG DADDY (*grins suddenly, wolfishly*). Jesus, I can't tell you! The sky is open! Christ, it's open again! It's open, boy, it's open!

BRICK looks down at his drink.

BRICK. You feel better, Big Daddy?

BIG DADDY. Better? Hell! I can breathe!—All of my life I been like a doubled up fist.

He pours a drink.

—Poundin', smashin', drivin'!—now I'm going to loosen these doubled-up hands and touch things easy with them. . . .

He spreads his hands as if caressing the air.

You know what I'm contemplating?

BRICK (*vaguely*). No, sir. What are you contemplating?

BIG DADDY. Ha ha!—*Pleasure!*—pleasure with women!

BRICK's smile fades a little but lingers.

—Yes, boy. I'll tell you something that you might not guess. I still have desire for women and this is my sixty-fifth birthday.

BRICK. I think that's mighty remarkable, Big Daddy.

BIG DADDY. Remarkable?

BRICK. *Admirable*, Big Daddy.

BIG DADDY. You're damn right it is, remarkable and admirable both. I realize now that I never had me enough. I let many chances slip by because of scruples about it, scruples, convention—crap. . . . All that stuff is bull, bull, bull!—It took the shadow of death to make me see it. Now that shadow's lifted, I'm going to cut loose and have, what is it they call it, have me a—ball!

BRICK. A ball, huh?

BIG DADDY. That's right, a ball, a ball! Hell!—I slept with Big Mama till, let's see, five years ago, till I was sixty and she was fifty-eight, and never even liked her, never did!

The phone has been ringing down the hall. BIG MAMA enters, exclaiming:

BIG MAMA. Don't you men hear that phone ring? I heard it way out on the gall'ry.

BIG DADDY. There's five rooms off this front gall'ry that you could go through. Why do you go through this one?

BIG MAMA makes a playful face as she bustles out the hall door.

Hunh!—Why, when Big Mama goes out of a room, I can't remember what that woman looks like—

BIG MAMA. Hello.

BIG DADDY. —But when Big Mama comes back into the room, boy, then I see what she looks like, and I wish I didn't!

Bends over laughing at this joke till it hurts his guts and he straightens with a grimace. The laugh subsides to a chuckle as he puts the liquor glass a little distrustfully down the table.

BIG MAMA. Hello, Miss Sally.

BRICK has risen and hobbled to the gallery doors.

BIG DADDY. Hey! Where you goin'?

BRICK. Out for a breather.

BIG DADDY. Not yet you ain't. Stay here till this talk is finished, young fellow.

BRICK. I thought it was finished, Big Daddy.

BIG DADDY. It ain't even begun.

BRICK. My mistake. Excuse me. I just wanted to feel that river breeze.

BIG DADDY. Set back down in that chair.

BIG MAMA's voice rises, carrying down the hall.

BIG MAMA. Miss Sally, you're a case! You're a caution, Miss Sally.

BIG DADDY. Jesus, she's talking to my old maid sister again.

BIG MAMA. Why didn't you give me a chance to explain it to you?

BIG DADDY. Brick, this stuff burns me.

BIG MAMA. Well, goodbye, now, Miss Sally. You come down real soon. Big Daddy's dying to see you.

BIG DADDY. Crap!

BIG MAMA. Yaiss, goodbye, Miss Sally. . . .

She hangs up and bellows with mirth. BIG DADDY groans and covers his ears as she approaches.

Bursting in.

Big Daddy, that was Miss Sally callin' from Memphis again! You know what she done, Big Daddy? She called her doctor in Memphis to git him to tell her what that spastic thing is! Ha-HAAAA!—And called back to tell me how relieved she was that—Hey! Let me in!

BIG DADDY has been holding the door half closed against her.

BIG DADDY. Naw I ain't. I told you not to come and go through this room. You just back out and go through those five other rooms.

BIG MAMA. Big Daddy? Big Daddy? Oh, big Daddy!—You didn't mean those things you said to me, did you?

He shuts door firmly against her but she still calls.

Sweetheart? Sweetheart? Big Daddy? You didn't mean those awful things you said to me?—I know you didn't. I know you didn't mean those things in your heart. . . .

The childlike voice fades with a sob and her heavy footsteps retreat down the hall. BRICK has risen once more on his crutches and starts for the gallery again.

BIG DADDY. All I ask of that woman is that she leave me alone. But she can't admit to herself that she makes me sick. That comes of having slept with her too many years. Should of quit much sooner but that old woman she never got enough of it—and I was good in bed . . . I never should of wasted so much of it on her. . . . They say you got just so many and each one is numbered. Well, I got a few left in me, a few, and I'm going to pick me a good one to spend 'em on! I'm going to pick me a choice one, I don't care how much she costs, I'll smother her in—minks! Ha ha! I'll strip her naked and smother her in minks and choke her with diamonds! Ha ha! I'll strip her naked and choke her with diamonds and smother her with minks and hump her from hell to breakfast. *Ha aha ha ha!*

MAE *(gaily at door).* Who's that laughin' in there?

GOOPER. Is Big Daddy laughin' in there?

BIG DADDY. Crap!—them two—*drips.* . . .

He goes over and touches BRICK's shoulder.

Yes, son. Brick, boy.—I'm—*happy!* I'm happy, son, I'm happy!

He chokes a little and bites his under lip, pressing his head quickly, shyly against his son's head and then, coughing with embarrassment, goes uncertainly back to the table where he set down the glass. He drinks and makes a grimace as it burns his guts. BRICK sighs and rises with effort.

What makes you so restless? Have you got ants in your britches?

BRICK. Yes, sir . . .

BIG DADDY. Why?

BRICK. —Something—hasn't—happened. . . .

BIG DADDY. Yeah? What is that!

BRICK *(sadly).* —the click. . . .

BIG DADDY. Did you say click?

BRICK. Yes, click.

BIG DADDY. What click?

BRICK. A click that I get in my head that makes me peaceful.

BIG DADDY. I sure in hell don't know what you're talking about, but it disturbs me.

BRICK. It's just a mechanical thing.

BIG DADDY. What is a mechanical thing?

BRICK. This click that I get in my head that makes me peaceful. I got to drink till I get it. It's just a mechanical thing, something like a—like a—like a—

BIG DADDY. Like a—

BRICK. Switch clicking off in my head, turning the hot light off and the cool night on and—

He looks up, smiling sadly.

—all of a sudden there's—peace!

BIG DADDY (*whistles long and soft with astonishment; he goes back to Brick and clasps his son's two shoulders*). Jesus! I didn't know it had gotten that bad with you. Why, boy, you're—alcoholic!

BRICK. That's the truth, Big Daddy. I'm alcoholic.

BIG DADDY. This shows how I—let things go!

BRICK. I have to hear that little click in my head that makes me peaceful. Usually I hear it sooner than this, sometimes as early as—noon, but—

—Today it's—dilatory. . . .

—I just haven't got the right level of alcohol in my bloodstream yet!

This last statement is made with energy as he freshens his drink.

BIG DADDY. Uh—huh. Expecting death made me blind. I didn't have no idea that a son of mine was turning into a drunkard under my nose.

BRICK (*gently*). Well, now you do, Big Daddy, the news has penetrated.

BIG DADDY. UH-huh, yes, now I do, the news has—penetrated.

BRICK. And so if you'll excuse me—

BIG DADDY. No, I won't excuse you.

BRICK. —I'd better sit by myself till I hear that click in my head, it's just a mechanical thing but it don't happen except when I'm alone or talking to no one. . . .

BIG DADDY. You got a long, long time to sit still, boy, and talk to no one, but now you're talkin' to me. At least I'm talking to you. And you set there and listen until I tell you the conversation is over!

BRICK. But this talk is like all the others we've ever had together in our lives! It's nowhere, nowhere!—it's—it's *painful*, Big Daddy. . . .

BIG DADDY. All right, then let it be painful, but don't you move from that chair!—I'm going to remove that crutch. . . .

He seizes the crutch and tosses it across room.

BRICK. I can hop on one foot, and if I fall, I can crawl!

BIG DADDY. If you ain't careful you're gonna crawl off this plantation and then, by Jesus, you'll have to hustle your drinks along Skid Row!

BRICK. That'll come, Big Daddy.

BIG DADDY. Naw, it won't. You're my son and I'm going to straighten you out; now that *I'm* straightened out, I'm going to straighten out you!

BRICK. Yeah?

BIG DADDY. Today the report come in from Ochsner Clinic. Y'know what they told me?

His face glows with triumph.

The only thing that they could detect with all the instruments of science in that great hospital is a little spastic condition of the colon! And nerves torn to pieces by all that worry about it.

A little girl bursts into room with a sparkler clutched in each fist, hops and shrieks like a monkey gone mad and rushes back out again as BIG DADDY *strikes at her.*

Silence. The two men stare at each other. A woman laughs gaily outside.

I want you to know I breathed a sigh of relief almost as powerful as the Vicksburg tornado!

There is laughter outside, running footsteps, the soft, plushy sound and light of exploding rockets.

BRICK *stares at him soberly for a long moment; then makes a sort of startled sound in his nostrils and springs up on one foot and hops across the room to grab his crutch, swinging on the furniture for support. He gets the crutch and flees as if in horror for the gallery. His father seizes him by the sleeve of his white silk pajamas.*

Stay here, you son of a bitch!—till I say go!

BRICK. I can't.

BIG DADDY. You sure in hell will, God damn it.

BRICK. No, I can't. We talk, you talk, in—circles! We get no where, no where! It's always the same, you say you want to talk to me and don't have a fuckin' thing to say to me!

BIG DADDY. Nothin' to say when I'm tellin' you I'm going to live when I thought I was dying?!

BRICK. Oh—*that!*—Is that what you have to say to me?

BIG DADDY. Why, you son of a bitch! Ain't that, ain't that—*important?!*

BRICK. Well, you said that, that's said, and now I—

BIG DADDY. Now you set back down.

BRICK. You're all balled up, you—

BIG DADDY. I ain't balled up!

BRICK. You are, you're all balled up!

BIG DADDY. Don't tell me what I am, you drunken whelp! I'm going to tear this coat sleeve off if you don't set down!

BRICK. Big Daddy—

BIG DADDY. Do what I tell you! I'm the boss here, now! I want you to know I'm back in the driver's seat now!

BIG MAMA rushes in, clutching her great heaving bosom.

BIG MAMA. Big Daddy!

BIG DADDY. What in hell do you want in here, Big Mama?

BIG MAMA. Oh, Big Daddy! Why are you shouting like that? I just cain't *stainnnnnnnd*—it. . . .

BIG DADDY (*raising the back of his hand above his head*). GIT!—outa here.

She rushes back out, sobbing.

BRICK (*softly, sadly*). Christ. . . .

BIG DADDY (*fiercely*). Yeah! Christ!—is right . . .

BRICK breaks loose and hobbles toward the gallery.

BIG DADDY jerks his crutch from under BRICK so he steps with the injured ankle. He utters a hissing cry of anguish, clutches a chair and pulls it over on top of him on the floor.

Son of a—tub of—hog fat. . . .

BRICK. Big Daddy! Give me my crutch.

BIG DADDY throws the crutch out of reach.

Give me that crutch, Big Daddy.

BIG DADDY. Why do you drink?

BRICK. Don't know, give me my crutch!

BIG DADDY. You better think why you drink or give up drinking!

BRICK. Will you please give me my crutch so I can get up off this floor?

BIG DADDY. First you answer my question. Why do you drink? Why are you throwing your life away, boy, like somethin' disgusting you picked up on the street?

BRICK (*getting onto his knees*). Big Daddy, I'm in pain, I stepped on that foot.

BIG DADDY. Good! I'm glad you're not too numb with the liquor in you to feel some pain!

BRICK. You—spilled my—drink . . .

BIG DADDY. I'll make a bargain with you. You tell me why you drink and I'll hand you one. I'll pour you the liquor myself and hand it to you.

BRICK. Why do I drink?

BIG DADDY. Yea! Why?

BRICK. Give me a drink and I'll tell you.

BIG DADDY. Tell me first!

BRICK. I'll tell you in one word.

BIG DADDY. What word?

BRICK. DISGUST!

The clock chimes softly, sweetly. BIG DADDY gives it a short, outraged glance.

Now how about that drink?

BIG DADDY. What are you disgusted with? You got to tell me that, first. Otherwise being disgusted don't make no sense!

BRICK. Give me my crutch.

BIG DADDY. You heard me, you got to tell me what I asked you first.

BRICK. I told you, I said to kill my disgust!

BIG DADDY. DISGUST WITH WHAT!

BRICK. You strike a hard bargain.

BIG DADDY. What are you disgusted with?—an' I'll pass you the liquor.

BRICK. I can hop on one foot, and if I fall, I can crawl.

BIG DADDY. You want liquor that bad?

BRICK (*dragging himself up, clinging to bedstead*). Yeah, I want it that bad.

BIG DADDY. If I give you a drink, will you tell me what it is you're disgusted with, Brick?

BRICK. Yes, sir, I will try to.

The old man pours him a drink and solemnly passes it to him.

There is silence as BRICK *drinks.*

Have you ever heard the word "mendacity"?

BIG DADDY. Sure. Mendacity is one of them five dollar words that cheap politicians throw back and forth at each other.

BRICK. You know what it means?

BIG DADDY. Don't it mean lying and liars?

BRICK. Yes, sir, lying and liars.

BIG DADDY. Has someone been lying to you?

CHILDREN (*chanting in chorus offstage*). We want Big Dad-dee! We want Big Dad-dee!

GOOPER *appears in the gallery door.*

GOOPER. Big Daddy, the kiddies are shouting for you out there.

BIG DADDY (*fiercely*). Keep out, Gooper!

GOOPER. 'Scuse *me!*

Big Daddy slams the doors after Gooper.

BIG DADDY. Who's been lying to you, has Margaret been lying to you, has your wife been lying to you about something, Brick?

BRICK. Not her. That wouldn't matter.

BIG DADDY. Then who's been lying to you, and what about?

BRICK. No one single person and no one lie. . . .

BIG DADDY. Then what, what then, for Christ's sake?

BRICK. —The whole, the whole—thing. . . .

BIG DADDY. Why are you rubbing your head? You got a headache?

BRICK. No, I'm tryin' to—

BIG DADDY. —Concentrate, but you can't because your brain's all soaked with liquor, is that the trouble? Wet brain!

He snatches the glass from BRICK'S *hand.*

What do you know about this mendacity thing? Hell! I could write a book on it! Don't you know that? I could write a book on it and still not cover the subject? Well, I could, I could write a goddam book on it and still not cover the subject anywhere near enough!!—Think of all the lies I got to put up with!—Pretenses! Ain't that mendacity? Having to pretend stuff you don't think or feel or have any idea of? Having for instance to act like I care for Big Mama!—I haven't been able to stand the sight, sound, or smell of that woman for forty years now!—even when I *laid* her!—regular as a piston. . . .

Pretend to love that son of a bitch of a Gooper and his wife Mae and those five same screechers out there like parrots in a jungle? Jesus! Can't stand to look at 'em!

Church!—it bores the bejesus out of me but I go!—I go an' sit there and listen to the fool preacher!

Clubs!—Elks! Masons! Rotary!—*crap!*

A spasm of pain makes him clutch his belly. He sinks into a chair and his voice is softer and hoarser.

You I *do* like for some reason, did always have some kind of real feeling for—affection— respect—yes, always. . . .

You and being a success as a planter is all I ever had any devotion to in my whole life!—and that's the truth. . . .

I don't know why, but it is!

I've lived with mendacity!—Why can't *you* live with it? Hell, you *got* to live with it, there's nothing *else* to *live* with except mendacity, is there?

BRICK. Yes, sir. Yes, sir there is something else that you can live with!

BIG DADDY. What?

BRICK (*lifting his glass*). This!—Liquor. . . .

BIG DADDY. That's not living, that's dodging away from life.

BRICK. I want to dodge away from it.

BIG DADDY. Then why don't you kill yourself, man?

BRICK. I like to drink. . . .

BIG DADDY. Oh, God, I can't talk to you. . . .

BRICK. I'm sorry, Big Daddy.

BIG DADDY. Not as sorry as I am. I'll tell you something. A little while back when I thought my number was up—

This speech should have torrential pace and fury.

—before I found out it was just this—spastic—colon. I thought about you. Should I or should I not, if the jig was up, give you this place when I go—since I hate Gooper an' Mae an' know that they hate me, and since all five same monkeys are little Maes an' Goopers.—And I thought, No!—Then I thought, Yes!—I couldn't make up my mind. I hate Gooper and his five same monkeys and that bitch Mae! Why should I turn over twenty-eight thousand acres of the richest land this side of the valley Nile to not my kind?—But why in hell, on the other hand, Brick—should I subsidize a goddam fool on the bottle?—Liked or not liked, well, maybe even—*loved!*—Why should I do that?—Subsidize worthless behavior? Rot? Corruption?

BRICK (*smiling*). I understand.

BIG DADDY. Well, if you do, you're smarter than I am, God damn it, because I don't understand. And this I will tell you frankly. I didn't make up my mind at all on that question and still to this day I ain't made out no will!—Well, now I don't *have* to. The pressure is gone. I can just wait and see if you pull yourself together or if you don't.

BRICK. That's right, Big Daddy.

BIG DADDY. You sound like you thought I was kidding.

BRICK (*rising*). No, sir, I know you're not kidding.

BIG DADDY. But you don't care—?

BRICK (*hobbling toward the gallery door*). No, sir, I don't care. . . .

He stands in the gallery doorway as the night sky turns pink and green and gold with successive flashes of light.

BIG DADDY. *WAIT!*—Brick. . . .

His voice drops. Suddenly there is something shy, almost tender, in his restraining gesture.

Don't let's—leave it like this, like them other talks we've had, we've always—talked around things, we've—just talked around things for some fuckin' reason, I don't know what, it's always like something was left not spoken, something avoided because neither of us was honest enough with the—other. . . .

BRICK. I never lied to you, Big Daddy.

BIG DADDY. Did I ever to *you?*

BRICK. No, sir. . . .

BIG DADDY. Then there is at least two people that never lied to each other.

BRICK. But we've never *talked* to each other.

BIG DADDY. We can *now.*

BRICK. Big Daddy, there don't seem to be anything much to say.

BIG DADDY. You say that you drink to kill your disgust with lying.

BRICK. You said to give you a reason.

BIG DADDY. Is liquor the only thing that'll kill this disgust?

BRICK. Now. Yes.

BIG DADDY. But not once, huh?

BRICK. Not when I was still young an' believing. A drinking man's someone who wants to forget he isn't still young an' believing.

BIG DADDY. Believing what?

BRICK. Believing. . . .

BIG DADDY. Believing *what?*

BRICK (*stubbornly evasive*). Believing. . . .

BIG DADDY. I don't know what the hell you mean by believing and I don't think you know what you mean by believing, but if you still got sports in your blood, go back to sports announcing and—

BRICK. Sit in a glass box watching games I can't play? Describing what I can't do while players do it? Sweating out their disgust and confusion in contests I'm not fit for? Drinkin' a coke, half bourbon, so I can stand it? That's no goddam good any more, no help—time just outran me, Big Daddy—got there first . . .

BIG DADDY. I think you're passing the buck.

BRICK. You know many drinkin' men?

BIG DADDY (with a slight, charming smile). I have known a fair number of that species.

BRICK. Could any of them tell you why he drank?

BIG DADDY. Yep, you're passin' the buck to things like time and disgust with "mendacity" and—crap!—if you got to use that kind of language about a thing, it's ninety-proof bull, and I'm not buying any.

BRICK. I had to give you a reason to get a drink!

BIG DADDY. You started drinkin' when your friend Skipper died.

Silence for five beats. Then BRICK makes a startled movement, reaching for his crutch.

BRICK. What are you suggesting?

BIG DADDY. I'm suggesting nothing.

The shuffle and clop of BRICK's rapid hobble away from his father's steady, grave attention.

—But Gooper an' Mae suggested that there was something not right exactly in your—

BRICK. (stopping short downstage as if backed to a wall). "Not right"?

BIG DADDY. Not, well, exactly *normal* in your friendship with—

BRICK. They suggested that, too? I thought that was Maggie's suggestion.

BRICK's detachment is at last broken through. His heart is accelerated; his forehead sweat-beaded; his breath becomes more rapid and his voice hoarse. The thing they're discussing, timidly and painfully on the side of BIG DADDY, fiercely, violently on BRICK's side, is the inadmissible thing that Skipper died to disavow between them. The fact that if it existed it had to be disavowed to "keep face" in the world they lived in, may be at the heart of the "mendacity" that Brick drinks to kill his disgust with. It may be the root of his collapse. Or maybe it

is only a single manifestation of it, not even the most important. The bird that I hope to catch in the net of this play is not the solution of one man's psychological problem. I'm trying to catch the true quality of experience in a group of people, that cloudy, flickering, evanescent—fiercely charged!—interplay of live human beings in the thundercloud of a common crisis. Some mystery should be left in the revelation of character in a play, just as a great deal of mystery is always left in the revelation of character in life, even in one's own character to himself. This does not absolve the playwright of his duty to observe and probe as clearly and deeply as he legitimately can: but it should steer him away from "pat" conclusions, facile definitions which make a play just a play, not a snare for the truth of human experience.

The following scene should be played with great concentration, with most of the power leashed but palpable in what is left unspoken.

Who else's suggestion is it, is it *yours*? How many others thought that Skipper and I were—

BIG DADDY (gently). Now, hold on, hold on a minute, son.—I knocked around in my time.

BRICK. What's that got to do with—

BIG DADDY. I said "Hold on!"—I bummed, I bummed this country till I was—

BRICK. Whose suggestion, who else's suggestion is it?

BIG DADDY. Slept in hobo jungles and railroad Y's and flophouses in all cities before I—

BRICK. Oh, *you* think so, too, you call me your son and a queer. Oh! Maybe that's why you put Maggie and me in this room that was Jack Straw's and Peter Ochello's, in which that pair of old sisters slept in a double bed where both of 'em died!

BIG DADDY. *Now just don't go throwing rocks at—*

Suddenly REVEREND TOOKER appears in the gallery doors, his head slightly, playfully, fatuously cocked, with a practised clergyman's smile, sincere as a bird call blown on a hunter's whistle, the living embodiment of the pious, conventional lie.

BIG DADDY gasps a little at this perfectly timed, but incongruous, apparition.

—What're you lookin' for, Preacher?

REVEREND TOOKER. The gentleman's lavatory, ha ha!—heh, heh

BIG DADDY (*with strained courtesy*). —Go back out and walk down to the other end of the gallery, Reverend Tooker, and use the bathroom connected with my bedroom, and if you can't find it, ask them where it is!

REVEREND TOOKER. Ah, thanks.

He goes out with a deprecatory chuckle.

BIG DADDY. It's hard to talk in this place.

BRICK. Son of a—!

BIG DADDY (*leaving a lot unspoken*). —I seen all things and understood a lot of them, till 1910. Christ, the year that—I had worn my shoes through, hocked my—I hopped off a yellow dog freight car half a mile down the road, slept in a wagon of cotton outside the gin—Jack Straw an' Peter Ochello took me in. Hired me to manage this place which grew into this one.—When Jack Straw died—why, old Peter Ochello quit eatin' like a dog does when its master's dead, and died, too!

BRICK. Christ!

BIG DADDY. I'm just saying I understand such—

BRICK (*violently*). Skipper is dead. I have not quit eating!

BIG DADDY. No, but you started drinking.

Brick wheels on his crutch and hurls his glass across the room shouting.

BRICK. YOU THINK SO, TOO?

Footsteps run on the gallery. There are women's calls.

Big Daddy goes toward the door.

Brick is transformed, as if a quiet mountain blew suddenly up in volcanic flame.

BRICK. You think so, too? You think so, too? You think me an' Skipper did, did, did!—sodomy!—together?

BIG DADDY. Hold—!

BRICK. That what you—

BIG DADDY. —ON—a minute!

BRICK. You think we did dirty things between us, Skipper an'—

BIG DADDY. Why are you shouting like that? Why are you—

BRICK. —Me, is that what you think of Skipper, is that—

BIG DADDY. —so excited? I don't think nothing. I don't know nothing. I'm simply telling you what—

BRICK. You think that Skipper and me were a pair of dirty old men?

BIG DADDY. Now that's—

BRICK. Straw? Ochello? A couple of—

BIG DADDY. Now just—

BRICK. —fucking sissies? Queers? Is that what you—

BIG DADDY. Shhh.

BRICK. —think?

He loses his balance and pitches to his knees without noticing the pain. He grabs the bed and drags himself up.

BIG DADDY. Jesus!—Whew . . . Grab my hand!

BRICK. Naw, I don't want your hand . . .

BIG DADDY. Well, I want yours. Git up!

He draws him up, keeps an arm about him with concern and affection.

You broken out in a sweat! You're panting like you'd run a race with—

BRICK (*freeing himself from his father's hold*). Big Daddy, you shock me, Big Daddy, you, you—shock me! Talkin' so—

He turns away from his father.

—casually!—about a—thing like that . . .

—Don't you know how people *feel* about things like that? How, how *disgusted* they are by things like that? Why, at Ole Miss when it was discovered a pledge to our fraternity, Skipper's and mine, did a, *attempted* to do a, unnatural thing with—

We not only dropped him like a hot rock!—We told him to git off the campus, and he did, he got!—All the way to—

He halts, breathless.

BIG DADDY. —Where?

BRICK. —North Africa, last I heard!

BIG DADDY. Well, I have come back from further away than that, I have just now returned from the other side of the moon, death's country, son, and I'm not easy to shock by anything here.

He comes downstage and faces out.

Always, anyhow, lived with too much space around me to be infected by ideas of other people. One thing you can grow on a big place more important than cotton!—is *tolerance!*—I grown it.

He returns toward Brick.

BRICK. Why can't exceptional friendship, *real, real, deep, deep friendship!* between two men be respected as something clean and decent without being thought of as—

BIG DADDY. It can, it is, for God's sake.

BRICK. —Fairies. . . .

In his utterance of this word, we gauge the wide and profound reach of the conventional mores he got from the world that crowned him with early laurel.

BIG DADDY. I told Mae an' Gooper—

BRICK. Frig Mae and Gooper, frig all dirty lies and liars!—Skipper and me had a clean, true thing between us!—had a clean friendship, practically all our lives, till Maggie got the idea you're talking about. Normal? No!—It was too rare to be normal, any true thing between two people is too rare to be normal. Oh, once in a while he put his hand on my shoulder or I'd put mine on his, oh, maybe even, when we were touring the country in pro-football an' shared hotel-rooms we'd reach across the space between the two beds and shake hands to say goodnight, yeah, one or two times we—

BIG DADDY. Brick, nobody thinks that that's not normal!

BRICK. Well, they're mistaken, it was! It was a pure an' true thing an' that's not normal.

MAE *(off stage).* Big Daddy, they're startin' the fireworks.

They both stare straight at each other for a long moment. The tension breaks and both turn away as if tired.

BIG DADDY. Yeah, it's—hard t'—talk.

BRICK. All right, then, let's—let it go. . . .

BIG DADDY. Why did Skipper crack up? Why have you?

BRICK looks back at his father again. He has already decided, without knowing that he has made this decision, that he is going to tell his father that he is dying of cancer. Only this could even the score between them: one inadmissible thing in return for another.

BRICK *(ominously).* All right. You're asking for it, Big Daddy. We're finally going to have that real true talk you wanted. It's too late to stop it, now, we got to carry it through and cover every subject.

He hobbles back to the liquor cabinet.
Uh-huh.

He opens the ice bucket and picks up the silver tongs with slow admiration of their frosty brightness.

Maggie declares that Skipper and I went into pro-football after we left "Ole Miss" because we were scared to grow up. . . .

He moves downstage with the shuffle and clop of a cripple on a crutch. As MARGARET did when her speech became "recitative," he looks out into the house, commanding its attention by his direct, concentrated gaze—a broken, "tragically elegant" figure telling simply as much as he knows of "the Truth":

—Wanted to—keep on tossing—those long, long!—high, high!—passes that—couldn't be intercepted except by time, the aerial attack that made us famous! And so we did, we did, we kept it up for one season, that aerial attack, we held it high!—Yeah, but—

—that summer, Maggie, she laid the law down to me, said, Now or never, and so I married Maggie. . . .

BIG DADDY. How was Maggie in bed?

BRICK *(wryly).* Great! the greatest!

BIG DADDY nods as if he thought so.

She went on the road that fall with the Dixie Stars. Oh, she made a great show of being the world's best sport. She wore a—wore a—tall bearskin cap! A shako, they call it, a dyed moleskin coat, a moleskin coat dyed red!—Cut up crazy! Rented hotel ballrooms for victory celebrations, wouldn't cancel them when it—turned out—defeat. . . .

MAGGIE THE CAT! Ha ha!

Big Daddy nods.

—But Skipper, he had some fever which came back on him which doctors couldn't explain and I got that injury—turned out to be just a shadow on the X-ray plate—and a touch of bursitis. . . .

I lay in a hospital bed, watched our games on TV, saw Maggie on the bench next to Skipper when he was hauled out of a game for stumbles, fumbles!—Burned me up the way she hung on his arm!—Y'know, I think that Maggie had always felt sort of left out because she and me never got any closer together than two people just get in bed, which is not much closer than two cats on a—fence humping. . . .

So! She took this time to work on poor dumb Skipper. He was a less than average student at Ole Miss, you know that, don't you?!—Poured in his mind the dirty, false idea that what we were, him and me, was a frustrated case of that ole pair of sisters that lived in this room, Jack Straw and Peter Ochello!—He, poor Skipper, went to bed with Maggie to prove it wasn't true, and when it didn't work out, he thought it *was* true!—Skipper broke in two like a rotten stick—nobody ever turned so fast to a lush—or died of it so quick. . . .

—Now are you satisfied?

Big Daddy has listened to this story, dividing the grain from the chaff. Now he looks at his son.

BIG DADDY. Are *you* satisfied?

BRICK. With what?

BIG DADDY. That half-ass story!

BRICK. What's half-ass about it?

BIG DADDY. Something's left out of that story. What did you leave out?

The phone has started ringing in the hall.

GOOPER (*off stage*). Hello.

As if it reminded him of something, Brick glances suddenly toward the sound and says:

BRICK. Yes!—I left out a long-distance call which I had from Skipper—

GOOPER. Speaking, go ahead.

BRICK. —In which he made a drunken confession to me and on which I hung up!

GOOPER. No.

BRICK. —Last time we spoke to each other in our lives . . .

GOOPER. No, sir.

BIG DADDY. You musta said something to him before you hung up.

BRICK. What could I say to him?

BIG DADDY. Anything. Something.

BRICK. Nothing.

BIG DADDY. Just hung up?

BRICK. Just hung up.

BIG DADDY. Uh-huh. Anyhow now!—we have tracked down the lie with which you're disgusted and which you are drinking to kill your disgust with, Brick. You been passing the buck. This disgust with mendacity is disgust with yourself.

You!—dug the grave of your friend and kicked him in it!—before you'd face truth with him!

BRICK. *His* truth, not *mine!*

BIG DADDY. His truth, okay! But you wouldn't face it with him!

BRICK. Who *can* face truth? Can *you?*

BIG DADDY. Now don't start passin' the rotten buck again, boy!

BRICK. How about these birthday congratulations, these many, many happy returns of the day, when ev'rybody knows there won't be any except you!

Gooper, who has answered the hall phone, lets out a high, shrill laugh; the voice becomes audible saying: "No, no, you got it all wrong! Upside down! Are you crazy?"

Brick suddenly catches his breath as he realized that he has made a shocking disclosure. He hobbles a few paces, then freezes, and without looking at his father's shocked face, says:

Let's, let's—go out, now, and—watch the fireworks. Come on, Big Daddy.

BIG DADDY moves suddenly forward and grabs hold of the boy's crutch like it was a weapon for which they were fighting for possession.

BIG DADDY. Oh, no, no! No one's going out! What did you start to say?

BRICK. I don't remember.

BIG DADDY. "Many happy returns when they know there won't be any"?

BRICK. Aw, hell, Big Daddy, forget it. Come on out on the gallery and look at the fireworks they're shooting off for your birthday. . . .

BIG DADDY. First you finish that remark you were makin' before you cut off. "Many happy returns when they know there won't be any"?—Ain't that what you just said?

BRICK. Look, now. I can get around without that crutch if I have to but it would be a lot easier on the furniture an' glassware if I didn' have to go swinging along like Tarzan of th'—

BIG DADDY. FINISH! WHAT YOU WAS SAYIN'!

An eerie green glow shows in sky behind him.

BRICK (*sucking the ice in his glass, speech becoming thick*). Leave th' place to Gooper and Mae an' their five little same little monkeys. All I want is—

BIG DADDY. "LEAVE TH' PLACE," did you say?

BRICK (*vaguely*). All twenty-eight thousand acres of the richest land this side of the valley Nile.

BIG DADDY. Who said I was "leaving the place" to Gooper or anybody? This is my sixty-fifth birthday! I got fifteen years or twenty years left in me! I'll outlive *you*! I'll bury you an' have to pay for your coffin!

BRICK. Sure. Many happy returns. Now let's go watch the fireworks, come on, let's—

BIG DADDY. Lying, have they been lying? About the report from th'—clinic? Did they, did they—find something?—*Cancer.* Maybe?

BRICK. Mendacity is a system that we live in. Liquor is one way out an' death's the other. . . .

He takes the crutch from BIG DADDY's loose grip and swings out on the gallery leaving the doors open.

A song, "Pick a Bale of Cotton," is heard.

MAE (*appearing in door*). Oh, Big Daddy, the field hands are singin' fo' you!

BRICK. I'm sorry, Big Daddy. My head don't work any more and it's hard for me to understand how anybody could care if he lived or died or was dying or cared about anything but whether or not there was liquor left in the bottle and so I said what I said without thinking. In some ways I'm no better than the others, in some ways worse because I'm less alive. Maybe it's being alive that makes them lie, and being almost *not* alive makes me sort of accidentally truthful—I don't know but—anyway—we've been friends . . .

—And being friends is telling each other the truth. . . .

There is a pause.

You told *me*! I told *you*!

BIG DADDY (*slowly and passionately*). CHRIST—DAMN—

GOOPER (*offstage*). Let her go!

Fireworks off stage right.

BIG DADDY. —ALL—LYING SONS OF—LYING BITCHES!

He straightens at last and crosses to the inside door. At the door he turns and looks back as if he had some desperate question he couldn't put into words. Then he nods reflectively and says in a hoarse voice:

Yes, all liars, all liars, all lying dying liars!

This is said slowly, slowly, with a fierce revulsion. He goes on out.

—Lying! Dying! Liars!

BRICK remains motionless as the lights dim out and the curtain falls.

CURTAIN.

ACT THREE

THERE IS NO LAPSE OF TIME. BIG DADDY IS SEEN LEAVING AS AT THE END OF ACT II.

BIG DADDY. ALL LYIN'—DYIN'!—LIARS! LIARS!—LIARS!

MARGARET enters.

MARGARET. Brick, what in the name of God was goin' on in this room?

DIXIE and TRIXIE enter through the doors and circle around MARGARET shouting. MAE enters from the lower gallery window.

MAE. Dixie, Trixie, you quit that!

GOOPER enters through the doors.

Gooper, will y' please get these kiddies to bed right now!

GOOPER. Mae, you seen Big Mama?

MAE. Not yet.

GOOPER and kids exit through the doors.
REVEREND TOOKER enters through the windows.

REVEREND TOOKER. Those kiddies are so full of vitality. I think I'll have to be starting back to town.

MAE. Not yet, Preacher. You know we regard you as a member of this family, one of our closest an' dearest, so you just got t' be with us when Doc Baugh gives Big Mama th' actual truth about th' report from the clinic.

MARGARET. Where do you think you're going?

BRICK. Out for some air.

MARGARET. Why'd Big Daddy shout "Liars"?

MAE. Has Big Daddy gone to bed, Brick?

GOOPER [*entering*]. Now where is that old lady?

REVEREND TOOKER. I'll look for her.

He exits to the gallery.

MAE. Cain'tcha find her, Gooper?

GOOPER. She's avoidin' this talk.

MAE. I think she senses somethin'.

MARGARET. (*going out on the gallery to* BRICK). Brick, they're goin' to tell Big Mama the truth about Big Daddy and she's goin' to need you.

DOCTOR BAUGH. This is going to be painful.

MAE. Painful things caint always be avoided.

REVEREND TOOKER. I see Big Mama.

GOOPER. Hey, Big Mama, come here.

MAE. Hush, Gooper, don't holler.

BIG MAMA (*entering*). Too much smell of burnt fireworks makes me feel a little bit sick at my stomach.—Where is Big Daddy?

MAE. That's what I want to know, where has Big Daddy gone?

BIG MAMA. He must have turned in, I reckon he went to baid.

GOOPER. Well, then, now we can talk.

BIG MAMA. What *is* this talk, *what* talk?

MARGARET appears on the gallery, talking to Doctor Baugh.

MARGARET. (*musically*). My family freed their slaves ten years before abolition. My great-great-grandfather gave his slaves their freedom five years before the War between the States started!

MAE. Oh, for God's sake! Maggie's climbed back up in her family tree!

MARGARET. (*sweetly*). What, Mae?

The pace must be very quick: great Southern animation.

BIG MAMA (*Addressing them all*). I think Big Daddy was just worn out. He loves his family, he loves to have them around him, but it's a strain on his nerves. He wasn't himself tonight, Big Daddy wasn't himself, I could tell he was all worked up.

REVEREND TOOKER. I think he's remarkable.

BIG MAMA. Yaisss! Just remarkable. Did you all notice the food he ate at that table? Did you all notice the supper he put away? Why he ate like a hawss!

GOOPER. I hope he doesn't regret it.

BIG MAMA. What? Why that man—ate a huge piece of cawn bread with molasses on it! Helped himself twice to hoppin' John.

MARGARET. Big Daddy loves hoppin' John.—We had a real country dinner.

BIG MAMA (*overlapping* MARGARET). Yaiss, he simply adores it! an' candied yams? Son? That man put away enough food at that table to stuff a *field* hand!

GOOPER (*with grim relish*). I hope he don't have to pay for it later on.

BIG MAMA (*fiercely*). What's *that*, Gooper?

MAE. Gooper says he hopes Big Daddy doesn't suffer tonight.

BIG MAMA. Oh, shoot, Gooper says, Gooper says! Why should Big Daddy suffer for satisfying a normal appetite? There's nothin' wrong with that man but nerves, he's sound as a dollar! And now he knows he is an' that's why he ate such a supper. He had a big load off his mind, knowin' he wasn't doomed t'—what he thought he was doomed to . . .

MARGARET. (*sadly and sweetly*). Bless his old sweet soul . . .

BIG MAMA (*vaguely*). Yais, bless his heart, where's Brick?

MAE. Outside.

GOOPER. —Drinkin' . . .

BIG MAMA. I know he's drinkin'. Cain't I see he's drinkin' without you continually tellin' me that boy's drinkin'?

MARGARET. Good for you, Big Mama!

She applauds.

BIG MAMA. Other people *drink* and *have* drunk an' *will* *drink*, as long as they make that stuff an' put it in bottles.

MARGARET. That's the truth. I never trusted a man that didn't drink.

BIG MAMA. *Brick? Brick!*

MARGARET. He's still on the gall'ry. I'll go bring him in so we can talk.

BIG MAMA (*worriedly*). I don't know what this mysterious family conference is about.

Awkward silence. BIG MAMA looks from face to face, then belches slightly and mutters, "Excuse me . . ."
She opens an ornamental fan suspended about her throat. A black lace fan to go with her black lace gown, and fans her wilting corsage, sniffing nervously and looking from face to face in the uncomfortable silence as MARGARET calls "Brick?" and BRICK sings to the moon on the gallery.

MARGARET. Brick, they're gonna tell Big Mama the truth an' she's gonna need you.

BIG MAMA. I don't know what's wrong here, you all have such long faces! Open that door on the hall and let some air circulate through here, will you please, Gooper?

MAE. I think we'd better leave that door closed, Big Mama, till after the talk.

MARGARET. Brick!

BIG MAMA. Reveren' Tooker, will *you* please open that door?

REVEREND TOOKER. I sure will, Big Mama.

MAE. I just didn't think we ought t' take any chance of Big Daddy hearin' a word of this discussion.

BIG MAMA. *I swan!* Nothing's going to be said in Big Daddy's house that he caint hear if he want to!

GOOPER. Well, Big Mama, it's—

MAE gives him a quick, hard poke to shut him up. He glares at her fiercely as she circles before him like a burlesque ballerina, raising her skinny bare arms over her head, jangling her bracelets, exclaiming:

MAE. *A breeze! A breeze!*

REVEREND TOOKER. I think this house is the coolest house in the Delta.—Did you all know that Halsey Banks's widow put air-conditioning units in the church and rectory at Friar's Point in memory of Halsey?

General conversation has resumed; everybody is chatting so that the stage sounds like a bird cage.

GOOPER. Too bad nobody cools your church off for you. I bet you sweat in that pulpit these hot Sundays, Reverend Tooker.

REVEREND TOOKER. Yes, my vestments are drenched. Last Sunday the gold in my chasuble faded into the purple.

GOOPER. Reveren', you musta been preachin' hell's fire last Sunday.

MAE [*at the same time to Doctor Baugh*]. You reckon those vitamin B12 injections are what they're cracked up t' be, Doc Baugh?

DOCTOR BAUGH. Well, if you want to be stuck with something I guess they're as good to be stuck with as anything else.

BIG MAMA [*at the gallery door*]. *Maggie, Maggie, aren't you comin' with Brick?*

MAE (*suddenly and loudly, creating a silence*). I have a strange feeling, I have a peculiar feeling!

BIG MAMA (*turning from the gallery*). What feeling?

MAE. That Brick said somethin' he shouldn't of said t' Big Daddy.

BIG MAMA. Now what on earth could Brick of said t' Big Daddy that he shouldn't say?

GOOPER. Big Mama, there's somethin'—

MAE. NOW, WAIT!

She rushes up to BIG MAMA *and gives her a quick hug and kiss.* BIG MAMA *pushes her impatiently off.*

DOCTOR BAUGH. In my day they had what they call the Keeley cure for heavy drinkers.

BIG MAMA. Shoot!

DOCTOR BAUGH. But now I understand they just take some kind of tablets.

GOOPER. They call them "Annie Bust" tablets.

BIG MAMA. *Brick* don't need to take *nothin'*.

BRICK *and* MARGARET *appear in gallery doors,* BIG MAMA *unaware of his presence behind her.*

That boy is just broken up over Skipper's death. You know how poor Skipper died. They gave him a big, big dose of that sodium amytal stuff at his home and then they called the ambulance and give him another big, big dose of it at the hospital and that and all of the alcohol in his system fo' months an' months just proved too much for his heart . . . I'm scared of needles! I'm more scared of a needle than the knife . . . I think more people have been needled out of this world than—

She stops short and wheels about.

Oh—here's Brick! My precious baby—

She turns upon BRICK *with short, fat arms extended, at the same time uttering a loud, short sob, which is both comic and touching.* BRICK *smiles and bows slightly, making a burlesque gesture of gallantry for* MARGARET *to pass before him into the room. Then he hobbles on his crutch directly to the liquor cabinet and there is absolute silence, with everybody looking at* BRICK *as everybody has always looked at* BRICK *when he spoke or moved or appeared. One by one he drops ice cubes in his glass, then suddenly, but not quickly, looks back over his shoulder with a wry, charming smile, and says:*

BRICK. I'm sorry! Anyone else?

BIG MAMA (*sadly*). No, son. I *wish* you wouldn't!

BRICK. I wish I didn't have to, Big Mama, but I'm still waiting for that click in my head which makes it all smooth out!

BIG MAMA. Ow, Brick, you—BREAK MY HEART!

MARGARET (*at same time*). Brick, go sit with Big Mama!

BIG MAMA. I just cain't staiiiiii-nnnnnnnd-it . . .

She sobs.

MAE. Now that we're all assembled—

GOOPER. We kin talk . . .

BIG MAMA. Breaks my heart . . .

MARGARET. Sit with Big Mama, Brick, and hold her hand.

BIG MAMA *sniffs very loudly three times, almost like three drumbeats in the pocket of silence.*

BRICK. You do that, Maggie. I'm a restless cripple. I got to stay on my crutch.

BRICK *hobbles to the gallery door; leans there as if waiting.*

MAE *sits beside* BIG MAMA, *while* GOOPER *moves in front and sits on the end of the couch, facing her.* REVEREND TOOKER *moves nervously into the space between them; on the other side,* DOCTOR BAUGH *stands looking at nothing in particular and lights a cigar.* MARGARET *turns away.*

BIG MAMA. Why're you all *surroundin'* me—like this? Why're you all starin' at me like this an' makin' signs at each other?

REVEREND TOOKER *steps back startled.*

MAE. Calm yourself, Big Mama.

BIG MAMA. Calm you'self, *you'self*, Sister Woman. How could I calm myself with everyone starin' at me as if big drops of blood had broken out on m'face? What's this all about, annh! What?

GOOPER *coughs and takes a center position.*

GOOPER. Now, Doc Baugh.

MAE. Doc Baugh?

GOOPER. Big Mama wants to know the complete truth about the report we got from the Ochsner Clinic.

MAE (*eagerly*). —on Big Daddy's condition!

GOOPER. Yais, on Big Daddy's condition, we got to face it.

DOCTOR BAUGH. Well . . .

BIG MAMA (*terrified, rising*). Is there? Something? Something that I? Don't—know?

In these few words, this startled, very soft, question, BIG MAMA reviews the history of her forty-five years with BIG DADDY, her great, almost embarrassingly true-hearted and simple-minded devotion to BIG DADDY, who must have had something BRICK has, who made himself loved so much by the "simple expedient" of not loving enough to disturb his charming detachment, also once coupled, like Brick, with virile beauty.

BIG MAMA has a dignity at this moment; she almost stops being fat.

DOCTOR BAUGH (*after a pause, uncomfortably*). Yes?—Well—

BIG MAMA. I!!!—want to—knowwwwww . . .

Immediately she thrusts her fist to her mouth as if to deny that statement. Then for some curious reason, she snatches the withered corsage from her breast and hurls it on the floor and steps on it with her short, fat feet.

Somebody must be lyin'!—I want to know!

MAE. Sit down, Big Mama, sit down on this sofa.

MARGARET. Brick, go sit with Big Mama.

BIG MAMA. *What is it, what is it?*

DOCTOR BAUGH. I never have seen a more thorough examination than Big Daddy Pollitt was given in all my experience with the Ochsner Clinic.

GOOPER. It's one of the best in the country.

MAE. It's THE best in the country—bar *none!*

For some reason she gives GOOPER a violent poke as she goes past him. He slaps at her hand without removing his eyes from his mother's face.

DOCTOR BAUGH. Of course they were ninety-nine and nine-tenths per cent sure before they even started.

BIG MAMA. Sure of what, sure of what, sure of—what?—what?

She catches her breath in a startled sob. Mae kisses her quickly. She thrusts Mae fiercely away from her, staring at the DOCTOR.

MAE. Mommy, be a brave girl!

BRICK (*in the doorway, softly*). "By the light, by the light, Of the sil-ve-ry mo-oo-n . . ."

GOOPER. Shut up!—Brick.

BRICK. Sorry . . .

He wanders out on the gallery.

DOCTOR BAUGH. But now, you see, Big Mama, they cut a piece off this growth, a specimen of the tissue and—

BIG MAMA. Growth? You told Big Daddy—

DOCTOR BAUGH. Now wait.

BIG MAMA (*fiercely*). You told me and Big Daddy there wasn't a thing wrong with him but—

MAE. Big Mama, they always—

GOOPER. Let Doc Baugh talk, will yuh?

BIG MAMA. —little spastic condition of—

Her breath gives out in a sob.

DOCTOR BAUGH. Yes, that's what we told Big Daddy. But we had this bit of tissue run through the laboratory and I'm sorry to say the test was positive on it. It's—well—malignant . . .

Pause.

BIG MAMA. —Cancer?! Cancer?!

DOCTOR BAUGH nods gravely. BIG MAMA gives a long gasping cry.

MAE AND GOOPER. Now, now, now, Big Mama, you had to know . . .

BIG MAMA. WHY DIDN'T THEY CUT IT OUT OF HIM? HANH? HANH?

DOCTOR BAUGH. Involved too much, Big Mama, too many organs affected.

MAE. Big Mama, the liver's affected and so's the kidneys, both! It's gone way past what they call a—

GOOPER. A surgical risk.

MAE. —Uh-huh . . .

BIG MAMA draws a breath like a dying gasp.

REVEREND TOOKER. Tch, tch, tch, tch, tch!

DOCTOR BAUGH. Yes it's gone past the knife.

MAE. *That's why he's turned yellow, Mommy!*

BIG MAMA. *Git away from me, git away from me, Mae!*

She rises abruptly.

I want Brick! Where's Brick? Where is my only son?

MAE. Mama! Did she say *"only son"*?

GOOPER. What does that make *me*?

MAE. A sober responsible man with five precious children!—*Six!*

BIG MAMA. I want Brick to tell me! Brick! Brick!

MARGARET. *(rising from her reflections in a corner).* Brick was so upset he went back out.

BIG MAMA. *Brick!*

MARGARET. Mama, let *me* tell you!

BIG MAMA. No, no, leave me alone, you're not my blood!

GOOPER. *Mama, I'm your son!* Listen to *me*!

MAE. Gooper's your son, he's your first-born!

BIG MAMA. Gooper never liked Daddy.

MAE *(as if terribly shocked).* That's not TRUE!

There is a pause. The minister coughs and rises.

REVEREND TOOKER *(to Mae).* I think I'd better slip away at this point.

Discreetly.

Good night, good night, everybody, and God bless you all . . . on this place . . .

He slips out.

Mae coughs and points at Big Mama.

GOOPER. Well, Big Mama . . .

He sighs.

BIG MAMA. It's all a mistake, I know it's just a bad dream.

DOCTOR BAUGH. We're gonna keep Big Daddy as comfortable as we can.

BIG MAMA. Yes, it's just a bad dream, that's all it is, it's just an awful dream.

GOOPER. In my opinion Big Daddy is having some pain but won't admit that he has it.

BIG MAMA. Just a dream, a bad dream.

DOCTOR BAUGH. That's what lots of them do, they think if they don't admit they're having the pain they can sort of escape the fact of it.

GOOPER *(with relish).* Yes, they get sly about it, they get real sly about it.

MAE. Gooper and I think—

GOOPER. Shut up, Mae! Big Mama, I think—Big Daddy ought to be started on morphine.

BIG MAMA. Nobody's going to give Big Daddy morphine.

DOCTOR BAUGH. Now, Big Mama, when that pain strikes it's going to strike mighty hard and Big Daddy's going to need the needle to bear it.

BIG MAMA. I tell you, nobody's going to give him morphine.

MAE. Big Mama, you don't want to see Big Daddy suffer, you know you—

Gooper, standing beside her, gives her a savage poke.

DOCTOR BAUGH *(placing a package on the table).* I'm leaving this stuff here, so if there's a sudden attack you all won't have to send out for it.

MAE. I know how to give a hypo.

BIG MAMA. Nobody's gonna give Big Daddy morphine.

GOOPER. Mae took a course in nursing during the war.

MARGARET. Somehow I don't think Big Daddy would want Mae to give him a hypo.

MAE. You think he'd want *you* to do it?

DOCTOR BAUGH. Well . . .

Doctor Baugh rises.

GOOPER. Doctor Baugh is goin'.

DOCTOR BAUGH. Yes, I got to be goin'. Well, keep your chin up, Big Mama.

GOOPER *(with jocularity).* She's gonna keep *both* chins up, aren't you, Big Mama?

Big Mama sobs.

Now stop that, Big Mama.

GOOPER *[at the door with Doctor Baugh].* Well, Doc, we sure do appreciate all you done. I'm telling you, we're surely obligated to you for—

DOCTOR BAUGH has gone out without a glance at him.

—I guess that doctor has got a lot on his mind but it wouldn't hurt him to act a little more human . . .

BIG MAMA sobs.

Now be a brave girl, Mommy.

BIG MAMA. It's not true, I know that it's just not true!

GOOPER. Mama, those tests are infallible!

BIG MAMA. Why are you so determined to see your father daid?

MAE. Big Mama!

MARGARET. (*gently*). I know what Big Mama means.

MAE (*fiercely*). Oh, do you?

MARGARET. (*quietly and very sadly*). Yes, I think I do.

MAE. For a newcomer in the family you sure do show a lot of understanding.

MARGARET. Understanding is needed on this place.

MAE. I guess you must have needed a lot of it in your family, Maggie, with your father's liquor problem and now you've got Brick with his!

MARGARET. Brick does not have a liquor problem at all. Brick is devoted to Big Daddy. This thing is a terrible strain on him.

BIG MAMA. Brick is Big Daddy's boy, but he drinks too much and it worries me and Big Daddy, and, Margaret, you've got to cooperate with us, you've got to co-operate with Big Daddy and me in getting Brick straightened out. Because it will break Big Daddy's heart if Brick don't pull himself together and take hold of things.

MAE. Take hold of *what* things, Big Mama?

BIG MAMA. The place.

There is a quick violent look between MAE and GOOPER.

GOOPER. Big Mama, you've had a shock.

MAE. Yais, we've all had a shock, but . . .

GOOPER. Let's be realistic—

MAE. —Big Daddy would never, would *never*, be foolish enough to—

GOOPER. —put this place in irresponsible hands!

BIG MAMA. Big Daddy ain't going to leave the place in anybody's hands; Big Daddy is *not* going to die. I want you to get that in your heads, all of you!

MAE. Mommy, Mommy, Big Mama, we're just as hopeful an' optimistic as you are about Big Daddy's prospects, we have faith in *prayer*—but nevertheless there are certain matters that have to be discussed an' dealt with, because otherwise—

GOOPER. Eventualities have to be considered and now's the time . . . Mae, will you please get my brief case out of our room?

MAE. Yes, honey.

She rises and goes out through the hall door.

GOOPER (*standing over BIG MAMA*). Now, Big Mom. What you said just now was not at all true and you know it. I've always loved Big Daddy in my own quiet way. I never made a show of it, and I know that Big Daddy has always been fond of me in a quiet way, too, and he never made a show of it neither.

MAE returns with GOOPER's brief case.

MAE. Here's your brief case, Gooper, honey.

GOOPER (*handing the brief case back to her*). Thank you . . . Of cou'se, my relationship with Big Daddy is different from Brick's.

MAE. You're eight years older'n Brick an' always had t' carry a bigger load of th' responsibilities than Brick ever had t' carry. He never carried a thing in his life but a football or a highball.

GOOPER. Mae, will y' let me talk, please?

MAE. Yes, honey.

GOOPER. Now, a twenty-eight-thousand-acre plantation's a mighty big thing t' run.

MAE. Almost singlehanded.

Margaret has gone out onto the gallery and can be HEARD calling softly to Brick.

BIG MAMA. You never had to run this place! What are you talking about? As if Big Daddy was dead and in his grave, you had to run it? Why, you just helped him out with a few business details and had your law practice at the same time in Memphis!

MAE. Oh, Mommy, Mommy, Big Mommy! Let's be fair!

MARGARET. Brick!

MAE. Why, Gooper has given himself body and soul to keeping this place up for the past five years since Big Daddy's health started failing.

MARGARET. Brick!

MAE. Gooper won't say it, Gooper never thought of it as a duty, he just did it. And what did Brick do? Brick kept living in his past glory at college! Still a football player at twenty-seven!

MARGARET. [*returning alone*]. Who are you talking about now? Brick? A football player? He isn't a football player and you know it. Brick is a sports announcer on T.V. and one of the best-known ones in the country!

MAE. I'm talking about what he *was*.

MARGARET. Well, I wish you would just stop talking about my husband.

GOOPER. I've got a right to discuss my brother with other members of MY OWN family, which don't include *you*. Why don't you go out there and drink with Brick?

MARGARET. I've never seen such malice toward a brother.

GOOPER. How about his for me? Why, he can't stand to be in the same room with me!

MARGARET. This is a deliberate campaign of vilification for the most disgusting and sordid reason on earth, and I know what it is! It's *avarice, avarice, greed, greed!*

BIG MAMA. *Oh, I'll scream! I will scream in a moment unless this stops!*

GOOPER has stalked up to MARGARET with clenched fists at his sides as if he would strike her. MAE distorts her face again into a hideous grimace behind MARGARET's back.

BIG MAMA (*sobs*). Margaret. Child. Come here. Sit next to Big Mama.

MARGARET. Precious Mommy. I'm sorry, I'm sorry, I—!

She bends her long graceful neck to press her

forehead to BIG MAMA'S *bulging shoulder under its black chiffon.*

MAE. How beautiful, how touching, this display of devotion! Do you know why she's childless? She's childless because that big beautiful athlete husband of hers won't go to bed with her!

GOOPER. You jest won't let me do this in a nice way, will yah? Aw right—I don't give a goddam if Big Daddy likes me or don't like me or did or never did or will or will never! I'm just appealing to a sense of common decency and fair play. I'll tell you the truth. I've resented Big Daddy's partiality to Brick ever since Brick was born, and the way I've been treated like I was just barely good enough to spit on and sometimes not even good enough for that. Big Daddy is dying of cancer, and it's spread all through him and it's attacked all his vital organs including the kidneys and right now he is sinking into uremia, and you all know what uremia is, it's poisoning of the whole system due to the failure of the body to eliminate its poisons.

MARGARET (*to herself, downstage, hissingly*). *Poisons, poisons! Venomous thoughts and words! In hearts and minds!—That's poisons!*

GOOPER (*overlapping her*). I am asking for a square deal, and, by God, I expect to get one. But if I don't get one, if there's any peculiar shenanigans going on around here behind my back, well, I'm not a corporation lawyer for nothing, I know how to protect my own interests.

BRICK enters from the gallery with a tranquil, blurred smile, carrying an empty glass with him.

BRICK. Storm coming up.

GOOPER. Oh! A late arrival!

MAE. Behold the conquering hero comes!

GOOPER. The fabulous Brick Pollitt! Remember him?—Who could forget him!

MAE. He looks like he's been injured in a game!

GOOPER. Yep, I'm afraid you'll have to warm the bench at the Sugar Bowl this year, Brick!

MAE laughs shrilly.

Or was it the Rose Bowl that he made that famous run in?—

Thunder.

MAE. The punch bowl, honey. It was in the punch bowl, the cut-glass punch bowl!

GOOPER. Oh, that's right, I'm getting the bowls mixed up!

MARGARET. Why don't you stop venting your malice and envy on a sick boy?

BIG MAMA. *Now you two hush, I mean it, hush, all of you, hush!*

DAISY, SOOKEY. Storm! Storm comin'! Storm! Storm!

LACEY. Brightie, close them shutters.

GOOPER. Lacey, put the top up on my Cadillac, will yuh?

LACEY. Yes, suh, Mistah Pollitt!

GOOPER (*at the same time*), Big Mama, you know it's necessary for me t' go back to Memphis in th' mornin' t' represent the Parker estate in a lawsuit.

MAE sits on the bed and arranges papers she has taken from the brief case.

BIG MAMA. Is it, Gooper?

MAE. Yaiss.

GOOPER. That's why I'm forced to—to bring up a problem that—

MAE. Somethin' that's too important t' be put off!

GOOPER. If Brick was sober, he ought to be in on this.

MARGARET. Brick is present; we're present.

GOOPER. Well, good. I will now give you this outline my partner, Tom Bullitt, an' me have drawn up—a sort of dummy—trusteeship.

MARGARET. Oh, that's it! You'll be in charge an' dole out remittances, will you?

GOOPER. This we did as soon as we got the report on Big Daddy from th' Ochsner Laboratories. We did this thing, I mean we drew up this dummy outline with the advice and assistance of the Chairman of the Boa'd of Directors of th' Southern Plantahs Bank and Trust Company in Memphis, C. C. Bellowes, a man who handles estates for all th' prominent fam'lies in West Tennessee and th' Delta.

BIG MAMA. Gooper?

GOOPER (*crouching in front of Big Mama*). Now this is not—not final, or anything like it. This is

just a preliminary outline. But it does provide a basis—a design—a—possible, feasible—*plan!*

MARGARET. Yes, I'll bet it's a plan.

Thunder.

MAE. It's a plan to protect the biggest estate in the Delta from irresponsibility an'—

BIG MAMA. Now you listen to me, all of you, you listen here! They's not goin' to be any more catty talk in my house! And Gooper, you put that away before I grab it out of your hand and tear it right up! I don't know what the hell's in it, and I don't want to know what the hell's in it. I'm talkin' in Big Daddy's language now; I'm his *wife*, not his *widow*, I'm still his *wife!* And I'm talkin' to you in his language an'—

GOOPER. Big Mama, what I have here is—

MAE (*at the same time*). Gooper explained that it's just a plan . . .

BIG MAMA. I don't care what you got there. Just put it back where it came from, an' don't let me see it again, not even the outside of the envelope of it! Is that understood? Basis! Plan! Preliminary! Design! I say—what is it Big Daddy always says when he's disgusted?

BRICK (*from the bar*). Big Daddy says "crap" when he's disgusted.

BIG MAMA (*rising*). That's right—CRAP! I say CRAP too, like Big Daddy!

Thunder.

MAE. Coarse language doesn't seem called for in this—

GOOPER. Somethin' in me is *deeply outraged* by hearin' you talk like this.

BIG MAMA. *Nobody's goin' to take nothin'!*—till Big Daddy lets go of it—maybe, just possibly, not—not even then! No, not even then!

Thunder.

MAE. Sookey, hurry up an' git that po'ch furniture covahed; want th' paint to come off?

GOOPER. Lacey, put mah car away!

LACEY. Caint, Mistah Pollitt, you got the keys!

GOOPER. Naw, you got 'em, man. Where th' keys to th' car, honey?

MAE. You got 'em in your pocket!

BRICK. "You can always hear me singin' this song, Show me the way to go home."

Thunder distantly.

BIG MAMA. Brick! Come here, Brick, I need you. Tonight Brick looks like he used to look when he was a little boy, just like he did when he played wild games and used to come home when I hollered myself hoarse for him, all sweaty and pink cheeked and sleepy, with his—red curls shining . . .

BRICK draws aside as he does from all physical contact and continues the song in a whisper, opening the ice bucket and dropping in the ice cubes one by one as if he were mixing some important chemical formula.

Distant thunder.

Time goes by so fast. Nothin' can outrun it. Death commences too early—almost before you're half acquainted with life—you meet the other . . . Oh, you know we just got to love each other an' stay together, all of us, just as close as we can, especially now that such a *black* thing has come and moved into this place without invitation.

Awkwardly embracing BRICK, she presses her head to his shoulder.

A dog howls off stage.

Oh, Brick, son of Big Daddy, Big Daddy does so love you. Y'know what would be his fondest dream come true? If before he passed on, if Big Daddy has to pass on . . .

A dog howls.

. . . you give him a child of yours, a grandson as much like his son as his son is like Big Daddy . . .

MARGARET. I know that's Big Daddy's dream.

BIG MAMA. That's his dream.

MAE. Such a pity that Maggie and Brick can't oblige.

BIG DADDY (*off down stage right on the gallery*). Looks like the wind was takin' liberties with this place.

SERVANT (*off stage*). Yes, sir, Mr. Pollitt.

MARGARET. (*crossing to the right door*). Big Daddy's on the gall'ry.

BIG MAMA has turned toward the hall door at the sound of BIG DADDY's voice on the gallery.

BIG MAMA. I can't stay here. He'll see somethin' in my eyes.

Big Daddy enters the room from up stage right.

BIG DADDY. Can I come in?

He puts his cigar in an ash tray.

MARGARET. Did the storm wake you up, Big Daddy?

BIG DADDY. Which stawm are you talkin' about— th' one outside or th' hullballoo in here?

GOOPER squeezes past Big Daddy.

GOOPER. 'Scuse me.

MAE tries to squeeze past BIG DADDY to join Gooper, but BIG DADDY puts his arm firmly around her.

BIG DADDY. I heard some mighty loud talk. Sounded like somethin' important was bein' discussed. What was the powwow about?

MAE (*flustered*). Why—nothin', Big Daddy . . .

BIG DADDY (*crossing to extreme left center, taking Mae with him*). What is that pregnant-lookin' envelope you're puttin' back in your brief case, Gooper?

GOOPER (*at the foot of the bed, caught as he stuffs papers into envelope*). That? Nothin,' suh—nothin' much of anythin' at all . . .

BIG DADDY. Nothin'? It looks like a whole lot of nothin'!

He turns up stage to the group.

You all know th' story about th' young married couple—

GOOPER. Yes, sir!

BIG DADDY. Hello, Brick—

BRICK. Hello, Big Daddy.

The group is arranged in a semicircle above BIG DADDY, MARGARET at the extreme right, then MAE and GOOPER, then BIG MAMA, with BRICK at the left.

BIG DADDY. Young married couple took Junior out to th' zoo one Sunday, inspected all of God's creatures in their cages, with satisfaction.

GOOPER. Satisfaction.

BIG DADDY (*crossing to up stage center, facing front*). This afternoon was a warm afternoon in spring an' that ole elephant had somethin' else on his mind which was bigger'n peanuts. You know this story, Brick?

Gooper nods.

BRICK. No, sir, I don't know it.

BIG DADDY. Y'see, in th' cage adjoinin' they was a young female elephant in heat!

BIG MAMA (*at Big Daddy's shoulder*). Oh, Big Daddy!

BIG DADDY. What's the matter, preacher's gone, ain't he? All right. That female elephant in the next cage was permeatin' the atmosphere about her with a powerful and excitin' odor of female fertility! Huh! Ain't that a nice way to put it, Brick?

BRICK. Yes, sir, nothin' wrong with it.

BIG DADDY. Brick says th's nothin' wrong with it!

BIG MAMA. Oh, Big Daddy!

BIG DADDY (*crossing to down stage center*). So this ole bull elephant still had a couple of fornications left in him. He reared back his trunk an' got a whiff of that elephant lady next door!—began to paw at the dirt in his cage an' butt his head against the separatin' partition and, first thing y'know, there was a conspicuous change in his *profile*—very *conspicuous*! Ain't I tellin' this story in decent language, Brick?

BRICK. Yes, sir, too fuckin' decent!

BIG DADDY. So, the little boy pointed at it and said, "What's that?" His mama said, "Oh, that's— nothin'!"—His papa said, "She's spoiled!"

BIG DADDY crosses to Brick at left.

You didn't laugh at that story, Brick.

BIG MAMA crosses to down stage right crying. MARGARET goes to her. MAE and GOOPER hold up stage right center.

BRICK. No, sir, I didn't laugh at that story.

BIG DADDY. What is the smell in this room? Don't you notice it, Brick? Don't you notice a powerful and obnoxious odor of mendacity in this room?

BRICK. Yes, sir, I think I do, sir.

GOOPER. Mae, Mae . . .

BIG DADDY. There is nothing more powerful. Is there, Brick?

BRICK. No, sir. No, sir, there isn't, an' nothin' more obnoxious.

BIG DADDY. Brick agrees with me. The odor of mendacity is a powerful and obnoxious odor an' the stawm hasn't blown it away from this room yet. You notice it, Gooper?

GOOPER. What, sir?

BIG DADDY. How about you, Sister Woman? You notice the unpleasant odor of mendacity in this room?

MAE. Why, Big Daddy, I don't even know what that is.

BIG DADDY. You can smell it. Hell it smells like death!

BIG MAMA sobs. BIG DADDY looks toward her.

What's wrong with that fat woman over there, loaded with diamonds? Hey, what's-you-name, what's the matter with you?

MARGARET (*crossing toward Big Daddy*).

She had a slight dizzy spell, Big Daddy.

BIG DADDY. You better watch that, Big Mama. A stroke is a bad way to go.

MARGARET. [*crossing to Big Daddy at center*]. Oh, Brick, Big Daddy has on your birthday present to him, Brick, he has on your cashmere robe, the softest material I have ever felt.

BIG DADDY. Yeah, this is my soft birthday, Maggie . . . Not my gold or my silver birthday, but my soft birthday, everything's got to be soft for Big Daddy on this soft birthday.

MAGGIE kneels before BIG DADDY at center.

MARGARET. Big Daddy's got on his Chinese slippers that I gave him, Brick. Big Daddy, I haven't given you my big present yet, but now I will, now's the time for me to present it to you! I have an announcement to make!

MAE. What? What kind of announcement?

GOOPER. A sports announcement, Maggie?

MARGARET. Announcement of life beginning! A child is coming, sired by Brick, and out of Maggie the Cat! I have Brick's child in my body, an' that's my birthday present to Big Daddy on this birthday!

BIG DADDY looks at BRICK who crosses behind BIG DADDY to down stage portal, left.

BIG DADDY. Get up, girl, get up off your knees, girl.

BIG DADDY helps Margaret to rise. He crosses above her, to her right, bites off the end of a fresh cigar, taken from his bathrobe pocket, as he studies MARGARET.

Uh-huh, this girl has life in her body, that's no lie!

BIG MAMA. BIG DADDY'S DREAM COME TRUE!

BRICK. JESUS!

BIG DADDY (*crossing right below wicker stand*). Gooper, I want my lawyer in the mornin'.

BRICK. Where are you goin', Big Daddy?

BIG DADDY. Son, I'm goin' up on the roof, to the belvedere on th' roof to look over my kingdom before I give up my kingdom—twenty-eight thousand acres of th' richest land this side of the valley Nile!

He exits through right doors, and down right on the gallery.

BIG MAMA (*following*). Sweetheart, sweetheart, sweetheart—can I come with you?

She exits down stage right.

MARGARET is down stage center in the mirror area. Mae has joined GOOPER and she gives him a fierce poke, making a low hissing sound and a grimace of fury.

GOOPER (*pushing her aside*). Brick, could you possibly spare me one small shot of that liquor?

BRICK. Why, help yourself, Gooper boy.

GOOPER. I will.

MAE (*shrilly*). Of course we know that this is—a lie.

GOOPER. Be still, Mae.

MAE. I won't be still! I know she's made this up!

GOOPER. Goddam it, I said shut up!

MARGARET. Gracious! I didn't know that my little announcement was going to provoke such a storm!

MAE. *That* woman isn't *pregnant!*

GOOPER. Who said she was?

MAE. *She* did.

GOOPER. The doctor didn't. Doc Baugh didn't.

MARGARET. I haven't gone to Doc Baugh.

GOOPER. Then who'd you go to, Maggie?

MARGARET. One of the best gynecologists in the South.

GOOPER. Uh huh, uh huh!—I see . . .

He takes out a pencil and notebook.
—May we have his name, please?

MARGARET. No, you may not, Mister Prosecuting Attorney!

MAE. He doesn't have any name, he doesn't exist!

MARGARET. Oh, he exists all right, and so does my child, Brick's baby!

MAE. You can't conceive a child by a man that won't sleep with you unless you think you're—

BRICK has turned on the phonograph, A scat song cuts MAE'S speech.

GOOPER. Turn that off!

MAE. We know it's a lie because we hear you in here; he won't sleep with you, we hear you! So don't imagine you're going to put a trick over on us, to fool a dying man with a—

A long drawn cry of agony and rage fills the house. MARGARET turns the phonograph down to a whisper. The cry is repeated.

MAE. Did you hear that, Gooper, did you hear that?

GOOPER. Sounds like the pain has struck.

GOOPER. Come along and leave these lovebirds together in their nest!

He goes out first. MAE follows but turns at the door, contorting her face and hissing at Margaret.

MAE. *Liar!*

She slams the door.

MARGARET exhales with relief and moves a little unsteadily to catch hold of BRICK'S arm.

MARGARET. Thank you for—keeping still . . .

BRICK. O.K., Maggie.

MARGARET. It was gallant of you to save my face!

He now pours down three shots in quick succession and stands waiting, silent. All at once he turns with a smile and says:

BRICK. *There!*

MARGARET. What?

BRICK. The *click* . . .

His gratitude seems almost infinite as he hobbles out on the gallery with a drink. We hear his crutch as he swings out of sight. Then, at some distance, he begins singing to himself a peaceful song. MARGARET holds the big pillow forlornly as if it were her only companion, for a few moments, then throws it on the bed. She rushes to the liquor cabinet, gathers all the bottles in her arms, turns about undecidedly, then runs out of the room with them, leaving the door ajar on the dim yellow hall. BRICK is heard hobbling back along the gallery, singing his peaceful song. He comes back in, sees the pillow on the bed, laughs lightly, sadly, picks it up. He has it under his arm as Margaret returns to the room. MARGARET softly shuts the door and leans against it, smiling softly at BRICK.

MARGARET. Brick, I used to think that you were stronger than me and I didn't want to be overpowered by you. But now, since you've taken to liquor—you know what?—I guess it's bad, but now I'm stronger than you and I can love you more truly! Don't move that pillow. I'll move it right back if you do!—Brick?

She turns out all the lamps but a single rose-silk-shaded one by the bed.

I really have been to a doctor and I know what to do and—Brick?—this is my time by the calendar to conceive?

BRICK. Yes, I understand, Maggie. But how are you going to conceive a child by a man in love with his liquor?

MARGARET. By locking his liquor up and making him satisfy my desire before I unlock it!

BRICK. Is that what you've done, Maggie?

MARGARET. Look and see. That cabinet's mighty empty compared to before!

BRICK. Well, I'll be a son of a—

He reaches for his crutch but she beats him to it and rushes out on the gallery, hurls the crutch over the rail and comes back in, panting.

MARGARET. And so tonight we're going to make the lie true, and when that's done, I'll bring the liquor back here and we'll get drunk together, here, tonight, in this place that death has come into . . .—What do you say?

BRICK. I don't say anything. I guess there's nothing to say.

MARGARET. Oh, you weak people, you weak, beautiful people!—who give up with such grace. What you want is someone to—

She turns out the rose-silk lamp.

—take hold of you.—Gently, gently with love hand your life back to you, like somethin' gold you let go of. I *do* love you, Brick, I *do*!

BRICK *(smiling with charming sadness).* Wouldn't it be funny if that was true?

THE END.

9

The Odd Couple

Play by Neil Simon (1927–)

*Directed by Mike Nichols with set designed by Oliver Smith, was
presented by Saint Subber at the Plymouth Theatre, N.Y.C., on March 10, 1965.*

CAST OF CHARACTERS

(In Order of Their Appearance)

SPEED . . . . .Paul Dooley
MURRAY . . . . .Nathaniel Frey
ROY . . . . .Sidney Armus
VINNIE . . . . .John Fiedler
OSCAR MADISON . . . . .Walter Matthau
FELIX UNGAR . . . . .Art Carney
GWENDOLYN PIGEON . . . . .Carole Shelley
CECILY PIGEON . . . . .Monica Evans

SCENES

An apartment on Riverside Drive. New York City.

THE ODD COUPLE

ACT I

Time

A warm summer night.

SCENE

The apartment of Oscar Madison's. This is one of those large eight-room affairs on Riverside Drive in the upper eighties. The building is about 35 years old and still has vestiges of its glorious past. High ceilings, walk-in closets and thick walls. We are in the living room with doors leading off to kitchen, bedrooms, and a bathroom, and a hallway to other bedrooms. Although the furnishings have been chosen with extreme good taste, the room itself, without the touch and care of a woman these past few months, is now a study in slovenliness. Dirty dishes, discarded clothes, old newspapers, empty bottles, glasses filled and unfilled, opened and unopened laundry packages, mail and disarrayed furniture abound. The only cheerful note left in this room is the lovely view of the New Jersey Palisades through its twelfth floor window. Three months ago, this was a lovely apartment.

AT RISE

The room is filled with smoke. A poker game is in progress. There are six chairs around the table but only four men are sitting. They are simply, Murray, ROY, SPEED and VINNIE. VINNIE, with the largest stack of chips in front of him, is nervously tapping his foot and keeps checking his watch. ROY is watching SPEED and SPEED is glaring at Murray with incredulity and utter fascination. Murray is the dealer. He slowly and methodically tries to shuffle. It is a ponderous and painful business. SPEED shakes his head in disbelief. This is all done wordlessly.

SPEED. (*Cups his chin in his hand and looks at Murray*) . . . Tell me, Mr. Maverick, is this your first time on the riverboat?

MURRAY. (*With utter disregard.*) You don't like it, get a machine. (*He continues to deal slowly.*)

ROY. Geez, it stinks in here.

VINNIE. (*Looks at his watch.*) What time is it?

SPEED. Again what time is it?

VINNIE. (*Whiny.*) My watch is slow. I'd like to know what time it is.

SPEED. (*Glares at him.*) You're winning ninety-five dollars, that's what time it is . . . Where the hell are you running?

VINNIE. I'm not running anywhere. I just asked what time it was. Who said anything about running?

ROY. (*Looks at his watch.*) It's ten-thirty.

(*Pause.* MURRAY *continues to shuffle.*)

VINNIE. (*Pause.*) I got to leave by twelve.

SPEED. (*Looks up in despair.*) Oh, Christ!

VINNIE. I told you that when I sat down. I got to leave by twelve. Murray, didn't I say that when I sat down? I said I got to leave by twelve.

SPEED. All right, don't talk to him. He's dealing. (*To* MURRAY.) Murray, you wanna rest for a while? Go lie down, sweetheart.

MURRAY. You want speed or accuracy, make up your mind. (*He begins to deal slowly.*)

(SPEED *puffs on his cigar angrily.*)

ROY. Hey, you want to do me a really big favor? Smoke towards New Jersey.

(SPEED *blows smoke at* ROY.)

MURRAY. No kidding, I'm really worried about Felix. (Points to empty chair.) He's never been this late before. Maybe somebody should call. (Yells Off.) Hey, Oscar, why don't you call Felix?

ROY. (Waves hand through smoke.) Listen, why don't we chip in three dollars apiece and buy another window. How the hell can you breathe in here?

MURRAY. How many cards you got, four?

SPEED. Yes, Murray, we all have four cards. When you give us one more, we'll all have five. If you were to give us two more, we'd have six. Understand how it works now?

ROY. (*Yells Off.*) Hey, Oscar, what do you say? In or out?

(*From Offstage we hear* OSCAR'S VOICE.)

OSCAR. (*Off.*) Out, pussy cat, out!

(SPEED *opens, and the* OTHERS *bet.*)

VINNIE. I told my wife I'd be home by one the latest. We're making an eight o'clock plane to Florida. I told you that when I sat down.

SPEED. Don't cry, Vinnie. You're forty-two years old. It's embarrassing. Give me two, . . . (*Discards.*)

ROY. Why doesn't he fix the air-conditioner? It's ninety-eight degrees and it sits there swearing like everyone else. I'm out. (*Goes to window and looks out.*)

MURRAY. Who goes to Florida in July?

VINNIE. It's off season. There's no crowds and you get the best room for one-tenth the price. No cards. . . .

SPEED. Some vacation. Six cheap people in an empty hotel.

MURRAY. Dealer takes four. . . . Hey, you think maybe Felix is sick? (*He points to empty chair.*) I mean he's never been this late before.

ROY. (*Takes laundry bag from armchair and sits.*) You know it's the same garbage from last week's game. I'm beginning to recognize things.

MURRAY. (*Throwing cards down.*) I'm out. . . .

SPEED. (*Showing hand.*) Two kings. . . .

VINNIE. Straight. . . . (*Shows hand and takes in pot.*)

MURRAY. Hey, maybe he's in his office locked in the john again. Did you know Felix was once locked in the john overnight? He wrote out his entire will on a half a roll of toilet paper! . . . Heee, what a nut!

(VINNIE *is playing with his chips.*)

SPEED. (*Glares at him as he shuffles cards.*) Don't play with your chips. I'm asking you nice, don't play with your chips.

VINNIE. (*To* SPEED.) I'm not playing. I'm counting. Leave me alone. What are you picking on me for? How much do you think I'm winning? Fifteen dollars!

SPEED. Fifteen dollars? You dropped more than that in your cuffs! (SPEED *deals a game of draw poker.*)

MURRAY. (*Yells Off.*) Hey, Oscar, what do you say?

OSCAR. (*Enters carrying a tray with beer, sandwiches, can of peanuts, and opened bags of pretzels and Fritos.*) I'm in! I'm in! Go ahead. Deal! (OSCAR MADISON *is 43. He is a pleasant, appealing man. He seems to enjoy life to the fullest. He enjoys his weekly poker game, his friends, his excessive drinking and his cigars. He is also one of those lucky creatures in life who even enjoys his work, a sportswriter for the New York Post. His carefree attitude is evident in the sloppiness of his household but it seems to bother others more than it does* OSCAR. *This is all not to say that* OSCAR *is without cares or worries. He just doesn't seem to have any.*)

VINNIE. Aren't you going to look at your cards?

OSCAR. (*Sets tray on side chair.*) What for? I'm gonna bluff anyway. (*Opens bottle of Coke.*) Who gets the Coke?

MURRAY. I get a Coke.

OSCAR. My friend Murray, the policeman, gets a warm Coke. (*He gives him the bottle.*)

ROY. (*Opens the betting.*) You still didn't fix the refrigerator? It's been two weeks now. No wonder it stinks in here.

OSCAR. (*Picking up his cards.*) Temper, temper. If I wanted nagging I'd go back with my wife. . . . (*Throws them down.*) I'm out. . . Who wants food?

MURRAY. What have you got?

OSCAR. (*Looks under bread.*) I got brown sandwiches and green sandwiches. . . . Well, what do you say?

MURRAY. What's the green?

OSCAR. It's either very new cheese or very old meat.

MURRAY. I'll take the brown.

(OSCAR *gives* MURRAY *a sandwich.*)

ROY. (*Glares at* MURRAY.) Are you crazy? You're not going to eat that, are you?

MURRAY. I'm hungry.

ROY. His refrigerator's been broken for two weeks. I saw milk standing in there that wasn't even in the bottle.

OSCAR. (*To* ROY.) What are you, some kind of a health nut? Eat, Murray, eat!

ROY. I've got six cards. . . .

SPEED. That figures. . . . I've got three aces. Misdeal.

(ALL *throw their cards in.* SPEED *begins to shuffle.*)

VINNIE. You know who makes very good sandwiches? Felix. Did you ever taste his cream cheese and pimento on date nut bread?

SPEED. (*To* VINNIE.) All right, make up your mind, poker or menus. (OSCAR *opens a can of beer, which sprays in a geyser over all PLAYERS and table. There is a hubbub as they ALL yell at OSCAR. He hands ROY the overflowing can, and pushes the puddle of beer under the chair. The PLAYERS start to go back to the game only to be sprayed by the beer again as OSCAR opens another can. There is another outraged cry as they try to stop OSCAR and mop up the beer on the table with a towel which is hanging on the standing lamp. OSCAR, undisturbed, gives them the beer and the bags of refreshments, and they finally sit back in their chairs. OSCAR wipes his hands on the sleeve of ROY'S jacket which is hanging on the back of the chair.*) Hey, Vinnie, tell Oscar what time you're leaving.

VINNIE. (*Like a trained dog.*) Twelve o'clock.

SPEED. (*To* OTHERS.) You hear? We got ten minutes before the next announcement. All right, this game is five-card stud. . . . (*Deals, and ad libs calling cards, ending with* MURRAY's *card.*) And a bullet for the policeman. . . . All right, Murray, it's your bet. (No answer.) Do something, huh?

OSCAR. (*Getting drink at bar.*) Don't yell at my friend Murray.

MURRAY. (*Throwing in coin.*) I'm in for a quarter.

OSCAR. (*Proudly looks in* MURRAY'S *eyes.*) Beautiful, baby, beautiful (*Sits down and begins to open can of peanuts.*)

ROY. Hey, Oscar, let's make a rule. Every six months you have to buy fresh potato chips. How can you live like this? Don't you have a maid?

OSCAR. (*Shakes head.*) She quit after my wife and kids left. The work got to be too much for her. . . . (*Looks on table.*) The pot's shy. Who didn't put in a quarter?

MURRAY. (*To* OSCAR.) You didn't.

OSCAR. (*Puts in money.*) You got a big mouth, Murray. Just for that, lend me twenty dollars.

(SPEED *deals another round.*)

MURRAY. I just loaned you twenty dollars ten minutes ago.

(ALL *join in a round of betting.*)

OSCAR. You loaned me *ten* dollars *twenty* minutes ago. Learn to count, pussy cat.

MURRAY. Learn to play poker, chicken licken! . . . Borrow from somebody else. I keep winning my own money back.

ROY. (*To* OSCAR.) You owe everybody in the game. If you don't have it, you shouldn't play.

OSCAR. . . . All right, I'm through being the nice one. You owe me six dollars apiece for the buffet.

SPEED. (*Dealing another round of cards.*) Buffet? Hot beer and two sandwiches left over from when you went to high school?

OSCAR. What do you want at a poker game, a tomato surprise? . . . Murray, lend me twenty dollars or I'll call your wife and tell her you're in Central Park wearing a dress.

MURRAY. You want money, ask Felix.

OSCAR. He's not here.

MURRAY. Neither am I.

ROY. (*Gives him money.*) All right, here. You're on the books for another twenty.

OSCAR. How many times are you gonna keep saying it? (*Takes money.*)

MURRAY. When are you gonna call Felix?

OSCAR. When are we gonna play poker?

MURRAY. Aren't you even worried? It's the first game he's missed in over two years.

OSCAR. The record is fifteen years set by Lou Gehrig in 1939! . . . I'll call! I'll call!

ROY. How can you be so lazy?

(*The PHONE rings.*)

OSCAR. (*Throwing cards in.*) Call me irresponsible, I'm funny that way. (*Goes to phone.*)

SPEED. Pair of sixes. . . .

VINNIE. Three deuces. . . .

SPEED. (*Throws up hands in despair.*) This is my last week. I get all the aggravation I need at home.

(OSCAR *picks up phone.*)

OSCAR. Hello! Oscar the Poker Player!

VINNIE. (*To* OSCAR.) If it's my wife tell her I'm leaving at twelve.

SPEED. (*To* VINNIE.) You look at your watch once more and you get the peanuts in your face. . . . (*To* ROY.) Deal the cards!

(*The game continues during* OSCAR's *phone conversation, with* ROY *dealing a game of stud.*)

OSCAR. (*Into phone.*) Who? . . . Who did you want, please? . . . Dabby? Dabby who? . . . No, there's no Dabby here . . . Oh, *Daddy*! (*To* OTHERS.) For crise sakes, it's my kid. (*Back into phone, he speaks with great love and affection.*) Brucey, hello, baby. Yes, it's Daddy! (*There is a general outburst of ad-libbing from the* POKER PLAYERS. *To* OTHERs.) Hey, come on, give me a break, willya? My five-year-old kid is calling from California. It must be costing him a fortune. (*Back into phone.*) How've you been, sweetheart? . . . Yes, I finally got your letter. It took three weeks . . . Yes, but next time you tell Mommy to give you a stamp. . . . I know, but you're not supposed to draw it on. . . . (*Laughs. To* OTHERS.) You hear?

SPEED. We hear. We hear. We're all thrilled.

OSCAR. (*Into phone.*) What's that, darling, . . . ? What goldfish? . . . Oh, in your room! . . . Oh, sure. Sure, I'm taking care of them. . . . (*He holds phone over chest.*) Oh, God, I killed my kid's goldfish! (*Back into phone.*) Yes, I feed them every day.

ROY. Murderer!

OSCAR. Mommy wants to speak to me? Right. . . . Take care of yourself, soldier. I love you.

VINNIE. (*Beginning to deal a game of stud.*) Ante a dollar. . . .

SPEED. (*To* OSCAR.) Cost you a dollar to play. You got a dollar?

OSCAR. Not after I get through talking to this lady. (*Into phone. False cheerfulness.*) Hello, Blanche. How are you? . . . Err . . . Yes. . . . I have a pretty good idea why you're calling. . . . I'm a week behind with the check, right? . . . *Four* weeks? That's not possible. . . . Because it's not possible. . . . Blanche, I keep a record of every check and I *know* I'm only *three* weeks behind! Blanche, I'm trying the best I can. . . . Blanche, don't threaten me with jail because it's not a threat. . . . With my expenses and my alimony, a prisoner takes home more pay than I do! . . . Very nice, in front of the kids. . . . Blanche, don't tell me you're going to have my salary attached, just say goodbye! . . . Goodbye! (*He hangs up. To* PLAYERS.) I'm eight hundred dollars behind in alimony so let's up the stakes. . . . (*Gets drink from poker table.*)

ROY. She can do it, you know.

OSCAR. What?

ROY. Throw you in jail. For non-support of the kids.

OSCAR. Never. If she can't call me once a week to aggravate me, she's not happy. (*Crosses to bar.*)

MURRAY. It doesn't bother you? That you can go to jail? Or that maybe your kids don't have enough clothes or enough to eat?

OSCAR. Murray . . . *Poland* could live for a year on what my kids leave over for lunch! . . . Can we play cards? (*Refills drink.*)

ROY. But that's the point. You shouldn't *be* in this kind of trouble. It's because you don't know how to manage anything. I should know, I'm your accountant.

OSCAR. (*Crossing to table.*) If you're my accountant, how come I need money?

ROY. If you need money, how come you play poker?

OSCAR. Because I need money.

ROY. But you always lose.

OSCAR. That's why I need the money! . . . Listen, *I'm* not complaining. *You're* complaining. I get along all right. I'm living.

ROY. Alone? In eight dirty rooms?

OSCAR. If I win tonight, I'll buy a broom.

(MURRAY *and* SPEFD *buy chips from* VINNIE, *and* MURRAY *begins to shuffle the deck for a game of draw.*)

ROY. That's not what you need. What you need is a wife.

OSCAR. How can I afford a wife when I can't afford a broom?

ROY. Then don't play poker.

OSCAR. (*Puts down drink, rushes to* Roy *and they struggle over the bag of potato chips, which rips showering* EVERYONE, *who* ALL *begin to yell at one another.*) Then don't come to my house and eat my potato chips!

MURRAY. What are you yelling about? We're playing a friendly game.

SPEED. Who's *playing?* We've been sitting here talking since eight o'clock.

VINNIE. Since *seven.* That's why I said I was going to quit at *twelve.*

SPEED. How'd you like a stale banana right in the mouth?

MURRAY. (*The peacemaker.*) All right, all right, let's calm down. . . . Take it easy. . . . I'm a cop, you know. I could arrest the whole lousy game. (*Finishes dealing cards.*) Four. . . .

OSCAR. (*Sitting at table.*) My friend Murray the Cop is right. Let's just play cards. And please hold them up, I can't see where I marked them.

MURRAY. You're worse than the kids from the PAL.

OSCAR. But you still love me, Roy, sweety, right?

ROY. (*Petulant.*) Yeah yeah.

OSCAR. That's not good enough. Come on, say it. In front of the whole poker game. "I love you, Oscar Madison."

ROY. You don't take any of this seriously, do you. You owe money to your wife, your government, your friends. . . .

OSCAR. (*Throws cards down.*) What do you want me to do, Roy, jump in the garbage disposal and grind myself to death? (*The* PHONE *rings. He goes to answer it.*) Life goes on even for those of us who are divorced, broke and sloppy. (*Into phone.*) Hello? Divorced, Broke and Sloppy. Oh, hello, sweetheart. (*He becomes very seductive and pulls phone to side and talks low, but still audibly to* OTHERS, *who turn and listen.*) I told you not to call me during the game. . . . I can't talk to you now. . . . You *know* I do, darling, . . . All right, just a minute. (*He turns.*) Murray, it's your wife. (*Puts phone on table and sits on sofa.*)

MURRAY. (*Nods disgustedly as he crosses to phone.*) I wish you were having an affair with her. . . . Then she wouldn't bother *me* all the time. (*Picks up phone.*) Hello, Mimi, what's wrong?

(SPEED *gets up, stretches, and goes into bathroom.*)

OSCAR. (*Woman's voice, imitating* Mimi.) What time are you coming home? (*Then imitating* MURRAY.) I don't know, about twelve, twelve-thirty.

MURRAY. (*Into phone.*) I don't know, about twelve, twelve-thirty? (ROY *gets up and stretches.*) Why, what did you want, Mimi? . . . "A corned beef sandwich and a strawberry malted!"

OSCAR. Is she pregnant again?

MURRAY. (*Holds phone over chest.*) No, just fat! (*There is the sound of a* TOILET *flushing, and after* SPEED *comes out of the bathroom,* VINNIE *goes in. Into phone again.*) What? . . . How could you hear that, I had the phone over my chest? . . . Who? . . . Felix? . . . No, he didn't show up tonight. . . . What's wrong? . . . You're kidding! . . . How should I know? . . . All right, all right, goodbye. . . . (*The* TOILET *flushes again, and after* VINNIE *comes out of the bathroom,* ROY *goes in.*) Goodbye, Mimi. . . . Goodbye. (*He hangs up. To* OTHERS.) Well, what did I tell you? I knew it!

ROY. What's the matter?

MURRAY. (*Pacing above the couch.*) Felix is missing!

OSCAR. Who?

MURRAY. Felix! Felix Ungar! The man who sits in that chair every week and cleans ashtrays. I told you something was up.

SPEED. (*At the table.*) What do you mean, missing?

MURRAY. He didn't show up for work today. He didn't come home tonight. No one knows where he is. Mimi just spoke to his wife.

VINNIE. (*In his chair at the poker table.*) *Felix?*

MURRAY. They looked everywhere. . . . I'm telling you he's missing.

OSCAR. Wait a minute. No one is missing for one day.

VINNIE. That's right. You've got to be missing for forty-eight hours before you're missing. The worst he could be is lost.

MURRAY. How could he be lost? He's forty-four years old and lives on West End Avenue. What's the matter with you?

ROY. (*Sitting in armchair.*) Maybe he had an accident.

OSCAR. They would have heard.

ROY. If he's laying in a gutter somewhere? Who would know who he is?

OSCAR. He's got ninety-two credit cards in his wallet. The minute something happens to him, America lights up.

VINNIE. Maybe he went to a movie. You know how long those pictures are today.

SPEED. (*Looks at* VINNIE *contemptuously.*) No wonder you're going to Florida in July. Dumb dumb dumb!

ROY. Maybe he was mugged?

OSCAR. For thirty-six hours? How much money could he have on him?

ROY. Maybe they took his clothes. I knew a guy who was mugged in a doctor's office. He had to go home in a nurse's uniform.

(OSCAR *throws a pillow from the couch at* ROY.)

SPEED. Murray, you're a cop. What do you think?

MURRAY. I think it's something real bad.

SPEED. How do you know?

MURRAY. I can feel it in my bones.

SPEED. (To OTHERS.) You hear? Bulldog Drummond.

ROY. Maybe he's drunk. Does he drink?

OSCAR. Felix? On New Year's Eve he has Pepto Bismal. . . . What are we guessing? I'll call his wife. (*He picks up phone.*)

SPEED. Wait a minute! Don't start anything yet. Just 'cause we don't know where he is doesn't mean *somebody else* doesn't. . . . Does he have a girl?

VINNIE. A what?

SPEED. A girl? You know. Like when you're through work early.

MURRAY. Felix? Playing around? Are you crazy? He wears a vest and galoshes.

SPEED. (*Gets up and moves towards* MURRAY.) You mean you automatically know who has and who hasn't got a girl on the side?

MURRAY. (*Moves to* SPEED.) Yes, I automatically know.

SPEED. All right, you're so smart. Have *I* got a girl?

MURRAY. No, you haven't got a girl. What you've got is what I've got. What you wish you got and what you got is a whole different civilization! . . . Oscar maybe has a girl on the side.

SPEED. That's different. He's divorced. That's not on the *side*. That's in the *middle*. (*Moves to table.*)

OSCAR. (*To them* BOTH *as he starts to dial.*) You through? 'Cause one of our poker players is missing. I'd like to find out about him.

VINNIE. I thought he looked edgy the last couple of weeks. (*To* SPEED.) Didn't you think he looked edgy?

SPEED. No. As a matter of fact, I thought you looked edgy. (*Moves Down Right.*)

OSCAR. (*Into phone.*) Hello. . . . Frances? . . . Oscar. I just heard.

ROY. Tell her not to worry. She's probably hysterical.

MURRAY. Yeah, you know women. (*Sits down on couch.*)

OSCAR. (*Into phone.*) Listen, Frances, the most important thing is not to worry. . . . Oh! (*To others.*) She's not worried.

MURRAY. Sure.

OSCAR. (*Into phone.*) Frances, do you have *any* idea where he could be? . . . He what? . . . You're kidding? . . . Why? . . . No, I didn't know . . . Gee, that's too bad. . . . All right, listen, Frances, you just sit tight and the minute I hear anything I'll let you know. . . . Right. . . . G'bye.

(*He hangs up. They* ALL *look at him expectantly. He gets up wordlessly and crosses to the table, thinking. They* ALL *watch him a second, not being able to stand it any longer.*)

MURRAY. Ya gonna tell us or do we hire a private detective?

OSCAR. They broke up!

ROY. Who?

OSCAR. Felix and Frances! They broke up! The entire marriage is through.

VINNIE. You're kidding?

ROY. I don't believe it.

SPEED. After twelve years?

(OSCAR *sits down at the table.*)

VINNIE. They were such a happy couple.

MURRAY. Twelve years doesn't mean you're a *happy* couple. It just means you're a *long* couple.

SPEED. Go figure it. Felix and Frances.

ROY. What are you surprised at? He used to sit there every Friday night and tell us how they were fighting.

SPEED. I know. But who believes Felix?

VINNIE. What happened?

OSCAR. She wants out, that's all.

MURRAY. He'll go to pieces. I know Felix. He's going to try something crazy.

SPEED. That's all he ever used to talk about. "My beautiful wife. My wonderful wife." What happened?

OSCAR. His beautiful, wonderful wife can't stand him, that's what happened.

MURRAY. He'll kill himself. You hear what I'm saying? He's going to go out and try to kill himself.

SPEED. (*To* MURRAY.) Will you shut up, Murray? Stop being a cop for two minutes. (*To* OSCAR.) Where'd he go, Oscar?

OSCAR. He went out to kill himself.

MURRAY. What did I tell you?

ROY. (*To* OSCAR.) Are you serious?

OSCAR. That's what she said. He was going out to kill himself. He didn't want to do it at home 'cause the kids were sleeping.

VINNIE. Why?

OSCAR. Why? Because that's Felix, that's why. (*Goes to bar and refills his drink.*) You know what he's like. He sleeps on the window sill. "Love me or I'll jump" . . . 'Cause he's a nut, that's why.

MURRAY. That's right. Remember he tried something like that in the army? She wanted to break off the engagement so he started cleaning guns in his mouth.

SPEED. I don't believe it. Talk! That's all Felix is, talk.

VINNIE. (*Worried.*) But is that what he said? In those word? "I'm going to kill myself"?

OSCAR. (*Pacing about the table.*) I don't know in what words. She didn't read it to me.

ROY. You mean he left her a note?

OSCAR. No, he sent a telegram.

MURRAY. *A suicide telegram?* . . . Who sends a *suicide telegram*?

OSCAR. Felix, the nut, that's who! . . . Can you imagine getting a thing like that? She even has to tip the kid a quarter.

ROY. I don't gel it. If he wants to kill himself, why does he send a telegram?

OSCAR. Don't you see how his mind works? If he sends a note, she might not get it 'til Monday and he'd have no excuse for not being dead. This way, for a dollar ten, he's got a chance to be saved.

VINNIE. You mean he really doesn't want to kill himself? He just wants sympathy.

OSCAR. What *he'd* really like is to go to the funeral and sit in the back. He'd be the biggest cryer there.

MURRAY. He's right.

OSCAR. Sure I'm right. . . .

MURRAY. We get these cases every day. All they want is attention. We got a guy who calls us every Saturday afternoon from the George Washington Bridge.

ROY. I don't know. You never can tell what a guy'll do when he's hysterical.

MURRAY. Nahhh. Nine out of ten times they don't jump.

ROY. What about the tenth time?

MURRAY. They jump. He's right. There's a possibility.

OSCAR. Not with Felix. I know him. He's too nervous to kill himself. He wears his seat belt in a drive-in movie.

VINNIE. Isn't there someplace we could look for him?

SPEED. Where? Where would you look? Who knows *where* he is?

(*The* DOORBELL *rings. They* ALL *look at* OSCAR.)

OSCAR. Of course! . . . If you're going to kill yourself, where's the safest place to do it? . . . With your friends!

(VINNIE *starts for door.*)

MURRAY. (*Stopping him.*) Wait a minute! The guy may be hysterical. Let's play it nice and easy. If *we're* calm, maybe *he'll* be calm.

ROY. (*Getting up and joining them*) That's right. That's how they do it with those guys out on the ledge. You talk nice and soft.

(SPEED *rushes over to them, and joins in the frenzied discussion.*)

VINNIE. What'll we say to him?

MURRAY. We don't say nothin'. Like we never heard a thing.

OSCAR. (*Trying to get their attention.*) You through with this discussion. Because he already could have hung himself out in the hall. (*To* VINNIE.) Vinnie, open the door!

MURRAY. Remember! Like we don't know nothin'.

(ALL *rush back to their seats and grab up cards, which they concentrate on with greatest intensity.* VINNIE *opens the door.* FELIX UNGAR *is there. About 44. His clothes are rumpled as if he had slept in them, and he needs a shave. Although he tries to act matter-of-fact, there is an air of great tension and nervousness about him.*)

FELIX. (*Softly.*) Hi, Vin! (VINNIE *quickly goes back to his seat and studies his cards.* FELIX *has his hands in his pockets, trying to be very nonchalant. Controlled calm.*) Hi, fellas. (*They* ALL *mumble hello, but do not look at him. He put his coat over the railing and crosses to the table.*) How's the game going? (*They* ALL *mumble appropriate remarks, and continue staring at their cards.*) Good! . . . Good! . . . Sorry I'm late. (FELIX *looks a little disappointed that no one asks "What?" . . . He starts to pick up a sandwich, changes his mind, and makes a gesture of distaste. He vaguely looks around.*) Any coke left?

OSCAR. (*Looking up from his cards.*) Coke? . . . Gee, I don't think so. . . . I've got a Seven-Up!

FELIX. (*Bravely.*) No . . . I felt like a Coke. I just don't feel like Seven Up . . . tonight! (*Stands watching the game.*)

OSCAR. What's the bet?

SPEED. You bet a quarter . . . it's up to Murray. . . . Murray, what do you say? (MURRAY *is staring at* Felix.) Murray ! . . Murray!

ROY. (*To* VINNIE.) Tap his shoulder.

VINNIE. (*Taps* MURRAY'S *shoulder.*) Murray!

MURRAY. (*Startled.*) What? What?

SPEED. It's up to you.

MURRAY. Why is it always up to me?

SPEED. It's not always up to you. It's up to you now. What do you do?

MURRAY. I'm in. I'm in. (*He throws in quarter.*)

FELIX. (*Moves to bookcase.*) Anyone call about me?

OSCAR. Er . . . not that I can remember. (*To* OTHERS.) Did anyone call for Felix? (*They* ALL *shrug and ad-lib "No."*) Why? . . . Were you expecting a call?

FELIX. (*Looking at books on shelf.*) No! . . . No! . . . Just asking. (*He opens book and examines it.*)

ROY. Er . . . I'll see his bet and raise it a dollar.

FELIX. (*Without looking up from book.*) I just thought someone might have called.

SPEED. It costs me a dollar and a quarter to play, right?

OSCAR. Right!

FELIX. (*Still looking at book . . . sing-song.*) But . . . if no one called, no one called. (*Slams book shut and puts it back.* ALL *jump at the noise.*)

SPEED. (*Getting nervous.*) What does it cost me to play again?

MURRAY. (*Angry.*) A dollar and a quarter! A dollar and a quarter! Pay attention, for crise sakes!

ROY. All right, take it easy. Take it easy.

OSCAR. Let's calm down, everyone, heh?

MURRAY. I'm sorry. I can't help it. (*Points to* SPEED.) He makes me nervous.

SPEED. I make you nervous. You make me nervous. You make everyone nervous.

MURRAY. (*Sarcastic.*) I'm sorry. Forgive me. I'll kill myself.

OSCAR. Murray! (*He motions with his head to* FELIX.)

MURRAY. (*Realizes his error.*) Oh! . . . Sorry.

(SPEED *glares at him. They all sit in silence a moment, until* VINNIE *catches sight of* FELIX *who is now staring out Upstage window. He quickly calls the* OTHERS' *attention to* FELIX.)

FELIX. (*Looking back at them from the window.*) Gee, it's a pretty view from here. . . . What is it, twelve floors?

OSCAR. (*Quickly crossing to the window and closing it.*) No, its only eleven. That's all. Eleven. It says twelve but it's really only eleven. (*He then turns and closes the other window as* FELIX *watches him,* OSCAR *shivers slightly.*) Chilly in here. (*To* OTHERS.) Isn't it chilly in here? (*Crosses back to table.*)

ROY. Yeah, that's much better.

OSCAR. (*To* FELIX.) Want to sit down and play? It's still early.

VINNIE. Sure. We're in no rush. We'll be here 'til three, four in the morning.

FELIX. (*Shrugs.*) I don't know . . . I just don't feel much like playing now.

OSCAR. (*Sitting at table*) Oh! . . . Well . . . what *do* you feel like doing?

FELIX. (*Shrugs.*) I'll find *something*. . . . (*Starts to walk toward other room.*) Don't worry about me. . . .

OSCAR. Where are you going?

FELIX. (*Stops in the doorway. He looks at* OTHERS *who are all staring at him.*) To the john.

OSCAR. (*Looks at others worried, then at* FELIX.) Alone?

FELIX. (*Nods.*) I always go alone! Why?

OSCAR. (*Shrugs.*) No reason! . . . You gonna be in there long?

FELIX. (*Shrugs, then says meaningfully, like the martyr.*) As long as it takes.

(*Then he goes into the bathroom and slams the door shut behind him. Immediately they* ALL *jump up and crowd about the bathroom door, whispering in frenzied anxiety.*)

MURRAY. Are you crazy? Letting him go to the john alone?

OSCAR. What did you want me to do?

ROY. Stop him! Go in with him!

OSCAR. Suppose he just has to go to the john?

MURRAY. Supposing he does? He's better off being embarrassed than dead!

OSCAR. How's he going to kill himself in the john?

SPEED. What do you mean, how? Razor blades, pills. Anything that's in there.

OSCAR. That's the *kids'* bathroom. The worst he could do is brush his teeth to death.

ROY. He could jump.

VINNIE. That's right. Isn't there a window in there?

OSCAR. It's only six inches wide.

MURRAY. He could break the glass. He could cut his wrists.

OSCAR. He could also flush himself into the East River. I'm telling you he's not going to try anything! (*Moves to table.*)

ROY. (*Goes to doorway.*) Shhh! Listen! He's crying. . . . (*There is a pause as* ALL *listen as* FELIX *sobs.*) You hear that. He's crying.

MURRAY. Isn't that terrible? . . . For God's sakes, OSCAR, do something! Say something!

OSCAR. What? What do you say to a man who's crying in your bathroom?

(*There is the sound of the* TOILET *flushing and* ROY *makes a mad dash back to his chair.*)

ROY. He's coming!

(*They* ALL *scramble back to their places.* MURRAY *gets mixed up with* VINNIE *and they quickly straighten it out.* FELIX *comes bock into room. But he seems calm and collected with no evident signs of having cried.*)

FELIX. I guess I'll be running along. (*He starts for the door.* OSCAR *jumps up. So do* OTHERS.)

OSCAR. Felix, wait a second.

FELIX. No! No! I can't talk to you. I can't talk to anyone.

(*They* ALL *try to grab him, stopping him near the stairs.*)

MURRAY. Felix, please. We're your friends. Don't run out like this.

(FELIX *struggles to pull away.*)

OSCAR. Felix, sit down. Just for a minute. Talk to us.

FELIX. There's nothing to talk about. There's nothing to say. It's over. Over. Everything is over. Let me go!

(*He breaks away from them and dashes into the Stage Right bedroom. They start to chase him and he dodges from the bedroom through the adjoining door into the bathroom.*)

ROY. Stop him! Grab him!

FELIX. (*Looking for an exit.*) Let me out! I've got to get out of here!

OSCAR. Felix, you're hysterical.

FELIX. Please let me out of here!

MURRAY. The john! Don't let him get in the john!

FELIX. (*Comes out of the bathroom into the room with* ROY *hanging onto him, and the others trailing behind.*) Leave me alone. Why doesn't everyone leave me alone?

OSCAR. All right, Felix, I'm warning you. . . . Now cut it out! (*Throws half-filled glass of water, which he has picked up from the bookcase, into* FELIX'S *face.*)

FELIX. It's *my* problem. I'll work it out. Leave me alone. . . . (Ohh, my stomach. (*He collapses in* ROY'S *arms.*)

MURRAY. What's the matter with your stomach?

VINNIE. He looks sick. Look at his face.

(ALL *try to hold him as they lead him over to the couch.*)

FELIX. I'm not sick. I'm all right. I didn't take anything, I swear. . . . Ohh, my stomach.

OSCAR. What do you mean you didn't take anything? What did you take?

FELIX. (*Sitting on couch.*) Nothing! Nothing! I didn't take anything. . . . Don't tell Frances what I did, please! . . . Oohh, my stomach.

MURRAY. He took something! I'm telling you he took something.

OSCAR. What, Felix? *What??*

FELIX. Nothing! I didn't take anything.

OSCAR. Pills? Did you take pills?

FELIX. No! No!

OSCAR. (*Grabbing* FELIX.) Don't lie to me, Felix. Did you take pills?

FELIX. No, I didn't. I didn't take anything.

MURRAY. Thank God, he didn't take pills.

(ALL *relax and take a breath of relief.*)

FELIX. Just a few, that's all.

(ALL *react in alarm and concern over pills.*)

OSCAR. He took pills.

MURRAY. How many pills?

OSCAR. What kind of pills?

FELIX. I don't know what kind. Little green ones. I just grabbed anything out of her medicine cabinet. . . . I must have been crazy.

OSCAR. Didn't you look? Didn't you see what kind?

FELIX. I couldn't see. The light's broken. Don't call Frances. Don't tell her. I'm so ashamed. So ashamed.

OSCAR. Felix, how-many-pills-did-you-take?

FELIX. I don't know. I can't remember.

OSCAR. I'm calling Frances.

FELIX. (*Grabs him.*) No! Don't call her. Don't call her. If she hears I took a whole bottle of pills . . .

MURRAY. *A whole bottle? A whole bottle of pills?* (*He turns to* VINNIE.) My God, call an ambulance!

(VINNIE *runs to the front door.*)

OSCAR. (*To* MURRAY.) You don't even know what *kind!*

MURRAY. What's the difference? He took-a-whole-bottle!

OSCAR. Maybe they were vitamins. He could be the healthiest one in the room! . . . Take it easy, will you?

FELIX. Don't call Frances. Promise me you won't call Frances.

MURRAY. Open his collar. Open the window. Give him some air.

SPEED. Walk him around. Don't let him go to sleep.

(SPEED *and* MURRAY *pick* FELIX *up and walk him around, while* ROY *rubs his wrists.*)

ROY. Rub his wrists. Keep his circulation going.

VINNIE. (*Running to bathroom to get a compress.*) A cold compress. Put a cold compress on his neck.

(*They sit* FELIX *in the armchair, still chattering in alarm.*)

OSCAR. One doctor at a time, heh? All the interns shut the hell up!

FELIX. I'm all right. I'll be all right. . . . (*To* OSCAR *urgently.*) You didn't call Frances, did you?

MURRAY. (*To* OTHERS.) You just gonna stand here? No one's gonna do anything? I'm calling a doctor. (*Crosses to phone.*)

FELIX. No! No doctor.

MURRAY. You *gotta* have a doctor.

FELIX. I don't need a doctor.

MURRAY. You gotta get the pills out.

FELIX. I got them out. I threw up before! . . . (*Sits back weakly.* MURRAY *hangs up the phone.*) Don't you have a root beer or a ginger ale?

(VINNIE *gives compress to* SPEED.)

ROY. (*To* VINNIE.) Get him a drink.

OSCAR. (*Glares angrily at* FELIX.) He threw them up!

VINNIE. Which would you rather have, Felix, the root beer or the ginger ale?

SPEED. (*To* VINNIE.) Get him the drink! Just get him the drink.

(VINNIE *runs into the kitchen as* SPEED *puts the compress on* FELIX'S *head.*)

FELIX. Twelve years. Twelve years we were married. Did you know we were married twelve years, Roy?

ROY. (*Comforting him.*) Yes, Felix. I knew.

FELIX. (*Great emotion in his voice.*) And now it's over. Like that it's over. That's hysterical, isn't it?

SPEED. Maybe it was just a fight. You've had lights before, Felix.

FELIX. No, it's over. She's getting a lawyer tomorrow. . . . *My* cousin. . . . She's using *my* cousin ! . . . (*He sobs.*) Whom am *I* going to get? . . .

(VINNIE *comes out of kitchen with glass of root beer.*)

MURRAY. (*Patting his shoulder.*) It's okay, Felix. Come on. Take it easy.

VINNIE. (*Gives glass to* FELIX.) Here's the root beer.

FELIX. I'm all right. Honestly. . . . I'm just crying. (*He puts his head down. They all look at him helplessly.*)

MURRAY. All right, let's not stand around looking at him. (*Pushes* SPEED *and* VINNIE *away.*) Let's break it up, heh?

FELIX. Yes, don't stand there looking at me. Please.

OSCAR. (*To* OTHERS.) Come on, he's all right. Let's call it a night.

(MURRAY, SPEED *and* ROY *turn in their chips at the poker table, get their coats and get ready to go.*)

FELIX. I'm so ashamed. Please, fellas, forgive me.

VINNIE. (*Bending to* FELIX.) Oh, Felix, we—we understand.

FELIX. Don't say anything about this to anyone, Vinnie. Will you promise me?

VINNIE. I'm going to Florida tomorrow.

FELIX. Oh, that's nice. Have a good time.

VINNIE. Thanks.

FELIX. (*Turns away and sighs in despair.*) We were going to go to Florida next winter. (*He laughs, but it's a sob.*) Without the kids! . . . Now they'll go without me.

(VINNIE *gets his coat and* OSCAR *ushers them all to the door.*)

MURRAY. (*Stopping at door.*) Maybe one of us should stay?

OSCAR. It's all right, Murray.

MURRAY. Suppose he tries something again?

OSCAR. He won't try anything again.

MURRAY. How do you *know* he won't try anything again?

FELIX. (*Turns to* MURRAY.) I won't try anything again. I'm very tired.

OSCAR. (*To* MURRAY.) You hear? He's very tired, He had a busy night. . . . Good night, fellows. . . .

(ALL *ad-lib goodbyes and leave. The door closes, but opens immediately and* ROY *comes back in.*)

ROY. If anything happens, Oscar, just call me.

(*He exits, and as door starts to close, it reopens and* SPEED *comes in.*)

SPEED. I'm three blocks away. I could be here in five minutes.

(*He exits, and as door starts to close it reopens and* VINNIE *comes back in.*)

VINNIE. If you need me I'll be at the Meridian Motel in Miami Beach.

OSCAR. You'll be the first one I'll call, Vinnie.

(VINNIE *exits. The door closes and then reopens as* MURRAY *comes back.*)

MURRAY. (*To* OSCAR.) You're sure?

OSCAR. I'm sure.

MURRAY. (*Loud to* FELIX *as he gestures to* OSCAR *to come to door.*) Good night, Felix. Try to get a good night's sleep. I guarantee you things are going to look a lot brighter in the morning. (*To* OSCAR, *sotto voce.*) Take away his belt and his shoe laces.

(*He nods and exits.* OSCAR *turns and looks at* FELIX *sitting in the armchair and slowly moves across the room. There is a moment's silence.*)

OSCAR. (*He looks at* FELIX *and sighs.*) Ohh, Felix, Felix, Felix, Felix!

FELIX. (*Sits with his head buried in his hands. He doesn't look up.*) I know, I know, I know, I know! . . . What am I going to do, OSCAR?

OSCAR. You're gonna wash clown the pills with some hot, black coffee. . . . (*He starts for kitchen, then stops.*) Do you think I could leave you alone for two minutes?

FELIX. No, I don't think so! . . . Stay with me, Oscar. Talk to me.

OSCAR. A cup of black coffee. It'll be good for you. Come on in the kitchen. I'll sit on you.

FELIX. Oscar, the terrible thing is, I think I still love her. It's a lousy marriage but I still love her. . . . I didn't want this divorce.

OSCAR. (*Sitting on arm of couch.*) How about some Ovaltine? You like Ovaltine? With a couple of fig newtons . . . or chocolate mallomars?

FELIX. All right, so we didn't get along. . . . But we had two wonderful kids . . . and a beautiful home. . . . Didn't we, Oscar?

OSCAR. How about vanilla wafers? . . . Or Vienna fingers? . . . I got everything.

FELIX. What more does she want? What does *any* woman want?

OSCAR. I want to know what you want. Ovaltine, coffee or tea. Then we'll get to the divorce.

FELIX. It's not fair, darnit! It's just not fair! (*He hangs his fist on the arm of the chair angrily and suddenly winces in great pain and grabs his neck.*) Ohh! Ohh, my neck. My neck!

OSCAR. What? What?

FELIX. (*He is up and paces in pain. He is holding his twisted neck.*) It's a nerve spasm. I get it in the neck. Ohh! Ohh, that hurts.

OSCAR. (*Rushing to help.*) Where? Where does it hurt?

FELIX. (*Stretches out arm like a halfback.*) Don't touch me! Don't touch me!

OSCAR. I just want to see where it hurts.

FELIX. It'll just go way. Just let me alone a few minutes. . . . Ohh! . . . Ohh!

OSCAR. (*Moving to couch.*) Lie down, I'll rub it. . . . It'll ease the pain.

FELIX. (*In wild contortions.*) You don't know how. It's a special way. Only Frances knows how to rub me.

OSCAR. You want me to ask her to come over and rub you?

FELIX. (*Yells.*) No! No! . . . We're getting divorced. She wouldn't want to rub me anymore. . . . It's tension. I get it from tension, I must be tense.

OSCAR. I wouldn't be surprised. How long does it last?

FELIX. Sometimes a minute, sometimes hours. . . . I once got it while I was driving. . . . I crashed into a liquor store. . . . Ohhh! Ohhh! (*He sits, painfully, on the couch.*)

OSCAR. (*Getting behind him.*) You want to suffer or do you want me to rub your stupid neck? (*He starts to massage it.*)

FELIX. Easy! Easy!

OSCAR. (*Yells.*) Relax. . . . Dammit, relax!

FELIX. (*Yells back.*) Don't yell at me! . . . (*Then quietly.*) What should I do? Tell me nicely.

OSCAR. (*Rubbing neck.*) Think of warm jello! . . .

FELIX. Isn't that terrible? I can't do it. . . . I can't relax. I sleep in one position all night. . . . Frances says when I die on my tombstone it's going to say, "Here Stands Felix Ungar." (*He winces.*) Oh! Ohh!

OSCAR. (*Stops rubbing.*) Does that hurt?

FELIX. No, it feels good.

OSCAR. Then say so. You make the same sound for pain or happiness. (*Starts to massage neck again.*)

FELIX. I know. I know. . . . Oscar—I think I'm crazy.

OSCAR. Well, if it'll make you feel any better. . . . I think so, too.

FELIX. I mean it. Why else do I go to pieces like this? Coming up here, scaring you to death. Trying to kill myself. What is that?

OSCAR. That's panic. You're a panicky person. You have a low threshold for composure. (*Stops rubbing.*)

FELIX. Don't stop. It feels good. . . .

OSCAR. If you don't relax I'll break my fingers. . . . (*Touches his hair.*) Look at this. . . . The only man in the world with clenched hair. . . .

FELIX. I do terrible things, Oscar. You know I'm a crybaby.

OSCAR. Bend over.

(FELIX *bends over and* OSCAR *begins to massage his back.*)

FELIX. (*Head down.*) I tell the whole world my problems.

OSCAR. (*Massaging hard.*) Listen, if this hurts just tell me because I don't know what the hell I'm doing.

FELIX. It just isn't nice, Oscar, running up here like this, carrying on like a nut.

OSCAR. (*Finishes massaging.*) How does your neck feel?

FELIX. (*Twists neck.*) Better. Only my back hurts. (*Gets up and paces, rubbing back.*)

OSCAR. What you need is a drink. (*He starts for bar.*)

FELIX. I can't drink. It makes me sick. I tried drinking last night.

OSCAR. (*At bar.*) Where *were* you last night?

FELIX. Nowhere. I just walked.

OSCAR. All night?

FELIX. All night.

OSCAR. In the rain?

FELIX. No. In a hotel. I couldn't sleep. I walked around the room all night. . . . It was over near Times Square. A dirty, depressing room. Then I found myself looking out the window. And suddenly . . . I began to think about jumping.

OSCAR. (*He has two glasses filled and crosses to* FELIX.) What changed your mind?

FELIX. Nothing. I'm still thinking about it.

OSCAR. Drink this. (*He hands him glass, crosses to the couch and sits.*)

FELIX. I don't want to get divorced, Oscar. I don't want to suddenly change my whole life. . . . (*Moves to couch and sits next to* OSCAR.) Talk to me, Oscar. What am I going to do? . . . What am I going to do?

OSCAR. You're going to pull yourself together. And then you're going to drink that Scotch and then you and I are going to figure out a whole new life for you.

FELIX. Without! Frances? Without the kids?

OSCAR. It's been done before.

FELIX. (*Paces Right.*) You don't understand, Oscar. I'm nothing without them. I'm *nothing!*

OSCAR. What do you mean, nothing? You're *something!* (FELIX *sits in armchair.*) A person! You're flesh and blood and bones and hair and nails and ears. You're not a fish. You're not a buffalo. You're *you!* . . . You walk and talk and cry and complain and eat little green pills and send suicide telegrams. No one else does that, Felix. I'm telling you, *you're-the-only-one-of-its-kind-in-the-world!* (*Goes to bar.*) Now drink that.

FELIX. Oscar, you've been through it yourself. What did you do? How did you get through those first few nights?

OSCAR. (*Pours drink.*) I did exactly what you're doing.

FELIX. Getting hysterical!

OSCAR. No, drinking! *Drinking!* (*Comes back to couch with bottle. Sits.*) I drank for four days and four nights. And then I fell through a window. I was bleeding but I was forgetting. (*He drinks again.*)

FELIX. How can you forget your kids? How can you wipe out twelve years of marriage?

OSCAR. You can't. When you walk into eight empty rooms every night it hits you in the face like a wet glove. But those are the facts, Felix. You've got to face it. You can't spend the rest of your life crying. It annoys people in the movies! . . . Be a good boy and drink your Scotch. (*Stretches out on couch with head near* FELIX.)

FELIX. I can imagine what Frances must be going through.

OSCAR. What do you mean, what *she's* going through?

FELIX. It's much harder on the woman, Oscar. She's all alone with the kids. Stuck there in the house. She can't get out like me. I mean where is she going to find someone now at her age? With two kids. Where?

OSCAR. I don't know. Maybe someone'll come to the door! . . . Felix, there's a hundred thousand divorces a year. There must be *something* nice about it. (FELIX *suddenly puts both his hands over his ears and hums quietly.*) What's the matter now? (*Sits up.*)

FELIX. My ears are closing up. I get it from the sinus. It must be the dust in here. I'm allergic to dust. (*Hums. Then gets up and tries to clear ears by hopping first on one leg then the other as he goes to the window and opens it.*)

OSCAR. (*Jumping up.*) What are you doing?

FELIX. I'm not going to jump. I'm just going to breathe. (*He takes deep breaths.*) I used to drive Frances crazy with my allergies. I'm allergic to perfume. For a while the only thing she could wear was my after shave lotion. . . . I was impossible to live with. It's a wonder she took it this long. (*He suddenly bellows like a moose. He does this strange sound another time.* OSCAR *looks at him dumbfounded.*)

OSCAR. What are you doing?

FELIX. I'm trying to clear my ears. You create a pressure inside and then it opens it up. (*He bellows again.*)

OSCAR. Did it open up?

FELIX. A little bit (*He rubs neck.*) I think I strained my throat. (*Paces about the room.*)

OSCAR. Felix, why don't you leave yourself alone? Don't tinker.

FELIX. I can't help myself. I drive everyone crazy. A marriage counselor once kicked me out of his office. He wrote on my chart, Lunatic! . . . I don't blame her. It's impossible to be married to me.

OSCAR. It takes two to make a rotten marriage. (*Lies back down on couch.*)

FELIX. You don't know what I was like at home. I bought her a book and made her write down every penny we spent. Thirty-eight cents for cigarettes, ten cents for a paper. Everything had to go in the book. And then we had a big fight because I said she forgot to write down how much the book was. . . . Who could live with any one like that?

OSCAR. An accountant! . . . What do I know? We're not perfect. We all have faults.

FELIX. Faults? Heh! . . . Faults. . . . We have a maid who comes in to clean three times a week. And on the other days, Frances does the cleaning. And at night, after they've both cleaned lip, I go in and clean the whole place again. I can't help it. I like things clean. Blame it on my mother. I was trained at five months old.

OSCAR. How do you remember things like that?

FELIX. *I* loused up the marriage. Nothing was ever right. I used to recook everything. The minute she walked out of the kitchen I would add salt or pepper. It's not that I didn't trust her, it's just that I was a better cook. . . . Well, I cooked myself out of a marriage. (*He bangs his head with the palm of his hand three times.*) *Goddamned idiot!* (*Sinks down in armchair.*)

OSCAR. Don't do that, you'll get a headache.

FELIX. I can't stand it, Oscar. I hate me. Oh, boy, do I hate me.

OSCAR. You don't hate you. You love you. You think no one has problems like you.

FELIX. Don't give me that analyst jazz. I happen to know I hate my guts.

OSCAR. Come on, Felix, I've never *seen* anyone so in love.

FELIX. (*Hurt.*) I thought you were my friend.

OSCAR. That's why I can talk to you like this. Because I love you almost as much as *you* do.

FELIX. Then help me.

OSCAR. (*Up on one elbow.*) How can I help you when I can't help myself? You think *you're* impossible to live with? Blanche used to say, "What time do you want dinner?" And I'd say, "I don't know. I'm not hungry." Then at three o'clock in the morning I'd wake her up and say, "Now!" . . . I've been one of the highest paid sports writers in the East for the past fourteen years and we saved eight and a half dollars—in

pennies! I'm never home, I gamble, I burn cigar holes in the furniture, drink like a fish and lie to her every chance I get, and for our tenth wedding anniversary, I took her to see the New York Rangers–Detroit Red Wings hockey game, where she got hit with a puck. And I *still* can't understand why she left me. That's how impossible *I* am!

FELIX. I'm not like you, Oscar. I couldn't take it living all alone. I don't know how I'm going to work. They've got to fire me. . . . How am I going to make a living?

OSCAR. You'll go on street corners and cry. They'll throw nickels at you! . . . You'll work, Felix, you'll work. (*Lies back down.*)

FELIX. You think I ought to call Frances?

OSCAR. (*About to explode.*) *What for?* (*Sits up.*)

FELIX. Well . . . talk it out again.

OSCAR. You've *talked* it all out. There are no words left in your entire marriage. When are you going to face up to it?

FELIX. I can't help it, Oscar, I don't know what to do.

OSCAR. Then listen to me. Tonight you're going to sleep here. And tomorrow you're going to get your clothes and your electric tooth brush and you'll move in with me.

FELIX. No, no. It's your apartment. I'll be in the way.

OSCAR. There's eight rooms. We could go for a year without seeing each other. . . . Don't you understand? I *want* you to move in.

FELIX. Why? I'm a pest.

OSCAR. I *know* you're a pest. You don't have to keep telling me.

FELIX. Then why do you want me to live with you?

OSCAR. Because I can't-stand-liv ing-alone, that's why! . . . For crying out loud. I'm proposing to you. What do you want, a ring?

FELIX. (*Moves to* OSCAR.) Well, Oscar, if yon really mean it, there's a lot I can do around here. I'm very handy around the house. I can fix things.

OSCAR. You don't have to fix things.

FELIX. I want to do *something*, Oscar. Let me do something.

OSCAR. (*Nods.*) All right, you can take my wife's initials off the towels. Anything you want.

FELIX. (*Beginning to tidy up.*) I can cook. I'm a terrific cook.

OSCAR. You don't have to cook. I eat cold cuts for breakfast.

FELIX. Two meals a day at home, we'll save a fortune. We've got to pay alimony, you know.

OSCAR. (*Happy to see* FELIX'S *new optimism.*) All right, you can cook. (*Throws pillow at him.*)

FELIX. (*Throws pillow back.*) Do you like leg of lamb?

OSCAR. Yes. I like leg of lamb.

FELIX. I'll make it tomorrow night. . . . I'll have to call Frances. She has my big pot.

OSCAR. *Will you forget Frances!* We'll get our own pots. Don't drive me crazy before you move in. (*The* PHONE *rings.* OSCAR *picks it up quickly.*) Hello? . . . Oh, hello, Frances!

FELIX. (*stops cleaning and starts to wave his arms wildly and whispers screamingly.*) I'm not here! I'm not here! You didn't see me. You don't know where I am. I didn't call. I'm not here. I'm not here.

OSCAR. (*Into phone.*) Yes, he's here.

FELIX. (*Pacing back and forth.*) How does she sound? Is she worried? Is she crying? What is she saying? Does she want to speak to me? I don't want to speak to her.

OSCAR. (*Into phone.*) Yes, he is! . . .

FELIX. You can tell her I'm not coming back. I've made up my mind. I've had it there. I've taken just as much as she has. You can tell her for me if she thinks I'm coming back she's got another thing coming. Tell her. Tell her.

OSCAR. (*Into phone.*) Yes . . . Yes, he's fine.

FELIX. Don't tell her I'm fine! You heard me carrying on before. What are you telling her that for? I'm not fine.

OSCAR. (*Into phone.*) Yes, I understand, Frances.

FELIX. (*Sits down next to* OSCAR.) Does she want to speak to me? Ask her if she wants to speak to me?

OSCAR. (*Into phone.*) Do you want to speak to him?

FELIX. (*Reaches for phone.*) Give me the phone. I'll speak to her.

OSCAR. (*Into phone.*) Oh. You don't want to speak to him.

FELIX. She doesn't want to speak to me?

OSCAR. (*Into phone.*) Yeah, I see. . . . Right. . . . Well, goodbye. (*He hangs up.*)

FELIX. She didn't want to speak to me?

OSCAR. No!

FELIX. Why did she call?

OSCAR. She wants to know when you're coming over for your clothes. . . . She wants to have the room repainted.

FELIX. Oh!

OSCAR. (*Pats* FELIX *on shoulder.*) Listen, Felix, it's almost one o'clock. (*Gets up.*)

FELIX. Didn't want to speak to me, huh?

OSCAR. I'm going to bed. Do you want a cup of tea with Fruitanos or Raisonettos?

FELIX. She'll paint it pink. She always wanted it pink.

OSCAR. I'll get you a pair of pajamas. You like stripes, dots, or animals? (*Goes into Downstage bedroom.*)

FELIX. She's really heartbroken, isn't she? . . . I want to kill myself and she's picking out colors.

OSCAR. (*In bedroom.*) Which bedroom do you want? I'm lousy with bedrooms.

FELIX. (*Up and moves towards bedroom.*) You know, I'm glad. Because she finally made me realize . . . it's over. It didn't sink in until just this minute.

OSCAR. (*Comes back with pillow, pillowcase, and pajamas.*) Felix, I want you to go to bed.

FELIX. I don't think I believed her until just now. My marriage is *really* over.

OSCAR. Felix, go to bed.

FELIX. Somehow it doesn't seem so bad now. I mean think I can live with this thing.

OSCAR. Live with it tomorrow. Go to bed tonight.

FELIX. In a little while. I've got to think. I've got to start rearranging my life. . . . Do you have a pencil and paper?

OSCAR. Not in a little while. Now! It's my house, I make up the bedtime. (*Throws pajamas to him.*)

FELIX. Oscar, please. . . . I have to be alone for a few minutes. I've got to get organized. Go on, you go to bed. . . . I'll—clean up. (*Begins picking up debris from floor.*)

OSCAR. (*Putting pillow in pillowcase.*) You don't have to clean up. I pay a dollar fifty an hour to clean up.

FELIX. It's all right, Oscar, I wouldn't be able to sleep with all this dirt around anyway. Go to bed. I'll see you in the morning. (*Puts dishes on tray.*)

OSCAR. You're not going to do anything big, are you, like rolling up the rugs?

FELIX. Ten minutes, that's all I'll be.

OSCAR. You're sure . . .?

FELIX. (*Smiles.*) I'm sure.

OSCAR. No monkey business?

FELIX. No monkey business. . . . I'll do the dishes and go right to bed.

OSCAR. Yeah. . . . (*Crosses up to his bedroom, throwing pillow into the Downstage bedroom as he passes. Closes his bedroom door behind him.*)

FELIX. (*Calls him.*) Oscar! (OSCAR *anxiously comes out of his bedroom and crosses to* FELIX.) I'm going to be all right! . . . It's going to take me a couple of days . . . but I'm going to be all right.

OSCAR. (*Smiles.*) Good! Well—good night, Felix.

(*He turns to go towards bedroom as* FELIX *begins to plump up pillow from the couch.*)

FELIX. Good night, Frances.

(OSCAR *stops dead.* FELIX, *unaware of his error, plumps another pillow as* OSCAR *turns and stares at* FELIX *with a troubled, troubled expression.*)

CURTAIN

ACT II

SCENE I

Time

Two weeks later. About 11:00 P.M.

At Rise

It is late in the evening and the poker game is in session again. VINNIE, ROY, SPEED, MURRAY and OSCAR are all seated at the table. FELIX'S chair is empty. There is one major difference between this scene and the opening poker game scene. It is the appearance of the room. It is immaculately clean. No, not clean. Sterile! Spotless! Not a speck of dirt can be seen under the ten coats of Johnson's GloCoat that have been applied in the last two weeks. No laundry bags, no dirty dishes, no half-filled glasses. Suddenly FELIX appears from the kitchen. He carries a tray with glasses and food and napkins. After putting the tray down, he takes the napkins one at a time, flicks them out to full length and hands one to every player. They take them with grumbling and put them on their laps. FELIX picks up a can of beer and carefully pours it into a tall glass, measuring it perfectly so that not a drop spills or overflows. With a flourish he puts can down.

FELIX. (*Moves to* MURRAY.) . . . An ice-cold glass of beer for Murray.

MURRAY. (*He reaches up for it.*) Thank you, Felix.

FELIX. (*Holds glass, back.*) Where's your coaster?

MURRAY. My what?

FELIX. Your coaster. The little round thing that goes under the glass.

MURRAY. (*Looks around on the table.*) I think I bet it.

OSCAR. (*Picks it up and hands it to* MURRAY.) I knew I was winning too much. Here!

FELIX. Always try to use your coaster, fellows. (*He picks up another drink from tray.*) Scotch and a little bit of water?

SPEED. (*Raises hand.*) Scotch and a little bit of water. (*Proudly.*) And I have my coaster. (*He holds it up for inspection.*)

FELIX. (*Hands him drink.*) I hate to be a pest, but you know what wet glasses do? (*Goes back to the tray and picks up and wipes a clean ashtray.*)

OSCAR. (*Coldly and deliberately.*) They-leave-litle-rings-on-the-table.

FELIX. (*Nods.*) Ruins the finish. Eats right through the polish.

OSCAR. (*To* OTHERS.) So let's watch those little rings, huh?

FELIX. (*Takes ashtray and plate with a sandwich from tray and crosses to table.*) And we have a clean ashtray for Roy. . . . (*Handing* ROY *ashtray.*) Aaaaand . . . a sandwich for Vinnie. (*Like a doting headwaiter, he skillfully places the sandwich in front of* VINNIE.)

VINNIE. (*Looks at* FELIX, *then at sandwich.*) Gee it smells good. What is it?

FELIX. Bacon, lettuce and tomato with mayonnaise on pumpernickel toast.

VINNIE. (*Unbelievingly.*) Where'd you get it?

FELIX. (*Puzzled.*) I made it. In the kitchen.

VINNIE. You mean you put in toast and cooked bacon? Just for me?

OSCAR. If you don't like it, he'll make you a meat loaf. Takes him five minutes.

FELIX. It's no trouble. Honest. I love to cook. . . . Try to eat over the dish. I just vacuumed the rug. (*Goes back to tray, stops.*) Oscar!

OSCAR. (*Quickly.*) Yes, sir?

FELIX. I forgot what you wanted. What did you ask me for?

OSCAR. Two three-and-a-half-minute eggs and some petit fours.

FELIX. (*Points to him.*) A double gin and tonic. I'll be right back. . . . (FELIX *starts out, then stops at a little box on the bar.*) Who turned off the Pure-A-Tron?

MURRAY. The what?

FELIX. The Pure-A-Tron! (*He snaps it back on.*) Don't play with this, fellows. I'm trying to get some of the grime out of the air.

(*He looks at them and shakes his head disapprovingly, and exist. They* ALL *sit in silence a few seconds.*)

OSCAR. Murray—I'll give you two hundred dollars for your gun.

SPEED. (*Throws his cards on table and gets up angrily.*) I can't take it any more. (*Hand on neck.*) I've had it up to here. In the last three hours we played four minutes of poker. I'm not giving up my Friday nights to watch cooking and housekeeping.

ROY. (*Slumped in his chair, head hanging down.*) I can't breathe. (*Points to Pure-A-Tron.*) That lousy machine is sucking everything out of the air.

VINNIE. (*Chewing.*) Gee, this is delicious. Who wants a bite?

MURRAY. Is the toast warm?

VINNIE. Perfect. And not too much mayonnaise. It's really a well-made sandwich.

MURRAY. Cut me off a little piece.

VINNIE. Give me your napkin. I don't want to drop any crumbs.

SPEED. (*Watches them, horrified, as* VINNIE. *carefully breaks sandwich over* MURRAY's *napkin. Then turns to* OSCAR.) Are you listening to this? Martha and Gertrude at the Automat. (*Almost crying in despair.*) What the hell happened to our poker game?

ROY. (*Still choking.*) I'm telling you that thing could kill us. They'll find us here in the morning with our tongues on the floor.

SPEED. (*Yells at* OSCAR.) Do something! Get him back in the game.

OSCAR. (*Rises, containing his anger.*) Don't bother me with your petty little problems. You get this one stinkin' night a week. I'm cooped up here with Mary Poppins twenty-four hours a day. (*Moves to window.*)

ROY. It was better before. With the garbage and the smoke, it was better before.

VINNIE. (*To* MURRAY.) Did you notice what he does with the bread?

MURRAY. What?

VINNIE. He cuts off the crusts. That's why the sandwich is so light.

MURRAY. And then he only uses the soft, green part of the lettuce. (*Chewing.*) It's really delicious.

SPEED. (*Reacts in amazement and disgust.*) I'm going out of my mind.

OSCAR. (*Yells towards kitchen.*) Felix! . . . Damn it, FELIX!

SPEED. (*Takes kitty box from bookcase, puts it on table, and puts money in.*) Forget it. I'm going home.

OSCAR. Sit down!

SPEED. I'll buy a book and I'll start to read again.

OSCAR. Siddown! Will you siddown! (*Yells.*) Felix!

SPEED. Oscar, it's all over. The day his marriage busted up was the end of our poker game. (*Takes his jacket from back of chair and crosses to door.*) If you find some real players next week, call me.

OSCAR. (*Following him.*) You can't run out now. I'm a big loser.

SPEED. (*With door open.*) You got no one to blame but yourself. It's all your fault. You're the one who stopped him from killing himself. (*He exits and slams door.*)

OSCAR. (*Stares at door.*) He's right! . . . The man is absolutely right. (*Moves to table.*)

MURRAY. (*To* VINNIE.) Are you going to eat that pickle?

VINNIE. I wasn't thinking of it. Why? Do you want it?

MURRAY. Unless you want it. It's your pickle.

VINNIE. No, no. Take it. I don't usually eat pickle.

(VINNIE. *holds plate with pickle out to* MURRAY. OSCAR *slaps the plate which sends the pickle flying through the air.*)

OSCAR. Deal the cards!

MURRAY. What did you do that for?

OSCAR. Just deal the cards. You want to play poker, deal the cards. You want to eat, go to Schrafft's. (*To* VINNIE.) Keep your sandwich and your pickles to yourself. . . . I'm losing ninety-two dollars and everybody's getting fat! (*He screams.*) Felix. . . .

(FELIX *appears in the kitchen doorway.*)

FELIX. What?

OSCAR. Close the kitchen and sit down. It's a quarter to twelve. I still got an hour and a half to win this month's alimony.

ROY. (*Sniffs*). What is that smell? Disinfectant! (*He smells cards.*) It's the cards. *He washed the cards!* (*Throws down cards, takes jacket from chair and moves above table. Puts money into kitty box.*)

FELIX. (*Comes to table with* OSCAR'S *drink, which he puts down, and then sits in his own seat.*) Okay. . . . What's the bet?

OSCAR. (*Hurrying to his seat.*) I can't believe it. We're gonna play cards again. (*He sits.*) It's up to Roy. . . . Roy, baby, what are you gonna do?

ROY. I'm going to get in a cab and go to Central Park. If I don't get some fresh air, you got yourself a dead accountant. (*Moves towards door.*)

OSCAR. (*Follows him.*) What do you mean? It's not even twelve o'clock.

ROY. (*Turns back to* OSCAR.) Look, I've been sitting here breathing lysol and ammonia for four hours! . . . Nature didn't intend for poker to be played like that. (*He crosses to door.*) If you wanna have a game next week . . . (*He points to* FELIX.) either Louis Pasteur cleans up *after* we've gone . . . or we play in the Hotel Dixie! Good night! (*He goes and slams door.*)

There is a moment's silence. OSCAR *goes back to table and sits.*)

OSCAR. We got just enough or handball!

FELIX. Gee, I'm sorry. Is it my fault?

VINNIE. No, I guess no one feels like playing much lately.

MURRAY. Yeah. I don't know what it is, but something's happening to the old gang. (*Goes to side chair, sits, and puts on shoes.*)

OSCAR. Don't you know what's happening to the old gang? It's breaking up. Everyone's getting divorced. . . . I swear, we used to have better games when we couldn't get out at night.

VINNIE. (*Getting up and putting on jacket.*) Well—I guess I'll be going, too. Bebe and I are driving to Asbury Park for the Weekend.

FELIX. Just the two of you, heh? Gee, that's nice! . . . You always do things like that together, don't you?

VINNIE. (*Shrugs.*) We have to. I don't know how to drive! . . . (*Takes all the money from the kitty box and moves to door.*) You coming, Murray?

MURRAY. (Gets up, takes jacket and moves towards door.) Yeah, why not? If I'm not home by one o'clock with a hero sandwich and a frozen eclair, she'll have an all-points out on me. . . . Ahhh, you guys got the life.

FELIX. Who?

MURRAY. (Turns back.) Who? . . . You! The Marx Brothers! Laugh laugh laugh. What have you got to worry about? . . . If you suddenly want to go to the Playboy Club to hunt Bunnies, who's gonna stop you?

FELIX. I don't belong to the Playboy Club.

MURRAY. I know you don't, Felix, it's just a figure of speech. . . . Anyway, it's not such a bad idea. Why don't you join?

FELIX. Why?

MURRAY. *Why?* Because for twenty-five dollars they give you a key—and you walk into Paradise. *My* keys cost thirty cents—and you walk into corned beef and cabbage. (He winks at him.) Listen to me. (Moves to door.)

FELIX. What are you talking about, Murray? You're a happily married man.

MURRAY. (Turns back on landing.) I'm not talking about *my* situation. . . . (Put's on jacket.) I'm talking about *yours!* . . . Fate has just played a cruel and rotten trick on you . . . so enjoy it! (Turns to go, revealing "PAL" letters sewn on back of his jacket.) C'mon, Vinnie.

(VINNIE waves goodbye and they both exit.)

FELIX. (Staring at door.) That's funny, isn't it, Oscar? . . . They think we're happy, . . . They really think we're enjoying this. . . . (Gets up and begins to straighten up chairs.). They don't know, Oscar. They don't know what it's like. (He gives a short, ironic laugh, tucks napkins under arm and starts to pick up dishes from table.)

OSCAR. I'd be immensely grateful to you, Felix, if you didn't clean up just now.

FELIX. (Puts /fishes on tray.) It's only a few things . . . (He stops and looks back at door.) I can't get over what Murray just said. . . . You know I think they really envy us. (Clears more stuff from table.)

OSCAR. Felix, leave everything alone. I'm not through dirtying up for the night. (Drops poker chips on floor.)

FELIX. (Puts dishes on tray.) But don't you see the irony of it? . . . Don't you see it, Oscar?

OSCAR. (Sighs heavily.) Yes, I see it.

FELIX. (Clearing table.) No, you don't. I really don't think you do.

OSCAR. Felix, I'm telling you I see the irony of it.

FELIX. (Pauses.) Then tell me. What is it? What's the irony?

OSCAR. (Deep breath.) The irony is—unless we can come to some other arrangement, I'm gonna kill you! . . . That's the irony.

FELIX. What's wrong? (Crosses back to tray, puts down glasses, etc.)

OSCAR. There's something wrong with this system, that's what's wrong. I don't think that two single men living alone in a big eight-room apartment should have a cleaner house than my mother.

FELIX. (Gets rest of dishes, glasses and coasters from table.) What are you talking about? I'm just going to put the dishes in the sink. You want me to leave them here all night?

OSCAR. (Takes his glass which FELIX has put on tray and crosses to bar for refill.) I don't care if you take them to bed with you. You can play Mr. Clean all you want. But don't make *me* feel guilty.

FELIX. (Takes tray into kitchen, leaving swinging door open.) I'm not asking you to do it, Oscar. You don't have to clean up.

OSCAR. (Moves up to door.) *That's* why you make me feel guilty. You're always in my bathroom hanging up my towels. . . . Whenever I smoke you follow me around with an ashtray. . . . Last night I found you washing the kitchen floor shaking your head and moaning, "Footprints, footprints"! (Paces Right.)

FELIX. (Comes back to table with silent butler into which he dumps the ashtrays; then wipes them carefully.) I didn't say they were yours.

OSCAR. (Angrily; sits Down Right in wing chair.) Well, they *were* mine, damn it. I have feet and they make prints. What do you want me to do, climb across the cabinets?

FELIX. No! I want you to walk on the floor.

OSCAR. I appreciate that! I really do.

FELIX. (*Crosses to telephone table and cleans ashtray there.*) I'm just trying to keep the place livable. I didn't realize I irritated you that much.

OSCAR. I just feel *I* should have the right to decide when my bathtub needs a going over with Dutch Cleanser. . . . It's the democratic way!

FELIX. (*Puts down silent butler and rag on coffee table and sits down on couch, glumly.*) I was wondering how long it would take.

OSCAR. How long *what* would take?

FELIX. Before I got on your nerves.

OSCAR. I didn't say you get on my nerves.

FELIX. Well, it's the same thing. You said I irritated you.

OSCAR. *You* said you irritated me. *I* didn't say it.

FELIX. Then what *did* you say?

OSCAR. I don't know *what* I said. What's the difference what I said?

FELIX. It doesn't make any difference. I was just repeating what I thought you said.

OSCAR. Well, don't repeat what you *thought* I said. Repeat what I *said!* . . . My God, that's irritating!

FELIX. You see! You *did* say it!

OSCAR. I don't believe this whole conversation. (*Gets up and paces above table.*)

FELIX. (*Pawing with a cup.*) Oscar, I'm—I'm sorry. I don't know what's wrong with me.

OSCAR. (*Paces Down Right.*) And don't pout. If you want to fight, we'll fight. But don't pout! Fighting *I* win. Pouting *you* win!

FELIX. You're right. Everything you say about me ix absolutely right.

OSCAR. (*Really angry, turns to* FELIX.) And don't give in so easily. I'm *not* always right. Sometimes *you're* right.

FELIX. You're right. I do that. I always figure I'm in the wrong.

OSCAR. Only this time you *are* wrong. And I'm right.

FELIX. Oh, leave me alone.

OSCAR. And don't sulk. That's the same as pouting.

FELIX. I know. I know. (*He squeezes cup with anger.*) Damn me, why can't I do one lousy thing right ? (*He suddenly stands up and cocks his arm back angrily about to hurl the cup against the front door, then thinks better of it and puts it down and sits.*)

OSCAR. (*Watching this.*) Why didn't you throw it?

FELIX. I almost did. I get so insane with myself sometimes.

OSCAR. Then why don't you throw the cup?

FELIX. Because I'm trying to control myself.

OSCAR. Why?

FELIX. What do you mean, why?

OSCAR. Why do you have to control yourself? You're angry, you felt like throwing the cup, why don't you throw it.

FELIX. Because there's no point to it. I'd still be angry and I'd have a broken cup.

OSCAR. How do you *know* how you'd feel? Maybe you'd feel *wonderful*. Why do you have to control every single thought in your head? . . . Why don't you let loose *once* in your life? Do something that you *feel* like doing—and not what you *think* you're supposed to do. Stop keeping books, Felix. Relax. Get drunk. Get angry. . . . C'mon, *break the Goddamned cup!*

(Felix *suddenly stands up and hurls the cup against the door, smashing it to pieces. Then he grabs his shoulder in pain.*)

FELIX. Oww! . . . I hurt my arm! (*Sinks down on couch, massaging his arm.*)

OSCAR. (*Throws up hands.*) You're hopeless? You're a hopeless mental case! (*Paces about the table.*)

FELIX. (*Grimacing with pain.*) I'm not supposed to throw with that arm. What a stupid thing to do.

OSCAR. Why don't you live in a closet? I'll leave your meals outside the door and slide in the papers. Is that safe enough?

FELIX. (*Rubbing arm.*) I used to have bursitis in this arm. I had to give up golf . . . Do you have a heating pad?

OSCAR. How can you hurt your arm throwing a cup? If it had coffee in it, that's one thing. But an *empty* cup . . . (*Sits in wing chair.*)

FELIX. All right, cut it out, Oscar. That's the way I am. I get hurt easily. I can't help it.

OSCAR. You're not going to cry, are you? I think all those tears dripping on the arm is what gave you bursitis.

FELIX. (*Holding arm.*) I once got it just from combing my hair.

OSCAR. (*Shaking his head.*) A world full of room-mates and I pick myself the Tin Man. (*Sighs.*) Oh well, I suppose I could have done worse.

FELIX. (*Puts rag and silent butler on bar. Takes chip box from bar and crosses to table.*) You're darn right, you could have. A *lot* worse.

OSCAR. *How?*

FELIX. What do you mean, how? How'd you like to live with Ten-thumbs Murray or Speed and his complaining? (*Gets down on his knees, picks up chips and puts them into box.*) Don't forget I cook and clean and take care of this house. I save us a lot of money, don't I?

OSCAR. Yeah, but then you keep me up all night counting it.

FELIX. (*Goes to table and sweeps chips and cards into box.*) Now wait a minute. We're not always going at each other. We have fun too, don't we?

OSCAR. (*Crosses to couch.*) *Fun?* Felix, getting a clear picture on Channel Two isn't my idea of whoopee.

FELIX. What are you talking about?

OSCAR. All right, what do you and I do every night? (*Takes off sneakers, dropping them on floor.*)

FELIX. What do we do? You mean after dinner?

OSCAR. That's right. After we've had your halibut steak and the dishes are done and the sink has been Brillo'd and the pans have been S.O.S.'d and the leftovers have been Saran-wrapped—what do we do?

FELIX. (*Finishes clearing table and puts everything on top of bookcase.*) Well, we read . . . we talk . . .

OSCAR. (*Takes off pants and throws them on floor.*) No, no. *I* read and *you* talk. . . . I try to work and you talk. . . . I take a bath and you talk. . . . I go to sleep and you talk. We've got your life arranged pretty good but I'm still looking for a little entertainment.

FELIX. (*Pulling Upstage kitchen chairs away from table.*) What are you saying? That I talk too much?

OSCAR. (*Sits on couch.*) No, no. I'm not complaining. You have a lot to say. What's worrying me is that I'm beginning to listen.

FELIX. (*Pulls table up into alcove.*) Oscar, I told you a hundred times, just tell me to shut up. I'm not sensitive. (*Pulls love seat down into room, and centers table between windows in alcove.*)

OSCAR. I don't think you're getting my point. For a husky man, 1 think I've spent enough evenings discussing tomorrow's menu. . . . The night was made for other things.

FELIX. Like what? (*Puts two dining chairs neatly at Left and Down of the table.*)

OSCAR. Like unless I get to touch something soft in the next two weeks, I'm in big trouble.

FELIX. You mean women? (*Puts two other dining chairs neatly at Right and Down of table.*)

OSCAR. If you want to give it a name, all right, women!

FELIX. (*Picks up two kitchen chairs and starts towards landing.*) That's funny. You know I haven't even *thought* about women in weeks.

OSCAR. I fail to see the humor.

FELIX. (*Stops.*) No, that's really strange. I mean when Frances and I were happy I don't think there was a girl on the street I didn't stare at for ten minutes. (*Crosses to Up Left kitchen door, pitches it open with back.*) I used to take the wrong subway home just following a pair of legs. . . . But since we broke up, I don't even know what a woman looks like. (*Takes chairs into kitchen.*)

OSCAR. Well, either I could go downstairs and buy a couple of magazines . . . or I could make a phone call.

FELIX. (*From the kitchen, as he washes dishes.*) What are you saying?

OSCAR. (*Crosses to humidor on small table Down Right and takes cigar.*) I'm saying let's spend one night talking to someone with higher voices than us.

FELIX. You mean go out on a date?

OSCAR. Ya . . .

FELIX. Oh, well, I—I can't.

OSCAR. Why not?

FELIX. Well, it's all right for you. But I'm still married.

OSCAR. (*Paces towards kitchen door.*) You can *cheat* until the divorce comes through!

FELIX. It's not that. It's just that . . . I have no—no *feeling* for it. I can't explain it.

OSCAR. Try!

FELIX. (*Comes to doorway with brush and dish in hand.*) Listen, I intend to go out. I get lonely, too. But I'm just separated a few weeks. Give me a little time. (*Goes back to sink.*)

OSCAR. There isn't any time left. I saw TV Guide and there's nothing on this week! (*Paces into and through kitchen and out kitchen door on landing to Down Right.*) What am I asking you? All I want to do is have dinner with a couple of girls. You just have to eat and talk. It's not hard. You've eaten and talked before.

FELIX. (*In kitchen.*) Why do you need me? Can't you go out yourself?

OSCAR. Because I may want to come back here. And if we walk in and find you washing the windows, it puts a damper on things. (*Sits Down Right.*)

FELIX. (*Pokes head out of kitchen.*) I'll take a pill and go to sleep. (*Back into kitchen.*)

OSCAR. Why take a pill when you can take a girl?

FELIX. (*Comes out with aerosol bomb held high over his head, and circles the room spraying it.*) Because I'd feel guilty, that's why. Maybe it doesn't make any sense to you, but that's the way I feel. (*Puts bomb on bar and takes silent butler and rag into kitchen. Places them on sink and busily begins to wipe refrigerator.*)

OSCAR. Look, for all I care you can take her in the kitchen and make a blueberry pie. But I think it's a lot healthier than sitting up in your bed every night writing Frances' name all through the

crossword puzzles. . . . just for one night, talk to another girl.

FELIX. (*Pushes love seat carefully in position Down Right and sits; weakening.*) But—who would I call? The only single girl I know is my secretary and I don't think she likes me.

OSCAR. (*Jumps up and crouches next to* FELIX.) Leave that to me. There's two sisters who live in this building, English girls. One's a widow, the other's a divorcee. They're a barrel of laughs.

FELIX. How do you know?

OSCAR. I was trapped in the elevator with them last week. (*Runs to telephone table, puts directory on floor, and gets down on knees to look for number.*) I've been meaning to call them but I didn't know which one to take out. This'll be perfect.

FELIX. What do they look like?

OSCAR. Don't worry. Yours is very pretty.

FELIX. I'm not worried. . . . Which one is mine?

OSCAR. The divorcee. (*Looking in book.*)

FELIX. (*Goes to* OSCAR.) Why do I get the divorcee?

OSCAR. I don't care. You want the widow? (*Circles number on page with crayon.*)

FELIX. (*Sitting on couch.*) No, I don't want the widow. I don't even want the divorcee. I'm just doing this for you.

OSCAR. Look, take whoever you want. When they come in the door, point to the sister of your choice. (*Tears page out of the book, runs to bookcase and hangs it up.*) I don't care. I just want to have some laughs.

FELIX. All right. All right.

OSCAR. (*Crosses to couch, sits next to* FELIX.) Don't say all right. I want you to promise me you're going to try to have a good time. Please, Felix. It's important. Say I promise.

FELIX. (*Nods.*) I promise.

OSCAR. Again!

FELIX. I promise!

OSCAR. And no writing in the book, a dollar thirty for the cab.

FELIX. No writing in the book.

OSCAR. No one is to be called Frances. It's Gwendolyn and Cecily.

FELIX. No Frances.

OSCAR. No crying, sighing, moaning or groaning.

FELIX. I'll smile from seven to twelve.

OSCAR. And this above all, no talk of the past. Only the present.

FELIX. And the future.

OSCAR. That's the new Felix I've been waiting for. (*Leaps up and prances Right.*) Oh, is this going to be a night. . . . Where do you want to go?

FELIX. For what?

OSCAR. For dinner. Where'll we eat?

FELIX. You mean a restaurant? For the four of us? It'll cost a fortune.

OSCAR. We'll cut down on laundry. We don't wear socks on Thursdays.

FELIX. But that's throwing away money. We can't afford it, Oscar.

OSCAR. We have to eat.

FELIX. (*Moves to* OSCAR.) We'll have dinner here.

OSCAR. *Here?*

FELIX. I'll cook. We'll save thirty, forty dollars. (*He goes to couch, sits, and picks up phone.*)

OSCAR. What kind of a double date is that? You'll be in the kitchen all night.

FELIX. No, I won't. I'll put it up in the afternoon. Once I get my potatoes in, I'll have all the time in the world. (*He starts to dial.*)

OSCAR. (*Pacing back and forth.*) What happened to the new Felix? . . . Who are you calling?

FELIX. Frances, I want to get her recipe for London broil. The girls'll be crazy about it.

(*He dials as* OSCAR *storms off towards his bedroom.*)

CURTAIN

ACT II

SCENE 2

Time

A few days later. About 8 o'clock.

At Rise

No one is on Stage. The dining table looks like a page out of House and Garden. It's set up for dinner for four, complete with linen tablecloth, candles and wine glasses. There is a floral centerpiece and flowers about the room, and crackers and dip on the coffee table. There are sounds of ACTIVITY in the kitchen. The front door opens and

Oscar enters with a bottle of wine in a brown paper bag, and his jacket over his arm. He looks about gleefully as he listens to the sounds from the kitchen. He puts the bag on the table and his jacket over the chair, Down Right.

OSCAR. (*Calls out. In a playful mood.*) I'm home, dear! (*He goes into his bedroom, taking off his shirt, and comes skipping out shaving with a cordless razor, and with a clean shirt and a tie over his arm, he is joyfully singing as he admires the table.*) Beautiful! Just beautiful! (*He sniffs, obviously catching the aroma from the kitchen.*) Oh, yeah. Something wonderful is going on in that kitchen. . . . (*He rubs hands gleefully.*) No, sir. There's no doubt about it. I'm the luckiest man on earth. (*Puts razor into his pocket, and begins to put on shirt. FELIX enters slowly from the kitchen. He's wearing a small dish towel as an apron. He has a ladle in one hand. He looks silently and glumly at OSCAR, crosses to the armchair and sits.*) I got the wine. (*Takes bottle out of the bag and puts it on the table.*) Batard Montrachet. Six and a quarter. You don't mind, do you, pussycat? We'll walk to work this week. (FELIX *sits glumly and silently.*) Hey, no kidding, Felix, you did a great job. One little suggestion? Let's come down a little with the lights . . . (*Switches of wall brackets.*) and up very softly with the music. (*He crosses to stereo in bookcase and picks up albums.*) What do you think goes better with London broil, Mancini or Sinatra? (FELIX *just stares ahead.*) Felix? . . .

What's the matter? (*Puts albums down.*) Something's wrong. I can tell by your conversation. (*Goes into bathroom, gets bottle of after shave lotion, comes out and puts it on.*) All right, Felix, what is it?

FELIX. (*Without looking at him.*) What is it? Let's start with what time do you think it is?

OSCAR. What time? I don't know. Seven-thirty?

FELIX. Seven-thirty? Try eight o'clock.

OSCAR. (*Puts lotion down on small table.*) All right, so it's eight o'clock. So? (*Begins to fix tie.*)

FELIX. So? . . . You said you'd be home at seven.

OSCAR. Is that what I said?

FELIX. (*Nods.*) That's what you said. "I will be home at seven" is what you said.

OSCAR. Okay, I said I'd be home at seven. And it's eight. So what's the problem?

FELIX. If you knew you were going to be late, why didn't you call me?

OSCAR. (*Pauses while making tie.*) I couldn't call you. I was busy.

FELIX. Too busy to pick up a phone? . . . Where were you?

OSCAR. I was in the office, working.

FELIX. (*Moves Down Left.*) Working? Ha!

OSCAR. Yes. Working!

FELIX. I called your office at seven o'clock. You were gone.

OSCAR. (*Tucking in shirt.*) It took me an hour to get home. I couldn't get a cab.

FELIX. Since when do they have cabs in Hannigan's bar?

OSCAR. Wait a minute. I want to get this down on a tape recorder . . . because no one'll believe me! . . . You mean now I have to call you if I'm coming home late for dinner?

FELIX. (*Crosses to* OSCAR.) Not *any* dinner. Just the ones I've been slaving over since two o'clock this afternoon . . . to help save *you* money to pay your wife's alimony.

OSCAR. (*Controlling himself.*) Felix . . . this is no time to have a domestic quarrel. We have two girls coming down any minute.

FELIX. You mean you told them to be here at eight o'clock?

OSCAR. (*Takes jacket and crosses to couch. Sits and takes some dip from coffee table.*) I don't remember what I said. Seven-thirty, eight o'clock. What difference does it make?

FELIX. (*Follows* OSCAR.) I'll tell you what difference. You told me they were coming at seven-thirty. You were going to be here at seven to help me with the hors d'oeuvres. At seven-thirty they arrive and we have cocktails. At eight o'clock we have dinner. It is now eight o'clock. *My-London-broil-is-finished!* If we don't eat now the whole damned thing'll be *dried out!*

OSCAR. Oh, God, help me.

FELIX. Never mind helping *you.* Tell Him to save the meat. Because we got nine dollars and thirty-four cents worth drying up in there right now.

OSCAR. Can't you keep it warm?

FELIX. (*Paces Right.*) What do you think I am, the Magic Chef? I'm lucky I got it to come out at eight o'clock. What am I going to do?

OSCAR. I don't know. Keep pouring gravy on it.

FELIX. What gravy?

OSCAR. Don't you have any gravy?

FELIX. (*Storms over to* OSCAR.) Where the hell am I going to get gravy at eight o'clock?

OSCAR. (*Gets up and moves Right.*) I thought it comes when you cook the meat.

FELIX. (*Follows him.*) When you *cook the meat?* You don't know the first thing you're talking about. You have to make gravy. It doesn't *come!*

OSCAR. You asked my advice, I'm giving it to you. (*Putting on jacket.*)

FELIX. Advice? (*He waves ladle in his face.*) You didn't know where the kitchen was 'til I came here and showed you.

OSCAR. You wanna talk to me, put down the spoon.

FELIX. (*Exploding in rage, again waving ladle in his face.*) Spoon? You dumb ignoramus. It's a ladle. You don't even know it's a ladle.

OSCAR. All right, Felix, get a hold of yourself.

FELIX. (*Pulls himself together, sits on love seat.*) You think it's so easy? Go on. The kitchen's all yours. Go make a London broil for four people who come a half hour late.

OSCAR. (*To no one in particular.*) Listen to me. I'm arguing with him over gravy.

(*The BELL RINGS.*)

FELIX. (*Jumps up.*) Well, they're here. Our dinner guests. I'll get a saw and cut the meat. (*Starts for kitchen.*)

OSCAR. (*Stopping him.*) Stay where you are!

FELIX. I'm not taking the blame for this dinner.

OSCAR. Who's blaming you? Who even *cares* about the dinner?

FELIX. (*Moves to OSCAR.*) I care. I take *pride* in what I do. And you're going to explain to them exactly what happened.

OSCAR. All right, you can take a Polaroid picture of me coming in at eight o'clock! . . . Now take off that stupid apron because I'm opening the door. (*Rips the towel off FELIX and goes to the door.*)

FELIX. (*Takes jacket from dining chair and puts it on.*) I just want to get one thing clear. This is the last time I ever cook for you. Because people like you don't even appreciate a decent meal. That's why they have T.V. dinners.

OSCAR. You through?

FELIX. I'm through!

OSCAR. Then smile. (OSCAR *smiles and opens the door. The GIRLS poke their heads through the door. They are BOTH in their young thirties and somewhat attractive. They are undoubtedly British.*) Well, hello.

GWENDOLYN. (*To OSCAR.*) Hallo.

CECILY. (*To OSCAR.*) Hallo.

GWENDOLYN. I do hope we're not late.

OSCAR. No, no. You timed it perfectly. Come on in. (*He points to them as they enter.*) Er, Felix, I'd like you to meet two very good friends of mine, Gwendolyn and Cecily—

CECILY. (*Pointing out his mistake.*) Cecily and Gwendolyn.

OSCAR. Oh, yes. Cecily and Gwendolyn . . . er . . . (*Trying to remember their last name.*) Er . . . Don't tell me. . . . Robin? . . . No, no. . . . Cardinal?

GWENDOLYN. Wrong both times. It's Pigeon!

OSCAR. Pigeon. Right. Cecily and Gwendolyn Pigeon.

GWENDOLYN. (*To* FELIX.) You don't spell it like Walter Pidgeon. You spell it like "Coo Coo" Pigeon.

OSCAR. We'll remember that if it comes up. . . . Cecily and Gwendolyn, I'd like you to meet my room-mate . . . and our chef for the evening . . . Felix Ungar.

CECILY. (*Holding hand out.*) Heh d'yew dew?

FELIX. (*Moving to her and shaking her hand.*) How do you do?

GWENDOLYN. (*Holding hand out.*) Heh d'yew dew?

FELIX. (*Stepping up on landing and shaking her hand.*) How do you do?

(*This puts him nose to nose with OSCAR, and there is an awkward pause as they look at each other.*)

OSCAR. Well, we did that beautifully. . . . Why don't we sit down and make ourselves comfortable?

(FELIX *steps aside and ushers the GIRLS down into the room. There is ad-libbing and a bit of confusion and milling about as they ALL squeeze between the armchair and the couch, and the PIGEONS finally seat themselves on the couch. OSCAR sits in the armchair, and FELIX sneaks past him to the love seat. Finally ALL have settled down.*)

CECILY. This is ever so nice, isn't it, Gwen?

GWENDOLYN. (*Looking around.*) Lovely. And much nicer than our flat. Do you have help?

OSCAR. Er, yes. I have a man who comes in every night.

CECILY. Aren't you the lucky one?

(CECILY, GWENDOLYN *and* OSCAR *all laugh at her joke.* OSCAR *looks over at* FELIX *but there is no response.*)

OSCAR. (*Rubs hands together.*) Well, isn't this nice? . . . I was telling Felix yesterday about how we happened to meet.

GWENDOLYN. Who's Felix?

OSCAR. (*A little embarrassed. Points to* FELIX.) He is!

GWENDOLYN. Oh, yes, of course. I'm so sorry.

(FELIX *nods that it's all right.*)

CECILY. You know it happened to us again this morning.

OSCAR. What did?

GWENDOLYN. Stuck in the elevator again.

OSCAR. Really? Just the two of you?

CECILY. And poor old Mr. Kessler from the third floor. We were in there half an hour.

OSCAR. No kidding? What happened?

GWENDOLYN. Nothing much, I'm afraid.

(CECILY *and* GWENDOLYN *both laugh at her latest joke, joined by* OSCAR. *He once again looks over at* FELIX, *but there is no response.*)

OSCAR. (*Rubs hands again.*) Well, this really is nice.

CECILY. And ever so much cooler than our place.

GWENDOLYN. It's like equatorial Africa on our side of the building.

CECILY. Last night it was so bad Gwen and I sat there in Nature's Own cooling ourselves in front of the open frig. Can you imagine such thing?

OSCAR. Er . . . I'm working on it.

GWENDOLYN. Actually, it's impossible to get a night's sleep. Cec and I really don't know what to do.

OSCAR. Why don't you sleep with an air-conditioner?

GWENDOLYN. We haven't got one.

OSCAR. I know, but we have.

GWENDOLYN. Oh you! I told you about that one, didn't I, Cec?

FELIX. They say it may rain Friday.

(*They* ALL *stare at* FELIX.)

GWENDOLYN. Oh?

CECILY. That should cool things off a bit.

OSCAR. I wouldn't be surprised.

FELIX. Although sometimes it gets hotter after it rains.

GWENDOLYN. Yes, it does, doesn't it?

(*They continue to stare at* FELIX.)

FELIX. (*Jumps up and, picking up ladle, starts for the kitchen.*) Dinner is served!

OSCAR. (*Stopping him.*) No, it isn't!

FELIX. Yes, it is!

OSCAR. No, it isn't! I'm sure the girls would like a cocktail first. (*To* GIRLS.) Wouldn't you, girls?

GWENDOLYN. Well, I wouldn't put up a struggle.

OSCAR. There you are. (*To* CECILY.) What would you like?

CECILY. Oh, I really don't know. (*To* OSCAR.) What have you got?

FELIX. London broil.

OSCAR. (*To* FELIX.) She means to drink. (*To* CECILY.) We have everything. And what we don't have, I mix in the medicine cabinet. What'll it be? (*Crouches next to her.*)

CECILY. Oh . . . a double vodka.

GWENDOLYN. Cecily . . . not before dinner.

CECILY. (*To the* MEN.) My sister . . . She watches over me like a mother hen. (*To* OSCAR.) Make it a *small* double vodka.

OSCAR. A small double vodka! . . . And for the beautiful mother hen?

GWENDOLYN. Oh . . . I'd like something cool. I think I would like to have a double Drambuie with some crushed ice . . . unless you don't have the crushed ice.

OSCAR. I was up all night with a sledge hammer. . . . I shall return! (*Goes to bar and gets bottles of vodka and Drambuie.*)

FELIX. (*going to him.*) Where are you going?

OSCAR. To get the refreshments.

FELIX. (*Starting to panic.*) Inside? What'll *I* do?

OSCAR. You can finish the weather report. (*He exits into kitchen.*)

FELIX. (*Calls after him.*) Don't forget to look at my meat! (*He turns and faces the* GIRLS. *He crosses to chair and sits. He crosses his legs* *nonchalantly. But he is ill at east and he crosses them again. He is becoming aware of the silence and he can no longer get away with just smiling.)* Er . . . Oscar tells me you're sisters.

CECILY. Yes. That's right. (*She looks at* GWENDOLYN.)

FELIX. From England.

GWENDOLYN: Yes. That's right. (*She looks at* CECILY.)

FELIX. I see. (*Silence. Then, his little joke.*) We're not brothers.

CECILY. Yes. We know.

FELIX. Although I am a brother. I have *a* brother who's a doctor. He lives in Buffalo. That's upstate in New York.

GWENDOLYN. (*Taking cigarette from her purse.*) Yes, we know.

FELIX. You know my brother?

GWENDOLYN. No. We know that Buffalo is upstate in New York.

FELIX. Oh! (*Gets up, takes cigarette lighter from side table and lights* GWENDOLYN'S *cigarette.*)

CECILY. We've been there! . . . Have you?

FELIX. No! . . . Is it nice?

CECILY. Lovely.

(FELIX *closes lighter on cigarette and turns to go back to chair, taking the cigarette, now caught in the lighter, with him. He notices cigarette and hastily gives it back to* GWENDOLYN, *stopping to light it once again. He puts lighter back on table and sits nervously. There is a pause.*)

FELIX. Isn't that interesting? . . . How long have you been in the United States of America?

CECILY. Almost four years now.

FELIX. (*Nods.*) Uh-huh. . . . Just visiting?

GWENDOLYN. (*Looks at* CECILY.) No! . . . We live here.

FELIX. And you work here too, do you?

CECILY. Yes. We're secretaries for Slenderama.

GWENDOLYN. You know. The Health Club.

CECILY. People bring us their bodies and we do wonderful things with them.

GWENDOLYN. Actually, if you're interested, we can get you ten per cent off.

CECILY. Off the price, not off your body.

FELIX. Yes, I see. (*He laughs, they* ALL *laugh. Suddenly shouts towards kitchen.*) Oscar, where's the drinks?

OSCAR. (*Offstage.*) Coming! Coming!

CECILY. What field of endeavor are you engaged in?

FELIX. I write the news for C.B.S.

CECILY. Oh! Fascinating!

GWENDOLYN. Where do you get your ideas from?

FELIX. (*He looks at her as though she's a Martian.*) From the news.

GWENDOLYN. Oh, yes, of course. Silly me. . . .

CECILY. Maybe you can mention Gwen and I in one of your news reports.

FELIX. Well, if you do something spectacular, maybe I will.

CECILY. Oh, we've done spectacular things but I don't think we'd want it spread all over the Telly, do you, Gwen?

(*They both laugh.*)

FELIX. (*He laughs too, then cries out almost for help.*) Oscar!

OSCAR. (*Offstage.*) Yeah yeah!

FELIX. (*To* GIRLS.) It's such a large apartment, sometimes you have to shout.

GWENDOLYN. Just you two baches live here?

FELIX. Baches? Oh, bachelors! We're not bachelors. We're divorced. That is, Oscar's divorced. I'm *getting* divorced.

CECILY. Oh. Small world. We've cut the dinghy loose too, as they say.

GWENDOLYN. Well, you couldn't have a *better* matched foursome, could you?

FELIX. (*Smiles weakly.*) No, I suppose not.

GWENDOLYN. Although technically, I'm a widow. I was divorcing my husband but he died before the final papers came through.

FELIX. Oh, I'm awfully sorry. (*Sighs.*) It's a terrible thing, isn't it? Divorce.

GWENDOLYN. It can be . . . if you haven't got the right solicitor.

CECILY. That's true, Sometimes they can drag it out for months. I was lucky. Snip, cut and I was free.

FELIX. I mean it's terrible what it can do to people. After all, what is divorce? It's taking two happy people and tearing their lives completely apart. It's inhuman, don't you think so?

CECILY. Yes, it can be an awful bother.

GWENDOLYN. But of course, that's all water under the bridge now, eh? . . . er . . . I'm terribly sorry, but I think I've forgotten your name.

FELIX. Felix.

GWENDOLYN. Oh, yes. Felix.

CECILY. Like the Cat.

(FELIX *takes wallet front his jacket pocket.*)

GWENDOLYN. Well, the Pigeons will have to beware of the cat, won't they? (*She laughs.*)

CECILY. (*Nibbles on a nut from the dish.*) Mmm, cashews. Lovely.

FELIX. (*Takes snapshot out of wallet.*) This is the worst part of breaking up. (*He hands picture to CECILY.*)

CECILY. (*Looks at it.*) Childhood sweethearts, were you?

FELIX. No, no. That's my little boy and girl. (CECILY *gives picture to* GWENDOLYN *and takes pair of glasses from her purse and puts them on.*) He's seven, she's five.

CECILY. (*Looks again.*) Oh! Sweet.

FELIX. They live with their mother.

GWENDOLYN. I imagine you must miss them terribly.

FELIX. (*Takes back picture and looks at it longingly.*) I can't stand being away from them. (*Shrugs.*) But—that's what happens with divorce.

CECILY. When do you get to see them?

FELIX. Every night. I stop there on my way home! . . . Then I take them on the weekends and I get them on holidays and July and August.

CECILY. Oh! . . . Well, when is it that you miss them?

FELIX. Whenever I'm not there. If they didn't have to go to school so early, I'd go over and make them breakfast. They love my French toast.

GWENDOLYN. You're certainly a devoted father.

FELIX. It's Frances who's the wonderful one.

CECILY. She's the little girl?

FELIX. No. She's the mother. My wife.

GWENDOLYN. The one you're divorcing?

FELIX. (*Nods.*) Mm! . . . She's done a terrific job bringing them up. They always look so nice. They're so polite. Speak beautifully. Never "Yeah!" Always "Yes." . . . They're such good kids. And she did it all. She's the kind of woman who—Ah, what am saying? You don't want to hear any of this. (*Puts picture back in wallet.*)

CECILY. Nonsense. You have a right to be proud. You have two beautiful children and a wonderful ex-wife.

FELIX. (*Containing his emotions.*) I know. I know. (*He hands* CECILY *another snapshot.*) That's her. Frances.

GWENDOLYN. (*Looking at picture.*) Oh, she's pretty. Isn't she pretty, Cecy?

CECILY. Oh, yes. Pretty. A pretty girl. Very pretty.

FELIX. (*Takes picture back.*) Thank you. (*Shows them another snapshot.*) Isn't this nice?

GWENDOLYN. (*Looks.*) There's no one in the picture.

FELIX. I know. It's a picture of our living room. We had a beautiful apartment.

GWENDOLYN. Oh, yes. Pretty. Very pretty.

CECILY. Those are lovely lamps.

FELIX. Thank you. (*Takes picture.*) We bought them in Mexico on our honeymoon. . . . (*He looks at picture again.*) I used to love to come home at night. (*He's beginning to break.*) That was my whole life. My wife, my kids . . . and my apartment. (*He breaks down and sobs.*)

CECILY. Does she have the lamps now, too?

FELIX. (*Nods.*) I gave her everything. . . . It'll never be like that again. . . . Never! . . . I—I—(*He turns head away.*) I'm sorry. (*He takes out a handkerchief and dabs eyes.* GWENDOLYN *and* CECILY *look at each other with compassion.*) Please forgive me. I didn't mean to get emotional. (*Trying to pull himself together. He picks up bowl from side table and offers it to* GIRLS.) Would you like some potato chips?

(CECILY *takes the bowl.*)

GWENDOLYN. You mustn't be ashamed. I think it's a rare quality in a man to be able to cry.

FELIX. (*Hand over eyes.*) Please. Let's not talk about it.

CECILY. I think it's sweet. Terribly terribly sweet. (*Takes potato chip.*)

FELIX. You're just making it worse.

GWENDOLYN. (*Teary-eyed.*) It's so refreshing to hear a man speak so highly of the woman he's divorcing! . . . Oh, dear. (*She takes out her handkerchief.*) Now you've got me thinking about poor Sydney.

CECILY. Oh, Gwen. Please don't. (*Puts bowl down.*)

GWENDOLYN. It was a good marriage at first. Everyone said so. Didn't they, Cecily? Not like you and George.

CECILY. (*The past returns as she comforts* GWENDOLYN.) That's right. George and I were never happy. . . Not for one single, solitary day. (*She remembers her unhappiness and grabs her handkerchief and dabs her eyes. ALL THREE are now sitting with handkerchiefs at their eyes.*)

FELIX. Isn't this ridiculous?

GWENDOLYN. I don't know what brought this on. I was feeling so good a few minutes ago.

CECILY. I haven't cried since I was fourteen.

FELIX. Just, let it pour out. It'll make you feel much better. I always do.

GWENDOLYN. Oh dear oh dear oh dear.

(ALL THREE *sit sobbing into their handkerchiefs. Suddenly* OSCAR *bursts happily into the room with a tray full of drinks. He is all smiles.*)

OSCAR. (*Like a corny M.C.*) Is ev-rybuddy happy? (*Then he sees the maudlin scene.* FELIX *and the* GIRLS *quickly try to pull themselves together.*) What the hell happened?

FELIX. Nothing! Nothing! (*He quickly puts handkerchief away.*)

OSCAR. What do you mean, nothing? I'm gone three minutes and I walk into a funeral parlor. What did you say to them?

FELIX. I didn't say anything. Don't start in again, Oscar.

OSCAR. I can't leave you alone for five seconds. Well, if you really want to cry, go inside and look at your London broil.

FELIX. (*He rushes madly into the kitchen.*) Oh, my gosh! Why didn't you call me? I told you to call me.

OSCAR. (*Giving drink to* CECILY.) I'm sorry, girls. I forgot to warn you about Felix. He's a walking soap opera.

GWENDOLYN. I think he's the dearest thing I ever met.

CECILY. (*Taking the glass.*) He's so sensitive. So fragile. I just want to bundle him up in my arms and take care of him.

OSCAR. (*Holds out* GWENDOLYN'S *drink. At this, he puts it back down on tray and takes a swallow from his own drink.*) Well, I think when he comes out of that kitchen you may have to.

(*Sure enough,* FELIX *comes out of the kitchen onto the landing looking like a wounded puppy. With a protective kitchen glove, he holds a pan with the exposed London broil. Black is the color of his true love.*)

FELIX. (*Very calmly.*) I'm going down to the delicatessen. I'll be right back.

OSCAR. (*Going to him.*) Wait a minute. Maybe it's not so bad. Let's see it.

FELIX. (*Shows him.*) Here! Look! Nine dollars and thirty-four cents' worth of ashes! (*Pulls pan away. To* GIRLS.) I'll get some corned beef sandwiches.

OSCAR. (*Trying to get a look at it.*) Give it to me! Maybe we can save some of it.

FELIX. (*Holding it away from* OSCAR.) There's nothing to save. It's all black meat. Nobody likes black meat! . . .

OSCAR. Can't I even look at it?

FELIX. No, you can't look at it!

OSCAR. Why can't I look at it?

FELIX. If you looked at your watch before you wouldn't have to look at the black meat now! Leave it alone! (*Turns to go back into kitchen.*)

GWENDOLYN. (*Going to him.*) Felix . . . Can *we* look at it?

CECILY. (*Turning to him, kneeling on couch.*) Please? (FELIX *stops in the doorway to kitchen. He hesitates for a moment. He likes them. Then he turns and wordlessly holds pan out to them.* GWENDOLYN *and* CECILY *inspect it wordlessly, and then turn away sobbing quietly. To* OSCAR.) How about Chinese food?

OSCAR. A wonderful idea.

GWENDOLYN. I've got a better idea. Why don't we just make pot luck in the kitchen?

OSCAR. A *much* better idea.

FELIX. I used up all the pots. (*Crosses to love seat and sits, still holding the pan.*)

CECILY. Well then, we can eat up in *our* place. We have tons of Horn and Hardart's.

OSCAR. (*Gleefully.*) That's the best idea I ever heard.

GWENDOLYN. Of course it's awfully hot up there. You'll have to take off your jackets.

OSCAR. (*Smiling.*) We can always open up a refrigerator.

CECILY. (*Gets purse from couch.*) Give us five minutes to get into our cooking things.

(GWENDOLYN *gets purse from couch.*)

OSCAR. Can't you make it four? I'm suddenly starving to death.

(*The* GIRLS *are crossing to door.*)

GWENDOLYN. Don't forget the wine.

OSCAR. How could I forget the wine?

CECILY. And a corkscrew.

OSCAR. *And* a corkscrew.

GWENDOLYN. And Felix.

OSCAR. No, I won't forget Felix.

CECILY. Ta ta!

OSCAR. Ta ta!

GWENDOLYN. Ta ta!

(*The* GIRLS *exit.*)

OSCAR. (*Throws a kiss at the closed door.*) You bet your sweet little crumpets, ta ta! (*He wheels around beaming and quickly gathers up the corkscrew from bar, the wine and the records.*) Felix, I love you. You've just overcooked us into one hell of a night. Come on, get the ice bucket. Ready or not, here we come. (*Runs to door.*)

FELIX. (*Sitting motionless.*) I'm not going!

OSCAR. What?

FELIX. I said I'm not going.

OSCAR. (*Crossing to* FELIX.) Are you out of your mind? . . . Do you know what's waiting for us up there? You've just been invited to spend the evening in a two bedroom hot-house with the Coo Coo Pigeon Sisters! What do you mean you're not going?

FELIX. I don't know how to talk to them. I don't know what to say. I already told them about my brother in Buffalo. I've used up my conversation.

OSCAR. Felix, they're crazy about you. They told me! One of them wants to wrap you up and make a bundle out of you. You're doing better than *I* am! Get the ice bucket. (*Starts for door.*)

FELIX. Don't you understand? I cried! I cried in front of two women.

OSCAR. (*Stops.*) And they *loved* it! I'm thinking of getting hysterical. (*Goes to door.*) Will you get the ice bucket?

FELIX. But why did I cry? Because I felt guilty. Emotionally I'm still tied to Frances and the kids.

OSCAR. Well, untie the knot just for tonight, will you!

FELIX. I don't want to discuss it any more. (*Starts for kitchen.*) I'm going to scrub the pots and wash my hair. (*Goes into kitchen and puts pan in sink.*)

OSCAR. (*Yelling.*) Your greasy pots and your greasy hair can wait. You're coming upstairs with me!

FELIX. (*In kitchen.*) I'm not! *I'm not!*

OSCAR. What am I going to do with two girls? Felix, don't do this to me. I'll never forgive you!

FELIX. I'm not going!

OSCAR. (*Screams.*) All right, damn you, I'll go without you! (*And he storms out the door and* *slams it. Then opens and he comes in again.*) Are you coming?

FELIX. (*Comes out of kitchen looking at magazine.*) No.

OSCAR. You mean you're not going to make any effort to change. . . . This is the person you're going to be . . . until the day you die.

FELIX. (*Sitting on couch.*) We are what we are.

OSCAR. (*Nods, then crosses to a window, pulls back drapes and opens window wide. Starts back to door.*) It's twelve floors, not eleven.

(*He walks out as FELIX stares at the open windows.*)

CURTAIN

ACT III

Time

The next evening about 7:30 PM.

At Rise

The room is once again set up for the poker game, with the dining table pulled Down Right, and the chairs set about it and the love seat moved back beneath the windows in the alcove. FELIX appears from the bedroom with a vacuum cleaner. He is doing a thorough job on the rug. As he vacuums around the table, the door opens and, OSCAR comes in wearing a summer hat and carrying a newspaper. He glares at FELIX, still arguing, and shakes his head contemptuously, as he crosses behind FELIX, leaving his hat on the side table next to the armchair, and goes into his bedroom. FELIX is not aware of his presence. Then suddenly the power stops on the vacuum as OSCAR has obviously pulled the plug in the bedroom. FELIX tries switching the ON button a few times, then turns to go back into bedroom. He stops and realizes what's happened as OSCAR comes back into the room. OSCAR takes a cigar out of his pocket and as he crosses in front of FELIX to the couch, lie unwraps it and drops the wrappings carelessly on the floor. He then steps up on the couch and walks back and forth mashing down the pillows. Stepping down, he plants one foot on the armchair and then sits on the couch, taking a wooden match from the coffee table, striking it on the table, and lighting his cigar, he flips the match onto the rug and settles back to read his newspaper. FELIX has watched this all in silence, and now carefully picks up the cigar wrappings and the match and drops them into OSCAR'S hat. He then dusts his hands and takes the vacuum cleaner into the kitchen, pulling the cord in after him. OSCAR takes the wrappings from the hat and puts them in the butt-filled ashtray on the coffee table. Then takes the ashtray and dumps it on the floor. As he once more settles dawn with his newspaper, FELIX comes out of the kitchen carrying a tray with steaming dish of spaghetti. As he crosses behind OSCAR to the table, he smells it "deliciously" and passes it close to OSCAR. to make sure OSCAR smells the fantastic dish he's missing. As FELIX sits and begins to eat, OSCAR takes can of aerosol spray from the bar, and circling the table sprays all about FELIX, puts can down next to him and goes back to his newspaper.

FELIX. (*Pushing spaghetti away.*) All right, how much longer is this gonna go on?

OSCAR. (*Reading his paper.*) Are you talking to me?

FELIX. That's right, I'm talking to you.

OSCAR. What do you want to know?

FELIX. I want to know if you're going to spend the rest of your life not talking to me. Because if you are, I'm going to buy a radio. (*No reply.*) Well (*No reply.*) I see. You're not going to talk to me. (*No reply.*) All right. Two can play at this game. (*Pause.*) If you're not going to talk to me, I'm not going to talk to you. (*No reply.*) I can act childish too, you know. (*No reply.*) I can go on without talking just as long as you can.

OSCAR. Then why the hell don't you shut up?

FELIX. Are you talking to me?

OSCAR. You had your chance to talk last night. I begged you to come upstairs with me. From now on I never want to hear a word from that shampooed head as long as you live. That's a warning, Felix.

FELIX. (*Stares at him.*) I stand warned. . . . Over and out!

OSCAR. (*Gets up taking key out of his pocket and slams it on the table.*) There's a key to the back door. If you stick to the hallway and your room, you won't get hurt. (*Sits back down on couch.*)

FELIX. I don't think I gather the entire meaning of that remark.

OSCAR. Then I'll explain it to you. Stay out of my way.

FELIX. (*Picks up key and moves to couch.*) I think you're serious. I think you're really serious. . . . Are you serious?

OSCAR. This is my apartment. Everything in my apartment is mine. The only thing here that's yours is you. Just stay in your room and speak softly.

FELIX. Yeah, you're serious. . . . Well, let me remind you that I pay half the rent and I'll go into any room I want. (*He gets up angrily and starts towards hallway.*)

OSCAR. Where are you going?

FELIX. I'm going to walk around your bedroom.

OSCAR. (*Slams down newspaper.*) You stay out of there.

FELIX. (*Steaming.*) Don't tell me where to go. I pay a hundred and twenty dollars a month.

OSCAR. That was off-season. Starting tomorrow the rates are twelve dollars a day.

FELIX. All right. (*He takes some bills out of his pocket and slams them down on table.*) There you are. I'm paid up for today. Now I'm going to walk in your bedroom. (*He starts to storm off.*)

OSCAR. Stay out of there! Stay out of my room!

(*He chases after him.* FELIX *dodges around the table as* OSCAR *blocks the hallway.*)

FELIX. (*Backing away, keeping table between them.*) Watch yourself! Just watch yourself, Oscar!

OSCAR. (*With a pointing finger.*) I'm warning you. You want to live here, I don't want to see you, I don't want to hear you and I don't want to smell your cooking. Now get this spaghetti off my poker table.

FELIX. Ha! Haha.

OSCAR. What the hell's so funny?

FELIX. It's not spaghetti. It's linguini!

(OSCAR *picks up the plate of linguini, crosses to the doorway, and hurls it into the kitchen.*)

OSCAR. Now it's garbage! (*Paces above couch.*)

FELIX. (*Looks at* OSCAR *unbelievingly. What an insane thing to do.*) You are crazy! . . . I'm a neurotic nut but you are crazy!

OSCAR. I'm crazy, heh? That's really funny coming from a fruitcake like you.

FELIX. (*Goes to kitchen door and looks in at the mess. Turns back to* OSCAR.) I'm not cleaning that up.

OSCAR. Is that a promise?

FELIX. Did you hear what I said? I'm not cleaning it up. It's your mess. (*Looking into kitchen again.*) Look at it. Hanging all over the walls.

OSCAR. (*Crosses up on landing and looks at kitchen door.*) I like it. (*Closes door and paces Right.*)

FELIX. (*Fumes.*) You'd just let it lie there, wouldn't you? Until it turns hard and brown and . . . yich. . . . It's disgusting. . . . I'm cleaning it up.

(*He goes into kitchen.* OSCAR *chases after him. There is the sound of a STRUGGLE and falling POTS.*)

OSCAR. (*Off.*) Leave it alone! . . . You touch one strand of that linguini—and I'm gonna punch you right in your sinuses.

FELIX. (*Dashes out of kitchen with* OSCAR *in pursuit. Stops and tries to calm* OSCAR *down.*) Oscar . . . I'd like you to take a couple of phenobarbital.

OSCAR. (*Points.*) Go to your room! . . . Did you hear what I said? Go to your room!

FELIX. All right . . . let's everybody just settle down, heh? (*He puts his hand on* OSCAR'S *shoulder to calm him but* OSCAR *pulls away violently from his "touch."*)

OSCAR. If you want to live through this night, you'd better tie me up and lock your doors and windows.

FELIX. (*Sits at table with great pretense of calm.*) All right, Oscar, I'd like to know what's happened.

OSCAR. (*Moves towards him.*) What's happened?

FELIX. (*Hurriedly slides over to the next chair.*) That's right. Something must have caused you to go off the deep end like this. What is it? Something I said? Something I did? Heh? What?

OSCAR. (*Pacing.*) It's nothing you said. It's nothing you did. It's you!

FELIX. I see. . . . Well that's plain enough.

OSCAR. I could make it plainer but I don't want to hurt you.

FELIX. What is it, the cooking? The cleaning? The crying?

OSCAR. (*Moving towards him.*) I'll tell you exactly what it is. It's the cooking, cleaning and crying. . . . It's the talking in your sleep, it's the moose calls that open your ears at two o'clock in the morning. . . . I can't take it any more, Felix. I'm crackin' up. Everything you do irritates me. And when you're not here, the things I know you're gonna do when you come in irritate me. . . . You leave me little notes on my pillow. I told you a hundred times, I can't stand little notes on my pillow. "We're all out of Corn Flakes. F.U." . . . took me three hours to figure out that F.U. was Felix Ungar. . . . It's not your fault, Felix. It's a rotten combination.

FELIX. I get the picture.

OSCAR. That's just the frame. The picture I haven't even painted yet. . . . I got a typewritten list in my office of the "Ten Most Aggravating Things You Do That Drive Me Berserk." . . . But last night was the topper. Oh, that was the topper. Oh, that was the ever loving lulu of all times.

FELIX. What are you talking about, the London broil?

OSCAR. No, not the London broil. I'm talking about those two lamb chops (*He points upstairs.*) I had it all set up with that English Betty Boop and her sister and I wind up drinking tea all night and telling them your life story.

FELIX. (*Jumps up.*) Oho! So that's what's bothering you. That I loused up your evening!

OSCAR. After the mood you put them in, I'm surprised they didn't go out to Rockaway and swim back to England.

FELIX. Don't blame me. I warned you not to make the date in the first place. (*He makes his point by shaking his finger in OSCAR'S face.*)

OSCAR. Don't point that finger at me unless you intend to use it!

FELIX. (*Moves in nose to nose with OSCAR.*) All right, OSCAR, get off my back. Get off! Off! (*Startled by his own actions, FELIX jumps back from OSCAR, warily circles him, crosses to the couch and sits.*)

OSCAR. What's this? A display of temper? I haven't seen you really angry since the day I dropped my cigar in your pancake batter. (*Starts towards the hallway.*)

FELIX. (*Threateningly.*) Oscar. . . . You're asking to hear something I don't want to say. But if I say it, I think you'd better hear it.

OSCAR. (*Comes back to table, places both hands on it, leans towards FELIX.*) If you've got anything on your chest besides your chin, you'd better get it off.

FELIX. (*Strides to table, places both hands on it, leans towards OSCAR. They are nose to nose.*) All right, I warned you. . . . You're a wonderful guy, OSCAR. You've done everything for me. If it weren't for you, I don't know what would have happened to me. You took me in here, gave me a place to live and something to live for. I'll never forget you for that. You're tops with me, Oscar.

OSCAR. (*Motionless.*) If I've just been told off, I think I may have missed it.

FELIX. It's coming now! . . . You're also one of the biggest slobs in the world.

OSCAR. I see.

FELIX. And completely unreliable.

OSCAR. Finished?

FELIX. Undependable.

OSCAR. Is that it?

FELIX. And irresponsible.

OSCAR. Keep going. I think you're hot.

FELIX. That's it. I'm finished. Now you've been told off. How do you like that? (*Crosses to couch.*)

OSCAR. (*Straightening up.*) Good. Because now I'm going to tell you off. . . . For six months I lived alone in this apartment. All alone in eight rooms. . . . I was dejected, despondent and disgusted. . . . Then you moved in. My dlearest and closest friend. . . . And after three weeks of close, personal contact—I am about to have a nervous breakdown! Do me a favor. Move into the kitchen. Live with your pots, your pans, your ladle and your meat thermometer. . . . When you want to come out, ring a bell and I'll run into the bedroom. (*Almost breaking down.*) I'm asking you nicely, Felix. . . . As a friend. . . . Stay out of my way! (*And he goes into the bedroom.*)

FELIX. (*Hurt by this; then remembering something. Calls after him.*) Walk on the paper, will you? The floors are wet. (OSCAR *comes out of the door. He is glaring maniacally, as he slowly strides back down the hallway.* FELIX *quickly puts the couch between him and* OSCAR.) Awright, keep away. Keep away from me.

OSCAR. (*Chasing him around the couch.*) Come on. Let me get in one shot. You pick it. Head, stomach, or kidneys.

FELIX. (*Dodging about the room.*) You're gonna find yourself in one sweet law suit, Oscar.

OSCAR. It's no use running, Felix. There's only eight rooms and I know the short cuts.

(*They are now poised at opposite ends of the couch.* FELIX *picks up a lamp for protection.*)

FELIX. Is this how you settle your problems, Oscar? Like an animal?

OSCAR. All right. You wanna see how I settle my problems. I'll show you. (*Storms off into* FELIX'S *bedroom. There is the sound of falling objects and he returns with a suitcase.*) I'll show you how I settle them. (*Throws suitcase on table.*) There! That's how I settle them!

FELIX. (*Bewildered, looks at suitcase.*) Where are you going?

OSCAR. (*Exploding.*) Not me, you idiot! You. You're the one who's going. I want you out of here. Now! Tonight! (*Opens suitcase.*)

FELIX. What are you talking about?

OSCAR. It's all over, Felix. The whole marriage. We're getting an annulment! Don't you understand? I don't want to live with you any more. I want you to pack your things, tie it up with your Saran Wrap and get out of here.

FELIX. You mean actually move out . . . ?

OSCAR. Actually, physically and immediately. I don't care where you go. Move into the Museum of Natural History. (*Goes into kitchen. There is the crash of falling* POTS *and* PANS.) I'm sure you'll be very comfortable there. You can dust around the Egyptian mummies to your heart's content. But I'm a human living person. (*Comes out with stack of cooking utensils which he throws into the open suitcase.*) All I want is my freedom. Is that too much to ask for? (*Closes it.*) There. . . . You're all packed.

FELIX. You know, I've got a good mind to really leave.

OSCAR. (*Looking to the heavens.*) Why doesn't he ever listen to what I say? Why doesn't he hear me? I know I'm talking. . . . I recognize my voice.

FELIX. (*Indignantly.*) Because if you really want me to go, I'll go.

OSCAR. Then go. I want you to go, so go. When are you going?

FELIX. When am I going, huh? Boy, you're in a bigger hurry than Frances was. . . .

OSCAR. Take as much time as she gave you. I want you to follow your usual routine.

FELIX. In other words you're throwing me out.

OSCAR. Not in other words. Those are the perfect ones. (*Picks up suitcase and holds it out to* FELIX.) I am throwing you out.

FELIX. All right. . . . I just wanted to get the record straight. Let it be on your conscience. (*Goes into his bedroom.*)

OSCAR. What . . . ? What . . . ? (*Follows him to bedroom doorway.*) Let what be on my conscience?

FELIX. (*Comes out pulling on jacket, goes by Oscar.*) That you're throwing me out. (*Stops and turns back to him.*) I'm perfectly willing to stay and clear the air of our differences. . . . But you refuse, right?

OSCAR. (*Still holding suitcase.*) Right. . . . I'm sick and tired of you clearing the air. That's why I want you to leave!

FELIX. Okay. . . . As long as I heard you say the words, "Get out of the house," . . . Fine. . . . But remember, what happens to me is your responsibility. Let it be on your head. (*Crosses to the door.*)

OSCAR. (*Follows him to door; screams.*) Wait a minute, damn it. Why can't you be thrown out like a decent human being? Why do you have to say things like, "Let it be on your head"? I don't want it on my head. I just want you out of the house.

FELIX. What's the matter, Oscar? Can't cope with a little guilt feelings—?

OSCAR. (*Pounding railing in frustration.*) Damn you. I've been looking forward to throwing you out all day long and now you even take the pleasure out of that.

FELIX. Forgive me for spoiling your fun, I'm leaving now . . . according to your wishes and desires. (*Starts to open the door.*)

OSCAR. (*Pushes by* FELIX *and slams the door shut. Stands between* FELIX *and the door.*) You're not leaving here until you take it back.

FELIX. Take what back?

OSCAR. "Let it be on your head." . . . What the hell is that, the Curse of the Cat People?

FELIX. Get out of my way, please.

OSCAR. Is this how you left that night with Frances? No wonder she wanted to have the room repainted right away. (*Points to* FELIX'S *bedroom.*) I'm gonna have yours dipped in bronze.

FELIX. (*Sits on back of couch with his back to* OSCAR.) How can I leave if you're blocking the door?

OSCAR. (*Very calmly.*) Felix, we've been friends a long time. For the sake of that friendship, please say, "Oscar, we can't stand each other, let's break up."

FELIX. I'll let you know what to do about my clothes. . . . Either I'll call . . . or someone else will. (*Controlling great emotion.*) I'd like to leave now.

(OSCAR, *resigned, moves out of the way.* FELIX *opens the door.*)

OSCAR. Where will you go?

FELIX. (*Turns in doorway and looks at him.*) Where? . . . (*He smiles.*) Oh, come on, Oscar. You're not really interested, are you? (*He exits.*)

(OSCAR *looks as though he's about to burst with frustration. He calls after* FELIX.)

OSCAR. All right, Felix, you win. (*Goes out into hall.*) We'll try to iron it out. Anything you want. Come back, Felix. . . . Felix ? Felix? Don't leave me like this.—You louse! (*But* FELIX *is gone.* OSCAR *comes back into the room closing the door. He is limp. He searches for something to ease his enormous frustration. He throws a pillow at the door, and then paces about like a caged lion.*) All right, Oscar, get a hold of yourself! . . . He's gone! Keep saying that over and over. . . . He's gone. He's really gone! (*He holds his head in pain.*) He did it. He put a curse on me. It's on my head. I don't know what it is, but something's on my head. (*The* DOORBELL *rings and he looks up hopefully.*) Please let it be him. Let it be Felix. Please give me one more chance to kill him.

(*Putting the suitcase on the sofa, he rushes to the door and opens it.* MURRAY *comes in with* VINNIE.)

MURRAY. (*Putting jacket on chair at table.*) Hey, what's the matter with Felix? He walked right by me with that "human sacrifice" look on his face again. (*Takes off shoes.*).

VINNIE. (*Laying jacket on love seat.*) What's with him? I asked him where he's going and he said, "Only Oscar knows. Only Oscar knows." Where's he going, Oscar?

OSCAR. (*Sitting at table.*) How the hell should I know? All right, let's get the game started, heh? Come on, get your chips.

MURRAY. I have to get something to eat. I'm starving. Mmm, I think I smell spaghetti. (*Goes into kitchen.*)

VINNIE. Isn't he playing tonight? (*Takes two chairs from dining alcove and puts them Downstage of table.*)

OSCAR. I don't want to discuss it. I don't even want to hear his name.

VINNIE? Who? Felix?

OSCAR. I told you not to mention his name.

VINNIE. I didn't know what name you meant. (*Clears table and places what's left from* FELIX'S *dinner on bookcase.*)

MURRAY. (*Comes out of the kitcken.*) Hey, did you know there's spaghetti all over the kitchen?

OSCAR. Yes, I know and it's not spaghetti, it's linguini.

MURRAY. Oh. I thought it was spaghetti. (*He goes back into the kitchen.*)

VINNIE. (*Taking poker stuff from bookcase and putting it on table.*) Why shouldn't I mention his name?

OSCAR. Who?

VINNIE. Felix. What's happened? Has something happened?

(SPEED *and* ROY *come in the open door.*)

SPEED. Yeah, what's the matter with Felix?

(SPEED *puts his jacket over a chair at the table.* ROY *sits in armchair.*) MURRAY *comes out of the kitchen with a six-pack of beer and bags of pretzels and chips. They all stare at* Oscar *waiting for an answer. There is a long pause and then he stands up.*)

OSCAR. We broke up! I kicked him out. It was my decision. I threw him out of the house. All right? . . . I admit it. Let it be on my head.

VINNIE. Let what be on your head?

OSCAR. How should I know? Felix put it there! Ask him! (*Paces Right.*)

Murray. He'll go to pieces. I know Felix. He's gonna try something crazy.

OSCAR. (*Turns to BOYS.*) Why do you think I did it? (MURRAY *makes a gesture of disbelief and moves to couch, putting down beer and bags.* OSCAR *moves to him.*) You think I'm just selfish? That I wanted to be cruel? I did it for you. . . . I did it for all of us.

ROY. What are you talking about?

OSCAR. (*Crosses to* ROY.) All right, we've all been through the napkins and the ashtrays and the bacon, lettuce and tomato sandwiches. . . . But that was just the beginning. Just the beginning. Do you know what he was planning for next Friday night's poker game? As a change of pace. Do you have any idea?

VINNIE. What?

OSCAR. A Luau! An Hawaiaan Luau! Spareribs, roast pork and fried rice. . . . They don't play poker like that in Honolulu.

MURRAY. One thing has nothing to do with the other. We all know he's impossible but he's still our friend and he's still out on the street, and I'm still worried about him.

OSCAR. (*Going to* MURRAY.) And I'm not, heh? I'm not concerned? I'm not worried? Who do you think sent him out there in the first place?

MURRAY. Frances!

OSCAR. What?

MURRAY. Frances sent him out in the first place. *You* sent him out in the second place. And whoever he lives with next will send him out in the third place. . . . Don't you understand? It's Felix. He does it to himself.

OSCAR. Why?

MURRAY. I don't know why. *He* doesn't know why. There are people like that. There's a whole tribe in Africa who hit themselves on the head all day long. (*He sums it all up with an eloquent gesture of resignation.*)

OSCAR. (*A slow realization of a whole new reason to be angry.*) I'm not going to worry about him. Why should I? He's not worrying about me. He's somewhere out on the streets sulking and crying and having a wonderful time. . . . If he had a spark of human decency he would leave us all alone and go back to Blanche. (*Sits down at table.*)

VINNIE. Why should he?

OSCAR. (*Picks up deck of cards.*) Because it's his wife.

VINNIE. No, Blanche is your wife. His wife is Frances.

OSCAR. (*Stares at him.*) What are you, some kind of wise guy?

VINNIE. What did I say?

OSCAR. (*Throws cards in air.*) All right, the poker game is over. I don't want to play any more. (*Paces Right.*)

SPEED. Who's playing? We didn't even start.

OSCAR. (*Turns on him.*) Is that all you can do is complain? Have you given one single thought to where Felix might be?

SPEED. I thought you said you're not worried about him?

OSCAR. (*Screams.*) I'm not worried, darnmit! I'm not worried. (*The DOORBELL rings. A gleeful* *look passes over* OSCAR'S *face.*) It's him. I bet it's him! (*The* BOYS *start to go for the door.* OSCAR *stops them.*) Don't let him in, he's not welcome in this house.

MURRAY. (*Moves towards door.*) Oscar, don't be childish. We've got to let him in.

OSCAR. (*Stopping him and leading him to the table.*) I won't give him the satisfaction of knowing we've been worrying about him. Sit down. Play cards. Like nothing happened.

Murray. But, Oscar—

OSCAR. Sit down. Everybody. . . . Come on. . . . Sit down and play poker.

(*They sit and* SPEED *begins to deal out cards.*)

VINNIE. (*Crossing to door.*) Oscar . . . .

OSCAR. All right, Vinnie, open the door.

(VINNIE *opens door. It is* GWENDOLYN *standing there.*)

VINNIE. (*surprised.*) Oh, hello. (*To* OSCAR.) It's not him, Oscar.

GWENDOLYN. How do you do? (*She walks into the room.*)

OSCAR. (*Crosses to her.*) Oh, hello, Cecily. Boys, I'd like you to meet Cecily Pigeon.

GWENDOLYN. Gwendolyn Pigeon. Please don't get up. (*To* OSCAR.) May I see you for a moment, Mr. Madison?

OSCAR. Certainly, Gwen. What's the matter?

GWENDOLYN. I think you know. . . . I've come for Felix's things.

(OSCAR *looks at her in shock and disbelief. He looks at the* BOYS, *then back at* GWENDOLYN.)

OSCAR. Felix. . . . My Felix?

GWENDOLYN. Yes. Felix Ungar. That sweet, tortured man who's in my flat at this moment pouring his heart out to my sister.

OSCAR. (*Turns to* BOYS.) You hear? I'm worried to death and he's up there getting tea and sympathy.

(CECILY *rushes in dragging a reluctant* FELIX *with her.*)

CECILY. Gwen, Felix doesn't want to stay. Please tell him to stay.

FELIX. Really, girls, this is very embarrassing. I can go to a hotel. . . . (*To* BOYS.) Hello, fellas.

GWENDOLYN. (*Overriding his objections.*) Nonsense. I told you, we've plenty of room, and it's a very comfortable sofa. Isn't it, Cecy?

CECILY. (*Joining in.*) Enormous. And we've rented an air-conditioner.

GWENDOLYN. And we just don't like the idea of you wandering the streets looking for a place to live.

FELIX. But I'd be in the way. Wouldn't I be in the way?

GWENDOLYN. How could you possibly be in anyone's way?

OSCAR. You want to see a typewritten list ?

GWENDOLYN. (*Turning on him.*) Haven't you said enough already, Mr. Madison? (*To* FELIX.) I won't take no for an answer. Just for a few days, Felix.

CECILY. Until you get settled.

GWENDOLYN. Please. Please say "Yes," Felix.

CECILY. Oh, please . . . we'd be so happy.

FELIX. (*Considers.*) Well . . . maybe just for a few days.

GWENDOLYN. (*Jumping with joy.*) Oh, wonderful.

CECILY. (*Ecstatic.*) Marvelous!

GWENDOLYN. (*Crosses to door.*) You get your things and come right up.

CECILY. And come hungry. We're making dinner.

GWENDOLYN. (*To* BOYS.) Good night, gentlemen, sorry to interrupt your bridge game.

CECILY. (*To* FELIX.) If you'd like, you can invite your friends to play in our flat.

GWENDOLYN. (To FELIX.) Don't be late. Cocktails in fifteen minutes.

FELIX. I won't.

GWENDOLYN. Ta ta.

CECILY. Ta ta.

FELIX. Ta ta.

(*The* GIRLS *leave.* FELIX *turns and looks at the* FELLOWS *and smiles as he crosses the room into the bedroom. The five* MEN *stare dumbfounded at the door without moving. Finally* MURRAY *crosses to the door.*)

SPEED. (*To the* OTHERS.) I told you. It's always the quiet guys.

MURRAY. Gee, what nice girls. (*Closes door.*)

(FELIX *comes out of the bedroom carrying two suits in a plastic cleaner's bag.*)

ROY. Hey, Felix, are you really gonna move in with them?

FELIX. (*Turns back to them.*) Just for a few days. Until I find my own place. . . . Well, so long, fellows. You can drop your crumbs on the rug again. (*Starts towards door.*)

OSCAR. Hey, Felix. Aren't you going to thank me?

FELIX. (*Stopping on landing.*) For what?

OSCAR. For the two greatest things I ever did for you. Taking you in and throwing you out.

FELIX. (*Lays suits over railing and goes to* OSCAR.) You're right, Oscar. Thanks a lot. Getting kicked out twice is enough for any man. . . . In gratitude, I remove the curse.

OSCAR. (*Smiles.*) Oh, bless you and thank you. Wicked Witch of the North.

(*They shake hands. The PHONE rings.*)

FELIX. Ah, that must be the girls.

MURRAY. (*Picking up phone.*) Hello. . . .

FELIX. They hate it so when I'm late for cocktails. (*Turning to BOYS.*) Well, so long.

MURRAY. It's your wife.

FELIX. (*Turning to* MURRAY.) Oh? Well, do me a favor, Murray. Tell her I can't speak to her now. But tell her I'll be calling her in a few days because she and I have a lot to talk about. And tell her if I sound different to her, it's because I'm not the same man she kicked out three weeks ago. Tell her, Murray, tell her.

MURRAY. I will when I see her. This is Oscar's wife.

FELIX. Oh!

MURRAY. (*Into phone.*) Just a minute, Blanche.

(OSCAR *crosses to phone, sits on arm of the couch.*)

FELIX. Well, so long, fellows. (*Shakes hands with the* BOYS, *takes suits and moves to door.*)

OSCAR. (*Into phone.*) Hello? . . . Yeah, Blanche. I got a pretty good idea why you're calling. You got my checks, right? . . . . Good. (FELIX *stops at the* door, *caught by* OSCAR'S *conversation. He slowly comes back into the room to listen, putting suits on railing, and sitting down on the arm of the armchair.*) So now I'm all paid up. . . . No, no, I didn't win at the track. I've just been able to save a little money. . . . I've been eating home a lot. (*Takes a pillow from couch and throws it at* FELIX.) Listen, Blanche, you don't have to thank me. I'm just doing what's right. . . . Well, that's nice of you, too. . . . The apartment? No, I think you'd be shocked. . . . It's in surprisingly good shape. . . . (FELIX *throws pillow back at* OSCAR.) Say, Blanche, did Brucey get the goldfish I sent him? . . . Yeah, well, I'll speak to you again soon, huh? . . . Whenever you want. I don't go out much any more. . . .

FELIX. (*Gets up, takes suits from railing and goes to door.*) Well, good night, Mr. Madison. If you need me again, I get a dollar-fifty an hour.

OSCAR. (*Makes gesture to stop* FELIX *as he talks on phone.*) Well, kiss the kids for me. Good night, Blanche. (*Hangs up and turns to* FELIX.) Felix?

FELIX. (*At opened door.*) Yeah?

OSCAR. How about next Friday night? You're not going to break up the game, are you?

FELIX. Me? Never! Marriages may come and go, but the game must go on. So long, Frances. (*He exits, closing door.*)

OSCAR. (*Yelling after him.*) So long, Blanche. (*The* BOYS *all look at* OSCAR *a moment.*) All right, are we just gonna sit around or are we gonna play poker?

ROY. We're gonna play poker.

(*There is a general hubbub as they pass out the beer, deal the cards, etc.*)

OSCAR. (*Standing up.*) Then let's play poker. (*Sharply to the* BOYS.) And watch your cigarettes, will you? This is my house, not a pig sty.

(*Takes the ashtray from the side table next to armchair, bends down and begins to pick up the butts. The BOYS settle down to play poker.*)

CURTAIN

10

Topdog/Underdog

Play by Suzan-Lori Parks (1963–)

THE PLAYERS

LINCOLN, *the topdog*
BOOTH (*aka 3-Card*), *the underdog*

A SPELL

An elongated and heightened (Rest). Denoted by repetition of figures' names with no dialogue. Has sort of an architectural look:

LINCOLN
BOOTH
LINCOLN
BOOTH

This is a place where the figures experience their pure true simple state. While no action or stage business is necessary, directors should fill this moment as they best see fit. [Brackets in the text indicate optional cuts for production.] (Parentheses around dialogue indicate softly spoken passages (asides; sotto voce)).

TOPDOG/UNDERDOG

Scene One

Thursday evening. A seedily furnished rooming house room. A bed, a reclining chair, a small wooden chair. Some other stuff but not much else. BOOTH, a black man in his early 30s, practices his 3-card monte scam on the classic setup: 3 playing cards and the cardboard playing board atop 2 mismatched milk crates. His moves and accompanying patter are, for the most part, studied and awkward.

BOOTH. Watch me close watch me close now: who-see-thuh-red-card-who-see-thuh-red-card? I-see-thuh-red-card. Thuh-red-card-is-thuh-winner. Pick-thuh-red-card-you-pick-uh-winner. Pick-uh-black-card-you-pick-uh-loser. Theres-thuh-loser, yeah, theres-thuh-black-card, theres-thuh-other-loser-and-theres-thuh-red-card, thuh-winner.

(Rest.)

Watch me close watch me close now: 3-Card-throws-thuh-cards-lightning-fast. 3-Card-that's-me-and-Ima-last. Watch-me-throw-cause-here-I-go. One-good-pickll-get-you-in, 2-good-picks-and-you-gone-win. See-thuh-red-ard-see-thuh-red-card-who-see-thuh-red-card?

(Rest.)

Dont touch my cards, man, just point to thuh one you want. You-pick-that-card-you-pick-a-loser, yeah, that-cards-a-loser. You-pick-that-card-that's-thuh-other-loser. You-pick-that-card-you-pick-a-winner. Follow that card. You gotta chase that card. You-pick-thuh-dark-deuce-thats-a-loser-other-dark-deuces-thuh-other-loser, red-deuce. thuh-deuce-of-heartsll-win-it-all. Follow thuh red card.

(Rest.)

Ima show you thuh cards: 2 black cards but only one heart. Now watch me now. Who-sees-thuh-red-card-who-knows-where-its-at? Go on, man, point to thuh card. Put yr money down cause you aint no clown. No? Ah you had thuh card, but you didnt have thuh heart.

(Rest.)

You wanna bet? 500 dollars? Shoot. You musta been watching 3-Card real close. Ok. Lay the cash in my hand cause 3-Cards thuh man. Thank you, mister. This card you say?

(Rest.)

Wrong! Sucker! Fool! Asshole! Bastard! I bet yr daddy heard how stupid you was and drank himself to death just cause he didn't wanna have nothing to do witchu! I bet yr mama seen you when you comed out and she walked away from you with thuh afterbirth still hanging from out twixt her legs. sucker! Ha Ha Ha! And 3-Card, once again. wins all thuh money!!

(Rest.)

What? Cops looking my way? Fold up thuh game, and walk away. Sneak outa sight. Set up on another corner.

(Rest.)

Yeah.

(Rest.)

Having won the imaginary loot and dodged the imaginary cops. BOOTH *sets up his equipment and starts practicing his scam all over again.* LINCOLN *comes in quietly. He is a black man in his later 30s. He is dressed in an antique frock coat and wears a top hat and fake beard, that is, he is dressed to look like Abraham* LINCOLN. *He surreptitiously walks into the room to stand right behind* BOOTH, *who engrossed in his cards, does not notice* LINCOLN *right away.*

BOOTH. Watch me close watch me close now: who-see-thuh-red-card-who-see-thuh-red-card? I-see-thuh-red-card. Thuh-red-card-is-thuh-winner. Pick-thuh-red-card-you-pick-uh-winner. Pick-uh-black-card-you-pick-uh-loser. Theres-thuh-loser-yeah-theres-thuh-black-card, theres-thuh-other-loser-and-theres-thuh-red-card, thuh-winner. Don't touch my cards, man, don't—

(Rest.)

Dont do that shit. Don't do that shit. Don't do that shit!

BOOTH, *sensing someone behind him, whirls around, pulling a gun from his pants. While the presence of* LINCOLN *doesn't surprise him, the* LINCOLN *costume does.*

BOOTH. And woah. man dont *ever* be doing that shit! Who thuh fuck you think you is coming in my shit all spooked out and shit. You pull that one more time I'll shoot you!

LINCOLN. I only had a minute to make the bus.

BOOTH. Bullshit.

LINCOLN. Not completely. I mean, its either bull or shit, but not a complete lie so it aint bullshit, right?

(*Rest.*)

Put yr gun away.

BOOTH. Take off the damn hat at least.

LINCOLN *takes off the stovepipe hat.* BOOTH *puts his gun away.*

LINCOLN. Its cold out there. This thing kept my head warm.

LINCOLN. Better?

BOOTH. Take off the damn coat too. Damn, man. Bad enough you got to wear that shit all day you come up in here wearing it. What my women gonna say?

LINCOLN. What women?

BOOTH. I got a date with Grace tomorrow. Shes in love with me again but she dont now it yet. Aint no man can love her the way I can. She sees you in that getup its gonna reflect bad on me. She coulda seen you coming down the street. Shit. Could be standing outside right now taking her ring off and throwing it on the sidewalk.

BOOTH *takes a peek out the window.*

BOOTH. I got her this ring today. Diamond. Well, diamondesque, but it looks just as good as the real thing. Asked her what size she wore. She say 7 so I go boost a size 6 and a half, right? Show it to her and she loves it and I shove it on her finger and its a tight fit right, so she cant just take it off on a whim, like she did the last one I gave her. Smooth, right?

BOOTH *takes another peek out the window.*

LINCOLN. She out there?

BOOTH. Nope. Coast is clear.

LINCOLN. You boosted a ring?

BOOTH. Yeah. I thought about spending my inheritance on it but—take off that damn coat, man, you make me nervous standing there looking like a spook, and that damn face paint, take it off. You should take all of it off at work and leave it there.

LINCOLN. I dont bring it home someone might steal it.

BOOTH. At least *take it off* there, then.

LINCOLN. Yeah.

(*Rest.*)

LINCOLN *takes off the frock coat and applies cold cream, removing the whiteface.*

LINCOLN. I was riding the bus. Really I only had a minute to make my bus and I was sitting in the arcade thinking, should I change into my street clothes or should I make the bus? Nobody was in there today anyway. Middle of week middle of winter. Not like on weekends. Weekends the place is packed. So Im riding the bus home. And this kid asked me for my autograph. I pretended I didnt hear him at first. I'd had a long day. But he kept asking. Theyd just done LINCOLN in history class and he knew all about him, he'd been to the arcade but, I dunno, for some reason he was tripping cause there was Honest Abe right beside him on the bus. I wanted to tell him to go fuck hisself. But then I got a look at him. A little rich kid. Born on easy street, you know the type. So I waited until I could tell he really wanted it, the autograph and I told him he could have it for 10 bucks. I was gonna say 5, cause of the LINCOLN connection but something in me made me ask for 10.

BOOTH. But he didnt have a 10. All he had was a penny. So you took the penny.

LINCOLN. All he had was a 20. So I took the 20 and told him to meet me on the bus tomorrow and Honest Abe would give him the change.

BOOTH. Shit.

LINCOLN. Shit is right.

(*Rest.*)

BOOTH. Whatd you do with thuh 20?

LINCOLN. Bought drinks at Luckys. A round for everybody. They got a kick out of the getup.

BOOTH. You shoulda called me down.

LINCOLN. Next time, bro.

(Rest.)

You making bookshelves? With the milk crates, you making bookshelves?

BOOTH. Yeah, a big bro, Im making bookshelves.

LINCOLN. Whats the cardboard part for.

BOOTH. Versatility.

LINCOLN. Oh.

BOOTH. I was thinking we dont got no bookshelves we dont got no dining room table so Im making a sorta modular unit you put the books in the bottom and the table top on top. We can eat and store our books. We could put the photo album in there.

BOOTH *gets the raggedy family photo album and puts it in the milk crate.*

BOOTH. Youd sit there. Id sit on the edge of the bed. Gathered around the dinner table. Like old times.

LINCOLN. We just gotta get some books but thats great, BOOTH, that's real great.

BOOTH. Dont be calling me BOOTH no more, K?

LINCOLN. You changing yr name?

BOOTH. May be.

LINCOLN

BOOTH

LINCOLN. What to?

BOOTH. Im not ready to reveal it yet.

LINCOLN. You already decided on something?

BOOTH. Maybe.

LINCOLN. You gonna call yrself something african? That be cool. Only pick something thats easy to spell and pronounce, man, cause you know, some of them african names. I mean, ok, Im down with the power to the people thing, but, no ones gonna hire you if they cant say yr name. And some of them fellas who got they african names, no one can say they names and they cant say they names neither. I mean, you dont want yr new handle to obstruct yr employment possibilities.

BOOTH

LINCOLN

BOOTH. You bring dinner?

LINCOLN. "Shango" would be a good name. The name of the thunder god. If you aint decided already Im just throwing it in the pot. I brought chinese.

BOOTH. Lets try the table out.

LINCOLN. Cool.

They both sit at the new table. The food is far away near the door.

LINCOLN

BOOTH

LINCOLN. I buy it you set it up. Thats the deal. Thats the deal, right?

BOOTH. You like this place?

LINCOLN. Ssallright.

BOOTH. But a little cramped sometimes, right?

LINCOLN. You dont hear me complain. Although that recliner sometimes BOOTH, man—no BOOTH, right—man, Im too old to be sleeping in that chair.

BOOTH. Its my place. You dont got a place. Cookie, she threw you out. And you cant seem to get another woman. Yr lucky I let you stay.

LINCOLN. Every Friday you say *mi casa es su casa.*

BOOTH. Every Friday you come home with yr paycheck. Today is Thursday and I tell you brother, its a long way from Friday to Friday. All kinds of things can happen. All kinds of bad feelings can surface and erupt while yr little brother waits for you to bring in yr share.

(Rest.)

I got my Thursday head on. Link. Go get the food.

LINCOLN *doesn't budge.*

LINCOLN. You dont got no running water in here, man.

BOOTH. So?

LINCOLN. You dont got no toilet you dont got no sink.

BOOTH. Bathrooms down the hall.

LINCOLN. You living in thuh Third World, fool! Hey, I'll get thuh food.

LINCOLN *goes to get the food. He sees a stray card on the floor and examines it without touching it. He brings the food over, putting it nicely on the table.*

LINCOLN. You been playing cards?

BOOTH. Yeah.

LINCOLN. Solitaire?

BOOTH. Thats right. Im getting pretty good at it.

LINCOLN. Thats soup and thats sauce. I got you the meat and I got me the skrimps.

BOOTH. I wanted the skrimps.

LINCOLN. You said you wanted the meat. This morning when I left you said you wanted the meat.

(Rest.)

Here man, take the skrimps. No sweat. *They eat. Chinese food from syrofoam containers, cans of soda, fortune cookies.* LINCOLN *eats slowly and carefully.* BOOTH *eats ravenously.*

LINCOLN. Yr getting good at solitaire?

BOOTH. Yeah. How about we play a hand after eating.

LINCOLN. Solitaire?

BOOTH. Poker or rummy or something.

LINCOLN. You know I dont touch thuh cards, man.

BOOTH. Just for fun.

LINCOLN. I dont touch thuh cards.

BOOTH. How about for money?

LINCOLN. You dont got to money. All the money you got I bring in here.

BOOTH. I got my inheritance.

LINCOLN. Thats like saying you dont got no money cause you aint never gonna do nothing with it so its like you dont got it.

BOOTH. At least I still got mines. You blew yrs.

LINCOLN

BOOTH

LINCOLN. You like the skrimps?

BOOTH. Ssallright.

LINCOLN. Whats yr fortune?

BOOTH. "Waste not want not." Whats yrs?

LINCOLN. "Your luck will change!"
BOOTH *finishes eating. He turns his back to* LINCOLN *and fiddles around with the cards, keeping them on the bed, just out of* LINCOLNs *sight. He mutters the 3-card patter under his breath. His moves are still clumsy. Every once and a while he darts a look over at* LINCOLN *who does his best to ignore* **BOOTH.**

BOOTH. ((((Watch me close watch me close now: who-see-thuh-red-card-who-see-thuh-red-card? I-see-thuh-red-card. Thuh-red-card-is-thuh-winner. Pick-thuh-red-card-you-pick-uh-winner. Pick-uh-black-card-and-you-pick-uh-loser. Theres-thuh-loser, yeah, theres-thuh-black-card, theres-thuh-other-loser-and-theres-thuh-red-card, thuh-winner! Cop C, Stick. Cop C! Go on—))))

LINCOLN. ((Shit.))

BOOTH. (((((((One-good-pickll-get-you-in, 2-good-picks-and-you-gone-win. Dont touch my cards, man, just point to thuh one you want. You-pick-that-card-you-pick-uh-loser, yeah, that-cards-uh-loser. You-pick-that-card-thats-thuh-other-loser. You-pick-that-card-you-pick-uh-winner. Follow-that-card. You-gotta-chase-that-card!)))))))

LINCOLN. You wanna hustle 3-card monte, you gotta do it right, you gotta break it down. Practice it in smaller bits. Yr trying to do the whole thing at once thats why you keep fucking it up.

BOOTH. Show me.

LINCOLN. No. Im just saying you wanna do it you gotta do it right and if you gonna do it right you gotta work on it in smaller bits, thatsall.

BOOTH. You and me could team up and do it together. We'd clean up, Link.

LINCOLN. I'll clean up—bro.

LINCOLN *cleans up. As he clears the food,* BOOTH *goes back to using the "table" for its original purpose.*

BOOTH. My new names 3-Card. 3-Card, got it? You wanted to know it so now you know it.

3-card monte by 3-Card. Call me 3-Card from here on out.

LINCOLN. 3-Card. Shit.

BOOTH. Im getting everybody to call me 3-Card. Grace likes 3-Card better than BOOTH. She says 3-Cards got something to it. Anybody not calling me 3-Card gets a bullet.

LINCOLN. Yr too much, man.

BOOTH. Im making a point.

LINCOLN. Point made, 3-Card. Point made.

LINCOLN *picks up his guitar. Plays at it.*

BOOTH. Oh, come on, man, we could make money you and me. Throwing down the cards. 3-Card and Link: look out! We could clean up you and me. You would throw the cards and I'd be yr Stickman. The one in the crowd who looks like just an innocent passerby, who looks like just another player, like just another customer, but who gots intimate connections with you, the Dealer, the one throwing the cards, the main man. I'd be the one who brings in the crowd, I'd be the one who makes them want to put they money down, you do yr moves and I do mines. You turn yr head and I turn the card—

LINCOLN. It aint as easy as all that. Theres—

BOOTH. We could be a team, man. Rake in the money! Sure thered be some cats out there with fast eyes, some brothers and sisters who would watch real close and pick the right card, and so thered be some days when we could lose money, but most of the days we would come out on top! Pockets bulging, plenty of cash! And the ladies would be thrilling! You could afford to get laid! Grace would be all over me again.

LINCOLN. I thought you said she was all over you.

BOOTH. She is she is. Im seeing her tomorrow but today we gotta solidify the shit twixt you and me. Big Brother Link and little brother BOOTH—

LINCOLN. 3-Card.

BOOTH. Yeah. Scheming and dreaming. No one throws the cards like you, Link. And with yr moves and my magic, and we get Grace and a girl for you to round out the posse. We'd be golden, bro! Am I right?

LINCOLN

LINCOLN

BOOTH. Am I right?

BOOTH. I dont touch thuh cards. 3-Card. I dont touch thuh cards no more.

LINCOLN

BOOTH

LINCOLN

BOOTH

BOOTH. You know what Mom told me when she was packing to leave? You was at school motherfucker you was at school. You got up that morning and sat down in yr regular place and read the cereal box while Dad read the sports section and Mom brought you yr dick toast and then you got on the damn school bus cause you didnt have the sense to do nothing else you was so into yr own shit that you didnt have the sense to feel nothing else going on. I had the sense to go back cause I was feeling something going on man, I was feeling something changing. So I—

LINCOLN. Cut school that day like you did almost every day—

BOOTH. She was putting her stuff in bags. She had all them nice suitcases but she was putting her stuff in bags.

(*Rest.*)

Packing up her shit. She told me to look out for you. I told her I was the little brother and the big brother should look out after the little brother. She just said it again. That I should look out for you. Yeah. So who gonna look out for me. Not like you care. Here I am interested in an economic opportunity, willing to work hard, willing to take risks and all you can say you shiteating motherfucking pathetic limpdick uncle tom, all you can tell me is how you dont do no more what I be wanting to do. Here I am trying to earn a living and you standing in my way. YOU STANDING IN MY WAY, LINK!

LINCOLN. Im sorry.

BOOTH. Yeah, you sorry all right.

LINCOLN. I cant be hustling no more, bro.

BOOTH. What you do all day aint no hustle?

LINCOLN. Its honest work.

BOOTH. Dressing up like some crackerass white man, some dead president and letting people shoot at you sounds like a hustle to me.

LINCOLN. People know the real deal. When people know the real deal it aint a hustle.

BOOTH. We do the card game people will know the real deal. Sometimes we will win sometimes they will win. They fast they win, we faster we win.

LINCOLN. I aint going back to that, bro. I aint going back.

BOOTH. You play Honest Abe. You aint going back but you going all the way back. Back to way back then when folks was slaves and shit.

LINCOLN. Dont push me.

BOOTH

LINCOLN

BOOTH. You gonna have to leave.

LINCOLN. I'll be gone tomorrow.

BOOTH. Good. Cause this was only supposed to be a temporary arrangement.

LINCOLN. I will be gone tomorrow.

BOOTH. Good.

BOOTH *sits on his bed* LINCOLN, *sitting in his easy chair with his guitar, plays and sings.*

LINCOLN. My dear mother left me, my fathers gone away

My dear mother left me and my fathers gone away

I dont got no money, I dont got no place to stay.

My best girl, she threw me out into the street

My favorite horse, they ground him into meat

Im feeling cold from my head down to my feet.

My luck was bad but now it turned to worse

My luck was bad but now it turned to worse

Dont call me up a doctor, just call me up a hearse.

BOOTH. You just made that up?

LINCOLN. I had it in my head a few days.

BOOTH. Sounds good.

LINCOLN. Thanks.

(Rest.)

Daddy told me once why we got the names we do.

BOOTH. Yeah?

LINCOLN. Yeah?

(Rest.)

He was drunk when he told me, or maybe I was drunk when he told me. Any way he told me, may not be true, but he told me. Why he named us both. Lincoln and Booth.

BOOTH. How come. How come, man?

LINCOLN. It was his idea of a joke.

Both men relax back as the light fades.

Scene Two

Friday evening. The very next day. BOOTH comes in looking like he is bundled up against the cold. He makes sure his brother isnt home, then stands in the middle of the room. From his big coat sleeves he pulls out one new shoe then another, from another sleeve come two more shoes. He then slithers out a belt from each sleeve. He removes his coat. Underneath he wears a very nice new suit. He removes the jacket and pants revealing another new suit underneath. The suits still have the price tags on them. He takes two neckties from his pockets and two folded shirts from the back of his pants. He pulls a magazine from the front of his pants. Hes clearly had a busy day of shoplifting. He lays one suit out on LINCOLNs easy chair. The other he lays out on his own bed. He goes out into the hall returning with a folding screen which he sets up between the bed and the recliner creating 2 separate spaces. He takes out a bottle of whiskey and two glasses, setting them on the two stacked milk crates. He hears footsteps and sits down in the small wooden chair reading the magazine. LINCOLN, dressed in street clothes, comes in.

LINCOLN. Taaaaadaaaaaaaa!

BOOTH. Lordamighty, Pa, I smells money!

LINCOLN. Sho nuff, Ma. Poppas brung home thuh bacon.

BOOTH. Bringitherebringitherebingithere

With a series of very elaborate moves LINCOLN *brings the money over to* BOOTH.

BOOTH. Put it in my hands. Pa!

LINCOLN. I want ya tuh smells it first. Ma!

BOOTH. Put in heath my nose then, Pa!

LINCOLN. Take yrself a good long whiff of them greenbacks.

BOOTH. Oh lordamighty Ima faint, Pa! Get me muh med-un!

LINCOLN *quickly pours two large glasses of whiskey.*

LINCOLN. Dont die on me. Ma!

BOOTH. Im fading fast, Pa!

LINCOLN. Thinka thuh children. Ma! Thinka thuh farm!

BOOTH. 1–2–3.

Both men gulp down their drinks simultaneously.

LINCOLN AND BOOTH: AAAAAAAAAAAAAAAAAAAAAH!

Lots of laughing and slapping on the backs.

LINCOLN. Budget it out man budget it out.

BOOTH. You in a hurry?

LINCOLN. Yeah. I wanna see how much we got for the week.

BOOTH. You rush in here and dont even look around. Could be a fucking A-bomb in the middle of the floor you wouldnt notice. Yr wife, Cookie—

LINCOLN. X-wife—

BOOTH.—could be in my bed you wouldnt notice—

LINCOLN. She was once—

BOOTH. Look the fuck around please.

LINCOLN *looks around and sees the new suit on his chair.*

LINCOLN. Wow.

BOOTH. Its yrs.

LINCOLN. Shit.

BOOTH. Got myself one too.

LINCOLN. Boosted?

BOOTH. Yeah, I boosted em. Theys stole from a big-ass department store. That store takes in more money in one day than we will in our whole life. I

stole and I stole generously. I got one for me and I got one for you. Shoes belts shirts ties socks in the shoes and everything. Got that screen too.

LINCOLN. You all right, man.

BOOTH. Just cause I aint good as you at cards dont mean I cant do nothing.

LINCOLN. Lets try em on.

They stand in their separate sleeping spaces, BOOTH *near his bed,* LINCOLN *near his recliner, and try on their new clothes.*

BOOTH. Ima wear mine tonight. Gracell see me in this and *she* gonna ask me tuh marry *her.*

(Rest.)

I got you the blue and I got me the brown. I walked in there and walked out and they didnt as much as bat an eye. Thats how smooth lil bro be, Link.

LINCOLN. You did good. You did real good, 3-Card.

BOOTH. All in a days work.

LINCOLN. They say the clothes make the man. All day long I wear that getup. But that dont make me who I am. Old black coat not even real old just fake old. Its got worn spots on the elbows, little raggedy places thatll break through into holes before the winters out. Shiny strips around the cuffs and the collar. Dust from the cap guns on the left shoulder where they shoot him, where they shoot me I should say but I never feel like they shooting me. The fella who had the gig before I had it wore the same coat. When I got the job they had the getup hanging there waiting for me. Said thuh fella before me just took it off one day and never came back.

(Rest.)

Remember how Dads clothes used to hang in the closet?

BOOTH. Until you took em outside and burned em.

(Rest.)

He had some nice stuff. What he didnt spend on booze he spent on women. What he didnt spend on them two he spent on clothes. He had some nice stuff. I would look at his stuff and calculate thuh how long it would take till I was big enough to fit it. Then you went and burned it all up.

LINCOLN. I got tired of looking at em without him in em.

(Rest.)

They said thuh fella before me—he took off the getup one day, hung it up real nice, and never came back. And as they offered me thuh job, saying of course I would have to wear a little makeup and accept less than what they would offer a—another guy—

BOOTH. Go on, say it. "White." Theyd pay you less than theyd pay a white guy.

LINCOLN. I said to myself thats exactly what I would do: wear it out and then leave it hanging there and not come back. But until then, I would make a living at it. But it dont make me. Worn suit coat, not even worn by the fool that Im supposed to be playing, but making fools out of all those folks who come crowding in for they chance to play at something great. Fake beard. Top hat. Dont make me into no LINCOLN. I was LINCOLN on my own before any of that.

The men finish dressing. They style and profile.

BOOTH. Sharp, huh?

LINCOLN. Very sharp.

BOOTH. You look sharp too, man. You look like the real you. Most of the time you walking around all bedraggled and shit. You look good. Like you used to look back in thuh day when you had Cookie in love with you and all the women in the world was eating out of yr hand.

LINCOLN. This is real nice, man. I dont know where Im gonna wear it but its real nice.

BOOTH. Just wear it around. Itll make you feel good and when you feel good yll meet someone nice. Me I aint interested in meeting no one nice, I mean, I only got eyes for Grace. You think she'll go for me in this?

LINCOLN. I think thuh tie you gave me'll go better with what you got on.

BOOTH. Yeah?

LINCOLN. Grace likes bright colors dont she? My ties bright, yrs is too subdued.

BOOTH. Yeah. Gimmie yr tie.

LINCOLN. You gonna take back a gift?

BOOTH. I stole the damn thing didnt I? Gimmie yrs! I'll give you mines.

They switch neckties. BOOTH *is pleased.* LINCOLN *is more pleased.*

LINCOLN. Do thuh budget.

BOOTH. Right. Ok lets see; we got 314 dollars. We put 100 aside for the rent. 100 a week times 4 weeks makes the rent and—

LINCOLN AND BOOTH: —we dont want thuh rent spent.

BOOTH. That leaves 214. We put aside 30 for the electric leaving 184. We put aside 50 for thuh phone leaving 134.

LINCOLN. We dont got a phone.

BOOTH. We pay our bill theyll turn it back on.

LINCOLN. We dont need no phone.

BOOTH. How you gonna get a woman if you dont got a phone? Women these days are more cautious, more waddacallit, more circumspect. You get a filly to give you her numerophono and gone is the days when she just gives you her number and dont ask for yrs.

LINCOLN. Like a woman is gonna call me.

BOOTH. She dont wanna call you she just doing a preliminary survey of the property. Shit, Link, you dont know nothin no more.

(Rest.)

She gives you her number and she asks for yrs. You give her yr number. The phone number of yr home. Thereby telling her 3 things: 1) you got a home, that is, you aint no smooth talking smooth dressing *homeless* joe; 2) that you is in possession of a telephone and a working telephone number which is to say that you got thuh cash and thuh wherewithal to acquire for yr self the worlds most revolutionary communication apparatus and you together enough to pay yr bills!

LINCOLN. Whats 3?

BOOTH. You give her yr number you telling her that its cool to call if she should so please, that is, that you aint got no wife or wife approximation on the premises.

(Rest.)

50 for the phone leaving 134. We put aside 40 for "medsin."

LINCOLN. The price went up. 2 bucks more a bottle.

BOOTH. We'll put aside 50, then. That covers the bills. We got 84 left. 40 for meals together during the week leaving 44, 30 for me 14 for you. I got a woman I gotta impress tonight.

LINCOLN. You didnt take out for the phone last week.

BOOTH. Last week I was depressed. This week things is looking up. For both of us.

LINCOLN. Theyre talking about cutbacks at the arcade. I only been there 8 months, so—

BOOTH. Dont sweat it man, we'll find something else.

LINCOLN. Not nothing like this. I like the job. This is sit down, you know, easy work. I just gotta sit there all day. Folks come in kill phony Honest Abe with the phony pistol. I can sit there and let my mind travel.

BOOTH. Think of women.

LINCOLN. Sometimes.

(Rest.)

All around the whole arcade is buzzing and popping. Thuh whirring of thuh duckshoot, baseballs smacking the back wall when someone misses the stack of cans, some woman getting happy cause her fella just won the ring toss. The Boss playing the barker talking up the fake freaks. The smell of the ocean and cotton candy and rat shit. And in thuh middle of all that, I can just sit and let my head go quiet. Make up songs, make plans. Forget.

(Rest.)

You should come down again.

BOOTH. Once was plenty, but thanks.

(Rest.)

Yr Best Customer, he come in today?

LINCOLN. Oh, yeah, he was there.

BOOTH. He shoot you?

LINCOLN. He shot Honest Abe, yeah.

BOOTH. He talk to you?

LINCOLN. In a whisper. Shoots on the left whispers on the right.

BOOTH. Whatd he say this time?

LINCOLN. "Does thuh show stop when no ones watching or does thuh show go on?"

BOOTH. Hes getting deep.

LINCOLN. Yeah.

BOOTH. Whatd he say, that one time? "Yr only yrself—"

LINCOLN. "—when no ones watching," yeah.

BOOTH. Thats deep shit.

(Rest.)

Hes a brother, right?

LINCOLN. I think so.

BOOTH. He know yr a brother?

LINCOLN. I dunno. Yesterday he had a good one. He shoots me, Im playing dead, and he leans in close then goes: "God aint nothing but a parasite."

BOOTH. Hes one *deep* black brother.

LINCOLN. Yeah. He makes the day interesting.

BOOTH

(Rest.)

Thats a fucked-up job you got.

LINCOLN. Its a living.

BOOTH. But you aint living.

LINCOLN. Im alive aint I?

(Rest.)

One day I was throwing the cards. Next day Lonny died. Somebody shot him. I knew I was next, so I quit. I saved my life.

(Rest.)

The arcade gig is the first lucky break Ive ever had. And Ive actually grown to like the work. And now theyre talking about cutting me.

BOOTH. You was lucky with thuh cards.

LINCOLN. Lucky? Aint nothing lucky about cards. Cards aint luck. Cards is work. Cards is skill. Aint never nothing lucky about cards.

(Rest.)

I dont wanna lose my job.

BOOTH. Then you gotta jazz up yr act. Elaborate yr moves, you know. You was always too stiff with it. You cant just sit there! Maybe, when they shoot you, you know leap up flail yr arms then fall down and wiggle around and shit so they gotta shoot you more than once. Blam! Blam! Blam! Blam!

LINCOLN. Help me practice. I'll sit here like I do it work and you be like one of the tourists.

BOOTH. No thanks.

LINCOLN. My paychecks on the line, man.

BOOTH. I got a date. Practice on yr own.

(*Rest.*)

I got a rendezvous with Grace. Shit she so sweat she makes my teeth hurt.

(*Rest.*)

Link, uh, howbout slipping me an extra 5 spot. Its the biggest night of my life.

LINCOLN

BOOTH

LINCOLN *gives* BOOTH *a 5er.*

BOOTH. Thanks.

LINCOLN. No sweat.

BOOTH. Howabout I run through it with you when I get back. Put on yr getup and practice till then.

LINCOLN. Sure.

BOOTH *leaves.* LINCOLN *stands there alone. He takes off his shoes, giving them a shine. He takes off his socks and his fancy suit, hanging it neatly over the little wooden chair. He takes his getup out of his shopping bag. He puts it on, slowly, like an actor preparing for a great role: frock coat, pants, beard, top hat, necktie. He leaves his feet bare. The top hat has an elastic band which he positions securely underneath his chin. He picks up the white pancake makeup but decides against it. He sits. He pretends to get shot, flings himself on the floor and thrashes around. He gets up, considers giving the new moves another try, but instead pours himself a big glass of whiskey and sits there drinking.*

Scene Three

Much later that same Friday evening. The recliner is reclined to its maximum horizontal position and LINCOLN lies there asleep. He wakes with a start. He is horrific, bleary eyed and hungover, in his full LINCOLN regalia. He takes a deep breath, realizes where he is and reclines again, going back to sleep. BOOTH comes in full of swagger. He slams the door trying to wake his brother who is dead to the world. He opens the door and slams it again. This time LINCOLN wakes up, as hungover and horrid as before, BOOTH swaggers about, its moves are exaggerated, rooster-like. He walks round and round LINCOLN making sure his brother sees him.

LINCOLN. You hurt yrself?

BOOTH. I had me "an evening to remember."

LINCOLN. You look like you hurt yrself.

BOOTH. Grace Grace Grace. *Grace.* She wants me back. She wants me back so bad she wiped her hand over the past where we wasn't together just so she could say we aint never been apart. She wiped her hand over our breakup. She wiped her hand over her childhood, her teenage years, her first boyfriend, just so she could say that she been mine since the dawn of time.

LINCOLN. Thats great, man.

BOOTH. And all the shit I put her through; she wiped it clean. And the Women I saw while I was seeing her—

LINCOLN. Wiped clean too?

BOOTH. Mister Clean, Mister, Mister Clean!

LINCOLN. Whered you take her?

BOOTH. We was over at her place. I brought thuh food. Stopped at the best place I could find and stuffed my coat with only the best. We had candlelight, we had music we had—

LINCOLN. She let you do it?

BOOTH. Course she let me do it.

LINCOLN. She let you do it without a rubber?

BOOTH. —Yeah.

LINCOLN. Bullshit.

BOOTH. I put my foot down—and she *melted*. And she was—thuh—she was something else. I dont wanna get you jealous, though.

LINCOLN. Go head, I dont mind.

BOOTH

(*Rest.*)

Well, you know what she looks like.

LINCOLN. She walks on by and the emergency room fills up cause all the guys get whiplash from lookin at her.

BOOTH. Thats right thats right. Well—she comes to the door wearing nothing but her little nightie, eats up the food I'd brought like there was no tomorrow and then goes and eats on me.

(*Rest.*)

LINCOLN. Go on.

BOOTH. I dont wanna make you feel bad, man.

LINCOLN. Ssallright. Go on.

BOOTH

(*Rest.*)

Well, uh, you know what she likes. Wild. Goodlooking. So sweet my teeth hurt.

LINCOLN. Sexmachine.

BOOTH. Yeah.

LINCOLN. Hotsy-Totsy.

BOOTH. Yeah.

LINCOLN. Amazing Grace.

BOOTH. Amazing Grace! Yeah. That's right. She let me do her how I wanted. And no rubber.

(*Rest.*)

LINCOLN. Go on.

BOOTH. You dont wanna hear the mushy shit.

LINCOLN. Sure I do.

BOOTH. You hate mushy shit. You always hated thuh mushy shit.

LINCOLN. Ive changed. Go head. You had "an evening to remember," remember? I was just here alone sitting here. Drinking. Go head. Tell Link thuh stink.

(*Rest.*)

Howd ya do her?

BOOTH. Dogstyle.

LINCOLN. Amazing Grace.

BOOTH. In front of a mirror.

LINCOLN. So you could see her. Her face her breasts her back her ass. Graces got a great ass.

BOOTH. Its all right.

LINCOLN. Amazing Grace!

BOOTH *goes into his bed area and takes off his suit, tossing the clothes on the floor.*

BOOTH. She said next time Ima have to use a rubber. She let me have my way this time but she said that next time I'd have to put my boots on.

LINCOLN. Im sure you can talk her out of it.

BOOTH. Yeah.

(*Rest.*)

What kind of rubbers you use, I mean, when you was with Cookie.

LINCOLN. We didnt use rubbers. We was married, man.

BOOTH. Right. But you had other women on the side. What kind you use when you was with them?

LINCOLN. Magnums.

BOOTH. Thats thuh kind I picked up. For next time. Grace was real strict about it.

While BOOTH sits on his bed fiddling with his box of condoms, LINCOLN sits in his chair and resumes drinking.

LINCOLN. Im sure you can talk her out of it. You put yr foot down and she'll melt.

BOOTH. She was real strict. Sides I wouldnt wanna be taking advantage of her or nothing. Putting my foot down and her melting all over thuh place.

LINCOLN. Magnums then.

(*Rest.*)

Theyre for "the larger man."

BOOTH. Right. Right.

LINCOLN *keeps drinking as BOOTH, sitting in the privacy of his bedroom, fiddles with the condoms, perhaps trying to put one on.*

LINCOLN. Thats right.

BOOTH. Graces real different from them fly-by-night gals I was making do with. Shes in school. Making something of herself. Studying cosmetology. You should see what she can do with a womans hair and nails.

LINCOLN. Too bad you aint a woman.

BOOTH. What?

LINCOLN. You could get yrs done for free. I mean.

BOOTH. Yeah. She got this way of sitting. Of talking. Everything she does is. Shes just so hot.

(*Rest.*)

We was together 2 years. Then we broke up. I had my little employment difficulty and she needed time to think.

LINCOLN. And shes through thinking now.

BOOTH. Thats right.

LINCOLN

BOOTH

LINCOLN. Whatcha doing back there?

BOOTH. Resting. That girl wore me out.

LINCOLN. You want some med-sin?

BOOTH. No thanks.

LINCOLN. Come practice my moves with me, then.

BOOTH. Lets hit it tomorrow, K?

LINCOLN. I been waiting. I got all dressed up and you said if I waited up—come on, man, they gonna replace me with a wax dummy.

BOOTH. No shit.

LINCOLN. Thats what theyre talking about. Probably just talk, but—come on, man. I even lent you 5 bucks.

BOOTH. Im tired.

LINCOLN. You didnt get shit tonight.

BOOTH. You jealous, man. You just jail-us.

LINCOLN. You laying over there yr balls blue as my boosted suit. Laying over there waiting for me to go back to sleep or black out so I wont hear you rustling thuh pages of yr fuck book.

BOOTH. Fuck you, man.

LINCOLN. I was over there looking for something the other week and theres like 100 fuck books under yr bed and theyre matted together like a bad fro, bro, cause you spunked in the pages and didnt wipe them off.

BOOTH. Im hot, I need constant sexual release. If I wasnt taking care of myself by myself I would be out there running around on thuh town which costs cash that I dont have so I would be doing worse: I'd be out there doing who knows what, shooting people and shit. Out of a need for unresolved sexual release. I'm a hot man. I aint apologizing for it. When I dont got a woman, I gotta make do. Not like you, Link. When you dont got a woman you just sit there. Letting yr shit fester. Yr dick, if it aint falled off yet, is hanging there between yr legs, little whiteface shriveled-up blank-shooting grub worm. As goes thuh man so goes thuh mans dick. Thats what I say. Least my shits intact.

(*Rest.*)

You a limp dick jealous whiteface motherfucker whose wife dumped him cause he couldnt get it up and she told me so. Came crawling to me cause she needed a man.

(*Rest.*)

I gave it to Grace good tonight. So goodnight.

LINCOLN.

(*Rest.*)

Goodnight.

LINCOLN

BOOTH

LINCOLN

BOOTH

LINCOLN

BOOTH

LINCOLN *sitting in his chair.* BOOTH *lying in bed. Time passes* BOOTH *peeks out to see if* LINCOLN *is asleep.* LINCOLN *is watching for him.*

LINCOLN. You can hustle 3-card monte without me you know.

BOOTH. Im planning to.

LINCOLN. I could contact my old crew. You could work with them. Lonny aint around no more but theres the rest of them. Theyre good.

BOOTH. I can get my own crew. I dont need yr crew. Buncha hasbeens. I can get my own crew.

LINCOLN. My crews experienced. We usedta pull down a thousand a day. Thats 7 G a week. That was years ago. They probably do twice, 3 times that now.

BOOTH. I got my own connections, thank you.

LINCOLN. Theyd take you on in a heartbeat. With my say. My say still counts with them. They know you from before, when you tried to hang with us but—wernt ready yet. They know you from then, but I'd talk you up. I'd say yr my bro, which they know, and I'd say youd been working the west coast. Little towns. Mexican border. Taking tourists. I'd tell them you got moves like I dreamed of having. Meanwhile youd be working out yr shit right here, right in this room, getting good and getting better every day so when I did do the reintroductions youd have some marketable skills. Youd be passable.

BOOTH. I'd be more than passable, I'd be the be all end all.

LINCOLN. Youd be the be all end all. And youd have my say. If yr interested.

BOOTH. Could do.

LINCOLN. Youd have to get a piece. They all pack pistols, bro.

BOOTH. I *got* a piece.

LINCOLN. Youd have to be packing something more substantial than that pop gun, 3-Card. These hustlers is upper echelon hustlers they pack upper echelon heat, not no Saturday night shit, now.

BOOTH. Whata you know of heat? You aint hung with those guys for 6, 7 years. You swore off em. Threw yr heat in thuh river and you "Dont touch thuh cards." I know more about heat than you know about heat.

LINCOLN. Im around guns every day. At the arcade. Theyve all been reworked so they only fire caps but I see guns every day. Lots of guns.

BOOTH. What kinds?

LINCOLN. You been there, you seen them. Shiny deadly metal each with their own deadly personality.

BOOTH. Maybe I *could* visit you over there. I'd boost one of them guns and rework it to make it shoot for real again. What kind you think would best suit my personality?

LINCOLN. You aint stealing nothing from the arcade.

BOOTH. I go in there and steal it I want to go in there and, steal I go in there and steal.

LINCOLN. It aint worth it. They dont shoot nothing but blanks.

BOOTH. Yea, like you. Shooting blanks.

(*Rest.*)

(*Rest.*)

You ever wonder if someones gonna come in there with a real gun? A real gun with real slugs? Someone with uh axe tuh grind or something?

LINCOLN. No.

BOOTH. Someone who hates you come in there and guns you down and gets gone before anybody finds out.

LINCOLN. I dont got no enemies.

BOOTH. Yr X.

LINCOLN. Cookie dont hate me.

BOOTH. Yr Best Customer? Some miscellaneous stranger?

LINCOLN. I cant be worrying about the actions of miscellaneous strangers.

BOOTH. But there they come day in day out for a chance to shoot Honest Abe.

(*Rest.*)

Who are they mostly?

LINCOLN. I dont really look.

BOOTH. You must see something.

LINCOLN. Im supposed to be staring straight ahead. Watching a play, like Abe was.

BOOTH. All day goes by and you never ever take a sneak peek at who be pulling the trigger.

Pulled in by his own curiosity, BOOTH *has come out of his bed area to stand on the dividing line between the two spaces.*

LINCOLN. Its pretty dark. To keep thuh illusion of thuh whole thing.

(Rest.)

But on thuh wall opposite where I sit theres a little electrical box, like a fuse box. Silver metal. Its got uh dent in it like somebody hit it with they fist. Big old dent so everything reflected in it gets reflected upside down. Like yr looking in uh spoon. And thats where I can see em. The assassins.

(Rest.)

Not behind me yet but I can hear him coming. Coming in with his gun in hand, thuh gun he already picked out up front when he paid his fare. Coming on in. But not behind me yet. His dress shoes making too much noise on the carpet, the carpets too thin. Boss should get a new one but hes cheap. Not behind me yet. Not behind me yet. Cheap lightbulb just above my head.

(Rest.)

And there he is. Standing behind me. Standing in position. Standing upside down. Theres some feet shapes on the floor so he knows just where he oughta stand. So he wont miss. Thuh gun is always cold. Winter or summer thuh gun is always cold. And when the gun touches me he can feel that Im warm and he knows Im alive. And if Im alive then he can shoot me dead. And for a minute, with him hanging back there behind me, its real. Me looking at him upside down and him looking at me looking like LINCOLN. Then he shoots.

(Rest.)

I slump down and close my eyes. And he goes out thuh other way. More come in. Uh whole day full. Bunches of kids, little good for nothings, in they school uniforms. Businessmen smelling like two for one martinis. Tourists in they theme park t-shirts trying to catch it on film. Housewives with they mouths closed tight, shooting more than once.

(Rest.)

They all get so into it. I do my best for them. And now they talking bout replacing me with uh wax dummy. It'll cut costs.

BOOTH. You just gotta show yr boss that you can do things a wax dummy cant do. You too dry with it. You gotta add spicy shit.

LINCOLN. Like what.

BOOTH. Like when they shoot you, I dunno, scream or something.

LINCOLN. Scream?

BOOTH *plays the killer without using his gun.*

BOOTH. Try it. I'll be the killer. Bang!

LINCOLN. Aaaah!

BOOTH. Thats good.

LINCOLN. A wax dummy can scream. They can put a voice-box in it and make it like its screaming.

BOOTH. You can curse. Try it. Bang!

LINCOLN. Motherfucking cocksucker!

BOOTH. That's good, man.

LINCOLN. They aint going for that, though.

BOOTH. You practice rolling and wiggling on the floor?

LINCOLN. A little.

BOOTH. Lemmie see. Bang!

LINCOLN *slumps down, falls on the floor and silently wiggles around.*

BOOTH. You look more like a worm on the sidewalk. Move yr arms. Good. Now scream or something.

LINCOLN. Aaaah! Aaaaah! Aaaah!

BOOTH. A little tougher than that, you sound like yr fucking.

LINCOLN. Aaaaaah!

BOOTH. Hold yr head or something, where I shotcha. Good. And look at me! I am the assassin! *I am* BOOTH!! Come on man this is life and death! Go all out!

LINCOLN *goes all out.*

BOOTH. Cool, man thats cool. Thats enough.

LINCOLN. Whatdoyathink?

BOOTH. I dunno, man. Something about it. I dunno. It was looking too real or something.

LINCOLN. They dont want it looking too real. I'd scare the customers. Then I'd be out for sure. Yr trying to get me fired.

BOOTH. Im trying to help. Cross my heart.

LINCOLN. People are funny about they LINCOLN shit. Its historical. People like they historical shit in a certain way. They like it to unfold the way they folded it up. Neatly like a book. Not raggedy and bloody and screaming. You trying to get me fired.

(*Rest.*)

I am uh brother playing LINCOLN. Its uh stretch for anyones imagination. And it aint easy for me neither. Every day I put on that shit. I leave my own shit at the door and I put on that shit and I go out there and I make it work. I make it look easy but its hard. That shit is hard. But it works. Cause I work it. And you trying to get me fired.

(*Rest.*)

I swore off them cards. Took nowhere jobs. Drank. Then Cookie threw me out. What thuh fuck was I gonna do? I seen that "Help Wanted" sign and I went up in there and I looked good in the getup and agreed to the whiteface and they really dug it that me and Honest Abe got the same name.

(*Rest.*)

Its a sit down job. With benefits. I dont wanna get fired. They wont give me a good reference if I get fired.

BOOTH. Iffen you was tuh get fired, then, well—then you and me could—hustle the cards together. We'd have to support ourselves somehow.

(*Rest.*)

Just show me how to do the hook part of the card hustle man. The part where the Dealer looks away but somehow he sees—

LINCOLN. I couldnt remember if I wanted to.

BOOTH. Sure you could.

LINCOLN. No.

(*Rest.*)

Night, man.

BOOTH. Yeah.

LINCOLN *stretches out in his recliner. BOOTH stands over him waiting for him to get up, to change his mind. But LINCOLN is fast asleep. BOOTH covers him with a blanket then goes to his bed, turning off the lights as he goes. He quietly rummages underneath his bed for a girlie magazine which, as the lights fade, he reads with great interest.*

SCENE FOUR

Saturday. Just before dawn. LINCOLN gets up. Looks around. BOOTH is fast asleep, dead to the world.

LINCOLN. No fucking running water.

He stumbles around the room looking for something which he finally finds: a plastic cup, which he uses as a urinal. He finishes peeing and finds an out of the way place to stow the cup. He claws at his LINCOLN *getup, removing it and tearing it in the process. He strips down to his t-shirt and shorts.*

LINCOLN. Hate falling asleep in this damn shit. Shit. Ripped the beard. I can just hear em tomorrow. Busiest day of the week. They looking me over to make sure Im presentable. They got a slew of guys working but Im the only one they look over every day. "Yr beards ripped, pal. Sure, we'll getcha new one but its gonna be coming outa yr say." Shit. I should quit right then and there. I'd yank off the beard, throw it on the ground and stomp it, then go straggle the fucking boss. Thatd be good. My hands around his neck and his bug eyes bugging out. You been ripping me off since I took this job and now Im gonna have to take it outa yr pay, motherfucker. Shit.

(*Rest.*)

Sit down job. With benefits.

(*Rest.*)

Hustling. Shit. I was good. I was great. Hell I was the be all end all. I was throwing cards like throwing cards was made for me. Made for me and me alone. I was the best anyone ever seen. Coast to coast. Everybody said so. And I never lost. Not once. Not one time. Not never. Thats how much them cards was mines. I was the be all end all. I was that good.

(*Rest.*)

Then you woke up one day and you didnt have the taste for it no more. Like something in you knew.—Like something in you knew it was time to quit. Quit while you was still ahead. Something in you was telling you.—But hells no. Not Link thuh stink. So I went out there and threw one more time. What thuh fuck. And Lonny died.

(*Rest.*)

Got yrself a good job. And when the arcade lets you go yll get another good job. I dont gotta spend my whole life hustling. Theres more to Link than that. More to me than some cheap hustle. More to life than cheating some idiot out of his paycheck or his life savings.

(*Rest.*)

Like that joker and his wife from out of town. Always wanted to see the big city. I said you could see the bigger end of the big city with a little more cash. And if they was fast enough, faster than me, and here I slowed down my moves I slowed em way down and my Lonny, my right hand, my Stickman, spanish guy who looked white and could draw a customer in like nothing else, Lonny could draw a fly from fresh shit, he could draw Adam outa Eve just with that look he had. Lonny always got folks playing.

(*Rest.*)

Somebody shot him. They dont know who. Nobody knows nobody cares.

(*Rest.*)

We took that man and his wife for hundreds. No, thousands. We took them for everything they had and every thing they ever wanted to have. We took a father for the money he was gonna get his kids new bike with and he cried in the street while we vanished. We took a mothers welfare check, she pulled a knife on us and we ran. She threw it but her aim werent shit. People shopping. Greedy. Thinking they could take me and they got took instead.

(*Rest.*)

Swore off thuh cards. Something inside me telling me—.But I was good.

LINCOLN

LINCOLN

He sees a packet of cards. He studies them like an alcoholic would study a drink. Then he reaches for them, delicately picking them up and choosing 3 cards.

LINCOLN. Still got my moves. Still got my touch. Still got my chops. Thuh feel of it. And I aint hurting no one, God. Link is just here hustling hisself.

(*Rest.*)

Lets see whatcha got.

He stands over the monte setup. Then he bends over it placing the cards down and moving them around. Slowly at first, aimlessly, as if hes just making little ripples in water. But then the game draws him in. Unlike BOOTH, LINCOLN patter and moves are deft, dangerous, electric.

LINCOLN. (((Lean in close and watch me now: who see thuh black card who see thuh black card I see thuh black card black cards thuh winner pick thuh black card thats thuh winner pick thuh red card thats thuh loser pick thuh other red card thats thuh other loser pick thuh black card you pick thuh winner. Watch me as I throw thuh cards. Here we go.)))

(*Rest.*)

(((Who see thuh black card who see thuh black card? You pick thuh red card you pick a loser you pick that red card you pick a loser you pick thuh black card thuh deuce of spades you pick a winner who sees thuh deuce of spades thuh one who sees it never fades watch me now as I throw thuh cards. Red losers black winner follow thuh deuce of spaces chase thuh black deuce. Dark deuce will get you thuh win.)))

Even though LINCOLN speaks softly, BOOTH wakes and, unbeknownst to LINCOLN, listens intently.

(*Rest.*)

LINCOLN. ((10 will get you 20, 20 will get you 40.))

(*Rest.*)

((Ima show you thuh cards: 2 red cards but only one spade. Dark winner in thuh center and thuh red losers on thuh sides. Pick uh red card you got a loser pick thuh other red card you got a loser pick thuh black card you got a winner. One good pickll get you in, 2 good picks and you gone win. Watch me come on watch me now.))

(Rest.)

((Who sees thuh winner who knows where its at? You do? You sure? Go on then, put yr money where yr mouth is. Put yr money down you aint no clown. No? Ah, you had thuh card but you didnt have thuh heart.))

(Rest.)

((Watch me now as I throw thuh cards watch me real close. Ok, man, you know which card is the deuce of spades? Was you watching Links lighting fast express? Was you watching Link cause he the best? So you sure, huh? Point it out first, then place yr bet and Linkll show you yr winner.))

(Rest.)

((500 dollars? You thuh man of thuh hour you thuh man with thuh power. You musta been watching Link real close. You must be thuh man who know thuh most. Ok. Lay the cash in my hand cause Link the man. Thank you, mister. This card you say?))

(Rest.)

((Wrong! Ha!))

(Rest.)

((Thats thuh show. We gotta go.))

LINCOLN *puts the cards down. He moves away from the monte setup. He sits on the edge of his easy chair, but he can't take his eyes off the cards.*
Intermission

SCENE FIVE

Several days have passed. Its now Wednesday night. BOOTH is sitting in his brand-new suit. The monte setup is nowhere in sight. In its place is a table with two nice chairs. The table is covered with a lovely tablecloth and there are nice plates, silverware, champagne glasses and candles.

All the makings of a very romantic dinner for two. The whole apartment in fact takes its cue from the table. Its been cleaned up considerably. New curtains on the windows, a doily-like object on the recliner. BOOTH sits at the table darting his eyes around, making sure everything is looking good.

BOOTH. Shit.

He notices some of his girlie magazines visible from underneath his bed. He goes over and nudges them out of sight. He sits back down. He notices that theyre still visible. He goes over and nudges them some more, kicking at them finally. Then he takes the spread from his bed and pulls it down, hiding them. He sits back down. He gets up. Checks the champagne on much melted ice. Checks the food.

BOOTH. Foods getting cold, Grace!! Dont worry man, she'll get here, she'll get here.

He sits back down. He goes over to the bed. Checks it for springiness. Smoothes down the bedspread. Double-checks 2 matching silk dressing gowns, very expensive, marked "His" and "Hers." Lays the dressing gowns across the bed again. He sits back down. He cant help but notice the visibility of the girlie magazines again. He goes to the bed, kicks them fiercely, then on his hands and knees shoves them. Then he begins to get under the bed to push them, but he remembers his nice clothing and takes off his jacket. After a beat he removes his pants and, in this half-dressed way, he crawls under the bed to give those telltale magazines a good and final shove. LINCOLN comes in. At first BOOTH, still stripped down to his underwear, thinks its his date. When he realizes its his brother, he does his best to keep LINCOLN from entering the apartment. LINCOLN wears his frock coat and carries the rest of his getup in a plastic bag.

LINCOLN. You in the middle of it?

BOOTH. What the hell you doing here?

LINCOLN. If yr in thuh middle of it I can go. Or I can just be real quiet and just—sing a song in my head or something.

BOOTH. The casas off limits to you tonight.

LINCOLN. You know when we lived in that 2-room place with the cement backyard and the frontyard with nothing but trash in it. Mom and

Pops would do it in the middle of the night and I would always hear them but I would sing in my head, cause, I dunno, I couldnt bear to listen.

BOOTH. You gotta get out of here.

LINCOLN. I would make up all kinds of songs. Oh, sorry, yr all up in it. No sweat, bro. No sweat. Hey, Grace, howyadoing?!

BOOTH. She aint here yet, man. Shes running late. And its a good thing too cause I aint all dressed yet. Yr gonna spend thuh night with friends?

LINCOLN. Yeah.

BOOTH *waits for* LINCOLN *to leave.* LINCOLN *stands his ground.*

LINCOLN. I lost my job.

BOOTH. Hunh.

LINCOLN. I come in there right on time like I do every day and that motherfucker gives me some song and dance about cutbacks and too many folks complaining.

BOOTH. Hunh.

LINCOLN. Showd me thuh wax dummy—hes buying it right out of a catalog.

(*Rest.*)

I walked out still wearing my getup.

(*Rest.*)

I could go back in tomorrow. I could tell him I'll take another pay cut. Thatll get him to take me back.

BOOTH. Link. Yr free. Dont go crawling back. Yr free at lase! Now you can do anything you want. Yr not tied down by that job. You can—you can do something else. Something that pays better maybe.

LINCOLN. You mean Hustle!

BOOTH. Maybe. Hey, Graces on her way. You gotta go.

LINCOLN *flops into his chair,* BOOTH *is waiting for him to move* LINCOLN *doesnt budge.*

LINCOLN. I'll stay until she gets here. I'll act nice. I wont embarrass you.

BOOTH. You gotta go.

LINCOLN. What time she coming?

BOOTH. Shes late. She could be here any second.

LINCOLN. I'll meet her. I met her years ago. I'll meet her again.

(*Rest.*)

How late is she?

BOOTH. She was supposed to be here at 8.

LINCOLN. Its after 2 a.m. Shes—shes late.

(*Rest.*)

Maybe when she comes you could put the blanket over me and I'll just pretend like Im not here.

(*Rest.*)

I'll wait. And when she comes I'll go. I need to sit down.

I been walking around all day.

BOOTH

LINCOLN

BOOTH *goes to his bed and dresses hurriedly.*

BOOTH. Pretty nice, right? The china thuh silver thuh crystal.

LINCOLN. Its great.

(*Rest.*)

Boosted?

BOOTH. Yeah.

LINCOLN. Thought you went and spent yr inheritance for a minute, you had me going I was thinking shit, BOOTH—3-Card—that 3-Cards gone and spent his inheritance and the gal is—late.

BOOTH. Its boosted. Every bit of it.

(*Rest.*)

Fuck this waiting bullshit.

LINCOLN. She'll be here in a minute. Dont sweat it.

BOOTH. Right.

BOOTH *comes to the table. Sits. Relaxes as best he can.*

BOOTH. How come I got a hand for boosting and I dont got a hand for throwing cards? Its sorta the same thing—you gotta be quick—and slick. Maybe yll show me yr moves sometime.

LINCOLN

BOOTH

LINCOLN

BOOTH

LINCOLN. Look out the window. When you see Grace coming, I'll go.

BOOTH. Cool. Cause youd jinx it, youd really jinx it. Maybe you being here has jinxed it already. Naw. Shes just a little late. You aint jinxed nothing.

BOOTH *sits by the window, glancing out, watching for his date.* LINCOLN *sits in his recliner. He finds the whiskey bottle, sips from it. He then rummages around, finding the raggedy photo album. He looks through it.*

LINCOLN. There we are at the house. Remember when we moved in?

BOOTH. No.

LINCOLN. You were 2 or 3.

BOOTH. I was 5.

LINCOLN. I was 8. We all thought it was the best fucking house in the world.

BOOTH. Cement backyard and a frontyard full of trash, yeah, dont be going down memory lane man, yll jinx thuh vibe I got going in here. Gracell be walking in here and wrinkling up her nose cause you done jinxed up thuh joint with yr raggedy recollections.

LINCOLN. We had some great times in that house, bro. Selling lemonade on thuh corner, thuh treehouse out back, summers spent lying in thuh grass and looking at thuh stars.

BOOTH. We never did none of that shit.

LINCOLN. But we had us some good times. That row of nails I got you to line up behind Dads car so when he backed out the driveway to work—

BOOTH. He came back that night, only time I ever seen his face go red, 4 flat tires and yelling bout how thuh white man done sabotaged him again.

LINCOLN. And neither of us flinched. Neither of us let on that itd been us.

BOOTH. It was at dinner, right? What were we eating?

LINCOLN. Food.

BOOTH. We was eating pork chops, mashed potatoes and peas. I remember cause I had to look at them peas real hard to keep from letting on. And I would glance over at you, not really glancing not actually turning my head, but I was looking at you out thuh corner of my eye. I was sure he was gonna find us out and then he woulda whipped us good. But I kept glancing at you and you was cool, man. Like nothing was going on. You was cooooool.

(Rest.)

What time is it?

LINCOLN. After 3.

(Rest.)

You should call her. Something mighta happened.

BOOTH. No man, Im cool. She'll be here in a minute. Patience is a virtue. She'll be here.

LINCOLN. You look sad.

BOOTH. Nope. Im just, you know, Im just—

LINCOLN. Cool.

BOOTH. Yeah, Cool.

BOOTH *comes over, takes the bottle of whiskey and pours himself a big glassful. He returns to the window looking out and drinking.*

BOOTH. They give you a severance package, at thuh job?

LINCOLN. A weeks pay.

BOOTH. Great.

LINCOLN. I blew it. Spent it all.

BOOTH. On what?

LINCOLN. —Just spent it.

(Rest.)

It felt good, spending it. Felt really good. Like back in thuh day when I was really making money. Throwing thuh cards all day and strutting and rutting all night. Didnt have to take no shit from no fool, didnt have to worry about getting fired in favor of some damn wax dummy. I was thuh shit and they was my fools.

(Rest.)

Back in thuh day.

(Rest.)

(Rest.)

Why you think they left us, man?

BOOTH. Mom and Pops? I dont think about it too much.

LINCOLN. I dont think they liked us.

BOOTH. Naw. That aint it.

LINCOLN. I think there was something out there that they liked more than they liked us and for years they was struggling against moving towards that more liked something. Each of them had a special something that they was struggling against. Moms had hers. Pops had his. And they was struggling. We moved out of that nasty apartment into a house. A whole house. I wernt perfect but it was a house and theyd bought it and they brought us there and everything we owned, figuring we could be a family in that house and them things, them two separate things each of them was struggling against, would just leave them be. Them things would see thuh house and be impressed and just leave them be. Would see thuh job Pops had and how he shined his shoes every night before he went to bed, shining them shoes whether they needed it or not, and thuh thing he was struggling against would see all that and just let him be, and thuh thing Moms was struggling against, it would see the food on the table every night and listen to her voice when she'd read to us sometimes, the clean clothes, the buttons sewed on all right and it would just let her be. Just let us all be, just regular people living in a house. That wernt too much to ask.

BOOTH. Least we was grown when they split.

LINCOLN. 16 and 13 aint grown.

BOOTH. 16s grown. Almost. And I was ok cause you were there.

(Rest.)

Shit man, it aint like they both one day both, together packed all they shit up and left us so they could have fun in thuh sun on some tropical island and you and me would have to grub in thuh dirt forever. They didnt leave together. That makes it different. She left, 2 years go by. Then he left. Like neither of them couldnt handle it no more. She split then he split. Like thuh whole family mortgage bills going to work thing was just

too much. And I dont blame them. You dont see me holding down a steady job. Cause its bullshit and I know it. I seen how it cracked them up and I aint going there.

(Rest.)

It aint right me trying to make myself into a one woman man just because she wants me like that. One woman rubber-wearing motherfucker. Shit. Not me. She gonna walk in here looking all hot and shit trying to see how much she can get me to sweat, how much she can get me to give her before she gives me mines. Shit.

LINCOLN

BOOTH

LINCOLN. Moms told me I shouldnt never get married.

BOOTH. She told me thuh same thing.

LINCOLN. They gave us each 500 bucks then they cut out.

BOOTH. Thats what Im gonna do. Give my kids 500 bucks then cut out. Thats thuh way to do it.

LINCOLN. You dont got no kids.

BOOTH. Im gonna have kids then Im gonna cut out.

LINCOLN. Leaving each of yr offspring 500 bucks as yr splitting.

BOOTH. Yeah.

(Rest.)

Just goes to show Mom and Pops had some agreement between them.

LINCOLN. How so.

BOOTH. Theyd stopped talking to each other. Theyd stopped *screwing* each other. But they had an agreement. Somewhere in there when it looked like all they had was hate they sat down and did thuh "split" budget.

(Rest.)

When Moms splits she gives me 5 hundred-dollar bills rolled up and tied up tight in one of her nylon stockings. She tells me to put it in a safe place, to spend it only in case of an emergency, and not to tell nobody I got it, not even you. 2 years later Pops splits and before he goes—

LINCOLN. He slips me 10 fifties in a clean handkerchief: "Hide this somewheres good, dont go blowing it, dont tell no one you got it, especially that BOOTH."

BOOTH. Theyd been scheming together all along. They left separately but they was in agreement. Maybe they arrived at the same place at the same time, maybe they renewed they wedding vows, maybe they got another family.

LINCOLN. Maybe they got 2 new kids. 2 boys. Different than us, though. Better.

BOOTH. Maybe.

Their glasses are empty. The whiskey bottle is empty too. BOOTH takes the champagne bottle from the ice tub. He pops the cork and pours drinks for his brother and himself.

BOOTH. I didnt mind them leaving cause you was there. Thats why Im hooked on us working together. If we could work together it would be like old times. They split and we got that room downtown. You was done with school and I stopped going. And we had to run around doing odd jobs just to keep the lights on and the heat going and thuh child protection bitch off our backs. It was you and me against thuh world. Link. It could be like that again.

LINCOLN

BOOTH

LINCOLN

BOOTH

LINCOLN. Throwing thuh cards aint as easy as it looks.

BOOTH. I aint stupid.

LINCOLN. When you hung with us back then, you was just on thuh sidelines. Thuh perspective from thuh sidelines is thuh perspective of a customer. There was all kinds of things you didnt know nothing about.

BOOTH. Lonny would entice folks into thuh game as they walked by. Thuh 2 folks on either side of ya looked like they was playing but they was only pretending tuh play. Just tuh generate excitement. You was moving thuh cards as fast as you could hoping that yr hands would be faster than yr customers eyes. Sometimes you won sometimes you lost what else is there to know?

LINCOLN. Thuh customer is actually called the "Mark." You know why?

BOOTH. Cause hes thuh one you got yr eye on. You mark him with yr eye.

LINCOLN

LINCOLN

BOOTH. Im right, right?

LINCOLN. Lemmie show you a few moves. If you pick up these yll have a chance.

BOOTH. Yr playing.

LINCOLN. Get thuh cards and set it up.

BOOTH. No shit.

LINCOLN. Set it up set it up.

In a flash, BOOTH clears away the romantic table setting by gathering it all up in the tablecloth and tossing it aside. As he does so he reveals the "table" underneath: the 2 stacked monte milk crates and the cardboard playing surface. LINCOLN lays out the cards. The brothers are ready. LINCOLN begins to teach BOOTH in earnest.

LINCOLN. Thuh deuce of spades is thuh card tub watch.

BOOTH. I work with thuh deuce of hearts. But spades is cool.

LINCOLN. Theres thuh Dealer, thuh Stickman, thuh Sides, thuh Lookout and thuh Mark. I'll be thuh Dealer.

BOOTH. I'll be thuh Lookout. Lemmie be thuh Lookout, right? I'll keep an eye for thuh cops. I got my piece on me.

LINCOLN. You got it on you right now?

BOOTH. I always carry it.

LINCOLN. Even on a date? In yr own home?

BOOTH. You never know, man.

(*Rest.*)

So Im thuh Lookout.

LINCOLN. Gimmie yr piece.

BOOTH *gives LINCOLN his gun. LINCOLN moves the little wooden chair to face right in front of the setup. He then puts the gun on the chair.*

LINCOLN. We dont need nobody standing on the corner watching for cops cause there aint none.

BOOTH. I'll be thuh Stickman, then.

LINCOLN. Stickman knows the game inside out. You aint there yet. But you will be. You wanna learn good, be my Sideman. Playing along with the Dealer, moving the Mark to lay his money down. You wanna learn, right?

BOOTH. I'll be thuh Side.

LINCOLN. Good.

   (Rest.)

First thing you learn is what is. Next thing you learn is what aint. You dont know what is you dont know what aint, you dont know shit.

BOOTH. Right.

LINCOLN

BOOTH

BOOTH. Whatchu looking at?

LINCOLN. Im sizing you up.

BOOTH. Oh yeah?!

LINCOLN. Dealer always sizes up thuh crowd.

BOOTH. Im yr Side, Link, Im on yr team, you dont go sizing up yr own team. You save looks like that for yr Mark.

LINCOLN. Dealer always sizes up thuh crowd. Everybody out there is part of the crowd. His crew is part of the crowd, he himself is part of the crowd. Dealer always sizes up thuh crowd.

LINCOLN *looks* BOOTH *over some more then looks around at an imaginary crowd.*

BOOTH. Then what then what?

LINCOLN. Dealer dont wanna play.

BOOTH. Bullshit man! Come on you promised!

LINCOLN. Thats thuh Dealers attitude. He *acts* like he dont wanna play. He holds back and thuh crowd, with their eagerness to see his skill and their willingness to take a chance, and their greediness to win his cash, the larceny in their hearts, all goad him on and push him to throw his cards, although of course the Dealer has been wanting to throw his cards all along. Only he dont never show it.

BOOTH. Thats some sneaky shit, Link.

LINCOLN. It sets thuh mood. You wanna have them in yr hand before you deal a hand, K?

BOOTH. Cool—K.

LINCOLN. Right.

LINCOLN

BOOTH

BOOTH. You sizing me up again?

LINCOLN. Theres 2 parts to throwing thuh cards. Both parts are fairly complicated. Thuh moves and thuh grooves, thuh talk and thuh walk, thuh patter and thuh pitter pat, thuh flap and thuh rap: what yr doing with yr mouth and what yr doing with yr hands.

BOOTH. I got thuh words down pretty good.

LINCOLN. You need to work on both.

BOOTH. K.

LINCOLN. A goodlooking walk and a dynamite talk captivates their entire attention. The Mark focuses with 2 organs primarily: his eyes and his ears. Leave one out you lose yr shirt. Captivate both, yr golden.

BOOTH. So them times I seen you lose, them times I seen thuh Mark best you, that was a time when yr hands werent fast enough or yr patter werent right.

LINCOLN. You could say that.

BOOTH. So, there was plenty of times—

LINCOLN *moves the cards around.*

LINCOLN. You see what Im doing? Dont look at my hands, man, look at my eyes. Know what is and know what aint.

BOOTH. What is?

LINCOLN. My eyes?

BOOTH. What aint?

LINCOLN. My hands. Look at my eyes not my hands. And you standing there thinking how thuh fuck I gonna learn how tuh throw thuh cards if I be looking in his eyes? Look into my eyes and get yr focus. Dont think about learning how tuh throw thuh cards. Dont think about nothing. Just look into my eyes. Focus.

BOOTH. Theyre red.

LINCOLN. Look into my eyes.

BOOTH. You been crying?

LINCOLN. Just look into my eyes, fool. Now. Look down at thuh cards. I been moving and moving and moving them around. Ready?

BOOTH. Yeah.

LINCOLN. Ok, Sideman, thuh Marks got his eye on you. Yr gonna show him its easy.

BOOTH. K.

LINCOLN. Pick out thuh deuce of spades. Dont pick it up just point to it.

BOOTH. This one, right?

LINCOLN. Dont ask thuh Dealer if yr right, man, point to yr card with confidence.

BOOTH *points.*

BOOTH. That one.

> *(Rest.)*

Flip it over, man.

LINCOLN *flips over the card. It is in fact the deuce of spades.* BOOTH *struts around gloating like a rooster.* LINCOLN *is mildly crestfallen.*

BOOTH. Am I right or am I right?! Make room for 3-Card! Here comes thuh champ!

LINCOLN. Cool. Stay focused. Now we gonna add the second element. Listen.

LINCOLN *moves the cards and speaks in a low hypnotic voice.*

LINCOLN. Lean in close and watch me now: who see thuh black card who see thuh black card I see thuh black card black cards thuh winner pick thuh black card thats thuh winner pick thuh red card thats thuh loser pick thuh other red card thats thuh other loser pick thuh black card you pick thuh winner. Watch me as I throw thuh cards. Here we go.

> *(Rest.)*

Who see thuh black card who see thuh black card? You pick thuh red card you pick a loser you pick that red card you pick a loser you pick thuh black card thuh deuce of spades you pick a winner who sees thuh deuce of spades thuh one who sees it never fades watch me now as I throw thuh cards. Red losers black winner follow thuh deuce of spades chase thuh black deuce. Dark deuce will get you thuh win. One good pickll get

you in 2 good picks you gone win. 10 will get you 20, 20 will get you 40.

> *(Rest.)*

Ima show you thuh cards: 2 red cards but only one spade. Dark winner in thuh center and thuh red losers on thuh sides. Pick uh red card you got a loser pick thuh other red card you got a loser pick thuh black card you got a winner. Watch me watch me watch me now.

> *(Rest.)*

Ok, 3-Card, you know which cards thuh deuce of spade?

BOOTH. Yeah.

LINCOLN. You sure? Yeah? You sure you sure or you just think you sure? Oh you sure you sure huh? Was you watching Links lighting fast express? Was you watching Link cause he the best? So you sure, huh? Point it out. Now, place yr bet and Linkll turn over yr card.

BOOTH. What should I bet?

LINCOLN. Dont bet nothing man, we just playing. Slap me 5 and point out thuh deuce.

BOOTH *slaps* LINCOLN 5, *then points out a card which* LINCOLN *flips over. It is in fact, again the deuce of spades.*

BOOTH. Yeah, baby! 3-Card got thuh moves! You didnt know lil bro had thuh stuff, huh? Think again, Link, think again.

LINCOLN. You wanna learn or you wanna run yr mouth?

BOOTH. Thought you had fast hands. Wassup? What happened tuh "Links Lightning Fast Express"? Turned into uh local train looks like tuh me.

LINCOLN. Thats yr whole motherfucking problem. Yr so busy running yr mouth you aint never gonna learn nothing! You think you something but you aint shit.

BOOTH. I aint shit. I am *The* Shit. Shit. Wheres thuh dark deuce? Right there! Yes. baby!

LINCOLN. Ok, 3-Card. Cool. Lets switch. Take thuh cards and show me whatcha got. Go on. Dont touch thuh cards too heavy just—its a light touch. Like yr touching Graces skin. Or, whatever, man, just a light touch. Like uh whisper.

BOOTH. Like uh whisper.

BOOTH moves *the cards around, in an awkward imitation of his brother.*

LINCOLN. Good.

BOOTH. Yeah. All right. Look into my eyes.

BOOTHs *speech is loud and his movements are jerky. He is doing worse than when he threw the cards at the top of the play.*

BOOTH. Watch-me-close-watch-me-close-now: who-see-thuh-dark-card-who-see-thuh-dark-card? I-see-thuh-dark-card. Here-it-is. Thuh-dark-card-is-thuh-winner. Pick-thuh-dark-card-and-you-pick-uh-winner. Pick-uh-red-card-and-you-pick-uh-loser. Theres-thuh-loser-yeah-theres-thuh-red-card, theres-thuh-other-loser-and-theres-thuh-black-card, truth-winner. Watch-me-close-watch-me-close-now: 3-Card-throws-thuh-cards-lightning-fast. 3-Card-thats-me-and-lma-last. Watch-me-throw-cause-here-I-go. See truth black card? Yeah? Who see I see you see thuh black card?

LINCOLN. Hahahahhahahahahahahah!

LINCOLN *doubles over laughing.* BOOTH *puts on his coat and pockets the gun.*

BOOTH. What?

LINCOLN. Nothing, man, nothing.

BOOTH. *What?!*

LINCOLN. Yr just, yr just a little wild with it. You talk like that on thuh street cards or no cards and theyll lock you up, man. Shit. Reminds me of that time when you hung with us and we let you try being thuh Stick cause you wanted to so bad. Thuh hustle was so simple. Remember? I told you that when I put my hand in my left pocket you was to get thuh Mark tuh pick thuh card on that side. You got to thinking something like Links left means my left some dyslexic shit and turned thuh wrong card. There was 800 bucks on the line and you fucked it up.

(*Rest.*)

But it was cool, little bro, cause, we made the money back. It worked out cool.

(*Rest.*)

So, yeah, I said a light touch, little bro. Throw thuh cards light. Like uh whisper.

BOOTH. Like Graces skin.

LINCOLN. Like Graces skin.

BOOTH. What time is it?

LINCOLN *holds up his watch.* BOOTH *takes a look.*

BOOTH. Bitch. *Bitch!* She said she was gonna show up around 8. 8-a-fucking-clock.

LINCOLN. Maybe she meant 8 *a.m.*

BOOTH. Yeah. She gonna come all up in my place talking bout how she *love* me. How she cant stop *thinking* bout me. Nother mans shit up in her nother mans thing in her nother mans dick on her breath.

LINCOLN. Maybe something happened to her.

BOOTH. Something happened to her all right. She trying to make a chump outa me. I aint her chump. I aint nobodys chump!

LINCOLN. Sit. I'll go to the payphone on the corner. I'll—

BOOTH. Thuh world puts its foot in yr face and you dont move. You tell thuh world tuh keep on stepping. But Im my own man, Link. I aint you.

BOOTH *goes out, slamming the door behind him.*

LINCOLN. You got that right.

After a moment LINCOLN *picks up the cards. He moves them around fast, faster, faster.*

Scene Six

Thursday night. The room looks empty, as if neither brother is home. LINCOLN comes in. He's fairly drunk. He strides in, leaving the door slightly ajar.

LINCOLN. Taaadaaaa!

(*Rest.*)

(*Rest.*)

Taadaa, motherfucker. Taadaa!

(*Rest.*)

BOOTH—uh, 3-Card—you here? Nope. Good. Just as well.

Ha Ha *Ha Ha Ha!*

He pulls an enormous wad of money from his pocket. He counts it, slowly and luxuriously, arranging and smoothing the bills and sounding the amounts under his breath. He neatly rolls up the money, secures it with a rubber band and puts it back in his pocket. He relaxes in his chair. Then he takes the money out again, counting it all over again, but this time quickly, with the touch of an expert hustler.

LINCOLN. You didnt go back, Link, you got back, you got it back you got yr shit back in thuh saddle, man, you got back in business. Walking in Luckys and you seen how they was looking at you? Lucky starts pouring for you when you walk in. And the women. You see how they was looking at you? Bought drinks for everybody. Bought drinks for Lucky. Bought drinks for Luckys damn dog. Shit. And thuh women be hanging on me and purring. And I be feeling that old call of thuh wild calling. I got more phone numbers in my pockets between thuh time I walked out that door and thuh time I walked back in than I got in my whole life. Cause my shit is *back.* And back better than it was when it left too. Shoot. Who thuh man? Link. Thats right. Purrrrring all up on me and letting me touch them and promise them shit. 3 of them sweethearts in thuh restroom on my dick all at once and I was *there* my shit was there. And Cookie just went out of my mind which is cool which is very cool. 3 of them. Fighting over it. Shit. Cause they knew I'd been throwing thuh cards. Theyd seen me on thuh corner with thuh old crew or if they aint seed me with they own eyes theyd heard word. Links thuh stink! Theyd heard word and they seed uh sad face on some poor sucker or a tear in thuh eye of some stupid fucking tourist and they figured it was me whod Just took thuh suckers last dime, it was me who had all thuh suckers loot. They knew. They knew.

BOOTH *appears in the room. He is standing behind the screen, unseen all this time. He goes to the door, soundlessly, just stands there.*

LINCOLN. And they was all in Luckys. Shit. And they was waiting for me to come in from my last throw. Cant take too many fools in one day, its bad luck, Link, so they was all waiting in there for me to come in thuh door and let thuh liquor start flowing and thuh music start going and let thuh

boys who dont have thuh balls to get nothing but a regular job and uh weekly paycheck, let them crowd around and get in somehow on thuh excitement, and make way for thuh ladies, so they can run they hands on my clothes and feel thuh magic and imagine thuh man, with plenty to go around, living and breathing underneath.

(Rest.)

They all thought I was down and out! They all thought I was some NoCount HasBeen LostCause motherfucker. But I got my shit back. Thats right. They stepped on me and kept right on stepping. Not no more. Who thuh man?! Goddamnit, who thuh—

BOOTH *closes the door.*

LINCOLN

BOOTH

(Rest.)

LINCOLN. Another evening to remember, huh?

BOOTH.

(Rest.)

Uh—yeah, man, yeah. Thats right, thats right.

LINCOLN. Had me a memorable evening myself.

BOOTH. I got news.

(Rest.)

What you been up to?

LINCOLN. Yr news first.

BOOTH. Its good.

LINCOLN. Yeah?

BOOTH. Yeah.

LINCOLN. Go head then.

BOOTH.

(Rest.)

Grace got down on her knees. Down on her knees, man.

Asked *me* tuh marry *her.*

LINCOLN. Shit.

BOOTH. Amazing Grace!

LINCOLN. Lucky you, man.

BOOTH. And guess where she was, I mean, while I was here waiting for her. She was over at her house watching tv. I'd told her come over Thursday and I got it all wrong and was thinking I said Wednesday and here I was sitting waiting my ass off and all she was doing was over at her house just watching tv.

LINCOLN. Howboutthat.

BOOTH. She wants to get married right away. Shes tired of waiting. Feels her clock ticking and shit. Wants to have a baby. But dont look so glum man, we gonna have a boy and we gonna name it after you.

LINCOLN. Thats great, man. That's really great.

BOOTH

LINCOLN

BOOTH. Whats yr news?

LINCOLN.

(Rest.)

Nothing.

BOOTH. Mines good news, huh?

LINCOLN. Yeah. Real good news, bro.

BOOTH. Bad news is—well, shes real set on us living together.

And she always did like this place.

(Rest.)

Yr gonna have to leave. Sorry.

LINCOLN. No sweat.

BOOTH. This was only a temporary situation anyhow.

LINCOLN. No sweat man. You got a new life opening up for you, no sweat. Graces moving in today? I can leave right now.

BOOTH. I don't mean to put you out!

LINCOLN. No sweat. I'll just pack up.

LINCOLN *rummages around finding a suitcase and begins to pack his things.*

BOOTH. Just like that, huh? "No sweat"?! Yesterday you lost yr damn job. You dont got no cash. You dont got no friends, no nothing, but you clearing out just like that and its "no sweat"?!

LINCOLN. You've been real generous and you and Grace need me gone and its time I found my own place.

BOOTH. No sweat.

LINCOLN. No sweat.

(Rest.)

K. I'll spill it. I got another job, so getting my own place aint gonna be so bad.

BOOTH. You got a new job! Doing what?

LINCOLN. Security guard.

BOOTH.

(Rest.)

Security guard. Howaboutthat.

LINCOLN *continues packing a few things he has. He picks up a whiskey bottle.*

BOOTH. Go head, take thuh med-sin, bro. You gonna need it more than me. I got, you know. I got my love to keep me warm and shit.

LINCOLN. You gonna have to get some kind of work, or are you gonna let Grace support you?

BOOTH. I got plans.

LINCOLN. She might want you now but she wont want you for long if you dont get some kind of job. Shes a smart chick. And she cares about you. But she aint gonna let you treat her like some pack mule while shes out working her ass off and yr laying up in here scheming and dreaming to cover up thuh fact that you don't got no skills.

BOOTH. Grace is very cool with who I am and where I'm a thank you.

LINCOLN. It was just some advice. But, hey, yr doing great just like yr doing.

LINCOLN

BOOTH

LINCOLN

BOOTH

BOOTH. When Pops left he didnt take nothing with him. I always thought that was fucked-up.

LINCOLN. He was a drunk. Everything he did was always half regular and half fucked-up.

BOOTH. Whyd he leave his clothes though? Even drunks gotta wear clothes.

LINCOLN. Whyd he leave his clothes whyd he leave us? He was uh drunk, bro. He—whatever, right? I mean, you aint gonna figure it out by thinking about it. Just call it one of thuh great unsolved mysteries of existence.

BOOTH. Moms had a man on thuh side.

LINCOLN. yeah? Pops had side shit going on too. More than one. He would take me with him when he went to visit them. Yeah.

(Rest.)

Sometimes he'd let me meet the ladies. They was all very nice. Very polite. Most of them real pretty. Sometimes he'd let me watch. Most of thuh time I was just outside on thuh porch or in thuh lobby or in thuh car waiting for him but sometimes he'd let me watch.

BOOTH. What was it like?

LINCOLN. Nothing. It wasn't like nothing. He made it seem like it was this big deal this great thing he was letting me witness but it wasn't like nothing.

(Rest.)

One of his ladies liked me, so I would do her after he'd done her. Oh thuh sly though. He'd be laying there, spent and sleeping and snoring and her and me would be sneaking it.

BOOTH. Shit.

LINCOLN. It was alright.

BOOTH

LINCOLN

LINCOLN *takes his crumpled Abe* LINCOLN *getup from the closet. Isnt sure what to do with it.*

BOOTH. Im gonna miss you coming home in that getup. I don't even got a picture of you in it for the album.

LINCOLN.

(Rest.)

Hell, I'll put it on. Get thuh camera get thuh camera.

BOOTH. Yeah?

LINCOLN. What thuh fuck, right?

BOOTH. Yeah, what thuh fuck.

BOOTH *scrambles around the apartment and finds the camera.* LINCOLN *quickly puts on the getup, including 2 thin smears of white pancake makeup, more like war paint than whiteface.*

LINCOLN. They didnt fire me cause I wasnt no good. They fired me cause they was cutting back. Me getting dismissed didnt have no reflection on my performance. and I was damn good Honest Abe considering.

BOOTH. Yeah. You look great man, really great. Fix yr hat. Get in thuh light. Smile.

LINCOLN. LINCOLN didnt never smile.

BOOTH. Sure he smiled.

LINCOLN. No he didnt, man, you seen thuh pictures of him. In all his pictures he was real serious.

BOOTH. You got a new job, yr having a good day, right?

LINCOLN. Yeah.

BOOTH. So smile.

LINCOLN. Snapshots gonna look pretty stupid with me—

BOOTH *takes a picture.*

BOOTH. Thisll look great in thuh album.

LINCOLN. Lets take one together, you and me.

BOOTH. No thanks. Save the film for the wedding.

LINCOLN. This wasnt a bad job. I just outgrew it. I could put in a word for you down there, maybe when business picks up again theyd hire you.

BOOTH. No thanks. That shit aint for me. I aint into pretending Im someone else all day.

LINCOLN. I was just sitting there in thuh getup. I wasnt pretending nothing.

BOOTH. What was going on in yr head?

LINCOLN. I would make up songs and shit.

BOOTH. And think about women.

LINCOLN. Sometimes.

BOOTH. Cookie.

LINCOLN. Sometimes.

BOOTH. And how she came over here one night looking for you.

LINCOLN. I was at Luckys.

BOOTH. She didn't know that.

LINCOLN. I was drinking.

BOOTH. All she knew was you couldnt get it up. You couldnt get it up with her so in her head you was tired of her and had gone out to screw somebody new and this time maybe werent never coming back.

(Rest.)

She had me pour her a drink or 2. I didnt want to. She wanted to get back at you by having some fun of her own and when I told her to go out and have it, she said she wanted to have her fun right here. With me.

(Rest.)

[And then, just like that, she changed her mind.

(Rest.)

But she'd hooked me. That bad part of me that I fight down everyday. You beat yrs down and its stays there dead but mine keeps coming up for another round. And she hooked the bad part of me. And the bad part of me opened my mouth and started promising her things. Promising her things I knew she wanted and you couldnt give her. And the bad part of me took her clothing off and carried her into thuh bed and had her, Link, yr Cookie. It wasnt just thuh bad part of me it was all of me, man,] I had her. Yr damn wife. Right in that bed.

LINCOLN. I used to think about her all thuh time but I don't think about her no more.

BOOTH. I told her if she dumped you I'd marry her but I changed my mind.

LINCOLN. I dont think about her no more.

BOOTH. You dont go back.

LINCOLN. Nope.

BOOTH. Cause you cant. No matter what you do you cant get back to being who you was. Best you can do is just pretend to be yr old self.

LINCOLN. Yr outa yr mind.

BOOTH. Least Im still me!

LINCOLN. Least I work. You never did like to work. You better come up with some kinda way to bring home the bacon or Gracell drop you like a hot rock.

BOOTH. I got plans!

LINCOLN. Yeah, you gonna throw thuh cards, right?

BOOTH. That's right!

LINCOLN. You a double left-handed motherfucker who dont stand a chance in all get out out there throwing no cards.

BOOTH. You scared.

LINCOLN. I'm gone.

LINCOLN goes to leave.

BOOTH. Fuck that!

LINCOLN. Yr standing in my way.

BOOTH. You scared I got yr shit.

LINCOLN. The only part of my shit you got is the part of my shit you think you got and that aint shit.

BOOTH. Did I pick right them last times? Yes. Oh, I got yr shit.

LINCOLN. Set up the cards.

BOOTH. Thought you was gone.

LINCOLN. Set it up.

BOOTH. I got yr shit and Ima go out there and be thuh man and you aint gonna be nothing.

LINCOLN. Set it up!

BOOTH hurriedly sets up the milk crates and cardboard top. LINCOLN throws the cards.

LINCOLN. Lean in close and watch me now: who see thuh black card who see thuh black card I see thuh black card black cards thuh winner pick thuh black card thats thuh winner pick thuh red card thats thuh loser pick thuh other red card thats thuh other loser pick thuh black card you pick thuh winner. Who see thuh black card who see thuh black card? You pick thuh red card you pick a loser you pick that red card you pick a loser you pick thuh black card thuh deuce of spades you pick a winner who sees thuh deuce of spades thuh one who sees it never fades watch me now as I throw thuh cards. Red losers black winner follow thuh deuce of spades chase thuh black deuce. Dark deuce will get you thuh win. 10 will get you 20, 20 will get you 40. One good pickll get you in 2 good picks and you gone win.

(Rest.)

Ok, man, wheres thuh black deuce?

BOOTH points to a card. LINCOLN flips it over. It is the deuce of spades.

BOOTH. Who thuh man?!

LINCOLN *turns over the other 2 cards, looking at them confusedly.*

LINCOLN. Hhhhh.

BOOTH. Who thuh man, Link?! Huh? Who thuh man, Link?!?!

LINCOLN. You thuh man, man.

BOOTH. I got yr shit down.

LINCOLN. Right.

BOOTH. "Right"? All you saying is "right"?

(Rest.)

You was out on the street throwing. Just today. Werent you? You wasnt gonna tell me.

LINCOLN. Tell you what?

BOOTH. That you was out throwing.

LINCOLN. I was gonna tell you, sure. Cant go and leave my little bro out thuh loop, can I? Didnt say nothing cause I thought you heard. Did all right today but Im still rusty, I guess. But hey—yr getting good.

BOOTH. But I'll get out there on thuh street and still fuck up, wont I?

LINCOLN. You seem pretty good, bro.

BOOTH. You gotta do it for real, man.

LINCOLN. I am doing it for real. And yr getting good.

BOOTH. I dunno. It didnt feel real. Kinda felt—well it didnt feel real.

LINCOLN. We're missing the essential elements. The crowd, the street, thuh traffic sounds, all that.

BOOTH. We missing something else too, thuh thing thatll really make it real.

LINCOLN. Whassat, bro?

BOOTH. Thuh cash. Its just bullshit without thuh money. Put some money down on thuh table then itd be real, then youd do it for real, then I'd win it for real.

(Rest.)

And dont be looking all glum like that. I know you got money. A whole pocketful. Put it down.

LINCOLN

BOOTH

BOOTH. You scared of losing it to thuh man, chump? Put it down, less you think thuh kid who got two left hands is gonna give you uh left hook. Put it down, bro, put it down.

LINCOLN *takes the roll of bills from his pocket and places it on the table.*

BOOTH. How much you got there?

LINCOLN. 500 bucks.

BOOTH. Cool.

(Rest.)

Ready?

LINCOLN. Does it feel real?

BOOTH. Yeah. Clean slate. Take it from the top. "One good pickll get you in 2 good picks and you gone win."

(Rest.)

Go head.

LINCOLN. Watch me now:

BOOTH. Woah, man, woah.

(Rest.)

You think Ima chump.

LINCOLN. No I dont.

BOOTH. You aint going full out.

LINCOLN. I was just getting started.

BOOTH. But when you got good and started you wasn't gonna go full out. You wasnt gonna go all out. Yon was gonna do thuh pussy shit, not thuh real shit.

LINCOLN. I put my money down. Money makes it real.

BOOTH. But not if I dont put no money down tuh match it.

LINCOLN. You dont got no money.

BOOTH. I got money!

LINCOLN. You aint worked in years. You dont got shit.

BOOTH: I got money.

LINCOLN. Whatcha been doing, skimming off my weekly paycheck and squirreling it away?

BOOTH. I got money.

(Rest.)

They stand there sizing each other up. BOOTH *breaks away, going over to his hiding place from which he gets an old nylon stocking with money in the toe, a knot holding the money secure.*

LINCOLN

BOOTH

BOOTH. You know she was putting her stuff in plastic bags? She was just putting her stuff in plastic bags not putting but shoving. She was shoving her stuff in plastic bags and I was standing in thuh doorway watching her and she was so busy shoving thuh shit she didnt see me. "I aint made of money," thats what he always saying. The guy she had on the side. I would catch them together sometimes. Thuh first time I cut school I got tired of hanging out so I goes home—figured I could tell Mom I was sick and cover my ass. Come in thuh house real slow cause Im sick and moving slow and quiet. He had her bent over. They both had all they clothes on like they was about to do something like go out dancing cause they was dressed to thuh 9s but at thuh last minute his pants had fallen down and her dress had flown up and theyd ended up doing something else.

(*Rest.*)

They didnt see me come in, they didnt see me watching them, they didnt see me going out. That was uh Thursday. Something told me tuh cut school thuh next Thursday and sure enough.—He was her Thursday man. Every Thursday. Yeah. And Thursday nights she was always all cleaned up and fresh and smelling nice. Serving up dinner. And Pops would grab her cause she was all bright and she would look at me, like she didnt know that I knew but she was asking me not to tell nohow. She was asking me to—oh who knows.

(*Rest.*)

She was talking with him one day, her sideman, her Thursday dude, her backdoor man, she needed some money for something, thered been some kind of problem some kind of mistake had been made some kind of mistake that needed cleaning up and she was asking Mr. Thursday for some money to take care of it. "I aint made of money," he says. He was putting his foot down. And then there she was 2 months later not

showing yet, maybe she'd got rid of it maybe she hadnt maybe she'd stuffed it along with all her other things in them plastic bags while he waited outside in thuh car with thuh motor running. She must a known I was gonna walk in on her this time cause she had my payoff—my *inheritance*—she had it all ready for me. 500 dollars in a nylon stocking. Huh.

He places the stuffed nylon stocking on the table across from LINCOLN*s money roll.*

BOOTH. Now its real.

LINCOLN. Dont put that down.

BOOTH. Throw thuh cards.

LINCOLN. I dont want to play.

BOOTH. Throw thuh fucking cards, man!!

LINCOLN.

(*Rest.*)

2 red cards but only one black. Pick thuh black you pick thuh winner. All thuh cards are face down you point out thuh cards and then you move them around. Now watch me now, now watch me real close. Put thuh winning deuce down in the center put thuh loser reds on either side then you just move thuh cards around. Move them slow or move them fast. Links thuh king he gonna last.

(*Rest.*)

Wheres thuh deuce of spades?

BOOTH *chooses a card and chooses correctly.*

BOOTH. HA!

LINCOLN. One good pickll get you in 2 good picks and you gone win.

BOOTH. I know man I know.

LINCOLN. I'm just doing thuh talk.

BOOTH. Throw thuh fucking cards!

LINCOLN *throws the cards.*

LINCOLN. Lean in close and watch me now: who see thuh black card who see thuh black card I see thuh black card black cards thuh winner pick thuh black card thats thuh winner pick thuh red card thats thuh loser pick thuh other red card thats thuh other loser pick thuh black card you pick thuh winner. Watch me as I throw thuh cards. Here we go.

(Rest.)

Ima show you thuh cards: 2 red cards but only one spade. Dark winner in thuh center and thuh red losers on thuh sides. Pick up red card you got a loser pick thuh other red card you got a loser pick thuh black card you got a winner. Watch me watch me watch me now.

(Rest.)

Who see thuh black card who see thuh black card? You pick thuh red card you pick a loser you pick that red card you pick a loser you pick thuh black card thuh deuce of spades you pick a winner who sees thuh deuce of spades thuh one who sees it never fades watch me now as I throw thuh cards. Red losers black winner follow thuh deuce of spades chase thuh black deuce. Dark deuce will get you thuh win.

(Rest.)

Ok, 3–Card, you know which cards thuh deuce of spades? This is for real now, man. You pick wrong Im in yr wad and I keep mines.

BOOTH. I pick right I got yr shit.

LINCOLN. Yeah.

BOOTH. Plus I beat you for real.

LINCOLN. Yeah.

(Rest.)

You think we're really brothers?

BOOTH. Huh?

LINCOLN. I know we *brothers,* but is we really brothers, you know, blood brothers or not, you and me, whatdubyathink?

BOOTH. I think we're brothers.

BOOTH

LINCOLN

BOOTH

LINCOLN

BOOTH

LINCOLN

LINCOLN. Go head man, wheres thuh deuce?

In a flash BOOTH *points out a card.*

LINCOLN. You sure?

BOOTH. Im sure!

LINCOLN. Yeah? Dont touch thuh cards, now.

BOOTH. Im sure.

The 2 brothers lock eyes. LINCOLN *turns over the card that* BOOTH *selected and* BOOTH, *in a desperate break of concentration, glances down to see that he has chosen the wrong card.*

LINCOLN. Deuce of hearts, bro. Im sorry. Thuh deuce of spades was this one.

(Rest.)

I guess all this is mines.

He slides the money toward himself.

LINCOLN. You were almost right. Better luck next time.

(Rest.)

Aint yr fault if yr eyes aint fast. And you cant help it if you got 2 left hands, right? Throwing cards aint thuh whole world. You got other shit going for you. You got Grace.

BOOTH. Right.

LINCOLN. Whassamatter?

BOOTH. Mm.

LINCOLN. Whatsup?

BOOTH. Nothing.

LINCOLN.

(Rest.)

It takes a certain kind of understanding to be able to play this game.

(Rest.)

I still got thuh moves, dont I?

BOOTH. Yeah you still got thuh moves.

LINCOLN *cant help himself. He chuckles.*

LINCOLN. I aint laughing at you, bro, Im just laughing. Shit there is so much to this game. This game is—there is just so much to it.

LINCOLN, *still chuckling, flops down in the easy chair. He takes up the nylon stocking and fiddles with the knot.*

LINCOLN. Woah, she sure did tie this up tight, didnt she?

BOOTH. Yeah. I aint opened it since she gived it to me.

LINCOLN. Yr kidding. 500 and you aint never opened it? Shit. Sure is tied tight. She said heres 500 bucks and you didnt undo thuh knot to get a look at the cash? You aint needed to take a peek in all these years? Shit. I woulda opened it right away. Just a little peek.

BOOTH. I been saving it.

(*Rest.*)

Oh. dont open it, man.

LINCOLN. How come?

BOOTH. You won it man. you dont gotta go opening it.

LINCOLN. We gotta see whats in it.

BOOTH. We *know* whats in it. Dont open it.

LINCOLN. You are a chump, bro. There could be millions in here! There could be nothing! I'll open it.

BOOTH. Dont.

LINCOLN

BOOTH

(*Rest.*)

LINCOLN. Shit this knot aint coming out. I could cut it, but that would spoil the whole effect, wouldnt it? Shit. Sorry.

I aint laughing at you Im just laughing. Theres so much about those cards. You think you can learn them just by watching and just by playing but there is more to them cards than that. And——. Tell me something, Mr. 3–Card, she handed you this stocking and she said there was money in it and then she split and you say you didnt open it. Howd you know she was for real?

BOOTH. She was for real.

LINCOLN. How you know. She coulda been jiving you, bro. Jiving you that there really *was* money in this thing. Jiving you big time. Its like thuh cards. And ooooh you certainly was persistent. But you was in such a hurry to learn thuh last move that you didnt bother learning thuh first one. That was yr mistake. Cause its thuh first move that separates thuh Player from thuh Played. And thuh

first move is to know that there aint no winning. It may look like you got a chance but the only time you pick right is when thuh man lets you. And when its thuh real deal, when its thuh real fucking deal, bro, and thuh moneys on thuh line, thats when thuh man wont want you picking right. He will want you picking wrong so he will make you pick wrong. Wrong wrong wrong. Ooooh, you thought you was finally happening. didnt you? You thought yr ship had come in or some shit, huh? Thought you was uh Player. But I played you, bro.

BOOTH. Fuck you. Fuck you FUCKYOU *FUCKYOU!!!*

LINCOLN. Whatever, man. Damn this knot is tough. Ima cut it.

LINCOLN *reaches in his boot, pulling out a knife. He chuckles all the while.*

LINCOLN. Im not laughing at you, bro, Im just laughing.

BOOTH *chuckles with him.* LINCOLN *holds the knife high, ready to cut the stocking.*

LINCOLN. Turn yr head. You may not wanna look.

BOOTH *turns away slightly. They both continue laughing.* LINCOLN *brings the knife down to cut the stocking.*

BOOTH. I popped her.

LINCOLN. Huh?

BOOTH. Grace. I popped her. Grace.

(*Rest.*)

Who thuh fuck she think she is doing me like she done? Telling me I dont got nothing going on. I showed her what I got going on. Popped her good. Twice. 3 times. Whatever.

(*Rest.*)

She aint dead.

(*Rest.*)

She werent wearing my ring I gived her. Said it was too small. Fuck that. Said it hurt her. Fuck that. Said she was into bigger things. *Fuck* that. Shes alive not to worry, she aint going out that easy, shes alive shes shes——

LINCOLN. Dead. Shes——

BOOTH. Dead.

LINCOLN. Ima give you back yr stocking, man. Here, bro—

BOOTH. Only so long I can stand that little brother shit. Can only take it so long. I'm telling you—

LINCOLN. Take it back, man—

BOOTH. That little bro shit had to go—

LINCOLN. Cool—

BOOTH. Like BOOTH went—

LINCOLN. Here, 3-Card—

BOOTH. That BOOTH shit is over. 3-Cards thuh man now—

LINCOLN. I'm a give you yr stocking back, 3-Card—

BOOTH. Who thuh man now, huh? Who thuh man now?! Think you can fuck with me, motherfucker think again motherfucker think again! Think you can take me like I'm just some chump some two lefthanded pussy dickbreath chump who you can take and then go laugh at. Aint laughing at me you was just laughing bunch uh bullshit and you know it.

LINCOLN. Here. Take it.

BOOTH. I aint gonna be needing it. Go on. You won it you open it.

LINCOLN. No thanks.

BOOTH. Open it open it open it open it. *OPEN IT!!!*

(*Rest.*)

Open it up, bro.

LINCOLN

BOOTH

LINCOLN *brings the knife down to cut the stocking. In a flash, BOOTH grabs LINCOLN from behind. He pulls his gun and thrusts into the left side of LINCOLNs neck. They stop there poised.*

LINCOLN. Dont.

BOOTH *shoots* LINCOLN. LINCOLN *slumps forward, falling out of his chair and onto the floor. He lies there dead.* BOOTH *paces back and forth, like a panther in a cage, holding his gun.*

BOOTH. Think you can take my shit? My shit. That shit was mines. I kept it. Saved it. All this while. Through thick and through thin. Through fucking thick and through fucking thin, motherfucker. And you just gonna come up in here and mock my shit and call me two lefthanded talking about how she coulda been jiving me then go steal from me? My *inheritance.* You stole my *inheritance,* man. That aint right. That aint right and you know it. You had yr own. And you blew it. You *blew it,* motherfucker! I saved mines and you blew yrs. Thinking you all that and blew yr shit. And I *saved* mines.

(*Rest.*)

You aint gonna be needing yr fucking money-roll no more, dead motherfucker, so I will pocket it thank you.

(*Rest.*)

Watch me close watch me close now: I'm a go out there and make a name for myself that don't have nothing to do with you. And 3-Cards gonna be in everybodys head and in everybodys mouth like Link was.

(*Rest.*)

I'm a take back my inheritance too. It was mines anyhow. Even when you stole it from me it was still mines cause she gave it to me. She didn't give it to you. And I been saving it all this while.

He bends to pick up the money-filled stocking. Then he just crumples. As he sits beside LINCOLNs *body, the money-stocking falls away.* BOOTH *holds* LINCOLNS *body, hugging him close. He sobs.*

BOOTH. *AAAAAAAAAAAAAAAAAAAAAAAH!!*

END OF PLAY